SAUDI ARABIA

SAUDI ARABIA

Sherifa Zuhur

 ABC-CLIO

Santa Barbara, California • Denver, Colorado • Oxford, England

Library of Congress Cataloging-in-Publication Data

Zuhur, Sherifa.
  Saudi Arabia / Sherifa Zuhur.
    p. cm. — (Middle East in focus)
  Includes bibliographical references and index.
  ISBN 978-1-59884-571-6 (hardcopy : alk. paper)—ISBN 978-1-59884-572-3 (ebook)
1. Saudi Arabia. I. Title.
  DS204.Z84   2011
  953.8—dc23   2011019833

ISBN: 978-1-59884-571-6
EISBN: 978-1-59884-572-3

15   14   13   12   11   1   2   3   4   5

This book is also available on the World Wide Web as an eBook.
Visit www.abc-clio.com for details.

ABC-CLIO, LLC
130 Cremona Drive, P.O. Box 1911
Santa Barbara, California 93116-1911

This book is printed on acid-free paper ∞

Manufactured in the United States of America

Contents

About the Author

Sherifa Zuhur is a professor of Islamic and Middle Eastern studies, history, and national security affairs, formerly of the Strategic Studies Institute, U.S. Army War College. She directs the Institute of Middle Eastern, Islamic and Strategic Studies and has written 17 books and monographs, including *Saudi Arabia: Islamism, Political Reform and the Global War on Terror*, and *Ideological and Motivational Factors in the Defusing of Radical Islamist Violence*. She was a member of a NATO research team focusing on antiterrorism and wrote white papers and book chapters such as "Decreasing Violence in Saudi Arabia and Beyond" (in Pick, Speckhard, and Jacuch, eds., 2010) about Saudi Arabia. She is a former president of the Association of Middle East Women's Studies and an editor of the *Review of Middle East Studies*, and she holds a BA in political science and Arabic and Arabic literature, an MA in Islamic studies, and a PhD in history, all from the University of California, Los Angeles.

Preface

All books are written at particular historical moments. Especially in nonfiction writing, special concerns that color media, governmental, or scholarly publications are reflected, if not in the author's intent, in the questions formulated by editors and readers. This is true of both contemporary and historical writings. I want to note that both immediate and uncertain political currents are now impacting Saudi Arabia's neighbors in the Middle East; the Tunisians have ousted their long-time president, the Egyptians have overthrown Hosni Mubarak and are trying to implement a democratic and pluralist political system, Yemeni president 'Ali 'Abdullah Saleh left Yemen for Saudi Arabia after months of protests when he was wounded in an attack, the Libyan revoutionaries have killed Colonel Mu'ammar Qadhdhafi, and Syrians, Bahrainis, Omanis, Moroccans, Algerians, and Jordanians are calling for reform or changes in government. Saudi Arabian efforts to organize protests were anticipated and repressed, but it seems unlikely that the country will remain untouched by the regional fever for political change.

My second prefatory note is a general one; one finds far too schizophrenic a treatment of Saudi Arabia at this historical juncture. Portraits are painted with great love or sharp distaste, so strong as to cover over a truer panorama. Saudi Arabia is far too often essentialized as an unchanging archaic and exotic desert monarchy whose primary importance to the Western world is oil and/or Islamic extremism. Over many years, I have found it fascinating that so many outspoken American critics of Saudi Arabia were consulted at expert meetings in Washington, DC, primarily on the basis of their profound dislike of the country, which some had never visited. On the other hand, diplomats to the country have often served as experts, as they had acquired information inaccessible to others.

Just as great antipathy for Saudi Arabia and all things Saudi is expressed in some circles, others are at turns defensive or nostalgic, or offer apologia without much useful analysis or comparative perspectives. Nothing is ever so black or white as Saudi Arabia has been painted! The polemical manner in which Saudi Arabia is covered makes it difficult for a reader to acquire basic familiarity with the country's features. Contemporary scholarship in the Arab and Muslim worlds is also divided on the question of Saudi Arabia, and the country's own scholars are often unfortunately bound by prudence, discipline, bonds of employment or kinship, or justifiable suspicions about the motives of outsiders. This has complicated my task. As a responsible scholar, I have to write about subjects such as political succession in Saudi Arabia and the potential for struggle over that issue. However, Saudi Arabian scholars and writers are not free to share their insights on that issue, at least not at this time. About a month before I wrote this preface, Mohammed al-Abdulkarim, a Saudi Arabian professor of law, was arrested for publishing an article on royal succession and the potential for struggles over power within the royal family. Hatoon al-Fassi, a Saudi Arabian historian, was warned off at first by her editor at a Saudi Arabian newspaper for her depiction of Arab governments' response to the Tunisian revolution (*KQED News*, January 26, 2011). Now, if Saudi Arabian intellectuals cannot speak or write freely, then, unfortunately, external reportage from Western sources far less familiar with the dynamics of Saudi Arabian or other Arab nations will continue to shape opinions about their country.

Ma fi mushkila! (No problem! A typical Saudi response and subtle recommendation to relax and lighten up!) This book does not pretend to remedy these bifurcated perspectives and the struggle over the nation's image. It is, however, intended as a guide to uncover information about the real, multifaceted modern nation using an interdisciplinary approach and resources. My background and professional interests in Islamic studies, politics, security issues, and other interests in music, poetry, popular culture, gender relations, political economy, and race helped me formulate thoughts in brief on these subjects, although I could only hurriedly mention many that are covered in depth elsewhere. The book's format required coverage of so many other topics in order to make sense of contemporary Saudi Arabia that the reader would be well advised to continue her or his exploration of this fascinating country with materials suggested in this work and others.

The first chapter, "Geography," introduces readers to the physical and environmental basis of the Kingdom of Saudi Arabia. This includes its climate, weather patterns, major land forms, water sources, fauna, flora, and the scientific understanding of oil formation. Much of the wonderful photography and scientific studies of the landscape, geology, and fauna have come from Saudi Aramco. The second chapter, "History," provides the essential details of Arabia's ancient past, the advent of Islam, and the area's condition in the premodern era. Greater emphasis is put on contemporary history for it will greatly aid in understanding the nuances of Saudi Arabia's politics, international relations, economic policies, and laws. The third chapter, "Government and Politics," begins with an overview of political structures and roles.

I added a section on Saudi Arabia's international relations with Arab, Muslim, and foreign partners because of my interests and daily involvement in such issues over the last decade. Also, I believe that to study a country in isolation, without considering the impact of subregional, regional, and global influences on it, and vice versa, can be misleading and is a type of essentialism.

The fourth chapter, "Economy," provides an introduction to the country's resources, oil and other industries, agriculture, labor situation, and financial structures. The fifth chapter, "Society," begins with a section on Islam, the reform movement of Muhammad ibn 'Abd al-Wahhab, and today's religious structures, with some attention to the functioning of Islamic law in Saudi Arabia. I have briefly mentioned other ideological trends at the end of the subsection. The second subsection, on social class and ethnicity, reveals that social divisions in Saudi Arabia take various forms. Some predate the oil boom and arose from tribal, geographic, or occupational affiliations and gender. Slavery played an important role in the Arabian Peninsula that has not yet been fully explored or described. Other divisions are modern, arising since King 'Abd al-'Aziz al-Sa'ud's creation of the nation and during its governance by his descendants, whether from the need for foreign labor, the youth bulge in Saudi Arabia's demography, or disputes over the appropriate role of religion in society. The next subsection deals with women's roles and history in Saudi Arabia and with marriage. As many international groups have accused Saudi Arabia of suppressing women's rights, it is important to understand which limitations have the greatest impact on women's lives and to note the intense value placed on family ties and cohesion. Education is the subject of the next subsection. This sector has greatly expanded due to governmental policy, and its quality must improve as well. Also, to echo Dr. Khalid Alnowaiser, "reforms depend on a tolerant and informed citizenry," and thus reforming religious education to seek the "advancement of the human race" (*Arab News*, January 10, 2011) rather than replicating "memorizers" is a key, albeit disputed, goal.

The sixth chapter, "Culture," is composed of subsections on the Arabic language and Saudi dialects; social etiquette; Arabian and Saudi Arabian literature of the past and present, including poetry and prose; visual art; photography and films; music, dance, and public ceremonies or performances; Saudi Arabian cuisine and food traditions; and leisure activities, including popular sports in the kingdom. Another subsection is on popular cultural traditions not treated earlier, including proverbs, folktales, and superstitions, 'urf (customary or tribal law), customary and Islamic medicine, herbology or ethnobotany, popular gatherings, and traditional dress and its construction, which differ by region. This is a part of the living Saudi Arabia that is being rapidly forgotten and may be in danger of being relegated to obscure anthropological studies or museum exhibits.

The final chapter, "Contemporary Issues," of the book concerns subjects that may be controversial or that are of particular interest today. Many of these can be viewed alternatively as new stages of development; reaffirmation of the rulers' promise of security to their subjects, who in turn promise loyalty but have yet to fully acquire civil rights and responsibilities; struggles over the definition of Saudi Arabian nationhood; or struggles emanating from global conflicts and alliances. This chapter sets out Saudi Arabia's defense capabilities and weapons capacity as opposed to its relatively small military. This high weapons to low defense manpower ratio is the very reason that the kingdom requires coordination with and backing by an external power (and has led to the extremists' claim that it is overly influenced by the United States). The rise of violent extremism in Saudi Arabia over the last decade and the government's counterterrorism efforts, which I have written about elsewhere, are then described. To some degree, this problem has spilled over into Yemen. The next subsection covers health issues in the kingdom as an aspect of national development. The development of women's capabilities is also discussed, as well as the role of the women in the royal family, who are often overlooked by the international press. Saudi Arabia's media establishment and government censorship are, along with human rights issues, lightning rods for international criticism. Human rights are considered in the broadest meaning of the term; therefore, the large numbers of impoverished and homeless persons and children are mentioned along with issues of criminal justice. My intent is primarily to direct the reader toward issues of contemporary concern that are documented and likely to generate further public policy efforts.

A glossary of Arabic terms used throughout the text has been provided, and readers are advised to turn to this section whenever puzzled by a repeated usage of an Arabic term. Saudi Arabia's major holidays are described, and a section on organizations in Saudi Arabia includes some bilateral organizations, business portals, important organizations of the Saudi Arabian government, and a few examples of charitable and humanitarian organizations. Some of the most important international organizations of which Saudi Arabia is a member are listed, and because political parties are forbidden in Saudi Arabia, a few of the country's opposition groups are also briefly described.

I have included a bibliography that is intended to represent the many issues covered in this volume; in addition, a brief listing of musical recordings is provided for those who are curious about that aspect of cultural production. There is a vast literature on Saudi Arabia, and I have excluded a great deal of the works in Arabic because this series is geared toward English-language readers (I do urge readers to try, if they can, to learn this remarkable language, because without it, they may be missing about 80 percent of the available information on Saudi Arabia and much of the nuance.) The sidebars include some items of particular interest, and tables and additional information that should help provide a more detailed picture of the country's status and development are included in the back matter.

Acknowledgments

A number of acknowledgments are in order, as I have acquired various intellectual and personal debts while working on this book. I thank ABC-CLIO editors Lynn Jurgensen, Evan Brown, and Christian Green, who brought this book to life; Spencer Tucker, who had previously convinced me to work with him on other large encyclopedia projects for ABC-CLIO; and the copyediting team.

I could never have undertaken this book without the generosity of many individuals, scholars, and officials who live in Saudi Arabia or are connected to the Saudi Arabian diplomatic corps. Among them I want to thank the perennially supportive Hassan al-Husseini, my former classmate and fellow Bruin Abdullah al-Askar, the faculty and members of the Diplomatic Institute in the Saudi Arabian Ministry of Foreign Affairs, Elizabeth Hall, Dr. Abdullah Musa Al-Tayer, Elham Al Ateeq, Afaf Alhamdan, Huda Al-Jeraisy, Dr. Abdulmohsin Al-Akkas, Mohamed Ayaz, Desmond Carr, Abdulrahman al-Hadlag, Khalil al-Khalil, Muhammad Al Eissa, Sherry Cooper, Kay Campbell, Nadia al-Baeshen, and others not named here. When I arrived at the U.S. Army War College, I was supposed to embark on a large research project on Iraq. My supervisor prevented me from writing what I had intended to write, and I decided to work on a brief study of Saudi Arabia and its significance to the U.S. defense and political sectors. My interests deepened, and I began a more detailed case study of the Islamist opposition movement in Saudi Arabia, only to be forbidden from publishing it there. They say that when God closes a door, he opens a window, and so other venues for my work presented themselves, allowing me to review many special materials on Saudi Arabia. As I explored Saudi Arabia's culture and circumstances, I felt strongly that the Saudi bashing in the U.S. media was impeding an understanding of that country, and I made an effort, supported by Lt. Gen. David Huntoon and certain War College faculty, to bring Amb. H. R. H. Prince Turki Al-Faysal Al-Sa'ud to speak twice to the entire class and our international fellows. My travel to the kingdom from 2005 through 2008 for research prior to this book was supported by the U.S. government; however, the standard disclaimer applies—the government is in no way responsible for those earlier research works, my opinions, or this book. Thanks are also due to Laurie Fenstermacher of the U.S. Air Force Research Laboratory, Anne Speckhard, Tom Pick, and others who encouraged me to pursue my "alternative" idea that Muslims may craft their own responses to terrorism and extremism, sometimes more effectively than external actors.

I have benefited greatly from the insights and published works of many specialists on Saudi Arabia, who include Donald Cole, Eleanor Doumato, Soraya Altorki, Gregory Gause, Abdullah al-Askar, Khalid al-Dakhil, Natana Delong-Bas, Tim Niblock, Kay Hardy Campbell, Gwen Okruhlik, William Ochenswald, David Commins, Madawi al-Rasheed, Thomas Hegghammer, Christopher Boucek, Anthony Cordesman, Nawaf Obaid, John Duke Anthony, Lisa A. Urkevitch, Stèphane Lacroix, the late Sadekka Arebi, and others named in the book. As'ad AbuKhalil and Mona Eltahaway are vociferous critics of the Saudi Arabian government (not its people), but their attention to certain issues was a very constructive starting point for my own review.

I want to thank my son, Jean-Paul, and my husband, Ahmed, for putting up with an intense period of writing and the uncertain conditions it has entailed, and I dedicate the book to them, my daughter, Natasha, and my mother, Margot, who has always supported the life of the mind and spirit.

CHAPTER 1

Geography

The Kingdom of Saudi Arabia is located on the Arabian Peninsula in southwestern Asia, lying to the north of Yemen and to the west and north of Oman and the United Arab Emirates. It sits to the south of the Syrian Desert and Iraq, Jordan, and Kuwait; its northern boundary runs from the Arabian (Persian) Gulf to the Gulf of Aqaba for about 870 miles (1,400 kilometers). The Red Sea is located on its west, and the Arabian Gulf to the east, as well as Bahrain and Qatar. The Red Sea is part of the Great Rift Valley, which extends northward to the Gulf of Aqaba and the Jordan River valley. The natural land border of Arabia in the past was the great Syrian Desert to the north, although today borders are also demarcated with its southern neighbors on the Arabian Peninsula.

The country is between 756,954 and 899,766 square miles (1,218,199 and 2,331,000 square kilometers). The Saudi Arabian government states that the Kingdom of Saudi Arabia is 2,217,949 square kilometers (856,356 square miles). The figures vary in different sources because the borders with Oman and the United Arab Emirates were not very precisely defined and had been disputed. The Saudi Arabian–Oman border runs through the Rub' al-Khali, the great desert known as the Empty Quarter. Saudi Arabia comprises about 80 percent of the Arabian Peninsula and is about one-fifth the size of the United States.

Its northern boundaries were negotiated in the Treaty of Muhammara in 1922 and the al-Uqayr Convention, which created a diamond-shaped neutral zone between Saudi Arabia and Iraq, covering about 7,000 square kilometers (2,702.715 square miles). That neutral zone was dissolved by agreement. The other divided zone, also diamond shaped, exists between Kuwait and Saudi Arabia, with each country governing its half.

The Saudi Arabian Flag. (Dreamstime.com)

THE FLAG OF SAUDI ARABIA

The flag of Saudi Arabia has its origins in the reform movement of Muhammad ibn 'Abd al-Wahhab and the warriors of the al-Sa'ud. The flag above was adopted as the standardized form in 1973.

The color green has always symbolized Islam. The flag of Saudi Arabia is a green banner inscribed in white with the *shahadah* (testimony of faith) "There is no God but God; and Muhammad is his Messenger." The sword was added to the flag in 1906 to symbolize the military successes of Islam and of 'Abd al-'Aziz al-Sa'ud, who by then controlled Najd and founded the Kingdom of Saudi Arabia. The royal emblem consists of two crossed swords underneath a palm tree.

Much of Saudi Arabia is desert or semiarid, and however fruits, vegetables, and flowers are grown in the northern and southwestern mountain regions. A decreasing *badu* (bedouin or nomadic) population lives in the desert areas. Historically, the country was sparsely populated, and three types of populations lived there: the bedouin, herders who traveled to let their flocks graze; small agricultural communities; and communities in the highlands. There was both hostility and a degree of interdependence between the tribal groups and the settled communities, because while the tribal groups could attack the settled peoples, they also needed various types of food from them. The tribal groups also competed fiercely with each other, and raiding and looting were customary features of their subsistence. The presence of these various types of populations with different cultural traditions and patterns gave rise to various leaders who tried to solidify local or regional power. This made the political unification of the peninsula extremely difficult, with two main exceptions: the initial Islamic conquest and the rise of the Wahhabi-Sa'udi movement.

The peninsula experienced desertification after the end of the last Ice Age some 15,000 years ago due to changes in the currents of the oceans, mountain formation in the Middle East, monsoon patterns, and, since then, global warming. However, the country's topography is extremely varied, ranging from different types of desert terrain and oases to mountains of up to 9,840 feet (3,000 meters) in the Asir region to the southwest. The Asir area is greener and more tolerable than other parts of the country in the summer months due to its elevation. Mountains extend down the western side of the peninsula from the Gulf of Aqaba to the Gulf of Aden. The northern part of the mountain range, the Red Sea Escarpment, is in the Hijaz region and extends to a gap near Mecca (Makkah). Then the southern part of these mountains extends down through Asir. The Tihamah lowlands are a 40-mile-wide area from the Asir coast to the mountain range. The mountains of the southwestern area rise to 9,000 feet in elevation. The western coastal area can be humid, in comparison to the dry heat of much of the country.

To the east of the Hijaz is the central Najd region, a plateau about 200 miles (320 kilometers) wide that slopes down from the west to the east, dropping from about 2,200 feet to 1,800 feet. A limestone escarpment is found in the middle of Najd near Riyadh, called Jabal Tuwayq, dotted by oases and salt marshes. To the east of Jabal Tuwayq is a long, narrow desert area, al-Dahna, extending 800 miles from the al-Nufud Desert in the north to the Rub' al-Khali desert in the south. To the east of Najd is the Eastern Province. The coast of the Eastern Province is composed of rocky and sandy lowlands extending to the shores of the Arabian or Persian Gulf. The gulf coastline is made up of *sabkha*s (salt flats), marshes, and sandy areas. The sea is quite shallow with reefs extending far out into the gulf. The eastern portion of Arabia is sometimes called al-Ahsa because of the large oasis by that name located there, which is really made up of two oases; one of these oases includes the city of al-Hofuf.

About 41 miles to the northeast of Medina lies the Harrat Khaybar volcano, at an elevation of 6,867 feet and covering about 150,694 square feet. The volcano was described by explorer and traveler Charles Doughty in his 1876 work, which was published in 1888 (Doughty 1968). The area is actually three lava fields—Harrat Khaybar, Harrat Ithnayn, and Harrat Kura—with another lava field, Harrat Rahat, lying about 15.5 miles to the south. Harrat Rahat is huge, two times the size of Lebanon. Scientists believe the volcanic activity of this field goes back millions of years; at least 13 eruptions have been chronicled. A world team of volcanologists and geologists mapped the *harrah* region, theorizing that a 373-mile- (600-kilometer-) long volcanic axis, the Medina-Mecca-Nufud line, lies under it. The geological mapping of the country shows another field in the north between Tuwayq and al-Qurayyat, extending into Jordan, and other *harrat* near al-Wahba and al-Bahah. The ashy summits of Jabal Bayda and Jabal Abyad are huge and starkly white. Under the *harrat*

PROVINCES OF SAUDI ARABIA

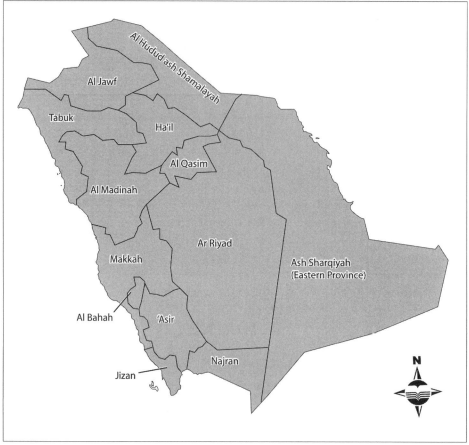

Provinces of Saudi Arabia. (ABC-CLIO): The transliteration of places and names in this map and other illustrations differs from the system used in this book.

lie tunnels called lava tubes. One of these, the Hibashi lava tube, has been studied by the National Space and Aeronautics Administration (NASA) as an example that helps them understand the lava tubes located under the planet Mars's basaltic plains (Harrigan 2006). Within the basaltic lava are minerals called xenochrysts or, commercially, peridots, gemstones now produced in this area.

Caves, sinkholes, tunnels, and caverns exist in the limestone areas of the Umm al-Radhuma formation, many of these at the edge of the al-Dahna Desert. The exploration of these geological formations was pioneered by Aramco's Max Steineke and Tom Barger and, later, by others including John Pint, a speleologist and writer, and through a project manned by the King Fahd University of Petroleum and Minerals and the Austrian Academy of Sciences (Pint 2003).

The limestone and dolomite of the Umm al-Radhuma formation were gradually created when the area was the ocean floor of a huge sea more than 60 million years ago. Over time, rain might flow into cracks in the stone, and its acidity ate away at the rock, forming cavities. During dry periods the underground water table receded

More than oil flows under the Arabian Peninsula. Here, volcanic lava beds (harrat in Arabic) in western Saudi Arabia. (Peter Harrigan/ Saudi Aramco)

even further, leaving some caves to fill with air and forming stalactites and stalagmites within them (Pint 2000, 27). At Ain Hit, in the Sulairy limestone formation near Ma'qalah to the northeast of Riyadh, there is a sinkhole called Dahl Hit, which continues into a series of water caves going down from the anhydrite layer into the limestone layer beneath. It was explored by cave diver Eric Bjurstrom (Bjurstrom 1997).

THE GEOLOGY OF PETROLEUM

The major theory explaining petroleum deposits is that they occur where very ancient organic matter, once zooplankton, or algae found on the bottom of a sea or lake, became fossilized. Then the fossilized matter was heated or subjected to pressure. (The alternative thesis is that petroleum is of abiogenic origin.) This material was buried under sediment, and that in turn created heat and pressure in a process called *diagenesis*. That turned the material into kerogen or, when even greater heat occurred, into hydrocarbons of a liquid or natural gas type. Usually, the oil or natural gas was trapped below the surface, in a porous variety of rock where it formed reservoirs. A less permeable kind of rock is usually above the reservoir, and one must drill through the rock to pump it out or inject water to pump out the oil.

The largest deposit of crude oil in the world, the Ghawar oil field is approximately 125 miles east of Riyadh and covers about 1.3 million acres. Ghawar produces about half of Saudi Arabia's light crude petroleum (more than 5 million barrels/day of 34 degrees API Arabian Light crude), totaling more than any other nation except for the United States and Russia (U.S. Energy Information Administration, 2010). The field has been divided into six areas—the Fazran, 'Ain Dar, Shedgum, 'Uthmaniyyah, Haradh, and Hawiyah—for the purposes of mapping and production (although they are not physically separated from each other). The source rock of the Ghawar oil field is the Tuwayq mountain formation. The oil-water contact of

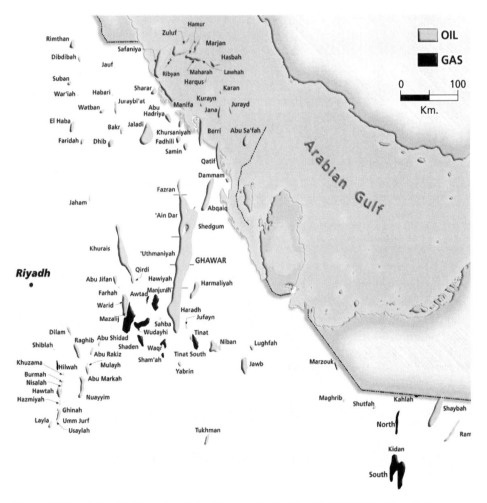

Map of Oil and Gas Fields in Saudi Arabia and the Arabian Gulf (2005). (Saudi Aramco World/SAWDIA)

the field is at a higher level on the western side than the eastern side. To the east of Ghawar is the Abqaiq oil field, which contains about 12 billion barrels. The other major Saudi Arabian oil fields are the Safaniyya/Khafji, Qatif, Shayba, and Zuluf fields (Greg Croft, Inc. n.d.; U.S. Energy Information Administration, 2010).

THE DESERTS

To the south of the Eastern Province is the sandy al-Jafurah Desert, which extends all the way to the Gulf at Dhahran and then to the south, where it merges into the Rub' al-Khali (Empty Quarter). The Rub' al-Khali is one of the world's largest sandy deserts, at 212,000 square miles. Here, there is very limited vegetation, and the annual precipitation is only about four inches. Daytime temperatures in the summer are often 113°F (45°C). The other major desert areas are al-Nafud to the north of Najd, which covers 20,000 square miles, and, to its north, the Syrian Desert. Some of the arable land in the Kingdom of Saudi Arabia lies in the oases of these deserts, such as Buraydah or al-Hofuf, which are heavily populated.

The three huge deserts historically isolated the region of the Najd on its northern, eastern, and southern sides. Located in the al-Nafud Desert are huge sand dunes, sometimes as high as 295 feet. To the south of al-Nafud is the al-Dahna area, which has sand mountains, reddish in color like the al-Nafud. This area covers an arc of about 78 miles, finally merging at the south with the Empty Quarter. The land formations of the Empty Quarter are extremely varied, with dunes and sand mountains,

Aerial view of sand dunes in the al-Nafud Desert, Saudi Arabia. (Dreamstime.com)

and the region is somewhat higher in the west, at about 1,969 feet, than in the east, where the elevation is only 591 feet.

Prior to large-scale oil production, the herding of animals and farming in the oases were the main means of sustenance in the interior regions; dates and Arabian horses were exported. In the Gulf and Red Sea region, pearl fishing, accomplished by means of slaves and credit-bound "free" laborers, was an important source of income until the pearl market collapsed about 1929. Date exports to the United States were negatively impacted by the rise of the date industry in California at about the same time (Hopper 2008, 27–28; Hopper 2010) although Saudi Arabia is today the world's second largest date producer. The taxes on pilgrims on the *hajj* were the only other major source of income for the local rulers and for the Saudi Arabian government in its early years.

The desert areas and lifestyle have impacted the language, literary heritage, and culture of Saudi Arabia. For instance, many words existed in the early dialects that distinguished different types of sand or terrain that are unique; wildlife such as *al-maha*, the oryx or Arabian antelope; and the domesticated camels and horses used by the nomads. However, today's urban environments in the country's capital, Riyadh, with few restrictions on construction, do not necessarily reflect many aspects of the desert heritage due to rapid urbanization and new living patterns.

Some features of traditional architecture, such as thicker walls, helped to soften or control the high temperatures, in contrast to modern concrete-block buildings (see Chapter 6, Architecture). Certain sectors of Saudi Arabian society want to spread an appreciation of the country's heritage and unique aspects of its former lifestyle and

Herd of camels outside the city of Riyadh, Saudi Arabia. (Dreamstime.com)

aesthetics and to retain or revive the social values that were supposed to accompany that heritage.

WATER

There are no rivers or lakes in Saudi Arabia. Wadis (valleys) may briefly surge with rivers following a rainfall. The water supply comes from rainfall, groundwater, and water that has been desalinated. In the Eastern Province and in the Jabal Tuwayq, many underground springs rise up into deep pools and are used to provide irrigation in the oases. In the Hijaz and Asir regions, springs are also common, as is well water, but water is less available and of poorer quality in the Najd and, naturally, in the desert areas. Saudi Aramco (Saudi Arabian Oil Company, formerly Aramco) was able to locate important aquifers in the northern and eastern areas of Saudi Arabia; the largest of these is called the Wasia.

The country has 1,553 miles of coastline along the Red Sea and the Arabian Gulf, which attract a wide variety of marine life. The Red Sea is quite deep, extending to 8,202 feet, while much of the Arabian Gulf is quite shallow. The Farasan Bank, part of Saudi Arabia's continental shelf off the Red Sea and containing 100 coral islets, and some of the islands of the Farasan archipelago are coral ecosystems. They have been reported on by Jacques Cousteau in the 1960s and by other divers (Bjurstrom, January/February 2000, 18–27). Some 250 types of coral have been recorded in the Red Sea, and coral reefs that shelter marine life are also found in the Arabian Gulf. At least 11 types of sea grass beds are found in the Red Sea and 3 types in the Arabian Gulf.

DESALINATION & ELECTRICITY

Somewhere between 50 percent and 70 percent of Saudi Arabia's drinking water is desalinated. As of 2010, the desalinated water is pumped through 4,157 kilometers of pipelines with 29 stations transporting water to 168 reservoirs with a capacity of up to 9.5 million cubic meters. But desalination is an expensive process which consumes 1.5 million barrels per day of oil equivalent energy, mostly gas. The technology of desalination improved and became less expensive; however, the Saudi Arabian minister of water and electricity explained that material and labor costs have increased, thus leading to rises in the price of desalinated water (*Emirates Business*, November 2009). However, this rose by an additional 1.0 mbd of actual crude in the hot summer of 2011, reducing net Saudi oil exports as not enough gas was available to desalinate water and generate electricity, especially for the Kingdom's high air conditioning usage. The government plans to build solar-powered desalination plants projected to reduce water and energy costs by 40 percent; the first plant is to be built at al-Khafji. Saudi Arabia plans to become an exporter of solar energy in the future. In addition, nanotech membranes are being considered as a way to improve desalination. An international center in nanotechnology is being established at the King Abdullah Institute at King Sa'ud University.

CLIMATE

The highest temperature recorded was at 124°F (51.1°C) in Dhahran in 1956. The lowest recorded temperature was at Turayf: 10.4°F (−12°C). The heat of the day drops to much lower temperatures at night. While summers are extremely hot, frost and snow can occur at higher elevations in the winter, but this occurs only once or twice every 10 years or so. The average winter temperature lies between 47°F and 68°F (8°C to 20°C), while during the hottest months, July and August, the average temperatures are above 105F, with low humidity in Najd and high humidity on the Red Sea coast. The Red Sea coastal areas are warm and humid year-round, rising in the south into the 40s Centigrade, while the Arabian Gulf coastal areas are cool in the winter (10-20s C) and hot and humid (30s to 40s C) in the summer. Strong winds carry sand storms from the northwest deserts to the Gulf coast. Rain occurs between January and May in the east and between November and January in the Jeddah area, and it can cause flash floods in the wadi (valley) areas.

Most of the Kingdom of Saudi Arabia is a true desert climate, with more extreme heat and dryness in the interior and more humidity and somewhat lower temperatures in the coastal areas on the Gulf and the Red Sea. In these areas, the humidity may create a mist or nighttime fog. The extremely high heat of the day in Najd, al-Qasim, and the deserts may far exceed the averages given earlier, at 113°F (45°C), and quite often going up to 129°F (54°C). In the winter, the same areas can be extremely cold due to the dryness of the climate. The Asir Province is affected by the change from the dry to the wet season, like areas of Africa and Asia; its monsoon season comes between May and October. Rainfall also occurs there and in parts of the Hijaz due to the higher mountain slopes. Very little rainfall occurs in the rest of the country, occurring often in storms.

From April to June, sandstorm conditions may develop, as low pressure mounts and the *shammal* (northerly) winds sweep over the northeastern coast. These conditions weaken in August and September. Humidity may increase in October and November, and storms can take place from December through February, with weather fronts typically passing from west to east, sometimes bringing dust in these months. Storms can also occur in March and April.

FAUNA

The Red Sea and the Arabian Gulf are home to 1,280 and 540 species of fish, respectively (Tasnee Petrochemicals 2005, Appendices 4 and 12). Endangered species of turtles and vulnerable species like the dugong (sea cow), the great white shark, and other sharks exist here.

Because the Arabian Peninsula was linked to Africa through an isthmus across the Red Sea in the Miocene period, different species were able to move between Africa and southwestern Asia. For instance, the common cat native to Egypt, the Nile Valley Egyptian, which is an ancient mixture between *Felix sylvestris lybica* (the wild cat) and the domestic cat, is also found in the Arabian Peninsula as well as the Sinai and Negev regions. In the highland areas of Arabia, one may find native ibex, wildcats, wolves, hyenas, and baboons. In addition, antelopes, bats, badgers, camels, foxes, gerbils, goats, hamsters, hyenas, jackals, leopards, mongooses, sheep, and shrews can be found in Saudi Arabia. Certain types of gazelles and oryx are particular to the region. The Arabian oryx became extinct in the 1970s; however, oryx and different varieties of gazelles have been reintroduced in the wildlife preserves. Between 67 and 100 species of lizards, 7 indigenous amphibians, and 45 to 53 species of snakes are present on the peninsula. (The lower numbers are provided in Appendix 4 of Tasnee Petrochemicals 2005.)

Many varieties of birds live in the highland areas and in the oases, or they touch down there as part of their annual migrations. At least 10 types of birds are native to Saudi Arabia, and falcons arrive in the winter. Other migrating species include *houbara*, kingfishers, owls, doves, ducks, geese, vultures, swallows, and warblers. Crows, sparrows, and black kites also live in the Kingdom of Saudi Arabia. The southern areas have even more types of birds, such as partridges, thrushes, woodpeckers, eagles, bustards, and goshawks. A royal decree established the National Commission for Wildlife Conservation and Development in 1986. This led to the designation of 17 wildlife reserves to protect the habitat of endangered species.

FLORA

The flora of Saudi Arabia is extremely diverse, although fewer varieties of plants may be found in the desert areas, geographically classified as the Saharo-Sindian regions. Even here, when there is rainfall, there are purple irises and bright red fruits on the *'abal* bush. Plants here adapt to little water and the high heat. While many sources describe the Arabian Peninsula as completely barren, Betty Vincett cataloged and photographed some 80 varieties of flowers in the 1970s (Vincett 1977). In the Eastern Province, there are drying winds and salty soil. Some 360 types of plants can be found, including weeds. Livestock graze on the *arfaj* bush, the *rimth* salt bush, and *tkumam*, a kind of grass. James Mandaville (1968) provides the Latin and Arabic plant names.

Traditional medicine in Saudi Arabia relies on many herbs, spices, and other mineral or natural substances that grow in different parts of the country, including anise for colic, indigestion, and coughs; alum and *habbat al-barakah* (nigella sativa, or black seed), to aid digestion and rheumatism; and cardamom, which also relieves indigestion and gas (Lebling 2006).

The high mountain ranges from Ta'if to Yemen actually possess temperate species that one could find in other areas of the world, including the white iris, the Ethiopian rose, and terrestrial orchids, which also grow in Africa. The Ethiopian

GLOSSARY OF ARABIC PLANT NAMES

'abal Calligonom comosum

'arfaj Rhanterium epapposum

ghada Haloxylon ammodendron

hambizan Emex spinosa

hamd several species of saltbushes of the family Chenopodiaceae

harmal Rhazya stricta

ja'dah Teucrium polium

kaftah Anastatica hierochuntica

kahil Arnebia decumbens

khuzama Horwoodia dicksoniae

kurraysh Glossonema edule

rak Salvadora persica

ramram Heliotropium ramosissimum

rimth Haloxylon salicornicum

rubahla Scorzonera papposa

samh Mesembryanthemum forskahlei

shary Citndlus colocynthis

thumam Panicum turgidum

'ushar Calotropis procera

Source: James Mandaville, "Flowers in the Sand." *Aramco World*, January/February 1968, 23–25.

rose (*Rosa abyssinica*) and the orchids may derive from the time when the peninsula was conjoined to Africa. Others, like the iris, might be found in other European or Asian highlands, and still other varieties, like thyme, are similar to their European or Asian temperate counterparts but have adapted in a specific form to their Arabian ecosystem (Larsen 1983).

ENVIRONMENT AND POLLUTION

Pollution exists to some degree in the large cities such as Riyadh and Jeddah due to automobile traffic. The greatest environmental problems came following the first Gulf War in 1991, when a huge, 8-million-barrel oil spill occurred, which has impacted areas of the Saudi Arabian coast, damaging plants, shallow areas, and sea life. This measurably affected areas at al-Jubayl, at the harbor, on Abu 'Ali island, and the beaches of the Gulf coastline. In addition, during the war, some 700 oil wells in

Kuwait burned or exploded, releasing pollution into the air and oil into the Kuwaiti desert. The particles from this pollution moved as far south as Riyadh, coating items left outdoors and soaking into the desert areas of northern Arabia.

HISTORIC AND MODERN DIVISIONS

Locations in ancient Arabia had different names in the past. One must therefore rely on historians to ascertain exactly which area was being discussed. Historians have disagreed about the country's divisions but generally present the peninsula as having been divided into the Tihamah lowlands, along the Red Sea coast; the Hijaz region; the al-'Arudh region, which included al-Yamamah and Bahrayn; Najd, al-Yaman; the Rub' al-Khali; and Oman. These were the names used by the historian al-Mada'ini, the genealogist Ibn Kalbi (d. 213 h./828 CE), and the religious scholar Ibn Abbas (d. 688). However, some historical sources differentiate only the Hijaz and Najd, as in the work of the geographer Ibn Hawqal (d. 977). Others wrote of the areas of Mecca, Medina, and al-Yamama as representing the three major regions of Arabia, as did al-Shaf'i (d. 810), the founder of an important school of Islamic law. For religious reasons, al-Yamama was included in discussions of the Hijaz because it had acknowledged the Islamic conquest under Muhammad. However, some geographers included al-Yamama within Najd, as that is its actual location (al-Askar 2002, 7–10).

Contemporary Saudi Arabia is divided into 13 *manatiq idariyyah* (administrative districts or emirates), and each of these is divided into *muhafazat*, or governates. There are 118 *muhafazat*, which include the regional capitals considered municipalities that have mayors and councils. The 13 *manatiq idariyyah* are Riyadh (159,074 square miles), al-Qasim (25,097 square miles), and Ha'il (40,111 square miles) in Najd in the center of the country; Tabuk (16,100 square miles), al-Madinah (66,796 square miles), Makkah (Mecca) (63,321 square miles), and al-Bahah (3,831 square miles) in the Hijaz in the western part of the country; al-Hudud al-Shamaliyyah (49,035 square miles) and al-Jawf (39,387 square miles) in the northern part of the country; Jizan (4,506 square miles), Asir (31,313 square miles), and Najran (45,946 square miles) in the southern part of the country; and al-Sharqiyyah (274,133 square miles) in the eastern part of the country. The regional capitals are Riyadh (in Riyadh province), Ha'il (Ha'il), Buraydah (in al-Qasim province), Tabuk (Tabuk), Medina (Madinah), Mecca (Makkah), al-Bahah (al-Bahah), Arar (al-Hudud al-Shamaliyyah), Sakaka (al-Jawf), Jizan (Jizan), Abha (Asir), Najran (Najran), and Dammam (al-Sharqiyyah).

Each region is known for its particular geographic features, natural resources, and specific history and cultural traditions. In the past, travel through the Arabian Peninsula was arduous, but, today, air, train, and road travel links the country and enables internal tourism. For instance, al-Bahah in the southwest is a holiday destination due to its mountains, valleys, forests, and agreeable climate. Asir is also a mountain region and the only area that features forests. Al-Abha also has a pleasant highland climate, and many national parks have been established here. Najran, in the southwest, has a desert climate, but heavy rains in the spring boost agriculture, as does the huge Najran Valley Dam. A great waterfall is located there. The Makkah region, including Jeddah and the holy city of Mecca, attracts the enormous annual pilgrimage, the *hajj*. Jeddah's port and airport are the gateways of the pilgrimage, and the city has long been a commercial center. Pilgrims also travel to the holy city of Medina in the Madinah region, which also includes the port and industrial city of Yanbu and the cities of Hanakiah, Badr, Khayber, and al-Mahd. Al-Ha'il in the Ha'il region in the north served as the transit point for pilgrimage caravans traveling overland. Other cities in this region expanded from smaller settlements due to their wheat, date, and other agricultural outputs. The Jizan region features plains, forests, and mountains, including the 11,000-foot Fifa Mountain. The region runs along the Red Sea coast and so includes at least 100 islands.

In al-Jawf in the north, the city of al-Jawf is famous for date and olive production. Tabarjal and Suwair, long agricultural centers, and the pre-Islamic city of Duma al-Jandal are also located in al-Jawf. The Northern Border (al-Hudud al-Shamali-yyah) region produces phosphates, and its residents raise and breed livestock. The Qasim region includes Buraydah, Unayzah, Bakariyah, and Darya. Buraydah and Unayzah were important agricultural centers, and the Ikhwan were settled here. (See Chapter 2, History.) The Eastern Province (Sharqiyyah) holds the heart of the petroleum industry at Dhahran, with the port of Ra's Tanura to the north and Dammam to its south; it is home to the industrial city of al-Jubayl, the historic area of al-Ahsa, and the oasis cities of Hofuf and Qatif. The Riyadh region is made up of plateaus and river valleys (wadis) and contains the huge capital city, Riyadh, the political and cultural center of the Kingdom of Saudi Arabia. Tabuk, to the northwest, has rich mineral deposits, and its cities relied on fishing, pearling, agriculture, and trade; and today, tourism is also important. Among the greatest challenges to Saudi Arabia has been the forging of a national identity from the many regional identities and loyalties that exist.

REFERENCES

Bjurstrom, Eric. "Dreaming of Farasan." *Aramco World,* 51, no. 1 (January/February 2000), 18–26.

Bjurstrom, Eric. "Diving in the Desert." *Aramco World*, July/August 1997.

Doughty, Charlies M. *Travels in Arabia Deserta*. Abridged by Edward Garnett. Gloucester, MA: Peter Smith, 1968.

Doumato, Eleanor. "Saudi Arabia, The Society and Its Environment." In *Saudi Arabia: A Country Study*, edited by Helen Chapin Metz, Federal Research Division, Library of Congress. Washington, DC: Library of Congress, 1993.

Greg Croft, Inc. "The Ghawar Oil Field." n.d. http://www.gregcroft.com/ghawar.ivnu

Harrigan, Peter. "Volcanic Arabia." *Saudi Aramco World*, March/April 2006, 2–13.

Hopper, Matthew. "Pearls, Globalization and the African Diaspora in the Arabian Gulf in the Age of Empire." Paper presented at the 124th Annual Meeting of the American Historical Association, San Diego, January 9, 2010.

Hopper, Matthew. "Slavery and the Slave Trades in the Indian Ocean and Arab Worlds: Global Connections and Disconnections." Paper presented at 10th Annual Gilder Lehrmann International Center Conference, Yale University, November 7–8, 2008.

Larsen, Torben B. "In the Alps of Arabia." *Aramco World*, July/August 1983, 16–21.

Lebling, Robert. "Natural Remedies of Arabia." *Saudi Aramco World,* 57, no. 5 (September/ October 2006), 12–21.

Mandaville, James. "Flowers in the Sand." *Aramco World*, January/February 1968, 23–25.

Pint, John. *The Desert Caves of Saudi Arabia*. London: Saudi Geological Survey and Stacey International, 2003.

Pint, John. "Saudi Arabia's Desert Caves." *Aramco World* 51, no. 2 (March/April 2000), 27–38.

Silsby, Jill. *Inland Birds of Saudi Arabia*. London: Immel, 1980.

U.S. Energy Information Administration. Independent Statistics and Analysis. "Saudi Arabia." 2010. http://www.eia.doe.gov/emeu/cabs/Saudi_Arabia/Oil.html

Vincett, Betty A. Lipscombe. *Wild Flowers of Central Arabia*. N.p.: Author, 1977. Distributed by E.W. Classey Ltd., Faringdon, Oxon, UK.

Vincett, Betty A. Lipscombe. *Animal Life in Saudi Arabia*. Cernusco, Italy: Garzanti Editore, 1982.

CHAPTER 2

History

TIMELINE

3200–1600 BCE—Dilmun civilization in modern-day Bahrain and nearby coastal areas.

900 BCE–542 CE—Sabaean civilization in southern Arabia.

420 BCE–105 CE—Nabataean kingdom in northern Arabia.

570—Muhammad ibn 'Abdullah, the Prophet of Islam, is born in Mecca (Makkah).

610—Muhammad receives the First Revelation at Mount Hira.

622—In the Hijrah (emigration) the Prophet Muhammad and the Muslims leave Mecca for Yathrib, renamed Medina (Madinah). The Islamic calendar is dated from this event.

624—Battle of Badr.

625—Battle of Uhud.

627—Battle of the Ditch.

630—Muslim conquest of Mecca.

632—Death of the Prophet Muhammad.

632–661—The Rashidun (Rightly Guided) Caliphate.

661–750—Ummayyad Caliphate; capital in Damascus.

17

750–1258—Abbasid Caliphate; capital in Baghdad.

930—Qarmatians attack Mecca and steal the Black Stone.

ca. 967—*Ashraf* (*sharif*s) gain control over Mecca.

1107–1291—The Crusades.

1170—Salah al-Din al-Ayyubi sends his brother to Mecca.

1182—Reynald de Châtillon, lord of Oultrejourdan, leads his knights on a raid in Taymah in the Hijaz.

1425—Mamluks have authority over Mecca.

1446—Al-Sa'ud ancestors establish Dir'iyyah, the capital of the first Sa'udi state.

1507—Portuguese capture Hormuz and set up Arabian outposts.

1517—Ottomans defeat Mamluks and assume authority over the Hijaz.

1541—Portuguese attack Jeddah (the date is given as 1542 in some sources). The town of Buraydah is founded.

1591—Ottomans gain authority in Hasa.

1631—Ottoman troops defeated in the Yemen revolt; they loot and brutalize population of Mecca and Medina.

1669—Banu Khalid uprising; they drive the Ottomans out of Hasa.

1744—Muhammad ibn 'Abd al-Wahhab moves to Dir'iyyah. 'Abd al-Wahhab and Muhammad ibn Sa'ud form alliance. Founding of the first Sa'udi state.

1744–1800—Sa'udi-Wahhabi forces battle to control Najd.

1794—Al-Sa'ud's forces capture Hasa.

1798—Ottomans begin offensive against the Sa'udi forces. Napoleon invades Egypt.

1801–1802—Sa'udi forces attack Karbala and expand into the Hijaz.

1803—Al-Sa'ud's forces conquer Mecca.

1813–1814—Egyptian forces end Sa'udi-Wahhabi rule in the Hijaz.

1818—Egyptian forces sack Dir'iyyah, ending the first Sa'udi state.

1824—Turki ibn Abdullah imposes Sa'udi rule in Riyadh, initiating the second Sa'udi state.

1830—Sa'udi authority spreads to Hasa.

1834—Turki assassinated; his son Faysal succeeds him and appoints 'Abdullah ibn Rashid governor of Ha'il the next year.

1837–1838—Faysal captured by Egyptians and sent to Cairo.

1840—Egyptians withdraw from Najd.

1843—Faysal returns to Riyadh and recovers control of Najd.

1868—Ottomans expand into Arabian Peninsula after Midhat Pasha becomes governor in Baghdad.

1871—Muhammad ibn Rashid takes Hasa from the al-Sa'ud.

1889–1891—Abd al-Rahman ibn Faysal ejects al-Rashid from Riyadh. Then the Rashidis defeat the al-Sa'ud, putting an end to the second Sa'udi state.

1893—The al-Sa'ud obtain sanctuary in Kuwait.

1901—A British firm obtains a concession to explore southwestern Persia for oil deposits.

1902—'Abd al-'Aziz (Ibn Sa'ud) conquers Riyadh and brings the Sa'udi family back from their exile in Kuwait.

1906—Ibn Sa'ud conquers Qasim.

1908—First major oil strike in Persia.

1912—The Ikhwan (Brotherhood) forms and Ibn Sa'ud establishes their first settlement.

1913—Ibn Sa'ud annexes al-Hasa and al-Qatif.

1914—The Sykes-Picot Treaty signed. The secret treaty assigned certain areas of the Middle East to British, French, and Russian control.

1915—Great Britain recognizes Ibn Sa'ud as ruler of Najd and Hasa in an Anglo-Sa'udi treaty. Lord McMahon corresponds with Sharif Husayn of Mecca, promising him an independent Arab nation if he aligns with the British against the Ottomans.

1916—Sharif Husayn of Mecca announces the Arab Revolt waged against the Ottoman forces and names himself king of the Arabs.

1917—Balfour Declaration issued by the British, promising the Zionists a Jewish state in Palestine.

1918—Ottoman Empire surrenders.

1920—The Treaty of Sèvres signed, formalizing the Mandatory Authority of Great Britain over Palestine, Iraq, and the Transjordan, and that of France over Syria and Lebanon.

1923—Transjordan becomes independent under Amir Abdullah, the son of Sharif Husayn. Major Frank Holmes obtains an oil concession for al-Ahsa.

1924—Ibn Sa'ud conquers Mecca.

1927—Ikhwan raids into Iraqi territory.

March 29, 1929—Ibn Sa'ud defeats the Ikhwan in the Battle of Sibillah. Ajman tribal federation revolts. Pearl exports sharply decline, as do date exports to the United States.

1930—Faysal al-Duwaysh , Ikhwan leader, gives himself up to the British in Kuwait, ending the Ikhwan revolt.

1932—Unification of Najd and the Hijaz; creation of the modern nation of Saudi Arabia. Discovery of oil in Bahrain by Standard Oil Company of California.

1933—Kingdom grants oil concession in al-Ahsa to California Arabian Standard Oil Company (CASOC, then known as SOCAL).

1934—Border war with Yemen; treaty of Ta'if ends that war.

May 1935—Assassination attempt on Ibn Sa'ud by three Yemeni former soldiers during the *hajj* in Mecca.

1936—Palestinians protest British support of the Zionist movement in Palestine with a major strike and three years of unrest known as the Great Revolt.

1938—Large-scale oil strike at Well Number Seven at Dammam Dome; commercial oil production begins.

1944—CASOC is renamed the Arabian American Oil Company (Aramco).

1945—Saudi Arabia becomes a member of the League of Nations.

1946—The Ministry of Defense is founded in Saudi Arabia.

1947—A British military mission is sent to Ta'if.

1948—State of Israel is declared; first Arab-Israeli War fought.

1949—Creation of the Hashemite Kingdom of Jordan.

1950—Jordan annexes the West Bank.

1952—Free Officers revolt in Egypt ends Egyptian monarchy. Gamal abd al-Nasser (Jamal abd al-Nasir) becomes president by 1954. Saudi Arabian occupation of a village in the Buraymi Oasis.

1953—Death of Ibn Sa'ud. His son Sa'ud succeeds him and rebuilds Nasiriyah Palace. Council of Ministers established. First strike by Aramco workers.

1954—King Sa'ud signs treaty with Nasser of Egypt.

1955—Egyptian military mission arrives to train the Saudi Arabian army. The U.S. Central Intelligence Agency (CIA) with help from Stavros Niarchos stir up news of a Saudi Arabian contract with Aristotle Onassis to build oil tankers to be controlled by the Sa'udi-Arabian Maritime Tanker Company, which would have taken over shipping from Aramco. International arbitration decides in Aramco's favor.

1956—Suez (also known as the Tripartite) War; Israel, France, and Great Britain attack Egypt.

1957—Riyadh University established; later named King Sa'ud University.

1958—Sa'udi plot against Nasser is made public. Prince Faysal takes over finances and administration of Saudi Arabian government.

1960—Formation of Organization of Petroleum Exporting Companies (OPEC).

1961—Free Princes Movement begins; these princes go into exile.

1962—Slavery in Saudi Arabia is abolished.

September 19, 1962—Imam Ahmad ibn Yahya of Yemen dies. An army-led rebellion overthrows his eldest son, al-Mansur Billah Muhammad al-Badr, a week later, touching off the Yemeni Civil War.

October 1962—Four Saudi Arabian aircraft crews defect to Egypt carrying arms for the rebels.

1963—Buraydah riots in response to establishment of a school for girls.

1964—King Sa'ud abdicates; Faysal becomes king.

1966—A series of bombs is set off by the opposition in Saudi Arabia.

1967—Second Arab-Israeli War; Israel takes over the West Bank, Gaza, East Jerusalem, and the Golan Heights.

1968—Saudi Arabia's Central Planning Organization created.

1970—Saudi Arabia's First Five-Year Development Plan begins.

1971—As Great Britain withdraws from the Gulf states, Iraq threatens Kuwait. Saudi Arabia helps negotiate a secret agreement to contain Iraq.

1972—Saudi Arabia gains 20 percent control of Aramco.

1973—Workers from the Philippines begin to travel to Saudi Arabia for employment.

March 13, 1973—Arab oil ministers agree in Tripoli to lift the embargo against the United States and to continue the embargo against the Netherlands and Denmark. However, Libya and Syria plan to continue the embargo.

October 6, 1973—Third Arab-Israeli (Ramadan or October) War.

October 8, 1973—OPEC demands price increase at Vienna meeting.

October 16, 1973—OPEC delegates in Kuwait announce unilateral price increase from $3.01 to $5.12 per barrel. After this, producers set price. In response to President Nixon's airlift to Israel and proposed $2.2 billion to Israel, King Faysal freezes oil shipments to the United States and other countries aiding Israel.

November 8, 1973—Secretary of State Henry Kissinger visits Riyadh and asks for an end to the embargo, but Faysal refuses.

November 21, 1973—Kissinger threatens countermeasures to a continuing embargo, and Oil Minister Yamani says that if the West takes countermeasures, Saudi Arabia would cut production by 80 percent.

1974—Construction of King Khalid Military City begins.

1975—King Faysal assassinated by Faysal ibn Musaid; Khalid becomes king.

1976—Saudi Arabia seeks to purchase U.S.-made F-15 fighter aircraft.

1978—U.S. Congress approves the sale of the F-15 aircraft to Saudi Arabia.

1979—Followers of Juhayman al-'Utaybi seize the Grand Mosque. Umm al-Qura University established. Soviets invade Afghanistan. Islamic Revolution of Iran. Khomeini returns there from France. Fifty-two Americans are taken hostage in U.S. embassy in Tehran.

March 1979—Camp David Accords signed. In response, Saudi Arabia severs relations with Egypt.

1979–1980—Shi'a unrest in the Eastern Province.

1980—The Fundamental or Basic Law is announced. Aramco converts to full Saudi Arabian ownership.

1981—The Gulf Cooperation Council (GCC) is formed on May 25.

1982—King Khalid dies; King Fahd succeeds him.

1983—Stock market created in Saudi Arabia. Bandar ibn Sultan is appointed ambassador to the United States.

1984–1985—Saudi Arabian government provides aid for the contras in Nicaragua. Muhammad ibn Fahd becomes the governor of the Eastern Province. Poet and minister Ghazi al-Ghosaybi (Qusaibi) is sacked after he publishes a poem critical of the king and his subordinates.

1985—Al-Yamamah arms deal with the United Kingdom is signed. Prince Sultan ibn Salman is part of the U.S. National Aeronautics and Space Administrations (NASA) *Discovery* flight orbiting the earth.

1986—Oil prices drop.

1987—Diplomatic relations with Egypt restored. Deaths of 402 pilgrims in incidents sparked by Iranian demonstrations during the *hajj.*

1988—Osama bin Laden (Usama bin Ladin) and other Arab supporters of the *mujahidin* are active in Afghanistan; Saudi Arabian Oil Company, known as Saudi Aramco, is established. Explosions occur at refinery at Ra's Tanura and in plant in Jubayl.

1989—Soviet forces withdraw from Afghanistan.

1990—Saddam Hussein (Husayn)'s Iraqi forces invade Kuwait, threatening Saudi Arabia.

1991—First Gulf War begins. U.S. and coalition troops arrive in Saudi Arabia. Poet Sadiq Mellalah is beheaded in Qatif for the crimes of blasphemy and apostasy. Saudi Arabian women protest the unwritten rule disallowing women from driving automobiles by staging a public demonstration in which they drove their own vehicles.

1992—Memorandum of Advice issued as part of "petition" movements.

1993—The liberal reform movement and the opposition group Committee for Defense of Legitimate Rights (CDLR) are declared illegal. Osama bin Laden and his followers are based in the Sudan.

December 1993—Majlis al-Shura (Consultative Council) is created.

1994—Uprising in Buraydah against government corruption. Saudi Arabian government strips Osama bin Laden of his citizenship.

1995—Osama bin Laden writes a letter to King Fahd complaining of waste and corruption, Saudi Arabia's reliance on Westerners for defense, and its lack of commitment to Islamic principles. He calls for fighters to expel Western military forces. Car bombing at National Guard facility in Riyadh kills five Americans and two Indians. King Khalid suffers a debilitating stroke, and Crown Prince 'Abdullah takes over de facto rule.

1996—Attack on Khobar Towers, Dhahran, by Saudi Arabian Hizballah, killing 19 military personnel and wounding 515.

1998—Bin Laden and al-Zawahiri issue a *fatwa* against foreign occupation of the Arabian Peninsula. Al-Qa'ida operatives bomb the U.S. embassies in Dar al-Salaam and Nairobi. Taliban refuse to extradite bin Laden to Saudi Arabia.

April 1999—Saudi Arabia has 112,500 Internet users and 45,000 online subscribers. Inauguration of the Shayba oil field in the Rub' al-Khali desert.

January 3, 2000—An al-Qa'ida cell fails in an attempted attack on the USS *The Sullivans* as it refuels in Yemen.

March 2000—Shots fired at a guard at the Russian embassy.

October 4, 2000—Saudi Arabian dissidents hijack an airplane to Iraq.

October 12, 2000—Al-Qa'ida bombs the USS *Cole* in Yemen, killing 17 and wounding 30. Treaty of Jeddah resolves the demarcations of the border between the Republic of Yemen and the Kingdom of Saudi Arabia.

May 2, 2001—A parcel bomb seriously injures a U.S. physician at a medical center at Khobar.

September 11, 2001—Suicide attacks in the United States kill 2,976. Fifteen of the 19 terrorists are said to be Saudi Arabian nationals. Operation Enduring Freedom is launched against the Taliban in Afghanistan.

October 6, 2001—A suicide bomber in al-Khobar kills two foreigners, including an American, and injures four.

October 11, 2001—A Molotov cocktail is thrown at a car carrying two Germans in Riyadh.

October 31, 2001—Saudi Arabian government freezes the assets of 66 persons and organizations believed to be sponsoring terrorism.

2002—Crown Prince 'Abdullah issues a plan for Arab peace with Israel. Fire in a girl's school kills 15 who are unable to escape due to interference by the HAIA (Hay'at al-Ma'ruf wa al-Nahaya 'an al-Munkar, or the Committee for the Promotion of Virtue and Prevention of Vice, known popularly as *mutawa'in*, or the religious police) because they did not want girls leaving the building without wearing their *abayas*. Three Saudi Arabian nationals are arrested in Morocco for planning an attack on ships in the Strait of Gibraltar. Then, seven Moroccans are arrested in connection with the same plot. Twenty are arrested in connection with a plot to attack Ra's Tanura.

April 2002—A demonstration by at least 2,000 in Dhahran against the Israeli attacks on the West Bank.

2003—The Saudi Arabian government recognizes poverty in the kingdom and begins a plan to address it.

February 5, 2003—Gunmen fire at a British employee of British Airways.

February 7, 2003—Eight gunmen fire on police in Riyadh, killing a Kuwaiti.

February 20, 2003—A gunman kills a British employee of an engineering company in Riyadh as he stops at a stoplight.

February 25, 2003—A bomb thrown at a Dammam McDonald's restaurant fails to explode.

March 2003—Operation Iraqi Freedom begins.

April 29, 2003—U.S. secretary of defense Donald Rumsfeld announces that the United States will withdraw military forces from Saudi Arabia except for a small training mission.

May 12, 2003—Terrorist bombings of three residential compounds that primarily housed foreigners in Riyadh kill 35 and wound 200. Later, the terrorists are identified as being part of al-Qa'ida fi Jazirat al-'Arabiyya (al-Qa'ida on the Arabian Peninsula, abbreviated as QAP or AQAP).

June 2003—First National (Meeting for Intellectual) Dialogue convenes.

July 21, 2003—Saudi Arabian security forces raid farms and houses in Riyadh and Qasim, capturing 16 suspected terrorists.

November 6, 2003—Two suspected terrorists blow themselves up in Mecca.

February 2004—244 pilgrims die in a stampede during the *hajj*.

April 21, 2004—Car bombing in Riyadh kills 5 and wounds 148. Council of Ministers issues an edict forbidding military and civil servants from protesting government policy.

May 1, 2004—Four gunmen attack the offices of ABB-Lummus (a contractor for ExxonMobil) in Yanbu, killing 5 (including 2 Americans, 2 Britons, and an Australian) and wounding 3 other employees. In a battle with security forces, 3 terrorists are killed and one is taken into custody; several police are killed and 19 wounded. Shooting also takes place at a Holiday Inn and a McDonald's. Terrorists also throw a pipe bomb at the International School in Yanbu.

May 22, 2004—Gunmen kill a German national in Riyadh.

May 30, 2004—Militants attack two housing compounds in Khobar (22 killed, 25 wounded).

June 2004—Third National Dialogue convenes and concerns Saudi Arabian women's issues.

June 6, 2004—Gunman kills a BBC journalist and wounds another.

June 8, 2004—Gunmen kill U.S. contractor for Vinnell Corporation in Riyadh.

June 12, 2004—Three militants kill a U.S. employee of Advanced Electronic Company in Riyadh. Militants abduct and later behead Lockheed employee Paul M. Johnson.

August 3, 2004—Militants kill an Irish civil engineer in his office in Riyadh.

September 15, 2004—Two gunmen kill a British employee of Marconi Communications in Riyadh.

September 26, 2004—Gunmen kill a French defense electronics worker in Jeddah.

December 2004—Two car bombs are set off in Riyadh. Security forces kill seven.

December 6, 2004—Attack on U.S. consulate in Jeddah kills five staff and five attackers.

February–April 2005—Nationwide municipal elections held.

August 2005—King Fahd dies. Crown Prince 'Abdullah becomes king.

September 2005—Clashes in Dammam result in deaths of five militants and three police officers.

November 2005—World Trade Organization agrees to admit Saudi Arabia as a member after 12 years of discussions.

January 2006—363 pilgrims die in a stampede during the stone-throwing ritual. Seventy-six pilgrims die in the collapse of a hostel in Mecca.

February 2006—Saudi Arabian forces foil attack at Abqaiq oil facility.

June 2006—Shoot-out between Saudi Arabian forces and militants kills six militants. Three Saudi Arabian detainees in Guantanamo commit suicide.

November 2007—A young woman known as the "Girl from Qatif," who was kidnapped and gang-raped by seven men (her male companion was also raped), is sentenced in the retrial of the case to six months in jail and a 200-stroke lashing, and her lawyer, Abd al-Rahman Lahem, had his license suspended. After international outcry over the case, King 'Abdullah issued a royal pardon for her. Founding session of the Allegiance Council.

February 4, 2007—French tourists are killed in a militant attack near the ruins of Mada'in Saleh.

April 2007—Large-scale terrorist plot is foiled and some 176 alleged terrorists are arrested.

May 30, 2007—A Saudi Arabian detainee in Guantanamo commits suicide.

July 2007—The HAIA are ordered not to detain suspects themselves but to turn them over to police.

November 2007—A gas-pipeline fire kills 40 workers.

December 2007—Another militant plot at the time of the *hajj* results in multiple arrests.

January 2008—Leader of al-Qa'ida in Yemen announces a new organization named al-Qa'ida fi Jazirat al-'Arabiyya, made up of his organization, the earlier one by the same name (AQAP) that had been based in Saudi Arabia, and the Yemen Soldiers Brigades.

February 2008—UN Special Rapporteur on Violence against Women, Yakin Ertürk, visits Saudi Arabia and makes recommendations concerning abuses against women.

April–July 2008—British High Court rules that UK government unlawfully dropped a corruption inquiry in December 2006 into the 1985 al-Yamamah defense agreement. The House of Lords reverses the court's decision.

July 2008—King 'Abdullah initiates the Interfaith Dialogue in Madrid.

December 2008—Oil prices drop from $147 to $40 per barrel.

February, April 2009—Interpol issues alerts for 85 men suspected of plotting attacks in Saudi Arabia. King 'Abdullah removes several conservatives from government—the head of the HAIA (religious police), the most senior judge, and a central bank head—and appoints the first woman deputy minister (of education), Norah al-Faiz. Saudi Arabian officials arrest 11 al-Qa'ida militants.

June 2009—U.S. president Barack Obama visits Saudi Arabia.

July 2009—A Saudi Arabian court issues verdicts for 330 on trial for terrorism, one of whom is sentenced to death. Prince Nayif ibn 'Abd al-'Aziz is named the second deputy prime minister. The *al-Nasr al-Sa'udi* ship is hijacked by Somali pirates, and the crew suffers from torture and exposure until arrangements are approved by the Saudi Arabian Monetary Agency (SAMA) to pay the ransom. Pirates have hijacked at least 83 ships in the Gulf of Aden since 2005.

August 2009—Saudi Arabian authorities arrest 44 with suspected ties to al-Qa'ida. Prince Mohammad bin Nayif, 27th deputy interior minister for security affairs, is lightly wounded in a suicide attack when a militant claimed he wanted to meet with him to discuss an amnesty.

September 2009—King Abdullah University for Science and Technology is inaugurated.

October 13, 2009—Two terrorists and one policeman are killed at a checkpoint.

November 2009—Following clashes at the Yemeni border, Saudi Arabian troops move in to hold a buffer zone in Yemen. The *Sirius Star*, a Saudi Aramco ship, is hijacked in the Indian Ocean. The worst floods in 27 years hit Jeddah, which has no sewage system, in late November. Official figures listed 122 deaths and 350 missing.

January 2010—Bombing attacks against Yemeni targets, described by government sources as the work of al-Qa'ida (meaning AQAP) but actually carried out against the Houthi rebels.

August 2010—Arrests of 44 militants.

September 2010—Thirteen women are permitted to attend 'Id al-Fitr festivities at the Prince 'Abd al-'Aziz ibn Musaid Sports Pavilion in Ha'il for the first time; a concrete boundary is erected to separate them from men.

October 2010—Militants operating in Qasim. U.S. officials confirm plans to sell about $60 billion in arms to Saudi Arabia.

November 2010—Arrests of 149 alleged members or conspirators with al-Qa'ida, including 124 Saudi Arabian nationals. Wikileaks reveals U.S. State Department officials' comments on Saudi Arabian leaders' desire for the United States to attack Iran and U.S. claims that Saudi Arabia sponsors global terrorism. King 'Abdullah spends two months in the United States undergoing back surgery and another month in Morocco for further recovery and physical therapy, returning to Saudi Arabia on February 23, 2011.

January 2011—Saudi Arabians must now apply for a license to start a blog, a personal website, or any form of e-publishing. They must be over 20 years of age, with a good high school or higher-education record. Tunisian revolutionaries, with the agreement of the army, overturn the regime of President Zine al-Abedin Bin Ali, who takes refuge in Saudi Arabia. In February, the Egyptian revolution of January 25th forces Hosni Mubarak to step down.

March 2011—A Saudi Revolution Facebook page set up in February calls for protests in March to demand a constitutional monarchy, legislative elections, and other changes. Protests take place in the eastern cities of Qatif and Dhahran, but heavy police presence discourages protesters in Riyadh, although one is arrested. On March 14, Saudi Arabian troops and police arrive in Bahrain to help the government suppress protests. On March 18, King 'Abdullah announced a package of cash grants, loans, raises, apartments and reforms meant to prevent political protests. He also announced 60,000 new jobs in the security forces.

May 1, 2011—U.S. Special Forces kill Osama bin Laden at a compound near Abbottabad, Pakistan.

May 15, 2011—Pakistani Taliban take credit for shooting Hassan Qahtani of the security department of the Saudi Arabian embassy in a revenge slaying in Karachi following the assassination of Osama bin Ladin.

May 23, 2011—Manal Sharif is arrested after she posts a video on the Internet showing herself driving in Khobar in protest of the ban on women drivers. Other women join in a driving protest.

Arabia's history predates Islam. Yet the Arabian Peninsula was the cradle of Islamic civilization, which radiated outward and was synthesized with other cultures and civilizations. Islam's roots in Arabian history and culture have influenced Muslims far beyond the boundaries of the peninsula. The modern nation of Saudi Arabia is named for the family of 'Abd al-'Aziz al-Sa'ud, known as Ibn Sa'ud, who recaptured Riyadh and led his warriors to establish a modern state in the twentieth century. The term *Arabia* derives from *'arab*, or Arab, which specifically meant the Arabic-speaking tribes and more generically those who had a nomadic lifestyle.

The Arabian Peninsula linked Africa and Asia through an isthmus at the Red Sea, traversed by various species. In ancient times, the climate was less arid, featuring grasslands and bush. At the end of the last Ice Age, some 15,000 years ago, the peninsula began to undergo desertification due to multiple causes, including changes in the currents of the oceans, mountain formation in the Middle East, monsoon patterns, and, since then, global warming. The first inhabitants of the Arabian Peninsula were Neolithic hunters and gatherers who left petroglyphs of animals on rocks throughout the country. As the area became increasingly drier, scientists believe that these people retreated to the oases and were succeeded by Semitic tribes who settled first in southern Arabia. The inscriptions and art on rock in Saudi Arabia are still being studied, for instance, at al-Jubbah, where settlements were already in place during the Middle Paleolithic period some 80,000 to 25,000 years ago (Harrigan 2002). By the middle of the third millennium BCE, the cultures of Arabia were in contact with Mesopotamia, and the west coast of Arabia was linked to Egypt (Bowersock in Hayes, ed., 1992, 19).

In the interior of Arabia, life changed sometime between 3000 and 2500 BCE when the camel was domesticated and could be employed as a pack animal on the trading routes, and when irrigation for agriculture began. Trade provided income for early merchants, while agriculture sustained others. The third major group were nomadic herders. The Arabian Peninsula was the crossroads of several ancient cultures. To its north, the Sumerian civilization developed in the Tigris-Euphrates Valley. The Sabaean Empire was located in what is today Yemen. Biblical references to the Queen of Sheba pertain to the ruler of this empire, but these are thought to be apocryphal, as Saba existed somewhat later in history. Saba was at its height from 900 BCE to 542 CE; it possessed a strong army and produced frankincense and myrrh. The Sabaeans constructed the Ma'rib Dam, which constrained the Adhannah River. The Romans referred to this area as Arabia Felix (happy Arabia) for its prosperity, contrasting with the perilous, dry Arabia Deserta of the interior. When the dam collapsed in 542, Saba's inhabitants began to leave the area.

Archaeologists believe the civilization of Dilmun was located on the islands of Bahrain and Falaika, and along the eastern coast of Arabia between Kuwait and Bahrain. Dilmun, referred to as the "place where the sun rises" or the "land of the living" in early texts, was thought to be the Garden of Eden and was identified as such in the "Archaic Texts" of Uruk-Warka in Iraq (from the late fourth millennium BCE), in Akkadian as "Tilmun", and also in texts from Ebla in Syria. A tablet found at Dilmun refers to it as Elysium, whose inhabitants supposedly possessed the secret of eternal youth. It is referred to in the Mesopotamian saga of Gilgamesh (Zuhur in Melis, ed., 2004). Dilmun thrived between 2100 and 1600 BCE and became a burial site, or necropolis. Thousands of burial mounds remain today (Wynbrandt 2004, 10). The northwestern walled towns of al-Tayma, al-'Ula, and al-Jawf, and an irrigation system at al-Qurayyah, were built by the later second millennium (Bowersock 1992,

Ruins of the ancient civilization of Dilmun in contemporary Bahrain. (Arthur Thévenart/ Corbis)

29). Other relics, such as the stone pillars, which are in line with the rising and setting sun at Rajajil, date to about 4000 BCE. Literary references to early peninsular civilizations called 'Ad and Thamud, and to their destruction, are found in the Qur'an. According to some accounts, Thamud was a tribe of giants, and like 'Ad, its people were early monotheists who wavered from that faith and were killed when they rejected a miracle shown to them by their prophet, Saleh. In the interior of the Arabian Peninsula was Qaryat al-Fau, the capital of the Kingdom of Kinda, an urban and literary society where texts in the South Arabian language, written in the Musnad script's separate, block-like letters (see Chapter 6, section on language), have been discovered (Bowersock 1992, 26; al-Ansary 1982).

The Nabataeans, Arabs who spoke Arabic but used an Arabicized form of Aramaic as their written script (Bowersock 1992, 28), were established in the northern Arabian Peninsula with their capitals at Petra and Bosra in Syria. The Nabataeans moved into the Hijaz, the Negev, and Transjordan from elsewhere in the peninsula and became vassals of Rome after the Romans conquered their allies, the Parthians. The Nabataeans constructed buildings and tombs at Mada'in Saleh in the Hijaz, a site that has recently been excavated further (Harrigan 2007), and minted their own coins. The Roman annexation of the Nabataeans' area is also preserved in the relics of the caravan city at the oasis of Palmyra in Syria (Tadmur). This stood as a buffer against the Sassanians, who moved in after the death of Queen Zenobia (Az-Zabba) of Palymra in 272. Marcus Julius Philippus, who had become the Roman emperor in 244 CE, was an Arab and is variously described as being from the Syrian Hawran or the Lajah (the volcanic area close to the Hawran). His actual name was Elagabalus (for the god al-Jabal) (Bowersock 1992, 32; Ruedy in Hayes, ed., 1992, 43).

The Arabian Peninsula was also invaded by the Ethiopians and was influenced by the struggle between the earlier Arabian rulers of southern Arabia and these invaders, along with the Arabs' Sassanian allies, and also by the struggle between the Romans, or Byzantines, and the Sassanians. The Ghassanid tribal confederation, made up of the Saleh and the Bani Ghassan, allied itself with Byzantium, whereas the Lakhmid confederation was allied with the Sassanians. The other important alliance was the linkage of the Nabataeans with the Romans, as already mentioned.

In 30 CE, the Roman Gallus led an army to conquer Arabia, but his army retreated two years later. The Sassanian king, Aradashir, invaded Arabia in 225 CE, and King Shapur II invaded in 310 CE. After that, the Sassanians relied on their clients, the Lakhmids, to battle the client tribes of the Byzantines, who ruled the eastern half of the Roman Empire. Around 300 CE, Christianity was established in Abyssinia (Ethiopia), and the Abyssinians invaded southern Arabia in 525 CE and then sent an army by sea to conquer Yemen, ruled by the Himyarites, the dominant group in South Arabia (110–525 CE). Following their conquest of Yemen and the Himyarites, the new Abyssinian rulers established Christianity there and tried to discourage the tribal pilgrimage to the Ka'ba (a holy site devoted to the worship of the local pantheon of gods and goddesses), aiming to divert it to Sana'a (this ancient fortified city is the capital of contemporary Yemen). The second Abyssinian (Negashi) viceroy, Abraha, declared war. Abraha, mounted on a giant white elephant, and his army marched on Mecca in 570 CE. The Meccans fled, but during the rule of Abraha's successor, the people in the area suffered. Eventually, the Himyarites convinced the Sassanians, a Persian dynasty, to invade Arabia. The Sassanians extended their rule through Yemen, Oman, and Hadramaut, although their ruler Maadi-Kareb was killed by the Abyssinians, who took over and then once again were defeated by a Sassanian invasion (Simon 1998, 87–89). During this period, the Quraysh tribe continued to dominate Mecca. While the Sassanians ruled the peninsula, Christianity, Judaism, and Arab polytheism were all permitted and practiced.

The Lebanese scholar Kamal Salibi has postulated that the biblical Judaic kingdom of Israel was actually located in Arabia, specifically in the Asir region, as evidenced by place-names in the ancient Hebrew language. As Jerusalem (in Palestine) is referred to as the "daughter of Jerusalem," this would imply the existence of a Jerusalem in Arabia (Salibi 1985, 2007). Salibi, a well-respected scholar, does not comment on the implications for the modern states of Israel and Saudi Arabia, although some of his readers and critics have done so. If correct, his thesis might explain the large numbers of Jews in the Arabian Peninsula, specifically in Yemen, generally thought to have migrated from the north. Certain scholars of the ancient period have also refuted Salibi's theories for other reasons, arguing that if the Assyrians conquered the ancient Hebrew state, there should be geohistorical evidence in neo-Assyrian sources supportive of Salibi's thesis; that evidence has not been found (Hjelm 2009).

Mecca had become a religious and trading center prior to the rise of Islam. Its religious significance in Islam is traced back to Ibrahim (Abraham), who, according to Islam, is the forefather of the Muslims and the Jews. Ibrahim brought his Egyptian slave and wife Hajar (Hagar) and his son Isma'il (Ishmael) to the area. When Ibrahim left them and returned to his wife Sarah, Hajar set out to look for water. She ran back and forth seven times between the two hills of Safa and Marwah, looking for water. Her thirsty son, Isma'il, scraped his foot on the land, and the water sprang forth that is known as the well of Zamzam, or simply Zamzam (Muslim pilgrims try to reenact Hajar's movements and to drink from Zamzam in the ritual known as *sa'y*.) The waters of Zamzam attracted nomads, who settled there. Ibrahim became a monotheist and a prophet according to both Judaism and Islam, and he rejected the polytheists' idols erected to their deities. He returned to the area where Mecca is now located and was instructed to build a shrine to the one God. According to one Muslim tradition, the Ka'ba, which houses the Black Stone at Mecca, was built by the first human, Adam; or (according to some other traditions), it was built by angels. Ibrahim and his son Isma'il rebuilt the Ka'ba on its original foundations. Violence was forbidden in a 20-mile area surrounding the Ka'ba, making it a sanctuary, or *haram*, for traveling pilgrims. However, early peoples forsook the one and only God and again worshipped stone idols representing the ancient divinities at the Ka'ba. In the pre-Islamic era, the pilgrimage to the Ka'ba was held in the month of Dhu al-Hija. Fighting was forbidden then; in fact, it was prohibited during three sacred months, including the month of Ramadan.

The Prophet of Islam, Muhammad ibn 'Abdullah ibn 'Abd al-Mutallib, was born in 670 CE, and descended from the clan of Hashim of the Quraysh. The Quraysh tribe arrived in Mecca sometime in the fifth century and came to control the area and its pilgrimage following their leader Qusay's conquest of the region. Trade routes traversed the Arabian Peninsula, connecting it to Syria in the north and Mesopotamia. The population consisted of nomadic and settled peoples, the *badu* and the *hadhar*. The *badu* often engaged in warfare over their rights to obtain water for their herds or for territorial control. The *hadhar* concluded treaties to prevent the *badu* raids, paying them off in produce. The Arab tribes in the Hijaz, Saudi Arabia's western province, were primarily polytheistic, although some had converted to Judaism and to Christianity. As well, there were individuals identified by the word *hanif*, who preached the worship of one God only.

THE RISE OF ISLAM

The Qur'an, the holy text of Islam, was revealed to Muhammad ibn 'Abdullah, the prophet of Islam, and the seal of prophecy (meaning that he bore the final divine message). His father had died before his birth, and his mother died when he was a young child. He traveled with his uncle along the trade routes. Muhammad was later employed by a wealthy woman, Khadija, and handled her caravans and affairs. She married him when he was about 25 years old; she was 15 years his senior. Years later, when he had retreated to meditate on Mount Hira, a common custom of the men of Mecca, he received an oral revelation delivered by the angel Gabriel while meditating. He feared initially that this experience signaled the onset of madness, but Khadija convinced him otherwise and became his first convert to Islam, supporting his mission to recite and spread these revelations publicly, which he began to do in 613. The revelations called for worshipping the one God, Allah, exclusively; ending the practice of female infanticide and immoral customs; and living according to a code of social justice and reverence for Allah.

As Muhammad's followers increased in Mecca, the leaders of the Quraysh grew angry because the strict monotheism he preached threatened their dominance and the lucrative pilgrimage to the Ka'ba. The Meccans persecuted the early Muslims (literally, "those who submit to Allah"), who had no family protectors highly placed among the Quraysh. Muhammad sent some of his followers to Ethiopia for their safety.

When Muhammad's uncle, Abu Talib, died in 619, Muhammad became more vulnerable to persecution or even death at the hands of the Quraysh leaders. He and his followers emigrated from Mecca in 622 CE in the Hijrah (emigration), which is counted as the first year in the Muslim calendar, to the oasis of Yathrib. The people of Yathrib had invited him to come there to help settle the battles between those allied with the warring tribes of al-Khazraj and al-'Aws, as they could not resolve the dispute themselves. Yathrib came to be called Madinat al-Nabi (the city of the Prophet), known as Medina. At Medina, Muhammad led the Muslims religiously and politically, as a lawmaker and arbiter, and in a series of wars against the Meccans and their tribal allies. He continued to receive revelations, which were later collected into the Qur'an, Islam's holy book. The Ansar (helpers), Medinan nonemigrants, pledged to help the Muslims defend the city together with the *muhajirun* (emigrants) against the Quraysh. Also in Medina were three Jewish tribes: the Banu Qaynuqa,

Banu al-Nadir, and Banu Qurayza. A commonly held view is that the Jews of the Hijaz traveled there following their expulsion from the Holy Land by the Romans more than 500 years previously, in contrast with Salibi's thesis mentioned earlier.

Initially, Muhammad hoped the Jews of Medina would welcome his message. Accounts show that his prophecy was foretold by certain figures and that the two monotheistic traditions shared many principles, both ethical and symbolic. A document known as the Treaty or Constitution of Medina specified that the Muslims—emigrants and Ansar—as well as the Jews would be loyal and engage in war together, and that the Jews would maintain their religion and the Muslims theirs (Guillaume 1955, 231–235). Nonetheless, the Jewish religious leaders rejected Muhammad and his claim to prophecy according to Ibn Ishaq (Muhammad ibn Ishaq ibn Yasar ibn Khiyar, ca. 704–767 CE; Guillaume 1955, 242). Jewish-Muslim relations disintegrated primarily due to political tensions. The Meccans were determined to defeat the Muslims at Medina, and the Jewish tribes conspired with them. In the spring of 624, the Meccans learned that the Muslims planned to raid a caravan led by Abu Sufyan. Abu Sufyan was among the Prophet Muhammad's fiercest opponents in Mecca and was responsible for the initial extreme cruelty toward and attacks on Muslims and for their exile.

At this time, the Qur'anic revelations ordered the Muslims to engage in jihad (struggle) "on the path of God" yet also counseled peace when possible (Aboul-Enein and Zuhur 2004). The ensuing Battle of Badr, between a Meccan army of 1,000 men and a force of only 313 *sahaba,* other *muhajirun* (emigrants) and Ansar of Medina,

Depiction of a scene in the Battle of Badr (624 CE) as rendered by a Persian painter. (Bilkent University)

was a great victory for the Muslims. Under Muhammad's leadership, the Muslims also fought in the Battle of Uhud (625) and the Battle of the Ditch (627), a siege of Medina.

The Prophet Muhammad expelled the Banu Qaynuqa in response to a series of events. These included an incident in which a Jewish man tripped a Muslim woman or tore her garments so that her private parts showed. He was killed in an ensuing melée. Then, in revenge, a Muslim was killed by the Jewish crowd. When the Prophet Muhammad went to ask for the blood money (*dhiyya*, the payment due according to '*urf*, customary law) for the life of the Muslim man from the tribe who had killed him, the tribe stalled. As the tribesmen stalled and delayed, they planned to assassinate the Prophet. Another issue was an attempted poisoning of Muhammad and the treachery of a Jewish poet who went to meet with the Quraysh and incited them to war with Muhammad (through his poetry). After this period of friction, Muhammad expelled the Banu al-Nadir (Ibn Ishaq, 1964, 2000 or 2009 437–439). The third tribe, the Banu Qurayza, allied themselves with the Meccans just prior to the Battle of the Ditch. Muhammad tried to communicate with the Banu Qurayza to keep them on his side but to no avail. Following the siege of Medina, the Meccans retreated, leaving the Banu Qurayza on their own. Their punishment was put to an arbiter who had been fatally wounded. The arbiter demanded revenge, ruling that all the men were to be killed and the women and children enslaved. After this, war was waged on the Jews of Khaybar in 628, although they were permitted to remain there and pay a tax in crops from their lands. Muhammad's Jewish wife, Safiyya, a captive of the battle of Khaybar, retained privileges for her family. Some challenge the accounts given by Ibn Ishaq via others writing a century or more later (the Muslim historian Muhammad ibn Jarir al-Tabari [d. 923] also gives his version of Ibn Ishaq's biography), in part because one source was interviews with the descendants of those massacred by the Muslims, who are thought to have been embittered by these events. Also, Ibn Ishaq's account is second-hand through the work of Abu Muhammad 'Abd al-Malik ibn Hisham, known as Ibn Hisham (d. 833), who edited and recensed Ibn Ishaq's biography or *sira* of the Prophet Muhammad (and/or Tabari; Guillaume marks the sections from Tabari with a T, which he appends to Ibn Hisham's account). The Prophet Muhammad's agreement with the Jews was overturned by the caliph 'Umar, who expelled the Jews from the Hijaz, but accounts differ on their dispersal, and whether it was complete. Some indicated that the Jews of Khaybar relocated to Jericho and later Tiberias, or to Kufa (probably an incorrect thesis), and some sources indicated that at least some Jews remained in the area (Bornstein-Makovetsky 2008 [based on Braslavi's stance in the publication's first edition]; Pirenne 1958, 33, 76, 215ff).

In Medina, Muslim ritual and practice was established; whereas the Muslims had initially prayed toward Jerusalem, their *qibla* (prayer direction) shifted to Mecca (Ibn Ishaq, 2000, 258). A chanter gave the call to prayer (*adhan*), in contrast to the Christian ringing of bells (and the Jews' use of the ram's horn). The first *mu'adhdhin* was Bilal, an Ethiopian born in Mecca, a former slave freed by Abu Bakr (see the following) and one of the *sahaba* (Companions of the Prophet) considered extremely loyal to Muhammad and his nephew 'Ali ibn Abu Talib. Bilal possessed a beautiful voice.

After the Meccans broke the truce of Hudaybiyya they had previously signed with the Muslims, the latter marched on them and retook Mecca. Muhammad ordered the cleansing and removal of the idols from the Ka'ba. After the capture of Mecca in 630, Abu Sufyan, the Muslims' most vociferous foe, converted to Islam. By that time, many other tribes and groups had recognized Muslim authority or converted to Islam. In 632, Muhammad performed the *hajj* (pilgrimage) to Mecca. Islam thereafter spread in all directions, as the Muslim armies fought and defeated the Sassanians, the allies of the Eastern Roman Empire, and moved northward and westward into Egypt.

MUSLIM DYNASTIES

The Prophet Muhammad died in 632. By then, nearly the entire Arabian Peninsula recognized Muslim authority. A council of leaders in Medina met to choose a successor to the Prophet, who was known as the *khalifa* (caliph; literally, "successor" [of the Prophet]). They could not agree on a candidate. Some supported a leader from the powerful house of Ummayya from within the Quraysh clan, while others preferred 'Ali ibn Abu Talib, the Prophet's cousin and son-in-law, because he was the closest male relative of the Prophet, who had no living sons. The council settled instead on Abu Bakr al-Siddiq, Muhammad's father-in-law, who ruled as caliph until his death in 634. During this period, several tribes renounced Islam, and the Muslims battled and defeated them in the Wars of Ridda (apostasy). The caliph 'Umar succeeded Abu Bakr and ruled until 644, a period of military victories over Damascus and Jerusalem, as well as triumph over the Sassanians in the Battle of Nahavand in 641. 'Umar was killed by a Persian Christian captive. The next caliph, 'Uthman, further expanded the Muslim Empire and was responsible for the recension and arrangement of the Qur'an. Caliph 'Uthman became unpopular with some of his subjects. Accused of nepotism, he was murdered by a group led by Muhammad ibn Abu Bakr. 'Ali ibn Abu Talib was then named the caliph in Medina, although his rule was contested by Mu'awiyya, governor of Syria and cousin to 'Uthman. 'Uthman's murderers had been supporters of 'Ali, whereas the Prophet Muhammad's wife 'A'isha opposed 'Ali. This issue of succession ignited the first Muslim civil war, or *fitnah*, from 656 to 661. Eventually, the two sides agreed to arbitration, but when the tribunal decided neither should rule, 'Ali refused to abide by that decision and assumed the office of caliph in Kufa in southern Iraq. Meanwhile, Mu'awiyya declared himself caliph in 661, ruling over a much larger swath of territory than did 'Ali. One group, the Khawarij, or seceders, had supported 'Ali, but they contended that he had been mistaken to agree to arbitration in the first place, and one of them assassinated 'Ali in 662. Mu'awiyya, who established the Ummayyad Caliphate, eventually controlled the Holy Cities of Mecca and Medina and, with his main power base in Syria, insisted on recognition of his designated successor.

This shifted the center of Muslim imperial power away from the Arabian Peninsula to the Fertile Crescent region: first to Syria and later, under the Abbasid caliphs, to Baghdad. However, as a result of the conflicts in the Ummayyad period, regionally and religiously motivated movements arose in Arabia. The Khawarij (Kharijite) movement, which had espoused strong opposition to or death for those who failed to uphold the Prophet's teachings, was adopted in Yamama in 680, when the Khariji leader Najda bin 'Amr of the Banu Hanifa drove out the Ummayyad officials (al-Askar 2002, x, 133). However, this Khariji state collapsed about 10 years later, although the sect survived on the coast of the Arabian Gulf, evolving, somewhat moderated, into the Ibadi sect of Islam (Smyth in Metz, ed., 1993, 11–12).

When Mu'awiyya died in 680, his son Yazid claimed the caliphate. His succession was contested by Husayn, the son of 'Ali, who went from Medina to Iraq, where he had more support, in order to organize his followers, known in English as the 'Alids and later as the Shi'a Muslims (Shi'at 'Ali, or party of 'Ali). An Ummayyad army massacred Husayn and 70 of his followers at Karbala in 680. This event is commemorated by today's Shi'a Muslims as the religious holiday of 'Ashura on the 10th day of the month of Muharram. When Husayn was killed, a revolt began in Medina, which Yazid suppressed. Then he besieged Mecca. Yazid died during this siege, and his son, Mu'awiyya II, died only 40 days later.

Two claimants to the Ummayyad Caliphate arose. One of them, 'Abdullah ibn Zubayr, established his rule in Mecca. The Arabs had long been divided between the Qays tribal confederation and the Kalb confederation. Their enmities remained a part of politics during the Muslim expansion. In this case, the Qays backed Ibn Zubayr; however, the Kalb tribal confederation supported the other claimant, Marwan ibn al-Hakam (622–685). The Kalb prevailed, and Marwan was named caliph in 684, solidifying control of the Ummayyad Caliphate in other new areas of conquest. Nevertheless, Ibn Zubayr continued to rule in Arabia, and he defeated another rebel in Iraq, al-Mukhtar ibn Abi 'Ubayd al-Thaqafi (622–687). Al-Mukhtar was born in Ta'if, grew up in Medina under the Prophet Muhammad's rule, and sought to avenge Husayn ibn 'Ali until he was killed. Marwan's son, 'Abd al-Malik, finally defeated Ibn Zubayr at Mecca, reportedly destroying the Ka'ba. As caliph, 'Abd al-Malik made Arabic the official language of the empire and built the Dome of the Rock and rebuilt the al-Aqsa mosque in Jerusalem (al-Haram al-Sharif), intending to siphon away pilgrimage traffic to Mecca. Under 'Abd al-Malik and Walid I (r. 705–715), the Islamic conquests resumed; parts of Egypt were reconquered, and Carthage was taken. The Muslim armies crossed the Straits of Gibraltar in 711 and had conquered Spain by 716. Under the caliph Hisham (r. 724–743), the Muslim armies reached Tours in what is now France. To the east, the Muslim armies reached the Indus River by 710.

The Ummayyad caliphs were eventually overthrown by the Abbasids, followers of a descendant of the Prophet Muhammad's uncle. The Abbasid Caliphate lasted in name from 750 to 1258 CE. However, the Abbasid Caliphate was limited in practice by decentralization and the growing power of its own army commanders, resulting in the growth of independent dynasties from about the 10th century. In addition, the Abbasids faced serious economic problems and two invasions by Mongol armies. The Abbasids built their own new capital at Baghdad. Medina remained important as a center of Islamic learning and jurisprudence for some time. The various dynasties coterminous with the Abbasids sought to show their authority over the pilgrimage to and local rulers of Mecca. This was true of the Fatimid dynasty, ruling from Egypt, which influenced, or controlled, the Hijaz in western Arabia until its demise.

LATER MUSLIM DYNASTIES AND THE ARABIAN REGION

During the Crusades, a period when European leaders battled to establish and hold small states in the Near East, Salah al-Din al-Ayyubi (known as Saladin in the West), the great Muslim general, who was half Kurdish, reestablished Muslim rule throughout historic Syria and farther down into the Sinai Peninsula and Egypt. He replaced the governor of Mecca with his brother. However, Reynald de Châtillon, the lord of Oultrejourdan, one of the previously mentioned small Crusader states, moved into the Hijaz in 1182 and attacked an Arab caravan. Reynald then ordered ships to be carried overland from the Dead Sea to the Gulf of Aqaba. With a force of 1,000 men, he attacked Muslim pilgrims traveling by ship along the Red Sea coast, thus threatening Mecca and Medina and their Muslim supervision. This was a great offense to Salah al-Din, who canceled his truce with the Crusaders. Without the truce, Reynald was impelled to withdraw from the Hijaz in order to defend Oultrejourdan (Sabini 1981, 18–19), thus removing the threat to the Holy Cities of Mecca and Medina.

Salah al-Din and his descendants, the Ayyubids, reigned over the Holy Cities from Egypt. Local leaders who claimed descent from the Prophet, known as the *ashraf* (singular, *sharif*), competed with each other to obtain local control over the Hijaz. The ruler of Yanbu, Sharif Qitada, sent forces to Mecca in 1201, while that city's *amir* (prince, or leader) was making the *'umrah* (the lesser pilgrimage; it is briefer than the rites of the *hajj* and may be performed at other times of the year). He and his descendants held authority over the Holy Cities thereafter, although they acknowledged foreign rulers as needed, first acquiescing to the rulers of Cairo and later the Ottomans. Over time, the Ayyubids were replaced in Egypt by the Mamluk ruling dynasties. The Mamluks maintained a representative in Mecca and, like the *ashraf*, were responsible for ensuring that the Holy Cities were accessible to the pilgrims. The Hijaz benefited from the trade and cultural diversity of the pilgrim traffic.

The Ottoman Turks fought against and defeated the Mamluk armies in Egypt and Syria in 1517 during the reign of the Ottoman sultan Selim I (1513–1520). Selim, known as the Grim, claimed to be the protector of the Holy Cities of Mecca and Medina, and like other important Muslim rulers, his authority was acknowledged by the mentioning of his name in the Friday public prayers. The grand *sharif* (*sharif* being the title given at that time to the *ashraf*, or descendants of the Prophet, who were guardians of the Holy Cities) dispatched his son to give Selim the keys to the Ka'ba.

The Ottomans stationed troops in the Hijaz and refurbished the Holy Cities. The Ottomans wanted greater control over the Arabian Peninsula and attempted to attain it through the *ashraf*. They appointed their own *ashraf* to that end. After conquering Baghdad in 1534, the Ottomans were able to move into and occupy Hasa,

Al-Musmak Fort in Riyadh, Saudi Arabia, 2009. (Dreamstime.com)

installing their own governor, Fatih Pasha, after 1591 (Wynbrandt 2004, 101–102); they thereby gained more control over eastern Arabia.

In the 15th and 16th centuries, the Portuguese attacked the Arabian coastline, landed there, and built their own fortresses. At that time, influenced by the philosophy of the Inquisition, they considered the Arabs to be heretics. The Ottomans were supposed to defend the peninsula against such conquests. Some adventurers, or captives, called *renegados*, found their way to the Arabian Peninsula. One such figure was Ludovico de Varthema, who described the Hijaz, Khaybar, the Holy Cities, and the pilgrimage (Sabini 1981, 24–25). The Portuguese (like the English) became interested in the goods and possibilities of the East and the Arabian Peninsula.

Frequently, friction arose between the indigenous and foreign powers in the Hijaz. For instance, because the Ottoman troops were often paid late, they revolted in Mecca and Medina in 1631 after returning from a defeat in Yemen, looting the shops and attacking local residents. It has been observed that over the years, thanks to the pilgrimage and the connection of Muslim rulers to it, the Hijaz was always more influenced by external forces than was Najd, to the east. The Hijaz represented a larger economy, again because of the pilgrimage, but it was more vulnerable to foreign or syncretic influence. That became a significant rationale for the political and religious reform movement that was to develop from the teachings of the Najdi reformer Muhammad ibn ʿAbd al-Wahhab.

MUHAMMAD IBN 'ABD AL-WAHHAB
AND THE FIRST SA'UDI STATE

Muhammad ibn 'Abd al-Wahhab (1702–1792), who was born in 'Uyaynah in 1702 or 1703, came from a distinguished family of Hanbali religious scholars and judges (following the religious "school" or teachings of Ahmad ibn Hanbal al-Shaybani) and was a descendant of the Prophet Muhammad (de Corancez 1995, 5). His father was the *qadi* (judge) of 'Uyaynah. He had to leave his hometown after local leaders became concerned with his public preachings and admonishments to strive for a true *tawhid*, or absolute monotheism. He studied in Medina, with Shaykh 'Abdullah ibn Ibrahim ibn Sayf and Shaykh Muhammad Hayat al-Sindi. These two scholars emphasized the content of hadith, *ijtihad*, and the need for social reform, and they were admirers of Taqi al-Din ibn Ahmad Ibn Taymiyya's (1263–1328) work (Voll 1975, 32–39). Ibn Taymiyya, a scholar and teacher of Hanbali law, lived during the Mongol attacks on the Mamluks and was famous for supporting jihad against them since they followed their own legal code, the *yasa*, and not *shari'ah*. He was also known for his opposition to *kalam*, rational, philosophical argumentation of points of religion, and for his theological positions, including opposition to the belief in the intercession (*shafa'*) of saints and holy figures. 'Abd al-Wahhab is often accused of establishing an extreme sect of Islam and of being a devotee of Ibn Taymiyya; however, at least one scholar, Natana Delong-Bas (2004, 17–21), has countered that Ibn Taymiyya would have been but one of the sources 'Abd al-Wahhab read. Even more important, his mission was a reform movement rather than the formation of a new sect (Commins 2006; de Corancez 1995, 5). 'Abd al-Wahhab also traveled to Basra to study. His preaching against wrongful rituals may derive instead from that experience (Commins 2006, 12). He was, according to the chroniclers who supported the Wahhabi reform movement, exiled from Basra and struggled in the summer heat to reach al-Zubayr; he then returned to Huraymila, his father's home (Ibn Ghannam 1961). There he wrote his seminal essay, *Kitab al-Tawhid*, which attacked Muslim practices he considered heretical or polytheistic. His ideas spread widely, but he refrained from preaching until after his father's death in 1740 (Delong-Bas 2004, 22–23). From these ideas arose the reform movement, known outside of Saudi Arabia as Wahhabiyya (Wahhabism), which owes its importance to the successful political fortunes of the Sa'udi family. Information about 'Abd al-Wahhab's life and reform movement came from his supporters, Husayn ibn Ghannam (d. 1810) and 'Uthman ibn Bishr (d. 1873) (Ibn Ghannam 1381; Ibn Bishr, n.d.; also see Facey 1997, 33–45). He denounced sexual immorality and held that syncretic practices such as tomb or grave visitation, occasions when Muslims prayed for their holy men or women to intercede on their behalf with Allah, and also the traditions of other Islamic sects were innovations, or *bid'a*. These innovations lacked precedents in the tradition of the first Islamic generations. While others had protested against syncretism in Islam, 'Abd al-Wahhab further argued that these practices or beliefs were sinful and had to be punished because they granted importance to ideas or persons other than the Qur'an and Allah and so constituted *shirk* (polytheism). His rulings were strict, usually classical interpretations of the *shari'ah* (it is not true, as some claim, that the followers of 'Abd al-Wahhab reject all previous interpretations and schools of legal thought, only that they consider the possibility of creating new positions in *fiqh*, or jurisprudence, where necessary), and he called for active, militant jihad, fighting of Islam's enemies. His views gained admirers and detractors; his followers called themselves *muwahiddun* (monotheists). His enemies and those outside of his movement dubbed them Wahhabis.

'Abd al-Wahhab began a preaching campaign in support of the ruler of al-'Uyaynah, 'Uthman ibn Hamid ibn Mu'ammar, whose aunt 'Abd al-Wahhab married. 'Abd al-Wahhab then initiated a campaign of chopping down trees considered sacred by the locals. He then destroyed a monument over the tomb of Zayd ibn al-Khattab, a Companion of the Prophet Muhammad. He condemned a woman who admitted committing adultery to death by stoning. In response to his growing appeal in the area, the religious scholars attacked him, attempting to defame him. His protector, Ibn Mu'ammar, was forced to expel him, so he traveled to the town of Dir'iyyah (Delong-Bas 2004, 24–35). After the wife of Muhammad ibn Sa'ud, the leader of the al-Sa'ud tribe and ruler of Dir'iyyah, became acquainted with 'Abd al-Wahhab's ideas, Ibn Sa'ud invited him to become that town's *qadi* in 1744. The two swore an oath that they would strive to create an Islamic state (Smyth in Metz, ed., 1993, 15; al-Tihami in al-Sammari, ed., 2010). This alliance of the al-Sa'ud and 'Abd al-Wahhab's family, later known as the al-Shaykh, has endured from the first Sa'udi realm until today.

Al-Sa'ud began to expand his territory soon after 'Abd al-Wahhab's arrival in Dir'iyyah. He challenged other tribes in Najd, as his forces called for an end to popular syncretic and Shi'a observances. They attacked the town of Riyadh, farther into Najd. In 1764, the lords of Hasa and Najran mounted a combined resistance to the Sa'udi warriors, but the leaders from Najran decided to come to terms with al-Sa'ud. Ibn Sa'ud died in 1865 and was succeeded by his son 'Abd al-'Aziz (r. 1765–1803). 'Abd al-'Aziz would send an emissary to the tribes carrying a Qur'an and a sword, and his message, according to de Corancez (1995, 9), read:

> Abd el Aziz to the tribe of ***. Hail! Your duty is to believe in the book I send you. Do not be like the idolatrous Turks, who give God a human intermediary. If you are true believers, you shall be saved; otherwise, I shall wage war on you.

Under his command, the Sa'udi-Wahhabi forces captured Qatif, and then Hasa and Bahrain, and forced the sultan of Muscat to pay tribute. They reached the Rub' al-Khali (the Empty Quarter) and then tried moving into Hadhramaut without success. Tribes in Asir joined them, and they took the Tihamah lowlands and points on the coast of Yemen. They also moved to the north through the Iraqi and Syrian deserts and sacked Karbala with its important shrine to Husayn ibn 'Ali in 1801 (Safran 1985, 10–11). That shrine was guarded by a *mutasallim* (assistant governor) sent by the pasha of Baghdad. The slaughter of all the townsmen and pregnant women in the town, and the plunder of the shrine, greatly disturbed the authorities in Baghdad and Fath 'Ali, shah of Persia (de Corancez 1995, 21). The Sa'udi-Wahhabi forces then began advancing toward the cities of Mecca and Medina to the west. Those resisting them at the town of Ta'if were massacred in 1802. Mecca surrendered in 1803, although not Jeddah, which withstood a siege (de Corancez 1995, 29–30). Sharif Ghalib retook Mecca when 'Abd al-'Aziz retreated. The Sa'udi-Wahhabi forces had attacked shrines and images in Mecca and rejected the pilgrims from Egypt and Syria, calling them idol worshipers. Meanwhile, 'Abd al-'Aziz was assassinated by a Persian who sought revenge for the massacre of his sons in Karbala.

The Sa'udi unification of rule in the Arabian Peninsula under the banner of 'Abd al-Wahhab's followers, with its emblem of the *shahada*, or proclamation of the faith, challenged the authority of the Ottoman Empire, whose sultan obtained tribute from the peninsula, and rights over the Holy Cities. However, the Ottomans were too militarily weak to mount a campaign to the Hijaz, so they called on Muhammad 'Ali Pasha, their commander and viceroy in Egypt.

Muhammad 'Ali Pasha sent a force to the peninsula under his son Tusun in 1816, and these troops gained Mecca and Medina. The al-Sa'ud moved back to Najd. Then, Muhammad 'Ali sent forces to defeat them conclusively, a process that took two years before al-Dir'iyyah surrendered in 1818. Muhammad 'Ali sought recognition from the Ottoman Porte that he and his descendants would be permanent rulers of Egypt and so involved himself in other reconquests of Ottoman territories, notably Syria. The Egyptian forces sent several of the al-Sa'ud family into exile and forced 'Abdullah ibn Sa'ud ibn Muhammad to go to Istanbul, where he was executed. They destroyed the settlement of Dir'iyyah, sent troops to different parts of the peninsula, and set up a garrison at al-Qatif. In the Hijaz, they reestablished the rule of the *ashraf*, who had exercised authority over Mecca and the surrounding area prior to the Sa'udi-Wahhabi victory there.

THE SECOND SA'UDI REALM (1824–1891)

Muhammad 'Ali Pasha believed his Egyptian forces had completely routed the Sa'udis and withdrew from Najd. However, an escaped member of the Sa'udi family, Turki ibn 'Abdullah, who hid for two years, recaptured al-Dir'iyyah in 1821, then Riyadh and the rest of Najd by 1824, ruling until 1834. This revival owed much to the tenacity of tribal loyalties, aptly manipulated by the al-Sa'ud leadership. Their followers demonstrated their dedication to 'Abd al-Wahhab's teachings as well. By acknowledging the Sa'udi ruler as imam, they collected the tribute demanded by Islam and described their forays as jihads (Smyth in Metz, ed., 1993, 18).

Muhammad 'Ali and the succeeding khedives of Egypt could not retake the peninsula and were defeated in 1827 by British and French forces. However, they instigated another member of the Sa'ud family, Mishari, to assassinate Turki in 1834. Mishari was then defeated by Faysal ibn Turki. He then confronted opposition from the Banu Khalid, and the rulers of Bahrain and Qatar refused to recognize the Sa'udis. The Ottomans, backed by the Egyptians, continued to press for income, which they received through the *ashraf*. The Egyptians also tried to manipulate the al-Sa'ud against each other, doing so successfully when they marched on Najd in 1836 and supported a pretender, Khalid, a cousin of Faysal, and eventually shipped Faysal off to Cairo. The Egyptians' hopes of firmly ruling the peninsula were dashed by the Europeans, who in 1839 forced Muhammad 'Ali to agree to hereditary rule solely of Egypt.

Khalid was edged out by 'Abdullah ibn Thunayyan from the family of Muhammad ibn Sa'ud, who became the imam of Riyadh but was then jailed and poisoned by Faysal ibn Turki, who had returned from Egypt. Faysal then reigned from 1843 to 1865 over a smaller area than the first Sa'udi "kingdom" but this area was more cohesive and accepted by other forces and more flexible (Safran 1985, 16). Faysal unsuccessfully attempted to convince the British to ally with him against the Ottomans, and he then tried to advance into Oman, but the British bombarded Dammam and Hofuf in response. This second Sa'udi realm came to an end due to quarrels between Faysal's heirs, 'Abdullah and Sa'ud. The Ottomans were able to claim the province of Hasa in 1871, imprisoning 'Abdullah, who then escaped but had to recognize Turkish authority over the Eastern Province. After losing control of Asir, and numerous changes in authority between these brothers and their other two brothers, 'Abd al-Rahman and Muhammad, Muhammad ibn Rashid (originally from Ha'il) sent a force against Riyadh to free 'Abdullah and then set up a Rashidi governor there. The Rashidi governor quelled an attempt by the nephews of 'Abdullah to raid Kharj in 1888. Nevertheless, Ibn Rashid dismissed that governor (Salim ibn Subhan) and appointed 'Abd al-Rahman al-Sa'ud in his place, but 'Abd al-Rahman revolted in 1890. Unable to withstand a siege of Riyadh by Ibn Rashid, 'Abd al-Rahman was confirmed governor of Riyadh and some nearby areas (but was not independent of Ibn Rashid). In a second revolt, Ibn Rashid crushed the rebels in 1891 in the battle of Mulayda, and 'Abd al-Rahman fled to the desert and eventually to Kuwait.

In the next resurgence of the al-Sa'ud family, some historians observe that the British, concerned over their own dominance in the Persian Gulf, accommodated the al-Sa'ud, even while supporting other allies like the al-Rashid family and the *sharif* of Mecca.

'ABD AL-'AZIZ (IBN SA'UD) AND THE FORGING OF SAUDI ARABIA

The creation of Saudi Arabia is attributed to the determination and leadership of Ibn Sa'ud, or 'Abd al-'Aziz 'Abd al-Rahman Faysal al-Sa'ud (ca. 1876–1951), the son of 'Abd al Rahman and the first king of Saudi Arabia. No record of 'Abd al-'Aziz's birth was kept. Some historians estimate it occurred 1876, while others proffer 1880 or 1882, in Riyadh, probably on November 26 (Hamza). His mother was Sara bint Ahmad al-Sudayri, the daughter of a powerful tribal leader. While he was a boy, his family, the rulers of Riyadh in the central province of Najd, fled from their rivals, the al-Rashid family, in 1891. His family spent about two years with the Murrah bedouin at Yabrin, a period that acquainted 'Abd al-'Aziz with the lifestyle, language, and skills of the bedouin. In 1894 or 1895, the al-Sa'ud clan took refuge in Kuwait.

'Abd al-'Aziz married for the first time when he was 16 or 17. At that point, the al-Sa'ud were so poor they could hold his wedding only when its costs were covered by a friendly merchant. He later married many times and sired at least 43 sons and

King 'Abd al-'Aziz ibn 'Abd al-Rahman Faysal al-Sa'ud in 1949. Founder and first king of Saudi Arabia from 1932–1953, he was also known as Ibn Sa'ud. (Library of Congress)

20 daughters. His sons succeeded him as the kings of modern Saudi Arabia, and his other family members comprise such a large group with special privileges that they are like an entire elite social class rather than merely a family.

In 'Abd al-'Aziz's youth, Arabia was not united. The Hashemite (Hashimite) family, the sons of Sharif Husayn of Mecca, came to control the Hijaz, to the west, and the al-Rashid family battled the Sa'uds in their original Najdi homelands. The Mubarak family of Kuwait fought the al-Rashid near Ha'il, along with their bedouin allies and the al-Sa'ud, in 1901. The al-Rashid were involved in plans to counterattack Mubarak when the young 'Abd al-'Aziz took advantage of their distraction to set out for Riyadh with a force of only 40 companions. That force swelled to 200, then decreased to about 60, who rode off with him into the Rub' al-Khali (the Empty Quarter) during Ramadan so that his enemies would think they had disappeared. He then rode back to Riyadh and attacked the Rashidi governor at the Musmak fortress, which served as the city's garrison, thereby recapturing Riyadh in January 1902.

'Abd al-'Aziz (who became known internationally as Ibn Sa'ud) and his tribal warriors, the Ikhwan (literally, "the Brothers" or "Brethren"), then embarked on a series of conquests to regain his family's territory, beginning with the territory of Najd.

He combined military advances with negotiations and also made alliances with key tribes and settled clans through marriages. By 1913, Ibn Sa'ud was able to focus farther east and pushed the Ottomans from al-Hasa Province. He aimed to make himself a key ally of the British, something that empire needed in order to carry out their military plans in Mesopotamia during World War I. The British signed a treaty of friendship with Ibn Sa'ud on December 26, 1915, recognizing him as the ruler of Najd and its dependent territories. The British agreed to protect him and began paying him an annual subsidy of £5,000 in gold and money for arms, which he needed badly at that time. For his part, Ibn Sa'ud agreed he would not oppose the British government in a war or attack the other Gulf sheikhdoms the British were supporting.

Sultan Abdulhamid of the Ottoman Empire had built a railway line into the Hijaz, connecting Damascus and Medina, which was inaugurated in that Holy City on September 1, 1908. This had been considered a difficult, and nearly impossible, task, yet it began in 1900 and reached Maan in 1904 (Nicholson 2005, 2–46). The railway also extended into a Haifa-Dar'a branch, with additional service to Bosra and Suwaida and from Haifa to Acre. The railway began to be a target for the tribes who opposed Ottoman control of the Hijaz. The British sought to manipulate these sentiments against the Ottomans and supported Sharif Husayn of Mecca in the Arab revolt against the Ottomans during World War I. Although 'Abd al-'Aziz did not fight the Ottomans as Sharif Husayn and his son did, neither did he support the Ottoman sultan in the war, and he was able to fight the al-Rashid clan, who had supported the Ottomans. In 1917, the British political emissary Harry St. John Philby arrived in Arabia to make certain that Ibn Sa'ud would not attack Britain's ally, Sharif Husayn of Mecca, and to convince him to attack the *sharif* of Ha'il, who was an Ottoman ally (Brown 1999, 2–3).

At the close of World War I, Ibn Sa'ud controlled central Arabia, and his advances on the al-Rashid at Ha'il resulted in their defeat in 1921. Then, since the war had ended, he moved against the Hashemites in the Hijaz. The Ikhwan defeated Sharif Husayn's armies at Turabah, and that battle convinced some in the British government that the *sharif* was not sufficiently strong to be their mainstay. The *sharif*, who had received a British subsidy during the Arab revolt, was now quite desperate for funds and had imposed various unpopular taxes on the Hijazis. On March 5, 1924, Sharif Husayn proclaimed that he was the caliph of the Muslims, another unpopular move. The Ikhwan were angered by the *sharif*'s claim, and although Ibn Sa'ud had initially cautioned them against marching on the Holy Cities, he decided to attack Ta'if. Sharif Husayn's eldest son abandoned the city on the night of September 4, 1924 (Lacey 1981, 187); the Ikhwan took over and carried out a terrible massacre. Sharif Husayn appealed to the British, but they did not respond. So, the leaders of Jeddah proposed that Sharif Husayn would abdicate, and he did so on October 3, 1924 (Lacey 1981, 189), leaving with a British escort to Aqabah and then to Cyprus.

The Ikhwan then moved on to Mecca. 'Abd al-'Aziz followed in December. Some resistance by Sharif 'Ali bin Husayn continued, and while the merchants of Jeddah were opposed to Sa'udi rule, they eventually had to accede. 'Abd al-'Aziz formed a *majlis al-shura*, a consultative council, to rule Mecca with him, greatly facilitating his control over the pilgrimage. Medina then surrendered, and finally Jeddah,

CAPTAIN SHAKESPEAR AND IBN SA'UD'S ARABIA

Captain William Henry Irvine Shakespear(1878–1915), a British political agent posted in Kuwait, was the first Briton to meet 'Abd al-'Aziz al-Sa'ud and impressed him in subsequent meetings as "the greatest Englishman he had ever known" (Harrigan 2002, 20). Shakespear was born in Bombay, educated at Sandhurst, and served in the Devonshire Regiment and also the Bengal Lancers of the Indian Army. He had learned Arabic by the time he met 'Abd al-'Aziz, and he enjoyed exploring the country and photography. His photographs of Shaykh Mubarak of Kuwait and 'Abd al-

Portrait of William Henry Irvine Shakespear. (Royal Geographical Society)

'Aziz were the first photographic images of the latter. Shakespear argued that the British should acknowledge 'Abd al-'Aziz al-Sa'ud as the ascending force in the region, but the British were not at first prepared to do so. As Ibn Sa'ud conquered more territory and drove the Ottomans from the Gulf region, Shakespear was authorized to meet with Ibn Sa'ud officially and discuss a treaty. Shakespear then planned a long expedition in Arabia and met with Ibn Sa'ud along his 1,200-mile route in Riyadh. After the onset of World War I, Shakespear returned on special assignment to 'Abd al-'Aziz and was killed in battle by the Shammar fighters of Ibn Rashid, who were fighting 'Abd al-'Aziz and his Ikhwan (Harrigan 2002).

whose leaders proposed that 'Abd al-'Aziz become the ruler of Hijaz and the Najd as a united entity (Lacey 1981, 200). By the 1930s, 'Abd al-'Aziz also controlled the Asir and Najran regions. Faysal, son of 'Abd al-'Aziz, had led the challenge against Sharif Husayn and was made the governor of the Hijaz.

Ibn Sa'ud faced serious challenges from his own supporters, the Ikhwan warriors, who continued to raid where they had opportunities and protested all innovations, from the telephone lines to the way that the *hajj* was observed in 1926, when their attacks ended in 40 deaths. When they could not attack and plunder in the Hijaz, they returned to Najd and began to raid up into Iraqi territory in 1927. Ibn Sa'ud had the political sense to realize that he must control the Ikhwan, despite their major role in his conquest of Arabia. In his attempts to communicate with them, he was stung by the contempt of the Ikhwan leaders. He met with one of their leaders in an effort to reach an agreement but to no avail. 'Abd al-'Aziz was victorious over the Ikhwan in the Battle of Sibillah on March 29, 1929, and then in several more battles. After these defeats, the Ikhwan leader, Faysal al-Duwaysh, sought refuge for the women in his family, first in Kuwait and then in Iraq. At first, these requests were refused, but then H.R.P. Dickson, the British political agent in Kuwait, provided an escort (Powell 1982, 77). Al-Duwaysh's life was pardoned by 'Abd al-'Aziz, but he died in prison in Riyadh. The Ikhwan retreated to their *hudhur*, or settlements, in Najd (Lacey 1981; Powell 1982, 77). In 1932, the Kingdom of Saudi Arabia was formally created.

After formally announcing the Kingdom of Saudi Arabia, Ibn Sa'ud faced many problems including a revolt in the northern Hijaz in which the Transjordanians and Egyptians had a hand, a revolt in Asir, and a border conflict with Yemen that led to war. Most pressing was a financial crisis due indirectly to the worldwide depression, which had caused a decrease in pilgrimage revenues (Safran 1985, 60). An American, Charles Crane, had offered Ibn Sa'ud a free geological survey and visited the Kingdom of Saudi Arabia in 1931. Another invitee, mining engineer Karl Twitchell, noted geological signs of oil in 1932. Standard Oil of California (SOCAL) had discovered oil in Bahrain, and their geologist, Fred Davies, met with Twitchell. In 1933, SOCAL's lawyer and Saudi Arabia's 'Abdullah al-Sulayman, the minister of finance, began to negotiate an agreement granting rights to explore and develop oil resources in return for rents and a loan (Chevron n.d. [ca. 2007]). SOCAL created California Arabian Standard Oil Company (CASOC) to carry out the concession granted by the king, and CASOC/SOCAL established a base at Jubayl, where they explored the Dammam Dome (Lacey 1981, 244–245). In 1933, SOCAL paid a rent of $35,000, plus it offered loans of $210,000 and $140,000 in the first and second years. Saudi Arabian *'ulama*, religious leaders, bitterly protested Ibn Sa'ud's decision to permit infidels into the kingdom, who they believed would corrupt its citizens (Mumayiz 1963, 229), but Ibn Sa'ud overruled them. He was able to obtain some $700,000 when the war with Yemen was settled, but he still needed funds.

When the oil company discovered oil in 1938, Ibn Sa'ud was able to collect $32 million (Safran 1985, 61). However, this new source of income as well as the pilgrimage was once again impacted when the hostilities of World War II began. The United States offered financial aid at CASOC/SOCAL's urging, and the British sent food shipments.

KINGS OF SAUDI ARABIA

The Kingdom of Saudi Arabia was created in 1932. Histories of Saudi Arabia refer to this period from 1932 as the Third State or the Third Realm, as it was preceded by two other periods of al-Sa'ud dominance. What follows is a list of the kings:

* King 'Abd al-'Aziz ibn 'Abd al-Rahman ibn Faysal ibn Turki al-Sa'ud
Born: January 15, 1876 (other sources list 1880)
Died: November 9, 1953
Son of Sara bint Ahmad al-Sudayri
Known as Ibn Sa'ud
Reigned from 1932 to 1953

* King Sa'ud ibn 'Abd al-'Aziz al-Sa'ud
Born: January 12, 1902
Died: February 23, 1969
Became crown prince in 1933
Reigned from 1953 to November 1964, when he was deposed (his brother governed for a period in 1962)

* King Faysal ibn 'Abd al-'Aziz al-Sa'ud
Born: 1903
Died: March 25, 1975
Reigned from 1964 to 1975

* King Khalid ibn 'Abd al-'Aziz al-Sa'ud
Born: 1912
Died: June 13, 1982
Reigned from 1975 to 1982

* King Fahd ibn 'Abd al-'Aziz al-Sa'ud
Born: March 16, 1921 (other sources give the year of birth as 1922 or 1923)
Died: August 1, 2005
Son of Hussah bint Ahmad al-Sudayri
Reigned from 1982 to 2005

* King 'Abdullah ibn 'Abd al-'Aziz al-Sa'ud
Born: August 1, 1924
Crown prince from 1982 to 2005
King from 2005 to the present

During World War II, King 'Abd al-'Aziz joined the Allied cause, as he had been an ally of Great Britain for decades and, thereafter, an ally of the United States. Other areas of the Middle East were heavily impacted by the Axis propaganda, mainly because of the desire for independence on the part of the Mandate populations (those ruled under the Treaty of Paris by French or British mandates in Syria, Lebanon, Palestine, Iraq, and Transjordan), Egyptians, and other North Africans. At the close of the war, oil revenues again accrued, reaching $10 million in 1946, $53 million in 1948, and $212 million in 1952, but Saudi Arabian debt and budgetary problems continued for some time. Ibn Sa'ud suffered from painful arthritis, and his health declined quickly.

Ibn Sa'ud pursued a greater alliance with the United States for other reasons; he distrusted Great Britain, which he believed had encouraged his enemies, the Hashemite rulers. He was concerned about the Greater Syria scheme proposed by King 'Abdullah of Transjordan to unite Syria, Lebanon, and Palestine, and also by the Fertile Crescent plan of Nuri Sa'id Pasha (prime minister of Iraq), wherein Iraq, Syria, Transjordan, and Palestine would unite. He met with President Franklin D. Roosevelt on the USS *Quincy* on February 14, 1945, a meeting that marked the formal starting point of the long alliance between the United States and Saudi Arabia. In that meeting, the Americans had hoped to obtain 'Abd al-'Aziz's agreement to an increase in Jewish settlement in Palestine, a policy that ruler had outspokenly and consistently disputed. 'Abd al-'Aziz on the other hand, wanted arms and aid from the United States and promises that it would not support either Hashemite scheme.

On the question of Palestine, Saudi Arabia's leaders argued for the rights of the Palestinians on the basis of self-representation even before Israel's emergence. Ibn Sa'ud and his sons Faysal and Fahd argued vociferously with U.S. officials on this point, but they were confronted with a much stronger American commitment to Israel from President Truman's time on (see Chapter 3, Government and Politics). Although Saudi Arabia resisted and fought communism, as did the United States, it greatly opposed the creation of the state of Israel in 1948 and what the Saudi Arabians considered an unfair American commitment to Israel at the expense of the Palestinians. Saudi Arabia shared its view of Israel's creation and of the need for a just solution to the Palestinian refugee problem with other Arab governments.

In the post–World War II period, a U.S. military and training mission was launched and began to develop the Saudi Arabian armed forces. This came about via Assistant Secretary of State George McGhee's memorandum of April 1950, which offered a friendship treaty; provided loans and technicians, military aid, and a military training mission; and included an agreement by which the Americans would lease the Dhahran air base. Ibn Sa'ud did not immediately agree to the Dhahran lease but did so in June 18, 1951.

'Abd al-'Aziz died in Ta'if on November 9, 1953. His eldest surviving son, Sa'ud, succeeded him as king. Many of the histories of Ibn Sa'ud focus on his personal charisma, which waned only with his health, and include anecdotes concerning his generosity and the dependence of a large number of people on his largesse. This personal identification of the state with its leader and his own fortunes was a legacy somewhat at odds with the development of a government bureaucracy that continued to serve and represent the royal family but also a large and growing nation.

KING SA'UD IBN 'ABD AL-'AZIZ

The reign of King Sa'ud was a troubled one. Problems emanated not only from the personal failings of Sa'ud and his excesses but also from his enmeshment in regional and international tensions stemming from the rise of Arab nationalism as a response to Western colonialism. In addition, the lack of separation between Saudi Arabia's state and its ruler, and between the finances of each, was inherited by Sa'ud, who came up against a younger generation determined to create more viable institutions for a growing country. As experts have pointed out, Saudi Arabia was reacting in this period to new Western policies toward the Middle East in general and to the conflict among Arab and Middle Eastern nations, which Malcolm Kerr (1971) has dubbed "the Arab cold war."

Sa'ud ibn 'Abd al-'Aziz was born January 12, 1902, and died on February 23, 1969, serving as king from 1953 until he was formally deposed in 1964. He became his father's heir when his elder brother, Turki (1900–1919), died in the influenza pandemic of 1918–1919. Following King Sa'ud's rule, the order of royal succession shifted to a brother-to-brother pattern rather than passing from father to son.

In 1952, the year prior to his accession, the Egyptian Free Officers revolted and overthrew the Egyptian monarchy, establishing a republic. At first, the Free Officers were headed by General Muhammad Naguib, a senior officer, but within two years, Colonel Gamal Abd al-Nasser (Jamal 'abd al-Nasir) bested Naguib. Over the next several years, Nasser presented new ideas of populism and Arab solidarity to Egypt and the Arab world. If Arab nations united, they could defeat the forces that sought to exploit them. Later, he proposed ideals of Arab socialism. To some degree, King Sa'ud was caught up and enamored with the Arab nationalist ideals, or their popularity, although he eventually realized that Nasser's goals also involved opposition to monarchies such as his own. Nasser garnered great disapproval from Great Britain because he wanted to liberate Egypt and the entire region from the British strategic and economic sphere. Some American, British, and other Western officials also took a dim view of Nasser because of his populism and because he obtained weapons and support from the Soviet bloc when he could not get them from the West. Nasser's own voice could be heard over Radio Cairo, but his ideas also entered the Kingdom of Saudi Arabia through foreign educators and workers in Saudi Arabia and through the military cooperation established between the two countries. In 1955, an army mutiny broke out in Ta'if, and it was suspected that Egypt was involved in some way (Lacey 1981, 313). King Sa'ud crushed the mutineers and set up a Royal Guard as well as a force known as the White Army (for their white *thobes* [long garments]), which became Saudi Arabia's National Guard. The same year, the U.S. Central Intelligence Agency, with some assistance from the Greek shipping tycoon Stavros Niarchos, spread news about a Saudi contract with Aristotle Onassis to build oil tankers to be controlled by the Saudi-Arabian Maritime Tanker Company, which would have taken over shipping from Aramco. International arbitration decided in Aramco's favor.

Nasser nationalized the Suez Canal in 1956 and flew to consult with King Sa'ud only a few days before Great Britain, France, and Israel launched the Tripartite, or Suez, War, against Egypt. Huge crowds greeted Nasser, first at Dhahran and then in Riyadh, which concerned King Sa'ud, as did the ensuing war. The conflict made Nasser even more popular with the Arab masses. Although Sa'ud supported Nasser, he realized the war placed Saudi Arabia's foreign relations with the West on a tenuous plane. Arab nationalists in Saudi Arabia were critical of the American lease of Dhahran's air base, and Sa'ud terminated that arrangement.

American Point Four economic aid had been extended to certain developing countries under the 1950 Act for International Development with the intent of discouraging communism, or at least encourage neutral or nonaligned development. (The Nonaligned Movement of Third World Nations, formed in Belgrade in 1961, which called for no binding alliances with Western- or Eastern-bloc nations, was the creation of Yugoslavian president Josip Tito, Indian prime minister Jawaharlal Nehru, Egyptian president Nasser, Ghana's president Kwame Nkrumah, and Indonesian president Sukarno. The U.S. government, deeply engaged by that time in the Cold War, was actually rather hostile to the Nonaligned Movement, but, at this earlier stage, it hoped to bring Middle Eastern countries into its orbit or create neutrality sufficient to encourage aid proposals that might lead to firmer alliances.) Point Four aid was implemented through the Technical Cooperation Administration, it brought technicians to Saudi Arabia and Saudi Arabian students to the United States. However, Point Four aid to Saudi Arabia had ceased in 1954. The U.S. Secretary of State, John Foster Dulles, had already toured the region, promoting the Northern Tier agreement since the Egyptians and Israelis had opposed an Arab regional alliance with the United States. Dulles's goal was also to stave off Soviet influence, ideally through strengthening a "northern tier" of anticommunist states—Turkey, Iran, Iraq, and Pakistan. He wanted the United States' Arab allies to join in as well, but the United States was not to be a direct member of the alliance, making it more problematic for Saudi Arabia. Nasser greatly opposed this proposal (later known as the Baghdad Pact and signed by Great Britain, Turkey, Iran, Iraq, and Pakistan in 1955). He and King Sa'ud exerted efforts to discourage Jordan from signing the pact, which angered Dulles.

When Great Britain, France, and Israel attacked Egypt in the Suez War of 1956, Sa'ud offered a loan to Egypt equal to $10 million and severed relations with Great Britain and France (Smyth in Metz, ed., 1993, 209). The United States condemned the attack on Egypt, even though they were concerned by Nasser's populism and increasing influence in the region.

Later, after his country's relations with Egypt had become more tenuous, King Sa'ud agreed to the renewal of the Americans' lease of the air base at Dhahran in a meeting with President Eisenhower in the United States in 1957 (Smyth in Metz, ed., 1993, 29). On this first visit of a Sa'udi ruler to the United States, Sa'ud was denounced by Mayor Robert F. Wagner of New York for being anti-Catholic and anti-Jewish. However, President Eisenhower honored him by meeting him personally on the airfield and pitching his "Eisenhower Doctrine"—that the king would serve as a force of moderation and support American aims in the region. For this, King Sa'ud received an additional $180 million in economic aid.

The Kingdom of Saudi Arabia had a long way to go in terms of human development. Health, education, and social welfare were all impacted by low literacy rates (only 15 percent for men and 2 percent for women by 1970). Public secondary schools for males had been set up in 1951. Sa'ud's government had established a Ministry of Education in 1954, and the first nonreligious college, Riyadh University, was started in 1957 and later named King Sa'ud University.

By 1957, Sa'ud was widely accused of overspending on his palace's construction, payments to the tribes, personal luxuries, and the establishment of his new forces. The riyal, Saudi Arabia's currency, had to be devalued by 1958. The royal family also disliked the way he had promoted his own supporters and sons instead of his brothers in the royal family. He had made his son Fahd chief of his private office and by 1957 made him minister of defense. His son Muhammad was in charge of his bodyguard, his son 'Abdullah headed the royal farms and gardens, his son Musa'id was given the command of the royal palace guards, his son Khalid was put at the head of the National Guard, and his son Sa'ad was in charge of the Private Guard. In making these appointments, he passed over many more senior qualified family members. Sa'ud and his most powerful and intellectual brother, Faysal, were in disaccord over the structure of the government and Faysal's role. Sa'ud had done away with the office of prime minister and was acting as his own prime minister, although Faysal was deputy prime minister (al-Rasheed 2002, 108; Safran 1985, 91).

Along with the financial crisis and concern over Sa'ud's impact on succession, there was a huge scandal as a result of the king's falling out with Nasser. In May 1957, Saudi Arabian authorities discovered evidence of an assassination plot being planned by the Egyptian military attaché in Jeddah. Even though Nasser sent a representative who swore that the leader knew nothing of the plot, Sa'ud planned a counterassassination (Lacey 1981, 317). Syria and Egypt had established a union in 1958 that was to last only three years. Colonel Abd al-Hamid Sarraj of Syria revealed in March 1958 that Sa'ud had paid for Syrian influence within this new government and for Sarraj to carry out a coup that was to destroy the union known as the United Arab Republic; he was also supposed to arrange Nasser's assassination. He offered proof in the form of photocopies, checks, and details in a news conference. Nasser began blasting the Saudi Arabian government over Radio Cairo. Due to all of the preceding problems, King Sa'ud was forced to turn over foreign, financial, and internal affairs to Faysal by his brothers' decision, although he remained king.

Faysal assumed these responsibilities but faced a financial crisis with only 317 riyals in available cash, and the National Commercial Bank refused him a loan. He did his best to resurrect the government's finances and administration. Still, Sa'ud continued to maneuver in an effort to regain his kingly authority. There was also opposition from a group of young princes headed by Talal ibn 'Abd al-'Aziz, who had insisted on constitutional reforms that Faysal had not enacted, and also from young nonroyal reformers. Sa'ud manipulated this group to support him but then did not follow through on reforms. In 1960, the king refused to sign a budget that Faysal had prepared, and Saʿud decided to represent a note that Faysal had written in protest as being his resignation. Faysal's control over finances was given over to Prince Talal. Saʿud eventually got rid of the liberal princes, and soon after that, Egypt's propaganda against Saudi Arabia (and all monarchies) became even more strident with the failure of the United Arab Republic, the union between Egypt and Syria.

In this period, the Organization of Petroleum Exporting Countries (OPEC) was created in 1960. In 1959, the first Arab Petroleum Congress had convened in Cairo. Following the Suez Crisis, in February 1959, the oil companies known as the Seven Sisters (Standard Oil of New Jersey, later Esso; Royal Dutch Shell; British Petroleum, later BP; Standard Oil of New York, later ExxonMobil; Texaco; Gulf Oil; and Standard Oil of California) had decided to cut oil prices from the $2.12 per barrel they had risen to. No consultation was held with the oil-producing countries whose incomes were thus sharply hit. When this scenario repeated itself in 1960, as Esso (Standard Oil of New Jersey) decided to cut prices and the rest of the Seven Sisters followed suit, the producing nations decided to act. Saudi Arabia's participation in the cartel was approved by Prince Faysal, and the initiative owed much to ʿAbdullah al-Tariki, who became oil minister. Al-Tariki had carefully studied the ways that Aramco extracted profits in a theoretical 50/50 split, although what the Aramco side paid Saudi Arabia was tax deductible for the Americans as a so-called local income tax. Al-Tariki traveled to Venezuela to observe a different production model, and he urged his government to engage Saudi Arabians at every stage of production, for they had been heretofore excluded from management, including the senior level. He and the other oil-producing members protested the oil companies' decision to slash prices in 1960 without any consultation with the oil-producing countries. The oil companies initially refused to deal with OPEC, headed by Fuʾad Rouhani (Lacey 1981, 328–333). However, the solidarity of the cartel held and eventually empowered the member countries. Saudi Arabia's participation was viewed with nationalist pride.

At this still politically delicate stage, one of the previously active liberal princes, Prince Talal, defected and caused embarrassment to the al-Saʿud when he broadcast his opposition to his brothers from exile, calling for a constitutional democracy under a monarchy in Saudi Arabia. Some of his brothers supported him, but his passport was revoked.

In 1962, Faysal formed a cabinet while Saʿud was overseas for medical treatment. Faysal brought his half brothers and allies, Fahd and Sultan, into the government but not the sons of his brother Saʿud. He proposed a reform program that included a new Basic Law, the abolition of slavery, and the formation of a judicial council. There were large numbers of slaves in Saudi Arabia and the Gulf states. According to Bernard Lewis (1990) and others, the British had pressed the Ottomans to end slavery, and in an 1857 *firman* (royal decree), the Ottomans had prohibited the trade in black slaves (an order to emancipate Christian slaves was issued in 1830), excluding the Hijaz from the prohibition. The exception came about due to a revolt against the Ottomans that was unleashed when a leader of the *ʿulama* issued a *fatwa* against the Ottomans for this decree (Lewis 1990, 80–81). It seems curious that many of the British sources characterized Arabian slavery as not being linked to production (instead, they either attributed it to Islam or attempted to unify descriptions of the forms of slavery that provided military personnel [like the *mamalik* or Janissaries] along with household and agricultural slavery), yet slaves played a crucial role in date and pearl production on the Arabian Peninsula (Hopper 2006, 2010). Abolition came in Saudi Arabia just a few weeks after a similar prohibition in Yemen. Faysal paid for the manumission of some 4,000 slaves. The various reforms Faysal intended were challenged and took time, and when Sa'ud returned, he rejected the entire reform plan. Nevertheless, Faysal eventually proceeded with these plans with the support of U.S. president John F. Kennedy's administration.

A complicating factor was the outbreak of the Yemeni Civil War in northern Yemen. The Egyptians supported the republicans against the traditional religious leader and monarch of Yemen, the imam, and they made a claim to the Saudi Arabian province of Asir. The republicans had about 30,000 troops, and they countered royalist advances by bombing Saudi Arabian territory. The Saudi Arabian strategy in this war was in part to involve the Americans and British as opponents of Egypt, along with the Jordanians. After the Egyptian bombings, President Kennedy ordered U.S. fighter planes to fly over Riyadh and Jeddah. The war continued as Egypt was unable to best the royalists, even with a buildup to 40,000 troops. Yet Saudi Arabia was equally incapable of ousting the Egyptians and the republicans.

Sa'ud threatened to mobilize the Royal Guard against Faysal in 1963, after Faysal ordered that receptions in Sa'ud's honor in the Hijaz be scaled down due to cost. Faysal, in turn, ordered that the National Guard be deployed. Senior princes demanded compromise; the *'ulama* were called in and backed Faysal, ordering that he should take over power due to Sa'ud's poor health. Nonetheless, Faysal agreed that Sa'ud should represent his country and travel to a 1964 Arab summit meeting in Cairo. When Sa'ud returned, he wrote to Faysal demanding that his rights as king be restored as his health had improved. However, senior members of the family had reached the limits of their patience, and Faysal's supporters approached the mufti of Jeddah and then met with the *'ulama*. The Jeddah *'ulama* met with other clerics from elsewhere in the Kingdom of Saudi Arabia, who issued a *fatwa* to fully empower Prince Faysal to rule and yet retain Sa'ud as king. King Sa'ud mobilized his personal guard and the Royal Guard, while Faysal ordered the National Guard to surround the royal palace. However, the Royal Guard refused to leave. The group of senior princes of the al-Sa'ud, who are known as the *ahl al-hal wa al-'aqd* (the people who bind and loose), met and signed a petition that alluded to the *fatwa*. However, Sa'ud declined a ceremonial position and was then forced to agree to abdicate on March 28, 1964. Sa'ud left Saudi Arabia for Switzerland. He was invited to live in Egypt in 1966 and died in Athens, Greece, in 1969.

THE REIGN OF FAYSAL IBN 'ABD AL-'AZIZ

Faysal ibn 'Abd al-'Aziz (1903–1975), the fourth son of King 'Abd al-'Aziz ibn Sa'ud, became king on November 2, 1964, after Sa'ud was finally induced to abdicate. Faysal introduced various plans for Saudi Arabia's economic, social, and industrial development. From the outset of his rule, when Saudi Arabia's finances were still limited, revenue rose enormously. During his rule, Saudi Arabia's oil revenues grew

King Faysal ibn 'Abd al-'Aziz, who reigned from 1964 to 1975. King Faysal made many improvements in the Saudi Arabian government, infrastructure, and education. (National Archives and Records Administration)

from $334 million in 1960 to $22.5 billion in 1974, allowing the king to institute generous benefits to Saudi Arabian citizens, including free medical care and education through the postgraduate level. The government was also able to subsidize utilities, certain food items, water, and rents (Willbanks 2008; Beling 1980).

Faysal began a program to modernize the army and establish a more extensive air defense system under his brother Sultan, who became defense minister and minister of aviation. His other modernizations and reforms encompassed the educational sector, industry, and governmental administration, through the revamping of centralized planning, utilization of the oil revenues, and the introduction of various infrastructures and technologies. Doing so brought about very negative reactions at times from the conservative *'ulama* and equally conservative elements of the population. *Conservative* is not a sufficiently evocative term to convey the mix of former Ikhwan, those opposed to Westernizing influences, *salafists* (who call for a return to the spirit of the first three generations of Islam), and a more contemporary, ardent, and politicized iteration, now dubbed *neosalafists*. Such elements had protested the introduction of the radio under Ibn Sa'ud, and others were adamant against the establishment of television, including one of the king's nephews, Khalid ibn Musa'id al-Sa'ud. Khalid was killed in 1966 when, according to some accounts, he and his cohorts attacked a television studio or participated in a riot or demonstration (Smyth in Metz, ed., 1993). His father claimed he was merely a bystander and asked for vengeance against the authority who had killed his son, but Faysal denied it. Prince Musa'id bitterly attacked the king, and he and his family left the Kingdom of Saudi Arabia (Powell 1982, 276–277).

Under Faysal, spending on education rose to 10 percent of the total budget. He increased support to King 'Abd al-'Aziz University in Jeddah, established the University of Petroleum and Minerals in Dhahran, and opened and funded vocational centers and elementary and secondary schools. Faysal, in support of the initiatives of his wife, Iffat al-Thunayan, did a great deal to introduce and expand education for women. Because of opposition to female education and any deleterious effects it might have on women's morals, the schools were placed under religious supervision instead of the education ministry. Conservatives were highly opposed to the education of women outside their homes, and even though the monarch and his wife also found support for women's education, they had to accommodate interference by the *'ulama* and public opposition. In 1963, strong opposition to the education of girls broke out in Buraydah, and forces were sent to dispel it (Lacey 1981, 364; Hamdan 2005, 48). According to Robert Lacey (1981, 369), the headmistress, installed "by force," had only her own daughter as a pupil in the first year of the school (see Chapter 5, section on education).

Security was threatened in the Eastern Province in 1967 by bomb attacks that were thought to emanate from an underground political opposition that had taken the name the Union of the Arabian Peninsula. Seventeen Yemeni citizens were tried and executed in March 1967 on terrorism charges. The Yemeni government and the exiled former king Sa'ud protested these executions (Powell 1982, 278).

Following a deadlock at a 1965 conference at Harad in Yemen, hostilities had resumed between the Yemeni republicans and the royalists and, therefore, between the Egyptian and the Saudi Arabian forces. The Egyptian troops remained in Yemen, and this war effort was detrimental to Egypt, which was ill prepared for the outbreak of war with Israel in 1967; Yemen was even regarded as its Vietnam (Aboul Enein 2004). King Faysal and President Nasser signed an agreement in Khartoum on August 31, 1967, to peacefully resolve the conflict in Yemen. The settlement involved an aid payment to Egypt, whose military infrastructure had been badly damaged during the 1967 war. Saudi Arabia, responsible for about £50 million (out of £135 million), would make payment after Egyptian troops were withdrawn from Yemen (Fraser 1980, 115–116).

The Saudi Arabian government was also concerned by other leftist movements in southern Arabia and border conflicts. Meanwhile, the Egyptians supported Yemen nationalists who began a terrorist campaign against the British in Aden (later South Yemen) in 1963. The British withdrew in 1967. A new Marxist faction of South Yemen's National Front regime announced the creation of the People's Democratic Republic of Yemen in 1969. The border conflicts with Qatar were solved in 1965; conflicts with Iran over rights in the Gulf were concluded in 1968 in the Continental Shelf Agreement (Smyth in Metz, ed., 1993, 33). A dispute over the Buraymi Oasis meant that Saudi Arabia did not recognize the formation of the United Arab Emirates in 1971. That particular dispute was solved after Faysal's death in 1975.

Saudi Arabia supported the Arab states in the Six-Day, or June War of 1967, and Faysal was extremely troubled by Israel's victory and subsequent occupation of the West Bank and the Gaza Strip. Even before the war, three bombs exploded near the U.S. embassy and the U.S. Military Training Mission in Riyadh on June 2 to protest U.S. support for Israel, and anti-Israeli and anti-American demonstrations were held at Ra's Tanura and Dhahran. The Saudi Arabians arrested many protesters and exiled several hundred Palestinians. Sources disagree about Saudi Arabia's stance; some claim that Faysal's strong statements in support of jihad for the Muslim cause in 1967 were simply face-saving rhetoric in the Arab arena (Ciorciari 2005, 1), whereas others describe the aims of supporting Palestine and yet maintaining as amicable relations as possible with the United States as consistent themes in Saudi Arabian foreign policy. A short-lived effort at an oil boycott following the conflict foreshadowed the far more effective effort in 1973.

In his regional policy, Faysal while still crown prince had supported Nasser's Arabism, but with the increase of Saudi Arabian–Egyptian hostilities, he moved in a different direction once he was king, calling on Islamic leaders worldwide to unite. His idea of Islamic leadership was almost counterintuitive in an era when socialist and leftist philosophies had taken hold in many parts of the Arab world, and it predated the massive religious revival that began in the mid- to late 1970s. He convened an important meeting following widespread Muslim alarm when Michael Dennis Rohan, an Australian, set fire to the al-Aqsa mosque in Jerusalem in August 1969. This galvanized country representatives to meet in Rabat in September 1969 as a pan-Islamic body.

King Faysal appointed his brother Khalid as crown prince and first deputy prime minister. Khalid's elder brother, Muhammad ibn 'Abd al-'Aziz, and other princes gave up their claim to succession in order to support this move to stabilize the leadership. However, Khalid was not thought to be politically ambitious, as Faysal himself had been under the rule of his brother Sa'ud. In 1967, Faysal created the position of second deputy prime minister for Prince Fahd ibn 'Abd al-'Aziz, who was the minister of the interior, since Faysal needed more assistance than Khalid, who suffered from a heart condition, could provide. Faysal was able to avoid the factional schisms that had occurred under King Sa'ud, but some clashes were still inevitable between the two stronger leaders in this triad. When Faysal and Fahd had disputes in the aftermath of various unsuccessful plots against the government, Fahd left Saudi Arabia for over six months from October 1969 to May 1970.

The increasing hostilities in the War of Attrition concerned Saudi Arabia, with Israel and Egypt exchanging air strikes. There was a coup in Sudan, a foiled coup attempt in Saudi Arabia, and, in Faysal's view, Arab radicalism was only growing stronger. People's Democratic Republic of Yemen (PDRY, also known as South Yemen) was ideologically opposed to Saudi Arabia, and a radical movement in Oman was making headway. Faysal had been arguing that the United States should support the United Nations (UN) Resolution 242, which called for Israeli withdrawal from the occupied territories of the West Bank and the Gaza Strip. But his efforts, and U.S.-Soviet efforts to reach an agreement, had been rejected by Nasser. The United States issued a very similar plan, the Rogers Plan, which Israel rejected. Soon after, Nasser called for an Arab summit in Rabat and for the use of an oil boycott against the supporters of Israel. Nasser criticized the Saudi Arabian rulers for their close relations to the United States (Safran 1985, 140–141). After further superpower negotiations, a ceasefire in the War of Attrition was arranged and went into effect on August 7, 1970. The next month, Nasser died, and Saudi relations with Egypt improved when Anwar al-Sadat became president.

King Faysal had established the Central Planning Organization in 1968, and, as the Ministry of Planning, it orchestrated the first Five Year Plan and oversaw enormous changes in the economy brought about by oil income. The king had realized that the country must modernize, create more infrastructure, and educate its citizens so they could be productive rather than relying on the state for income. The plan focused on urban areas where more skilled labor was to be found—Riyadh, Jeddah, and al-Khobar. The rural population was not greatly affected but, after 1973, began to migrate to the urban areas (Mackey 1987, 43–44).

When the United States strongly supported and assisted Israel in 1973, in the next war between Israel and the Arabs, Faysal withdrew Saudi Arabian oil from the world markets, with the support of other OPEC nations. This precipitated a rise in the price of oil and limited the supplies available to the American and European markets. Many of the allocations of the first Five Year Plan could not be spent, and instead revenues were converted to gold or foreign reserves. With the launching of the Second Economic Development Plan in 1975, the country was still facing huge challenges with its significant port congestion, underdeveloped infrastructure, and citizenry requiring education and job training (Mackey 1987, 44–45).

Saudi Arabia encountered new currents in regional politics. Following challenges to its authority, the Jordanian government battled the Palestinian militias, forcing them out in 1969 in what was known as Black September. The Palestinian commandos resolved to continue battling to regain their land, resorting to hijackings and hostage seizures in the early 1970s after many had fled to Lebanon. This spurred the Arab countries to rein them in, which was basically accomplished by 1974. Hafiz al-Asad assumed power in Syria and ameliorated relations with Saudi Arabia, permitting the repair of the Tapline (the Trans-Arabian Pipeline, the largest oil pipeline when it was constructed, which transported Saudi Arabian oil to Sidon, Lebanon, was intended to go through Palestine, but once Israel was established, a different route went through Jordan and the Golan Heights of Syria; see Chapter 3, Government and Politics), ceasing support of revolutionary organizations elsewhere in the peninsula, opposing Iraq, and signing a trade and economic treaty with the Kingdom of Saudi Arabia (Safran 1985, 144). Meanwhile, in July 1972, Sadat ordered the 21,000 Soviet advisers and military in Egypt to leave and retreated from a planned union with Colonel Mu'ammar Qadhdhafi of Libya. In addition to strengthening its hand vis-à-vis radical forces in the region, Saudi Arabia had become a regional and even a world leader when confronting the United States for the first time during the oil embargo. The Kingdom of Saudi Arabia chose to not significantly reduce the increase in oil prices set at Tehran. Oil prices would continue to increase, even though the country has since deliberately acted to control prices for the benefit of Western economies time and time again.

Following a dramatic series of meetings and U.S. and Saudi Arabian counterstatements, Secretary of State Henry Kissinger's comments that he would not rule out the use of military force against oil producers were they to engage in "strangulation" were published in *Business Week* in January 1975 (Safran 1985, 174). Arab states responded harshly, but, meanwhile, the United States signed a contract to send 60 F-5E/F fighters to Saudi Arabia, and plans to train the Saudi Arabian National Guard were undertaken.

On March 25, 1975, King Faysal was shot and killed by his nephew, Prince Faysal ibn Musa'id, an event that shocked and traumatized the Kingdom of Saudi Arabia. Some claimed that the young prince had some involvement in drugs (he was arrested when a student in Colorado for selling LSD and hashish), but another common explanation in Saudi Arabia was that he sought revenge for the death of his elder brother who had been killed by security forces back in 1966. The assassin was found guilty and was executed in Riyadh in June 1975.

THE REIGN OF KHALID IBN 'ABD AL-'AZIZ

King Khalid, born in 1912, ruled from 1975 until his death in 1982. The collective leadership of the al-Sa'ud family resumed under his reign, whereas King Faysal had, for the most part, exercised power far more on his own, while balancing different factions within the royal family. Khalid became king immediately after Faysal's death; Fahd was appointed crown prince and first deputy prime minister, while Prince 'Abdullah ibn 'Abd al-'Aziz, the commander of the National Guard, became second deputy prime minister. Khalid's brother, Muhammad, was among his key advisers. In the first several years of Khalid's reign, Saudi Arabia witnessed some continuity to the policies set by King Faysal. The Second Economic Plan was implemented, although with a much larger and more ambitious scope than the First Five-Year Economic Plan. Other elements of policy were responsive to changes in regional relations; for instance, Iraq, which Saudi Arabia had viewed with suspicion and some animosity in the 1960s and 1970s, due to its regional designs, moderated its behavior toward Saudi Arabia to some degree after 1975. On the other hand, during Khalid's rule, the Islamic Revolution in Iran brought in a government that at first broadcast its intent to mount challenges to other regimes and then broadcast verbal challenges to the Sa'udi royal family in its role as guardian of the Holy Cities.

Saudi Arabia, along with Syria and Egypt, took a role in attempting to intervene in the Lebanese Civil War, which had broken out in 1975 and was initially waged between the forces of the Lebanese National Movement and the Palestinians versus the Lebanese Front, which was made up of Maronite militias including the Phalangists and the National Liberal Party. Following Syria's military intervention into the conflict to bolster the Christian militias, a peace conference was convened in Riyadh in October 1976. This announced an end to the war, which nevertheless continued on until its formal end with the Ta'if Accords (when Lebanese politicians and others convened in Saudi Arabia to negotiate and finalize the agreement), although fighting and assassinations continued on informally into the early 1990s.

Saudi Arabia remained supportive of the Palestinian cause and was a funder of the Palestine Liberation Organization (PLO). Significantly, the Saudi Arabian government had reconciled with President Sadat of Egypt as the leftist, or radical, threats in the region appeared to decrease. The Saudi Arabian government supported Egyptian participation in peace negotiations so that Israel would return Egyptian and Syrian land that had been seized since 1967, including the Sinai Peninsula, and provide justice to the Palestinians. Unfortunately, of these goals, only the return of the Sinai was agreed to, and, without the threat of the large Egyptian army facing it, Israel would not offer the Palestinians anything for many years. Sadat traveled to Israel on November 19, 1977, and addressed the Israeli Knesset the next day, declaring his intention for peace with that country. The Saudi Arabian government and its people were not supportive of a separate peace between Egypt and Israel but had rather hoped for terms conducive to a comprehensive peace that were not so limited in their prospects for Palestinian sovereignty. On December 5, 1977, Algeria, Iraq, Syria, and South Yemen had condemned Sadat's visit to Israel. The incoming Israeli government under Menachem Begin by no means supported any efforts for Palestinian sovereignty, and Begin had an essentially different approach and demeanor than Sadat. President Jimmy Carter was determined to exploit this opportunity for peace, and Israel and Egypt accepted the terms of the agreement at Camp David. Saudi Arabia, however, opposed this initiative and severed relations with Egypt following the 1979 Camp David Accords (Hooglund in Metz, ed., 1993, 225). Apparently, Fahd was not supportive of the decision to sever relations with Egypt but did not prevail in the leadership's decision on the matter. Saudi Arabian aid to Egypt was cut off, the Arab League offices in Cairo were closed, and Gulf tourism to Egypt decreased for some years.

The Gulf region was impacted by the Islamic Revolution in Iran in 1979. The movement against the shah had strengthened in the previous year, and the shah left Iran in mid-January 1979. Ayatollah Ruhollah Khomeini, an Iranian religious leader who had been exiled to Iraq and then France, returned in February, and the shah's government soon collapsed. A group of Khomeini's followers seized the American embassy staff on November 4, 1979, and held them hostage for more than a year. Soon after this, the Kingdom of Saudi Arabia was shaken by a violent seizure of the Masjid al-Haram, the Grand Mosque at Mecca.

On November 20, the first day of the Hijrah year 1400, Juhayman ibn Muhammad ibn Sayf al-'Utaybi captured the Grand Mosque with a force of armed followers (various sources claim there were anywhere from 200–300 to 1,300–1,500 followers). He had planned to seize the king and other royals at prayer, but they were not present. Some of the many individuals attending the morning prayers were released, but 130 were held hostage. Despite a news blackout at the time, quite a few hostages have written accounts of the event. Juhayman al-'Utaybi called for all present to recognize his brother-in-law Muhammad al-Qahtani as the Mahdi, the leader who is supposed to appear prior to the Day of Judgment according to Muslim belief. He attacked the al-Sa'ud family for its corruption and called for an end to foreign influence (Mackey 1987, 230–231; Trofimov 2007). Juhayman had been influenced by the *salafi* movement, al-Jama'ah al-Salafiyya al-Muhtasiba, which called for a return to the spirit of the righteous ancestors (*salaf*) and rejection of *bid'a* and corruption. There have been peaceful *salafis* as well as violent activists; however, Juhayman al-'Utaybi and his 'Utaybi cohorts (many but not all of the renegades were from this tribe) were militant. The incident took everyone by surprise; Crown Prince Fahd was in Tunis, and King Khalid appeared utterly shocked. The *'ulama* were convened to issue a *fatwa* permitting force to be used in the sanctuary, because it is forbidden to fight in a *haram* (protected place). A siege began. The rebels were finally ousted, and at least 63 (according to other sources, 68) were executed. The incident deeply troubled the nation's rulers as it highlighted their vulnerabilities. Also, the antiroyalist claims of the rebels could be likened to those of the anti-shah Iranians (Smyth in Metz, ed., 1993, 40) and reminded everyone of the *salafi* Ikhwan's previously muzzled violence. Moreover, Juhayman's tribe, the 'Utayba, were a very large group and a source of recruits for the National Guard.

About two weeks after the siege, Shi'a riots and demonstrations took place in Qatif in the Eastern Province. Many were arrested and some were killed as 20,000 National Guard troops moved in to deal with these disturbances. In response to the charges of unfit government levied by the 'Utaybi rebels, the Saudi Arabian government promised to install a *majlis al-shura*, a consultative council (although its establishment came much later). Also, the Shi'a disruptions caused the government to acknowledge discrimination and discontent in the eastern provinces and set about addressing them (see Chapter 3, Government and Politics).

Saudi Arabia's Shi'a comprise about 40 percent of the population of al-Sharqiyyah, the eastern oil-rich province of the kingdom, and make up 10 to 15 percent of the indigenous Saudi Arabian population. The claim of Wahhabi preachers that the Shi'a were renegade-apostates has led to discrimination against them in Saudi Arabia, or measures intended to limit public outrage or persecution against them. Their public rites were restricted; for example, the tradition of holding a lamenting parade on Ashura, which commemorates the death of Husayn, son of 'Ali, at the hands of the Ummayyads, was not permitted (Zuhur 2005, 15). The Shi'a usually repeat the final line of the *adhan*, the call to prayer, and other minor differences with Sunni practice drew the ire of Sunni purists in Saudi Arabia. Shi'a Saudi Arabian were excluded from the military and government service until recently. Yet they have been employed by Aramco since its early days in the Eastern Province, and many have risen in status through their positions in the company.

The Soviet deployment of the 40th Army into Afghanistan took place on December 24, 1979. Saudi Arabia lent its support to an Islamic response to the Soviet invasion, the *mujahidin*, whose call for the primacy of jihad in the form of war fighting, set the stage for Islamist jihadists like Osama bin Laden, who fought in Afghanistan and then began plotting against Saudi Arabia and the West.

Many observers of Saudi Arabia note that following the takeover of the Grand Mosque, stricter measures with respect to religious conservatives were adopted, particularly restrictions on women. In 1980, an uproar arose when a film about an al-Saʿud family scandal was released in Europe. It covered the execution of Princess Mishael in 1977, when she was 19 years old. The princess was the granddaughter of Prince Muhammad ibn Abd al-Aziz. She had traveled to Lebanon for her studies and fell in love with Khalid Muhallal, nephew of the Saudi Arabian ambassador to Lebanon. They returned to Saudi Arabia, continued their relationship, and then attempted to flee the country. The princess faked her own death, but they were caught at the airport. She admitted to adultery although some accounts claim she need not have. According to the royal family, she was executed to demonstrate their honor and compliance with Islamic law, but there were complaints that she was shot (not an Islamic punishment), while her lover was decapitated. In the aftermath of the incident, travel restrictions were imposed on all women (Lacey 1981, 462). A British director and reporter, Antony Thomas, made a movie based on these events, entitled *Death of a Princess*. Once it was screened, the British ambassador to Saudi Arabia was recalled, and the Saudi Arabian government pressured then-acting U.S. secretary of state Warren Christopher to cancel broadcasts of the film on PBS. Thomas was told by some Saudi Arabians he should never have made the film, but he saw that the story had captivated the imagination of many Arabs. Crude pictures of dogs were printed in the Saudi Arabian newspapers and labeled as the dirty British in response to the controversy over the film, according to Ali al-Ahmed, himself a critic of the Saʿudi royal family. (Al-Ahmed and Thomas were interviewed in a PBS *Frontline* retrospective on the impact of *Death of a Princess*; PBS 2005). The Saudi Arabians were especially offended by a scene that showed other princesses picking up men, another smear on their cultural code of honor (Lacey 1981, 462–463); this was a commonplace circumstance reported to Thomas by a trusted respondent (PBS 2005)

In 1980, the Basic Law of Saudi Arabia, pertaining to governance, was created. King Khalid presided over other important Arab summits in Taʾif and Mecca and the creation of the Gulf Cooperation Council (GCC), made up of the rulers of Bahrain, Kuwait, Qatar, the Kingdom of Saudi Arabia, the United Arab Emirates, and the Sultanate of Oman. The GCC was intended to further cooperation and coordination on security issues, as well as economic and developmental aspects. Security experts believe that, in the decades since, the GCC has not developed interoperability as it should have nor met its goal of collective security and that it continues to exhibit strong rivalries (Cordesman and Obaid 2004, 1). The GCC countries were concerned by Iran's influence or potential strategic threats, not only from outside their small countries but also from within them. They often regarded their Shiʿa population suspiciously, for instance, in Bahrain, which had a Shiʿa majority, after the organization Islamic Front for the Liberation of Bahrain was broken up by police in 1981. More recently, in the spring of 2011, the Bahraini government has claimed that demonstrators for democracy in Bahrain are a pro-Iranian threat, which may explain Saudi Arabia's military support of the Bahraini effort to put down the demonstrations.

Four military cities were constructed with assistance from the U.S. Army Corps of Engineers in the 1970s and 1980s: Khamis Mushayt, Tabuk, Asad Military City at al-Kharj, and King Khalid Military City at Batin, which began functioning in 1985.

In September 1980, Iraq attacked Iran in the opening salvos of the Iran-Iraq War. This conflict shifted to the Gulf by 1986, and Iranian attacks impacted Saudi Arabian shipping from 1984 to 1987. Saudi Arabia remained neutral in the conflict but provided financial support to Iraq in loans and grants worth several billion dollars, and the Iranians viewed Saudi Arabia's financial backing of Iraq as a basis for hostility. The Iranians also decried the system of monarchy in Saudi Arabia, calling it un-Islamic (Hooglund in Metz, ed., 1993, 192). Also, the two countries conflicted over the numbers and behavior of the Iranian pilgrims on the *hajj*. More than 400 pilgrims died in 1987 (about two-thirds of them Iranian) after Saudi Arabian security forces suppressed a demonstration. As a result, Saudi Arabia banned such demonstrations, and Iranians attacked the Saudi Arabian embassy and beat several diplomats there, one of whom died (Hooglund in Metz, ed., 1993, 217). Other important shifts under King Khalid's reign were decisions to diversify Saudi Arabia's economy and efforts to build up industry and also agriculture.

In August 1981, Crown Prince Fahd proposed an eight-point plan for solving the Arab-Israeli conflict. This was based on Israeli withdrawal to the 1948 boundaries, the dismantling of post-1967 Israeli settlements, promises of freedom of worship for all religious groups at the holy sites in Israel/Palestine, guarantees of the right of return for Palestinians or compensation for those who did not want to return, and an independent Palestinian state with Jerusalem as its capital, with a transitional UN authority over the West Bank and the Gaza Strip until that state was declared. Some suggest that Fahd's proposal was aimed at securing the sale of airborne warning and control systems (AWACS) and F-15s by the United States, which a House of Representatives majority and 56 senators had opposed. Certainly the plan was unlikely to be accepted by either the United States or Israel (Safran 1985, 332–333), but perhaps this interpretation cynically misses the Saudi Arabian commitment to Arab unity that was expressed in the Fahd Plan.

On October 6, 1981, an Islamist radical in the Egyptian army, Khalid Islambuli, assassinated President Sadat. Those opposed to the Camp David Accords, such as Syria, Libya, and the PLO, pressed Egypt to rescind its separate peace with Israel. Yet the Saudi Arabian leadership restrained these pressures on the new president of Egypt, Hosni Mubarak.

King Khalid died on June 14, 1982, after a brief illness and was succeeded by his brother Fahd, the crown prince. Fahd had already been responsible for many decisions and had served as minister of education and minister of the interior.

SAUDI ARABIA UNDER KING FAHD

Fahd ibn 'Abd al-'Aziz al-Sa'ud was king from 1982 until his death in 2005. His half brother Crown Prince and First Vice Prime Minister 'Abdullah ibn 'Abd al-'Aziz al-Sa'ud served as regent for him from January 1996, when he suffered a massive stroke, until his death. Major decisions were made by a group of senior princes under Fahd's rule, and at least two princes other than 'Abdullah weighed in significantly: his full

King Fahd ibn 'Abd al-'Aziz al-Sa'ud photographed January 1987. King Fahd reigned from 1982 to 2005. (Peter Turnley/Corbis)

brothers Prince Sultan ibn 'Abd al-'Aziz, minister of defense and civil aviation and second vice prime minister, and Prince Nayif ibn 'Abd al-'Aziz, the minister of the interior. Fahd's birth year is given as 1922 or 1923; he was the 11th son of Ibn Sa'ud and the eldest of the Sudayri Seven, as the sons that Hussah bint Ahmad al-Sudayri had with King 'Abd al-'Aziz are sometimes called (see Chapter 3, Government and Politics). Another of his full brothers is Salman bin 'Abd al-'Aziz, the governor of Riyadh. Fahd had supported his elder half brother Faysal and had served as the minister of education from 1953 to 1960 and the minister of the interior from 1962 to 1975. He was an active leader in King Khalid's government and served as a de facto prime minister when King Khalid was in poor health.

The al-Yamama arms deal, a huge long-term sale, was concluded in 1985, bringing in £43 billion to BAE Systems of the United Kingdom and its partners and providing aircraft and weapons to Saudi Arabia. Saudi Arabia had turned to the United Kingdom for weapons because such a large purchase would likely have been disapproved, or aircraft sales limited, by the U.S. House of Representatives and Senate, due to many members' support for Israel. Margaret Thatcher, the British prime minister, had lobbied hard for the deal. BAE Systems was later sued in the United States, and the Serious Fraud Office (SFO) in the United Kingdom launched an investigation into corruption and bribery in the deal in 2004, but the SFO dropped the case. The High Court ruled against the SFO, but the House of Lords backed the SFO's decision in 2008, arguing that British citizens would be at risk if Saudi Arabia's cooperation in counterterrorism was compromised (*Independent*, July 31, 2008). Then in March 2010, the SFO was barred from dropping the case, following action by two charities. Meanwhile, BAE agreed to a settlement with the U.S. Department of Justice, including a $400 million fine for conspiracy to make false statements and payments in Saudi Arabia, Hungary, and other countries where it acquired arms sales contracts. The SFO dropped a separate case in 2006 that concerned payments made by Prince Bandar (*Independent*, March 3, 2010).

Under King Fahd, Saudi Arabia experienced a drop in oil revenues in 1982 and then a steeper drop in 1986. This essentially resulted from overproduction, which had impacted the oil market, but the bust would over time yield to another boom in prices.

Several technocratic nonroyal reformers earned the wrath of some princes, like popular reformer Ghazi al-Ghosaybi, the minister of health, a nonroyal and a poet. Prior to his dismissal, al-Ghosaybi published a poem in protest in the newspaper *al-Jazirah*; the poem was implicitly directed at the king and began: "Why should I go on singing when there are a thousand slanderers and backbiters going between you and me" (Mackey 1987, 388; also see Chapter 6, section on literature). Then, Ahmad Zaki Yamani, the minister of oil since 1962, who had played a powerful role in the 1973 oil embargo, fell from power in 1986. Oil prices had declined, and when OPEC met in 1986, Fahd had called for more production and a price of $18 a barrel, but Yamani had refused. Meanwhile, in 1983, the Saudi Arabian stock exchange was created. Foreigners could not invest, except for GCC members after 1984.

In 1982 King Fahd formally adopted the honorific title Custodian of the Two Holy Mosques, although the Sa'udi royal family had been exercising this role for decades. In the 1980s, perhaps as a response to growing neosalafism, or even to the attempted takeover at Mecca, stricter Islamic policies were followed.

Saudi Arabia continued to support the concepts of Arab unity and Islamic unity while still opposing the radicalism it had battled earlier in the century. Therefore, the disintegration of Lebanon in its lengthy civil war was of great concern to Saudi Arabia, which had now assumed a regional leadership role. In 1981, the Israeli air force's attacks on Beirut killed 300 and injured some 800 people. Philip Habib, working with Saudi Arabia, managed to forge a deal between Israel and the PLO for a ceasefire (Safran 1985, 331). This did not hold, and in 1982, Israel again invaded the country. As Israel began cleansing Beirut of Palestinians, the terrible massacres by Christian militias, let into the Palestinian refugee camps, Sabra and Chatilla, by the Israeli army, horrified the Saudi Arabian public. In 1989, Saudi Arabia hosted the surviving politicians of the Lebanese parliament at a summit in Ta'if, where formal accords ended the Lebanese Civil War.

Troops from the United Kingdom and other Coalition forces gather for review by King Fahd of Saudi Arabia during the First Gulf War. (Department of Defense)

THE GULF WAR

The Iraqi Republican Guard Forces Command invaded Kuwait on August 2, 1990, and Iraq claimed Kuwait as its 19th province. King Fahd agreed to permit U.S. and international coalition troops to stage operations from Saudi Arabia. During the initial campaign, Operation Desert Shield, forces began to assemble in the kingdom to defend the country if necessary and to enforce sanctions against Iraq (Freedman and Karsh 1993). The next phase of the engagement, Operation Desert Storm, began on January 17, 1991, and lasted for 43 days. During the war, Iraq fired SCUDS (ground-fired tactical missiles) at Saudi Arabia. After a concentrated air assault, a three-pronged ground attack began (initially called Desert Sword, then Desert Sabre), and Kuwait was retaken. Whether or not Iraq would really have invaded Saudi Arabia, the threat to the oil fields was certainly too great to withstand and the war greatly weakened Saddam Hussein. Saudi Arabia provided up to 100,000 personnel, and Prince Khalid ibn Sultan ibn 'Abd al-'Aziz was named commander of the Joint Forces (co-commander with U.S. General H. Norman Schwarzkopf) with the rank of lieutenant general. The Joint Forces consisted of troops from 34 countries, including the Arab nations of Saudi Arabia, Syria, Egypt, Bahrain, Morocco, Oman, Qatar, and the United Arab Emirates. During the ground campaign of the war, Prince Khalid commanded the Joint Forces Command North, composed of troops from Syria, Egypt, and Saudi Arabia, and the Joint Forces Command East, composed of units from the GCC member states. The Gulf War cost Saudi Arabia about $55 billion.

REACTIONS TO THE GULF WAR

Saudi Arabia was displeased by Yemen's declared neutrality in the Gulf War and quite upset with Jordan. Jordan had close historic and economic ties with Iraq and would not join the coalition against Saddam Hussein. Aid was withdrawn from both countries following the war. Because the PLO had sided with Saddam Hussein, the Saudi Arabian government cut off relations and aid to the organization, and the many thousands of Palestinians who had resided in Kuwait were expelled following the Gulf War.

Although Saudi Arabians did not support the Iraqi invasion of Kuwait, many nevertheless opposed the use of Saudi Arabia as a staging ground for Western troops. Osama bin Laden, for one, complained vociferously. The Western presence also aggravated the religious police (*mutawaʻin*). These employees and volunteers with the Committee for the Promotion of Virtue and Prevention of Vice, the modern-day equivalent of the medieval *muhtasib* (a state official who could enforce penalties at the level of *taʼzir*, the second-most serious class of crimes; see the Glossary), had to be reined in by royal edict. Additionally, during the Gulf War, a group of 45 Saudi Arabian women staged a protest against the unofficial ban on women's driving. They drove off together in their vehicles, leaving their male drivers behind. Many were fired from their jobs, and Shaykh ʻAbd al-ʻAziz ibn al-Baz, the country's most senior religious official, issued a *fatwa* in response to this polarizing incident. The *fatwa* officially banned women's driving.

In this period, the *sahwa* (Awakening, the local term that reflected the ongoing regionwide Islamic Awakening movements and activities which some scholars attribute to the Muslim Brotherhood as if the Saudi Arabian Islamists would not have become militant without their example (Lacroix, 2011)) preachers Salman al-Awda and Safar al-Hawali became increasingly popular for their criticism of the government's alliance with the West. They had become well known through the circulation of taped sermons and through live appearances. Shaykh al-Awda hailed from a village not far from the city of Buraydah, once a hotbed of Ikhwan activity, where farmers had protested the late delivery of subsidies. He preached about socioeconomic ills and decried normalization with Israel (al-Hawali 1991; Fandy 1991, 69–113). Another figure, Saʻid al-Ghamidi, attacked liberals and liberal ideas in Saudi Arabia. The government encouraged a countermovement under different preachers such as Shaykh Rabiʻ al-Madkhali (Zuhur 2005, 26).

A petition submitted to King Fahd in December 1990 called for the long-promised establishment of a consultative assembly, the revival of municipal courts, independence of the judiciary, equality of the citizenry, greater media freedom, women's participation, and educational reform (Kechichian 2001, 196–197). Some intellectuals and university students, attracted by the outspokenness of the Awakening movement, were involved in a different petition, the Letter of Demands, signed by more than 400 religious figures calling for heightened observance of Islamic mores. These two initiatives displayed the highly divided Saudi Arabian society in the post–Gulf War period. In 1992, a group of clerics produced a Memorandum of Advice, which also called for stricter observance of Islamic law and the cutting off of Saudi Arabia's relations with Western nations. Senior clerics were asked to decry the Memorandum, and al-Baz did so, but seven other senior clerics would not comply. The Awakening preachers were arrested and not released until later in the 1990s. In 1993 and 1996, two Islamist oppositionist groups emerged and then operated in exile, respectively, the Committee for the Defense of Legitimate Rights and the Movement for Islamic Reform (Zuhur 2005, 27–28; Teitelbaum 2000, 63–65).

At least partly in response, King Fahd proclaimed the Basic System of Government and promised to set up the long-awaited Majlis al-Shura, or Consultative Council. In 1993, he decreed the formal division of the Kingdom of Saudi Arabia into 13 administrative districts, and in December of that year 60 members of the Majlis al-Shura and its chairman were appointed by the king.

In 1994, uprisings by several thousand protesters against government corruption took place in Buraydah, once again expressing *neosalafi* views. Hundreds or possibly thousands were arrested. In that same year, the Saudi Arabian government stripped Osama bin Laden of his Saudi Arabian citizenship, and bin Laden relocated his operations to the Sudan. A car bombing targeted the facility housing the U.S. Army Materiel Command's Office of the Program Manager for the Saudi Arabian National Guard in Riyadh in 1995. Three of those executed for that crime were "Afghan" or "Bosnian" Arabs, identified as such because they had traveled to Afghanistan or Bosnia to fight, part of the global jihad. Scholars have described the "global jihad" as the internationalization of jihad beyond any one single target whether one of the "near enemy" (co-opted Muslim rulers) or the "far enemy" (Western opponents of Muslims).

After King Fahd suffered a stroke, Crown Prince 'Abdullah took over the leadership. Fahd later had gallbladder surgery, and 'Abdullah was increasingly acting as regent. Fahd retreated for extended periods to his estate in Marbella, Spain. 'Abdullah reshaped the cabinet, appointing 15 new members out of 29 cabinet positions, many of whom had professional experience (Obaid 2000, 11).

In 1996, a massive truck bomb killed 19 Americans and injured 345 at the Khobar Towers in Dhahran. A group known as (Saudi Arabian) Hizballah was responsible, although the American inquiry and indictment emphasized suspicions of Iran and Lebanese Hizballah (one of its members was involved) to a greater degree than did the Saudi Arabian government (Clarke 2005; Cordesman 2003, 196–206; Unger 2004).

Saudi Arabia's foreign policy began to shift. The Taliban seized Kabul, Afghanistan, in 1996. In 1997, Saudi Arabia recognized them but, the next year, accused the Taliban of providing shelter to Osama bin Laden and broke off relations with the Taliban in 2001. The Kingdom of Saudi Arabia achieved a rapprochement with Iran after Muhammad Khatami was elected in May 1997. Crown Prince 'Abdullah visited Tehran for the Organization of the Islamic Conference summit, and first Akbar Hashemi Rafsanjani, the former Iranian president, and then Khatami visited Riyadh. Iran agreed to cooperate with an OPEC production cutback, which greatly increased Saudi Arabian revenues (Obaid 2000, 60–61, 80). Domestic reforms also continued, with the expansion of the Majlis al-Shura in 1997 to 90 members and then, in 2001, to 120 members.

THE WAR ON TERRORISM AND THE GLOBAL WAR ON TERROR

On August 7, 1998, bombs hit the American embassies in Tanzania and Kenya, which were traced to the far-flung al-Qa'ida network. According to some, it was clear that al-Qa'ida had declared war on the United States—if not in this attack, then in the one on the USS *Cole* in Yemen. But the Saudi Arabian rulers disclaimed responsibility for bin Laden, whom they had stripped of citizenship some years previously. The Kingdom of Saudi Arabia was startled by the news that 15 of the 19 terrorists who hijacked American airplanes on September 11, 2001, were Saudi Arabians. The American media, authors, and pundits launched attacks on Saudi Arabia's purported sponsorship of terrorism to an extent never before seen as the Federal Bureau of Investigation (FBI) rounded up Saudi Arabian citizens in the United States (Eilts 2001). Saudi Arabians, and indeed most Arabs, were denied visas, and quite a few Saudi Arabians who had settled in the United States relocated back to their country. Saudi-bashing continued in a political environment led by U.S. neoconservatives and was matched by Saudi Arabian antipathy to American policies. As the United States began to plan a war against Iraq, the Saudi Arabian foreign minister said that the kingdom would not allow the United States to launch strikes from its soil even if the United Nations approved an attack.

Beginning in 2003, Saudi Arabia's citizenry was terrified by a wave of violent attacks within the kingdom, which were attributed to al-Qa'ida fi Jazirat al-'Arabiyyah (al-Qa'ida on the Arabian Peninsula, a group separate from, although similar in aims, to al-Qa'ida in Afghanistan and Pakistan). A bomb exploded in a home in Riyadh on March 18, 2003. This premature explosion led authorities to discover an enormous arms stockpile. A gun battle between the police and extremists took place in Riyadh on May 6, following a raid. Six days later, 12 suicide bombers attacked residential compounds in Riyadh on May 12, just prior to a planned visit by Secretary of State Colin Powell, killing 35 people, wounding 200, and signaling a crisis on Saudi Arabian soil. Many clashes followed, suggesting the presence of 10 or more cells of al-Qa'ida fi jazirat al-'arabiyyah (al-Qa'ida on the Arabian Peninsula). Hideouts were discovered in various parts of the country, and the leader of al-Qa'ida on the Arabian Peninsula, Yusuf al-'Uyayri, was killed by security forces (Zuhur 2005, 35). Another suicide attack took place at the al-Muhayya residential compound on November 8, 2003, killing 17. A group or cell identified as the Haramayn Brigades began battling security forces (see Chapter 7, Contemporary Issues).

At the same time, public protests against the Saudi Arabian government grew in September and October, resulting in arrests. Yet, in November, the Majlis al-Shura obtained greater legislative powers. The struggle between the Saudi Arabian citizenry and the government was not the cause of the ongoing reforms; rather, ruler-led, not citizen-sparked, reforms have been ongoing. Yet the latter popular movements continued and represented two camps—salafist and Islamist, and liberals, and some combinations (Lacroix 2005).

The terrorist groups pushed back against the counterterrorism campaign, killing some officers in gun battles, others in a car bombing. In May 2004, the Yanbu offices of a Swiss company were penetrated by militants, who moved freely around the installation, killing Westerners. On May 31, gunmen charged into an office and then through a housing compound in al-Khobar, killing 22 foreigners. In June, an Irish cameraman for the BBC, Simon Cumbers, was killed in Riyadh, and his colleague, Frank Gardner, was seriously wounded. Lone Westerners were attacked in Riyadh. For the first time since the drop in oil prices in the 1980s, many foreigners decided to leave the kingdom. An American employee of Lockheed Martin, Paul M. Johnson Jr., was beheaded by the self-proclaimed Fallujah Brigade, of the al-Qa'ida on the Arabian Peninsula, horrifying many Saudi Arabian citizens. The police reported that they had killed 'Abd al-'Aziz al-Muqrin, a leader of that group, along with three other leading militants, on June 19, 2004, and then offered a largely unsuccessful amnesty to militants. Another group of militants targeted the U.S. consulate in Jeddah, where five staff and four attackers were killed in December 2004, and more car bombs exploded in Riyadh.

Municipal elections were held countrywide from February to April 2005, sparking interest in political participation. Women were not permitted to vote or stand for election, and the two most frequent excuses given were (a) that too many women lacked identity cards (identity cards were issued in 2001 with a guardian's permission; however, many women decline to be photographed) and arrangements had not been made for female voting facilities; and (b) that the country was not yet ready for their participation as conservative protests against female suffrage might be overwhelming (Zuhur, Personal Interviews, 2005–2008). The government launched an Islamic antiterrorist campaign. The campaign included billboard advertisements, poster conferences where religious figures argued against militance using arguments based on Islamic precepts, and television dramas that addressed the background of militance and its presence in local communities. Also, the government began an experiment staffed by psychologists, other social scientists, and religious experts in "reeducating" detainees suspected of being linked to the militants. The voluntary counseling program was intended to correct wrongful notions of jihad and *takfir* (the action of declaring a Muslim to be a non-Muslim, or infidel, because of their sins) and antipathy to non-Muslims; to repatriate former militants alienated from their country, families, or communities; and to provide employment and other support to graduates of the program (Zuhur 2010).

King Fahd died of pneumonia in Riyadh on August 1, 2005. At the time of his death, Fahd was considered one of the richest men in the world, with a personal fortune worth more than $20 billion. Fahd was succeeded by his brother, Crown Prince 'Abdullah.

THE REIGN OF KING 'ABDULLAH

'Abdullah ibn 'Abd al-'Aziz al-Sa'ud was born in Riyadh in 1924 and educated at the Princes' School at the royal court. His mother comes from the al-Rashid family of the Shammar tribe. He became the mayor of Mecca in 1950, deputy defense minister in 1963, and the second deputy prime minister in 1975. He was the commander of the Saudi Arabian National Guard since 1963. He then became crown prince in 1982; the acting ruler of Saudi Arabia from 1995 to 2005 and then became king in 2005.

King 'Abdullah led the campaign against the ongoing internal terrorist threat. Soon after his brother's death, clashes with Islamist jihadists occurred in September in Dammam, in which three police and five gunmen were killed. In February 2006, militants planned a suicide bomb attack at the oil-processing installation of Abqaiq, but authorities stopped them. Further shoot-outs took place, including one in June 2006. After months of surveillance, a large-scale plot involving 172 members of seven terror cells was disrupted at the end of April 2007. Saudi Arabian officials said these operatives planned to attack military bases and oil refineries and that some of those arrested had been training as pilots in an unspecified "troubled country" (Associated Press, April 28, 2007). A large-scale plot timed to take place during the 2007 *hajj* (pilgrimage) season in December was also foiled, with arrests made in various Saudi Arabian cities (*Al-Arabiyya*, December 21, 2007; *Arab News*, December 23, 2007; Zuhur 2010).

By 2008, Saudi Arabian officials estimated that as many as 4,000 persons had been questioned and several thousand detained for suspicions of terrorist activity, many of whom had returned from jihad campaigns outside of Saudi Arabia. The officials had frozen financial transfers to suspicious charities, and they mounted an Internet surveillance and interactive project called the Sakinah (Tranquility) campaign in order to ferret out and actively debate Internet recruitment to violence online (Zuhur 2010).

In April 2008, another group of militants was captured, and, in July 2009, the courts issued verdicts against at least 330 persons on trial for terrorism. In August 2009, 44 more persons were arrested or detained on terrorism charges. On August 28, 2009, the deputy minister of the interior, Prince Muhammad ibn Nayif, survived a suicide bomber's attack at his home in Jeddah that killed the bomber, Abdullah Hassan al-Asiri. Al-Asiri had previously fled to Yemen but then pretended he was going to surrender himself to Prince Muhammad. Then, he set off the PETN (plastic explosive) bomb hidden in his underwear (Bergen 2009). In 2009, al-Qa'ida on the Arabian Peninsula announced its membership in a new consortium based in Yemen, perhaps as a way of maintaining visibility outside of the kingdom. Saudi Arabia has supported attacks against al-Qa'ida in Yemen and has also engaged in aerial bombings against the Houthi movement, a tribal opposition to President Saleh (see Chapter 3, Government and Politics), while allegedly acting against al-Qa'ida. However, the Saudi Arabian al-Qa'ida movement is still active, although the media have tended to downplay its presence in Saudi Arabia and have focused markedly on the threat in Yemen. Violent plots continued to be discovered through 2010. The arrests of 149 al-Qa'ida suspects in three networks, as well as seizures of arms and $600,000 worth of cash, took place in late November 2010 (*Huffington Post*, November 26, 2010). In early January 2011, the Saudi Arabian government identified 47 militants it wants to arrest, some of whom are in other countries, and sought assistance from Interpol (*Bloomberg News*, January 9, 2011).

On May 1, 2011, U.S. Special Forces killed Osama bin Laden in a compound in the area of Abbotabad, Pakistan. Although the other al-Qa'ida movements are not directly controlled by the original movement, the assassination surely had a symbolic effect on militants elsewhere, including Saudi Arabia. Saudi Arabia was thought to be part of the security cooperation necessary to locating bin Laden, and the country was targeted soon after in attacks by Pakistani Taliban, one of which killed a security official working for the Saudi Arabian embassy in Karachi. On May 5, Khalid Hadal al-Qahtani, who was on a list of most-wanted terrorists, surrendered to the Saudi Arabian security authorities. On that same day, a U.S. drone airplane killed two AQAP members in an attack in southern Yemen that was intended to eliminate a Saudi Arabian AQAP leader.

Despite the continuing concerns about terrorism, 'Abdullah has initiated important reforms in the kingdom. In 2005, Saudi Arabia joined the World Trade Organization, which has been opening the country to joint or conglomerate ventures. In 2007, he ordered changes in the judicial system and stepped in to prevent miscarriages of justice in several high-profile cases, such as that of the rape victim known as the Qatif Girl and one in which a father married off an eight-year-old child whom a judge then denied the right to divorce (see Chapter 5, section on women). In that same year, 'Abdullah issued an order barring the religious police from carrying out their own detentions.

Saudi Arabia's regional policies have importantly impacted Lebanon and the Palestinians. Former Lebanese prime minister Rafiq al-Hariri, who had been close to Saudi Arabia's rulers, was assassinated in 2005. Saudi Arabia backed the political party headed by his son Sa'd al-Hariri, the Future Party, and helped to pressure Syria to withdraw from the country. Saudi Arabia was extremely disturbed by the 2006 Israeli war on Lebanon, supposedly directed at Hizballah, and Prince Sa'ud al-Faysal called for the United States to arrange a ceasefire, an entreaty that was not heeded nor supported by U.S. secretary of state Condoleezza Rice, U.S. ambassador to the United Nations John Bolton, or President George W. Bush. Saudi Arabia supported compromise measures aimed at resolving Lebanese factional disputes (see Chapter 3, Government and Politics). However, behind the scenes, it appears that Saudi Arabia exerted and called for a great deal of pressure against Hizballah, despite the party's alliance with non-Muslims, that is, General Michel Aoun's supporters. In 2011, the outbreak of protests against the government of Bashar al-Asad has been strongly supported by certain Lebanese elements and Syrian expatriates, and Saudi Arabia's generally pro-American, anti-Hizballah policies may be important to both countries.

The Saudi Arabian stance on the lengthy division and conflict between the Palestinian parties Hamas and Fatah has differed from the U.S. position. The Saudi Arabian rulers invited both Palestinian parties to Mecca to establish an agreement after fratricidal fighting broke out. The agreement unfortunately did not solve the conflict, in part because Israel and the United States refused to accept the legitimacy of the elected Hamas government and encouraged, or even armed, Fatah and other elements against Hamas. The Saudi Arabian position has been that the Palestinians, like the Lebanese, must achieve a national unity government. An agreement was forged between the two groups in the spring of 2011, encouraged by the army leadership of the new Egyptian government, and many Saudi Arabians approve of this advent (although Israel and the United States have threatened Fatah that it must not continue its hard-won alliance with Hamas).

Under 'Abdullah, Saudi Arabia has continued to strengthen its relationship with other Muslim nations and its support of Islamic causes. While the West has critiqued Saudi Arabia for spreading terrorism through bolstering Islamic identity (Hanley

2003) or being a "problematic ally to the U.S. in the war on extremism" (National Commission on Terrorist Attacks upon the United States 2004), the Saudi Arabian view is that educational, developmental, and peaceful aspects of Islamic alliances are possible and positive and that it has fully cooperated in suppressing the spread of terrorism. While relations with the United States have greatly improved since the attacks of September 11, the two countries did not see eye to eye on U.S. aims and tactics in Iraq or its stance toward Iran. They had strongly hoped President Barack Obama would recast these aspects of U.S. foreign policy as suggested during his political campaign, but some were dubious about the U.S. withdrawal from Iraq because of the potential for chaos there. However, the United States maintains a very strong profile in Iraq, and many Saudi Arabians (not necessarily the government) will also be relieved if a withdrawal with a similar continuing presence is arranged in Afghanistan.

Saudi Arabia has upheld goals for Saudization of the workforce throughout its economic planning. Nonetheless, a sizable foreign workforce remains in Saudi Arabia, made up of Asians, Westerners, and Arabs, including about a million Egyptians. Numerous Asian world nationals have come from Bangladesh, India, Pakistan, Nepal, the Philippines, and elsewhere. International bodies have voiced considerable concern regarding the treatment of foreign workers in the Kingdom of Saudi Arabia. The aim of Saudization is to educate and prepare Saudi Arabian employees and professionals to be employed in the place of foreign workers. However, foreign non-Western workers are far cheaper to house and less likely to demand higher incomes, due to the sponsorship system and the depressed labor conditions in their own countries. Overall, this situation and its defects remain an area for reform by King 'Abdullah's government.

'Abdullah's own administration highlighted four main areas of accomplishment: (1) a stress on educational reform and the establishment of many universities; (2) his efforts on behalf of Arab-Israeli peace, beginning with the Arab Peace Initiative, which he announced in March 2002, calling for a Palestinian state with the return of pre-1967 territory and efforts to end inter-Palestinian strife as in the Hamas-Fatah agreement forged in Saudi Arabia in 2007, which unfortunately broke down when Hamas learned that a Fatah uprising was to be launched against them in Gaza; (3) economic development, the achievement of certain milestones in Saudization (jobs now acquired by Saudi Arabians), and the building of six economic cities; and (4) the fostering of dialogue. King 'Abdullah has called for dialogue among Saudi Arabians as during the municipal elections, between Muslim religious sects, and concerning the issue of women, and with representatives of Christianity, Buddhism, Islam, and Judaism in an International Conference for Dialogue organized by the Muslim World League at the king's initiative from July 16–18, 2008, in Madrid, Spain (*Ekklesia*, July 17, 2008; *Sharq al-Awsat*, July 22, 2008). In 2009, he inaugurated the King Abdullah University of Science and Technology at Thuwal, about 80 kilometers (approximately 50 miles) north of Jeddah. In February 2009, King 'Abdullah appointed the first woman cabinet member: a woman deputy minister of girl's education, Norah al-Fayez. He dismissed the head of the Commission for the

Promotion of Virtue and Prevention of Vice, known as the *mutawaʿin*, and also fired the high-ranking judge Saleh al-Luhaydan, who had declared it *halal* (Islamically permitted) to kill the owners of television programs whose content was not Islamic. Supporters believe these actions confirm Abdullah's reforming mission, yet detractors were still critical (Jones 2009).

In November 2009, Saudi Arabian troops moved in to enforce a buffer zone in northern Yemen after a series of clashes with Yemeni groups. The Yemeni government was cooperating with the United States, and apparently with the Saudi Arabian government, but had not defeated the Houthi rebels or the AQAP branch operating in Yemen with some coordination with the Saudi Arabia–based AQAP groups, as explained earlier (see also Chapter 7, Contemporary Issues). With the release of classified embassy reports through Wikileaks, certain stances of the Saudi Arabian, American, and Yemeni governments became public knowledge. For instance, Americans were conducting the bombings in Yemen, instead of the Yemeni air force (with coordination and approval from Saudi Arabia) but the Yemeni government publicly lied about this; and that the Saudi Arabian leadership had been extremely concerned by and hostile to Iran's acquisition of nuclear technology despite various conciliatory statements to the contrary by the Saudi Arabian Foreign Ministry. Overall, these disclosures underscored the close alliance between Saudi Arabia and the United States but also points of tension coming from differing prioritizations of national security.

At the time of writing, a wave of political oppositions has swept the Arab world in Tunisia, Egypt, Libya, Syria, Bahrain, Yemen, and Oman, and also in Morocco, Jordan, and to a much lesser degree Saudi Arabia. Saudi Arabia's policies toward some of these countries will be affected, and it has witnessed large demonstrations in its eastern cities. Many observers believed that the huge package of cash grants, loans, raises, apartments, and reforms announced by King ʿAbdullah in mid-March 2011 was intended to stave off discontent in Saudi Arabia. The creation of 60,000 new jobs in the security sector also indicates concern over political stability. Perhaps the potential for popular revolutions elsewhere will hasten the speed of political and social transformation in Saudi Arabia. For now, the royal family remains firmly in control and a buffer between the more conservative elements of the population and those who would welcome swifter and more substantive reforms.

REFERENCES

Aboul-Enein, Youssef. "The Egyptian-Yemen War: Egyptian Perspectives on Guerilla Warfare." *Infantry Magazine*, January–February 2004. http://findarticles.com/p/articles/mi_m0IAV/is_1_93/ai_n6123802/?tag=content;col1

Aboul-Enein, Youssef, and Sherifa Zuhur. *Islamic Rulings on Warfare*. Carlisle, PA: Strategic Studies Institute, 2004.

al-Ansary, Abd al-Rahman. *Qaryat al-Fau: A Portrait of Pre-Islamic Civilization in Saudi Arabia*. Riyadh, Saudi Arabia: Riyadh University Press, 1982.

Armstrong, H. C. *Lord of Arabia*. London: Arthur Barker, 1934.

al-Askar, Abdullah. *Al-Yamama in the Early Islamic Era*. Reading, UK: Ithaca Press, in association with the King Abdul Aziz Foundation for Research and Archives, KSA, 2002.

Ayoub, Mahmoud. *The Qur'an and Its Interpreters: The House of Imran*. Albany: State University of New York Press, 1992.

Beling, William A., ed. *King Faisal and the Modernization of Saudi Arabia*. Boulder, CO: Westview Press, 1980.

Bergen, Peter. "Similar Explosive on Plane Used in Saudi Attack." *CNN.com*, December 27, 2009.

Bornstein-Makovetsky, Leah (based on Braslavi, Joseph, from the 1st edition). "Khaybar." In *Encyclopedia Judaica*, 2nd ed., editor-in-chief, Fred Sko. Macmillan, Gale Group, 2008.

Bowersock, G. W. "The Arabs before Islam." In *The Genius of Arab Civilization: Source of Renaissance*, edited by John Hayes. New York: New York University Press, 1992, 17–34.

Brown, Anthony Cave. *Oil, God, and Gold: The Story of Aramco and the Saudi Kings*. Boston: Houghton Mifflin, 1999.

Al-Bukhari (Muhammad ibn Isma'il ibn Ibrahim ibn al-Mughira ibn Barizbah al-Bukhari). *Sahih Bukhari*. Translated by M. Muhsin Khan. Vol. 5, Book 59 (Military Expeditions Led by the Prophet), nos. 285–749. Available online by the University of Southern California, Center for Muslim Jewish Engagement, 2007. http://www.usc.edu/schools/college/crcc/engagement/resources/texts/muslim/hadith/bukhari/059.sbt.html

Chevron. "Chevron and Saudi Arabia/Chevron wa al-Mamlakah al-'Arabiyyah al-Sa'udiyyah." Riyadh, Saudi Arabia: Arabian Chevron, n.d. [ca. 2007].

Ciorciari, John D. "Saudi-U.S. Alignment after the Six Day War." *Middle East Review of International Affairs* 9, no. 2 (June 2005). http://meria.idc.ac.il/journal/2005/issue2/jv9no2a1.html

Clarke, Richard. "Interview with Richard Clarke." "The Man Who Knew." Produced and directed by Michael Kirk. *Frontline*. Public Broadcasting Service, March 20, 2002. http://www.pbs.org/wgbh/pages/frontline/shows/knew/interviews/clarke.html

Commins, David Dean. *The Wahhabi Mission and Saudi Arabia*. London: I. B. Tauris, 2006.

Cordesman, Anthony H., and Nawaf Obaid. *Saudi National Security: Military and Security Services—Challenges and Developments*. Full Report. Washington, DC: Center for Strategic and International Studies, Draft, September 29, 2004.

Cordesman, Anthony H. *Saudi Arabia Enters the Twenty-First Century: The Political, Foreign Policy, Economic, and Energy Dimensions*. London: Center for Strategic and International Studies; Westport, CT: Praeger, 2003.

de Corancez, Louis Alexandre Olivier. *The History of the Wahabis from Their Origin until the End of 1809*. Translated by Eric Tabet. Reading, UK: Garnet, 1995.

De Gaury, Gerald. *Arabia Felix*. London: George Harrap, 1947.

Delong-Bas, Natana J. *Wahhabi Islam: From Revival and Reform to Global Jihad*. Oxford, UK: Oxford University Press, 2004.

Eilts, Hermann F. "U.S.-Saudi Relations after the September 11 Debacle." *American Diplomacy*, November 22, 2001.

Ekklesia. "Madrid Inter-Faith Summit Highlights Global Problems and Possibilities." July 17, 2008.

Facey, William. *Dir'iyyah and the First Saudi State.* London: Stacey International, 1997.

Fandy, Mamoun. "Strategic Dimensions of the Interfaith Dialogue." *Al-Sharq al-Awsat,* July 22, 2008. http://www.aawsat.com/english/news.asp?section=2&id=13477

Fandy, Mamoun. *Saudi Arabia and the Politics of Dissent.* New York: Palgrave, 1991.

Farsy, Fouad. *Custodian of the Two Holy Mosques: King Fahd bin Abdul Aziz.* New York: Knight Communications, 2001.

Fraser, T. G. *The Middle East 1914–1979.* London: Edward Arnold, 1980. Contains a reprinting of the Resolutions of the Khartoum Conference, September 1, 1967, 115–116.

Freedman, Lawrence, and Efraim Karsh. *The Gulf Conflict, 1990–1991: Diplomacy and War in the New World Order.* Princeton, NJ: Princeton University Press, 1993.

Guillaume, A. *The Life of Mohammed: A Translation of Ibn Ishaq's Sirat Rasul Allah.* Oxford, UK: Oxford University Press 1955; reissued Pakistan, 1967.

Hamdan, Amani. "Women and Education in Saudi Arabia: Challenges and Achievements." *International Education Journal* 6, no. 1 (2005), 42–64.

Hanley, Delinda. "Saudi Bashing: Who's behind It and Why." *Washington Report on Middle East Affairs,* March 2003, 20–21.

Hawali, Safar al-. *Haqa'iq hawl 'Azmat al-Khalij.* Cairo: Dar Makka al-Mukarrama, 1991.

Harrigan, Peter. "New Pieces of Mada'in Saleh's Puzzle." *Saudi Aramco World* 58, no. 4 (July/August 2007), 14–23.

Henderson, Simon. *After King Fahd: Succession in Saudi Arabia.* Washington, DC: Washington Institute for Near East Policy, 1994.

Hjelm, Ingrid. "The Assyrian Evidence: A Reply to Salibi's Questions Regarding Assyrian Sources for Their Campaigns in Palestine and the Existence of a Bît Humria in Palestine in the Iron II." *Scandinavian Journal of the Old Testament* 23, no. 1 (May 2009), 7–22.

Hodgson, Marshall. *The Venture of Islam: The Classical Age of Islam.* Chicago: University of Chicago Press, 1974.

Holden, David, and Richard Johns. *The House of Saud.* New York: Holt, Rinehart and Winston, 1982.

Hopper, Mathew S. "Pearls, Globalization and the African Diaspora in the Arabian Gulf in the Age of Empire." Paper presented at the 124th Annual Meeting of the American Historical Association, San Diego, January 9, 2010.

Hopper, Mathew S. "The African Presence in Arabia: Slavery, the World Economy, and the African Diaspora in Eastern Arabia, 1840–1940." PhD diss., University of California, Los Angeles, 2006.

Hoyland, Robert. *Arabia and the Arabs: From the Bronze Age to the Coming of Islam.* London and New York: Routledge, 2001.

Ibn Bishr, 'Uthman. *'Unwan al-majd fi tarikh Najd.* Riyadh, Saudi Arabia: Maktabah al-Riyadh al-Hadithah, n.d.

Ibn Ghannam, Husayn. *Rawdat al-afkar wa al-afham li-murtad hal al-imam wa-ta'dad ghazawat dhawi al-Islam.* Riyadh, 1381h.

Ibn Ghannam, Husayn. *Tarikh Najd.* Cairo, 1961.

Ibn Ishaq. *The Life of Muhammad, Apostle of Allah*. Translated by Edward Rahatsek. Abridged and introduced by Michael Edwards. London: The Folio Society, 1964.

Ibn Ishaq. *al-Sira al-nabawiyya*. Edited by Ahmad Farid al-Mizyadi. 2 vols. 2nd ed. Beirut: Dar al-Kutub al-'Ilmiyya, 2009.

Ibn Ishaq. *Sirat Rasul Allah li-Ibn Ishaq/Ibn Hisham: al-fatrah al-Makkiyah: tahlil naqdi lil-nass.* Edited by Mahmud Ali Murad. Dar al-Hilal, 2000.

Ibrahim, Mahmood. "Social and Economic Conditions in Pre-Islamic Mecca." *International Journal of Middle East Studies* 14, no. 3 (1982), 343–358.

Jones, Toby. "Saudi Arabia's Silent Spring." *Foreign Policy*, February 2009. http://www.foreignpolicy.com/story/cms.php?story_id=4718

al-Juhany, Uwaidah M. *Najd before the Salafi Reform Movement: Social, Religious and Political Conditions in the Three Centuries Preceding the Rise of the Saudi State*. Reading, UK: Ithaca, 2002.

Kechichian, Joseph. *Succession in Saudi Arabia*. New York: Palgrave, 2001.

Kerr, Malcolm. *The Arab Cold War: Gamal Abd al-Nasir and His Rivals 1958–1970*. London: Oxford University Press, 1971.

Kostiner, Joseph. "Regulating Arab Politics (Part I): The War of the Summits." *Tel Aviv Notes*, March 26, 2009.

Lacey, Robert. *Inside the Kingdom: Kings, Clerics, Modernists, Terrorists and the Struggle for Saudi Arabia*. New York: Viking Penguin, 2009.

Lacey, Robert. *The Kingdom*. London: Hutchinson, 1981.

Lacroix, Stéphane. *Awakening Islam*. Translated by George Holoch. Cambridge, MA: Harvard University Press, 2011.

Lacroix, Stéphane. "Islamo-Liberal Politics in Saudi Arabia." In *Saudi Arabia in the Balance*, edited by Paul Aarts and Gerd Nonneman. London: Hurst, 2005, 35–56.

Lewis, Bernard. *Race and Slavery in the Middle East: An Historical Enquiry*. New York: Oxford University Press, 1990.

Lings, Martin. *Muhammad: His Life Based on the Earliest Sources*. Rochester, VT: Inner Traditions International, 1983.

Mackey, Sandra. *The Saudis: Inside the Desert Kingdom*. New York: New American Library, 1987.

al-Mumayiz, Amin. *Al-Mamlakah al-'Arabiyyah kama 'ariftuha: Mudhakkirat diblumasiyyah.* Beirut, Lebanon, 1963.

National Commission on Terrorist Attacks upon the United States. "Executive Summary." In *The 9/11 Commission Report.* National Commission on Terrorist Attacks upon the United States, 2004. http://www.911commission.gov/report/911Report_Exec.htm

Nicholson, James. *The Hejaz Railway*. London: Stacey International; Riyadh, Saudi Arabia: Al-Turath, 2005.

Obaid, Nawaf E. *The Oil Kingdom at 100: Petroleum Policymaking in Saudi Arabia*. Washington, DC: Washington Institute for Near East Policy, 2000.

Philby, H. St. J. B. *Arabian Jubilee*. London: Robert Hale, 1952.

Pirenne, J. *A la découverte de l'Arabie*. Paris: Le livre contemporaine, 1958.

Powell, William. *Saudi Arabia and Its Royal Family*. Secaucus, NJ: Lyle Stuart, 1982.

Public Broadcasting Service. "2005 Update: Death of a Princess: Interview with Ali al-Ahmed" and "Interview with Antony Thomas." Producers, Jim Gilmore and ?Greg Barke; associate producer, Catherine Wright; editor, Shady Hartshorne. *Frontline*, April 19, 2005. http://www.pbs.org/wgbh/pages/frontline/shows/princess/interviews/

Ramadan, Tariq. *In the Footsteps of the Prophet*. New York: Oxford University Press, 2007.

al-Rasheed, Madawi. "Saudi Arabia and the Palestine War: Beyond Official History." In *The War for Palestine: Rewriting the History of 1948 War*, edited by Eugene Rogan and Avi Shlaim. 2nd ed. Cambridge: Cambridge University Press, 2007, 228–247.

Al-Rasheed, Madawi. *A History of Saudi Arabia*. Cambridge: Cambridge University Press, 2002.

Rentz, George, and William Facey. *The Birth of the Islamic Reform Movement in Saudi Arabia: Muhammad ibn Abd al-Wahhab 1703/4–1792 and the Beginning of Unitarian Empire in Saudi Arabia*. London: Arabian Publishers, 2004.

Ruedy, John. "Philip the Arab." In *The Genius of Arab Civilization: Source of Renaissance*, edited by John Hayes. New York: New York University Press, 1992, 42–44.

Sabini, John. *Armies in the Sand: The Struggle for Mecca*. London: Thames and Hudson, 1981.

Safran, Nadav. *Saudi Arabia: The Ceaseless Quest for Security*. Cambridge, MA: Belknap Press of Harvard University Press, 1985.

Salibi, Kamal. *Who Was Jesus? Conspiracy in Jerusalem.* London: Tauris Parke, 2007.

Salibi, Kamal. *The Bible Came from Arabia*. London: Jonathan Cape, 1985.

Smyth, William. "The Historical Setting." In *Saudi Arabia: A Country Study*, edited by Helen Chapin Metz. Washington, DC: Library of Congress, 1993.

Teitelbaum, Joshua. *Holier Than Thou: Saudi Arabia's Islamic Opposition.* Washington, DC: Washington Institute for Near East Policy, 2000.

Al-Tihami, Nuqra. "Muhammad ibn Abd al-Wahhab and His Call for Monotheism." In *A History of the Arabian Peninsula*, edited by al-Fahd Semmari and translated by S. Jayyusi. London: Palgrave Macmillan, 2010, 91–104.

Trofimov, Yaroslav. *The Siege of Mecca: The Forgotten Uprising in Islam's Holiest Shrine and the Birth of Al Qa'ida*. New York: Random House, 2007.

Unger, Craig. *House of Bush, House of Saud: The Secret Relationship between the World's Two Most Powerful Dynasties*. New York: Scribner, 2004.

Van der Meulen, Daniel. *The Wells of Ibn Saud*. New York: Praeger, 1957.

Vassiliev, Alexei. *The History of Saudi Arabia*. London: Saqi Books, 1998.

Voll, John. "Muhammad Hayya al-Sindi and Muhammad 'Abd al-Wahhab: An Analysis of an Intellectual Group in Eighteenth-Century Madina." *Bulletin of the School of Oriental and African Studies* 38 (1975), 32–39.

Willbanks, James H. "Faysal, King of Saudi Arabia." In *The Encyclopedia of the Arab-Israeli Conflict*, edited by Spencer Tucker. 4 vols. Santa Barbara, CA: ABC-CLIO, 2008, Vol. 2, 435–436.

Wynbrandt, James. *A Brief History of Saudi Arabia*. New York: Facts on File, 2004.

Zuhur, Sherifa. "Radicalization and Deradicalization in Saudi Arabia." In *Home-Grown Terrorism: Understanding and Addressing the Root Causes of Radicalisation among Groups with an Immigrant Heritage in Europe*, edited by Thomas M. Pick, Anne Speckhard, and Beatrice Jacuch. Amsterdam: IOS, with NATO Public Diplomacy Division, 2010, 74–98.

Zuhur, Sherifa. Personal interviews conducted in Riyadh, Dir'iyyah, Jeddah, London, and Washington, DC, 2005–2008.

Zuhur, Sherifa. *Saudi Arabia, Islamic Threat, Political Reform and the Global War on Terror*. Carlisle Barracks, PA: Strategic Studies Institute, U.S. Army War College, 2005.

Zuhur, Sherifa. "Arabs and Arab Culture." In *Nazar, Photography and Visual Culture of the Arab World*, edited by Wim Melis. Leeuwarden, the Netherlands: Stichting Fotografie Noorderlicht, 2004, 22–24 in English and 14–16 in Arabic.

CHAPTER 3

Government and Politics

The Saudi Arabian government is a dynastic and hereditary monarchy headed by the al-Sa'ud family. Sources critical of the kingdom claim it is an absolute monarchy because political parties are not permitted and it lacks an elected legislative body. Others contend that the king's power is limited, and the government relies on the creation of consensus, "not authoritarianism," and on "pragmatism, rather than ideology" (Cordesman 2003, 132). Under the first three kings since the modern nation's foundation ('Abd al-'Aziz al-Sa'ud, Sa'ud ibn 'Abd al-'Aziz, and Faysal ibn 'Abd al-'Aziz), ultimate power was wielded by the ruler and a group of senior princes, who weighed in on, or initiated, action. An informal structure, the *ahl al-hal wa-l-'aqd*, composed of the senior princes of the different branches of the al-Sa'ud family, sometimes met as a larger council, as they did during the crisis of 1964 (Lacey 1981, 354). This type of decision making still functions, but all areas of government have expanded, and the matter of succession was regulated and delegated to a new body, the Bay'ah, or Allegiance, Council. Even with the rise of "royal technocrats"—junior princes serving in government and nonroyal professional advisers—Gerd Nonneman (2005, 337), a scholar of Saudi Arabia, believes that the senior royal princes exercise the strongest decision-making role in Saudi Arabia, including that of the king.

Since the creation of the Majlis al-Shura, the Consultative Council, the government may be characterized as a consultative monarchy. *Shura* (consultation) is an Islamic requirement of government; it is also an Arab and bedouin tradition. Through consultation, the ruler better serves the ruled. Many key governmental positions are held by members of the royal family, and a primary root of political and governmental actions is to ensure the continuing primacy of the royal family.

Prominent advisers to the king have offices in the Royal Diwan (the King's Court), as does the king. The Council of Ministers is the principal executive structure of government, advising the king, who must approve its decisions. He is also advised by the Majlis al-Shura. This body existed early in the modern state's history and was revived under King Fahd ibn 'Abd al-'Aziz, who also decreed a Majlis al-Shura law (08 27, 1412 h.) The Majlis al-Shura was expanded under King 'Abdullah ibn 'Abd al-'Aziz after 2005, and it includes a wide range of advisers and opinions.

Saudi Arabia proclaims it is governed by the Qur'an and the sunna, or tradition of the Prophet Muhammad. The kingdom observes Islamic law. Saudi Arabia does not have a constitution per se, although it possesses a Basic Law. King Fahd promulgated the Basic Law following the First Gulf War in 1992. Consisting of nine chapters and 83 articles, it is similar to a constitution in that it sets out basic principles of government and explains the duties and rights of various bodies and of the state and its citizens. The Basic Law is constructed so as not to violate *shari'ah*, as do the man-made laws of other Muslim states, according to the *salafiyya* (religious purists who call for a return to the spirit of the first three generations of Islam). The Basic Law explains that the two official holidays of Saudi Arabia are the religious feasts—the 'Id al-Fitr, which concludes Ramadan, and the 'Id al-Adha, the feast of the sacrifice. In addition, Saudi National Day is held annually. Because the kingdom follows the Islamic lunar calendar, which moves backward 10 days each year, this holiday was held on September 23 in 2010.

The Basic Law has been criticized by external observers because it does not grant key rights of individuals such as those guaranteed in the U.S. Constitution—rights to belief, expression, assembly, or political participation (Hooglund in Metz, ed., 1993, 193). The law nevertheless issues various important guarantees to its citizens in the chapter "Rights and Duties":

Article 26:
The State shall protect human rights in accordance with Islamic Shari'ah.

Article 27:
The State shall guarantee the right of its citizens and their families in an emergency or in case of disease, disability and old age. Likewise it shall support the social security system and encourage individuals and institutions to contribute to charitable pursuits.

Article 28:
The State shall provide job opportunities to all able-bodied people and shall enact laws to protect both the employee and the employer.

Article 29:
The State shall foster sciences, arts, and culture. It shall encourage scientific research, shall preserve Arab and Islamic heritage and shall contribute to Arab, Islamic and human civilization.

Article 30:
The State shall provide public education and shall commit itself to the eradication of illiteracy.

Article 31:
The State shall be solicitous for promoting public health and shall provide medical care to every citizen.

Article 36:
The State shall ensure the security of all its citizens and expatriates living within its domains. No individual shall be detained, imprisoned or have his actions restricted except under the provisions of the law.

Article 37:
Houses are inviolable. They shall not be entered without the permission of their owners, nor shall they be searched except in cases specified by the law. (Basic Law 1992; SAMIRAD 2010)

These passages serve as a vital covenant between the state and its people.

Saudi Arabian governance was nearly synonymous with the first king and his advisers. This lack of structure and personal politics led to a dissolute and uncontrolled period in the 1940s, when overspending was rampant, according to the first American ambassador, J. Rives Childs (Childs 1969, 156, cited in Lippman 2004, 102). Thanks to the oil boom in the 1970s, a different type of governmental dilemma emerged, as foreign entrepreneurs rushed to the kingdom, sometimes resulting in corruption or questionable developmental projects. Since then, the government has continued planning public policy and development and adjusting its goals as necessary.

THE KING

Saudi Arabia's government is the administration and structure that serves and preserves the Saudi Arabian citizenry and also the al-Sa'ud family's authority. The legitimate governing rights of the al-Sa'ud date back to the First Kingdom of Saudi Arabia. That legitimacy is both religious and political, resting on the alliance struck between Muhammad ibn Sa'ud (1710–1765) and the religious reformer Muhammad ibn 'Abd al-Wahhab (1703–1787) (see Chapter 2, History). Ibn Sa'ud vowed to support 'Abd al-Wahhab and to impose his beliefs while expanding his tribe's political power. He swore he would stand by him "even if the whole of Najd came tumbling down over us" (AbuKhalil 2004, 66). 'Abd al-Wahhab preached loyalty and obedience to Sa'udi rule, as long as they did not order a "violation to Allah's will" (AbuKhalil 2004, 62). 'Abd al-Wahhab issued this support because of Ibn Sa'ud's leadership of the jihad and also because of his typically conservative reading of Islamic law, in which sedition is a grave sin. Therefore, numerous sources mention

Saudi Arabia's foundation resting on two "houses"—the House of Sa'ud and the House of al-Shaykh. The al-Shaykh descendants have been important religious clerics in the modern government of Saudi Arabia. All but one of the grand muftis (the highest religious office appointed by the government, a mufti is a religious scholar who can issue *fatawa*, or legal responses—plural of *fatwa*) of Saudi Arabia have derived from this family; that exception was Grand Mufti 'Abd al-'Aziz ibn 'Abdullah ibn Baz (1912–1999), an extremely important and influential religious scholar.

Tim Niblock has described a model for political power in Saudi Arabia in which policy processes, conditioning factors, and circles of support interact. Within it, he enlists differing possible types of legitimacy (Niblock 2006, 9). Besides the historical and religious claims for legitimacy, one may consider personal charisma as a source of legitimacy. This sort of legitimacy is often attributed to King 'Abdullah, who has been called visionary, disciplined, and impatient with those who needlessly grovel. He is pro-reform and anticorruption and has overcome personal limitations. (Lacey 2009, 180–203). The king, whom Robert Lacey has described as "an old man in a hurry," was frustrated with the delays in the construction of the new King Abdullah University of Science and Technology (KAUST), which would benefit his citizens (Lacey 2009, 330–332). This shows how the king's dedication to his country is a part of his personal legitimacy and fits what Niblock terms "eudaenomic legitimacy," that which meets the popular needs of citizens.

The Saudi Arabian monarchs cannot claim legitimacy on democratic/structural grounds as they are not elected (Niblock 2006, 12–13). When I interviewed or conversed with many Saudi Arabians in the period between 2005 and 2008, they stressed the royal family's ability to mediate between differing trends in society and prevent the more conservative and even radical groups from running over other constituents. The same observers noted that the royal family was adept at avoiding liberal demands by overemphasizing the threat that conservatives pose to their society (Personal Interviews, Riyadh, Jeddah, Washington, DC, and other locations, 2005–2008). The rulers have also been intolerant of overt demands with timetables, those that invoked previous enemies, or those that gave the impression of being dictated by an external agenda, such as those of the reformers who called for a constitutional monarchy in late December 2003 and were arrested in March 2004 (Glosmeyer in Aarts and Nonneman, eds., 2005, 228–229; Lacroix in Aarts and Nonneman, eds., 2005, 54–55; and see Chapter 5, section on religion).

King 'Abd al-'Aziz al-Sa'ud returned the al-Sa'ud family to political dominance as an ally of Great Britain. His political fortunes rested on foreign policy as much as on the foundational alliance with the Wahhabi religious reform movement. That basis of his legitimacy might have been eroded when he battled against his own Ikhwan warriors in the late 1930s (see Chapter 2, History). Since 'Abd al-'Aziz's reining in of the Ikhwan took place during the final stages of state consolidation and he possessed other strong allies, he was able, despite this disturbing experience, to retain his legitimacy.

King 'Abd al-'Aziz had named his son Sa'ud as crown prince, but he had not established any protocol for royal succession. Severe problems did arise under King Sa'ud's rule, as a result of his financial management, his ouster of senior princes and recalcitrance to accept collective family decisions, his dalliance with Nasserist principles, and his opposition to management by his brother Faysal ibn 'Abd al-'Aziz. Hence, the coordination of the senior members of the royal family was crucial in the resolution of these problems. Sa'ud also sowed seeds of discord in the royal family by promoting some of his 53 sons to positions of greater power than their seniority or expertise warranted, which led them to be referred to as "little kings" (see Chapter 2, History; also Kechichian 2001, 28). The other sons of 'Abd al-'Aziz were not content with this challenge to their status in the royal family. While the main rationale for actions against King Sa'ud, culminating in the al-Sa'ud's 1964 decision to replace him with his brother Faysal (see Chapter 2, History) and resulting in his abdication, was mismanagement, these political tensions were also important. The general principle established was that brothers would succeed each other, in preference to sons succeeding their fathers. Certain kings' sons, such as those of King Faysal and King Fahd, were placed in prominent positions or worked their way upward in government; other princes—the sons of Khalid—have not played such public roles.

Direct power has been held by the sons of 'Abd al-'Aziz, but his nine brothers were on occasion deeply involved in family politics. For instance, 'Abdullah (1900–1976) and Musa'id (b. 1922) initially attempted to mediate in the struggle between King Sa'ud and his brother Faysal, and they later supported Faysal (Kechichian 2001, 32).

During King Faysal's reign, the king's role was expanded to include both head-of-state and head-of-government functions. This had not been the case under King Sa'ud because of the tensions he had created with his family; therefore, it was possible for much of his rule to describe Sa'ud as the head of state, whereas Faysal had served as the head of government during certain periods. Faysal officially declared this change in the king's role in a royal decree. He made other decisions regarding succession, asking his brothers to observe birth order to help stabilize the succession, although some princes who were ahead in the birth order stepped out of the way or were asked to step out of the way of Faysal's successor, Khalid. He also established the country's national development plans and set up the Ministry of Justice to oversee the religious courts. Faysal was responsible for many other aspects of expansion and modernization; he opposed communism and supported pan-Islamic positions and institutions. When King Faysal was assassinated in 1975, there might have been another political crisis, but he had already designated Khalid to follow him. Khalid was acknowledged by the senior princes, and his younger brother, Fahd, was designated crown prince.

Since 1986, the king of Saudi Arabia has been referred to as the Custodian of the Two Holy Mosques, a title that emphasizes the Islamic duty of the monarch, which he fulfills for all Muslims, not only the citizens of Saudi Arabia. Gregory Gause has suggested that this title was taken at that particular time to "blunt the Iranian revolutionary contention that monarchy is an un-Islamic form of government" (1994, 30). The king again asserted Saudi Arabia's particular Islamic leadership role after the Gulf War, perhaps because of the strong internal disapproval of hosting Western troops on Saudi Arabian soil. Islamic opposition in Saudi Arabia became more widespread and was more active than liberal forms of opposition. It broke with the Saudi Arabian cultural preference for keeping dissension private with the issuance

LINE OF SUCCESSION IN SAUDI ARABIA

Succession to the throne in Saudi Arabia has passed from brother to brother among the sons of King 'Abd al-'Aziz al-Sa'ud; however, certain princes have given up their right to succession in favor of others. King 'Abdullah ibn 'Abd al-'Aziz's creation of new procedures for succession (see Government) would enable succession to pass to the next generation of princes.

After battling colon cancer for some years, the crown prince, Sultan ibn 'Abd al-'Aziz died October 22, 2011. He was born in 1928, and had been minister of defense and aviation since 1962. His successor as crown prince is Nayif ibn 'Abd al-'Aziz, born in 1934, minister of the interior since 1975. There is no agreement on who might follow Prince Nayif in the line of succession, as it is not an automatic process. The new Allegiance Council initiated by King 'Abdullah lends more formality to the process and acknowledges that the age of possible successors and poor health to the point of incapacity must be considered. Foreign observers believe other factors are tenure in government, acceptance by the 'ulama, tribal affiliations, support from the most powerful members of the al-Sa'ud family, and support from the general public, including the powerful commercial elites. A selection from among the remaining sons of King 'Abd al-'Aziz (shown in birth order) might include

'Abd al-Rahman ibn 'Abd al-'Aziz, b. 1931 (vice minister of defense and aviation since 1979)

Muta'ib ibn 'Abd al-'Aziz, b. 1931 (retired minister for municipal and rural affairs, 1975–2009)

Badr ibn 'Abd al-'Aziz, b. 1933 (deputy commander of the Saudi Arabian National Guard since 1968). Prince Badr was one of the Free Princes who went into exile but was rehabilitated by King Faysal.

Salman ibn 'Abd al-'Aziz, b. 1939 (governor of Riyadh since 1962)

Sattam ibn 'Abd al-'Aziz, b. 1941 (deputy governor of Riyadh since 1968)

Ahmad ibn 'Abd al-'Aziz, b. 1942 (vice minister of the interior since 1975)

Muqrin ibn 'Abd al-'Aziz, b. 1945 (former governor of Ha'il and Madinah Province, director-general of Saudi intelligence since 2005)

Under the terms of the Allegiance Council, it is also possible that princes of the third generation could be selected, possibly:

Sa'ud al-Faysal, b. 1941 (foreign minister since 1975)

Turki al-Faysal, b. 1945 (former ambassador and former director-general, General Intelligence Directorate, 1977–2001)

Khalid al-Faysal, b. 1941 (former governor of Asir, governor of Makkah Province since 2007)

In 2010 there were speculations that health problems might cause Foreign Minister Sa'ud al-Faysal to step down and be replaced by his brother Turki and that Crown Prince Sultan would step down as minister of defense and aviation, to be replaced by his son Khalid (Henderson, NPR, October 12, 2010); so his death and the confirmation of Prince Nayef as his successor was not a surprise.

of a public letter in 1991 signed by 453 *'ulama* (clerics) and Islamic activists. The letter called for more "seriousness" and attention to *shari'ah*. This was followed by an even more strenuous call for reform in 1992 (Gause 1994, 34; Zuhur 2005a, 26–27). The government was offended and concerned by the public nature of this criticism as much as by its content. Ever since, Islamic opposition has been a key factor in Saudi Arabian politics.

The country's Islamic leadership role remains an important legitimating factor, but it has evolved and brought new challenges. Managing and guaranteeing the safety of the millions of pilgrims on the *hajj* is a grave responsibility of the government. The volume of pilgrims has expanded greatly thanks to the advent of air travel, so that it requires extraordinary efforts, improvement of facilities, and international agreements with pilgrim-based nations via the Organization of the Islamic Conference (discussed in the following and in Chapter 5, section on religion). The pilgrimage could be the occasion for foreign policy threats or internal ones to emerge. King 'Abd al-'Aziz survived several assassination attempts, one while he was on *'umrah*, the minor pilgrimage. Stampeding and deaths and injuries due to trampling have marred some pilgrimages, for example, in 2006, and the swine flu epidemic required special measures in 2009. When Iranian pilgrims used the occasion to protest the authority of the Sa'udi family rulers in the 1980s (see the following), the incident paralyzed relations between the two countries. An plot attributed to al-Qa'ida on the Arabian Peninsula and other militants was discovered during the 2007 pilgrimage and foiled (Riedel and Saab 2008, 37).

King 'Abdullah is currently both the head of state and the head of government, acting as the prime minister as well as the ultimate ruler. The Saudi Arabian king is also commander in chief of the armed forces, and he appoints all diplomats and ambassadors. If the king is incapacitated, the crown prince will take on these functions; King 'Abdullah ruled in all but name for about 10 years, after his brother Fahd became seriously ill. Hence, the most recent transition from crown prince to king was less politically eventful than Sa'ud's accession.

The king is expected to initiate legislation. He sets the tone for the type of changes and development intended for the country. The king has not always acted as prime minister; there have been periods when a crown prince or designated prince has done so, as under the rule of King Sa'ud. As the sons of 'Abd al-'Aziz have become increasingly elderly, the king has not always served as head of state; twice a crown prince has done so.

Concerns over succession caused King Fahd, who ascended to the throne in 1982, to issue another royal decree in 1992. This decree affirmed that the king of Saudi Arabia would name a crown prince and could also remove him. The crown prince would henceforth not automatically become the king, but he would be the provisional ruler until either he was approved via the process known as the *bay'ah*, or oath of allegiance, and placed on the throne, or a different al-Sa'ud was so enthroned. In the same Basic Law of 1992, it is specified that only the sons of 'Abd al-'Aziz or his sons' sons have the "dynastic right" to become ruler (Basic Law, 1992).

Some observers of Saudi Arabia have emphasized the stability of succession in the royal family; others point to the great threat that instability would pose to the oil industry and the West. One theory has been that full brothers in the family have tended to cleave more strongly to each other. A powerful group of full brothers became known as the Sudayri Seven (the sons of Ibn Sa'ud and Hussah al-Sudayri, a member of a prominent Najdi family): the late King Fahd (1921–2005); Prince Sultan ibn 'Abd al-'Aziz (b. 1926), the late crown prince; Prince 'Abd al-Rahman ibn 'Abd al-'Aziz (b. 1931), vice minister of defense; Minister of the Interior (since 1975) Prince Nayif (b. 1933); Prince Turki ibn 'Abd al-'Aziz (b. 1934); Prince Salman ibn 'Abd al-'Aziz (b. 1936), governor of Riyadh; and Prince Ahmad ibn 'Abd al-'Aziz (b. 1940), vice minister of the interior. Although the princesses of the royal family are usually absent from the political literature, they have great influence, as do the full sisters of the Sudayri Seven, Princesses Latifa, al-Jawahara, and Jawahir (see also Chapter 7, Contemporary Issues).

A royal decree announced in October 2006 formally established a committee of Sa'udi princes, the Allegiance (Bay'ah) Commission, who will determine succession in the future. A year later, the king announced the Allegiance Commission Law, providing detailed rules for succession as well as for the constitution and conduct of the commission. Succession will be handled in the following manner: When a king dies, the commission is to meet and confirm the crown prince as king. That new king will send the name of a proposed crown prince to the commission within 10 days of taking

Members of the Saudi Arabian royal family at a press conference in New York, May 10, 1945. From left to right (seated): Prince Fahd ibn 'Abd al-'Aziz, Prince Faysal ibn 'Abd al-Aziz, Prince Muhammad ibn 'Abd al-Aziz. Standing (left to right) are Prince 'Abdullah al-Faysal (son of Prince Faysal) and Prince Nawwaf ibn 'Abd al-Aziz.

office, or he may ask the commission to appoint a crown prince (al-Badi, February 14, 2008). The Bay'ah Commission has the right to reject the ruler's choice of a crown prince and to install a crown prince even if the ruler does not approve of him (T. al-Sa'ud 2006). Should the ruler or the crown prince, or both fall ill, or be unable to serve, the commission has the power to refer the health issue to a medical committee that should swiftly issue a confidential report on the health of the ruler. If, for some reason, he is incapacitated, the medical committee would provide certification of his condition. The administration of the government would pass to the Transitional Ruling Council, and the commission would determine a successor (al-Badi, February 14, 2008). This new system of determining succession will not be fully implemented until Crown Prince Nayif becomes king.

The former deputy defense minister and governor of Mecca, Prince Mishaal ibn 'Abd al-'Aziz was appointed the chairman of the commission at the end of 2007 (Abdul Ghafour, December 11, 2007). The commission's members are Prince Miteb, Prince Abdul Rahman, Prince Talal, Prince Badr, Prince Turki, Prince Nayif, Prince Fawaz, Prince Salman, Prince Mamdouh, Prince 'Abdul Ilah, Prince Sattam, Prince Ahmed, Prince Mashhour, Prince Hadhlool, and Prince Muqrin, all sons of King 'Abd al-'Aziz. Additional members are Prince Muhammad ibn Sa'ud, Prince Khalid al-Faysal, Prince Muhammad ibn Sa'ad, Prince Turki ibn Faysal, Prince Muhammad ibn Nasser, Prince Faysal ibn Bandar, Prince Sa'ud ibn 'Abd al-Mohsen, Prince Muhammad ibn Fahd, Prince Khalid ibn Sultan, Prince Talal ibn Mansour, Prince Khalid ibn 'Abdullah, Prince Muhammad ibn Mashari, Prince Faysal ibn Khalid, Prince Badr ibn Muhammad, Prince Faysal ibn Thamir, Prince Mishaal ibn Majid, Prince 'Abdullah ibn Musa'id, Prince Faysal ibn Abd al-Majid, and Prince 'Abd al-'Aziz ibn Nawwaf.

The aim of these reforms is to maintain consensus within the royal family and the nation concerning the transfer of the highest power from the sons of 'Abd al-'Aziz to his grandsons, barring some unforeseen shift in the political basis of the kingdom.

KING 'ABDULLAH

King 'Abdullah ibn 'Abd al-'Aziz was born on August 1, 1924, the son of 'Abd al-'Aziz and Fahda bint 'Asi al-Shraim of the Shammar tribe, who had previously been married to the Amir Sa'ud, the Rashidi leader. 'Abdullah had acted as the de facto ruler of Saudi Arabia ever since 1996, when Fahd suffered a major stroke, and he became king in 2005. 'Abdullah was the commander of the Saudi Arabian National Guard for many years and stepped down from that responsibility only in 2010. The king has been married nine times, and he has 15 sons and 20 daughters according to one source (Datarabia.com). 'Abdullah has overseen the political and security responses to the militant Islamist attacks in Saudi Arabia since May 12, 2003. He has done so through counterinsurgency, antiterrorism campaigns, criminal trials, and a religious reeducation program. He has shaped the nation's response to international concerns and sharp attacks from the United States concerning Saudi Arabia's connection with Islamist terrorism since 2001.

King 'Abdullah has donated generously to various causes, establishing the King Abdulaziz Library in Riyadh and a library in Casablanca, Morocco. He worked to establish the King Abdullah University of Science and Technology (KAUST), a graduate institute along the lines of the Massachusetts Institute of Technology, dedicated to producing superior graduate education and research in the sciences, and gave $10 billion to its endowment fund. He also established the King Abdullah University in Azad Jammu/Kashmir in Pakistan. He donated $50 million in cash and $10 million in relief supplies for the victims of the 2008 earthquake in Szechuan, China, and supported the cost of surgeries performed in Riyadh to separate conjoined twins. As crown prince, he repeatedly attempted to change the U.S. stance on the Israeli-Palestinian issue, as he strongly supported Palestinian rights to sovereignty. As king or crown prince, 'Abdullah has met with American presidents Gerald Ford, George H.W. Bush, Bill Clinton, George W. Bush, and Barack Obama, as well as many other heads of state.

KING 'ABDULLAH'S SONS IN OFFICIAL POSITIONS

In much of the earlier political literature on Saudi Arabia, a great deal of attention was given to the brothers known as the Sudayri Seven, the brothers of King Fahd, and their sons in government. King 'Abdullah's sons, listed here, may also play a leading role in the future of Saudi Arabia and have served in the government:

Khalid ibn 'Abdullah, a businessman, formerly western commander for the Saudi Arabian National Guard (SANG)

Miteb ibn 'Abdullah, commander of SANG (since November 17, 2010), formerly SANG vice commander, and president of King Khaled Military Academy

'Abd al-'Aziz ibn 'Abdullah, adviser to the king (formerly to the court of the crown prince)

Mishaal ibn 'Abdullah, governor of Najran (since 2009), formerly minister plenipotentiary in the foreign ministry

Faysal ibn 'Abdullah, president of the Saudi Red Crescent Society, also a businessman

Turki ibn 'Abdullah, wing commander, Saudi Arabian Royal Air Force

THE CROWN PRINCE

At the time this book was written, Crown Prince Sultan ibn 'Abd al-'Aziz al-Sa'ud (b. 1926) was the minister of defense and aviation and the inspector general of the kingdom, as well as deputy prime minister, but he died in October of 2011 and his successor, Prince Nayif was confirmed as crown prince. Prince Sultan was the son of King 'Abd al-'Aziz and Princess Hussah bint Ahmad ibn Muhammad al-Sudayri. Prince Sultan had served for many years as a government official. Like his brothers

French President Nicolas Sarkozy (center) in a meeting with Saudi Arabia's Crown Prince and Defense Minister Sultan ibn 'Abd al-'Aziz al-Sa'ud (left) and King 'Abdullah (right) on January 13, 2008. (AP/Wide World Photos)

he was educated at the Prince's School at the royal court. He was appointed the governor of Riyadh in 1947. He became the minister of agriculture in 1953 and the minister of defense and aviation in 1962. He has overseen the development of Saudi Arabia's military forces, with the exception of the National Guard, which was for many years King 'Abdullah's responsibility. Somewhat similar to 'Abdullah's vision for the National Guard, Sultan has paid attention to the military's education and human development. He has been ill with colon cancer since 2004. According to the precedent set by King Faysal back in 1967, when he appointed Fahd (Safran 1985, 217), there is a second deputy prime minister, Prince Nayif, the longtime minister of the interior.

As the crown prince is the future king, the fortunes of his offspring are important. In February 2010, the king's son Turki, who is a pilot with the Royal Saudi Air Force, married a daughter of Khalid ibn Sultan, the deputy defense minister; she is the granddaughter of the crown prince.

THE ROYAL DIWAN

The Royal Diwan houses the primary executive office of the king and his main advisers on domestic politics, religious affairs, and international relations. In addition to the king, those who have offices in the Diwan include the chamberlain of the court; the chief of protocol; the Office of Bedouin Affairs; the Committee for the Promotion of Virtue and Prevention of Vice, known as the HAIA (Hay'at al-Ma'ruf wa al-Nahaya 'an al-Munkar or, more colloquially, as the *mutawa'in*); the Department of Religious Research, Missionary Activities and Guidance; and others. Extremely influential *'ulama* of the country are represented here. The king conducts many routine matters from this office, such as the drafting and promulgation of royal decrees. He convenes his *majlis* here. (A *majlis* is literally a "sitting" or meeting. Members of the royal family, officials, businessmen, and tribal leaders are expected to hold such open meeting sessions regularly.) The purpose of the *majlis* is to provide Saudi Arabia's citizens an opportunity to make requests of the king, on private matters or those with a public aspect. Under King Khalid and King Fahd, a requestor would submit a written petition and provide an explanation and would then return for the monarch's response (Hooglund in Metz, ed., 1993, 298–299). The crown prince has his own *diwan* with an office and *majlis* maintained by its own administration.

THE COUNCIL OF MINISTERS

The Council of Ministers is the main executive body of the government and was established by King 'Abd al-'Aziz in 1953. The king appoints the Council of Ministers every four years. King Fahd presented the bylaws of the council in 1993. The Council of Ministers drafts domestic, international, economic, financial, educational, and defense policies and manages all general affairs overseen by the state. This council passes laws that are proposed by the king, the deputy prime minister, or key ministers. The king's ratification of such laws is necessary for them to take effect, and they may not contradict *shari'ah*. In fact, political practice is such that the king may pass laws or amend them without bringing them to the council. The council also creates taxes and makes decisions on the sale, lease, or use of government property (Carnegie Endowment for International Peace and Fundacion par las Relaciones Internacionales y el Dialogio Exterior [FRIDE] n.d. [ca. 2007], 4). The council meets weekly—at the time of writing, these meetings are scheduled on Mondays—and the king or the crown prince presides. The council members have remained consistent for many years; the number of ministers of state without portfolio who attend has risen from three to five; and the secretary general for the Commission of Tourism, being at the rank of a minister, now attends. Currently, the council lists its members as

- Prime Minister, the King
- First Deputy Prime Minister, who is the Crown Prince
- Minister of Agriculture
- Minister of Civil Service
- Minister of Commerce and Industry
- Minister of Communications and Information Technology
- Minister of Culture and Information
- Minister of Economy and Planning

- Minister of Education
- Minister of Finance
- Minister of Foreign Affairs
- Minister of Hajj
- Minister of Health
- Minister of Higher Education
- Minister of Interior
- Minister for Islamic Affairs, Endowment, Da'wah and Guidance
- Minister of Justice
- Minister of Labor
- Minister of Municipal and Rural Affairs
- Minister of Petroleum and Mineral Resources
- Minister of Social Affairs
- Minister of Transport
- Minister of Water and Electricity
- Ministers of State (five)
- Secretary General of the Supreme Commission for Tourism (SAMIRAD 2010)

Others who hold ministerial rank and are represented on the council are the governor of the Saudi Arabian Monetary Agency, the commander of the Saudi Arabian National Guard, and the head of the General Petroleum and Mineral Organization. As in many other countries, the Ministry of Defense and the Ministry of the Interior, which is responsible for security inside of the kingdom, are particularly important institutions. These ministries and some others are headed by members of the royal family; other royals are also appointed to deputy minister positions. However, non-royals also serve as members of the council or as ministers. In 2009, a woman was appointed as one of the ministers, the deputy minister of education. The governors of provinces of Saudi Arabia hold the rank of minister and are involved in the council through the Ministry of the Interior. The Ministry of Justice links the Supreme Judicial Council to this body. Since there is no tradition of political parties in Saudi Arabia, individuals do not ascend to government posts through party leadership as occurs in the United States or Europe, but many hold advanced degrees, as do key personnel advising them or serving as deputies.

THE MAJLIS AL-SHURA

The Majlis al-Shura, or Consultative Council, refers to *shura*, the Muslim practice of consultation by the ruler. This allows for decisions to reflect collective understandings, strengthens consensus, and helps to avoid tyranny or mishap so long as those consulted have the right to be critical. King 'Abd al-'Aziz first formed a Shura

Shaykh Muhammad ibn Jubayr in the grand reception hall of the Majlis al-Shura, the Consultative Council which he chaired, in Riyadh, Saudi Arabia in 1997. (AP/Wide World Photos)

Council of the Hijaz in 1927. A Majlis al-Shura was later enlarged to 20 members and presided over by Prince Faysal. During the rule of King Sa'ud, the council ceased to meet, but the concept was revived under King Fahd (Cordesman 2003, 134). Liberal and Islamist trends had been calling for the council to be reestablished; it was announced in 1991 under the authority of the Basic Law and in Royal Decree No. 91 of March 1992, which is referred to as the Majlis al-Shura, or Shura Council Law. The council first met in 1993. Members serve for four years. They are chosen by the king and must be Saudi Arabian nationals, "well known for uprightness and competence," and not less than 30 years of age (Majlis al-Shura Law). About half of the membership should be newly appointed as each new Majlis is formally convened. The Majlis al-Shura consists of a general assembly and committees with at least five members. The membership expanded to 90 in 1997, to 120 in 2001, and to 150 in 2005, at which time it was also permitted to move beyond a purely advisory role. The Majlis has the power to examine and discuss the economic plans and to draft, examine, reject, or amend laws. Its decisions rest on an absolute majority. The Majlis al-Shura's decisions proceed to the Council of Ministers for approval. If both groups agree, and the king assents, the measure or action is taken. If one group dissents, the king decides on the outcome.

The Majlis al-Shura, which meets biweekly, has consisted of appointed businessmen, professionals, academic scholars, government officials, and clan and religious leaders, who received a salary of 20,000 Saudi Arabian riyals in 2010. There are currently six women on the Majlis al-Shura, which is headed by 'Abdullah ibn

Muhammad al-Shaykh. Although the media reported in October 2003, and again in 2005, that a proportion of the Majlis's members would be elected, this had not yet occurred by 2011. Several Majlis members have stated that if elections were held, they personally would not have been elected—in other words, they felt that the rulers were more liberal in their selection process than the electorate may be (Zuhur, Personal Interviews, 2005–2008). The Majlis is now housed at Yamamah Palace in Riyadh.

The 12 committees of the Majlis are the

- Islamic and Judicial Affairs and Human Rights Committee
- Social, Family, and Youth Affairs Committee
- Economic Affairs and Energy Committee
- Educational and Scientific Research Affairs Committee
- Security Affairs Committee
- Cultural and Informational Affairs Committee
- Foreign Affairs Committee
- Health and Environmental Affairs Committee
- Transportation, Communications, and Information Technology Committee
- Water and Public Facilities and Services Committee
- Administration, Human Resources, and Petitions Committee

The Majlis was accepted as a member of the Inter-Parliamentary Union (a global association of national parliaments) in 2003. It now fulfills some parliamentary functions as it is able to consider draft laws without prior submission to the king. It serves as a parliament symbolically and diplomatically, as when the prime minister of India, Dr. Manmohan Singh, was invited to speak on Saudi Arabian–Indian relations in 2010 (Press Information Bureau, Government of India, March 1, 2010).

JUDICIARY AND LEGAL SYSTEM

The Ministry of Justice administers the *shari'ah* (Islamic) courts of the country. The minister acts as a chief justice in some instances, and the Supreme Judicial Council reviews legal decisions, gives opinions, and approves all capital sentences and sentences for serious (*hadd*) crimes that are punished by amputation or stoning. In 2009, the minister of justice was Dr. Muhammad ibn 'Abd al-Kareem al-'Eissa.

It is often claimed there is no habeas corpus in the kingdom, and sometimes individuals are detained for a lengthy period without charge. However, the practice of detention without charge contravenes the Statute of Principles, Temporary Confinement, and Preventive Detention (November 11, 1983), which states that individuals must be charged within three days (Carnegie Endowment for International Peace and FRIDE n.d. [ca. 2007], 6). Courts are in four tiers: limited or summary courts, general courts, courts of appeal, or appellate courts to the district courts, which are headed by panels of three judges. The cases are divided into matters of criminal law, matters of personal status (*ahwal shakhsiyyah*, or family law), and all other matters. Above the appellate courts, which are normally the final level of appeal, the Supreme Judicial Council could weigh in, or the king could issue a pardon or remove a sentence (see Chapter 5, section on religion and thought for additional information). In addition, the Board of Grievances hears commercial cases, tax disputes, and contract violations. The Ministry of Justice disciplines judges. However, the judges are supposed to possess independence with reference to their rulings. A Committee on Conflicts of Jurisdiction exists. Also important is the 20-member Council of Senior Islamic Scholars, which serves in an advisory capacity to the king and his cabinet and which frames legal principles for the use of lower-court judges.

Saudi Arabia's interpretation and usage of Islamic law has become a highly politicized issue in the world media. The world media often inject misunderstandings about the difference between *shari'ah* (divine law, or the theory and intention of Islamic law) and *fiqh* (jurisprudence, which is man made), and strict penalties and capital punishment are targets of criticism. When the media have reported on cases with a public interest—as in the Qatif Girl rape case, involving a woman who was raped and then punished by judges along with her male companion in this incident for being in a situation where she was alone with a man, or the divorce suit brought on behalf of an eight-year-old girl (see Chapter 5, section on women)—and an international outcry ensued, the government has responded to the perceived or actual injustice. Yet, in other cases, as with the executions of migrant workers, international reaction made no difference to the outcome. Saudi Arabians as well as others are perturbed by the degree of variation in judges' interpretations and sentences. Some of the judiciary have been angered by the reportage on their cases, regarding it as an attack on their office as well as the country, although quite a few reporters and lawyers disagreed (Sidiya, February 23, 2010). The issue was considered in the National Intellectual Dialogue in 2011 because editors of media articles are subject to fines, and yet reportage of social issues is considered the press's duty. The kingdom's publication law (Article 73) appears to restrict coverage, but there is a loophole: "It is not legal to publish investigations or court hearings related to personal issues or other (issues) unless an authorization is taken from the concerned authorities" (Sidiya, February 23, 2010). Trials are supposed to be public; however, those of the alleged terrorists have not been open to the public (see also Chapter 5, section on religion and law).

CIVIL SERVICE BOARD AND INDEPENDENT AGENCIES

The Civil Service Board presided over the Civil Service Bureau until 1999, making decisions about the employees of all of the ministries with respect to recruitment, personnel, pay rates, and grade classifications in a greatly expanded bureaucracy. The Civil Services Ministry was then created in 1999. Civil servants could receive training in their own ministries or at the Institute of Public Administration and could bring complaints to a board of grievances.

The Audit Bureau can monitor the accounts of various government offices. Other separate organizations are the Central Department of Statistics, the Meteorology and Environmental Protection Agency, the Saudi Arabian Standards Organization, and the Saudi Ports Authority.

REGIONAL AND MUNICIPAL GOVERNMENT

The king appoints regional governors and the members of provincial councils. The minister of the interior appoints local administrators. Most of the governors are members of the royal family. The governors, who may have deputies, supervise the recruitment to the Saudi Arabian National Guard and the local police. Each holds an open *majlis* at which residents may present petitions.

In 2003, the king approved municipal consultative councils. Half of the council members were to be elected by popular vote, and these elections took place in 2005. Elections are being held again in 2011. The councils primarily deal with the municipalities' provision of services, development, and planning. The elections became a matter of great national and international interest, and electioneering took place in *majlis* settings.

THE *'ULAMA*

The *'ulama* (literally, those who possess religious knowledge ['*ilm*], scholars, and teachers of religion) fulfill an important official task in politics and in religion in Saudi Arabia as an additional legitimizing force (see Chapter 5, section on religion and law). Many sources on Saudi Arabia attribute the prominence of the *'ulama* to the legacy of intermarriage and political ties between the houses of al-Sa'ud and al-Shaykh, but the relationship of the *'ulama* to political leadership goes far back in Islamic history and is not reserved to Saudi Arabia. The linkage involves newer groups of *mutawa'a*, religious specialists who saw a reversal of their misfortunes in the 19th century in Ibn Sa'ud's new state (al-Rasheed 2002, 55–57). Their resurgence had various results, from the hostilities between the Ikhwan and the regime, to delicate maneuvering to gain acceptance of technological innovations or foreign influence. But the state also created institutions that employed the *'ulama* and made it possible to regulate their activities. Currently, their alliance with the al-Sa'ud could be weakening, as some infer (Commins 2006), and require a reinterpretation of the Wahhabi reform ideals, although that interpretation may be just one of several post-9/11 responses. Some analysts suggest that perhaps the *'ulama*'s ineffective efforts at political opposition may now be adapting to the reforming impulses of the present. Others perceive the strength of the *sahwa* (Islamic awakening) in Saudi Arabia to have been profound and identify its members as a cohesive group, one in which the *'ulama* remain very important. Although they have been coopted by the government to refrain from severe criticism (Lacroix 2011), they can and do block reform efforts.

The following are official religious institutions that are part of the government: The Board of Senior 'Ulama was established in 1971 and is composed of the most senior *'ulama* and headed by the grand mufti. It issues *fatawa* on key matters. The Permanent Committee for Scientific Research and Legal Opinion carries out research, supports the efforts of the Board of Senior 'Ulama, and issues private *ifta'* (responses, or *fatawa*—specific religious opinions). The Office of the Grand Mufti manages the grand mufti's activities as he heads both the Board of Senior 'Ulama and the Permanent Committee for Scientific Research and Legal Opinion (CRLO).

The Supreme Council of Islamic Affairs (al-Majlis al-'A'la lil-Shu'un al-Islamiyyah) rules on matters requiring multiple *'ulama* opinions and is in charge of domestic Islamic matters. This Council reviews judgments carrying death sentences and some other major crimes, constructs general principles and judicial precedents, and examines *shari'ah* questions involving principles which are referred to the Council. The Council for Islamic Mission and Guidance (Majlis lil-Da'wah wa al-Irshad) is in charge of Muslims and mosques abroad. Both were established within a few days of each other in 1994, and some sources suggest that the government moved to create these institutions to control the mosques and "bypass the [independent] *'ulama*" (Bachar et al. 2006, 15) or as one of the responses to the Islamist opposition movement (Kostiner 1997), which gave the *'ulama* "a more active role in government" (Bachar et al. 2006, 14).

While the preceding institutions employ about 100 *'ulama*, the Ministry of Islamic Affairs employs thousands of clerics. The educational system and the Ministry of Education are also sources of employment for the *'ulama*. In Saudi Arabia, many students gravitate to Islamic studies and consequently to the religious fields upon graduation.

The government has been obliged to respond to dissonant voices from conservative and also oppositionist clerical views that have countered various modernization efforts. They have opposed many reforms and perceived "innovations" under the first two Saudi Arabian kings and the reforms supervised by King Faysal. There was another wave of clerical concerns in the wake of the Juhayman al-'Utaybi attack on the Grand Mosque at Mecca, and then in the 1990s. Most recently, the clerical establishment responded to post-2003 violence by Islamic radicals, although some clerics have supported the *mujahidin* where foreign armies fought them in Afghanistan and Iraq. Meanwhile, various strands of the *'ulama* confronted the desire of liberals to open employment and grant voting and driving rights to women. Further, some have supported a reduction of the absolute authority of the royal family and an increase in the political rights of citizens.

The *'ulama* establishment is not necessarily or inherently the source of all Islamic opposition. That has a populist base in Saudi Arabia in many instances. On the contrary, the scholarly establishment has called for and been part of a state-centered Islamic leadership and, for that reason, stands accused of compliance, passivity, or being a ruler-dominated *'ulama*. Yet certain clerical elements are not included in that establishment and some have often pushed back against the government's reforms.

FAMILY AND TRIBAL INFLUENCES

Estimates of the size of the al-Sa'ud family vary, from 25,000 (probably a low estimate as they were counted at 20,000 in 1992) up; or, counting only males descended from Faysal ibn Turki, the grandfather of King 'Abd al-'Aziz, they are estimated at 6,000 or more (4,000 in 1992). Succession to the position of king was limited to the sons of 'Abd al-'Aziz, 22 of whom are now living. Succession was then extended to the grandsons of 'Abd al-'Aziz, providing a pool of some 150 princes. External observers of Saudi Arabia have emphasized divisions within the royal family or speculated about the forces for unity or division within the royal family, but little is actually known outside of Saudi Arabia about these dynamics. Historical examples of schisms include the Free Princes movement, a group of King 'Abd al-'Aziz's younger's sons, led by Talal ibn 'Abd al-'Aziz. The Free Princes demanded reforms and liberalization and left for Egypt, returning to the kingdom at the request of Faysal ibn 'Abd al-'Aziz. The sons of King Sa'ud followed their father into exile when he abdicated in favor of Faysal. In addition, several groups in the Al Faysal branch (the sons of King Faysal) have been particularly important. The seven sons of Hussah al-Sudayri and King 'Abd al-'Aziz, including King Fahd, who were dubbed the Sudayri Seven (see the preceding), used to meet weekly at a family dinner and conferred with each other. The minister of defense, Prince Sultan, and the governor of Riyadh, Prince Salman, were Fahd's closest political advisers. In addition, they have half brothers through 'Abd al-'Aziz's offspring from other Sudayri women.

The Thunayan clan, a branch of the al-Sa'ud, included King Faysal's favorite wife, Iffat; while the Jiluwi clan descended from a brother of Faysal ibn Turk. The mother of King Khalid and his brother, Prince Muhammad, were from the Jiluwi branch. The al-Kabir clan may be traced back to 'Abd al-'Aziz's first cousin, Sa'ud al-Kabir, and his wife Nura, a sister of 'Abd al-'Aziz. While not in the line of succession, Muhammad ibn Sa'ud was an important prince (Hooglund in Metz, ed., 1993) due to seniority. Analyzing the royal family around full-brother groupings is not particularly useful in understanding all of its members, for although the current king, 'Abdullah, had no full brothers, it would be foolish to assume he had no important alliances within the royal family. In addition, his power and abilities were developed during long service as head of the National Guard and as crown prince. It is also misleading to associate certain figures entirely with religiosity or opposition to progress, as Michael Doran (a Princeton PhD with neoconservative views who was invited to

---

GRANDSONS OF KING 'ABD AL-'AZIZ AL-SA'UD

Succession will eventually pass to the grandsons of 'Abd al-'Aziz al-Sa'ud (unless the democracy movement or some other unforeseen shift in politics completely transforms the political system of Saudi Arabia, as happened in Iraq in 1958 and 2003 and in Tunisia, Egypt, Yemen, and Libya in 2011). Many, but not all, have served in positions of great responsibility in the government. The following are among those better known to the world outside Saudi Arabia.

PRINCE SA'UD AL-FAYSAL IBN 'ABD AL-'AZIZ

Prince Sa'ud al-Faysal ibn 'Abd al-'Aziz is the son of King Faysal (his name is frequently transliterated as Al Faisal), born in 1942. He has served as minister of foreign affairs since 1975. He obtained a degree in economics from Princeton University in 1964. He served as the deputy minister of oil for petroleum policy and as chairman of the Supreme Council's Specialized Committee on Foreign Investments. He is credited as the organizing force behind the Ta'if Accords (1989) ending the Lebanese Civil War and the coordination of policies with Crown Prince 'Abdullah to meet the terrorist challenge to the kingdom and deal with the severe criticism of Saudi Arabia abroad following 9/11. He is said to be deeply committed to a just solution to the Arab-Israeli conflict.

PRINCE TURKI AL-FAYSAL IBN 'ABD AL-'AZIZ

Prince Turki al-Faysal (Al Faisal) ibn 'Abd al-'Aziz is the son of King Faysal, born on February 15, 1945. He attended the Lawrenceville School in New Jersey and Georgetown University. He became the director-general of the General Intelligence Directorate in 1977 and was responsible for modernizing that agency. He became the ambassador of Saudi Arabia to the United Kingdom and Ireland in 2002 and ambassador to the United States from 2005 until his resignation on February 2, 2007. He is a founder of the King Faisal Foundation, chairman of the King Faisal Center for Research and Islamic Studies in Riyadh, and co-chair of the C-100 (Council of 100 Leaders) Group.

PRINCE KHALID IBN SULTAN IBN 'ABD AL-'AZIZ

Prince Khalid ibn Sultan ibn 'Abd al-'Aziz, born on September 23, 1949, is Sultan's eldest son. He attended the Royal Military Academy at Sandhurst in the United Kingdom and programs at the U.S. Army's Command and General Staff College and the U.S. Air War College at Maxwell Air Force Base in Alabama. He obtained a master's degree from Auburn University. He was lieutenant general and commander of the joint forces and theater of operations during the 1991 Gulf War and was promoted to the rank of field marshal following the war. He rejoined the government in 2001 as deputy minister of defense and aviation and inspector general for military affairs.

PRINCE BANDAR IBN SULTAN

Prince Bandar ibn Sultan, born in 1949, is the son of Prince Sultan ibn 'Abd al-'Aziz. He has been the president of the National Security Council since 2005 and served as ambassador to the United States from 1983 to 2005. Bandar's mother was a young Libyan servant and concubine to Prince Sultan, and he came to live with his grandmother Princess Hussah at age 11. He attended the Royal Air Force College at Cranwell and served in the Royal Saudi

Air Force for 17 years. He received a master's degree in international public policy at Johns Hopkins University. He was on an extended leave from 2009 to November 2010, when he returned to Saudi Arabia.

PRINCE WALID IBN TALAL

Prince Walid ibn Talal ibn 'Abd al-'Aziz, born on March 7, 1955, is a nephew of King 'Abdullah and a grandson of Riyad al-Solh, Lebanon's first prime minister. He owns most of the Kingdom Holding Company, and his net worth is estimated at $19.4 billion. With degrees from Menlo College and the Maxwell School, Syracuse University, Prince Walid has hired women to work in his own companies in professions from which they are excluded elsewhere in Saudi Arabia and notably the first female Saudi Arabian pilot. He is not considered a likely candidate to succeed to the throne.

join the U.S. National Security Council under President George W. Bush) did when he depicted Prince Nayif, as a force of religious conservatism and retrogression in contrast with then Crown Prince 'Abdullah (depicted as a force of progress) (Doran 2004). More often, the king is portrayed as a skillful mediator "between conflicting elements of society," an excellent reason for his convening of the National Dialogue Forums (Glosmeyer in Aarts and Nonneman, eds., 2005, 226). These forums were another first in the kingdom, whereby representatives were encouraged to discuss pressing matters of interest related to the nation's development.

To manage domestic affairs, the Saudi Arabian government has consulted and relied on local elites, although governors were often members of the royal family. The tribes remain a very important part of Saudi Arabian politics; they numbered among the Ikhwan following Ibn Sa'ud and have been very important in the Saudi Arabian National Guard (SANG). The most prominent tribes were the Bani Khalid, Harb, al-Murrah, Mutayr, Qahtan, Shammar, 'Anayzah, 'Utayba, Ajman, al-Dawasir, Amarat, Awazim, Bani Malik, Bani Yam, Dahamsha, Dhufir, Huwaytat, Mutafiq, and Ruwalla; there are many others as well (Hooglund in Metz, ed., 1993, 209; Zuhur, Personal Interviews, 2005–2008; Kostiner 1998, 143–155; Kostiner 1991).

Most of the tribes have become settled or sedentary in a gradual process similar to that which occurred throughout the Middle East; only about 5 percent remain pastoral. Sedentarization created various issues around land rights. Acknowledging tribal structures and asserting their cultural influence is part of the state's discourse on Saudi Arabia's *turath*, or cultural legacy (Gause 1994, 27).

Commercial elites were important to the regime, especially prior to the large influx of oil income. The al-Qusaibi, Alireza, Ba Kashab, Bin Laden, Jamjum, Kaki, Nasi, Juffali, Olayan, Nasif, al-Rajhi, and Sulayman families helped by loaning money to the government early on. Other important families emerged later as entrepreneurial entities including the Khashoggi, Ojjeh, Pharaon, and Kamil families. As Eric Hooglund has pointed out, other nonroyals rose politically and socially as technocrats into key ministerial and government positions, but they paid a price when their policies alienated certain Sa'udi princes. He was alluding to the fall of Ghazi al-Qusaibi (often shown as al-Ghosaybi), once minister of health; Ahmad Zaki Yamani, formerly minister of oil; and 'Abd al-'Aziz Qurayshi, once head of the Saudi Arabian Monetary Agency Board (Hooglund in Metz, ed., 1993, 210).

NATIONAL (MEETING FOR INTELLECTUAL) DIALOGUE

King 'Abdullah inaugurated the first National Meeting for Intellectual Dialogue in June 2003. The meetings, known as the National Dialogue, are intended to enhance communication and solving of the nation's problems. Only clerics were invited to the first National Dialogue; however, these included Shi'a, Isma'ili (the Isma'iliyya are a branch of the Shi'a but distinct from Saudi Arabia's larger Twelver or Ja'fari Shi'a of eastern Saudi Arabia), and Maliki (a different school of Islamic jurisprudence, as contrasted with the more dominant Hanbali school) leaders alongside Sunni leaders who follow 'Abd al-Wahhab's ideas. Safar al-Hawali, one of the *neosalafi* Awakening Shaykhs, declined to attend a meeting that included Shi'a of Saudi Arabia, as he considers them religious heretics, but another Awakening Shaykh, Salman al-Awdah, attended (Lacey 2009, 271). Some women were invited to attend the Second National Dialogue meeting, although they met separately from the men, communicating with them via closed-circuit television. The idea of meeting in different areas of the country was discussed at the initial Dialogue meetings and has been implemented.

The Third National Dialogue meeting in June 2004 addressed women's issues, and the participants resolved that women should be able to work and further their education, at college or university, without needing the permission of their *mahram* (guardian). They recommended that courts should be established with female judges to rule on women's issues (a highly controversial issue as many male clerics have rejected any woman's right to become a judge). Also, they called for a public transportation system that would benefit women who cannot afford to hire drivers (Lacey 2009, 325–326) and are therefore unable to travel to work or study. The National Dialogue sessions have also discussed religious extremism and moderation, youth issues, relations with non-Muslims, the educational system, labor issues, and national unity. They have been criticized because advisory recommendations made in the sessions are not necessarily acted on (SUSRIS [interview with Rachel Bronson] April 27, 2006) but praised for introducing topics that are "open targets" for free speech and for giving the participants standing in civil society (Bronson in SUSRIS, 2007). However, free expression has also been punished, as in 2006 when a Najrani woman, Fatima al-Tisan, spoke out about the disenfranchisement of Isma'ili Saudi Arabians and was soon fired from her job at the Ministry of Education (Worth, October 20, 2010). The National Dialogue session in Najran in April 2010, attended by 70 delegates, discussed ways to improve health care in the kingdom. The theme of the National Meeting for Intellectual Dialogue in 2011 concerns dialogue between the media and society.

DOMESTIC POLITICAL ISSUES

Domestic political issues concern many topics taken up in the National Dialogue, as well as competition for government resources, the growing class divisions among Saudi Arabians on the basis of income, regional tensions with the politics, beliefs, or cultural customs of the central region, Najd, and an ongoing counterterrorism program. King 'Abdullah has enacted many reforms and has indicated a gradual path, estimated to require 20 years, to a political system with an elected legislature and a political life with a greater role for citizenry. The nature and measures of change to be implemented are controversial. This is because Saudi Arabian society is divided into extremely conservative, less conservative, and liberal sectors. Also, the potential of National Dialogue sessions appears increasingly symbolic in the context of regional instability; for in each case of challenged governments—in Tunisia, Egypt, Yemen, Syria etc. National Dialogues have been announced to stave off radical change, and failed in some cases to forestall it.

Political parties are not permitted in the kingdom. The Arab Socialist Action Party and the Communist Party of Saudi Arabia did exist in the past but were subject to harassment and arrests and disbanded in the 1990s. An illegal Green Party of Saudi Arabia exists, although its 2009 website has been dismantled; it espoused political goals similar to those in a Western country, calling for a secular constitution. Other groups exist such as the Muslim Brotherhood and Hizb al-Tahrir, but not as parties. An active opposition wants a more faithfully Islamic government and opposes the al-Sa'ud alliance with the United States—but their opposition activity is illegal. In the spring of 2011, the Islamic Ummah party, which represents the views of *sahwa* (Islamic Awakening) supporters and calls for an end to the absolute authority of the Saudi Arabian monarchy, was established. The 10 founders of the party were all arrested as of June 11, but other party supporters remain. It is important to note that some strands of opposition to the government have spoken out against the government; others have refrained; still others are in exile, notably in London.

In the 2005 municipal elections, a fairly large number of conservative, or Islamist, candidates prevailed, suggesting that broader elections for the legislature might bring more conservatives to power than liberals. Women campaigned unsuccessfully for participation, but even that activity was positive in raising awareness of their status and informing the public about potential female candidates such as the historian Hatoon al-Fassi and others. Despite promises to the contrary, women are also excluded from standing in the 2011 elections or voting. The King has promised women the vote for the 2015 elections.

Provincial development can involve heavy politicking. The areas of Abha, Asir, the Eastern Province, and the Hijaz have sometimes protested that Saudi Arabia's policies reflected Najd and the attitudes and customs of those originating there. In addition, Saudi Arabia's Shi'a minority has been a political concern since the 1970s. Discrimination against the Shi'a went hand in hand with neglect of the areas where they were a majority. To some extent, Aramco impacted the Eastern Province, employing large numbers of Shi'a and paying for many projects that were necessary to establish the company's functionality.

In 1980, following Shi'a demonstrations, mentioned later, the deputy minister of the interior, Amir Ahmad ibn 'Abd al-'Aziz, designed a comprehensive plan to develop the Eastern Province, and the government ordered a large development project for al-Qatif. However, 30 years later, the Shi'a still lack proportional representation in government or leadership. Only three members of the Majlis al-Shura are from this minority, although they did win local offices in the 2005 municipal elections. In the spring of 2011, following pro-democracy movements in other Arab nations that sought the ouster of long-standing dictators like Hosni Mubarak, Zein al-Abedin bin 'Ali (who fled to Saudi Arabia), Mu'ammar Qadhdhafi, 'Ali 'Abdullah Saleh (also in Saudi Arabia at the time of writing), and Bashar al-Asad, Saudi Arabian pro-democracy activists announced protests in the kingdom on Facebook. Demonstrations and riots in the eastern cities of al-Qatif and al-Hofuf were far larger than the protests in Riyadh, in part because of the precedent set in this region. In addition to calls against discrimination, Shi'a protesters in Saudi Arabia called for the withdrawal of Saudi Arabian forces from Bahrain.

King 'Abdullah has supported measures to improve relations between the Sunni majority and Saudi Arabia's Shi'a minority. The Shi'a intermittently demanded freedom of worship in the past, so that they could build mosques, print religious books, and carry out religious rites according to their own custom. Opposition mostly came from Saudi Arabia's religious conservatives and neosalafists, who declare the Shi'a heretical. Hence, the policies disallowing 'Ashura parades and preventing the call to prayer (*adhan*) from being delivered in the Shi'a version (in which a certain line of the *adhan* is repeated, the final phrase "La illaha il-Allah,"; as this repetition is not performed by Sunni Muslims, it is a target for those who argue against specific exclusive Shi'a practices and ideas) were aimed at containing public strife, much as Christians were expected to keep all prayer private and as invisible as possible. In 1979, this red line was breached by activists of the Shirazi trend who had developed teaching centers in the Gulf region by then, who announced their intended demonstrations ahead of time. They threatened Aramco workers and challenged the al-Sa'ud rule in the demonstrations, known as the Muharram of 1400 (Louër 2008, 163–165) or Intifadhat (the uprising of) Muharram 1400. Except for one cleric, the Shirazi leadership went into exile, and many were imprisoned. King Fahd appointed his son Muhammad to take the Shi'a problem in hand in 1984, and he released many of these prisoners. During the Gulf War, the Shi'a of the Eastern Province, and even those leaders in exile, were loyal to the Saudi Arabian government, refusing advances by Saddam Hussein. Today, the aims of the community are different, more aimed at integration. Erasing discrimination will require changes in the thinking of fellow Saudi Arabians as much as patronage from the king, due to the anti-Shi'a rhetoric of many neosalafists (see Chapter 5, section on religion, for more discussion).

Other hotly debated domestic issues are women's rights (see Chapter 5, section on women and marriage) and employment issues, including the large number of foreign, primarily Asian, workers. Clearly, state support will be necessary in further reforms, hopefully to include suffrage and women's rights to stand for office. The push to employ Saudi Arabian citizens, including women and their future prospects, comes up against the more profitable importation of foreign workers. These dynamics have a great impact on labor issues and, like many other aspects of domestic policy, are difficult to understand without a comprehensive view of Saudi Arabia's economy and also its foreign policy.

FOREIGN POLICY

Saudi Arabia's foreign policy evolved in the pre–oil production era and featured Great Britain as security guarantor; that role was later transferred to the United States. In part, the shift occurred naturally because Great Britain faced great economic difficulties following World War II and had relinquished some of its international influence. However, at the same time, some Anglo-American competition remained at the commercial level within the Gulf region. Saudi Arabia's foreign policy initially grew to support state consolidation, and next to secure the nation and prevent challenges to the regime and, subsequently, the petroleum industry. Foreign policy initiated and strengthened certain relationships to preserve Saudi Arabia's stewardship of the *hajj* (pilgrimage) and secure the country from any threats to its own integrity or to pilgrims during the pilgrimage period. Beyond this, Islamic leadership has proven a strong tool for advancing Saudi Arabia's interests in the region, although this was not the case at midcentury.

Saudi Arabia has supported Arabism and its own sovereign and national interests but not the secular antimonarchist Arab nationalism of the revolutionary mode supported at one time by the countries of Egypt, Syria, and Iraq. The al-Sa'ud have firmly opposed communism and attacks on other Muslims, including those by Israel on the Palestinians and Muslim holy places in Palestine. Finally, it opposes terrorism by Muslims through an active security and counterterrorist force and also ideologically, by promoting Islamic moderation, supporting an Islamic legal stance against terrorism, and promoting respect for the authority of Islamic rulers.

Saudi Arabia's Relations with Yemen

When the Wahhabi movement on the Arabian Peninsula was contained by Egyptian forces for the Ottoman Turks, they allowed the traditional ruler of northern Yemen, the Zaydi Imam, to govern that area. Meanwhile, Great Britain had occupied the port of Aden in 1839. Aden became a Crown Colony, and the other southern Yemeni areas were under a protectorate. After World War I, Imam al-Nasir al-Din Allah Ahmad ibn al-Mutawakkil 'Ala Allah Yahya (Imam Ahmad ibn Yahya) fought the British to the south and the Saudi Arabians to the north. 'Abd al-'Aziz al-Sa'ud unsuccessfully attempted to conquer Yemen in 1934. He survived an assassination attempt by Yemeni killers, and serious territorial disputes between the two countries continued.

Following Imam Yahya's death on September 9, 1962, his son Imam Muhammad al-Badr succeeded him. Then, an army uprising overthrew Imam al-Badr, declaring the Yemen Arab Republic. Imam al-Badr escaped, gathered tribal forces, and received aid from the Saudi Arabian government against the republicans. The conflict continued; Gamal abd al-Nasser's government backed the republicans and sent troops and aircraft, miring itself into a Vietnam-like situation (Aboul-Enein 2004). When Egypt finally withdrew, it faced a disastrous defeat in the Six-Day War with Israel in 1967. In that year, Aden and the former protectorate of South Yemen formed the People's Democratic Republic of Yemen (PDRY), which adopted

Marxist ideology and policies. When thousands fled northward in 1971, Saudi Arabia backed dissidents against the PDRY. Meanwhile, the PDRY strengthened its ties with the Soviets as well as Cuban, Chinese, and East German advisers.

'Ali 'Abdullah Saleh became president in 1978, and fighting resumed between the North and the South in 1979. Following several violent shifts in leadership in the south, the unification of the two Yemens was achieved, an event that Saudi Arabia had opposed. Yemen is the only country on the Arabian Peninsula not included in the Gulf Cooperation Council (GCC), which results from Saudi Arabian insistence, due to its republican form of government. Gause, a specialist in Gulf affairs, notes Saudi Arabia's strong influence over North Yemen due to the two nations' political and structural commonalities, including their Islamic outlook (Gause 1990, 160). If Saudi Arabia had been less influential in Yemen, North Yemen might more easily have withstood Saudi Arabia's pressures against unity (Badeeb 1986, 95, 104).

Since Yemen's unification, Saudi Arabia continued to give support to certain tribal leaders in the North and strongly supported the Saleh government until the democracy movement of 2011 began, even then trying ensure a peaceful departure for Saleh (which he rejected, he left only after being injured in a bombing). Saudi Arabia also strengthened salafist Yemeni tribal elements, which led, perhaps inadvertently, to the creation of a haven for al-Qa'ida on the Arabian Peninsula.

Saudi Arabia's expulsion of a million and a half Yemeni nationals in the wake of the Gulf War negatively impacted Yemen's economy. In 2000, a new border agreement with Saudi Arabia was concluded with the Treaty of Jeddah (Whitaker, trans., June 12, 2000). The agreement includes three areas: the coastline to the Jabal al-Thar; the land border from there eastward, in which 17 sets of coordinates were determined; and respective maritime rights (Whitaker, July 1, 2000).

During the Gulf War, U.S. General H. Norman Schwarzkopf decided Yemen was strategically important, and it became a naval reloading and fueling point for the United States. The American ships attracted al-Qa'ida, which launched a suicide attack on the USS *Cole* in October 2000. This, together with the concerns raised by the September 11, 2001, attacks resulted in cooperation among the American, Saudi Arabian, and Yemeni counterterrorism programs and officials. Even so, there was another attempted ship bombing, and eight of the suspects of the USS *Cole* bombing escaped from prison in 2003 (two were recaptured).

The Houthi rebellion, or al-Sa'adah conflict, expanded in 2004 after government troops killed its leader, Shaykh Husayn Badr al-Din al-Houthi, and tried to crush resistance. Fighting resumed in 2005, and Saudi Arabia, which had long sponsored tribes that fought the Houthis, embarked on bombings against the rebels in 2009. In 2008, a series of al-Qa'ida attacks took place. The originally Saudi Arabia–based al-Qa'ida fi Jazirat al-'Arabiyyah (QAP) joined forces with two other militant salafist organizations in Yemen. An agent of this QAP group pretended to seek mediation and then attempted to kill Deputy Minister of the Interior Prince Muhammad ibn Nayif during Ramadan in 2009. Then, a Christmas Day bombing attempt on a U.S. airliner revealed that the Nigerian would-be bomber had made contacts with al-Qa'ida in Yemen (Bergen, December 27, 2009).

Border issues remained, along with disputes about a barricade Saudi Arabia had begun to build along the Yemeni–Saudi Arabian border. The border was being traversed daily, according to Saudi Arabia, by scores of illegal Yemeni immigrants, Somalis and Ethiopians. The Saudi Arabian government related its support against the Houthi rebellion to the terrorist threat, which was not, in fact, as large or imminently threatening as the Saleh government made it out to be. Indeed, Yemenis complained bitterly about the corruption of the Saleh government and its manipulation of foreign assistance. In addition, the Americans, who were coordinating with Saudi Arabia concerning Yemen, were concerned by unsubstantiated claims that the Houthis had support from Iran (Murphy, November 14, 2009), and that was further reason to back Saleh. Saudi Arabian troops went after the Houthi rebels, moving into Yemen and forcing the rebels out in early 2010 (Murphy, January 27, 2010). Despite Saudi Arabian and American support for the Saleh regime, in 2011 several months of massive demonstrations culminated in some violence; an attack wounded the president (as well as other governmental officials) severely, and he left Yemen for treatment in Saudi Arabia on June 4, 2011, and was not expected to return to Yemen again in a presidential capacity (Whitaker, June 5, 2011) for three months returning to huge protests and inter-Yemeni fighting.

Saudi Arabia and Yemen have long been linked economically, and not as equal partners. Yemeni immigration to Saudi Arabia had brought about two million Yemenis into the country before the Gulf War, many of whom worked in low-paying construction jobs. However, Yemen, unlike Saudi Arabia, developed many private structures, whereas its national banks and the state itself weakened, and it drew income from tariffs and foreign aid (Chaudhry 1989, 1997; Okruhlik and Conge 1997).

A Saudi Arabian soldier stands on top of Mt. Dowd on January 27, 2010, a strategic position that was recaptured from the Houthi rebels of Yemen the previous week. Mt. Dowd is in Jizan province.

Given Yemen's rather dire economic situation, it is likely that the post-Saleh situation will continue to rely on remittances from Yemeni immigrants in Saudi Arabia and elsewhere in the world.

Osama bin Laden's Yemeni father made his fortune early in the construction boom in Saudi Arabia and acquired Saudi Arabian citizenship. Countless other Yemenis traveled to Saudi Arabia on the pilgrimage. Recently, illegal immigration into Saudi Arabia has increased because of the limited employment opportunities in Yemen. The settlement of naturalized Yemeni immigrants has more recently been occurring in Najran, contributing to *salafi* and Sunni-Isma'ili tensions in that area. The Isma'ili residents of Najran contend that the government wants to alter the sectarian balance somewhat, just as Saddam Hussein effected in Kirkuk by settling non-Kurds there.

Saudi Arabia's Relations with Iraq

Saudi Arabia shares history, land, and people with Iraq. Numerous tribes extend over the border (Trench, ed., 1996), including the Shammar tribe, which numbers at least 1 million members in Saudi Arabia and about 2.5 million in Iraq. Many Saudi Arabians traveled to Iraq, grew up there, or studied there due to family and cultural ties. The Shi'a of Saudi Arabia have religious and intellectual linkages to the Iraqi holy cities. In addition, both nations became oil producers, and a fair amount of competition and political scrapping infighting emerged between the British in Iraq and Aramco in Saudi Arabia (Brown 1999).

Until 1958, Iraq was ruled by the descendants of Sharif Husayn of Mecca: the Hashemites, once rivals of the al-Sa'ud. Following the revolution of 1958, when the Iraqi monarchy was overthrown, Sa'udi-Iraqi relations were often hostile as a consequence of direct disputes, ideological differences, and competition for influence in the region. However, the Iraqi government had begun to modify and soften its attacks in 1975, and a closer relationship formed in response to the emergent Islamic Republic in Iran following the overthrow of Shah Muhammad Reza Pahlavi. The Saudi Arabian government formulated several conflicting policy goals from 1979 to 1982—they wanted to rely on Iraq to offset Iranian power without antagonizing Iran and to appease Iran without angering Iraq; moreover, they needed the Americans to vouchsafe their security without angering Arab nations that had opposed Camp David (Safran 1985, 353).

After the Iran-Iraq War began, Saudi Arabia declared neutrality yet supported Iraq. Saudi Arabia was concerned by Iranian victories early in 1982 and tried to convince the Egyptians to intervene militarily. The Syrians were urging support of the Iraqis and then reversed their position, deploying Syrian forces on their borders with Iraqi, cutting off the Iraqi oil flow through their country, and sending arms to Iran. The Egyptians then declined to intervene. Iran began a major advance. Finally, Saudi Arabian concerns were allayed when the Iraqis pushed back the Iranian attacks (Safran 1985, 373–385). By the war's end, Saudi Arabia had supplied an estimated $25 to $30.9 billion in grants and low-interest loans to Iraq.

Despite Kuwait's similar support for Iraq during the war, Iraq pressed claims against Kuwait and invaded the country in August 1990. This invasion shocked the

Sa'udi royal family and the Saudi Arabian government. It feared an Iraqi advance into the kingdom. It was the ultimate test of Saudi Arabia's trust in the United States. The U.S. and coalition forces used Saudi Arabia's air bases to stage strikes against Iraq. Iraq fired Scud missiles at Riyadh and other Saudi Arabian cities. The war was unpopular with many Saudi Arabians, as with other Arab populations, because Iraq was an Arab-led Muslim country. After many years of the constant promotion of Arab unity, an inter-Arab war countered popular sentiments. The government turned to the *'ulama*, who issued a *fatwa* that essentially permitted the presence of foreign troops on Saudi Arabian soil in defense of the Muslim community there.

Operation Desert Shield lasted from August until January 1991 and was followed by Operation Desert Storm. Desert Shield was a defensive staging operation that was vital to the success of Operation Desert Storm; it allowed for the assembly of sufficient troops and supplies to defend Saudi Arabia if deterrent actions failed. Thanks to Desert Shield, the military coalition was prepared, in a little more than a month, to defend Saudi Arabia and thereafter to attack Iraq.

Operation Desert Storm, the coalition's air campaign, was conducted from January 15 to February 17, 1991. More than 44,000 combat sorties were conducted, dropping more than 84,000 tons of bombs, crippling the Iraqi response. A ground advance achieved the final blows against the Iraqi forces (Cordesman and Wagner 1996; Freedman and Karsh 1993). Major-General Prince Khalid ibn Sultan, the commander of the Joint Forces, wrote his own account of the war with author Patrick Seale. His account is unique in providing a view of behind-the-scenes diplomacy including inter-Arab politics prior to the Gulf War and divergences between American and Saudi Arabian goals, as well as details of the battle of Khafiji and certain blunders during the war (Khaled bin Sultan 1995).

The Gulf War led to the expulsion of Yemenis working in Saudi Arabia and a cessation of relations with the Palestine Liberation Organization (PLO) because of Yasir 'Arafat's support of Iraq. It also led to internal opposition. Certain clerics were unconvinced by the official *fatwa* and believed the alliance with the United States and hosting of foreign troops were wrong and against Islamic law encouraged other Saudi Arabians to oppose the presence of Western troops and political influence on the Saudi Arabian government. Their criticisms continued for many years in sermons, actions, demonstrations, letters, and official memoranda. The ultimate counterresponse to the hue and cry over the illicitness of the American presence was the United States' withdrawal from its military missions in Saudi Arabia (although the United States remains involved in numerous training endeavors such as the Saudi War College).

During the Gulf War, the Americans followed orders developed by Ambassador Chas Freeman prohibiting alcohol, sexy magazines, and T-shirts on women. Non-Muslim religious services were to be held where Saudi Arabian citizens could not see them, and the U.S. military forces passed the *mutawa'in*'s inspection (Lippman 2004, 304–305). Nevertheless, certain failures occurred, from leaked photos of female entertainment to the troops to news of excessive civilian deaths in Iraq, to breaches of Saudi Arabian custom. Prince Khalid agreed to having female U.S. troops be part of the mission; among them were female soldiers who were permitted to drive. Saudi Arabian conservatives were outraged when that same year a group of 41 Saudi Arabian women staged a driving demonstration. The conservatives gathered en masse outside the Dar al-Ifta' to put pressure on the government (bin Baz, January 14, 2011) and publicly accused these Saudi Arabian women of defying their culture, trying to transform Saudi Arabia into the United States, and encouraging sin. The women were fired from their jobs and not allowed to travel out of the country (although bin Baz, the Grand Mufti, helped several to recover their positions later). The incident increased criticism against the government for allowing foreign troops to operate from Saudi Arabia. Despite this, Operation Desert Storm was a success from Saudi Arabia's perspective. But it heightened the resolve of Osama bin Laden and other radicals to rid Saudi Arabia completely of its foreigners and alliance with the United States.

The Iraqi government railed against the Saudi Arabian government as U.S. attacks were staged during the 1990s. However, Saudi Arabia was not in favor of the 2003 invasion of Iraq and did not support the effort. On November 5, 2004, 26 well-known Saudi Arabian clerics signed a *fatwa* in support of Iraqi resistance against the U.S. military there. A disputed number of Saudi Arabians traveled to Iraq to join the resistance against the United States and the new Iraqi government. Some were linked directly with al-Qa'ida in Iraq. The Saudi Arabian government then strengthened its border security and detained or charged many of those who had gone to fight in Iraq.

Saudi Arabia was concerned that American imposition of a federal system in Iraq, or protracted civil war, would further endanger the region. However, Saudi Arabia is a charter member of the International Compact with Iraq and part of the Expanded Iraq Neighbors meetings. Even though Iraq's leading political coalition was made up primarily of Shi'a Islamist parties, which dominated government under Prime Minister Nuri al-Maliki, Saudi Arabia has assumed that Iraq will pursue policies independent from Iran, and this assumption has proven true.

Saudi Arabia's Relations with Iran

Saudi Arabia's relations with Iran shifted from a quasi-alliance and rivalry in the Gulf with the Pahlavi regime to confrontation upon the rise of Ayatollah Ruhollah Khomeini's government. Saudi Arabia's leaders understood from the Islamic Revolution in Iran that liberalization and modernization could backfire in an Islamist form. Iran, a much more populous nation, with the largest military force in the Gulf, was obviously threatening to Saudi Arabia and its oil production. It also challenged Saudi Arabia on the basis of leadership in the Islamic world. Iran sends a large number of pilgrims to the *hajj*, and their demonstrations and protests proved troublesome after the Islamic Revolution. Also, Saudi Arabia had witnessed rising tensions with its Shi'a population in the Eastern Province immediately following Juhayman al-'Utaybi's 1979 takeover of the Grand Mosque.

Yet Saudi Arabia's Iran policy has not replicated that of the United States. One can explain this in various ways. One view considers it the practical reaction of a wealthier yet more vulnerable nation. Alternatively, some experts hold that in view of the United States' abandonment of the shah, the Saudi Arabians had reason to wonder if the United States would be a reliable ally (Chubin and Tripp 1996 and 2005). This causes them to act more cautiously, expanding their options.

The two nations have approached oil policies differently; it is often argued that Iran needs oil income more urgently and so pushes for higher pricing. They have vied with each other over regional and subregional policy, clashing in Lebanon, and over Iraq. Also, Iran has been suspect in activism by Shi'a Muslim populations in the GCC states. Iran believes that Saudi Arabia plays a strong role in opposition to the central government in Baluchistan and among Arabs in Khuzestan (Wehry et al. 2009, x).

Saudi Arabia and Iran were linked by the early rivalries of British and American oil development. By the time Great Britain withdrew from the Gulf in 1971, the shah of Iran had embarked on various efforts to enhance his influence, including dispatching Iranian troops to Oman to extinguish the Dhofar Rebellion. The shah and the Saudi Arabian government had in common a basic antipathy to communist and leftist elements, and both had alliances with the United States.

With the Islamic Revolution in Iran, Saudi Arabian–Iranian relations deteriorated. Iran was fearful of a counterrevolution and concerned by Saudi Arabia's support of Iraq, despite its declared neutrality in the Iran-Iraq War. In response to the war, the GCC was formed, and Iran viewed this teaming up of Arab monarchies and sheikhdoms as a hostile gesture. Because Saudi Arabia had invited the United States into the Gulf in its efforts to boost its defense and military power, Iran was directly antagonized and yet constrained. Otherwise, it might have responded differently to

Opening of the Gulf Cooperation Council (GCC) consultative summit in Riyadh, Saudi Arabia, May 11, 2010. Shown here are (from left to right) Bahraini King Hamad ibn Isa al-Khalifa, UAE Vice-President and Prime Minister, Shaykh Muhammad ibn Rashid al-Maktoum, Saudi Arabian King 'Abdullah ibn 'Abd al-'Aziz, Kuwaiti Emir Sabah al-Ahmad al-Sabah, Qatari Emir Shaykh Hamad ibn Khalifa al-Thani, and Omani Deputy Prime Minister Fahd ibn Mahmoud al-Saeed. (AP/Wide World Photos)

attacks by two Saudi Arabian war planes in 1984 and the U.S. downing of a passenger jet in 1988 (Chubin and Tripp 2005, 11).

Revolutionary rhetoric in Iran called for an end to the Sa'udi monarchy, charging the royal family with corruption and improper stewardship of the Holy Cities. The initial zeal in Iran to spread the Islamic Revolution to the entire region gradually abated, as it was not practicable, but this hostile discourse remained active. During the 1980s, Iranian pilgrims directly confronted Saudi Arabia's rulers when they demonstrated and shouted slogans against them during the *hajj* rites. The Saudi Arabian authorities tried to enforce rules whereby the demonstrators were confined to specific areas. In the summer of 1987, more than 400 pilgrims, about two-thirds of these Iranian, died after Saudi Arabian security forces attempted to halt a demonstration in Mecca. This led to stricter Saudi Arabian regulations and also to attacks on the Saudi Arabia's embassy in Tehran, resulting in the death of one official. In 1988 Saudi Arabia severed diplomatic relations with Iran, and Iranian pilgrims returned to the *hajj* only in 1991.

For Iran, Saudi Arabia's subsequent enmity to Iraq during the First Gulf War was somewhat reassuring. On the other hand, the war invited the U.S. military even more deeply into the role of security guarantor in the Gulf on behalf of Saudi Arabia. Following the Gulf War, a number of conflicts arose. Calls for religious and political rights for the Shi'a in the Eastern Province heightened in the Intifadhat (uprising of) 1400. A Qatari–Saudi Arabian dispute in 1992 elicited Iranian support for Qatar; it pledged to send 30,000 troops. An attempted coup by Islamist Shi'a in Bahrain was dismantled by that government in 1996. In the same year, the bombings of the U.S. Air Force barracks in Dhahran at the Khobar Towers took place. U.S. government officials insisted that Iran was responsible, but the bombers were a cell of the Saudi Arabian Hizballah, and no direct Iranian link was established. Iran had provided a certain degree of support to the Saudi Arabian Hizballah, which published a journal in Beirut from 1991 to 1995, *Risalat al-Haramayn* (Fürtig 2002; Ibrahim 2007, 195). The two nations differed in their actions in Afghanistan. Saudi Arabia had funded the *mujahidin*. Iran opposed the emergent Taliban and preferred the Northern Alliance.

The various bilateral differences were deflected by a policy of accommodation between then-Crown Prince 'Abdullah and President Rafsanjani, beginning in 1997 with their meeting in Pakistan and continuing with the Iranian president's visit to Saudi Arabia in 1999. They made various agreements concerning security, the pilgrimage, and drug trafficking and cooperated again in the post-9/11 period regarding al-Qa'ida (Keynoush 2007).

Tensions also arose because the Shi'a minorities in Saudi Arabia and the Gulf have been treated as a potential fifth column, accused of being more loyal to Shi'ism or Iran than their own country. Additionally, the numerous attacks on Shi'a Muslim pilgrims, and political and clerical attacks on Shi'ism in Iraq, sent shock waves through the region. Salafists in Saudi Arabia strongly attacked the Shi'a Muslims in statements and *fatawa*. Senior clerics at Qum explicitly attacked Wahhabis for their violence to the Shi'a (Wehry et al. 2009, 29–40). Some accommodation was achieved in 2007, when both Iranian and Saudi Arabian officials agreed to monitor highly sectarian and divisive *fatawa* issued by clerics and with Ayatollah Khamene'i's symbolic declaration of 2009 as a year of Islamic solidarity and national unity (Wehry et al. 2009, 38, 40).

The Islamic Revolution did impact the Middle East; Sunni Islamists detested Shi'ism but held many of the same ideals as Iranians, preferring Islamic government and law, and some likewise embraced activism to bring about these conditions. Yet most Islamist parties in the Arab world rejected the Khomeinist proposal of *vilayat-e faqih* (rule of the cleric). The populism of Khomeini's ideology troubled Saudi Arabia (al-Mani in Suweidi, ed., 1996), as it called into question a monarchy's right to govern the holy cities. Still, Iran's Islamic Revolution heralded the Sudanese coup led by Omar al-Bashir and the National Islamic Front, an Islamist-dominated government in post-Saddam Iraq, and a moderate Islamist leadership in republican Turkey. Nonetheless, monarchs and traditional *amirs* continued to rule in the Gulf. When Mahmoud Ahmadinejad, leading a wave of Iranian neoconservatism, was elected president of Iran, U.S.-Iranian relations deteriorated. Ahmadinejad was admired for his anti-Americanism in the Arab world and in Iran for being a genuine, modest, or "plain" leader giving voice to Islamic-Iranian nationalism (Zuhur 2006). His oral support for Hizbullah of Lebanon and Hamas continued as Saudi Arabia was pressed by Washington to intervene to the disadvantage of these two groups and Iranian influence in the region, which they believed to have increased with regime change in Iraq.

Saudi-Iranian relations are deeply impacted by U.S.–Saudi Arabian relations, especially since the demise of Saddam Hussein and in light of Iranian claims to pursue their rights to a nuclear program. In the first year of Barack Obama's administration, the United States mirrored its Cold War strategy when it had championed Saudi Arabia as a force against Egypt's Abd al-Nasser and Arab socialism (Kerr 1976; Zuhur 2005b, 46–47). The United States also exaggerated a Sunni-Shi'a division of the Islamic world, in which Saudi Arabia was supposed to undo Iran's ambitions (Wehry et al. 2009). The United States includes Saudi Arabia in this endeavor, along with Arab nations it considers "moderates," like Jordan and Egypt.

A Saudi Arabian–Iranian rivalry is also useful for the United States in its approach to the global War on Terror. However, the United States loudly opposed Islamic "theocracy," demonizing rule by the cleric and use of Islamic law in general. If this was applicable to Iran, it was hard to see why Saudi Arabia's claim to be an Islamic government and use of Islamic law were not to be criticized. Indeed, that came about following 9/11.

As part of the wave of pro-democratic and revolutionary activity in the Arab world in 2011, demonstrations broke out in Bahrain. Saudi Arabia's military intervention there to put down the demonstrations was sharply criticized in the Iranian media, as the entire set of events have a strong sectarian content, being that the demonstrators are Shi'a but the Bahraini government, like the Saudi Arabian troops, are Sunni. The Saudi Arabian–Iranian rivalry may appear in the "new" Middle East, if these same trends continue in Syria and other Arab countries.

Saudi Arabia's Relations with Egypt

Saudi Arabia and Egypt clashed politically from Abd al-Nasser's ascension until Anwar al-Sadat's succession. Nasser's use of propaganda against the kingdom on Radio Cairo and in the press was one manifestation of this rivalry. Another was the previously mentioned Saudi Arabian and Egyptian embroilment in Yemen, with the Egyptians supporting the republicans, while Saudi Arabia supported the

loyalists. These differences were exploited by Egypt following 'Abd al-'Aziz's demise and led to a plot for an attempted assassination of Nasser involving Sa'udi
and Syrian officials, and also many other incidents (see Chapter 2, History). Some
of the Sa'udi royal family, many young technocrats, and some in the military were
influenced by or at least receptive to the popularity of Arab nationalism, and they
embraced challenges to the rule of the al-Sa'ud. At the same time, the ideas of anti-
imperialism, and national control and sovereignty, impacted even King Sa'ud, who
vacillated between polices for a time. Also, while Egypt was truly a regional leader
in this period, it lost some regional influence due to the wane of Nasserism, and the
Camp David agreement, whereas Saudi Arabia's impact in the region has grown.

When the union between Egypt and Syria ended, Nasser issued increasingly ideological attacks on the forces he thought were to blame, the political influence of the
al-Sa'ud, imperialism, and comprador elites (who served Western commercial and
political interests) among them. These attacks and the stances taken by the Syrian and
Iraqi governments led Saudi Arabia to increase its alliance with the United States.

Egypt received Saudi Arabian aid after its great losses as a result of the Six-Day
War in 1967 and also following the Ramadan War of 1973. It also received aid for
nonmilitary development. The Saudi Fund for Development, established in 1975,
helped to provide infrastructure for the water system in Cairo as well as $50 million
for the Egyptian reconstruction of the Suez Canal cities of Isma'iliyya and Suez
(*Aramco World*, September–October 1977; *Aramco World*, November–December
1979 [entire issue], including Lawton 1979). During these years, as President Sadat
consolidated his power, Saudi Arabian–Egyptian relations became more amicable.
Sadat ordered the exodus of Soviet advisers from Egypt and mended relations with
Syria. Saudi Arabia's position during the oil embargo of 1973 was designed to help
the Arab and Palestinian cause, and thus Egypt as well. For similar reasons, Saudi
Arabian defense funding to Egypt was viewed in Washington and Tel Aviv as serious
strategic challenge (Jabber in Kerr and Yassin, eds., 1982).

The oil boom brought greater numbers of Gulf Arabs to Egypt in the summers.
They could pay high rents which drove up property prices and some indulged themselves in nightclubs and casinos, some married young girls for a summer (or less),
which created a degree of resentment and dependence. The Saudi Arabian government objected to the signing of the Camp David Accords on September 17, 1978.
The accords, signed by Sadat and Israeli prime minister Menachem Begin and witnessed by President Jimmy Carter, involved two frameworks, one of which led to
a peace treaty between Israel and Egypt, signed in 1979. Saudi Arabia opposed the
Israeli-preferred tactic of pursuing separate peace treaties with Arab nations, and
this treaty did not provide justice for the Palestinians. Egypt was ousted from the
Arab League, lost its aid from Saudi Arabia, and turned even further to the West in
consequence. Relations were restored by 1987, although, in the interim, Saudi Arabia
had continued to be influential, indirectly abetting the growth of Islamist societies
and sentiment in Egypt and supporting various Islamic endeavors. Egypt sent forces
to participate in the coalition efforts in Saudi Arabia during the Gulf War.

Egyptian labor has contributed much in Saudi Arabia since 1971, when laws were
changed to favor emigration. About 10 percent of Egypt's population works abroad,

nearly 48 percent of them in Saudi Arabia. Unskilled labor accounts for a large portion of those hired, but today, a higher percentage of skilled workers, professionals, and service employees are recruited. To counter displacement by Asian labor, the Egyptian government instituted a ministry for emigration.

The heightening of Islamism in Egypt was partially attributed to return emigrants from the Gulf or the example of Saudi Arabian salafism (see the preceding, the glossary, and Chapter 5, section on religion and law). This contributed to a homegrown salafism in Egypt, particularly since the 1990s, as seen in the popularity of purist religious messages, themes, and preachers and increasing attacks against Egyptian Christians. The government challenged extremism by periodically repressing Egypt's most well-organized opposition, the Muslim Brotherhood, but it issued no direct onslaught against salafism.

As of 2010, Saudi Arabia had been the largest Arab donor to Egypt, even with the interruption in aid already mentioned. However, the ordinary Egyptian does not know that Saudi Arabia gives money to his country; hence, the foreign-policy influence is more on the government than on the populace. Books critical of the Saudi Arabian government were consistently on the censored list (euphemistically termed "removed from circulation") issued by the Egyptian Ministry of Information. These were among a list of 500+ titles including publications about Islam or Islamic matters by authors with non-Muslim names, books critical of the Egyptian government, and books whose titles mention gender or sexual issues. With the Egyptian January 25th Revolution of 2011, Hosni Mubarak was ousted from power. The ideas of the young revolutionaries or elements in the army may impact Egypt's foreign policy; certainly there has been new rhetoric and actions, including the opening of the border to Gaza at Rafah and more criticism of Saudi Arabia due to the rulers' repression of demonstrations in Saudi Arabia and Bahrain. In tensions between salafist-oriented groups in Egypt and new liberal parties, accusations about Saudi Arabia's role in encouraging salafism is seen, particularly in the pro-liberal press in Egypt. Egyptian and Saudi Arabian leaders have been pressed by the United States to mitigate various situations involving the Palestinians, and the Arab-Israeli issue remains the crux of many of their difficulties and differences. The young Egyptians who sparked the 2011 revolution want to cool relations with Israel. Some of the human rights activists held a large protest at the Saudi Arabian embassy in May 2011 because they felt that Saudi Arabia, and specifically Prince Walid ibn Talal, was interfering with their efforts to put former president Hosni Mubarak on trial (*Islâmi Davet*, May 9, 2011).

Saudi Arabia's Relations with the GCC States

Saudi Arabia's relations with the smaller Arabian states were shaped by competitive relations due to tribal rivalries, the influence of Great Britain, oil policy, and mutual security concerns involving Iran, Iraq, and the United States. Saudi Arabia has had some significant border disputes with GCC countries, some of which have been settled.

In 1992, Saudi Arabia took the lead in forming the GCC, along with Bahrain, Kuwait, Oman, Qatar, and the United Arab Emirates. The permanent seat of the GCC is in Saudi Arabia. Each member has insufficient military power to protect itself from Iran or Iraq, although for different reasons. The smaller sheikhdoms were too small to protect their oil fields; Saudi Arabia was too vast with too limited a population (although this is changing) and had deliberately built a smaller military to limit the possibility of insurrection. Therefore, the GCC sought to limit first Iran, and then Iraq, from overpowering them in the 1970s and 1980s (Anthony in Adams, ed., 1988). This observation has remained true from the 1990s on.

Saudi Arabia's Relations with Qatar

Qatar hosts U.S. military forces and has become increasingly open to international entities at a time when U.S. military forces have withdrawn from Saudi Arabia. Sometimes Saudi Arabians have expressed fears that the United States can operate more easily from the GCC states and may manipulate them against the kingdom. However, Qatar is also home to the *al-Jazeera* satellite television channel, which frequently targets Saudi Arabia and U.S. Middle East policies. Qatari foreign policy has more stringently opposed Israel, appeased Iran, and been more supportive of Hamas than Saudi Arabia has in recent years. Following the December 2008–January 2009 war on Gaza, a Doha summit was convened to which Ahmadinejad, Bashar al-Asaad, Hamas's Khalid Mishaal, and Iraqi vice-president Tariq al-Hashemi were invited. It coincided with an alternative summit in Riyadh (Wehry et al. 2009, 50–51).

Saudi Arabia's Relations with Oman

Oman and Saudi Arabia clashed over rights to the Buraymi Oasis, an area with nine villages. Ibn Sa'ud had ordered Prince Turki ibn 'Abdullah al-Ataishan to seize the Buraymi Oasis in 1952 despite the sultan of Muscat and Oman's claims to the area. Aramco had supported Saudi Arabia's claim to the Buraymi Oasis because of its own designs on the holdings of the Anglo-Persian Oil Company near the village of Fuhud. Aramco supplied Saudi Arabia with documentation for its historical claim, and the matter was given to a tribunal. Efforts to bribe the tribunal were later revealed. British officers overseeing the forces of the shaykh of Abu Dhabi retook the Buraymi Oasis in 1955, forcing the Saudi Arabian police to withdrew, and they were followed by a 350-man Scottish regiment, the Cameron Highlanders. Aramco knew it had been drawn into a struggle with the British (Brown 1999, 207–213), but the U.S. government did not press the Saudi Arabian claim. An agreement was forged in 1974. In the subsequent Dhofar Rebellion, the sultan of Oman received assistance from the shah of Iran and Saudi Arabia.

Sultan Qabus ibn Sa'id gradually opened the country from the isolation it experienced under Sultan ibn Taymur. His government, like Saudi Arabia's, has been pro-Western. On January 17, 2011, antigovernment and pro-democracy demonstrations broke out in Oman as part of what is being termed the Arab Awakening, or Arab Spring of 2011, a wave of protest movements.

Saudi Arabia's Relations with Kuwait

The Ottoman Empire established the outlines of the modern states bordering the Gulf, from Iraq and Kuwait to Qatar. Kuwait has allowed entry to various enemies of the al-Sa'ud, from the Rashidi family to the Ikhwan leaders. However, Saudi Arabia's actions in the Gulf War demonstrated Saudi Arabian–Kuwaiti mutual interests.

Kuwait has a large Shi'a population and considers itself vulnerable to Iran. As in Saudi Arabia, some Kuwaiti elements deplored the Western military presence in the Gulf. In 2005, a group called the Peninsula Lions Brigades, allegedly linked to al-Qa'ida, fought battles with police in Kuwait City, killing four police and eight attackers, including two Saudi Arabians. Six individuals who planned attacks against the U.S. army Camp Arifjan (a forward logistics base) in August 2009 were arrested. Kuwait has shared and coordinated information on Islamist radical activists with Saudi Arabia. However, in Kuwait, democratization is proceeding more swiftly than in Saudi Arabia, resulting in some conservative backlash in Kuwait as well as actions against critics of Saudi Arabia or conservative Muslim policies. For instance, a Saudi Arabian cleric, Muhammad al-'Uraifi, was banned from entering Kuwait due to protests by Shi'a members of parliament in Kuwait. In response, 100 leading Kuwaiti clerics signed a petition to lift the ban (*Kuwait Times*, January 16, 2010). The late Egyptian Qur'an scholar Nasr Abu Zayd, identified with the liberal, anti-apostasy cause, and Saudi Arabian historian Madawi al-Rasheed, who has been critical of the Sa'udi rulers, were scheduled to speak in Kuwait in 2010. However, they were both denied travel permissions.

Saudi Arabia's Relations with Bahrain

The Bahraini government's claims that Iran has designs on the island mask political dissatisfaction with the government and discrimination against its citizenry and reflect the historical relationship between the island nation and Iran. Bahrain's indigenous population is about two-thirds Shi'a Muslim, but its ruling family and elites are Sunni. An Iranian-sponsored coup linked to the Islamic Front for the Liberation of Bahrain was discovered in December 1981. The police believed the group planned to assassinate Bahraini officials and attempt to overthrow the government. Other incidents followed just as the war on tankers took place during the Iran-Iraq War. Another period of unrest and demonstrations in Bahrain occurred in the mid-1990s, and then on February 14, 2011, very large antigovernment demonstrations began. Very severe violence against demonstrators was cataloged, and some international observers believed that the United States did not support the protesters as they claimed to in Tunisia and Egypt, because of the stationing of the U.S. Fifth Fleet in Bahrain and strong Saudi Arabian support for the Bahraini government.

Bahrain is now closer to Saudi Arabia than it was in the past. In 1986, Saudi Arabia mediated a serious dispute between Bahrain and Qatar over the Bahraini claim to Zubarah, Hawar, and islands south of Zubarah. At that time, Bahrainis constructing a Coast Guard station were kidnapped by Qataris; a truce was reached but then failed when Qatar went to the International Court of Justice in the Hague. The King Fahd Causeway, a 15-mile- (24-kilometer-) long highway bridge, links Bahrain to Saudi Arabia, providing easy access to Saudi Arabian drivers who may spend a weekend there or even reside in Bahrain.

After weeks of demonstrations, 1,000 Saudi Arabian troops along with tanks and vehicles moved into Bahrain on March 13, 2011, to support the Khalifa government along with other GCC forces. If the al-Khalifa rulers of Bahrain were to be further politically challenged, the Saudi Arabian government will likely continue to lend force to that government because it fears the spread of sectarian violence or larger demonstrations into Saudi Arabia.

Saudi Arabia's Relations with the United Arab Emirates

The United Arab Emirates, like Saudi Arabia, was shaken by the Iraqi invasion of Kuwait, realizing the weakness of the GCC's deterrent and defensive capabilities. It supported the coalition's actions against Iraq. Similarly to Saudi Arabia, it opposed the U.S. invasion of Iraq in 2003. The Emirates are somewhat more liberal than Saudi Arabia; parts of the country have attracted Saudi Arabian investments, and Saudi Arabians travel there frequently. Although Saudi Arabian–Emirati relations are generally good, there are disputes concerning maritime rights. In March 2010 an incident in which the navy of the Emirates fired on a small Saudi Arabian patrol vessel was reported in the foreign press (*Telegraph*, March 26, 2010).

Some Islamist militant activities have been tracked to the United Arab Emirates, and the country also sent troops in March 2011 to protect the rulers of Bahrain from the political threat posed by demonstrators.

Outside of politics, the United Arab Emirates have much in common with Saudi Arabia. The Emirates have made efforts similar to Saudi Arabia to reach out to Muslims worldwide and to encourage scholarship in Islamic studies and on Muslims. The Emirates are also concerned by the populist democratic protests of the Arab Spring.

Saudi Arabia's Relations with the United States

Saudi Arabian–American relations are key to Saudi Arabia's foreign and defense policies and also many of its oil policies to date. The United States became involved in Saudi Arabia through its commercial interest in oil and through commercial actors that are directly and indirectly linked with the U.S. government, initially Aramco and later many other companies. Aramco's explorations helped to keep the government of Ibn Sa'ud afloat and were able to keep out British commercial interests. Aramco also provided much of the country's early infrastructure, as it needed a working port, housing, hospitals, roads, and imported American labor. In addition, its leadership served as unofficial country representatives (Brown 1999; Lippman 2004).

Ibn Sa'ud had depended on the British for security guarantees, but with his decision to grant oil rights to the Americans, he expected and hoped for this assistance from the United States. In 1943, President Franklin Roosevelt declared the defense of Saudi Arabia to be a key interest of the United States. Military missions were sent to

Saudi Arabia and renewed for decades. The U.S. Army Corps of Engineers built an airfield at Dhahran and other facilities, including the King Khalid Military City (built between 1974 and 1987), the largest project ever completed by the corps (Bronson 2008). Even after the withdrawal of all but 500 troops, American contractors continue to train and hire personnel for the Saudi Arabian defense sectors. The military-aid relationship has been questioned periodically by various U.S. congressional members, who countered or cancelled various weapons sales on the grounds that Saudi Arabia might use these weapons against Israel (Hooglund in Metz, ed., 1993, 223).

Saudi Arabia and the United States signed a mutual defense agreement in 1951 under which the United States was entitled to create a permanent Military Training Mission in the kingdom. The U.S. secretary of state, John Foster Dulles, considered Nasser to be very dangerous and thought that his promotion of Arab nationalism was dangerous to U.S. interests. Then after Nasser's request to the United States for arms was ignored, Dulles thought his purchase of Eastern-bloc arms and an influx of Soviet advisors even more ominous. Nasser's Arab nationalist messages, and the strength of leftist parties and later the Ba'th in Iraq and Syria, caused consternation in Saudi Arabia and Washington. President John F. Kennedy sent off squadrons of fighters to Saudi Arabia to fend off Egyptian air attacks in 1963. Similarly, when the Iran-Iraq War began, President Carter permitted Saudi Arabia to borrow AWACs (airborne warning and control systems) monitoring craft and crews. The Saudi Arabian–American alliance withstood the pressures of different stances on Israel and the Palestinians. Yet Saudi Arabia noted that sponsors of Israel were among its strongest critics in the United States.

In the 1970s, the oil boom resulted in business expansions and construction in the kingdom that employed tens of thousands of Americans. Aramco embarked on a huge eight-year project to capture and utilize natural gas that had heretofore been flared off as waste, and it needed to bring in 30,000 workers. American companies constructed buildings at Riyadh University, classrooms for the Saudi Navy, the headquarters of the National Commercial Bank, military housing, a hospital in Ta'if, residential areas for the industrial city of Yanbu, and an ethylene plant there, all in 1980. In the same year, they were involved in training programs for industries, fire crews, and naval crews, and they also handled air traffic control. The U.S. Congress intervened and investigated the paying of bribes to foreign officials. This process revealed that some companies like the Whitaker Corporation, which operated hospitals in the kingdom, successfully operated and prospered without breaking any U.S. laws, since payments to nongovernmental officials were legal (Lippman 2004, 161, 164–165).

The U.S.–Saudi Arabian Joint Economic Commission (JECOR) was established in 1974 and ceased in 2000. It was managed by the U.S. Treasury Department and ran entirely on Saudi Arabian funds, except for one program for solar energy development, which received U.S. funds. It was independent of the U.S. embassy until about 1989 and provided assistance in numerous aspects of development and governmental management, from statistics collection and compilation to the running of national parks, desalinization, customs administration, audits, highway administration, agricultural development, training of tax auditors, and university-level educational exchanges (Lippman 2004, 168–178). Depending on one's perspective, the program could be critiqued for fostering a dependent, cliental relationship between Saudi Arabians and Americans or praised for accomplishing its achievement of building capability.

The United States followed through on its security commitment to the kingdom when it sent 400,000 troops there following the Iraqi invasion of Kuwait. The 1991 Gulf War was a confluence of U.S. intent to forcibly contain Saddam Hussein and Saudi Arabian fears that their small military (like the other small militaries of the GCC states) would be overrun by Iraq. The enormous U.S. presence in Saudi Arabia garnered many Arab critics, including Islamic opposition in the kingdom. Following the Gulf War, Saudi Arabia made a request to purchase $20 billion of equipment from the United States. The administration remonstrated that Congress would disapprove of the package, and so the request was made in stages.

The September 11, 2001 attacks on the twin towers of the World Trade Center, carried out by 19 Arab Muslim hijackers, including Saudi Arabians, plunged Saudi Arabian–American relations into a crisis. Saudi Arabians were horrified by the attacks, but the public and media response in the United States involved such sweeping condemnations against the kingdom, its royal family, and religion, and against Muslims and Arabs in general, that they were offended. Many had been educated in the United States in the years when some 30,000 students per year traveled west. Now, visitor and student visas were withheld, as well as visas requested for medical reasons (large numbers of student visas were eventually issued in 2007). Even the staunchest Saudi Arabian supporters of the United States were treated like potential terrorists. A lawsuit was filed against members of the royal family for complicity in the 9/11 attacks. The U.S. government demanded reforms in Saudi Arabia and an admission of its role in spreading religious fundamentalism globally. The U.S. government also asked the kingdom to take specific measures to control donations and financial links to terrorists. Some demands took shape in the Saudi Arabian Accountability Act presented by both the U.S. House of Representatives and Senate in 2007.

Saudi Arabia disagreed with the U.S. attacks in Afghanistan and with the United States' announced intent to make war on Iraq. Despite Saudi Arabia's refusal to join the coalition forces invading Iraq in 2003, the United States was permitted to launch aircraft from the kingdom in support of Operation Iraqi Freedom. Simultaneously, on February 27, 2003, a gradual withdrawal of U.S. troops from Saudi Arabia was announced. At the end of April, the Combined Air Operations Center was moved from Prince Sultan Air Base to the al-Udeid Air Base in Qatar. About 4,500 U.S. troops went from Saudi Arabia to Qatar, leaving only about 500 at Eskan village near Riyadh. This engendered musings by Saudi Arabians, who were not consulted regarding the withdrawal, that the United States now preferred to rely on the smaller GCC countries (Zuhur, Personal Interviews 2005–2008).

In 2003 terrorist attacks in Riyadh and subsequent attacks on the country (see Chapter 7, Contemporary Issues) convinced many Saudi Arabians that an Islamist terrorist threat was real and urgent and required a national response. Westerners working in the kingdom were targeted, like Simon Cumbers and Frank Gardner, a journalist and photographer who worked for the BBC. Paul Marshall Johnson, a helicopter engineer who lived in Saudi Arabia and worked for Lockheed Martin, was kidnapped on June 15, 2004, at a fake police checkpoint near Riyadh by individuals who called themselves al-Qa'ida in the Arabian Peninsula. The group demanded the release of its members who were in Saudi Arabian prisons within 72 hours. Just three days later, Johnson was beheaded by the group, which videotaped his murder. For the first time in many decades, large numbers of workers attached to companies based in Saudi Arabia returned to the United States. Relations began to improve again by 2007, as, by then, many terrorists had been captured and quite a few of the measures adopted and reforms begun by King 'Abdullah addressed U.S. and international criticisms of the kingdom.

Saudi Arabia, the Question of Palestine, and Israel

King 'Abd al-'Aziz first corresponded with the British government concerning Palestine. His letters claim that he did not support the Palestinian rebels of the 1936 uprising (although he did). They aver his loyalty to Great Britain and express concern over Jewish emigration and over any Jordanian control over Palestinian territory, especially Jerusalem; this last arose from his lengthy rivalry with the Hashemites (al-Rasheed in Rogan and Shlaim, eds., 2007, 231–233; also see Burdett 1999). Similarly, 'Abd al-'Aziz's subsequent correspondence with the U.S. government showed his opposition to Zionist expansion in Palestine and the partition plan and his concerns about U.S. support for Israel. President Truman hinted he would reverse President Roosevelt's commitment to a more neutral position when he wrote to the king of the persecution of the Jews and the refugees' need for a homeland. King 'Abd al-'Aziz replied, "I believe that your honor will agree that there is not a single people on this earth who would agree to have a foreign people come into their country, outnumber them and take control of everything" and concluded, "I ... expect that your honor will reconsider the position you had adopted and find a just solution to the plight of those refugees which would secure their safety in other countries around the world without a transgression against a calm people living peacefully in their own country" (Letter dated November 1, 1946, in al-Qabesi, ed., 1998, 222–223). In response, *Mahrajanat al-jihad* (festivals of jihad) were held in 1947. At these events as many as 200,000 Saudi Arabians signed up to fight in Palestine (Abu Aliyya 1999, 321), although they did not actually fight in the war of 1948.

After a huge number of Palestinians were driven from their homeland in 1948, Saudi Arabia offered them support and attempted to convince the United States to address their rights. In the Saudi Arabian government's analysis, the Palestinian issue, and the United States' uncritical support of Israel, was a significant cause of Arab discord and the chaotic politics of the next three decades. The defeat of the Arab (mainly Egyptian) forces in 1967 was perceived as the failure of Arab states to overcome Israel and led to a period of radical activities, hostage seizures, and bombings. These were mostly discontinued by the mid-1970s. Saudi Arabia's efforts in the oil boycott of 1973 were aimed at U.S. support of Israel, and perhaps, if the boycott had continued, it might have achieved its goal.

Saudi Arabia contributed financially to the PLO in the 1980s. In return for this aid, it expected to moderate PLO actions. Islamist Palestinian student groups coalesced in Kuwait and Saudi Arabia during this period, eventually emerging as Hamas. Relations with the PLO had been cut off when 'Arafat supported Saddam Hussein during the Gulf War, due to Hussein's courtship of the PLO in the several years prior to the war. Relations between Saudi Arabia and the PLO were later restored. The

Oslo Accords (officially the Declaration of Principles on Interim Self-Government Arrangements) set in motion 'Arafat's return and the Fatah Party's dominance until Hamas's electoral win in 2006. Then, Saudi Arabia was forced to reassess its Palestinian policies, as Israel revisited iron-fist policies against the Palestinians.

Meanwhile, in 2005 and 2006, Saudi Arabia was accused of supporting Hamas financially, which its ambassador to the United States, 'Adel Jubeir, has denied. Americans alleged that private donors in Saudi Arabia contributed to the movement (Congressional Research Service [CRS] and Library of Congress 2006, 9). Although then U.S. secretary of state Condoleezza Rice accused Hamas of lacking a commitment to peace, Prince Sa'ud, the foreign minister, rejected the U.S. idea that Saudi Arabia should cut off relations with the Palestinian National Authority due to the election of Hamas (CRS and Library of Congress 2006, 10). Saudi Arabia communicates with and supports Hamas as a legitimate leadership; however, the United States and Israel refuse to do so. Therefore, some U.S leaders demanded that Saudi Arabia interface solely with Mahmoud 'Abbas, leader of the Palestinian National Authority. Saudi Arabia's position is that the Palestinians must determine their own leadership and that the Kingdom must play a role to contain the inter-Palestinian rivalries between Fatah and Hamas. King 'Abdullah therefore invited both movements to Mecca for eight days of meetings resulting in the February 8, 2007 Mecca Agreement. Hostilities broke out again between the two groups, and another agreement was signed

---

EXCERPT FROM KING 'ABDULLAH'S SPEECH TO THE ARAB LEAGUE SUMMIT, 2002, CONCERNING THE ARAB PEACE INITIATIVE

King 'Abdullah offered a comprehensive peace initiative to Israel by the Arab nations at a summit meeting in Beirut in 2002, when he was Crown Prince. His offer was ignored by Israel at that time as the Israelis began a massive invasion of the West Bank. His wording acknowledges the former military struggle for Palestinians' rights but emphasizes the need for peace.

"In spite of all that has happened and what still may happen, the primary issue in the heart and mind of every person in our Arab Islamic nation is the restoration of legitimate rights in Palestine, Syria and Lebanon... . We believe in taking up arms in self-defense and to deter aggression. But we also believe in peace when it is based on justice and equity, and when it brings an end to conflict. Only within the context of true peace can normal relations flourish between the people of the region and allow the region to pursue development rather than war. In light of the above, and with your backing and that of the Almighty, I propose that the Arab summit put forward a clear and unanimous initiative addressed to the United Nations security council based on two basic issues: normal relations and security for Israel in exchange for full withdrawal from all occupied Arab territories, recognition of an independent Palestinian state with al-Quds al-Sharif as its capital, and the return of refugees" (*New York Times*, March 27, 2002).

in Yemen in 2008. Reconciliation talks continued in 2010. Fatah and Hamas leaders signed an agreement to form a National Unity government on April 27, 2011. The new post-Mubarak army-led Egyptian government had brokered the deal. This endeavor is supported by most in Saudi Arabia but is opposed by the United States and Israel.

Saudi Arabia's relations with Israel have remained hostile, both in the lack of diplomatic relations and in substantial counterinformation in each country. Saudi Arabia did not support the Camp David agreement because it held that a series of separately forged peace agreements would weaken the Arab and Palestinian positions and fail to provide the comprehensive agreements necessary to address the Palestinian refugee problem or meet Israel's demands for security. Some of the strongest critics of Saudi Arabia in the United States have been supporters of Israel, including members of Congress. The kingdom has accepted the principle of a two-state solution for many years. Saudi Arabia proposed the King Fahd Plan in August 1981, known as the Fez initiative (see Chapter 2, History), which included eight points: Israeli withdrawal from all territory occupied in 1967; dismantling of Israeli settlements; a guarantee of freedom of worship for all at the holy sites in Jerusalem; rights of return for Palestinians and compensation for those who did not want to return; transitional government of the West Bank and Gaza Strip by the United Nations for a few months; an independent Palestinian state with Jerusalem as its capital; peace for all states in the region; and a guarantee of the peace plan from the United Nations.

Another peace initiative was announced by then-crown prince 'Abdullah in 2002 and was reiterated after he became king. These included that Israel would withdraw from the occupied territories of the West Bank and the Gaza Strip, that the Palestinians would be entitled to East Jerusalem as their capital, and the Arab nations would recognize Israel and agree to nonhostilities. In 2005, Saudi Arabia announced an end to its previous boycott on Israeli goods, as that would counter a principle of the World Trade Organization.

Prince Turki al-Faysal invited Avi Shlaim, an Oxford professor and British-Israeli revisionist historian, to Riyadh, where Shlaim said he did not encounter any harsh anti-Israeli rhetoric. Shlaim supports the King 'Abdullah initiative but fears that Israel's Netanyahu and his American allies have been able to keep the world's focus on Iran rather than on solutions to the Arab-Palestinian conflict (*Jordan Times*, January 14, 2011).

Saudi Arabia's Relations with Jordan

Due to their early warring with the Hashemites, whom they drove out of the Hijaz, the al-Sa'ud have on occasion suspected the Hashemite rulers of Jordan of encouraging irredentism in the kingdom. The two countries became much closer politically after 1955, when both began to feel the sting of Nasser's regional policies and propaganda and due to their economic relationship. Saudi Arabia provided very substantial development funds and grants to Jordan consisting of millions of dollars to build the Husayn Thermal Power Station, develop 'Aqaba's port infrastructure and thermal station, and build Jordan University, UNRWA (United Nations Relief and

Work Agency for Palestinian Refugees in the Near East) schools, the Zarqa-Ghor road, and many other projects. The kingdom also employed thousands of Jordanians, many of whom were actually Palestinians. Because of Jordan's large Palestinian population, Saudi Arabia's relations with the PLO were important to Jordan in mediations following the Black September crisis of 1970.

Saudi Arabia treated Jordan as an important means of creating a secure buffer zone to its north and of attaining cooperation on interregional smuggling and in its Arab relations (Brand 1994, 87–120). When the Iraqi forces invaded Kuwait and Saudi Arabia called on the Arab nations to support the coalition, Jordan refused to do so and declared neutrality. Saudi Arabia cut off grants and aid to Jordan. Jordan obtained oil in the 1990s primarily from Iraq, but since 2003, it has imported oil from Saudi Arabia at market rates and under certain concessions.

Saudi Arabian Relations with Lebanon

Saudi Arabians became involved in Lebanon initially through Hussein 'Uwayni (1900–1970), an adviser to King 'Abd al-'Aziz. 'Uwayni was sent by Amin Rihani, a visitor to Saudi Arabia in 1924–1925, to mediate between Ibn Sa'ud and Sharif 'Ali, then king of the Hijaz. The mediation failed, but 'Uwayni became close to Ibn Sa'ud and wealthy through various types of commercial ventures. He represented French interests in the kingdom and eventually rose to become the prime minister of Lebanon (Traboulsi in Al-Rasheed, ed., 2008, 65–69).

In these years, Saudi Arabia sought political means to resist King 'Abdullah of Jordan's plan for Greater Syria and Nuri Sa'id Pasha's Greater Fertile Crescent plan and to oppose leftists and Nasserists in Lebanon. While 'Uwayni was prime minister, he tried to discourage supporters of Nasser in Lebanon (AbuKhalil in Al-Rasheed, ed., 2008, 85) and supported an anticommunist policy, encouraging Lebanon's signing of the Point Four agreement with the U.S. government (Traboulsi 2008, 76). 'Uwayni helped obtain support for an agreement permitting the Aramco subsidiary Tapline and Bechtel Corporation to build a 1,750-kilometer pipeline across Syria and Lebanon to connect Saudi Arabia to Banyas, Syria, and Tripoli, Lebanon. The Lebanese parliament ratified an agreement with Tapline, but the Syrian parliament refused, leading to the Husni Za'im coup in Syria in March 1949. Thereafter, the Tapline agreement was ratified, and Syria agreed to an armistice with Israel. Za'im announced that Syria would unite with Iraq, but Saudi Arabia and Egypt moved quickly, offering him $6 million to unite with their countries instead (Traboulsi in al-Rasheed, ed., 2008, 76–77). Za'im was soon killed, in August 1949, by Colonel Sami Hinnawi, who took over and rolled back movement on Tapline and talks with Israel (Saunders 1996, 11).

The al-Sa'ud family became powerful in the Arabic-language media industry, once centered in Lebanon. They published the *al-Hayat* newspaper, which later moved to London. Other ties were strengthened through higher education and labor migration. The media have had a strong influence in Lebanese internal conflicts and also on the Arab world in general.

Saudi Arabian leaders repeatedly attempted to mediate throughout the lengthy Lebanese Civil War, for instance, between the PLO and the Syrians, and they responded to Syria's recalcitrance by withdrawing the Saudi Arabian brigade stationed in the Golan since 1973 (Safran 1985, 250). Saudi Arabia's leaders were enraged by the Israeli invasion of Lebanon and the siege of Beirut in 1982. U.S. Secretary of State Alexander Haig resigned when Fahd pressured President Reagan to call on Israel to desist, and repeated his effort, as Haig felt these actions undermined his own plan to ensure foreign withdrawals from Lebanon (Safran 1985, 347–350). The long, complicated war resulted in an increase in sectarianism as well as in Syrian influence in Lebanon. At the end of that crisis, the Lebanese legislature was invited to Ta'if in the Hijaz and negotiated the Ta'if Accords in 1989.

Another notable figure enhancing Saudi Arabia's influence in Lebanon (and then in Syria) was Prime Minister Rafiq al-Hariri, a self-made businessman who became wealthy in Saudi Arabia and was an adviser to the al-Sa'ud family on Lebanese affairs. Al-Hariri was close to Hafez al-Asad and influential in Damascus and Riyadh. He was assassinated in a bombing of his motorcade on February 15, 2005. Most assert that Syrians, or Lebanese elements working for Syria (individuals associated with Hizbullah), planned his assassination because he had begun maneuvering to attain a Syrian withdrawal from Lebanon. Saudi Arabia pressed Syria to agree to an international tribunal investigating the circumstances of al-Hariri's assassination. Saudi Arabia strongly supported al-Hariri and, following his death, his son Sa'd, who led the Future Party of Lebanon, amid U.S.-sponsored efforts that resulted in Syrian withdrawal. Their combined efforts also targeted Hizbullah and the followers of General Aoun, who comprised roughly half of the country's population and demanded enhanced political rights as an opposition. As'ad AbuKhalil holds that Saudi Arabia acted in this way in Lebanon because of its linkages with the Bush administration and that it could do so in the absence of a strong Arab rival (AbuKhalil in al-Rasheed, ed., 2008, 92–95). I suggest that elements of the Saudi Arabian government were protective of Syria because of feared U.S. expansionism in the period from 2005 to 2008, when some U.S. officials were arguing for regime change in Syria to follow that in Iraq (Zuhur, Personal Interviews 2005–2008).

In the summer of 2006, Saudi Arabia criticized Hizbullah's actions in kidnapping and killing Israelis in a border village, which sparked the 2006 Israeli war on Lebanon. Yet the Saudi Arabian foreign minister then formally requested that President Bush intervene with the Israelis to halt large-scale casualties in Lebanon. Saudi Arabia supported a national unity government in Lebanon in the political struggle emerging at the time of Michel Suleiman's ascendance to president. Rumors concerning Saudi Arabia's involvement in Lebanon are difficult to assess: These include charges that the United States and al-Hariri's Future Party funneled money to a Sunni Islamist group called Fateh al-Islam, which fought against the Lebanese Army in May and June 2007 in the Nahr al-Bared Palestinian refugee camp. Other Syrian claims made in 2010 are that the United States and Saudi Arabia have tried unsuccessfully to sponsor anti-Hizbullah Shi'a pockets in Lebanon, so far in vain, or funded Subhi Tufayli, a former Hizbullah leader, who had led the Revolt of the Hungry against the prevailing Hizbullah leadership, as a counterweight to Hassan Nasrullah's leadership.

In 2008, a Lebanese former television show host who traveled to the kingdom for the *'umrah*, the minor pilgrimage, was arrested by the religious police and charged with sorcery. On television, he had made predictions, acting as a psychic, and the Saudi Arabian court in Medina sentenced him to death in December 2009. The Lebanese minister of justice asked for a stay of execution, granted in 2010 by the Saudi Arabian High Court, which recommended a new trial and deportation (Naharnet. com, November 11, 2010). Other "cultural" clashes have emerged concerning the popularity of Lebanese musical contest reality shows and other entertainment venues with younger Saudi Arabians.

Saudi Arabian Relations with Syria

Saudi Arabia and Syria were on opposing sides of the Arab Cold War waged between pro-Western monarchies and republican progressive Arab states during Nasser's era. The secularist and republican aspects of Ba'thism countered Saudi Arabia's ideas of governance and legitimacy. Gradually, however, relations improved, and the Saudi Arabian government had a significant role in Syria through economic aid. Syria allied with Iran due to its fractious politics with neighboring Iraq. This alliance was problematic to Saudi Arabia through the years of the Iran-Iraq War. Later on, especially with the events of the Gulf War, that Syrian stance did not discourage Saudi Arabia's relations with Syria, although the Western press has frequently over-emphasized Saudi Arabian antipathy to Iranian influence in Syria, at least since 2003.

A significant number of Saudi Arabian tourists travel to Syria in the summers, which increased during the years of the Lebanese Civil War. Many Syrians reside in Saudi Arabia, and Saudi Arabian businessmen own real estate and shares in service, tourist, and industrial projects in Syria. Saudi Arabia is Syria's largest trading partner (*Syrian Arab News Agency*, March 10, 2010). This current trend is long-standing, despite ideological differences (and the fact that Syria is far from being Saudi Arabia's largest trading partner). Imports from Saudi Arabia made up an average of 55.83 percent of Syria's imports from 1974 to 1982 (Zuhur 1986, table 7).

The Syrian government attempted to destroy its Islamist front, which included the Muslim Brotherhood. Up to 30,000 people were massacred in the city of Hama in 1982, and many of those Syrians with Islamist ties, or opposed to the government, fled to Saudi Arabia and other Gulf states. A revival, or new growth, of Islamism has taken place in Syria since the early 1990s, and Saudi Arabian and Kuwaiti donors to religious buildings and funding are evident in Syria.

U.S.-Syrian relations deteriorated after the 2003 regime change in Iraq but even more so following the withdrawal from Lebanon, the 2006 war on Lebanon, and the attempted isolation of Iran. The United States has generally attributed the worsening relations on these issues to Saudi Arabia, but perhaps this fracture is not seen similarly in Riyadh and Damascus. Syria banned the Sa'udi-owned *al-Sharq al-Awsat* newspaper in 2007, and the Sa'udi-owned *al-Hayat* was banned in October 2008. However, in 2009, King 'Abdullah announced an initiative to restore Arab unity, which translated into new diplomatic initiatives and visits to Syria.

Protests broke out in Syria after the revolutions in Egypt and Tunisia, and with the violent governmental response, the protesters who had begun by calling for more democracy are at the time of writing demanding the ouster of Bashar al-Asad and his government. Such a situation presents another strong regional challenge to the Saudi Arabian government and may alter Syrian–Saudi Arabian relations in the long run.

BROADER SAUDI ARABIAN FOREIGN POLICY

A substantial and special feature of the Saudi Arabian government is its relations with Muslim countries throughout the world. One arm of these endeavors concerns management of the *hajj* through the Organization of the Islamic Conference (OIC), first established in 1969, with its permanent secretariat in Jeddah. The OIC is the second-largest intergovernmental organization with 57 member nations (see Chapter 5, section on religion).

Saudi Arabia's Islamic foreign policies, emphasized under King Faysal, led it to oppose the Soviet occupation of Afghanistan and to fund the *mujahidin* there. Saudi Arabia supported Islamization policies in other states, such as Pakistan or the state of Kelantan in Malaysia, and backed political figures such as Nawaz Sharif of Pakistan, who lived for eight years in exile in the kingdom. This general policy has strengthened Saudi Arabia's relationship with other nations with large Muslim populations like Indonesia and Malaysia. Saudi Arabia has granted large amounts of aid to Bangladesh, Somalia, and Pakistan primarily because they are Islamic nations, and the Pakistani military were, during the 1980s, often seconded to the Saudi Arabian armed forces (Metz, ed., 1993, 227). Somali immigrants, on account of the long civil war, have been treated differently than others who make their way illegally to Saudi Arabia, for example, the Ethiopians (who have often entered Yemen illegally and then try to cross into Saudi Arabia).

The Institute of Islamic and Arabic Studies (referred to as LIPIA for Lembaga Ilmu Pengetahuan Islam dan Arab), founded in 1980 in Jakarta, Indonesia, graduated hundreds of students. Some were recruited to continue their Islamic studies in Saudi Arabia, where, like Saudi Arabian students and other young people, they joined the jihad in Afghanistan. This resulted in an Indonesian *salafi* generation who were anti-Shi'a, politicized, and opposed to earlier Islamic institutions. With Saudi Arabian financial support, they established new institutions in the early 1990s, producing cassette tapes and books for their *da'wah* effort (Hasan in Al-Rasheed, ed., 2008, 268–273). Saudi Arabia is often accused of funding salafism in Thailand, Malaysia, Vietnam, and Cambodia—as well as in South Asia, Europe, Africa, and the United States—although the process is often similar to that described for Indonesia, motivated by actors in the second country.

European nations are dependent on the pricing of oil set by Saudi Arabia, even though they import a greater share of crude from Norway and the Russian Federation (Aarts, Meertens, and van Duijne in Al-Rasheed, ed., 2008, 140–141). Lower oil prices and availability of crude for Europe, Saudi Arabia's spending on commodities, and Europe and Saudi Arabia's mutual desire for resource stability characterizes their relationship (Aarts, Meertens, and van Duijne in Al-Rasheed, ed., 2008). Post-9/11 European criticisms of the kingdom, from neoconservative and left-liberal stances, increased and were directed at the kingdom's lack of democracy, women's rights, and secularism, but they also reflected political changes in Europe, including anti-immigrant movements. This did not damage economic relations, but the Saudi Arabian diplomatic response was to assert its ongoing reforms and changes and its determination to remain an Islamic country (S. al-Sa'ud, February 19, 2004). Tensions reemerged with a conflict over cartoons lampooning the Prophet Muhammad published in a Danish newspaper in September 2005, resulting in the recall of the Saudi Arabian ambassador to Denmark and an unofficial boycott of Danish food imports. Many additional concerns about extremism emerged in England, Scotland, France and other countries, but a better understanding of the dynamics of terrorism has been gaining.

Saudi Arabia is a major donor of international aid. It is the single largest Arab donor to Egypt and second only to the United States in donations to Asia, including Iraq and Afghanistan. However, much of the aid given is not reported online, or information is unavailable, as with other donors. Humanitarian aid was the main share of Saudi Arabian support to Afghani refugees in Pakistan and other activities in Afghanistan. The kingdom does not view the aid given as a premise for shared policies or "the spread of Wahhabism" as its enemies have charged (see Chapter 5, section on religion).

Saudi Arabian Relations with Russia

Saudi Arabia has opposed communism since the Kingdom of Saudi Arabia was established. It cut off diplomatic relations and closed its legation in Moscow in 1938. In the region around Saudi Arabia, the Communist Party has been a political force in Syria, Egypt, Iraq, the Sudan, and Yemen, and also among Palestinians. Saudi Arabia had concerns that some of its own citizens might be influenced. Russia stood in the background of the Arab Cold War, providing aid to the more radical republican states in contrast with the alliances that Saudi Arabia sought with the West. However, since the collapse of the Soviet Union, communism is no longer seen as a primary threat by Saudi Arabia. Instead, Saudi Arabia has established relations with Russia and most of the former Soviet republics and is particularly interested in those with large Muslim populations. Saudi Arabia must take note of Russia because it is a competing oil producer and exporter of natural gas and, at the same time, also an oil consumer. In September 2003, then Crown Prince 'Abdullah made an official visit to Russia. Russia also hopes to improve its relations with the Islamic world since the days of its policy conflicts with Saudi Arabia in the Arab world, notably over Afghanistan.

Saudi Arabia's Relations with China

China is important to Saudi Arabia as an oil consumer, second in the world only to the United States. Former diplomats to Saudi Arabia have, in conversation and in print, referred to the Saudi Arabian "marriage with China," or that China is a "second wife" to Saudi Arabia. The Chinese presidents visited Saudi Arabia in 1999 and 2000, and King 'Abdullah traveled first to China and then to India in 2006. Some

CHRONOLOGY OF AID OR HUMANITARIAN ASSISTANCE PROVIDED BY SAUDI ARABIA IN 2010

December 1, 2010	Saudi Arabian medical team arrives in Rawalpindi
November 23, 2010	Pakistan receives 350 tons of dates from Saudi Arabian king
November 17, 2010	Sacrificial meat is distributed in Pakistan
October 22, 2010	Fifth Saudi Arabian relief convoy heads to Pakistan
October 19, 2010	Saudi Arabia sends 71 tons of humanitarian aid to Chad
October 15, 2010	Mauritania and International Development Bank sign two loan agreements
October 15, 2010	Dr. Nizar Madani describes $358,198,994 and $700 million of aid and efforts for Pakistan at aid conference in Belgium
October 14, 2010	Saudi Arabia's medical team arrives in Pakistan
October 12, 2010	Prince Nayif sends 5,000 tents worth 2.21 million riyals to Pakistan
October 10, 2010	Saudi Arabia continues distributing food baskets in Pakistan
October 7, 2010	King 'Abdullah gives $20 million for reconstruction of Mauritanian city
October 6, 2010	IDB approves more than $772 million to finance new projects
September 24, 2010	Saudi Arabian campaign distributes 7,000 food baskets in Pakistan
September 23, 2010	Saudi Arabian relief camp in Pakistan expands
September 21, 2010	30 doctors from King Faisal Hospital arrive in Pakistan
September 17, 2010	King Abdullah International Foundation for Charity established
September 12, 2010	Saudi Arabian camp for Pakistani flood victims opens
September 9, 2010	Humanitarian aid shipment arrives in Pakistan
September 7, 2010	Saudi Arabian assistance for Pakistani flood relief exceeds $240 million
September 2, 2010	First relief plane of Custodian of the Two Holy Mosques Campaign arrives in Pakistan
September 2, 2010	Saudi Arabian medical team arrives in Islamabad, Pakistan
September 1, 2010	Saudi Arabian team rescues 463 people in Pakistan
September 1, 2010	Saudi Arabian food aid distributed in Peshawar, Pakistan
August 30, 2010	700 tons of foodstuff are sent to Pakistan
August 30, 2010	Second field hospital is dispatched to Pakistan

August 29, 2010	AGFUND donates $100,000 for victims of Pakistani floods
August 28, 2010	Medical team arrives in Pakistan to aid flood victims
August 27, 2010	Crown prince gifts 100 tons of dates to Pakistanis
August 26, 2010	Saudi Arabian medical team arrives in Pakistan
August 25, 2010	Saudi Arabian Consulate in Istanbul distributes two tons of dates from Crown Prince
August 24, 2010	Saudi Arabian envoys hand over dates to Turkey and Cameroon
August 23, 2010	Kingdom sends field hospitals, rescue teams to Pakistan
August 20, 2010	22 Saudi planes have delivered relief supplies to Pakistan
August 19, 2010	Saudi Arabia donates $80 million for Pakistani flood relief
August 17, 2010	King 'Abdullah donates SR 20 million to Pakistani relief campaign
August 17, 2010	First day of national campaign to help Pakistan flood victims raises SR 77 million
August 17, 2010	Kingdom to host 2,000 Palestinian pilgrims
August 17, 2010	Saudi Arabian humanitarian airlift to Pakistan continues
August 16, 2010	King's Campaign for the Relief of the Pakistani People starts today
August 16, 2010	Saudi Popular Campaign provides financial assistance to Lebanon
August 16, 2010	More Saudi Arabian relief arrives in Pakistan
August 15, 2010	Saudi Arabian relief planes continue to arrive with relief supplies for Pakistan
August 13, 2010	Saudi Arabia delivers tents, dates to Senegal
August 12, 2010	IDB extends $11 million in relief aid for flood victims in Pakistan
August 11, 2010	Ninth and tenth Saudi Arabian relief planes arrive in Pakistan
August 9, 2010	Sixth, seventh, and eighth Saudi Arabian relief planes arrive in Pakistan
August 7, 2010	Saudi Arabia continues relief airlift for Pakistani flood victims
August 7, 2010	Saudi Arabia is leading MENACA aid donor
August 7, 2010	Ministry of Health announces the death of one of the separated Iraqi conjoined twins
August 6, 2010	100 tons of Saudi Arabian dates given to the Philippines
August 6, 2010	Saudi Arabian Ambassador to Pakistan visits areas hit by flooding

August 5, 2010	Saudi Arabian humanitarian aid arrives in Pakistan
August 5, 2010	150 tons of Saudi Arabian dates delivered to Pakistan
August 3, 2010	Crown Prince Sultan provides Palestinian refugees with 15 tons of dates
July 27, 2010	The International Islamic Relief Organization, Saudi Arabia (IIROSA) has dug 5,745 wells in Asia and Africa
July 27, 2010	Mauritania receives 200 tons of Saudi dates
July 24, 2010	Saudi Arabia gifts Yemen with 150 tons of dates
July 16, 2010	Operation to separate Iraqi conjoined twins begins
July 11, 2010	Saudi Arabia provides Jordan with 150 tons of dates
July 8, 2010	UNRWA (United Nations Relief and Work Agency for Palestinian Refugees in the Near East) spokesman lauds Saudi assistance to Palestinian refugees
July 6, 2010	Kingdom provides financial aid to help rebuild Ivorian Parliament
July 1, 2010	Saudi Fund for Development has provided over $8.23 billion in foreign grants since 1975
June 28, 2010	King 'Abdullah addresses G-20 summit
June 23, 2010	Foreign ministers of the Gulf Cooperation Council vow to support Yemeni development
June 20, 2010	Saudi Arabia provides the United Nations High Commissioner for Refugees (UNHCR) $10 million grant for Pakistani relief
June 15, 2010	Saudi Arabia transfers $15.4 million to Palestinian Finance Ministry
June 15, 2010	King orders transportation of Iraqi conjoined twins to Saudi Arabian hospital
June 12, 2010	Cameroon receives 90 tons of Saudi Arabian dates
June 9, 2010	Saudi campaign sends 11 generators to Lebanon
June 4, 2010	Saudi Arabian medical team performs 30 open-heart surgeries on Yemeni patients
June 3, 2010	Saudi Arabian humanitarian aid convoy heads for Gaza
June 2, 2010	Saudi Arabia provides dates for World Food Program (WFP) in Cameroon
June 1, 2010	Saudi Arabia will chair UNRWA Advisory Commission
May 25, 2010	Saudi Arabian medical team performs heart surgeries in Yemen
May 23, 2010	Third shipment of Saudi flour aid heads to Gaza

May 22, 2010	Yemeni president announces Saudi Arabian–financed water project
May 18, 2010	Saudi Arabia provides WFP in Yemen with 1,013 tons of dates
May 12, 2010	Second convoy of 268 tons of Saudi Arabian flour (part of 2,000 tons total) to Gaza
May 12, 2010	Kingdom funds five humanitarian projects in Aceh, Indonesia
May 5, 2010	IDB expands activities with India and will fund Indian-Muslim institutions
April 30, 2010	Jordanian conjoined twins successfully separated
April 29, 2010	Kingdom sends 342 tons and 90 tons of dates to Egypt and Mauritania, respectively
April 29, 2010	Saudi Fund for Development provides a soft loan of $20 million to Cuban maternity hospitals
April 27, 2010	Development of 18 vocational institutes sponsored by the Saudi Development Fund in Yemen is monitored
April 15, 2010	Saudi Arabia sends 750 tons of flour to Gaza
April 14, 2010	Saudi Development Fund grants $40 million loan for Jordanian power station
April 9, 2010	Syrian conjoined twins separated in Riyadh
April 6, 2010	Saudi Arabia delivers $500,000 for food supplies to Bangladesh
April 2, 2010	Saudi Arabia gives $2 million for Darfur peacekeepers
April 2, 2010	King 'Abdullah orders treatment of Palestinian conjoined twins
March 17, 2010	IDB approves $333.9 million in new grants
March 16, 2010	The WFP in Syria receives 450 tons of dates as gift from Saudi Arabia's king
March 15, 2010	Prince Sultan accepts award in Algiers for disability center
March 11, 2010	Arab ministers of health meet in Cairo and provide $100,000 to the Palestinian and Somali Ministries of Health and review reports on swine flu
March 3, 2010	Saudi Arabia provides $1.33 million for Côte d'Ivoire Islamic center and societies
March 1, 2010	Kingdom funds $114.8 million in Yemeni development projects
February 23, 2010	IDB extends $5 million for Haitian school reconstruction
February 5, 2010	Saudi Arabia contributes $5 million to the Carter Center's Guinea Worm Eradication Program
February 2, 2010	IDB approves $196.4 million for development projects
January 30, 2010	Saudi Arabia finances $4.36 million for renovation of Bangladesh's national mosque

January 28, 2010	Saudi Arabia pledges $150 million in aid for Afghanistan
January 25, 2010	Kingdom donates $50 million for Haiti earthquake relief
January 21, 2010	Gulf Cooperation Council appropriates $164 million for Gaza projects
January 16, 2010	Organization of Petroleum Exporting Countries Fund announces $500,000 in relief aid for Haiti
January 15, 2010	AGFUND donates $100,000 to support relief efforts in Haiti (Information adapted from that provided by the Saudi Arabian government on its embassy websites and SAMIRAD)

saw this outreach as a response to Washington's declarations that the kingdom had not reformed itself sufficiently. Saudi Arabia's interests in its relations to China are primarily oil sales and arms purchases. Arms purchases date back to the 1980s, when the Saudi Arabians imported CSS-2 intermediate-range ballistic missiles. Now, they are interested in upgrading them (Pant 2006). The Chinese have also been interested in Saudi Arabia as a market for their manufactured goods.

Saudi Arabia's international relations and foreign policy are an important aspect of political life in that nation. Maintaining its own security and dominance in the Arabian Peninsula and Middle East region are major drivers of these policies. However, Saudi Arabian officials know that the world is changing rapidly and that they must do more than react to circumstances. Therefore, the pursuit of diplomacy and forging of good relations are part of their preparation for the unknown future.

REFERENCES

Abdul Ghafour, P. K. "Mishaal Named Arab Commission Chairman." *Arab News*, December 11, 2007.

Aboul-Enein, Youssef. "The Egyptian-Yemen War: Egyptian Perspectives on Guerilla Warfare." *Infantry Magazine*, January–February 2004.

Abu Aliyya, Abulfatah. *al-Mamlakah al-'Arabiyyah al-Sa'udiyyah wa Qadiyat Falastin.* Riyadh, Saudi Arabia: al-Dara (King Abdulaziz Foundation for Research and Archives), 1999.

AbuKhalil, As'ad. "Determinants and Characteristics of the Saudi Role in Lebanon: The Post-Civil War Years." In *Kingdom without Borders: Saudi Political, Religious and Media Frontiers*, edited by Madawi Al-Rasheed. New York: Columbia University Press, 2008, 79–98.

AbuKhalil, As'ad. *The Battle for Saudi Arabia: Royalty, Fundamentalism and Global Power.* New York: Seven Stories, 2004.

Altorki, Soraya. "The Concept and Practice of Citizenship in Saudi Arabia." In *Gender and Citizenship in the Middle East*, edited by Suad Joseph. Syracuse, NY: Syracuse University Press, 2000.

Anscombe, Frederick. *The Ottoman Gulf: The Creation of Kuwait, Saudi Arabia and Qatar.* New York: Columbia University Press, 1997.

Anthony, John Duke. "The Gulf in Its Contemporary Setting." In *The Middle East*, edited by Michael Adams. New York: Facts on File, 1988.

Bachar, Shmuel, Bar Shmuel, Rachel Machtiger, and Yair Minzili. *Establishment Ulama and Radicalism in Egypt, Saudi Arabia and Jordan.* Washington, DC: Hudson Institute, Series 1, Paper 4, December 2006.

Badeeb, Saeed M. *The Saudi-Egyptian Conflict over North Yemen, 1962–1970.* Boulder, CO: Westview, 1986.

al-Badi, Awadh. "Institutionalizing Hereditary Succession in Saudi Arabia's Political Governance System: The Allegiance Commission." *Arab Reform Initiative*, February 14, 2008. http://arab-reform.net/.

Bahgat, Gawdat. "Foreign Investment in Saudi Arabia's Energy Sector." *Middle East Economic Survey* XLVII, no. 34 (August 23, 2004).

Basic Law. (1992). SAMIRAD (Saudi Arabia Market Information Resource). http://saudinf.com/main/c541f.htm. Last visited March 29, 2010.

bin Baz, Ahmad. Interview, "Change and Reform Don't Come without a Price." *The Saudi*, January 14, 2011.

Bergen, Peter. "Similar Explosive on Plane Used in Saudi Attack." *CNN.com*, December 27, 2009.

Brand, Laurie A. *Jordan's Inter-Arab Relations: The Political Economy of Alliance-Making.* New York: Columbia University Press, 1994.

Bronson, Rachel. *Thicker Than Oil: America's Uneasy Partnership with Saudi Arabia.* New York: Oxford University Press, 2008.

Brown, Anthony Cave. *Oil, God, and Gold: The Story of Aramco and the Saudi Kings.* New York: Houghton-Mifflin, 1999.

Burdett, A.L.P., ed. *King Abdul Aziz: Diplomacy and Statecraft 1902–1953.* 4 vols. Cambridge: Cambridge Archive Editions, Cambridge University Press, 1999.

Carnegie Endowment for International Peace and Fundacion par las Relaciones Internacionales y el Dialogio Exterior (FRIDE). *Arab Political Systems: Baseline Information and Reforms—Saudi Arabia.* n.d. [ca. 2007].

Chaudhry, Kiren Aziz. *The Price of Wealth: Economies and Institutions in the Middle East.* Ithaca, NY: Cornell University Press, 1997.

Chaudhry, Kiren Aziz. "The Prince of Wealth: Business and State in Labor Remittance and Oil Economies." *International Organization* 43 (1989), 101–145.

Childs, J. Rives. *Foreign Service Farewell: My Years in the Near East.* Charlottesville: University of Virginia, 1969.

Chubin, Shahram, and Charles Tripp. *Iran-Saudi Arabia Relations and Regional Order.* Adelphi Paper 304. First published by International Institute for Strategic Studies, 1996. Reprinted New York: Routledge, 2005.

Commins, David Dean. *The Wahhabi Mission and Saudi Arabia.* London: I. B. Tauris, 2006.

Congressional Research Service (CRS) and Library of Congress. "Saudi Arabia: Current Issues and U.S. Relations." *Congressional Research Survey Issue Brief* Alfred B. Prados. Updated February 24, 2006. http://www.fas.org/sgp/crs/mideast/IB93113.pdf.

Cordesman, Anthony H. *Saudi Arabia Enters the Twenty-First Century: The Political, Foreign Policy, Economic, and Energy Dimensions.* London: Center for Strategic and International Studies; Westport, CT: Praeger, 2003.

Cordesman, Anthony H., and Abraham R. Wagner. *The Lessons of Modern War.* Vol. 4, *The Gulf War.* Boulder, CO: Westview Press, 1996.

Doran, Michael Scott. "The Saudi Paradox." *Foreign Affairs*, January/February 2004, 35–51.

Freedman, Lawrence, and Efraim Karsh. *The Gulf Conflict, 1990–1991: Diplomacy and War in the New World Order.* Princeton, NJ: Princeton University Press, 1993.

Fürtig, Henner. *Iran's Rivalry with Saudi Arabia between the Gulf Wars.* Reading, UK: Ithaca, 2002. (Reprinted in 2006.)

Gause, Gregory F., III. *Oil Monarchies: Domestic and Security Challenges in the Arab Gulf States.* Washington, DC: Council on Foreign Relations, 1994.

Gause, Gregory F., III. *Saudi-Yemeni Relations: Domestic Structures and Foreign Influence.* New York: Columbia University Press, 1990.

Glosmeyer, Iris. "Checks, Balances and Transformations in the Saudi Political System." In *Saudi Arabia in the Balance*, edited by Paul Aarts and Gerd Nonneman. London: Hurst, 2005; New York: New York University Press, 2006, 214–233.

Hasan, Noorhaidi. "Saudi Expansion, the Salafi Campaign and Arabized Islam in Indonesia." In *Kingdom without Borders: Saudi Political, Religious and Media Frontiers*, edited by Madawi Al-Rasheed. New York: Columbia University Press, 2008, 263–282.

Hooglund, Eric. "Government and Politics." In *Saudi Arabia: A Country Study*, edited by Helen Chapin Metz, Federal Research Division, Library of Congress. Washington, DC: Library of Congress, 1993.

Jabber, Paul. "Oil, Arms, and Regional Diplomacy: Strategic Dimensions of the Saudi-Egyptian Relationship." In *Rich and Poor States in the Middle East: Egypt and the New Arab Order*, edited by Malcolm H. Kerr and Yassin, El Sayed. Boulder, CO: Westview, 1982, 415–448.

Kechichian, Joseph A. *Succession in Saudi Arabia.* New York: Palgrave, 2001.

Kerr, Malcolm H. *The Arab Cold War 1958–1964: A Study of Ideology in Politics.* London: Oxford University Press, 1965.

Kerr, Malcom H., and Yassin, El Sayed, eds. *Rich and Poor States in the Middle East: Egypt and the New Arab Order.* Boulder, CO: Westview; Cairo: American University in Cairo Press, 1982.

Keynoush, Banafsheh. "The Iranian-Saudi Arabian Relationship: From Ideological Confrontation to Pragmatic Accommodation." PhD diss., Fletcher School, Tufts University, 2007.

Kostiner, Joseph. "The Role of Tribal Groups in State Expansion and Consolidation." In *Changing Nomads in a Changing World*, edited by Joseph Ginat and Anatoly Khazanov. Brighton, UK: Sussex Academic Press, 1998, 143–155.

Kostiner, Joseph. "State, Islam and Opposition in Saudi Arabia: The Post Desert-Storm Phase." *Middle East Review of International Affairs* 1, no. 2 (July 1997). http://meria.idc. ac.il/journal/1997/issue2/jv1n2a8.html

Kostiner, Joseph. "Transforming Dualities: Tribes and State Formation in Saudi Arabia." In *Tribe and State Formation in the Middle East*, edited by Philip S. Khoury and Joseph Kostiner. Berkeley: University of California Press, 1991, 226–253.

Lacey, Robert. *Inside the Kingdom: Kings, Clerics, Modernists, Terrorists and the Struggle for Saudi Arabia*. New York: Viking Penguin, 2009.

Lacey, Robert. *The Kingdom*. New York: Harcourt Brace Jovanovich, 1981.

Lacroix, Stéphane. "Islamo-Liberal Politics in Saudi Arabia." In *Saudi Arabia in the Balance*, edited by Paul Aarts and Gerd Nonneman. London: Hurst, 2005, 35–56.

Lacroix, Stéphane. "Saudi Islamists and the Potential for Protest." *Foreign Policy*, June 2, 2011.

Lawton, John. "Arab Aid." *Saudi-Aramco World* 30, no. 6 (November/December 1979). http://www.saudiaramcoworld.com/issue/197906/arab.aid-how.it.s.spent.htm

Lippmann, Thomas W. *Inside the Mirage: America's Fragile Partnership with Saudi Arabia*. Boulder, CO: Westview, 2004.

Long, David. E. *The United States and Saudi Arabia: Ambivalent Allies*. Boulder, CO: Westview, 1985.

Louër, Laurence. *Transnational Shia Politics: Religious and Political Networks in the Gulf*. New York: Columbia University Press, 2008.

Majlis al-Shura Law. Ministry of Foreign Affairs, Kingdom of Saudi Arabia. 27/08/1412h. http://www.mofa.gov.sa

al-Mani, Saleh. "The Ideological Dimension in Saudi-Iranian Relations." In *Iran and the Gulf: A Search for Stability*, edited by Jamal S. al-Suwaidi. Abu Dhabi, United Arab Emirates: Emirates Center for Strategic Studies and Research, 1996, 158–174.

Murphy, Caryle. "View from Mt. Doud: Saudi Arabia Says Offensive against Yemeni Rebels Over." *Christian Science Monitor*, January 27, 2010.

Murphy, Caryle. "Analysis: What Is behind Saudi Offensive in Yemen." *Globalpost*, November 14, 2009.

Niblock, Tim. *Saudi Arabia: Power, Legitimacy, Survival*. New York: Routledge, 2006.

Nonneman, Gerd. "Determinants and Patterns of Saudi Foreign Policy—Omni-Balancing and 'Relative Autonomy' in Multiple Environments." In *Saudi Arabia in the Balance*, edited by Paul Aarts and Gerd Nonneman. London: Hurst and Co., 2005, 315–351.

Okruhlik, Gwenn and Conge, Patrick. "National Autonomy, Labor Migration and Political Crisis: Yemen and Saudi Arabia." *Middle East Journal* 51, no. 4 (Autumn 1997), 554–565.

Pant, Harsh V. "Saudi Arabia Woos China and India." *Middle East Quarterly*, Fall 2006, 45–52.

Press Information Bureau, Government of India. "Prime Minister's Address to the Majlis al-Shura." March 1, 2010.

al-Qabesi, Mohyddin, coll. and ed. *The Holy Quran and the Sword: Selected Addresses, Speeches Memoranda and Interviews by HM The Late King Abdul Aziz al-Saud*. Riyadh: Saudi Desert House for Publishing and Distribution, 1998.

al-Rasheed, Madawi. "Saudi Arabia and the Palestine War: Beyond Official History." In *The War for Palestine: Rewriting the History of 1948 War*, edited by Eugene Rogan and Avi Shlaim. 2nd ed. Cambridge: Cambridge University Press, 2007, 228–247.

Al-Rasheed, Madawi. *A History of Saudi Arabia.* Cambridge: Cambridge University Press, 2002.

Riedel, Bruce, and Bilal Y. Saab. "Al Qa'ida's Third Front." *Washington Quarterly*, 31, no. 2 (Spring 2008), 33–46.

Safran, Nadav. *Saudi Arabia: The Ceaseless Quest for Security.* Cambridge, MA: Belknap Press of Harvard University Press, 1985.

SAMIRAD (Saudi Arabian Market Information Resource). March 26, 2010. http://www.saudinf.com/

al-Sa'ud, Saud al-Faisal ibn 'Abd al-'Aziz. "Saudi-European Relations: Towards a Reliable Partnership." Brussels: European Policy Center, February 19, 2004.

al-Sa'ud, Turki al-Faisal ibn 'Abd al-'Aziz. "Saudi Arabian Constitutional Evolution." Keynote address at the 15th Annual Arab-US Policymakers Conference, Washington, DC, October 30, 2006. Available at SUSRIS (Saudi-U.S. Relations): http://www.saudi-us-relations.org/articles/2006/ioi/061106-turki-succession.html

Saunders, Bonnie. *The United States and Arab Nationalism: The Syrian Case, 1953–1960.* Westport, CT: Praeger, 1996.

Sidiya, Fatima. "Experts Divided over Media Coverage of Court Cases." *Arab News*, February 23, 2010.

Ibn Sultan, HRH General Khaled (with Patrick Seale). *Desert Warrior: A Personal View of the Gulf War by the Joint Forces Commander.* London and New York: Harper Collins, 1995.

SUSRIS. "The Time is Now in Saudi Arabia. A Conversation with Rachel Bronson." SUSRIS. April 27, 2006. http://www.susris.com/articles/2006/interviews/060427-bronson-interview-complete.html

Traboulsi, Fawwaz. "Saudi Expansion: The Lebanese Connection, 1924–1952." In *Kingdom without Borders: Saudi Political, Religious, and Media Frontiers*, edited by Madawi Al-Rasheed. New York: Columbia University Press, 2008, 65–78.

Trench, R., ed. *Gazetteer of Arabian Tribes.* 18 vols. Farnham Commons, Buckinghamshire, UK: Cambridge Archive Editions (Cambridge University Press dist.), 1996.

U.S. Commission on International Religious Freedom. "Saudi Arabia." 2010 Annual Report May 2009. http://www.uscirf.gov/countries/1414.html?task=view

Wehry, Frederick, Theodore W. Karasik, Alireza Nader, Jeremy Ghez, Lydia Hansell, and Robert A. Guffey. *Saudi-Iranian Relations since the Fall of Saddam: Rivalry, Cooperation and Implications for U.S. Policy.* Washington, DC: Rand Corporation (National Security Research Division), 2009.

Whitaker, Brian. "Saleh Is Gone. What Next for Yemen?" *Guardian.co.uk*, June 5, 2011. http://www.guardian.co.uk/commentisfree/2011/jun/05/yemen-saleh

Whitaker, Brian. "The Yemeni-Saudi Border Treaty." July 1, 2000. Available at http://www.al-bab.com/yemen/ border/00629.htm

Whitaker, Brian, trans. "Treaty of Jiddah." June 12, 2000. Available at http://www.al-Bab.com/yemen/pol/int5/htm

Worth, Brian F. "Najran Journal: Muslim Sect Sees Struggle through Christian Lens." *New York Times/International Herald Tribune*, October 20, 2010. http://www.nytimes.com/2010/10/21/world/middleeast/21saudi.html

Zuhur, Sherifa. "Orgoglio Iraniano" [Iranian pride]. *Revista di Intelligence* Anno II, no. 3 (September 2006), 14–25.

Zuhur, Sherifa. Personal interviews with named and anonymous respondents. Jeddah, Riyadh, Washington, DC, London, etc., 2005–2008.

Zuhur, Sherifa. *Saudi Arabia: Islamism, Political Reform and the Global War on Terror*. Carlisle, PA: Strategic Studies Institute, 2005a.

Zuhur, Sherifa. *The Middle East: Politics, History, and Neonationalism*. Carlisle, PA, and Philadelphia: Institute of Middle Eastern, Islamic, and Diasporic Studies (distributed by Ingrahm), 2005b.

Zuhur, Sherifa. "A Preliminary View of Intraregional Trade in the Middle East, 1974–1982." Los Angeles, 1986.

CHAPTER 4

Economy

OVERVIEW

Saudi Arabia's economic productivity is largely based on its sale of petroleum and its by-products, which have made it the largest and strongest economy in the Middle East region. Oil income impacted the nation's development, enabling numerous areas of expansion and subsidies. Simultaneously, the oil industry has complicated Saudi Arabia's foreign relations, domestic policies, and global impact. Since oil profits had to be invested and the entire country developed with a view toward the future, when oil may be depleted, the government and individual investors likewise encountered various conditions that both advanced and restricted their goals.

Saudi Arabia has been diversifying its industrial output and spending on human capital in education and training toward these goals. It has experimented technologically with agriculture, sometimes despite strong external criticism because of the cost of certain projects. All countries present unique ratios of labor and arable land. In some cases, they amass capital from valuable resources moving from a peripheral to a semi-peripheral status in the world economy (Wallerstein 1974). Saudi Arabia has dealt with its labor deficit (in the period prior to strong population growth) by importing workers from the Arab and non-Arab developing world and also from the West.

Western scholars and observers were critical of Saudi Arabia's centralized economic planning and state subsidies in decades past for different reasons. Supporters of economic liberalism argued that state subsidies can heighten debt (although Saudi Arabia could afford such measures, whereas some countries arguably could not) and increase dependence on the state. Some aspects of their critiques emanate from the

Saudi Arabians view the Aramco Mobile Oil exhibit, a traveling educational exhibition about the petroleum industry with audiovisual elements held in a three-tent pavilion covering 7,000 square feet. (Khalil Abou El-Nasr/Saudi Aramco)

vulnerability felt in the West due to its need for oil. Others are iterated because of a belief that the private sector must never be confined by national economic policies and are not particularly concerned with the impact of economics on the political stability of the Saudi Arabian government. Additionally, and particularly during the 2008 U.S. presidential elections, many pundits and politicians spoke out against Western dependence on petrochemicals derived from Saudi Arabia or other "countries hostile to us"—choosing to forget the lengthy U.S.–Saudi Arabian alliance and drawing on American economic insecurity and concerns over rising oil prices. Other critics have written about the oil industry as a family business of the Sa'udi royals, which entrenches their power. This is an insufficient and troublesome characterization of the largest economy in the Middle East today. In addition to politically motivated criticisms, many scholars and observers viewed the private sector as the appropriate vehicle of industrialization (Evans 1995) and warn of a predatory state as the alternative (Cypher and Dietz 1997, 226). Consequently, many of the most detailed economic assessments of Saudi Arabia's reforms in Western languages are predicated on the idea that the private sector should behave as it does in a country like the United States and that the state should be a less controlling and powerful entity than it became in Saudi Arabia (as in Turkey, Iran, and Egypt—for all have developed very large public sectors). Saudi Arabia is, however, a developing nation, if semi-peripheral, under a very different set of circumstances than the United States.

The kingdom possesses 25 percent of the world's oil reserves. It has the largest capacity for crude oil production in the world, estimated in 2009 at about 11 million bar-

Petroleum tanks in Dhahran, Saudi Arabia. (Corel)

rels/day (U.S. Energy Information Administration). Actual crude output exceeded Saudi Arabia's Organization of Petroleum Exporting Countries (OPEC) quota in 2010 due to domestic demand for crude oil; it pumped an average of 8.4 million barrels a day that year (*Bloomberg*, January 4, 2011). Oil income, as well as the shift from pastoral to settled forms of tenure, has profoundly altered the country and its citizens' lives.

In many brief studies, reports, and statements, Saudi Arabia has been misrepresented as an undeveloped sandy desert formerly inhabited solely by nomads, who are dazed by their sudden wealth and who are lazy or disdain manual labor. This inaccurate portrayal contrasts with a history of labor-intensive agriculture and regional and long-distance trade complementing the husbandry, or herding and animal raising, and sales by the bedouin and *jamamil* (caravaneers who might sell camels and then carry in goods for sale). Date production and the pearl industry of the Gulf were other sources of pre-oil income, but they had been dependent on slave labor. These along with the income from annual pilgrimage also broadened the ethnic and social composition of the kingdom, albeit mostly in the Hijaz and on the eastern coast.

Once OPEC asserted more control over oil pricing, and prices rose following the boycott of 1973 (see Chapter 2, History); the first oil boom, referred to as the *tufrah*, greatly impacted the country. Since then, price rises and contractions have impacted economic planning, employment, and development and have also fostered expansion.

Saudi Arabia's modern oil-based economy outperforms many others in the Middle East in terms of gross domestic product (GDP) and growth. In comparison to Nigeria, the world's eighth-largest oil producer, where many people live on less than

$2 a day (and where the oil companies had a freer hand) or the small nations of Kuwait—with a population of 3.52 million, 2.36 million of whom are non-"Kuwait" (Kuwait. Fact Sheet. U.S. Department of State, 2011), and a per-capita GDP of $51,700 in 2010 ("Kuwait," *CIA World Factbook 2010*)—and Brunei—with a population of 395,027 and per-capita GDP estimated at $50,300 in 2010 (*CIA World Factbook*)—Saudi Arabia's population of 25,731,776 (2010 est., which includes 5,576,076 nonnationals) brings its GDP per capita to $24,400 in 2010. That average is far lower than the U.S. GDP of $47,400 per capita in 2010 or the United Kingdom's $35,100 per capita. The average in Saudi Arabia covers the wealthy and a substantial poverty-stricken or near-poor sector of the population. Thus, Saudi Arabia remains a developing nation that grew very swiftly and built a great deal of fairly new infrastructure and housing dating at least from the first oil boom. New challenges Saudi Arabia faces are its own increasing population, which is consuming more energy, and the shifting global situation, in which China and India are poised to be the world's largest nations and energy consumers.

At the modern nation's founding, the government treasury was synonymous with the personal wealth of Ibn Sa'ud, the country's first king. Economic, financial, and taxation systems had to be established along with a fairly large bureaucracy and civil service. The numbers of Saudi Arabians employed in the national government has greatly increased ever since. Economic resources devoted to the building of infrastructure have also addressed the particular geography of the country and the needs of the petroleum industry. Construction and industry were staffed with foreign labor, bringing along another bevy of economic and development issues. Until the end of the 1980s, the government's financial and other sectors were also staffed with foreigners in some cases. Legal and defense sectors continue to employ foreigners.

Saudi Arabia nationalized its petroleum industry and other economic sectors relatively late as compared to other neighboring countries. Much of its planning and reforms since 2000 have been in an opposite direction, privatizing and making the economy compliant with the rules and goals of the World Trade Organization (WTO), which Saudi Arabia joined in 2005.

ECONOMIC PLANNING

Saudi Arabia's centralized economic planning has tended to repeat certain key goals and programs, and it has also been impacted by the boom and bust cycles resulting from increases and falls in the price of oil. However, even with a recent boom until 2008, followed by a period of contraction, the impetus for reforms remained strong. These were necessary in the country's quest for membership in the WTO and the encouragement of business and trade thereafter.

The First (1970–1975) and Second (1975–1980) official national five-year Development Plans focused on improving infrastructure but also on building educational facilities. Highways were built, electricity was provided, and seaports were constructed or expanded. During the Third five-year Development Plan (1980–1985), the budget for health, social services, and education was expanded and the cities of

Jubayl and Yanbu were constructed. Education and training were also important areas of planning in the fourth economic development plan (1985–1990) because of the expansion of the population. It was important to build and expand colleges and universities so that students could pursue higher education in the kingdom. More emphasis was put on encouraging private investment and joint ventures between public and private companies, both of which benefited from government financing programs. During the Fifth Plan (1990–1995), coinciding with the Gulf War and its aftermath, the budget allocated more funds toward defense facilities and an increased emphasis on Saudization. The Sixth Development Plan (1996–2000) continued to emphasize education and training, Saudization, and control of government costs. The Seventh Plan (2000–2005) focused on greater economic growth in the private sector and continued its focus on Saudization and economic diversification, meaning development of sectors outside of oil production. The Eighth Plan (2005–2010) continued to focus on economic diversification; it called for establishing new colleges and universities to encourage new technical specializations, advancing women's interests in society and the economy, building tourism, and promoting privatization. The Ninth Economic Development Plan (2010–2014), as approved by the Supreme Economic Council, is supposed to further the country's long-term economic strategy to reach certain goals by 2025. One aspect is to develop six new economic cities in different parts of the country under a National Spatial Strategy (*UNDP News Room*, July 8, 2010). The plan is to improve quality-of-life issues and continue an emphasis on education and training. Under this plan spending will increase 67 percent increase from the previous five-year plan, up to a total of 1,444 billion Saudi riyals (*Saudi Gazette*, August 10, 2010).

Saudi Arabia has also experienced a challenge in investing its oil income appropriately, and it has examined and experimented with different forms of economic diversification in the industrial and agricultural sectors. The increase in its development plan in the current cycle is possible because of a large surplus in the budget. The basic monetary unit is the Saudi Arabian riyal. The U.S. dollar was equal to 3.7502 Saudi Arabian riyals in mid-January 2011. The riyal is a strong currency for the region.

Saudi Arabia is a founding member of the Organization of Petroleum Exporting Countries (OPEC) and became a member of the WTO in December 2005. It ranks 109th in the world in wealth, and although it is the strongest economy in the Middle East, as noted earlier, its per-capita GDP is lower than that of the United States. However, in the United States, citizens do not receive free health care or college educations, and subsidies to the poor are sharply limited; therefore, when comparing the two countries these forms of spending (considered human investment in Saudi Arabia) should be kept in mind. Saudi Arabia is the largest aid donor to other countries in the Middle East; its economic output has created political influence through aid and, more important, through trade.

As an Islamic country, Saudi Arabia is bound by certain economic principles expressed in law and tradition. Simultaneously, it is very much a part of a world economy that operates via profit-oriented principles. Muslims are required to support the poor and indigent, and, therefore, government policies must uphold such

Ministers and delegates of the Organization of Petroleum Exporting Countries (OPEC) gather on June 21, 2000 to discuss crude oil production levels. (AP/Wide World Photos)

ideals. Muslims are not supposed to charge interest on loans; interest is referred to as *riba'*, or usury. However, different business practices allowed for certain substitute charges and for payments on investments in what one might term shared projects. As a consequence, Islamic banking has developed, which follows various practices to give investors confidence that Islamic law is not being violated. Islamic banks and investment tools are more popular and frequently utilized than in some other countries, although conventional banking exists as well; currently, foreign banks are expanding their presence in the kingdom. *Shari'ah*-compliant bonds (*sukuk*) are available and are now a growing market.

One of the fundamental pillars of Islam is *zakat*, a voluntary form of charity that should comprise 2.5 percent of one's income and assets. Every Muslim is required to give *zakat* unless he is destitute, and the most blessed form is anonymous giving. This allows for the recycling of wealth and prevention of dire poverty. In practice, it is difficult to enforce what is voluntary or to track anonymous philanthropy. Charitable giving is considered virtuous but has traditionally taken place privately in requests by individuals to other individuals, perhaps impeding, or delaying, the state's role in addressing poverty. The Saudi Arabian government, concerned by poor and underdeveloped areas, including those within Riyadh, is systemizing social services. It also sought to control the abuse of donations made to mosques and other Islamic organizations, particularly after 2003, because these were alleged to have been used by terrorists.

Islam forbids speculation, profiting on speculation, and gambling. In addition, the laws of inheritance are supposed to dissolve partnerships at death and prevent a person from disinheriting his legal heirs; about two-thirds of one's estate must go to the heirs. One could set up a foundation or endowment with the other portion of one's estate, known as a *waqf*, to support a public service like a fountain or a library. Such properties, *awqaf*, come under special rules; like the Western legal category of *mortmain* which could not be claimed by the state and was endowed in perpetuity, and was not supposed to be subsumed under the ruler or government.

Local or distant rulers and merchants benefited from the lucrative pilgrim influx to the Hijaz, a major reason for the Ottoman Empire's efforts to defeat the Wahhabi forces on the peninsula. The pilgrimage is an enormous source of income, not only in Saudi Arabia but also for the private sector in countries where pilgrims originate. The *hajj*, which now brings in nearly 2.5 million people, is regulated through an international organization. Muslims also travel to the holy cities for the *'umrah*, or lesser pilgrimage. Saudi Arabia has not had a large share of tourism outside of its pilgrim trade but has recently formulated plans to foster tourism apart from the pilgrimage.

Other particular local economic features of note include money transfers made outside of banks, especially by foreign workers from South Asia; these are sometimes referred to as *hawala*. The worker typically pays the *hawaladar*, who telephones or electronically contacts his counterpart in the home country, who pays out cash to the worker's family. Such transfers cannot be easily traced and have also been criticized as a means, or potential means, of terrorist funding, although terrorist activity has not been traced to the foreign-labor sector in the kingdom.

The social and economic systems of the bedouin, the cultivators, and the pre-modern merchants, and of marriage payments and arrangements, all underlie the modern economy. In premodern times, the bedouin herded their animals exclusively and supplemented their needs by selling some animals or by raiding, or they made arrangements with cultivators for produce, for instance, dates. Their mode of production had already been impacted by the late 1960s, when anthropologist Donald Cole and sociologist Saad Eddin Ibrahim studied the al-Murrah and other bedouin tribes. Cole wrote that the sale of an animal was only an occasional event and that most food was grown for self-consumption (67.8 percent); only 3.5 percent was produced exclusively for selling (Cole 1975, 130) . He makes another point, that relatively few people (at the time he was writing) are productive, because herding requires little labor; at the same time herding "does not now and probably never has" met the subsistence needs of the nomads (Cole 1975, 131). Of the 10 families he studied, 8 had a member employed in the National Guard who drew a salary and met the families' needs; a third of his and Ibrahim's larger sample was employed by the government (Cole 1975, 131; Ibrahim and Cole 1978). These results were taken to mean that these family groups were unproductive or that it was difficult to instill a productive ethic in those who could subsist without it. Other anthropologists have shown that the bedouin had rarely relied entirely on herding and took Cole to task for wrongly depicting the bedouin household as unproductive (Fabietti 1990). Underlying this debate was the fact that the bedouin had been suffering economically in the period prior to certain government subsidies.

Much has happened since then with the economy's rapid growth, rises in prices, changes in consumption patterns, and new aspirations spurred by education. The same al-Murrah raise livestock for collectors, but their entire world has changed, as Cole later described (2006).

Agriculture is estimated at 3.2 percent (*CIA World Factbook 2010*) of the modern economy; however, in the prestatistical past, it may have comprised something like 60 percent of the pre-oil economy of specific population centers, and it remains very important in many areas. Modern industry (excluding agriculture) is 60.4 percent of the economy, and services are 36.4 percent (estimates for 2009 in *CIA World Factbook 2010*). The entire Saudi Arabian labor force (primarily men) is 6.922 million, and a rather startling number—80 percent—of the labor force are non–Saudi Arabians. This labor force is employed 6.7 percent in agriculture, 21.4 percent in industry, and 71.9 percent in services (*CIA World Factbook 2010*). If more currently unemployed Saudi Arabian men and women had jobs, they would occupy a larger share of the labor market, and the foreign labor force might not be as high.

INDUSTRY

Agriculture

In the traditional agriculture (*al-zira'ah al-taqlidiyyah*) of Saudi Arabia's oases like al-'Unayzah and Ha'il in Najd, farmers harvested dates, figs, pomegranates, melons, watermelons, wheat, millet, barley, alfalfa, squash, peppers, eggplant, okra, black-eyed peas, watercress, onions, leeks, cumin, coriander, and fenugreek. Wheat planting and date harvesting and processing were important collective activities, and the crops were used sometimes as payment. During the last 30 years, modern mechanical pumps reduced the labor needed to obtain water, as they replaced the traditional camel-drawn (or human-drawn) pulleys that draw well water in the *sawani* method. Many important aspects of new planning have emerged; some traditional types of land tenure have ceased, and the land is now primarily farmed by foreign workers. Crops are more intensively wheat, barley (subsidized by the government as a fodder crop), and potatoes. New fruits, animals, and other enterprises have also been introduced. Barley was instituted because the bedouin began raising more sheep after Saudi Arabia's unification. The additional sheep degraded the grazing lands, which also suffered from droughts. On one farm in al-'Unayzah, 30,000 fruit trees were planted in 1986—oranges, tangerines, Egyptian peaches, pomegranates from Ta'if, apricots, Spanish lemons, and American olives. Not far away, another farmer, inspired by travel to Syria, introduced fish farms (Altorki and Cole 1989, 42, 170–171). In Asir, where the steep highlands require terraced farming, wheat, cotton, coffee, indigo, ginger, and dates are grown. Roses are cultivated in the mountain wadis of Ta'if, not as a floral product, but to make *attar* (rose water) for use in cooking and fragrances (Pint 2005).

Farmer holding harvested vegetables, Saudi Arabia. (Tor Eigeland/Saudi Aramco)

In the pre-petroleum era, fishing and pearl diving, and the related industry of ship-building, were important in the Gulf and the Red Sea, but the natural-pearl industry was essentially killed off by the cultured-pearl industry by 1932. Slave labor was essential to pearling and date production (Hopper 2010); however, pearling declined in the 1930s, and date exports were challenged when California began cultivating that crop. Slave labor was abolished in 1962. The pearl diving industry created a seasonal workforce that greatly influenced popular culture in the Gulf region (see Chapter 6, section on music).

For decades, foreign labor has been utilized in agriculture, construction, domestic service, white-collar professional jobs, service positions, hotels, the legal and medical professions, nursing, education, and the oil industry. The proportion of foreign labor is disputed, but the international group Human Rights Watch (2010a) believes that 8 million foreign workers from Asian and other Arab countries are employed in Saudi Arabia. An official policy of Saudization projects its reduction through additional education, training, and incentives for Saudi Arabian workers; however, some structural features impede Saudization, for instance, the restriction of various fields to males only.

SAMPHIRE AND SEAWATER IRRIGATION

Saudi Arabian experiments with wheat farming were very successful but were criticized for the subsidies needed to promote the program and for their high water usage. Could seawater be used for irrigation? At Ra's al-Zawr in Saudi Arabian's northeastern region, samphire (*Salicornia bigelovii*) was grown commercially, irrigated with seawater, by the Arabian Saline Water Technology Company, also known as Behar. Samphire is eaten as a salad green or vegetable (it is called "poor man's asparagus" in Britain), yields oil, and can be used as animal feed. The project began in Saudi Arabia in 1993–1994. Samphire was chosen because it can thrive in salty soil and brackish water. Samphire was developed in Sonora, Mexico, as a potential challenger to soybean and safflower oil. Although it likes salt, it must still be overwatered to flush out salt (Clark 1994). The Behar project ended due to lack of demand. Recently, a experimental *Salicornia* plantation has been started in Abu Dhabi, United Arab Emirates, with the intent of cultivating samphire as an agrofuel for airplanes (InterPress Service, February 15, 2010).

Land Tenure

Undeveloped land is termed *'ardh baydha'* and was used for grazing. Grazing areas were reserved for particular tribes or townships under the *hima* system, and no one could cut vegetation in such areas. Outside such grazing areas, if someone cultivated land, then he could obtain freehold ownership (*mulk hurr*) if he could prove that the land was previously barren. The new cultivating landholder could sell the land, and his family could inherit it (Altorki and Cole 1989, 35). Or land could be granted a ruler through *iqta'* (a land grant, as elsewhere in the formerly Ottoman lands). When landholders went into debt, their land could be repossessed, usually by moneylenders or merchants. Another way of obtaining land was to lease it via contract—a form known as *subrah*. Freehold land could become part of a *waqf*, or an endowment, which changed the status of the land, because the state could not claim it, but it could be leased (Altorki and Cole 1989, 36–38). Sharecropping also took place, with peasants (*falalih*) working the land; and paying for seeds, fertilizer, and animals; and providing the labor on land owned by merchants, for example, who received a share of the crops.

Animal Husbandry and Trading

The bedouin raised animals that required grazing areas. However, many were agro-pastoralists; that is, they were not exclusively pastoralists but also seasonally engaged in agriculture. An additional boost to the income of the tribal groups was the sale of specialized animals, such as racing camels or horses. These commanded good prices; however, such sales might be only occasional. Alternatively, pastoralists simply

Saudi Arabian farmer uses cattle to till soil. (Tor Eigeland/Saudi Aramco)

acquired milk and meat from their herds. As in other parts of the Middle East and the Horn of Africa, the pastoralist or agropastoralist bedouin moved from certain areas to others in different seasons of the year. Each tribe, or animal owner, including the members of the Sa'udi royal family, was identified through special marks or designs branded onto the animals, known as *wasm*. Such markings were also replicated in bedouin weaving patterns (Hilden, n.d.). Traditional occupations such as that of the *jammal*, or caravaneer, have been relinquished in contemporary times. The *jammal* might typically have traveled to Damascus or Egypt to sell animals and would return with goods for sale. Others, known as *'uqaylin*, engaged in long-distance trade and also frequently worked abroad. The lifestyle and income of all of these groups were impacted with the introduction of automobiles and trucks; the latter replaced animals and ending the *jamamil* activities by and large.

Petroleum and Natural Gas

Saudi Arabia is the world's largest supplier of oil. The Ministry of Oil and Petroleum Resources develops all of the country's oil policies and projects. Deputy ministers report to the minister of oil, as does the country's representative to OPEC. Although the actual longevity of Saudi Arabian oil reserves is disputed—and thus no one knows for certain how long this economic situation will last—for the foreseeable future, or some 30 years, it is expected that production will continue at the current levels. As stated at the outset of this chapter, crude oil production increased in 2010.

This, in turn, made oil a more economical fuel than many of the more expensive alternatives under debate. On the other hand, Saudi Arabia is consuming an increasing share of its own fuel. To balance the dominant role of petrochemicals in the country's economy, planners have been encouraging the growth of the private sector and encouraged the kingdom's accession to the WTO. Six economic cities or zones have been constructed, and the country is emphasizing scientific and technological studies in the new King Abdullah University for Science and Technology. Some oil is possessed by Saudi Arabia and also Kuwait under the Neutral Territory, which was previously managed by a Japanese company. Other products like natural gas and petrochemicals are produced in the kingdom.

The history of the oil industry is fascinating and confusing. While oil excavation took place in the United States—in Pennsylvania and in California early in the 20th century—as in the world markets, the first scenarios saw wildcatting, in which investors rushed to pump oil until the commodity lost value, which occurred swiftly. This was the sort of situation that the giant companies that eventually formed sought to avoid. The oil industry came to be dominated by a few gigantic personalities who created companies that were able to fend off competitors, control the costs of transportation, and fight regulation (Pelletiere 2001; Yergin 1991; Kirk 2000). The great advantage of oil in the Arabian Gulf region rested on political, economic, and geological specifics. In this part of the world, companies could gain concessions for entire areas without dealing with individual landowners but only with the ruling *shaykhs* and, in Saudi Arabia, like in Kuwait, with the king. Oil companies were interested in excavating in the region, for geologists knew that oil was likely to be found there because of the naptha fires from oil seeping up to the surface, which had attracted the interest of visitors for centuries. In 1932, oil was discovered in Bahrain. In May 1933, the Saudi Arabian government agreed that Standard Oil of California (SOCAL) could explore Saudi Arabia for oil. This was undertaken by California Arabian Standard Oil Company (CASOC), a subsidiary of SOCAL. In 1936, the Texas Oil Company bought half of this concession and operated as the California Texas Oil Company. In Dammam, one well began producing more than 1,500 barrels a day in 1938, after nearly four years of unsuccessful efforts. In 1944, the company's name became the Arabian American Oil Company, known as Aramco. By 1948, the company was owned by Standard Oil of New Jersey, Socony Vacuum, SOCAL, and the Texas Oil Company. Aramco ran the company as it wished and set prices; however, it began to share the profits with the Saudi Arabian government and wrote off Saudi Arabia's share as a U.S. tax deduction.

In 1973, following U.S. support for Israel during the Ramadan (or October or Yom Kippur) War, the Saudi Arabian government acquired a 25 percent share of Aramco, increased the share to 60 percent by 1974, and finally acquired full control of Aramco by 1980. In November 1988, the company changed its name from Arabian American Oil Company to Saudi Arabian Oil Company, also known as Saudi Aramco.

Aramco built infrastructure in the Eastern Province and transported oil by tanker vessels from Ra's Tanura and Ju'aymah. In 1981, the company embarked on an east-west pipeline linking the eastern oil fields to Yanbu. This pipeline was not as heavily used as tanker traffic but was important in case of disruption in the Arabian (or Persian) Gulf. It boosted output, even more so with its expansion in 1987. In 1993, the Saudi Arabian government decreed that Saudi Aramco would merge with Samarec, the company responsible for refining oil. Ever since, the company has refined and distributed oil within the kingdom and ships oil internationally via its subsidiary, Vela International Marine, Limited, based in Dubai in the United Arab Emirates. Other subsidiaries are Aramco Services Company of Houston, Saudi Petroleum International, Saudi Petroleum Overseas (located in London), Aramco Services Company of the Netherlands, Bolanter Corporation, Pandlewood Corporation, and Saudi Aramco Total Refining and Petrochemical Company.

Aramco's senior management and engineers were nearly all Americans as recently as the 1970s, and foreign control over the kingdom's natural resources was disturbing to Saudi Arabia for various reasons. Even following nationalization, American nationals remained on as executives until 1988 (Obaid 2000, 41). The company has been very successful under Saudi Arabian management.

Today, Saudi Aramco is a huge company with a value estimated at $781 billion in 2006 (*Financial Times*). It manages more than 100 oil and gas fields and produces about 3.4 billion barrels of oil a year. It is the largest producer of oil and liquefied petroleum gas and the ninth-largest producer of natural gas in the world (Obaid 2000, 23; http://www.saudiaramco.com, 2010). Its headquarters are in Dhahran, and its chief current rival is ExxonMobil. Saudi Aramco also operates the Master Gas System, a hydrocarbon complex. It employed 54,441 people in 2008, including geologists and geophysicists who continue to explore for oil and more than 500 engineers and scientists. It maintains two research and development facilities, identified as Upstream and Downstream (and which pertain to the differing processes of these two stages), and a variety of subsidiary companies are related to Saudi Aramco.

KEY OFFICIALS IN SAUDI ARAMCO

Saudi Aramco's leading administrators were the following as of 2011:

Khalid al-Falih, CEO, president, and director

Saleh S. al-'Aidh, Senior Vice President for Engineering and Project Management.

al-Khalid G. al-Buainain, Senior Vice President for Downstream Operations, 'Abdulaziz F. al-Khayal, Senior Vice President for Industrial Relations, David B. Kultgen, General Counsel and Secretary

Amin H. Nassar, Senior Vice President for Upstream Operations for 'Abdullatif A. Othman, Senior Vice President for Finance

'Abdulrahman F. al-Wuhaib, Senior Vice President for Operations Services (Saudi Aramco,

---

Source: http://www.saudiaramco.com/en/home.html#our-company%257C%25

Selected and Recently Appointed Executives

Khaled A. al-Buraik, Vice President of Saudi Aramco Affairs

Dawood M. al-Dawood, Vice President of Marketing, Supply and Joint Venture Coordination

Zuhair A. al-Hussain, Vice President of Drilling and Workover

Majid Y. al-Mugla, Vice President of Project Management

Ahmad A. al-Sa'adi, Vice President of Pipelines, Distribution and Terminal Operations

Saad A. al-Turaiki, Vice President of Southern Area Oil Operations

Mu'tassim al-Maashouq, for Business Development

Khalid al-Dabbagh, Treasurer

Sources: Saudi Aramco, and *Reuters Africa*, November 6, 2010.

Saudi Aramco Board of Directors, August 2010–2013

Minister of Petroleum and Mineral Resources H.E. Ali I. al-Naimi, Chairman

H.E. Dr. Ibrahim A. al-'Assaf, Member

H.E. Dr. Mohammed I. al-Suwaiyel, Member

H.E. Dr. Abdul Rahman A. al-Tuwaijri, Member

H.E. Dr. Khaled S. al-Sultan, Member

Sir Mark Moody-Stuart, Member

Peter L. Woicke, Member

David J. O'Reilly, Member

President and CEO of Saudi Aramco Khalid A. al-Falih, Member

Abdulaziz F. al-Khayyal, Member

Salim S. al-'Aidh, Member

Amin H. Nasser, Member

Source: Royal Embassy of Saudi Arabia, Washington, DC, and *Financial Times*, November 6, 2010.

ExxonMobil is the largest publicly traded corporation in the world and had earnings of $19,420 million in 2009 due to falling oil prices. The company had previously been estimated as having a total worth of US$500 billion. The company's earnings and income have increased since as oil prices rose. Its current (July 2011) book value is 2.68. The company owns about 40 percent of the world's oil and is an extremely important corporation in the kingdom, as well as in the production of natural gas. ExxonMobil, like Saudi Arabia, expects an increase in the demand for petrochemicals in Asia and has been building projects in China, Singapore, Saudi Arabia, and Qatar to that end. In conjunction with the Saudi Arabian Basic Industries Corporation (SABIC) it is studying ways to supply rubber, polymers, and carbon black from its joint ventures in the country (ExxonMobil Corporation 2007).

Chevron was one of the original Aramco partners, and it continues to provide services to the kingdom. In addition, it transports crude from the kingdom to its refineries. Chevron has also been involved in technology transfer, the provision of asphalt for sports facilities, and, along with its Saudi Arabian partner Xenel, the formation of the Saudi (electrical) Cable Company. In addition, it operated the Saudi Arabian Maritime International Transport Company (1978–1987) to transport oil and is involved in civil engineering in the kingdom. Saudi Chevron Petrochemical, in a joint venture with the Saudi Industrial Venture Capital Group, constructed a Jubayl plant that blends motor gasoline and also produces cyclohexane and benzene. Arabian Chevron, Inc. maintains its offices in Riyadh (Arabian Chevron 2007).

Saudi Aramco has contributed greatly to the country's infrastructure, and ExxonMobil, Saudi Aramco, and other oil companies are involved in environmental research and donate toward humanitarian causes. For example, ExxonMobil made a donation of 5 million Saudi Arabian riyals (today this has a value of $1.333 million) toward disability research in 2005 (*Arab News*, May 20, 2005). The oil sector is currently managed in the Saudi government through particular structures such as the Petroleum Preparatory Committee and under the Ministry of Petroleum and Mineral Resources. The ministry oversees the activities of Saudi Aramco, Saudi Texaco, Aramco Gulf Operation Ltd., and the Saudi Arabian Mining Company, as well as the Saudi Geological Survey.

When questioned about the political volatility of the region and what that means for production, in 2008, oil company representatives expressed differing views: strong concerns that no war should break out with Iran or confidence that any conflict would be brief and that facilities could swiftly shut down and weather it. At that time,

Saudi Arabian men converse in front of an advertisement at the 2007 OPEC summit in Riyadh. (AP/Wide World Photos)

at least one representative explained that conflicts in Arab countries not immediately neighboring Saudi Arabia were not all that important to the then-booming economy, as these were the "hinterlands." (Zuhur 2005–2008; also see Chapter 7, Contemporary Issues) The major companies may feel somewhat differently about the current wave of protests and regime changes in the region. As important as the oil companies are to Saudi Arabia, the country's participation in OPEC granted it far more control over the corporate giants and the industry. When OPEC was first created, Aramco refused even to speak to the fledgling cartel, considering the company's role in pricing to be without challenge (Lacey 1981). OPEC is based in Vienna, Austria. OPEC's member states—Algeria, Angola, Iran, Iraq, Kuwait, Libya, Nigeria, Qatar, Saudi Arabia, the United Arab Emirates, and Venezuela (Indonesia and Ecuador are former members, and Iraq's production is still so low that it plays a minor role)—often disagree politically and economically as individual countries, but they have learned to operate together to their benefit. When the cartel agrees to cut output, then prices rise. The opposite lesson was learned in the years of an oil glut when production was increased in the early 1980s, and prices fell.

Prior to the establishment of a ministry for oil, the U.S.-educated 'Abdullah al-Tariki began his career at the Directorate for Oil and Mining Affairs and became director-general of petroleum and mineral affairs in 1954. He served as the first minister of petroleum and mineral resources (1960–1962). His career exemplifies the rapid transformation of Saudi Arabians, for his father was a camel and caravan owner. Al-Tariki set out to study Venezuela's behavior vis-à-vis oil companies and how it obtained control over each process in the industry. In September 1960, the Venezuelan oil minister Juan Pablo Pérez Alfonzo and al-Tariki organized a meeting in Baghdad, at which Saudi Arabia, Venezuela, Iran, Iraq, and Kuwait were represented, to discuss methods of increasing oil prices. Then, in response to quotas imposed by the United States on Venezuela and Persian Gulf oil exporters, OPEC was cofounded by Tariki and Pérez. The Arab members of OPEC also joined the Organization of Arab Petroleum Exporting Countries (OAPEC) in the wake of the June, or Six-Day, War of 1967. Following the 1973 Ramadan War between Israel and the Arab states, the Arab members of OPEC called for an oil embargo against the United States and Western Europe. The embargo was eventually called off by the Saudi Arabian government but not before creating a panic and oil rationing in the United States and Europe.

OPEC's aim is to maintain moderate oil prices that are not so high as to discourage global dependence on the oil market. When oil prices rose in the 1980s, non-OPEC oil supplies were sought out and rapidly expanded, contributing to a drop in oil prices. OPEC assigned production quotas in response; however, profits continued to slide. Certain other OPEC members produced more than their quotas, and Saudi Arabia had to cut production even further so long as it sold at official prices. In 1986 Saudi Arabia switched to a new method called *netback pricing*, which benefited its oil purchasers and allowed it to regain market share (Mohamedi in Metz, ed., 1993, 150). OPEC raised its quotas, and Saudi Arabia insisted on its allocation of 25 percent of the output, which later rose to 35 percent after Iraq's invasion of Kuwait. The United Arab Emirates and Kuwait overproduced prior to 1990; Iraq threatened to invade

Kuwait and dominated the 1990 OPEC meeting (Mohamedi in Metz, ed., 1993, 145–146). With the Iraqi invasion and U.S. intervention in the Gulf in Operation Desert Storm, Saudi Arabia obtained more of its objectives in OPEC.

Even so, market and corporate forces, as well as politics, continue to influence Saudi Arabia as an oil economy. The Saudi Arabian–American alliance was said to lie behind Saudi Arabia's role in moderating prices, which actually was part of the country's long-term strategy. However, in 1998–1999, OPEC and other oil-producing countries campaigned to cut production and increase prices, and Saudi Arabia participated, regarding this as a logical economic strategy for the country. Minister of Petroleum and Mineral Resources ʻAli al-Naʻimi was a chief advocate for subsequently maintaining a higher price, according to Nawaf Obaid, whereas those who urged a larger market share rather than higher prices were led by the deputy minister, Prince ʻAbd al-ʻAziz Salman, even though the latter had played a strong role in the 1998 agreement to make higher prices the official policy. Obaid makes the point that the leaders of the oil policy-making community are not price hawks or doves in any extreme sense, as the question of price versus market share has been debated, very publicly, for years (Obaid 2000, 19).

Saudi Arabia produces various types of crude oil that vary in their sulfur content, from Arab Super Light (produced at the Hazmiyah and Ghinah fields) to Arab Heavy (found at Manifa). The super-light oil is being pumped and depleted more rapidly throughout the global oil market, which means that refineries will eventually produce more of the heavier oil. The changes necessary to deal with higher sulfur content may produce higher costs and possibly delays (Cordesman and al-Rodhan 2006, vol. 2, 188, 194).

The management of the oil sector in the Saudi Arabian government has undergone professionalization and also relies on its negotiations with the oil companies and other OPEC nations. In 2000, the Supreme Council for Petroleum and Mineral Affairs was established by royal decree. It included the king, the then-Crown Prince ʻAbdullah; Prince Saʻud al-Faysal, the minister of foreign affairs; engineer ʻAli al-ʻNaimi, the minister of petroleum and mineral resources; Dr. Ibrahim al-Assaf, the minister of finance and national economy; Dr. Hashim Yamani, the minister of industry and electricity; Khaled al-Ghosaybi, the minister of planning and acting minister of post, telephone, and telegraph; Dr. Mutlib al-Nafisah, minister of state and secretary-general of the Supreme Council; Dr. Saleh al-Adhel, president of King Abdulaziz City for Science and Technology; ʻAbd al-ʻAziz al-Rashid, former deputy minister of finance; and ʻAbdullah Jumah, the president and CEO of Saudi Aramco (Obaid 2000, 21–29). The council has more authority than the previous Supreme Petroleum Council, overseeing Saudi Aramco, electing its board of directors, determining oil and gas production levels, and granting joint venture arrangements (Obaid 2000, 21).

The basic equation of profit maintenance in the oil industry is access to and control over the resource and regulation of production and prices. The industry mostly consists of giant corporations that obtain their profits without hindrance in places like Equatorial Guinea and Nigeria (Maass 2009), but different obstacles have been present in the Middle East, what with the nationalist goals determined by the Saudi

Arabians, who, after years of deferring to the oil company executives, demanded their nation's fair share. With the OPEC boycott, the power of the oil cartel became apparent, and eventually Aramco had to defer to OPEC after initially ignoring it. Saudi Arabia's goals through OPEC were nationalization and control throughout the production process, although Americans retained executive positions in the company for many years.

Another feature of the oil industry was its economic impact during boom and bust cycles. The first boom, or *tufrah*, had an incredibly strong effect on the economy, changing certain social features forever. The boom spurred construction, and many obtained credit to build new houses. Car imports tripled, and the U.S. ambassador, James Akins, wrote that the sky was "black with vultures" with "get-richer-quicker" schemes (Lacey 1981, 422).

Prices rose again in the late 1970s, first in response to the Iranian revolution. The attack by 700 rebels led by al-'Utaybi at the Grand Mosque in Mecca and the Soviet Union's invasion of Afghanistan also produced significant shocks in Saudi Arabia. At the 1979 OPEC meeting, the Saudi Arabian position was against raising prices because they worried about rates of inflation and exchange and were concerned that high prices would stimulate the search for alternative fuels (Yergin 1991, 703). Oil supply channels were disrupted, and stock and oil prices rose higher and higher after President Carter embargoed imports of Iranian oil into the United States. Inflation became a problem worldwide, and the oil "bubble" was unsustainable. As a result, OPEC lowered the price per barrel from $34 to $29 in 1983 (Yergin 1991, 720). OPEC members other than Saudi Arabia argued for higher production quotas, but the kingdom agreed to act as a "swing producer"—pumping more or less to keep prices down but ensure supplies. The embargo on Saddam Hussein in 1990 and then the Gulf War unleashed another crisis in terms of prices. But quite a few believe that the Gulf War was actually supported by the United States and Saudi Arabia, either to prevent Saddam Hussein from gaining more control over OPEC or to gain control over Iraq, not only to ensure access to Saudi Arabia's oil but also to prevent pricing challenges beyond U.S. control from arising, as had happened in the late 1970s. This logic sees the 2003 invasion of Iraq as furthering the same interests (Pelletiere 2001; Maass 2009).

Another oil boom took place more recently, up through 2007 and 2008, but then prices contracted and then rose again following the regional turmoil of the spring of 2011. Each of the contractions caused changes in the country's pursuance of its development plans; most recently, these plans have been expanded due to the large surplus of $28.9 billion during 2010. This allowed the government to raise its expenditure allocations by 8 percent to SR 580 billion, intended to encourage economic growth but not at so steep a rate as to encourage overspending. The surplus was attributed to higher oil prices and lowered oil capital expenditures from Saudi Aramco. The government also reduced its domestic debt by 25.8 percent (domestic debt is now at 10.2 percent of GDP, as compared to over 80 percent in 2003; John Sfakianakis, personal communication, December 20, 2010; also see Reuters on Arabian.Business. com, December 26, 2010.)

The literature on Saudi Arabia's petroleum sector reflects certain polemics. First, its early history was largely constructed by and reflects American oil interests. Even though Frank Holmes of New Zealand (known as Abu al-Naft [the father of oil] in Bahrain) was the true discoverer of oil, that fact has been obscured in accounts of the industry (even in Yergin's 1991 work, he is a minor figure). One researcher located Holmes's correspondence with Karl Twitchell, the Holmes-Amin Rihani correspondence and other documentation to establish this fact (Keating 2005, 9–10). At stake was the concept of rights to oil profits, whereby American commercial development trumped the United Kingdom's earlier governorship and initial claims. The Saudi Arabians (and Bahrainis, Kuwaitis, Emiratis, etc.) could and eventually did assert rights on the basis of national sovereignty. Earlier Western contentions in the literature that Arab states had no right to use the "oil weapon" reflected conflicting political and commercial interests and also this history of discovery and exploitation.

Ever since the 1973 war and in response to the increases in oil booms, Western and particularly American politicians have argued, in virtually every campaign speech, that their nation must become less dependent on imported oil. The 2008 U.S. presidential campaign featured promises to search for alternatives to fossil fuels and reduce the United States' dependency on what was largely understood to mean Arab oil producers, that is, Saudi Arabia. Similar discourse exists in Europe where higher oil prices are paid. Earlier literature often criticized Saudi Arabia for being a "social welfare state" (Hooglund in Metz, ed., 1993) for covering its citizens' basic economic needs and providing subsidies to them thanks to its oil profits. The liberal-capitalist tradition in economic studies of the kingdom decried the state's role in centralized planning or that state spending and planning were intended to enrich and entrench the royal family (Chaudhry 1997). More recent literature continues to promote and

Supertankers loading oil in Saudi Arabia. (Corel)

prefer private sector growth with longtime observer Giacomo Luciani arguing that the Saudi Arabian private sector is expanding appropriately (Luciani in Aarts and Nonneman, eds., 2006). Meanwhile, others like Tim Niblock and Monica Malik argue that only big businesses or certain others enjoyed access to the government (2007, 147–149). They disagree with Gwenn Okruhlik's claims for the importance of municipal chambers of commerce (1992, 320–321), which have been active and which serve political as well as economic interests. It seems to me, based on visits from 2005 to 2008, that the chambers of commerce indeed proved a vehicle for liberal influence in the government, contrary to Niblock and Malik's claim.

An entire genre of books warn that oil will be depleted, that production levels cannot remain as high as the Saudi Arabian government contends (Simmons 2005), or that the thirst for oil has driven American foreign policy. For example, it is claimed that former vice president Dick Cheney and former president George W. Bush had unnaturally close ties with the kingdom that overrode American concerns about terrorism (Unger 2004; Maass 2009). These polemics shed little light on the Saudi Arabian economy. Oil company executives who spoke with this author in 2008 predicted

Workers inspect an oil pipeline in Saudi Arabia. (Saudi Aramco World/ SAWDIA)

that at least 30 more years of oil production lie ahead. By that time, Saudi Arabia's past, current, and future investments will hopefully have built an alternative basis for the economy and provide another source of energy, possibly nuclear.

Other Industries

The largest nonoil company is SABIC, founded in 1976. It produces fertilizers, polymers, petrochemicals, and steel. This huge company brought in profits of approximately $5.8 billion in 2008. SABIC founded its own *sukuk* (singular, *sakk*) company, which issues bonds that are compliant with Islamic law. There are some disputes among Islamic scholars about *sukuk*. In general, they are supposed to represent ownership in assets or ventures that accrue profits; payments from them should represent after-cost profits; and the value paid at the maturity of the *sakk* should be its current value.

Water consumption is a serious concern in Saudi Arabia; aquifers, which are nonrenewable sources, were being depleted. Desalinization plants have increased in number and capacity, but water usage has continued to grow. As a result, major contracts have been awarded for desalinization and water projects. Allowing international companies to set up reuse facilities for wastewater in Saudi Arabia is being discussed, as one of the many ideas for expanding water availability in the kingdom (*Bawaba Business*, July 6, 2010).

Other industries include Saudi Arabia's transportation sector, which includes SAUDIA (the national airline) and the railways. The country has 865 miles of railways and 137,554 miles of roadways, which includes 2,418 miles of expressways. The Saudi Public Transportation Company operates buses throughout the country, now much easier to drive through since the construction of expressways and highways, such as the Trans-Arabian Highway (which connects the country's largest cities from east to west) and a causeway connecting Saudi Arabia with Bahrain. Saudi Arabian merchant marine vessels number 62. Seventy-one other vessels are registered in other countries. The building and management of seaports have been essential to the country's trade and oil exports, including the ports of Jeddah, al-Dammam, al-Jubayl and Yanbu al-Sinaiyah.

Air travel was essential in Saudi Arabia because of the difficulty of traveling long distances by road. Moreover, many of the pilgrims on the *hajj* travel by air, making up a large proportion of the estimated more than 2.5 million *hajj* pilgrims. Saudi Arabia has 217 airports, 81 of which have paved runways, and 9 heliports (*CIA World Factbook 2010*). SAUDIA is based in Jeddah and as of 2010 operated flights to more than 70 global destinations. The hub airports in Saudi Arabia are King Khalid International Airport in Riyadh and King Fahd International Airport in Dammam, which opened for commercial travel in 1999. SAUDIA is the second-largest carrier in the Middle East, behind Emirates Airlines. The privatization of SAUDIA began in 2006. It has had a monopoly on domestic air travel. Many Saudi Arabians believe that competition from other Gulf airlines would improve service, and they complain of overbooked flights or the inability to obtain tickets even when flights are half empty on domestic routes (*Arab News*, January 15, 2011). Far more international flights now arrive in Saudi Arabia than previously. Women are not permitted to be pilots on SAUDIA; however, Prince Walid ibn Talal, the owner of Kingdom Industries, made news in 2004 when he hired a female pilot, Hind Hanadi, to work for his company.

Saudi Arabia's telecommunication business has also expanded very rapidly, as has cellular and wireless service. In 2008, 4.1 million telephone lines and 36 million mobile cellular phones were in use (*CIA World Factbook 2010*). The largest national provider is the Saudi Telecom service, which also offers Internet access, and there are many other providers of mobile and Internet service. Government-run television operated four channels as of 2010, and the satellite market has opened the country to a multitude of television stations and companies. There were an estimated 7.7 million Internet users in 2008 and an estimated 11,400,000 in 2011.

The national radio service, located in Riyadh, is the Broadcasting Service of the Kingdom of Saudi Arabia. This service also offers shortwave radio, as does the BBC and Voice of America. Twelve Web-based FM radio channels operate from Riyadh and two from Khobar, and three satellite radio channels were available as of 2010.

THE PRIVATE SECTOR AND THE STATE

The private sector is being encouraged under official Saudi Arabian planning. One vehicle is the group of 26 Saudi Arabian Chambers of Commerce, which are elected bodies and federated under the Council of Saudi Chambers of Commerce and Industry. They are intended to aid and support investors and provide information on possible bids. The council is also linked to bilateral business councils such as the Saudi-Japanese Business Council and the Saudi-Ukrainian Business Council.

The private sector is creating wealth for Saudi Arabian as well as foreign companies and businesspersons. The *Arabian Business* 2009 Rich List (similar to *Forbes*'s magazine's Rich List but surveying Arabs) ranked Prince al-Walid bin Talal bin 'Abd al-'Aziz at the top of the list (not due to his royal, but his business standing), estimating his net worth at $18 billion. Shaykh Mohammad ibn 'Isa al-Jabir, who is primarily involved in the travel and hospitality industry, ranks second, with a net worth of $9.7 billion. Ranked fourth is Muhammad al-Amoudi, whose primary industry is in energy and whose net worth is estimated at $8.8 billion. The bin Laden family, whose primary industry is construction, is ranked seventh at $7.1 billion. In the eighth spot is the 'Olayan family, whose primary industry is in banking and finance and whose net worth is estimated at $6.9 billion. Ranked 22nd is the al-Zamil family, with a net worth estimated at $3.5 billion (ArabianBusiness.com 2010). Of these, Prince al-Walid ibn Talal is a well-known investor in the West. Educated in the United States, he bought a large amount of shares in Citicorp in the 1990s and bailed out Citibank when it experienced financial difficulties. He holds other investments in Apple Inc., AOL, Motorola, and News Corporation Limited; various hotel chains; a 10 percent holding in EuroDisney; and a 9 percent investment in Rotana Group, the large entertainment company (described in Chapter 6, section on music).

Despite the gains of such giants of business, nearly 90 percent of private-sector business owners in Saudi Arabia operate small to medium-sized enterprises. Their main complaints are the handicaps of strict regulations, lack of access to credit, and lack of data and information that would help startups (Bundagji 2005).

Crafts

Traditional and modern crafts in Saudi Arabia include animal husbandry for racing, falconry, bread baking (*farranah*), spice dealing (*'attarah*, frequently seen in Mecca and Medina, which includes traditional remedies), and the making of sandals, prayer beads, jewelry, and, in the past, gunpowder. The production of Islam-related books and educational materials is an important and specialized profession, as well as pilgrimage-related activities like the guides for *hajj* groups. Men's and women's clothing is produced in the kingdom, but some items, chiefly men's cotton robes, are imported from Oman, while synthetics and embroidered textiles come from India.

Palm trees produced various local crafts; women wove palm fronds into rugs and fans. Hats (*tafash*), rope, brooms, and matting are also made from palm fronds by rural men and women (Colyer-Ross 1981, 122–123). Women also fashioned the *maksar*, or camel litter, which was based on a tamarisk or pomegranate wood frame, then covered with gazelle skins and decorated with shells, cloth, and pieces of mirror. Stonecutting was once a major trade in the area of Jawf, and sculpture and pottery were important (Colyer-Ross 1981, 119–121). Metal crafts were made in the peninsula, along with armor, weapons, and coffeepots and utensils. Leather goods were also made, including storage bags, camel bags, and belts (Topham 1981).

Weaving was a highly developed craft in the past, and spinning to produce the thread was a necessary skill. In addition to woven textiles, garments, and rugs, embroidery was a very important craft today replaced with ready-made machine embroidered items. Earlier hand-produced items and the techniques used to produce them have been documented and photographed as well as items imported from Syria and Persia (Colyer-Ross 1981, 124–138; Hilden 2010).

Other handicrafts are based on local traditions, and some are important to traditional architecture, for instance, the tradition of mud-brick building, which has been championed by Prince Sultan ibn Salman al-Sa'ud, who restored his farmhouse at al-'Udhaybah with this technique. It is also known to the students of Egyptian architect Hassan Fahmy (Facey 1997, 1999). A special tradition still exists in the brilliant geometric painted frescoes or murals that decorate homes in the Asir region, carried out by master craftsmen (Mauger 1996). Both of these traditions stand in contrast to the far more common cement-block construction of rapidly expanding cities and towns. Other crafts and traditional products are displayed and sold annually at the Jinadiriyya Festival.

Pilgrimage Income and Tourism

The political economy of the annual pilgrimage is a unique aspect of life in Saudi Arabia. An enormous number of people travel each year for the *hajj*, bringing income into the economy. The government has had to invest in the infrastructure necessary to transport, house, and maintain security during this period and, to a lesser extent, during Ramadan, when it is popular to perform the lesser pilgrimage, or the *'umrah*. Political arrangements with all countries sending pilgrims are also necessary. In the past, it was customary for Muslim pilgrims who wanted to pursue Islamic studies to remain on in the kingdom. The pilgrimage visa does not allow for that possibility today; however, the burden of regulation is on the state, and some still overstay their visas. Other external tourism is still extremely limited; the government hopes to expand it as well as internal tourism. Saudi Arabia's unique historical and geographic sites would make it a very interesting destination.

LABOR

In addition to the labor functions coming from pastoral and agricultural-pastoral life, merchants traders, and those in occupations arising from the pilgrimage such as guides were historically important in the kingdom. In the 1940s, an industrial working class formed. This was mostly made up of the Shi'a workers employed by the oil industry in the Eastern Province. In the 1950s, merchant families became more important as they were able to import key goods and obtain contracts for buildings and new businesses.

The foreign workforce expanded throughout the 1960s with 60,000 foreign workers in 1962/1963, rising to 722,050 in 1970. At this point, many of the foreign workers were Arabs, some were Westerners, and others were from South Asia. During the Third Development Plan, government planners hoped that foreign labor would grow only 0.2 percent per year, but foreign labor is cheaper for employers, and according to Niblock and Malik Saudi Arabian productivity fell (Niblock and Malik 2007, 92) in spite of the expansion of educational opportunities. Reducing the foreign workforce and expanding the Saudi Arabian working population has remained a goal ever since. From 2000 to 2007, the entire labor force expanded by 1 million, mostly outside the oil industry, in services, construction, and electricity. More Saudi Arabian citizens were employed, but the number of non–Saudi Arabians working in the kingdom actually rose (Niblock and Malik 2007, 198–199). Only about 19 percent of the Saudi Arabian citizenry is employed; unemployment is thus a serious economic and social issue. The current indigenous labor force is 6.922 million, while the estimated population is 29,207,277 (the figure given in 2010 by the United States was only 25,731,776, but other, higher figures are provided in other sources. One should note that a large proportion of the Saudi Arabian population is under the age of 15 (38 percent, according to some statistics, and over 50 percent in other sources). Restrictions on women's employment also impact the labor sector, and the other major factor to remember is the importation of foreign labor. In addition, there is some casual, or informal, employment (unreported) and unpaid family labor; however, it is the large amount of foreign labor that is of concern, and it tends to be reported at different levels in different sources. For 2009, American sources reported that 80 percent of the labor force was made up of non–Saudi Arabian nationals (*CIA World Factbook 2010*). For several decades, Saudi Arabia has been the number-one destination of many Asian workers, for example, from the Philippines, Pakistan, and Bangladesh. Non–Saudi Arabian Arabs also continue to work in Saudi Arabia.

The labor force is employed primarily in services (71.9 percent), followed by industry (21.4 percent) and agriculture (6.7 percent). The unemployment rate is given at only 11.8 percent for 2008; however, this is based on the employment of Saudi Arabian males, and unemployment is estimated at 25 percent in other sources (*CIA World Factbook 2010*). Unemployment among the younger generation is readily discussed in the kingdom. Parents comment about their children's search for work despite their excellent educational qualifications. Or they complain about the very poor wages offered in certain jobs, which would not cover the expenses of a young man trying to save for marriage or the cost of a driver for a young woman employee. Foreign labor is brought in at lower wages than it would cost to employ Saudi Arabian labor in certain occupations, and the foreign workers are housed cheaply. It is claimed that commercial agents often violate foreign workers' rights—because they

Asian and African immigrants live under a bridge in the city of Jeddah in 2009. Some have overstayed their visas after arriving as pilgrims, others have escaped employers, still others no longer have sponsors. (Omar Salem/AFP/Getty Images)

sponsor workers' visas, frequently hold their passports, and sometimes withhold wages. The government of Saudi Arabia is targeted by international agencies for this situation since it is in the position to help regulate it.

Human Rights Watch (HRW) acknowledged that the Majlis al-Shura (Consultative Council) granted some rights to foreign workers who are employed as servants and domestic workers, estimated at about 1.5 million under the new law; however, they are still subject to abuse and are unable to leave their places of employment or hold their own passports. Asian embassies report thousands of complaints each year from domestic workers who are forced to work 15 to 20 hours a day, seven days a week, and are denied their salaries. Domestic workers frequently endure forced confinement, food deprivation, and severe psychological, physical, and sexual abuse (Human Rights Watch 2010b).

It is difficult for foreign workers to pursue criminal cases against their employers, sometimes because they are returned to their home countries. Human Rights Watch mentions various examples like that of an Indonesia woman, Keni binti Carda, whose employer burned her and pulled her teeth out. Unfortunately, once repatriated, she could not issue a formal complaint.

Many workers are illiterate and speak little Arabic; the agents who bring them into the country may hold their passports, charge them for their travel, and refuse to pay them. In 2007, Saudi Arabia revised its labor law to improve conditions for migrant workers; for example, increasing their annual leave from 15 to 21 days and to 30 days for those who served for five years. Muslim workers must have their hours reduced to 36 hours per week during Ramadan. However, the revised law also allows an employer to increase work hours beyond eight hours a day with the Ministry of Labor's permission or to reduce it to seven hours (*Arab News*, September 25, 2007). In addition, new rules punished labor trafficking with sentences of up to 15 years (Human Rights Watch 2010b).

Nevertheless, workers at Jadawel International, a Saudi Arabian company in Dhahran, complained to Human Rights Watch that those requiring medical treatment could not leave the compound, because the company had not renewed their residency permits. Further, workers said their wages were five months in arrears, and others said they had never been paid in a timely manner. The workers enacted a two-day work stoppage in April 2010 (Human Rights Watch 2010b). This was not the only company violating labor laws; 200 Filipino workers protested wage withholding at the al-Arab Contracting Company in February 2010 (*Business.com*, February 8, 2010). Five hundred Nepalese workers threatened a strike at a work site in Mecca but called it off when promised a resolution (*Yahoo Business*, May 10, 2010).

Strikes, collective bargaining, and unions are not permitted in Saudi Arabia. When the first labor protests broke out at Aramco in 1953, there were no formal laws on such issues. Workers were responding to the conditions in which they were housed, their treatment, and their pay, which was greatly to that of Western foreign workers. After their demands were first raised, 13,000 Saudi Arabian workers walked out, and there were even riots (*Time*, November 2, 1953), which happened again in 1956 (Niblock and Malik 2007, 33). At that time, there was some suspicion that leftist or worker-oriented views were spreading into Saudi Arabia, a form of political consciousness especially troublesome to employers. Some of the authors who chronicled

Aramco's history or their own experiences admitted the double standards permitted excellent housing for Western workers as compared to poor conditions for Saudi Arabian employees (Brown 1999; Lippman 2004; Vitalis 2009).

Saudization is the name of the official policy intended to result in the employment of more Saudi Arabians in place of foreign workers. It has impacted the service industries and is gradually being enacted in other sectors, for example, the health industry and education, which are two areas important to women's employment. Saudization creates various dilemmas for employers, such as meeting higher salary demands, which may impact their profit margins, and different regulatory procedures. An initial argument was that Saudi Arabians were not as qualified as some technically trained foreign workers, managers, or supervisorial staff. In some industries, education and training have overcome these differences, but in other areas (for instance, in services like hotels), it appears that Saudi Arabian managerial and supervisorial staff are employed, but additional foreign workers accomplish some of their duties. In other areas, such as the health industry (for example, nursing), there were differences in salaries, living conditions, and status that are being addressed through special protocols. Overall, Saudization increases costs for employers. In less-skilled occupations, such as the many workers brought in for construction, the policy is far less likely to impact employment (Lunde 2004).

In certain fields of employment, the hiring of foreign workers is a long-standing practice, not only in Saudi Arabia but in the countries of the Gulf Cooperation Council (GCC) as a whole or even more widely in the region. The hiring of foreign teachers, nurses, doctors, and oil-sector employees on rotating contracts strengthened employers' control over employees. As more Saudi Arabians were employed within the oil industry, many Americans continued to work in the kingdom. The advent of local terrorism and attacks on foreign workers in 2003–2004, as in the attacks at al-Khobar or the kidnapping and beheading of Paul Johnson, created a degree of panic and caused some who had spent most of their careers in the kingdom to retire or return to the West. Predictably, the government was eager to contain these breaches of security and ensure the safety of foreigners as well as their own citizens, which has largely been accomplished (see Chapter 7, Contemporary Issues).

Long-standing debates over women's employment come from social, cultural, and religious attitudes, official policies of segregating—or separating—women from men, and some restrictions within the educational system. On the one hand, this could, and will in the future, create jobs for women who provide services to other women, but, on the other, until women are permitted to work in different sectors, that effect is limited.

One area where women have worked in a mixed environment is in health services, but education, for instance, is segregated. Also, women are restricted at present from studying petroleum engineering and are excluded from military service and employment by the military or security services, except for a section of the Saudi Arabian National Guard. In some cases, it may be difficult for women to obtain higher academic degrees outside of the kingdom, which grants a degree of prestige, because of the overwhelming expectation that they marry, ideally by a certain age. This is why the inclusion of women in the new King Abdullah University for Science and Technology is so important.

Conservatives have attacked governmental initiatives to employ women in the service sectors, arguing that contact between men and women would take place, that women would be endangered by men, or that women should not "take men's jobs." These attacks make it difficult for women to move into new areas of employment. That women would be endangered by men is the main argument against permitting women to drive. That restriction also impacts their employment, because they must have a private vehicle and driver to reach their offices or places of work, a cost that may consume a large portion of their salary.

The government understands and respects the depth of cultural socialization, and, due to the rules of segregation, another factor impeding women's employment had concerned the difficulty of obtaining government permits and permissions, since some offices lacked windows (or desks) that served women (and where they may line up without being in proximity to men). The government did announce the provision of women's desks at all offices. These are not yet operating as well as they might, but they are a move in the right direction. The recent appointment of a woman deputy minister in the government is thought to signal encouragement for women's employment, as are announcements that women advocates (attorneys) will be permitted to practice. Women attorneys now work for legal groups, but men must present briefs. Some women are dubious about the pace of progress, because previous announcements that women were to be employed in the Foreign Ministry were first watered down by the added statement that they might be employed first as secretaries; in addition, these changes have not yet occurred.

In 2010 the general manager of the Jeddah labor office, Qusai al-Filali, announced that Saudi Arabian women will soon be allowed to work as cashiers. United Azizia Panda, which operates more than 100 supermarkets in the country, began a trial program for 16 women cashiers in one of its HyperPanda Jeddah stores (Handley 2010). These announcements elicited protests from conservatives and support for women's employment from others, even though women must be 26 or older, be divorced or widowed, observe Islamic dress requirements (wearing *'abaya* and veils, not the Panda uniform), and work in a sectioned-off women-only or family section of the market. In the *suqs*, some women have always sold goods, but in the newer stores and malls, only small numbers of women sell items in women-only establishments (*Arab News*, August 26, 2010).

Social and cultural expectations that women will manage the domestic responsibilities have also been impacted by the importation of foreign domestic labor. Not everyone can afford to hire such labor, but it became sufficiently prevalent as to spark two types of debates: one concerning the abuses of domestic laborers and the other concerning some families' relinquishing of parenting to maids and other caregivers. Since domestic labor takes place inside private homes, workers are vulnerable in a way they might not be elsewhere.

TRADE AND FINANCE

Saudi Arabia's balance of trade is considered positive as its exports have outstripped imports despite a fall in oil prices since 2008. In 2009, its exports were estimated at $180.5 billion, while 2008 exports were $313.4 billion. These figures were even higher in 2010. Ninety percent of Saudi Arabian exports are petroleum or petroleum-related products (*CIA World Factbook 2010*). Saudi Arabia's nonoil exports came to 8.9 billion riyals by April 2009 (on April 15, 2009, 1 SAR = 0.26668 USD), 5.8 billion riyals of which was from plastics and petrochemicals, which were primarily imported by GCC countries, followed by China (Reuters, July 3, 2010). The largest trading partners for Saudi Arabia's petroleum exports are the United States, which purchases 17.2 percent of the yearly output); South Korea at 10.2 percent; India at 5.9 percent; Taiwan at 4.6 percent; and Singapore at 4.4 percent. In the same period, Saudi Arabia's imports came to $86.61 billion and consisted primarily of machinery, equipment, food, chemicals, textiles, cattle, and motor vehicles. The United States provided the largest share of Saudi Arabia's imports at 12 percent; followed by China, 10.4 percent; Germany, 7.3 percent; South Korea, 5.1 percent; Italy, 4.7 percent; and the United Kingdom, 4 percent. Saudi Arabia's current account balance was estimated at $24.56 billion in 2009, down from $132.6 billion the previous year.

Saudi Arabia's exports are very important to Arab economies, although the income from these exports is far less crucial to Saudi Arabia than that from its exports to world markets. Today, Saudi Arabia is Egypt's largest Arab trading partner, and it has been one of Syria's largest trading partners, Arab or otherwise, since the 1980s. The United Arab Emirates is Saudi Arabia's largest Arab trading partner for its exports (Zuhur 1988; United Nations 2010a, 2010b).

Saudi Arabia's trade with the United States has also involved arms purchases, a politically sensitive aspect of trade that helps uphold the alliance between the two countries. In most years, a gap exists between the value of the arms ordered and those actually delivered, and purchases include not only weaponry and aircraft but also construction and support services. The Gulf War heightened Saudi Arabia's sense of vulnerability and arms purchases; however, reduced oil incomes restricted buying in the 1990s until production cuts again improved country finances. Saudi Arabia has also purchased arms from the United Kingdom and China (see Chapter 7, Contemporary Issues).

Saudi Arabia's investors benefited from the creation of the stock exchange (al-Tadawul), which helped make capital available as well. The Capital Market Authority operated informally in Saudi Arabia beginning in the 1950s until 2003. In 2003 the Capital Market Law was issued in Royal Decree No. 30. Five full-time commissioners were appointed by royal decree, and the Central Market Authority formally established the Tadawul. The stock market most recently peaked in 2006, when its (Tadawul) All Share Index reached 21,000 and a value of $745 billion. Many Saudi Arabians invested, some taking out loans to do so, and then the index fell. The companies that performed best were those in petrochemicals or communications (Niblock and Malik 2007, 217–220). In March 2010, the first Saudi Arabian fund on the Tadawul open to foreign investors was launched; however, they had to have a Saudi Arabian bank account, so direct investment has been limited (*Wall Street Journal*, May 17, 2010). Swap agreements were offered since 2008 through certain brokerages.

At the end of 2010, the Tadawul was at 6,620.75 points, gaining 489.99 points over the previous year. The total value of shares traded was $202.45 billion, less than in the previous year. An example of one of the Saudi Arabian joint stock companies is

Ma'aden, formed in March 1997, which has promoted the gold business, has operated five gold mines, and has branched out into phosphate, aluminum, and other
projects. The market value of publicly traded shares at the end of 2009 was $318.7
billion (*CIA World Factbook 2010*).

Public debt was estimated at 20.3 percent of GDP in 2009, and inflation was
estimated at 5 percent (*CIA World Factbook 2010*). The debt has now been reduced
to 10.3 percent of GDP according to the latest financial information. The country's
reserves of gold and foreign currency were estimated at $410.3 billion at the end of
December 2009. The first two figures reflect some change in a conservative society in
which cash spending is the norm and the use of credit is fairly new. Also, the costs of
certain products, often, but not always, imported goods, are extremely high.

Prior to 2000, foreign investment in the kingdom required a Saudi Arabian partner of at least 25 percent; the investor was required to boost development or technology transfer. The Foreign Capital Investment Committee normally required
51 percent Saudi Arabian ownership. Then, the Law on Foreign Direct Investment
was enacted, allowing for 100 percent foreign-owned companies. Also, they could
acquire land for their activities and for their employees. The Saudi Arabian General
Investment Authority (SAGIA) was to rule on applications by investors within 30
days, thus speeding up the bureaucratic process. An example of the foreign investment promoted through such measures was Alcoa's 2009 arrangement with Ma'aden
to build an aluminum refinery and smelter estimated at a value of $10.8 billion; the
project will begin in 2013–2014.

TAXATION

Numerous sources claim that Saudi Arabia had developed a taxation system but
abandoned it with the first oil boom. In fact, Saudi Arabian citizens are required to
pay *zakat* amounting to 2.5 percent of their income and assets, excluding real estate,
or 2.5 percent of an estimated profit of 15 percent of gross receipts. The Department
of Zakat and Income Tax governs taxation in the kingdom and provides information on a variety of complex topics and treaties. Beyond *zakat*, taxes apply to business income, and non–Saudi Arabian and non-GCC nationals are taxed on business
income in relation to the percentage they hold in a business. If non–Saudi Arabians
own rental real estate, they are taxed 5 percent of the gross rental income. Individuals
do not pay a capital gains tax on the sale of property.

Taxation on corporations depends as well on whether the entity is owned by a
Saudi Arabian or GCC national or by a foreigner from a non-GCC country and also
on the amount of profits. If not owned by a Saudi Arabian or GCC national, then
the company must pay a 25 percent tax on its profits if it makes up to 100,000 Saudi
riyals per year and also must pay capital gains tax (though the company is usually
exempted from paying any home-country tax on amounts taxed by the kingdom).
The taxed amount is 20 percent up from the minimum of 100,000 Saudi riyals to SAR
500,000 and rises to 30 percent on profits of more than SAR 1,000,001. Expenses
for income generation are deductible in calculating the corporation's income. If the

corporation is GCC based, then it pays a *zakat* tax at 2.5 percent (again, based on an estimated profit of 15 percent of gross receipts). Joint-venture companies also exist and are taxed; however, the foreign entity may be granted a tax holiday of up to five years by the Saudi Arabian government. SAGIA is the agency that promotes foreign and domestic investors and therefore must carefully consider the impact of taxation policies.

INVESTMENT

In 1971 the Public Investment Fund (PIF) was established to provide financing to commercial projects that could not be undertaken by the private sector. Applications for financing are made to the Secretariat of the Public Investment Fund and reviewed by its directors. The PIF has established five fully owned companies, including the Saudi Rail Road Company and the Security Exchange Company known as the Tadawul (stock exchange). It had also funded 37 national companies by 2008 and a number of bilateral companies with Arab partners.

As of 2008, the PIF had committed 82,828 million Saudi riyals in loans for refineries in the kingdom as well as to those which export; storage tanks for petroleum products; lubricant refining and processing; iron, steel, fertilizer, and petrochemical factories; pipelines for crude oil and other petroleum products; railroad, water, and electricity projects; a plan for pilgrim accommodations; aircraft purchases for Saudi Arabian Airlines Corporation; and other projects (PIF 2010).

Foreign investment in Saudi Arabia has gone through several phases. Following the initial period of the petroleum industry's expansion, investment in the kingdom was restricted in various ways, until the Foreign Investment Law of April 2000 was approved. At that time, the General Committee for Investment, intended to supervise all private and public investment, was set up under the Supreme Economic Council. The goal of the new law was to attract foreign capital in the interest of diversifying the Saudi Arabian economy (El Sheikh 2003, 22). Other changes meant that foreign companies could sponsor their own employees and own 100 percent of their projects established in the kingdom. These liberalizations were important to the country's accession to the WTO in 2005.

All foreign investment requires a license and may not be engaged in under the name of a Saudi Arabian national. Foreign companies are restricted from 22 areas of operation; for instance, they are not permitted to engage in "upstream activities," which include petroleum exploration, drilling, and production. However, they may engage in upstream gas and mining services. They are not allowed to produce clothing, machinery, or military equipment in the kingdom. Companies are not to provide services to the media, security, educational, military, and retail or distribution sectors. However, when based outside the kingdom, some companies contract with foreign employees who work on a contractual basis in some of these sectors, for instance, in the area of military education. In the past, foreign businesspersons, particularly those with less experience in the Kingdom of Saudi Arabia, generally considered it very difficult to do business there. Official rules and regulations were complex, it took time to obtain permissions and licenses, and many needed to rely on local contacts to understand procedures. The country's rating in this regard has greatly improved according to certain business publications.

BANKING AND FINANCIAL SYSTEMS

As of 2004, the International Monetary Fund judged the Saudi Arabian banking system to be modest but sophisticated and noted that reforms were underway. Eleven commercial banks held about half of the banking assets. In addition, all commercial banks hold universal banking licenses and manage mutual investment funds. Other entities exist in the financial system, three of which are autonomous government institutions—the PIF (mentioned earlier), the General Organization for Social Insurance (GOSI), and the Pension Fund. These manage securities and provide foreign and domestic investments. The Saudi Arabian Monetary Agency manages some of their investments. There are also five specialized credit institutions, all of which extend interest-free loans for public policy purposes (in areas such as housing, agriculture, or industry), and one of these is the aforementioned PIF.

Public ownership is fairly extensive, exceeding 20 percent in five banks and reaching 79 percent in one bank. Foreign bank participation is mainly through substantial equity positions as opposed to majority shareholdings. Six banks have foreign equity stakes of 20 percent or more. Assets of the joint Saudi Arabian–foreign banks accounted for 49 percent of total banking sector assets at the end of 2003, compared with 53 percent in 1998. One interesting feature of banking in Saudi Arabia is the presence of banks for women. The Saudi Arabian National Commercial Bank opened women-only branches in Riyadh and Jeddah in 1980. That bank later opened a special center for women with high-value accounts. A blog devoted to women's banking noted that women control 21 percent of the country's private investments and nearly a fifth of all mutual funds. They outnumber men as new stock investors and also invest in real estate ("Banking on Women," 2010). These observations echoed those of Mona Aboelnaga Kanaan, an investment banker reporting at an international meeting, along with the fact that banking in Saudi Arabia operates to segregate women's money from their husbands' and family members' investments, male bankers' misconceptions that women do not understand investments, and the potential for women to benefit more highly from investments (National Committee on American Foreign Policy, 2005). Sometimes, exceptions are made for women—for example, Nahid Taher heads the Gulf One Investment Bank, which she organized. Taher rose from a position as an economist at the National Commercial Bank; she was the only woman among the 4,000 employees at the bank's headquarters (Andleman 2006).

The GOSI, the Pension Fund, and the PIF have equity ownership in the banking sector. Insurance companies, leasing companies, and licensed money changers make up only 0.3 percent of the financial system (International Monetary Fund based on information from 2004, released 2006, 10). All of the commercial banks offer *shari'ah*-compliant products; however, some offer only such transactions, and others segregate them. Interbank transfers go through the Saudi Arabian Riyal Interbank Express (SARIE) system. A new mortgage market has been developing due to the demand for housing. As one would expect, the financial system is impacted by revenues from oil sales, which rise and fall according to demand and pricing.

ECONOMIC OUTREACH AND AID

Saudi Arabia granted approximately 5.3 percent of its GNP in aid up to 1993 and probably has been giving amounts equal to that since then. As already described, *zakat* is required of all Muslims and should be used to aid the needy and also to promote Islamic study and worship. At the same time, the philanthropic goals required by Islam were promoted through Saudi Arabia's efforts, beginning with King Faysal, to enhance Muslim solidarity on an international level.

The Islamic Development Bank (IDB) was established in 1975. Its goal was to bolster economic development in Muslim countries that are members of the Organization of the Islamic Conference (OIC) as well as Muslim communities outside of these countries. The shareholders of the bank are members of the OIC. The IDB set up the Islamic Corporation for the Development of the Private Sector (ICD) in 1999, the focus of which is on development and strengthening ties between business sectors in Muslim countries. Its initial capital was $1 billion, and spent half of this in its activities until 2008, when that capital base was increased to $2 billion. Within Saudi Arabia, the ICD set up the Iwan Real Estate Development Company and the Anfal Stock Exchange. Investment opportunities have also been opened in Muslim republics of the Russian Federation and in Africa (*Sharq al-Awsat*, May 2, 2010). Apart from the ICD, the IDB, based in Jeddah, is active in development projects. The IDB financed $180 million for road upgrades, school construction, and teacher-training projects in Uzbekistan in 2010 and signed a memorandum with the African Development Bank on December 21, 2010, to jointly fund $1 million worth of projects. The IDB offered two loans totaling $58 million to Mauritania in 2010 for a potable water project and the building of a new roadway. The IDB also offered $5 million in aid to Haiti in 2010 to reconstruct its schools after the devastating earthquake there.

The IDB offers charitable and development funds in addition to the commercial ventures already mentioned, and these are not given only to the citizens of its member states. It has a scholarship fund for academically talented but needy Muslims from nonmember states for university study in Saudi Arabia. This began with 53 students from India, Kenya, and Sri Lanka in 1983–1984. The program now includes many fields of study (not only in Saudi Arabia's large Islamic studies programs) and also funds students for study in other OIC member states. As a member state of the OIC, Saudi Arabia also contributes to the ongoing and emergency needs of Muslim nations. For example, in 2010, Pakistan was hit by the worst floods in its history to date. The OIC announced donations of $1 billion to Pakistan; the contributions came, according to Ekmelledin Ihsanaglu, the head of the OIC, from member states, nongovernmental organizations, institutions within the OIC, and donors who pledged through telethons in Saudi Arabia and also in Turkey, Kuwait, Qatar, and the United Arab Emirates. In 2011, the OIC is expected to create an Emergency Relief Fund (*Rohama.org*, August 30, 2010).

International Aid and Loans

Saudi Arabia is the largest donor of foreign aid after the United States. It is difficult to provide an accurate snapshot of this aid as some of it is granted through international agencies like the World Bank or the OIC (as already described) or agencies of the United Nations (UN), while other actions are reported separately or are not part of Saudi Arabia's official announcements. In addition to governmentally granted aid, large private donors, such as Prince Walid ibn Talal, give important contributions to specific projects, for instance, in Indonesia and other countries. By October 2010, Saudi Arabia had sent five convoys of humanitarian aid, including food and tents, to Pakistan and a total of $354,198,994 in aid and relief had been given to help the flood victims of 2010. In addition, $200 million was transferred to Pakistan's Central Bank, a $100 million loan was given for flood assistance, $200 million in credit was extended by the Saudi Development Fund (SDF), and $120 million had been allocated for Pakistan's energy sector. In addition, the SDF had granted funds to UN relief organizations for Pakistan (Madani, 3rd Friends of Pakistan Conference, reported by Embassy of Saudi Arabia, October 15, 2010).

King 'Abdullah gave $20 million to the SDF to fund the rebuilding of Tintan City in Mauritania, which had been destroyed by flooding. The king also provided aid to rebuild the Parliament Building of Côte d'Ivoire (Ivory Coast), which had been destroyed in a fire. The Saudi Popular Fund for the Relief of Lebanon gave $40,000 to the mufti of Lebanon to rehabilitate a health center. Saudi Arabia funded five projects in Aceh, Indonesia, in 2010, at a cost of more than $4.8 million. Saudi Arabia donated $2 million to the African peacekeeping forces in Darfur. Saudi Arabia also donated $5 million to the Carter Center's Guinea Worm Eradication Program in Africa.

In September 2010, Saudi Arabia provided $100 million to the Palestinian Authority (to the Abbas/Fayad government) to help meet its enormous financial deficit. As a point of reference, U.S. secretary of state Hillary Clinton granted a 2010 year-end grant of $150 million to Abbas; other categories of U.S. assistance are in rule-of-law aid, to the United Nations Relief and Works Agency for Palestinian Refugees in the Near East (UNRWA), and separately to schools (*Bloomberg*, November 10, 2010). A convoy brought 2,000 tons of flour to Gaza in May 2010 as part of the Campaign of the Custodian of Two Holy Mosques King 'Abdullah ibn 'Abd al-'Aziz for the Relief of the Palestinian People in Gaza.

The SDF gave $200 million to Morocco to fund an express train project (*Embassy of Saudi Arabia*, Washington, DC, December 10, 2010). In addition, institutions such as the Prince Salman Center for Disability Research were active in the region; that institute received an award in Algeria and donated the prize money back again. In addition, operations were performed in Saudi Arabia on Palestinian and Iraqi conjoined twins in 2010, and they offered the surgery to Algerian conjoined twins in 2011. A medical team offered some 50 heart surgeries in Yemen in January 2011.

What will Saudi Arabia's economy look like in the future? Certainly, the efforts in human development—providing higher education and training to its youth—will help the country continue the progress it has made.

REFERENCES

Aarts, Paul, and Gerd Nonneman, eds. *Saudi Arabia in the Balance: Political Economy, Society, Foreign Affairs*. New York: New York University Press, 2006.

Ahmed, Osama Saad. "Diversification through Industrialization: The Saudi Experience." In *Change and Development in the Gulf*, edited by Abbas Abdelkarim. London: Macmillan, 1999.

Alajaji, Adel Abdullah. "Obstacles to the Employment of Male Saudi University Graduates by the Private Sector." PhD diss., George Washington University, 1995.

Altorki, Soraya, and Donald P. Cole. *Arabian Oasis City: The Transformation of 'Unayzah*. Austin: University of Texas Press, 1989.

Andleman, David A. "Arabian Diary: From Banking to Racing." *Forbes.com*, February 15, 2006.

Arabian Chevron. *Chevron wa al-Mamlakah al-'arabiyyah al-sa'udiyyah*. Riyadh, Saudi Arabia: Arabian Chevron, 2007.

Bakr, Mohammed A. *A Model in Privatization: Successful Change Management in the Ports of Saudi Arabia*. London: London Center of Arab Studies, 2001.

"Banking on Women." *Birds on the Blog*. May 10, 2010. http://www.birdsontheblog.co.uk/banking-on-women/.

Bronson, Rachel. *Thicker Than Oil: America's Uneasy Partnership with Saudi Arabia*. New York: Oxford University Press, 2006.

Brown, Anthony Cave. *Oil, God, and Gold: The Story of Aramco and the Saudi Kings*. New York: Houghton-Mifflin, 1999.

Bundagji, Fatin Youssef. "Small Businesses and Market Growth in Saudi Arabia." *Arab News*, September 4, 2005.

Central Intelligence Agency (CIA). *World Factbook*. 2010 and 2011. (In some cases, the *Factbook* displays 2010 information.) https://www.cia.gov/library/publications/the-world-factbook/#

Chaudhry, Kiren Aziz. *The Price of Wealth: Economies and Institutions in the Middle East*. Ithaca, NY: Cornell University Press, 1997.

Clark, Arthur C., and Muhammad Tahlawy, eds. Pledge, Thomas et al., contributing eds., and Facey, William, et al., contributing authors. *A Land Transformed: The Arabian Peninsula, Saudi Arabia and Saudi Aramco*. Dhahran, Saudi Arabia, and Houston, TX: Aramco Services, 2006.

Cole, Donald P. "New Homes, New Occupations, New Pastoralism: Al Murrah Bedouin 1968–2003." In *Nomadic Societies in the Middle East and North Africa Entering the Twentieth Century*, edited by Dawn Chatty. Leiden, the Netherlands: Brill, 2006, 370–392.

Cole, Donald P. "Bedouin and Social Change in Saudi Arabia." In *Change and Development in Nomadic and Pastoral Societies*, edited by John G. Galaty and Philip Carl Salzman. Leiden, the Netherlands: Brill, 1981, 128–149.

Cole, Donald P. "Pastoral Nomads in a Rapidly Changing Economy: The Case of Saudi Arabia." In *Social and Economic Development in the Arab Gulf*, edited by Tim Niblock. New York: St. Martin's, 1980, 106–121.

Cole, Donald P. *Nomads of the Nomads: The Al Murrah Bedouin of the Empty Quarter*. Chicago: Aldine, 1975.

Colyer-Ross, Heather. *The Art of Arabian Costume: A Saudi Arabian Profile*. Fribourg, Switzerland: Arabesque Commercial, 1981.

Congressional Research Service. Albert B. Prados (Author) *Saudi Arabia: Current Issues and U.S. Relations*. Washington, DC: Congressional Research Service, Foreign Affairs, Defense and Trade Division, Library of Congress, February 24, 2006.

Cordesman, Anthony H., and Khalid R. Al-Rodhan. *The Changing Dynamics of Energy in the Middle East*. 2 vols. Westport, CT: Praeger Security International, 2006.

Cypher, James M., and James L. Dietz. *The Process of Economic Development*. London: Routledge, 1997.

El Sheikh, Fath al-Rahman Abdalla. *The Legal Regime of Foreign Private Investment in Sudan and Saudi Arabia*. Cambridge: Cambridge University Press, 1984 and 2003.

Evans, Peter. *Embedded Autonomy: States and Industrial Transformation*. Princeton, NJ: Princeton University Press, 1995.

ExxonMobil Corporation. *2007 Summary Annual Report*. Irving, TX: ExxonMobil Corporation, 2008.

Fabietti, Ugo. "Between Two Myths: Underproductivity and Development of the Bedouin Domestic Group." *Cahiers Sciences et Humanites* 26, nos. 1–2 (1990), 237–253.

Facey, William. "Al-'Udhaibat: Building on the Past." *Aramco World* 50, no. 3 (July/August 1999), 32–46.

Facey, William. *Back to Earth: Adobe Building in Saudi Arabia*. Riyadh, Saudi Arabia: Al Turath and St. Martin's, 1997.

Handley, Paul. "Saudi Supermarket Breaks Taboo with Women Cashiers." *Zawya.com*, August 25, 2010.

Hertog, Steffan. "Segmented Clientelism: The Political Economy of Saudi Economic Reform Efforts." In *Saudi Arabia in the Balance: Political Economy, Society, and Foreign Affairs*, edited by Paul Aarts and Gerd Nonneman. London: Hurst, 2005, 111–143.

Hilden, Joy Totah. *Bedouin Weaving of Saudi Arabia and Other Countries*. London: Arabian Publishing; Oakfield, CT: David Brown, 2010.

Hilden, Joy May (Totah) "The Use of Wasm (Animal Brands) in Beduin Weavings." BeduinWeaving.com, n.d. http://www.beduinweaving.com.

Hopper, Mathew S. "Pearls, Globalization and the African Diaspora in the Arabian Gulf in the Age of Empire." Paper presented at the 124th Annual Meeting of the American Historical Association, San Diego, January 9, 2010.

Hopper, Mathew S. "The African Presence in Arabia: Slavery, the World Economy, and the African Diaspora in Eastern Arabia, 1840–1940." PhD diss., University of California, Los Angeles, 2006.

Human Rights Watch. "Saudi Arabia: Events of 2009." 2010a. http://www.hrw.org.

Human Rights Watch. "Saudi Arabia: Free Trapped Workers." April 23, 2010b. http://www.hrw.org.

Ibrahim, Saad Eddin and Donald P. Cole. *Saudi Arabian Bedouin: An Assessment of Their Needs*. Cairo: American University in Cairo, 1978.

International Monetary Fund. "Saudi Arabia: Financial System Stability Assessment, Including Reports on Observance of Standards and Codes on the Following Topics, Monetary and Financial Policy Transparency, Banking Supervision and Payment Systems." IMF Country Report No. 06/199, June 2006.

Keating, Allison. *Mirage: Power, Politics and the Hidden History of Arabian Oil*. Amherst, NY: Prometheus Books, 2005.

Kirk, Anthony. *A Flier in Oil: Adolph B. Spreckels and the Rise of the California Petroleum Industry*. San Francisco: California Historical Society, 2000.

Krimly, Rayed. "The Political Economy of Adjusted Priorities: Declining Oil Revenues and Saudi Fiscal Policies." *Middle East Journal* 53, no. 2 (Spring 1999), 254–267.

Lacey, Robert. *Inside the Kingdom: Kings, Clerics, Modernists, Terrorists and the Struggle for Saudi Arabia*. New York: Viking Penguin, 2009.

Lacey, Robert. *The Kingdom*. New York: Harcourt Brace Jovanovich, 1981.

Lawton, John. "Arab Aid." *Aramco World* 30, no. 6 (November/December 1979). http://www.saudiaramcoworld.com/issue/197906/arab.aid-how.it.s.spent.htm

Lippman, Thomas W. *Inside the Mirage: America's Fragile Partnership with Saudi Arabia*. Boulder, CO: Westview, 2004.

Long, David. "The Hajj and Its Impact on Saudi Arabia and the Muslim World." *Saudi-Arabian Forum*, February 2003. Reposted on Saudi-U.S. Relations Information Service website, December 16, 2007, http://www.saudi-us-relations.org/articles/2007/ioi/071216-long-hajj.html

Lunde, Paul. "Saudization: A Useful Tool in the Kingdom's Battle against Unemployment?" *Journal of South Asian and Middle Eastern Studies* 27, no. 3 (Spring 2004).

Maass, Peter. *Crude World: The Violent Twilight of Oil*. New York: Alfred A. Knopf, 2009.

Malik, Monica, and Tim Niblock. "Saudi Arabia's Economy: The Challenge of Reform." In *Saudi Arabia in the Balance: Political Economy, Society, and Foreign Affairs*, edited by Paul Aarts and Gerd Nonneman. London: Hurst, 2005, 85–110.

Marcel, Valérie. *Oil Titans: National Oil Companies in the Middle East*. London: Chatham House, 2006.

Mauger, Thierry. *Impressions of Arabia: Architecture and Frescoes of the Asir Region*. Paris: Flammarion-Pere Casto, 1996.

Ministry of Planning, Kingdom of Saudi Arabia. *Eighth Development Plan, 2005–2009*. Riyadh, Saudi Arabia: Ministry of Planning, 2005.

Ministry of Planning, Kingdom of Saudi Arabia. *Seventh Development Plan 2000–2004*. Riyadh, Saudi Arabia: Ministry of Planning, 2000.

Mohamedi, Fareed, "Economics." In *Saudi Arabia: A Country Study*, edited by Helen Chapin Metz, Federal Research Division, Library of Congress. 1993. (First edition 1992, based on the Nyrop, ed., of the same name.)

Moinuddin, Hassan. *The Charter of the Islamic Conference and Legal Framework of Economic Cooperation among Its Member States*. New York: Oxford University Press, 1987.

al-Naqeeb, Khaldoun Hasan. *Society and State in the Gulf and Arabian Peninsula*. Translated by L. M. Kenny. London: Routledge, 1990.

National Committee on American Foreign Policy. *Summary and Recommendations from the Roundtable on Arab Women and the Future of the Middle East.* New York: National Committee on American Foreign Policy, 2005. http://www.ncafp.org/articles/05 percent20Arab percent20Women percent20Mideast percent20Rept percent204–05.pdf

Niblock, Tim, with Monica Malik. *The Political Economy of Saudi Arabia.* London: Routledge, 2007.

Obaid, Nawaf E. *The Oil Kingdom at 100: Petroleum and Policymaking in Saudi Arabia.* Washington, DC: Washington Institute for Near East Policy, 2000.

Okruhlik, Mary G. "Debating Profits and Political Power: Private Business and Government in Saudi Arabia." PhD diss., University of Texas, Austin, 1992.

Pelletiere, Stephen. *Iraq and the International Oil System: Why America Went to War in the Gulf.* Westport, CT: Praeger, 2001.

Pint, Susana. "The Roses of Taif." Desert Caves Project. 2005. http://www.saudicaves.com/saudi/roses.html.

Pryor, Stephen D. "Learning from the Saudi Arabian Model: Innovating through Energy Transition." Speech to the Global Competitiveness Forum, Riyadh, Saudi Arabia, January 24, 2010.

Public Investment Fund, Ministry of Finance, Kingdom of Saudi Arabia. 2010. http://www.mof.gov.sa/en/docs/ests/sub_invbox.htm.

Romahi, Mohamed A. *The Saudi Arabian Economy: Policies, Achievements and Challenges.* New York: Springer, 2005.

Simmons, Matthew. *Twilight in the Desert: The Coming Saudi Oil Shock and the World Economy.* Hoboken, NJ: John Wiley, 2005.

Topham, John. *Traditional Crafts of Saudi Arabia.* London: Stacey International, 1981.

Unger, Craig. *House of Bush, House of Saud: The Secret Relationship between the World's Two Most Powerful Dynasties.* New York: Scribner, 2004.

United Nations. "Saudi Arabia." *World Statistics Pocketbook.* 2010a. http://data.un.org.

United Nations. "Syria." *World Statistics Pocketbook.* 2010b. http://data.un.org.

United States Energy Information Administration. Saudi Arabia, Background and Information. 2010. Available at http://www.fas.org/sgp/crs/mideast/RL33533.pdf.

Vitalis, Robert. *America's Kingdom: Mythmaking on the Saudi Oil Frontier.* New York: Verso, 2009.

Wallerstein, Immanuel. *Semi-Peripheral Countries and The Contemporary World Crisis.* New York: Academic Press, 1974.

Yergin, Daniel. *The Prize: The Epic Quest for Oil, Money, and Power.* New York: Touchstone (Simon and Schuster), 1991.

CHAPTER 5

Society

Religion and Law

The official religion of Saudi Arabia is Islam. The majority of Muslims in the kingdom belong to the Sunni division of Islam. Ten to fifteen percent are Shi'a Muslims, primarily of the Ja'fari legal tradition, while a smaller minority of somewhere between 300,000 and 700,000 are indigenous Isma'ili Muslims, a different variety of Shi'ism. An unknown but small number of Sunni Muslims follow philosophical, theological, or legal traditions other than the majority Hanbali Sunni group, including followers of the legal tradition of Anas ibn Malik, known as the Maliki school (*madhhab*), and Sufi Muslim traditions. Non–Saudi Arabian Muslims may also follow the Shafi'i or Hanafi legal traditions.

Shi'a Islam developed from a dispute over political leadership. Following 'Ali ibn Abu Talib's assassination (see Chapter 2, History), his son Husayn disputed the caliph Mu'awiyya's leadership and the right of his son, Yazid, to succeed him when Mu'awiyya died. Mu'awiyya's Ummayyad troops killed Husayn at Karbala, but his followers, the Party of 'Ali (Shi'at 'Ali), even in defeat, rejected the legitimacy of the Ummayyads, and a serious revolt against Yazid broke out in Medina. Over time, the Shi'a Muslims came to hold distinct beliefs about leadership, such as the authority of the imamate (*a'ima*); imams are leaders with charismatic power who designated their successors. One branch of the Shi'a believe that their Twelfth Imam (who disappeared into occultation) will return, while others recognize a different descent order of imams. The Twelver Shi'a in Saudi Arabia commemorate the death of Husayn at Karbala on 'Ashura, but they have been forbidden to publicly celebrate the holiday and follow a different school of *shari'ah* than their Sunni compatriots. Many of the

Shi'a and Khawarij groups (early advocates of 'Ali) settled in the Arabian Gulf. As well, northern Yemen is home to the Zaydi Shi'a Muslims.

The majority of Sunni Muslims in Saudi Arabia, including the state-employed clerics and scholars and educational institutions, follow the legal school of Ahmad ibn Hanbal (d. 855 CE/241h.). Most of these are guided by the teachings of Muhammad ibn 'Abd al-Wahhab (1703–1791), the 18th-century preacher who allied with the Sa'ud family, and the socioreligious movement he inspired. These are called *muwahhidun* (monotheists) or, outside of Saudi Arabia, Wahhabiyya, anglicized as Wahhabis. The tribal supporters who fought to uphold Muhammad al-Sa'ud and spread 'Abd al-Wahhab's ideas were revived in the Ikhwan, or brotherhood, by Ibn Sa'ud.

The legal school (*madhhab*) of Ahmad ibn Hanbal (780–855), which is prevalent in Saudi Arabia, differs from the Shaf'i, Maliki, and Hanafi *madhahib*. Ibn Hanbal was a firm Traditionist, relying on the Qur'an and hadith. He gathered the *Musnad al-Imam Ahmad*, a six-volume collection of *ahadith*. Ibn Hanbal also issued *fatawa* (legal decisions), which his students collected. He based his decisions on the Qur'an and the *sunnah*, the *fatawa* of the Prophet's Companions in Medina (unless they contradicted the Qur'an or *sunnah*, the hadith of the Companions, and after that the weaker hadith, and then, only if necessary, *qiyas* (reasoning by analogy). Ibn Hanbal survived a great philosophical and theological clash that took place in his lifetime. He opposed the movement of the *mutakallimun* (those who used logic in a form of argumentation called *kalam*) and withstood that movement's inquisition and torture (Hurvitz 2002, 1–21). He provided some reconciliatory positions on questions that had divided Muslims by creating an order of preference for the Companions of the Prophets, defending the caliph's right to choose his successor, and calling for obedience to the imam, as long as he met his duties (Abdul Rauf in Cornell, ed., 2007, 200). He opposed Shi'i and Khariji claims that essentially detracted from the legitimacy of the ruling caliphs, and responded to such claims using the preceding points. When the followers of 'Abd al-Wahhab came to dominate the Arabian Peninsula in 1773 by capturing Riyadh, the Hanbali school became the official legal stance of the al-Sa'ud and, eventually, today's Saudi Arabia. The Wahhabiyya are, however, willing to reject a Hanbali interpretation, if they can prove it wrong; and they exercise *ijtihad*, or juristic interpretation, a source of Islamic law that the other Sunni schools ceased to use in the 10th century.

Two to three million non-Muslims work in the Kingdom of Saudi Arabia: Christians, Buddhists, Hindus, and others. Christians and Jews (and Samaritans and the Sabeans) are called the *ahl al-kitab*, or "People of the Book," as they possess a scripture, a divine message, and believe in Allah, the One God. As *ahl al-kitab*, they must be allowed to follow their own religion. Yet they must abide by the principles of Islamic law while living in Saudi Arabia and not involve any Muslims in sinful activity. Non-Muslims may not worship publicly; this is meant to discourage any violence against them by the salafists or other conservatives. They may not proselytize and must abide by the aspects of Islamic law that are enforced as public policy. Most of the time, authorities permit them to worship in private homes, but anything that could be construed as tools for proselytizing, such as the importing of Bibles, is punished. It is claimed that Jews are not allowed to travel to Saudi Arabia; however, this is untrue. Saudi Arabia does not recognize Israel, not because it is a Jewish state, but rather because of its illegal occupation of Palestinian territory and ill treatment of Palestinians since 1948.

In certain circles religious antipathy to non-Muslims increased during the 1990s, and this intolerance along with political resentment of the West was manifested in the attacks by al-Qa'ida on foreigners in Saudi Arabia (see Chapter 7, Contemporary Issues). Religious justification for such attacks was related to the insistence on *al-wala' wa-l-bara'*, a call to cleave to Muslims and stay far from non-Muslims. While this phrase comes from the Qur'anic call to support the Muslim community, it became a favorite stance of extremists in order to emphasize in-group status and strife between Muslims and non-Muslims. It was not at all evident in the attitude of generations of Saudi Arabians who studied and sometimes resided abroad. The Qur'an states unambiguously that some Christians are righteous; however, other verses refer to battles early in Islam's history and speak of the enmity of nonbelievers toward believers. This has created a type of religious chauvinism that the government began to address in 2007. Before the rise, or resurgence, of militant salafism in Saudi Arabia, the question of whether Muslims should engage in *hijrah* (immigration) to the West had been answered by 'Abd al-'Aziz Siddiq, who said that residence in the West for education and employment was permitted and that the position that the countries bound in pacts with Muslim nations no longer needed to be designated as *dar al-kufr* (the lands or domain of unbelief) for the reasons of ensuring Muslim safety ('Abd al-'Aziz Siddiq 1985, 51, 12–13).

Saudi Arabia is wrongly labeled a theocracy and accused of merging religion and politics. This is far from the ideal in Islam. In the earliest decades of Muslim rule, the caliphs of the Ummayyad and Abbasid empires claimed religious legitimacy. A religious class of scholars eventually asserted their independence from the rulers

An historic edition of the Qur'an, the holy book of Muslims. (Larry Sampas)

during the 10th and 11th centuries. These are the *'ulama* (those who possess *'ilm*, or religious knowledge), and they may be trained to issue *fatawa*, teach (see section on education in this chapter), and guide Muslims. They were generally not supposed to involve themselves in politics and had the right to criticize the political leadership if it violated religious principles or was unjust. As historian Peter von Sivers has explained, "caesaropapism" was rejected in Islam (von Sivers 1992, 255). The caliphs and, beginning in the 10th century, the sultans or other rulers were supposed to govern in accordance with Islamic law and consult with the *'ulama*. There is no central authority or pope in Islam, nor can any ruler declare simultaneous political and religious leadership.

The message of Islam is conveyed in the Qur'an, the word of Allah, delivered in Arabic by the angel Gabriel to the Prophet Muhammad in a series of revelations over 23 years. The language of the Qur'an is considered the most beautiful and perfect possible, based on the "high" Arabic of the seventh century. It was forbidden to translate the Qur'an, and translations cannot convey the rhythms and emphasis of its language. Translations have been carried out, but they are entitled "interpretations" and often add explanatory notes.

Following the *mihna* (inquisition) in Ibn Hanbal's era, the winning faction declared that the Qur'an was "uncreated"—meaning it was not written by human beings. Literary analysis of the Qur'an displays poetic and rhetorical forms of that age (see Chapter 6, section on literature), and, indeed, the Prophet Muhammad's enemies in Mecca "classed him with the poets and soothsayers, who in the common belief were inspired by genii (*jinn*)" (Gibb 1974, 35), a claim he rejected. After Muhammad and his followers left for Yathrib (Medina) in the *hijrah* (emigration) in 622 CE (see Chapter 2, History), they established their rituals and rules of social interaction and war as interpreted from the Qur'anic verses (Ibn Ishaq as given in Guillaume 1955). The Qur'an insists on social justice, monotheism, and ethical and social practice, which distinguished the Muslims from their native families in Mecca. The Muslims were still endangered by the Meccans and fought with them, bearing the Qur'an as a standard.

The first revelation of the Qur'an to Muhammad ibn 'Abdullah on Mount Hira began when the angel Gabriel commanded "Iqra'!" (Recite!) three times. Muhammad asked what he should "read," and the angel recited the first five *ayat* (verses, and also signs) of Surah 96. After a pause in revelation, the Qur'an was revealed in sections (singular, *surah*; plural, *surat*) over the course of 22 years until Muhammad's death. Passages that had direct relevance for the Prophet Muhammad and his followers led to the field of *asbab* (causes) of revelation in Qur'anic study and to the field of *naskh*, which examines abrogating and abrogated verses (verses that are contradicted by later verses). The 114 Qur'anic *surat* are arranged from longest to shortest in length, and *surat* are identified according to whether they were revealed in Mecca or in Medina. The Prophet's Companions and some of his wives had collections of the Qur'an, and other collections were made. Eventually, seven valid readings of the Qur'an were accepted (Ayoub 1992; Goldziher 1970; al-Sa'id 1975).

The Qur'an's theological importance is twofold, in its declaration of monotheism and guidance concerning human accountability. God, or Allah, is declared to be perfect, merciful, omnipotent, and all-knowledgeable (57:33). He is One and not a trinity, and his qualities are described in 99 names. The duty of every person is to submit to Allah, and that is the action of *islam*. Human beings must obey Allah's commands and be true to them in intent as well as deed, not acting merely to avoid punishment or when it is easy or convenient. Muslims must treat and interact with others as Allah commands, in a righteous and moral manner. Otherwise, they will be punished in hell, whereas if they follow the straight path, the way of Islam, their souls will proceed to paradise. Muslims believe in a Day of Judgment when all souls will be resurrected and held to account for themselves.

The Qur'an also serves as a source of *shari'ah* (Islamic law is the usual translation of this term, but actually it applied to *fiqh*; *shari'ah* is larger than interpreted law and encompasses the lifestyle or code of behavior and intent of Islam) and is studied for this specific reason, as well as being read by all Muslims and memorized if possible. That which is forbidden in the Qur'an is also forbidden in *fiqh*, Islamic jurisprudence. The exegesis of the Qur'an is called *tafsir*, and its interpretations have varied in different ways. The Qur'an contains references to texts and prophets of the Bible. This has sometimes confused Western readers; the Qur'an's affirmation of the previous revelations must be remembered.

The importance of the Qur'an and Islam in Saudi Arabia cannot be overemphasized. It is taught in all educational settings and is considered the country's constitution. The *shari'ah* and its goals of protecting life, intellect, property, belief, and inheritance are constantly brought into debates about the degree of change that can be tolerated in the kingdom. Living according to the *sunnah* of the Prophet is also an extremely important goal. Muslims do not worship the Prophet, yet many try to follow his example by repeating or performing supernumerary prayer or fasting, growing their beards because he wore one, wearing a shorter *thob* (robe) that reaches only to the ankle, using henna, and engaging in other customs popular with the *salafi* trend.

The teachings of Muhammad ibn 'Abd al-Wahhab and his followers have uniquely influenced Saudi Arabia. 'Abd al-Wahhab believed Qur'anic instruction should be required for all women as well as men, but that understanding of the text should be the goal of that instruction. Memorization, or parroting the teachings of others about the Qur'an, was insufficient. Ibn 'Abd al-Wahhab did not provide a full written *tafsir* (interpretation of the Qur'an), but he typically provided active interpretation in his discussions with his followers. Instead of citing other interpreters; he often chose a Qur'anic verse to discuss or cited one at the end of a discussion about a particular issue. The *'ulama* (clerics) of his time opposed his teaching methodology, just as he decried their reliance on memorization and blind imitation (*taqlid*). He also opposed the claims of those *ashraf* (descendants of the Prophet) who claimed to have esoteric knowledge of the Qur'an and who demanded deferential treatment from ordinary believers. Ibn 'Abd al-Wahhab also took issue with Sufi and Shi'i claims to esoteric knowledge (Delong-Bas 2004, 42–44). The institution of the *a'ima*, the charismatic leadership of specially designated imams beginning with Ibn 'Ali ibn Abu Talib, smacked of associationism to Ibn 'Abd al-Wahhab, as did the Shi'a's belief in the absent (*gha'ib*) Twelfth Imam. In this, Ibn 'Abd al-Wahhab was not unique; his anti-Shi'ism was prefaced by Ibn Taymiyya. He and his followers strongly opposed the Shi'a visitations to their leaders' graves and reverence for their masters, as well as ecstatic Sufi rituals, calling them an unlawful *bid'a* (innovation).

The King Fahd Complex for the Printing of the Holy Qur'an was established in 1982 in Medina to print officially recognized editions and translations of the Qur'an (at least 55 editions in 39 languages) and audiotapes of its recitations. The Ministry of Islamic Affairs, Endowments (*Awqaf*), *Da'wah*, and Guidance (see the following) supervises the complex, which contains the Qur'anic Studies Center, also dedicated to the preservation of Qur'ans, and a training and technical qualification center. (*Da'wah* is the "mission" of Islam, or education about Islam and propagation of its creed.) As part of the Islamic *da'wah* Saudi Arabia has distributed many editions of the Qur'an and other religious materials to Muslims elsewhere in the world; the country supports religious training, Qur'an memorization, and Islamic studies.

ISLAMIC LAW

Muslims must follow Islamic law, or *shari'ah*. In Saudi Arabia, law is a matter of religion and vice versa. The *shari'ah* is a complex, evolving body of rulings that has not been codified in Saudi Arabia. Some understanding of *shari'ah* is essential to understand the Saudi Arabian environment and religious process as well as the critiques levied against Saudi Arabia by external agencies like Amnesty International or Human Rights Watch.

The purpose of the *shari'ah* is to guide Muslims, who, if they are faithful to Allah's edicts, will attain paradise. Crimes that hurt the community are the most heinous, and those considered most severe are mentioned in the Qur'an. These may warrant a severe punishment called *hadd* (plural, *hudud*), such as stoning, or lashing for adultery or fornication, and these punishments were carried out in public to serve as an object lesson. Judges are supposed to operate via precedent, and a complex judicial system is overseen by the government.

The basis of Islamic legal judgments are found in the Qur'an, but where it offers no specific guidance, Muslims consult the *ahadith* (singular, *hadith*). These short texts relate the Prophet's practice, behavior, remarks, and beliefs, and sometimes those of his wives or Companions. They are preceded by a chain of transmitters (called an *isnad*), and the *isnad* are accordingly judged as being weak or sound depending on the persons in the chain of transmitters. Additionally, if there is a single occurrence of a particular hadith, it may be considered weak, whereas one that occurs multiple times may be judged "sound."

Other major Islamic legal principles are *qiyas*, or a type of analogy, in determining the licitness of any action or behavior, and the principle of *ijma'*, which means consensus. Some sources claim that the followers of Ibn 'Abd al-Wahhab do not use *ijma'* or state that Wahhabists reject the legal interpretations of the four classical legal schools. Although this claim has been made by certain leading scholars and opponents of Wahhabism (Asgari 2011), this is not an accurate version of Ibn 'Abd al-Wahhab's legal stance. Ibn 'Abd al-Wahhab defined *ijma'* in two particular ways. The first was as the consensus of the Companions of the Prophet, because they actually lived alongside the Prophet and could consult him. The second type of *ijma'* is that of legal scholars. 'Abd al-Wahhab found this type of consensus to be rare, and only when there was absolute agreement between the scholars did he invoke it and believe it incumbent on Muslims. He invoked this type of consensus, for instance, when he was trying to reform the prevalent bribery and corruption then practiced by some judges, in a question about repossessing the property of a debtor (Delong-Bas 2004, 98–99). The final methodology is *ijtihad*, a juristic interpretation. The Shi'a qualify certain jurists, *mujtahid*s, to use it, but Sunni schools other than Ibn Hanbal's stopped using it in the 10th century. When any legal question arises, a jurist capable of issuing a *fatwa* must consider the preceding sources of Islamic law to determine whether the action or issue in question is licit in Islam (*halal*) or unlawful (*haram*), neutral, recommended, or reprehensible.

ISLAMIC DUTIES

The basic rituals of Islam are practiced in Saudi Arabia. The five obligatory practices are often called the Five Pillars and include the testimony of faith (*shahadah*), which is the uttering of the phrase: "There is no God, but Allah; and Muhammad is his Messenger." The second requirement is the daily prayers (*salat*). Prayer is announced by a loud or broadcast call (*adhan*) at dawn, noon, midafternoon, sunset, and evening. While prayer is obligatory for all Muslims, in Saudi Arabia, businesses, schools, and institutions must cease all other activities at prayer time to allow employees or students to pray, which they do after ablutions called *wudu'*, facing Mecca. It is common to see individuals praying wherever they may be in Saudi Arabia, and the direction of

Pilgrims perform the noon prayer at the Prophet Muhammad's Mosque in Medina, Saudi Arabia, February 26, 2002. (AP/Wide World Photos)

prayer (*qibla*) is indicated on aircraft so that Muslims can orient themselves correctly. Attendance at the communal prayer on Friday, when a sermon is given, is obligatory for men but not for women.

The fast (*sawm*) of Ramadan, the ninth month of the Islamic calendar, is the third requirement. Nothing must pass the lips during daylight hours—no food, beverages, and no smoking of cigarettes; however, the fast is broken just after sunset. Fasting was practiced in pre-Islamic Arabia during three sacred months and also in the month of Rajab. Ramadan supplanted these fasts, and it is a religious obligation as compared to other supernumerary fasts. It is traditional in Saudi Arabia to break the fast by eating dates. The fasting month is a time for reflection, reading of the Qur'an, and gatherings of families and friends for an evening meal, called an *iftar*. Another meal (*suhur*) is served in the early morning hours before the dawn prayer. Numerous traditions are attached to Ramadan; for instance, the government may offer amnesties or release prisoners on this occasion, and gifts of money are given to employees, as they are at the Lesser Feast, or 'Id al-Fitr, which celebrates the end of the fasting month. In Saudi Arabia, fasting is considered obligatory, except for those who are ill, and no restaurants or food services are open in the daytime hours. Ramadan festivities have a carnival-like atmosphere in some parts of the Muslim world, and over the years, the month on the *hijri* calendar moves from the winter months to the summer months and back again. When Harry St. John Bridger Philby (known as Jack Philby or Shaykh 'Abdullah), then part of the British military intelligence and later an adviser to King 'Abd al-'Aziz, observed Ramadan in 1918, it came at the height of summer and there was a full 15 hours of fasting. The nights of Ramadan were spent praying rather than in festivities (Philby 1928, 3–7, 11–13, cited in Goitein 2006, 167). Muslims regard the last 10 days of Ramadan as particularly important. One of these nights is the *laylat al-qadr*, the Night of Power, the night on which the first revelation of the Qur'an was delivered.

Zakat, or charity, is the fourth pillar. It is a tax of 2.5 percent of a Muslim's income and assets and is supposed to support the poor and also promote Islamic institutions. A Department of Zakat operates in the Kingdom of Saudi Arabia. As explained in Chapter 4, Economics, *zakat* is considered a government requirement, not only a requirement of individuals, and thus it is an important feature of charity and philanthropy abroad and at home. Mosques typically have a box for *zakat* offerings; however, after concerns about terrorists who allegedly took these funds and coupons, safer measures for *zakat* were to be instituted.

The fifth pillar of Islam is the *hajj*, a mandatory pilgrimage at least once in a lifetime to the Holy City of Mecca and its environs in the western province of the Hijaz. During the *hajj*, pilgrims follow rules of ritual purification and don special clothing. Numerous beliefs about the *hajj* rituals are bolstered by the *ahadith* (Lazarus-Yafeh in Hawling, ed., 2006, 24–30). Muslims believe, and are told by their local imams in other parts of the world, that the sins of those who pray in Mecca will be erased or that a prayer made at the Black Stone (of the Ka'ba) and its circumambulation count for thousands of prayers made elsewhere. The Ka'ba is a cube-shaped building in the center of the Grand Mosque in Mecca, considered Allah's house on earth. The prophet Ibrahim (Abraham) and his son Isma'il (Ishmael) rebuilt it on the founda-

Muslim pilgrims perform their final circumambulation around the Ka'ba at the Grand Mosque, November 30, 2009. In the foreground a man raises his palms in supplication. (AFP/Getty Images)

tions of a Ka'ba first erected by Adam or angels. Muhammad cleansed the Ka'ba of pagan idols. It was henceforth the center of Islamic pilgrimage, and Muslims face it during prayer. The *hajj* gives Muslims a sense that their lives are related to their fate in the hereafter, and it unites them as Muslims in a common visit to God's house. Philosophers, religious leaders, and modern reinterpreters of Islam have all written about the meaning of the *hajj*.

The water of the Zamzam spring near Mecca is considered holy, and pilgrims drink it. Pilgrims attempt (but do not succeed due to the crowds) to kiss the Black Stone, which will rise like a bride on the Day of Judgment. Muslims believe that if they die before their return home, they are assured of paradise. The preceding rituals can be shortened because of the extreme overcrowding, and even if one is missed (such as not being able to hit a pillar, spend the entire night at Muzdalifa, or kiss the Black Stone), the pilgrimage is still valid (Bianchi 2004, 9, 10–16).

As there is great demand by Muslims to participate in *hajj*, the annual influx of pilgrims has strongly impacted Saudi Arabia's economics and politics. The government of Saudi Arabia, namely the king and the Sa'udi royal family, are considered and bear the title of the Guardians of the Holy Mosques (at Mecca and Medina). They are, in essence, the managers of the *hajj*. Under Ayatollah Khomeini, Iran tried to persuade other Muslim countries to put the control of the *hajj* under a shared Muslim apparatus. The Organization of the Islamic Conference (OIC), established by King Faysal, is an international body that meets and determines the quotas of pilgrims from different countries and the rules that guide their selection. The Asian

PERFORMANCE AND STAGES OF THE *HAJJ*

1. On the first day, the *ihram*, the clothing of a pilgrim is donned. Pilgrims enter the sacred area outside of Mecca. They chant the *talbiyya* (a greeting to Allah said in unison) on the way to Mecca. And they perform the *tawwaf* (circumambulation) of arrival around the Ka'ba before the eighth day of the *hajj*.

2. Pilgrims camp at Mina on the night of the eighth day of the pilgrimage.

3. All pilgrims assemble at the Plain of 'Arafat for the Day of Standing. This commemorates the Prophet Muhammad's address to the Muslims when he declaimed the final verses of the Qur'an a few months before he died when on his final pilgrimage. It is believed one's prayers reach Allah more easily here than anywhere else.

4. Pilgrims depart Arafat after sundown on the ninth day and then camp at the valley of Muzdalifa, where they each gather 70 pebbles to use the next day.

5. Pilgrims arrive in Mina on the 10th day, Dhu al-Hija. They throw the pebbles (stones) at three pillars representing Satan. This commemorates Ibrahim's throwing of stones at Satan when Satan tempted him to disobey Allah's command to sacrifice Isma'il. Today's pilgrims try to hit the first pillar before noon. Then they offer a sacrifice of an animal that represents Allah's allowing Ibrahim to sacrifice a ram instead of his son. The day is celebrated as 'Id al-Adha (the Feast of the Sacrifice), by all Muslims, whether they are on the *hajj* or not. The *ihram* is removed.

6. On the 10th or 11th day, the pilgrims return to Mecca and carry out a second *tawwaf*. Then they run back and forth seven times between the hills of al-Safa and al-Marwa to commemorate Isma'il's mother Hajar's frantic search for water. It culminated in her discovery of the waters of Zamzam.

7–9. Pilgrims travel between Mecca and Mina; all three pillars should be stoned; and pilgrims stay the night in Mina on the 11th to 13th nights.

10. On the 12th day or after, the *tawwaf* of farewell is performed at Mecca, and the pilgrims depart the *hajj* (Bianchi 2004, 9).

and African countries within the OIC supported Saudi Arabia's continued management of the *hajj*, but they demanded some internationalization of the process (Bianchi 2004, 5). Saudi Arabian pilgrims are permitted to attend the *hajj* during *hajj* season only once every five years in order to be fair to the international pilgrims. The government also issues visas for the lesser pilgrimage, the *'umrah*, so that those who cannot visit during the *hajj* season may visit during a less-crowded time. Going on the *'umrah* is considered *sunnah* (a deed blessed by the Prophet's practice but not required).

The responsibility for performing all of these duties falls on the individual, and observance varies. Travelers and those who are ill are exempted from prayer and fasting; menstruating women are exempt from fasting, and those who have recently given birth are not to pray. Those who are able, make up their days of fasting later.

Muslims who are infirm and cannot pray in the normal postures of bowing and prostrating themselves may sit on a chair and pray.

Unlike in Egypt or Jordan, where the governments have not generally permitted Muslims to enforce practice on others, in Saudi Arabia, the followers of 'Abd al-Wahhab believed it was the duty of the ruler (today, the state) to uphold the *hisba*—that is, to command the good and forbid the evil. In the service of the *hisba*, the HAIA (Hay'at al-Ma'ruf wa al-Nahaya 'an al-Munkar, the Committee for the Promotion of Virtue and Prevention of Vice), sometimes called the religious police, admonish believers about lax practice. There are other restrictions as well. Muslims must not drink alcohol, not simply as a forbidden substance but because it clouds alertness and judgment and makes it impossible to pray. Alcohol is therefore strictly forbidden in Saudi Arabia, and severe punishments are meted out to those who illegally import it. On the same grounds, drug use is forbidden. Pork is forbidden, as are gambling (although there are casinos in other Gulf countries) and sorcery or magic.

Modest behavior is required of both men and women. This is interpreted as requiring the segregation of men and women to prevent contact between unrelated men and women. This underlies the requirement for women to wear the *'abaya* over their clothing and cover their hair with a *shayla* or the *hijab* (or sometimes both). Some women also wear a face veil (*niqab*) and gloves. This is not a statement of fashion but one of religiosity. However, other women do not believe the face veil is required in Islam.

In addition to the pillars, the obligation of jihad, struggle in the cause of Allah, falls on Muslims. Because of contemporary violent Islamist movements' contention that jihad has been abandoned, it has become the subject of a new philosophical and religious debate extending far beyond Saudi Arabia (discussed in Chapter 7, Contemporary Issues). Jihad (or *jihad fi sabil Allah* [on the path of God]) has multiple meanings, including the struggle for Islam (*jihad al-akbar*) and the so-called lesser jihad, meaning the military or political struggle to defend Islam and Muslims from unbelievers. (Haarman in Hawling, ed., 2006, 307–314; Aboul-Enein and Zuhur 2004; Peters 1979) declared in certain periods on a yearly basis. The obligatory nature of the jihad played an important role in the founding of the first through the third Sa'udi states. It was supported by Ibn Taymiyya as the highest demarcation of belief next to the duty of prayer (*salat*) (Haarman in Hawling, ed., 2006, 307).

Shari'ah also governs criminal law (discussed under Law), economic transactions, and such matters of personal status as marriage, divorce, and inheritance. Precisely because matters of personal status must be regulated in accordance with *shari'ah* in Saudi Arabia, reforms concerning women's personal rights are quite a difficult prospect. Polygamy (the correct anthropological term is polygyny) is permitted, as is early marriage (there are many objections to the marriage of very young women, and a child marriage law may be supported by the government), and women's rights to divorce are limited by the judicial interpretation of *shari'ah*. These include quite narrow grounds for divorce, which must be granted by a judge if a woman initiates divorce, whereas a man's rights to divorce are less restrained. Polygamy is a psychological, an emotional, and sometimes an economic threat to women if husbands do not heed the

Qur'anic command to treat their wives equally. Unfortunately, divorced women are often unable to remarry, unless they agree to become second wives in Saudi Arabia, although this is not an Islamic ideal but a social trend. As there is a stigma and many limitations on unmarried women, this means that women also support the systems of thought undergirding polygamy.

Inheritance in Islam is set out to ensure that individuals cannot disinherit their own heirs and to provide equity among them. Ibn 'Abd al-Wahhab's influence was to emphasize classical rulings, for instance, that women must be able to inherit and not be denied their rights as they customarily were among the tribes. Property owners could set aside endowments and name their administrators and beneficiaries so long as their heirs could claim their due shares. These are called *awqaf*, and they are now administered by the government.

The final source of Islamic law, *ijtihad* (independent striving of the jurist), which was already mentioned, is controversial. Ibn 'Abd al-Wahhab was very intent on eradicating the practice of interpreting Islam by rote and blind imitation and consequently utilized his own *ijtihad* at times.

Some legal schools were also concerned, as were the Hanbalis, about a "mechanical application of analogy." Therefore, the Hanafi school also used *istishan* (or a preference of the jurist according to public interest), and the Maliki jurists elaborated on the idea of public interest (A. Yamani in Malik, ed., 1972, 54). Different jurists and legal schools vary in their reliance on particular principles. Generally, the Hanbali school adheres whenever possible to the Qur'an or the hadith, but when nothing is found to be applicable, their jurists can be more flexible than others in employing *ijtihad* to find a solution. One example is that the Hanbalis argue that all relatives who may inherit from someone who is ill or impoverished must provide care for them, but according to the Hanafi school only the nearest relatives are to care for them. Also, borrowing from the Maliki school, Hanbali jurists hold that minerals must not be controlled by private owners. (This latter idea has special relevance to Saudi Arabia.)

MUHAMMAD IBN 'ABD AL-WAHHAB

The legal thought and religious principles of Muhammad ibn 'Abd al-Wahhab strongly impacted Saudi Arabia. Most important, this came about because of the military expansion of Muhammad ibn Sa'ud (see Chapter 2, History), even though Ibn 'Abd al-Wahhab aimed for religious reform as a lifelong pursuit. Since he believed materialism was adopted in the lands governed by the al-Sa'ud family, once 'Abd al-'Aziz ibn Muhammad ibn Sa'ud came to power, Ibn 'Abd al-Wahhab stepped down from his position as his imam.

Ibn 'Abd al-'Wahhab's writing concerns *tawhid* (an absolute monotheism or unicity of God) and *shirk* (the idolatry he wanted Muslims to avoid). His treatise *Kitab al-Tawhid* defines and expands on this concept, outlining several types of *tawhid*: *tawhid al-rububiyya* means Allah's unique status of being the creator of the world and holding dominion over all of his creation; *tawhid al-ibada* refers to the idea that absolute monotheism or unicity must govern all aspects of worship of

Allah—that nothing and no one but he may be the object of worship; and *tawhid al-asma' wa al-sifat*, or monotheism of names and characteristics, means Allah's multiple names or attributes (*al-asma'*), such as the Generous or the Beneficent, that may be found in the Qur'an apply solely to Allah and may not be applied to rulers (Delong-Bas 2004, 57).

The greatest sins according to Ibn 'Abd al-Wahhab in *Kitab al-Kaba'ir* were *shirk* (polytheism or worship of any other than Allah), sheltering a perpetrator of a crime, cursing one's parents, and unjustly altering boundaries of land. Other terrible sins were engaging in sorcery, committing murder, living on *rib'a* (unlawful interest or usury [see Chapter 4, Economics]), robbing orphans, deserting jihad when the battle begins, and making false accusations about women's sexual behavior or reputation (Ibn 'Abd al-Wahhab, *Kitab al-Kaba'ir*, 35–36; also see Ibn 'Abd al-Wahhab 1398h).

Ibn 'Abd al-Wahhab was concerned about illicit innovations (*bid'ah*) that had crept into Islamic practice and beliefs, particularly those with "associationist" content—that is, where something other than Allah is worshipped. He opposed Muslims who prayed at graves or tombs, expanded these into shrines and mausoleums, or attached mosques to them. Many popular Sufi rituals were carried out at saints' tombs or celebrated their birthdays, and the Shi'a revered the sites where their leaders had perished. Both groups often sought intercession (*shaf'a*) by these figures with Allah, to plead for the soul of the supplicant (Delong-Bas 2004, 67–69). Natana Delong-Bas, who has studied Ibn 'Abd al-Wahhab's work in depth, does not believe that Ibn 'Abd al-Wahhab supported extremism; she writes that when the *'ulama* of Najd issued *fatawa* that those who engaged in tomb worship should be put to death, Ibn 'Abd al-Wahhab thought these injunctions too extreme (2004, 67). These positions had obvious consequences for all Muslims who visited the Holy Cities after the al-Sa'ud's conquest, and they provoked a reaction from *'ulama* who did not support Ibn 'Abd al-Wahhab and left Najd or Arabia. The Ottomans were greatly concerned by the rise of the Wahhabi movement and were determined to defeat it. Al-Jabarti, an Egyptian historian writing at the time, noted the Wahhabi massacre at Ta'if but seemed to approve of the Wahhabis' position on doctrine; he wrote that their takeover of the holy cities in 1803 and 1805 was peaceful and that they imposed order. At Medina, the warriors destroyed all the domes that had been erected over graves except the one at the tomb of the Prophet; they banned smoking, ordered people to attend prayer, and did away with then-current extortion of pilgrims (Commins 2006, 31).

In addition to Ibn 'Abd al-Wahhab's opposition to *taqlid* (blind imitation), his views concerning the Shi'a, jihad, and the identification of nonbelievers through a process called *takfir* were all important. Like others in the Hanbali school, Ibn 'Abd al-Wahhab opposed the Shi'a (he wrote about an extreme and early faction, the Rafidah) on the grounds that they violated *tawhid* on many points, including their tendency to allow their religious leaders great authority, their arguments against the first three caliphs in favor of leadership by 'Ali ibn Abi Talib, and their belief that the imams were infallible (Delong-Bas 2004, 85–86). On jihad, Ibn 'Abd al-Wahhab was close to the classical teachings about it; in *Kitab al-Jihad*, he held that its aim is religious, that it is a collective activity (unless certain circumstances prevail ('Abd al-Wahhab 1398h), and that jihad can be taken only after the nonbeliever has been invited to Islam and rejects it. He did not believe that the so-called Qur'anic verses of peace were abrogated by the sword verses (Delong-Bas 2004, 232–234), nor did he write about martyrdom. Moreover, he did not support jihad in the service of political gain.

Takfir means the identification of someone as an infidel. According to various scholars, the Wahhabists applied this to all who did not share their own interpretation of Islam (Commins 2006, 25; Algar 2002; Vali Nasr 2007); however, others do not agree that the Shaykh, Ibn 'Abd al-Wahhab, supported a state of permanent warfare of this type (Delong-Bas 2004, 242–243). A family member of the Shaykh, Sulayman ibn 'Abdullah ibn Muhammad (1785–1818), added some emphatic positions to the reform movement. He wrote that whoever is loyal to or pretends to believe in the religion of the idolators, or does not actively oppose them, is an infidel and that one could travel to the idolators' land only if one practiced Islam and did not befriend the idolators (Commins 2006, 33–37). These views had special meaning in the historic period that Sulayman lived through, when the supporters of the al-Sa'ud and the Ibn 'Abd al-Wahhab reform movement were conquered by the Egyptian-Ottoman forces and had to flee.

Ibn 'Abd al-Wahhab's family became known as Al-Shaykh, because of his position as religious adviser to Muhammad al-Sa'ud. His four sons all taught at Dir'iyyah. Essentially, his *da'wah*, or proselytizing mission and reform movement reshaped the *'ulama* of Saudi Arabia, as other schools or philosophies were replaced by his (Commins in Ayoob and Kosebalaban, eds., 2009, 40–45). This was true despite condemnations of Ibn 'Abd al-Wahhab by his own brother, Sulayman, and resistance to him from other *'ulama* at 'Uyaynah. Many of his descendants are part of the Saudi Arabian government. Also, it is extremely difficult to separate Ibn 'Abd al-Wahhab's impact from that of the Sa'udi political endeavor (despite Delong-Bas's efforts). Much of the polemics over al-Wahhabiyya have to do with its political nature and mission, more so than with its intended religious mission (al-Dakhil in Ayoob and Kosebalaban, eds., 2009, 23–35). Khalid al-Dakhil, a sociologist who supports political reform, makes the point that *shirk* (polytheism or polytheistic practices) was not so prevalent in Najd in this period; it could not be logically proven to be the true motivation for the Wahhabi mission. Rather, he infers that territorial expansionism was the goal. He also emphasizes that this movement arose from a settled, *hadhari*, or town-based milieu, which reflected several centuries of change in the Najd (al-Dakhil in Ayoob and Kosebalaban, eds., 2009, 33; al-Juhany 2002). Al-Dakhil refutes the claims of many scholars like Bernard Lewis, Bassam Tibi, and Ghassan Salame, who, he notes, are unfamiliar with Najdi history and so described al-Sa'ud and Ibn 'Abd al-Wahhab's movement as a tribal backward-looking one. This is true of many scholars; Vali Nasr claims that "Abdul Wahhab was a purist whose creed reflected the simple ways of the desert tribesman of Nejd'" (Vali Nasr 2006, 96). In fact, Ibn 'Abd al-Wahhab was a scholar from a settled town, and he found the desert tribesmen lax in religion and their adherence to *shari'ah* as compared to the townspeople.

Up until Ibn 'Abd al-Wahhab's mission, the *'ulama* in Najd had mostly written works of jurisprudence (al-Isa 1997, 87–100). During his era, Ibn 'Abd al-Wahhab wrote more than others; his work on jurisprudence follows along with prior tradition (as Delong-Bas [2004] basically shows); it was his ideas about doctrine, described both in the preceding and in the following, that were new.

Ibn 'Abd al-Wahhab and his followers are said to have opposed Sufism (mystical Islam) and Shi'ism and to have promoted violence in general. According to some, he did not violently oppose the more scriptural Sufi orders (Delong-Bas 2004), but in the Hijaz, the Sufi orders were mostly banned, though not entirely (Sedgwick 1997), and their leaders moved underground, teaching privately (Ochsenwald in Ayoob and Kosebalaban, eds., 2009, 78).

Ibn 'Abd al-Wahhab significantly promoted *da'wah*, or missionary activity that expanded the numbers of *'ulama* promoting his beliefs. After their defeat by the Egyptians and Ottomans, these *'ulama* had, in some cases, to flee and survive; they then revived and became the dominant order in the country. That historical process has created some resistance to external critique in today's *'ulama* (Commins in Ayoob and Kosebalaban, eds., 2009, 50). Second, the *da'wah* implies constant and international activities to "call" others to the correct Islam through education and other means.

Wahhabism became a synonym for *salafiyya* (a reform movement) over the 20th century although there are other actors in that movement. It was identified with violence initially because of the Ikhwan's excesses. It did influence the Muslim world; also, there were parallel movements. The movement of Sayyid Ahmad ibn Muhammad Irfan of Rai Barlei in India is credited with following similar ideas in opposing the *bid'ah* of "sufistic polytheists," and the Indian "Wahhabi" movement grew even after the Egyptian defeat of the first Sa'udi state (Ahmad 1994, 14–15). With the rise of Osama bin Laden's al-Qa'ida movement, many wrote increasingly about global *salafi* trends that may rely on influence from Saudi Arabia, although Osama bin Laden has incessantly opposed the Saudi regime. In caution, historian John Voll writes that "generic militance that is labeled as 'Wahhabi' is not the same as historical Wahhabism" (Voll in Ayoob and Kosebalaban, eds., 2009, 163). The latest round of scholarly polemics over Wahhabism appear to signal different beliefs about the linkage between the Saudi Arabian government and liberals and their Western scholarly allies and the more ardent of the Wahhabiyya—some appear to argue that Ibn 'Abd al-Wahhab's legacy was lacking in scholarly legitimacy or embroidered on by others (Commins 2006, 2009); conversely, others claim that his legacy is rooted in a classical tradition and capable of tolerance (Delong-Bas 2004, 2009) or that its root problem is an association with expanding state power (al-Dakhil 2009).

THE *'ULAMA*

The religious scholars of Saudi Arabia and their families are a large group in comparison to the situation in other countries (other nations with a large clerical presence include Iran). They numbered 7,000 to 10,000 in the early 1990s and possibly up to 20,000 today. Their numbers probably increased naturally and with the rise of the *sahwa*, or Islamic Awakening movement, and the emphasis on religious matters in Saudi Arabia following the 1979 takeover of the Grand Mosque. Many are employed by the government in Islamic education and other departments. Not all *'ulama* are legal

TABLE 5.1   The Council of Senior *'Ulama*

The following are among the most important of the official *'ulama* (clerics) serving in the government of Saudi Arabia as of 2009.

'Abdulaziz ibn 'Abdullah al-Ashaikh (chairman)

Saleh ibn Muhammad al-Lahaidan

Saleh ibn 'Abdulrahman al-Husayn

Saleh ibn Humaid

'Abdullah ibn Abdulmohsin al-Turki

'Abdullah ibn 'Abdulrahman al-Ghedyan

'Abdullah ibn Sulayman al-Manie

Saleh ibn Fouzan al-Fouzan

'Abdul Wahhab Abu Sulayman

'Abdullah ibn Muhammad al-Ashaikh

Ahmad Sirr Mubaraki

'Abdullah ibn Muhammad al-Mutlaq

Yaqub ibn 'Abdul Wahhab al-Bahussain

Abdul Karim ibn 'Abdullah al-Khodair

'Ali ibn 'Abbas Hakami

'Abdullah ibn Muhammad al-Khanayn

Muhammad al-Mukhtar Muhammad

Muhammad al-Ashaikh

Sa'd ibn Nasr ibn 'Abdullah al-Shathri

Qays al-Ashaikh Mubarak

Muhammad ibn 'Abd al-Karim 'Eissa

scholars; some are solely preachers or teachers, and some are appointed prayer leaders at particular mosques. Since 2003, the government has been very concerned about preaching that might support the claims of the Islamic opposition or support extremists elsewhere. Several programs have been held to reeducate preachers, who must be registered and are being monitored. Other points of tension arose when the supervision of girls' and women's education was returned to the Ministry of Education, and when King 'Abdullah made efforts to initiate religious dialogue. Some clerics and scholars oppose the views of other Muslim sects or fear that the influence of non-Muslims and official sponsorship of religious dialogue make it more difficult for them to continue opposing variant views and beliefs without consequences.

GOVERNMENTAL RELIGIOUS DEPARTMENTS

The Ministry for Islamic Affairs, Endowments (Awqaf), Da'wah, and Guidance is in charge of all Islamic matters in the kingdom except for the *hajj*. Its responsibilities include building and maintaining the mosques throughout the kingdom, monitoring the mosques' activities, and registering and administering the land and property held as *awqaf*. The minister of Islamic affairs, endowments, *da'wah*, and guidance as of 2010 was Shaykh Saleh ibn 'Abd al-'Aziz ibn Muhammad ibn Ibrahim al-Shaykh, who had served since 1999 in this position. The Ministry of the Hajj is responsible for the pilgrimage and in 2010 was headed by Dr. Fouad ibn 'Abd al-Salaam ibn Muhammad al-Farsy, who has been the minister of the *hajj* since 2005. The Ministry of Justice administers *shari'ah* and all legal and judicial matters for Saudi Arabian citizens. As described, this is a religious as well as a legal function. In 2009, King 'Abdullah appointed Dr. Muhammad ibn 'Abd al-Karim al-'Eissa as minister of justice and issued decrees to restructure the Supreme Court and the Council of Senior 'Ulama.

The Committee for the Promotion of Virtue and the Prevention of Vice (CPVPV) is popularly called the *mutawa'in* and officially termed the HAIA. This governmental department employs at least 3,500 religious officers and thousands of volunteers who claim to uphold the *hisba*, the command to order the good and forbid the evil. Until

---

HAJJ 2010

The *hajj* is the largest annual pilgrimage in the world. How many attended the 2010 *hajj*? We still don't really know. Saudi Arabians have been officially limited to attendance once every five years, and other countries have quotas for pilgrimage visas. Some sources said the Saudi government expected 3.4 million people over the *hajj* period; others said 2.8 million came, and some reported that up to 1 million or at least "tens of thousands" of unregistered pilgrims and squatters flocked to the pilgrimage as well, since they could move into the Plain of 'Arafat at night. From the United Kingdom alone, 25,000 pilgrims traveled.

The distinctive dress worn by pilgrims represents their equality and the sincerity of their intention to be pure and devoted to Allah and his rules for the *hajj*. The lowliest peasant and the wealthiest businessman wear the same dress, although the former may save for years for his *hajj*. This fact, and the amazing sight of Muslims from every corner of the world, of every color and language, has deeply impressed many. Pilgrims wear their *ihram* clothing and usually try to pray on the way to the *hajj*, even on the airplanes. Printed guides are published for pilgrims so they can prepare themselves to correctly perform the ritual. Human guides are also hired by different groups of pilgrims. European and American media sometimes cover the *hajj*, as when Michael Wolfe, an American Muslim, shared his *hajj* experience on the television program Frontline, including many of the vows, traditions, and explanations of the rite's practices and symbols. ("The Hajj, One American's Pilgrimage to Mecca," Nightline, ABC News. Part 1 / 2, 1997, 2010, http://www.youtube.com/watch?v=7dOlGoiGrSA). Saudi Arabians preparing for the *hajj* had many special traditions, some of which are now fading away. In Mecca, women used to prepare large quantities of *ma'mul*, a stuffed sweet pastry (usually stuffed with dates), to last the entire month.

Members of the HAIA (Committee for the Promotion of Virtue and Prevention of Vice, also known as religious police) while attending a training course in Riyadh on April 29, 2009. (Fahad Shadeed/Reuters/Corbis)

2007, they stopped, interrogated, and incarcerated individuals on their own, sometimes beating people, and there have been some fatalities. They were then ordered to allow the regular police to decide on charges. The *mutawa'in* enforce dress codes, the separation of men and women, and dietary rules, and they seize items they consider violations of religious doctrine, like CDs of music, iPods, films, Valentine's Day items (they consider this a pagan holiday), and many other items.

Grand Mufti

The grand mufti of Saudi Arabia as of 2010 was Shaykh 'Abd al-'Aziz ibn 'Abdullah ibn Muhammad al-Shaikh (b. 1940). He taught in various institutions, including the Faculty of Shari'ah at the Imam Muhammad ibn Sa'ud Islamic University in Riyadh, from 1971 to 1991. Like quite a few of the *'ulama*, he is blind. He became a member of the Council of Senior 'Ulama and of the Permanent Committee for Islamic Research and Fatawa in 1986 and became the deputy to the previous grand mufti, 'Abd al-'Aziz ibn 'Abdullah ibn Baz, in 1995. He has condemned suicide bombings and the 9/11 and London 7/7 attacks, and he also forbade Saudi Arabian youth from going abroad to engage in jihad because they were being exploited (Tariq Alhomayed, *al-Sharq al-Awsat*, October 2, 2007). He has firmly opposed al-Qa'ida but also decries the term *Wahhabist* for Saudi Arabian Muslims, and he has rebuked Iraqi prime minister Nuri al-Maliki for his statements about Saudi Arabian support for anti-Shi'ism. Like his predecessor, Shaykh ibn Baz, he often speaks on a popular radio show, "*Nur 'ala Darb*," and supports socially conservative stances, arguing that Saudi Arabian girls must guard their virtue and that they may be married as young as 10 to 12 years of age.

Council of Senior 'Ulama (Scholars)

The most prominent religious scholars serve on a Council of Senior 'Ulama established by King Faysal in 1971. The group has usually had 30 to 40 members. King Faysal and King Fahd used to meet weekly with those members who resided in Riyadh to provide a regular channel of communication between the rulers and the *'ulama*. When the Grand Mosque in Mecca was captured by Juhayman al-'Utaybi and his supporters, this council's approval was necessary for the state to launch operations against the group in that sacred space. Their approval was also sought when U.S. forces were invited to conduct operations in the kingdom prior to the Gulf War. The council is chaired by the grand mufti. Under the reforms of King 'Abdullah, the council now includes scholar representatives of the other *madhahib*, in addition to the Hanbali scholars, but no Shi'a *'ulama*.

Permanent Committee for Islamic Research and Fatawa
(Lajnah al-Da'imah lil-Buhuth al-'Ilmiyyah wa-l-Ifta')

The Permanent Committee for Islamic Research and Fatawa, sometimes identified in English as the Committee for Research and Legal Opinions (CRLO), is headed by scholars selected from the Council of Senior 'Ulama. Muslims can write to the committee and request a *fatwa* on matters important to them. The committee will not issue a *fatwa* unless a majority of members agree on it, and if the group is split, then the chair's view carries. The committee does not include opposition clerics; rather, it consists of the very important figures, Shaykh 'Abdullah ibn Qu'ud, Shaykh 'Abdullah ibn Munay, Shaykh Saleh al-Fawzan, and Shaykh 'Abd al-'Aziz al-Shaykh, who is the chair of the committee and grand mufti of the kingdom. The committee was formerly headed by Shaykh 'Abd al-'Aziz ibn Baz. Their rulings are not binding on all Muslims but are influential in Saudi Arabia. Some argue that their rulings, particularly on women's issues, are inappropriately harsh and illustrate undue influence by the *'ulama* and that, in some cases they are wrong (as when they state that a woman walking in front of a man [while he prays] or a woman's presence invalidates a man's prayers, or that a woman cannot be permitted to study at the university if her husband disagrees, or may be beaten) (Abou El Fadl 2001b).

SHI'A MUSLIMS IN SAUDI ARABIA

The Shi'a Muslims of Saudi Arabia are mostly concentrated in the Eastern Province. A small Shi'i community lives in Medina, known as the Nakhawila. Musta'li Isma'ili

Muslims, who form the Sulaymani branch of that sect, relocated to Yemen and Najran, Saudi Arabia. Their leader since 2005 has been the 52nd Da'i, 'Abdullah ibn Muhammad al-Makrami. The Sulaymanis struggled with the Zaydi Shi'a leaders of northern Yemen and at one time controlled an area in Hadhramaut. When Najran was annexed to Saudi Arabia, they remained, numbering perhaps between 300,000 and 400,000, but were more isolated than their Shi'a counterparts to the east. Their freedom of worship was restricted due to the Saudi Arabian promotion of *mutawa'in* to enforce compliance with Wahhabi standards. Reportedly, the Saudi Arabian government is currently settling Sunni Yemeni refugees—in large numbers—in Najran, which concerns the Sulaymanis (Nanji and Daftary in Cornell, ed., 2007, 239; U.S. Commission on International Religious Freedom 2009; Human Rights Watch 2008).

The Shi'a of the Eastern Province underwent attacks by the Ikhwan of Ibn Sa'ud in Hasa and then at Qatif and elsewhere. Ibn Sa'ud reined in the Ikhwan. The Shi'a were not self-governing but were permitted to conduct their own religious affairs (Louër 2008, 21–22). Their *'ulama* were in touch with scholars from Iraq and Iran and have typically arisen from the same scholarly families. With the Islamic Revolution in Iran in 1978 and 1979, tensions grew, especially after Khomeini preached against the House of al-Sa'ud and embarked on active propaganda to spread the revolution. In 1979, a Shi'a uprising on the heels of the Grand Mosque takeover, dubbed the Intifadhat (uprising) Muharram 1400, was brutally subdued by the National Guard (see Chapter 2, History). Some radical elements among the Shi'a, allegedly funded by Iran, formed a group called Hizbullah al-Hijaz, which was responsible for the Khobar bombing of 1996. Hizbullah retains a following; however, the vast majority of Shi'a do not advocate violent opposition and want greater representation and to assimilate into Saudi Arabian society. In February 2009, Shi'a attempting to celebrate the death of Muhammad and Hasan ibn 'Ali (who was buried along with the other imams) at al-Baqi' cemetery in Medina were attacked by Sunnis and security forces, setting off protests abroad and in the Shi'a towns of the Eastern Province. The Shi'a have called this the Intifadhat 1430 (Matthiesen 2009; also see Chapter 7, Contemporary Issues).

OTHER COMPETING IDEOLOGIES

The small number of remaining nomads are moving away from their own systems of thought, behavior, and beliefs. These range from aesthetic concepts and special terminology to tribal law (*'urf*) to traditional healing practices (see section on health in this chapter) and ideas about the cohesiveness of tribe and family (see subsection on society in this chapter). *'Urf* predated Islam, and, in some ways, it has been incorporated into *shari 'ah*, as well as sociocultural practices. Because of the need to rely on *ijma'*—consensus—as a source of adjudication, *'urf* or the existing practices were adopted to some degree. For instance, the second class of offenses under Islamic law may be punished through *qisas*. Here, the clan of a killed or injured tribesman (or -woman) was given the option of retaliating exactly in kind—no harsher—or receiving payment, called *dhiyya*, for the life taken or injured body part. Under Islamic law, the state may enact this punishment instead of the clan. Other tribal practices used to include swearing of oaths, tests of truthfulness, and the use of guarantors.

Sufism has existed in Saudi Arabia; however, its rites have been forbidden since the rise of the Wahhabiyya, even though it has continued to be practiced. Other popular beliefs concerned possession by spirits, and these were addressed through exorcism rituals, the *zar*, which is found throughout Egypt, eastern Africa, and the Arabian Peninsula. Such rituals are frowned on by the Wahhabiyya.

Modern political trends of thought like Nasirism, Baathism, Marxism, and subsidiary forms of Arab nationalism or Arab socialism had only a limited impact on Saudi Arabia because the government moved forcefully against such tendencies, using the security forces, foreign policy, media control, and other forms of dissuasion. The rulers were deeply concerned that such movements should not take hold. However, even a number of the al-Sa'ud princes defected—Talal, Badr 'Abd al-Muhsin, and Fawwaz ibn 'Abd al-'Aziz—and supported Nasser and a "free Saudi Arabia" (implying political freedom from the al-Sa'ud monarch). In contrast, Islamic diplomacy and emphasis on Saudi Arabia's Islamic mission has been the path preferred by the government under King Faysal and ever since.

Nevertheless, some aspects of Arab left philosophy, or antiroyalism, impacted the kingdom. In 1954 an attempted coup was discovered and revealed more antiroyalist activity. In 1962 two incidents involved four flight crews defecting to Egypt in October; then, in November, a group of pilots mounted another coup attempt. The pilots were members of the royal family, and they defected to Egypt. The regime grounded the air force (Kechichian 2008, 112–113) and was again threatened in 1969 by military supporters of antiroyalist groups, the Federation of Democratic Forces, the National Front for the Liberation of Saudi Arabia, and the Popular Democratic Front. Arab nationalism was believed to be encouraged by Arab expatriate workers, and many, although not all, were replaced with Asian workers. The concerns over the military became a debate over whether or not to professionalize and modernize the armed forces or to put more emphasis on strengthening the National Guard; these concerns were partially based on fears of political opposition arising from the military again. (Other opposition movements are discussed in Chapter 7, Contemporary Issues.)

All of this provides a background for two alternative philosophies of the present, one that we could call a reformist democratic movement and the other, the *sahwa*, or Islamic Awakening, whose advocates support greater democratization but have in mind a much different endpoint than the liberal reformers.

REFERENCES

'Abd al-Wahhab, Muhammad ibn. *Kitab al-Tawhid*. Translated by Ismail al-Faruqi. Kuwait City: al-Faisal Printing Company, 1986.

'Abd al-Wahhab, Muhammad ibn. "Kitab al-Jihad." In *Mu'allafat al-Shaykh al-Imam Muhammad ibn 'Abd al-Wahhab: al-Fiqh*. Vol. 2. Riyadh, Saudi Arabia: Jami'at al-Imam Muhammad ibn Sa'ud Islamiyyah, 1398h. (corresponds to 1977 or 1978).

'Abd al-Wahhab, Muhammad ibn. "Kitab al-Kaba'ir." In *Mu'allafat al-Shaykh al-Imam Muhammad ibn 'Abd al-Wahhab*. Vol. 1. Riyadh, Saudi Arabia: Jami'at al-Imam Muhammad ibn Sa'ud Islamiyyah, 1398h.

'Abd al-Wahhab, Muhammad ibn. "Kitab al-Nikah." In *Mu'allafat al-Shaykh al-Imam Muhammad ibn 'Abd al-Wahhab*. Vol. 2. Riyadh, Saudi Arabia: Jami'at al-Imam Muhammad ibn Sa'ud Islamiyyah, 1398h.

'Abd al-Wahhab, Muhammad ibn. "Kitab al-Tawhid." In *Mu'allafat al-Shaykh al-Imam Muhammad Ibn Abd al-Wahhab*. Vol. 1. Riyadh, Saudi Arabia: Jami'at al-Imam Muhammad ibn Sa'ud Islamiyyah, 1398h.

Abdul Rauf, Feisal. "What Is Sunni Islam?" In *Voices of Islam*. Vol. 1, *Voices of Tradition*, edited by Vincent Cornell. Westport, CT: Praeger, 2007.

Abou El Fadl, Khaled. *And God Knows the Soldiers: The Authoritative and Authoritarian in Islamic Discourses*. Lanham, MD: University Press of America, 2001a.

Abou El Fadl, Khaled. *Speaking in God's Name: Islamic Law, Authority and Women*. Oxford, UK: Oneworld, 2001b.

Aboul-Enein, Youssef, and Sherifa Zuhur. *Islamic Rulings on Warfare*. Carlisle, PA: Strategic Studies Institute, 2004.

Ahmad, Qeyamuddin. *The Wahhabi Movement in India*. New Delhi, India: Monohar, 1994.

Ahmed, Leila. *Women and Gender in Islam*. New Haven, CT: Yale University Press, 1992.

Alavi, Karima Diane. "Pillars of Religion and Faith." In *Voices of Islam*. Vol. 1, *Voices of Tradition*, edited by Vincent Cornell. Westport, CT: Praeger, 2007.

Algar, Hamid. *Wahhabism: A Critical Essay*. Oneonta, NY: Islamic Publications International, 2002.

Alhomayed, Tariq. "Saudi Arabia's Grand Mufti." *al-Sharq al-Awsat*, October 2, 2007. http://www.alarabiya.net/views/2007/10/03/39898.html

Armstrong, H. C. *Lord of Arabia*. London: Arthur Barker, 1934.

Asgari, Seyed Mohammad. "Islam: Reviewing Shiite-Sunni Relations in India: An Interview with Seyed Mohammad Asgari." Interviewed by Mahan Abedin. *Religioscope*, January 12, 2011. http://religion.info/english/interviews/article_513.shtml

Ayoob, Mohammed, and Hasan Kosebalaban, eds. *Religion and Politics in Saudi Arabia: Wahhabism and the State*. Boulder, CO: Lynne Rienner, 2009.

Ayoub, Mahmoud M. "The Qur'an: History of the Text." In *Encyclopedia of the Modern Islamic World*, edited by John Esposito. New York: Oxford University Press, 1995, Vol. 3, 385–387.

Bianchi, Robert. *Guests of God: Pilgrimage and Politics in the Islamic World*. Oxford, UK: Oxford University Press, 2004.

Bunt, Gary. *iMuslims: Rewiring the House of Islam*. Chapel Hill: University of North Carolina Press, 2009.

Commins, David Dean. *The Wahhabi Mission and Saudi Arabia*. London: I. B. Tauris, 2006.

Cook, Michael. "The Expansion of the First Saudi State: The Case of Washm." In *The Islamic World from Classical to Modern Times: Essays in Honor of Bernard Lewis*, edited by C. E. Bosworth, Charles Issawi, Roger Savory, and A. L. Udovitch. Princeton, NJ: Darwin, 1989.

Cornell, Vincent. "The Quran as Scripture." In *The Encylopedia of the Modern Islamic World*, edited by John Esposito. New York: Oxford University Press, 1995, Vol. 3, 387–394.

Delong-Bas, Natana. "Wahhabism and the Question of Religious Tolerance." In *Religion and Politics in Saudi Arabia: Wahhabism and the State*, edited by Mohammed Ayoob and Hasan Kosebalaban. Boulder, CO: Lynne Rienner, 2009.

Delong-Bas, Natana. *Wahhabi Islam: From Revival and Reform to Global Jihad*. Oxford, UK: Oxford University Press, 2004.

Edwards, Richard, and Sherifa Zuhur. "Sunni Islam." In *Encyclopedia of U.S. Wars in the Middle East*, edited by Spencer Tucker. Santa Barbara, CA: ABC-CLIO, 2010, 1176–1181.

Ende, W. "The Nakhawila: A Shi'ite Community in Medina, Past and Present." *Die Welt des Islams* 37, no. 3 (1997), 264–348.

Esposito, John L. *Islam: The Straight Path*. New York: Oxford University Press, 1991.

Fandy, Mamoun. *Saudi Arabia and the Politics of Dissent*. New York: St. Martin's, 1999.

Gibb, H.A.R. *Arabic Literature: An Introduction*. Oxford, UK: Oxford University Press, 1974.

Goitein, S. D. "Ramadan, the Muslim Month of Fasting." In *The Formation of the Classical Islamic World*, edited by Lawrence I. Conrad. Vol. 26, *The Development of Islamic Ritual*, edited by Gerald Hawling. Aldershot, UK, and Burlington, VT: Ashgate, 2006.

Goldziher, Ignacz. *Die Richtungen der islamischen Koranauslegung*. Leiden, the Netherlands: Brill, 1970. (Originally published in 1920.)

Guillaume, Alfred. *The Life of Muhammad: A Translation of Ishaq's Sirat Rasul Allah*. New York: Oxford University Press, 1955.

Habib, John S. *Ibn Saud's Warriors of Islam: The Ikhwan of Najd and Their Role in the Creation of the Saudi Kingdom, 1910–1930*. Atlantic Highlands, NJ: Humanities Press, 1978.

al-Hasan, Hamza. *al-Shi'a fi-l-Mamlakah al-'Arabiyyah al-Sa'udiyyah*. Beirut, Lebanon: Mu'assasat al-Baqi' li-Ihya' al-Turath, 1993.

al-Hashimi, Muhammad Ali. *The Ideal Muslim Society: As Defined in the Qur'an and Sunnah*. Riyadh, Saudi Arabia: International Islamic Publishing House, 2007.

Hawling, Gerald, ed. *The Development of Islamic Ritual*. Vol. 26 of *The Formation of the Classical Islamic World*, edited by Lawrence I. Conrad. Aldershot, UK, and Burlington, VT: Ashgate, 2006.

Hegghammer, Thomas. *Jihad in Saudi Arabia: Violence and Pan-Islamism since 1979*. Cambridge: Cambridge University Press, 2010.

Human Rights Watch. "The Ismailis of Najran: Second Class Citizens." September 22, 2008. http://www.hrw.org/en/reports/2008/09/22/ismailis-najran-0

Hurvitz, Nimrod. *The Formation of Hanbalism: Piety into Power*. London: RoutledgeCurzon, 2002.

Ibn Bishr, 'Uthman. *'Unwan al-majd fi tarikh Najd*. Riyadh, Saudi Arabia: Maktabah al-Riyadh al-Hadithah, n.d.

Ibn Ghannam, Husayn. *Tarikh Najd*. Edited by Nassar Al-Din Assad. Riyadh, Saudi Arabia: 'Abd al-'Aziz ibn Muhammad ibn Ibrahim al-Shaykh, 1982.

Ibn Ghannam, Husayn. *Rawdat al-afkar wa al-afham li-murtad hal al-imam wa-ta'dad ghazawat dhawi al-Islam*. Riyadh, 1381h.

Ibn Ghannam, Husayn. *Tarikh Najd*. Cairo, 1961.

Ibn Qasim, Abd al-Rahman ibn Muhammad, ed. *al-Durar al-saniya fi al-ajwiba al-najdiyya*. 12 vols. Riyadh, 1995.

Ibrahim, Fuad. *The Shiis of Saudi Arabia*. London: Saqi Books, 2007.

International Crisis Group. "The Shi'ite Question of Saudi Arabia." Report No. 45, Riyadh, Amman, and Brussels: International Crisis Group, September 2005. http://www.crisisgroup.org/en/regions/middle-east-north-africa/iran-gulf/saudi-arabia/045-the-shiite-question-in-saudi-arabia.aspx

al-Isa, Mayy bint 'Abd al- 'Aziz. *al-Haya al- 'ilmiyya fi Najd mundhu qiyam da 'wat al-Shaykh Muhammad ibn 'Abd al-Wahhab wa hatta nihayat al-dawla al-Sa 'udiyya al-'ula*. Riyadh, Saudi Arabia: Darat al-Malik 'Abd al-'Aziz, 1997.

Jones, Toby. "Saudi Arabia's Not So New Anti-Shi'ism." *Middle East Report* 242 (Spring 2007).

al-Juhany, 'Uwaidah M. *Najd before the Salafi Reform Movement: Social, Religious and Political Conditions in the Three Centuries Preceding the Rise of the Saudi State*. Reading, UK: Ithaca, 2002.

Kechichian, Joseph. *Faysal: Saudi Arabia's King for All Seasons*. Gainesville: University Press of Florida, 2008.

Lacroix, Stéphane. "Between Islamists and Liberals: Saudi Arabia's New 'Islamo-Liberal' Reformists." *Middle East Journal* 58, no. 3 (Summer 2004), 345–365.

Lazarus-Yafeh, Hava. "The Religious Dialectics of the Hadjdj." In *The Formation of the Classical Islamic World*, edited by Lawrence I. Conrad. Vol. 26, *The Development of Islamic Ritual*, edited by Gerald Hawling. Aldershot, UK, and Burlington, VT: Ashgate, 2006.

Long, David E. *The Hajj Today: A Survey of Contemporary Makkah Pilgrimage*. Albany: State University of New York, 1979.

Louër, Laurence. *Transnational Shia Politics: Religious and Political Networks in the Gulf*. New York: Columbia University Press, 2008.

Makky, Abdel Wahed. *Mecca: The Pilgrimage City: A Study of Pilgrim Accommodations*. London: Croom Helm, 1978.

Matthiesen, Toby. "The Shi'a of Saudi Arabia at a Crossroads." *Middle East Report Online*, May 6, 2009. http://www.merip.org/mero050609.html

Meijer, Roel, ed. *Global Salafism: Islam's New Religious Movement*. London: Hurst, 2009.

Moinuddin, Hassan. *The Charter of the Islamic Conference and Legal Framework of Economic Cooperation among Its Member States*. New York: Oxford University Press, 1987.

Nanji, Azim, and Farhad Daftary. "What Is Shiite Islam?" In *Voices of Islam*. Vol. 1, *Voices of Tradition*, edited by Vincent Cornell. Westport, CT: Praeger, 2007.

Nasr, Vali. *The Shia Revival: How Conflicts within Islam Will Shape the Future*. New York: W. W. Norton, 2007.

Ochsenwald, William. "Saudi Arabia." In *The Politics of Islamic Revivalism*, edited by Shireen Hunter. Bloomington: Indiana University Press, 1988, 105–115.

Ochsenwald, William. *Religion, Society and the State in Arabia: The Hijaz under Ottoman Control, 1840–1908*. Columbus: Ohio State University Press, 1984.

Peters, F. E. *The Hajj: The Muslim Pilgrimage to Mecca and the Holy Places*. Princeton, NJ: Princeton University Press, 1994, 1996.

Peters, Rudolph. *Islam and Colonialism: The Doctrine of Jihad in Modern History*. The Hague, the Netherlands: Mouton, 1979.

Rougier, Bernard, ed. *Qu'est-ce Que le Salafisme?* Paris: Presses Universitaires de France, 2008.

Rush, Alan, ed. *Records of the Hajj: A Documentary History of the Pilgrimage to Mecca*. Slough, UK: Archive Editions, 1993.

al-Sa'id, Labib. *The Recited Koran.* Translated by Bernard G. Weiss, M. A. Rauf, and Morroe Berger. Princeton, NJ: Darwin, 1975.

Salamah, Ahmad Abdullah. *Shia and Sunni Perspective on Islam: An Objective Comparison of the Shia and Sunni Doctrines Based on the Holy Quran and Hadith.* Jeddah, Saudi Arabia: Abul-Qasim Publication House, 1991.

Schacht, Joseph, ed. *The Legacy of Islam.* 2nd ed. Oxford, UK: Oxford University Press, 1974.

Sedgwick, Mark. "Saudi Sufis: Compromise in the Hijaz 1925–1940." *Die Welt des Islams* 37, no. 3 (1997), 349–368.

Sharif, M. M., ed. *History of Muslim Philosophy.* 2 vols. Wiesbaden, Germany, 1966.

Siddiq, 'Abd al-'Aziz. *Hukum al-iqama bi bilad al-kufr wa bayan wujubiha fi ba'd al-ahwal.* Tangier: Bughaz, 1985.

Smith, William Cantwell. *Islam in Modern History.* Princeton, NJ: Princeton University Press, 1957.

Snouck Hugronje, Christiaan. "The Meccan Feast" (An edited translation of C. Snouck Hurgronje, *Het Mekkaansche feest* [Leiden, the Netherlands: Brill, 1880]). In *The Formation of the Classical Islamic World,* edited by Lawrence I. Conrad. Vol. 26, *The Development of Islamic Ritual,* edited by Gerald Hawling. Aldershot, UK, and Burlington, VT: Ashgate, 2006, 239–290.

Steinberg, Guido. "The Shiites in the Eastern Province of Saudi Arabia, 1913–1953." In *The Twelver Shia in Modern Times: Religious Culture and Political History,* edited by Rainer Brunner and Werner Ende. Leiden, the Netherlands: Brill, 2001.

U.S. Commission on International Religious Freedom. *Annual Report of the United States Commission on International Religious Freedom.* May 2009.

al-'Uthaymin, Abd Allah Saleh. *Muhammad ibn 'Abd al-Wahhab: The Man and His Works.* London: I. B. Tauris, 2009.

von Sivers, Peter. "Islam in the Middle East and Africa." In *Encyclopedia of the Modern Islamic World,* edited by John Esposito. Oxford, UK: Oxford University Press, 1992, Vol. 2, 254–261.

Yamani, Ahmad Zaki. "Islamic Law and Contemporary Issues." In *God and Man in Contemporary Islamic Thought: Proceedings of the Philosophy Symposium Held at the American University of Beirut, February 6–10, 1967,* edited by Charles Malik. Beirut, Lebanon: American University of Beirut, 1972, 45–82.

Yamani, Maha A. Z. *Polygamy and Law in Saudi Arabia.* Reading, UK: Ithaca, 2008.

al-Yassini, Ayman. *Religion and State in the Kingdom of Saudi Arabia.* Boulder, CO: Westview, 1985.

Social Classes and Ethnicity

OVERVIEW

In Saudi Arabia, social class and ethnicity have not followed the precise lines of premodern and modern Western societies. Although there is a royal family and a distinction between the privileges of that family and those of other Saudi Arabian citizens, the family's preeminence derives from its tribal status and political success in unifying modern Saudi Arabia. The idea of royalty in Saudi Arabia is not that of kings who claim rule by divine right, as in early Europe. Instead, the royal family's higher political status was claimed through tribal conquest, and they must simultaneously meet traditional and tribal Islamic and modern expectations of governance. They possess special privileges and responsibilities and are subject to scrutiny and family censure. Some members have become extremely wealthy as a result of business activities, but the wealthiest groups in Saudi Arabia are actually a mixture of social elements.

Traditional differences in social status have arisen from geographic origins; tribal or nontribal and sedentary, partially sedentary or nonsedentary backgrounds; occupation; former slave or nonslave status; wealth or poverty; and gender. The differences between groups based on past or present modes of production were not perfectly distinct, as the families of tribal *amirs* began to see themselves separately from the bedouin at least by the early 1980s (Fernea 1987, 311).

Formal studies of Arabian society and anthropological studies are much scarcer than political studies. Early Western sources, anthropological studies of nomads, and other studies undertaken as part of the governmental development plans provide the most information, and different types of historical studies in Arabic provide other data and insights. The *sijilaat*, or court records, have been a very important source for understanding Ottoman-governed societies. The parallel for Arabia resides in arguments about certain key legal cases; more research on these would help us understand social relations through the lens of legal disputes.

BIAS IN SOCIAL INFORMATION

Travelers, missionaries, and adventurers who became famous in Europe for their memoirs of experiences in the East provided information about the groups and peoples they encountered and tended to generalize from them. These visitors came from highly stratified, patriarchal societies and viewed the Arabs as a race rather than an ethnicity. Although some of their descriptions, such as the Dutch scholar and government advisor Christiaan Snouke Hurgronje (1857–1936), who was permitted to go on the *hajj* to Mecca, were invaluable, as was his collection of then-current artifacts, he and others held individualistic and rather set theories about their subjects. Arab records of the time are not concerned with the matter of Arabians' ethnicity or race and social particularities but rather pertained to the impact of the Wahhabi reform movement. The lifestyle of the bedouin nomad fascinated and preoccupied Western adventurers (Blunt 1985; Burckhardt 1831; Doughty 1968; Burton 1907), as did the supposed inferiority of Eastern women and their veiling, presence in harems, segregation, and poor manners (Malmignati 1925; Hume-Griffith 1909). While the travelers' accounts are very useful as historical and anthropological records, many problems arise from their perceptions of the bedouin as a noble or a miserable savage. The aristocratic Blunts, a couple who traveled through Arabia and Mesopotamia, admired the Shammar tribe, comparing Ibn Rasheed with Richard III of England, whereas the Turkophobe Lady Blunt disliked Midhat Pasha, the Ottoman governor, because of his reforming zeal and greatly preferred the Arabs to the Persians or Shi'a (Melman 1992, 298–300). British diplomat Gertrude Bell, ambitious but far less racist than her compatriots, remained preoccupied with her purpose, writing that (being a woman) she could not travel like Richard Doughty, a well-known explorer of Arabia, nor race through the country without "a free hand to work at those things she cared about" (politics)—for "it's a bore being a woman when you are in Arabia" (Bell 2000, 74).

Women travelers tended to misunderstand the rarity of harems and see a false submissiveness in Arab women that blinded them to similar issues in their own society, which they carried with them (Mabro 1991, 1–3; Melman 1992, 16, 17). Polygamy brought forth "horror, disgust and pity" but was seen as exclusively Muslim, which it is not (Melman 1992, 198–199). These same themes recur whenever Saudi Arabian women are reviewed in mainstream Western media.

MODERN SOCIETAL STUDIES

A task of modern anthropologists of Saudi Arabian society is to make sense of these preoccupations and recenter studies on the issues that are of importance to their subjects. This can be seen in Soraya Altorki's work on upper-class women, Saddeka Arebi's studies of women writers, and Mai Yamani's survey of youth (Altorki 1986, 2003; Arebi 1994; Mai Yamani 2000) and in ongoing studies about the use of the Internet and social media.

Some efforts have been made to connect lack or loss of social status with tendencies toward opposition or militancy. Researchers have looked at self-provided data from the Saudi Arabian militant opposition, extracted from Internet postings (Hegghammer 2006), to see if there was a connection to geographic origin or tribal identity. In studies where the Saudi Arabian government provided data, these issues were apparently seen as highly sensitive (Ansary 2008), but they have been used to build a psychological program to retrain or reprogram that opposition in prison (see Chapter 7, Contemporary Issues). Put bluntly, it is possible that certain tribes such as the 'Utayba, some of whom were part of the 1979 uprising, could be targeted by militants, or individuals coming from disaffected regions of the country, because personal networks are usually part of recruitment. Also, those without jobs, university plans, or sufficient money to marry are likely to be disaffected, and so part of the government strategy has been to provide for these needs for those who leave a reeducation program in prison aimed at erasing militant tendencies (Zuhur 2010).

ETHNICITY VERSUS NATIONALITY

Ethnic divisions concern Arab or non-Arab backgrounds; however, this is less important than the dividing line of Saudi Arabian citizenship. Most Saudi Arabian citizens are Arabs, but some, an estimated 10 percent, are of African or Asian origin, often mixed with Arab lineage. The large size of the foreign worker community has meant a significant presence of non–Saudi Arabian Arabs or non-Arabs in the country, who lack the civil and political rights of citizens. What is important is *jinsiyya*, which means both origins and nationality; some groups may ignite negative feelings, but discrimination among Saudi Arabians on the basis of ethnicity is not common at all. Discrimination on the basis of religious sect, possibly geographic origin, or gender is far more common, although the general and the specific forms of any inequalities need to be understood.

TRIBALISM

Tribal affiliation goes back at least to the *jahilliya*, the pre-Islamic period. However, it has been subject to historical movements and changes. The *qabila*, or tribe, has come to mean tribes of noble blood who claimed to descend from 'Adnan or Qa-htan, the ancestors of the southern or northern Arabs. (This lineage is claimed not only by tribes in Saudi Arabia but also by those flung farther north and not only by Muslims.) *Qabyala*, or tribal status, is a very complex idea and pertains today to the former lifestyle of most members, as so few groups are living a purely pastoral lifestyle. Families trace descent through the father's line. In the past, manual labor as carried out by those mining gold, silver, antimony, and salt in al-Yamamah under the Ummayyad Caliphate was not as respected as the tribal lifestyle, and the Bahila people, who specialized solely in mining, were not regarded highly by other groups (al-Askar 2002, 37, 49, 50). Certain other occupations such as tanning hides would not be willingly chosen by those of tribal status. The separation between tribal and settled or agricultural groups is not as clear. Some Western scholars sharply divided in theory all *qabila* from *khadira* (nontribal free men). Yet historians also show us that many tribes were already practicing agriculture throughout the year, or part of the year, from the time of the Islamic conquest, such as the Banu Hazzam, Banu Tamim, one branch of the Banu Nadir, and the Banu Ka'b. In addition, tribal as well as nontribal people engaged in trade. Certain types of artisans were typically not *qabila*, but others might be. The *saluba*, tinkers and traders in the desert, were not *qabila*. It is not entirely clear that claims made in the modernization literature on Saudi Arabia—that the tribal people found work ignoble—were really based on fact. However, when Egyptian or Philippine laborers began to be imported to work on farms at relatively low wages, questions were asked as to why Saudi Arabians were not being hired.

ENDOGAMY

The *ashraf*, or those who claimed descent from the Prophet, were important in the Hijaz area (see Chapter 2, History), and some of them claimed the guardianship of the holy cities. Among the *ashraf*, as for all groups of tribal descent and others as well, endogamy (in-group marriage) was practiced and served to maintain social status. The preferred marriage partner was the father's brother's daughter (*bint 'amm*), but other female cousins through the father's line, or possibly the mother's line, might be considered as well. On the other hand, marriage was also used to stabilize relations between rival tribes and groups or between families that had allied in the past. Ibn Sa'ud married women from other clans of the al-Sa'ud, from a rival tribe, and from the al-Shaykh family.

TRIBAL VALUES

Tribal descent unites individuals and is the basis of social loyalty. If a member of the tribe is wronged, then a member of his or her lineage avenges him or her and pays out compensation to others who are wronged. Most tribal groups who still camped together in summertime considered themselves tribal members, and their animals were branded with the tribe's symbol. Donald Cole's 1968 study of the al-Murrah nomads showed that seven clans related patrilineally make up the tribe; however, the clans can add additional kin or claim relationships through marriages (Cole 1975, 1980). Many disputes arose over grazing and water rights. Certain grazing lands have been retained, but others have been given over to agriculture, based on claims of cultivation (see Chapter 4, Economy). Tribes that developed a water source usually claimed primary rights. They might travel to use it only once a year, so if another tribe claimed the water source or improved it, a clash developed. Tribal rights were fairly well allocated and understood by the beginning of the 20th century. They were altered in some areas with the establishment of the nation and were impacted later on by the loans available in the 1970s and thereafter (Altorki and Cole 1989).

RELIGIOUS ELITE

The *'ulama* (religious scholars) are another important social elite group constituted on the basis of occupation. The religious scholars serve as judges, preachers, notaries, educators, and authorities on Islamic doctrine. Many serve in the government, and Islamic education remains important in Saudi Arabia, whereas it has been displaced by modern educational systems elsewhere in the region (followed by a revival of new private Islamic educational institutes). In the literature on Saudi Arabian society that emphasized modernization, religious scholars tended to be juxtaposed with those with special technical or professional skills, who might make higher incomes. Muslims from international communities might remain in the Hijaz following pilgrimage, and some studied with particular scholars. This trend continued in the modern era, as students from certain countries with or without a tradition of higher Islamic learning wanted to study in the kingdom and could do so in the Islamic institutes or universities.

MERCHANTS

Merchants attained elite status through wealth, and being involved in trade did not detract from tribal status. However, merchants might come from other than tribal backgrounds. Traditional merchant families were located in the Hijaz and the Eastern Province as well as Najd. Some of these were originally from other parts of the world, and had relocated due to sea trade with Arabia, or resettled after coming to Arabia as pilgrims. New merchant and business groups from Najd have become more ascendant since the establishment of the modern kingdom. The modern business class is fairly distinct from the more traditional shop owner or merchant in several ways. Access to technology, knowledge of foreign languages, market study, and knowledge of changing opportunities mark the newer entrepreneurs. Long-distance traders and caravaneers were tribal people (see Chapter 4, Economy), but they have no place in the modern economy.

RELIGIOUS MINORITIES

The social status of minority religious groups, namely, the Shi'a Muslims of the Eastern Province, the Nakhawila of Medina, and the Isma'ilis, was lower than that of the majority Sunni group. This was complicated by the rise of opposition movements after 1979, because many became political prisoners. The Shi'a Muslims were increasingly drawn into government service and promised equity. Another opposition movement, the neosalafists, opposes rights for the Shi'a. Since the outset of militant opposition to the government in 2003, they now compose the majority of political prisoners but may not be categorized as such, since some are obviously guilty of bloodshed and others of complicity or conspiracy.

SLAVERY

Slavery was the outcome of war at the beginning of the Islamic era, and only later, in the premodern era, did it significantly involve the African slave trade. Slaves also came, as elsewhere in the Ottoman Empire, from other areas of the world (Circassia, the Caucasus, and so on), but this white slavery ended before the African slave trade did. Slaves were imported into Saudi Arabia until abolition in 1962. They may have made up as much as 10 percent of the population, an estimated 450,000 in the 1950s. They were very important in agricultural cultivation and in the pearl-diving industry of the Arabian Gulf and the Red Sea (Hopper 2006, 2010). Others were household servants and were usually brought up with their masters. The arguments over abolition in Saudi Arabia are best understood in a regional and international context, in which European pressure was brought to bear on the Ottoman sultan to end slavery; however, the Ottomans had not easily conquered the Arabian Peninsula and were not to retain control there. An 1857 Ottoman *firman* (edict) to end the slave trade in Africans was observed everywhere (orders to halt the Georgian and Circassian trade were issued in 1854 and 1855) except in the Hijaz, because the Ottoman sultan had good reason to anticipate a serious rebellion over the issue (Ochsenwald 1980; Lewis 1990, 80; Shehata 1997). In 1855, a group of merchants in Jeddah wrote to the *'ulama* about the regulations claiming they were anti-Islamic. When the governor of Hijaz sent a direct order to the *'ulama* and the *sharif*s in 1855, Shaykh Jamal issued a *fatwa* (at the instruction of the *sharif* of Mecca), which decreed that it was lawful to kill the Ottoman Turks since they were un-Islamic in banning the slave trade and other actions (Lewis 1990, 80).

Slavery (*'ubudiyya*) was permitted in Islam if the slave came from outside the *dar al-Islam* (lands of Islam) or was the child of existing slaves. A 1936 document, "Instructions Concerning the Trade in Slaves," indicates that slave dealers held documents for the slaves they purchased showing they were slaves in that other country at that time, that owners had to register their slaves, and that Saudi Arabians could not be enslaved (Lewis 1990, 167–169). Other forms of slavery (called elite slavery) have altered the ethnic pool in the Middle East, including the trade of Georgian and Circassian women who were purchased for marriage and the enslaved and converted groups who became warriors (*mamalik*) and members of the Ottoman administration. Such slavery contrasted with the use of slaves for plantation or household labor or for service as pearl divers or oarsmen on the Arabian Peninsula (Ze'evi 1995, 79–81; Lewis 1990). The pearl industry could not have been economically undertaken without slave labor (Hopper 2010). Slaves were also held by the bedouin and by the tribal leaders, and nearly each person that Bell (2000) encountered was served or accompanied by slaves. The slaves were therefore protected by the tribal system without being part of its social class. Some entered particular traditional occupations in the Hijaz, such as that of the watercarrier, but following abolition, all occupations and specializations opened to them.

RACIAL RELATIONS

Arguments over the degree of intermarriage between the races and its social meaning confront the fact that Islam proclaims the equality of believers and that dark complexions were considered equally worthy to light ones. The Qur'an proclaims: "O mankind, we have created you male and female, and appointed you races and tribes, so that you may know one another. Surely the noblest among you in the sight of God is the most godfearing of you" (49:13). In the Prophet Muhammad's final sermon while on pilgrimage, he stated, "All mankind is from Adam and Eve, an Arab has no superiority over a non-Arab nor a non-Arab has any superiority over an Arab; also a white has no superiority over black nor a black has any superiority over white except by piety and good action. You know that every Muslim is the brother of another Muslim." These messages are underscored in Prophetic hadith. Yet beliefs about social status sometimes contradicted this overall religious principle. The principle of *kafa'a*, or equality of status, could be used as a reason to refuse a groom (or, less often, a bride). In the Maliki school of law, this was intended to disqualify an impious spouse or one of bad character, but in the other schools it pertained to descent, wealth, and freedom (Lewis 1990, 86). Also, Muslim men were permitted to have concubines and had children with them, upon whom they could confer legitimacy. Even if these women were slaves, the children were then free. Some observers therefore argue that intermarriage has been very extensive and that race is not, for religious reasons, a distinguishing principle of social status the way that it is or has been in the United States. The Swiss traveler John Lewis Burckhardt remarked on the yellow-brown skin of the Meccans and Jeddawis, attributing it to intermarriage, frequently with Abyssinian concubines, whose children were equal to those of free Arabian women (Burckhardt 1972, 182–187; 1829, 243). Bernard Lewis, however, insists that the slaves left little mark on the Middle Eastern population (a broad statement) and speculates this is because the male slaves were eunuchs or married among their own kind (1990, 84); elsewhere, he states that it may be because of frequent manumission and frequent illness of the slaves (1990, 10). In these comments, one may surmise that he refers first to the slave eunuchs of the Ottoman court. Others wrote that only the *khadira* (nontribal people) intermarried with slaves and that debased their lineage (Doumato 1993, 62), but this idea appears contradicted by the frequent unions between members of elite and middle-class families and slaves, a notable example being that of Bandar ibn Sultan ibn 'Abd al-'Aziz. Similarly, Soraya Altorki, who provided the first anthropological study in English of modern Saudi Arabian urban women, reported the views of elite women in Jeddah. They explained that "good" descent meant the absence of slaves, *mawalid* (offspring of slaves and nonslaves), *takruni* (Africans), and Yemenis in one's family, and they attributed one attractive young woman's failure to marry to her mother's slave background (Altorki 1986, 16, 144).

Muslims are supposed to abhor racism or chauvinism by any one group, and the manumission of slaves was considered to be a good deed. It may be appropriate to understand the institution of slavery as a far-reaching economic system, just as it was in the Americas. The Saudi Arabian princes who fled to Egypt in 1962 included the presence of slavery in the kingdom in their criticisms of the Saudi Arabian rulers. They claimed that slaves were even put to work for the oil companies; the companies paid the slave's wages to his master. Slavery ended with more finality in Saudi Arabia than in the United States, where Jim Crow laws continued on until the civil rights movement of the 1960s (ironically, the same period when Saudi Arabian slaves were freed). The distinction of race between those of Arab and African origin is no longer a social marker among Saudi Arabians. However, it should be noted that beauty standards vary, from acceptance and appreciation of local features and coloring to a consistent identification with and desire for Western standards spread through the media. Highlighting, bleaching, or lightening of hair color, or straightening its frequently curly or frizzy texture to become "silky," is popular (although in Clairol's advertisement designed for Saudi Arabian women, a black hair dye is recommended [Zirinsky 2005, 83–87]). Skin bleaching, cosmetic surgery on noses, and emulation of tall, thin body types are fairly pervasive and speak to a racialization of beauty images (Hunter in Das Gupta, et al., eds., 2007, 313).

In addition, those who are not Saudi Arabian by nationality are exposed to some racist attitudes, and these include Africans and Asians. A well-known Saudi Arabian blogger (Saudi Jawa of the *Sandcrawler* blog) is of Javanese descent (*jawa* is the Saudi Arabian term for a person from Southeast Asia) and is a native of Mecca. He admits that there are racist attitudes in Saudi Arabia, but these are mitigated toward those of Saudi Arabian nationality as compared to foreign workers.

TRADITIONAL SOCIAL VALUES

Social values are said to derive from the noble tribal groups. *Muruwah*, or chivalry, meant devotion and loyalty to family, adhesion to certain norms of behavior, upholding of the honor of family and tribe, courage, self-sacrifice, generosity, and hospitality. It was expressed in the code of warfare between tribes as well as social relations outside of war. Some of these values carried over into Islamic society, but the ideal was loyalty to the brotherhood and sisterhood of Islam and an end to tribal feuding. Women represented the honor of their men, and violations of their sexual honor were punished by their male kin.

Because women must protect their sexual honor, segregation of women has been practiced by those economically able to do so. Devotion to society and the nation in the philanthropy practiced by their rulers, their creation of new institutions such as colleges and universities, and women's increasing educational and professional skills are all reasons that segregation by gender is beginning to break down in some circumstances, but it is being maintained in others.

Social and religious values combine in the case of philanthropy and charitable giving. Beyond this, people recognized those dependent on them economically—for business, the care of servants, unemployed family members, and the aged and poor people in the community. Upholding these social values as well as religious values imparts social status.

Other social values are changing as a result of the shift from extended family households to nuclear family households, which began in the 1970s. Women maintain reciprocal social relations (*wafa'*) through visits to networks of *wufyan* (formal networks) and *sudqan* (close friends), both for formal, invited occasions (*wu'ud*) and informal visits. But these now include unmarried women as well as married women. Women also now spend more time with their own husbands than in the past, just as it is now more common for spouses to share a bedroom. Sons are now raised together with daughters, and male servants may come into the female parts of the household (Altorki 1986, 32, 33 109–121). Women are now acquiring information through other means than their female networks, like television or, possibly, their workplaces and the Internet.

AGE

Age provides status to men as well as women. Deference is given to older family members, whether the father, grandfather, elder brother, or mother-in-law. A father typically decided what his children should study and whether they could travel for higher education, and a large percentage of families determined marriage partners for their sons and daughters.

The Sa'udi royal family is headed by its senior princes, most of whom are septuagenarians at least. While the aging power structure is aging, Saudi Arabian society as a whole is increasingly youthful, with a much lower median age than in Western countries. (Some sources claim that the population under 18 is higher than the following estimates.) The total estimated population of 28,686,633 includes 5,576,076 nonnationals. Since the nonnationals who are counted are all adults, this slightly skews measurements of the youth bulge. Other sources estimate far more foreign residents, at approximately 9.5 million. Out of the total (nationals and nonnationals), 38 percent are age 14 or younger, 59.5 percent are age 15 to 65, and only 2.5 percent are age 65 or older.

TABLE 5.2   Demographics

Total Population

28,686,633

country comparison to the world: 41

Note: This number includes 5,576,076 nonnationals (July 2010 est.).

Age Structure

0–14 years: 38% (male 5,557,453, female 5,340,614)

15–64 years: 59.5% (male 9,608,032, female 7,473,543)

65 years and over: 2.5% (male 363,241, female 343,750) (2010 est.)

Median Age

Total: 24.9 years

Male: 26 years

Female: 23.4 years (2010 est.)

* Males exceed females in each age category. Two reasons exist for this situation; one is the presence of foreign workers, who include more men than women. Also there is a preference for male children. It is possible that modern sex-selection techniques have had some impact, but it is also common for more boys to be born than girls (in many societies) and the infant mortality rate for boys is higher than for girls.

Source: "Saudi Arabia," *CIA World Factbook 2010.*

GENDER AND SOCIAL STATUS

Women who bore sons might have greater social status than others, depending on their children's achievement and closeness to them. Women who were childless might find themselves divorced, or their husband might take another wife. These consequences still pertain more than in the West but less so for some than in the past. Saudi Arabian women's fertility rate is 3.77 children per woman. This shows quite a reduction from the past. In the premodern period, women "without men" existed; this was a primary rationale for women's necessary work, but marriage was considered the norm.

The section on women later on in this chapter discusses many of the restrictions women face in the kingdom. They are not, however, automatically of lower status than men. Rather, much depends on other aspects of their social location. In general, the sexes are seen as complementary, and gender differences are biologically based. Gradually, women have argued, in some cases, against the belief that they are not capable of certain types of work, but they have accepted situations where they will work in segregated circumstances until conditions change. Many people differentiate between the status quo and the ideal role of women in either an authentic or an enlightened Muslim society. As the trends toward religiosity increased and the conservatives and neosalafists gained more adherents in Saudi Arabia, the debates over women's status heightened. Some women called for a refusal of the reforms Western feminists wanted for them. Sohaila Zain al-Abedin, a prominent Saudi Arabian essayist, supported the wearing of the *hijab* (Islamic head covering) in addition to the *abaya*, domesticity for women, and segregation, and she opposed sexual permissiveness. However, she simultaneously opposed the abuse of Islamic privileges like polygamy (Zain al-Abedin 1982; Arebi 1994, 236–239).

MODERNIZATION AND SOCIETY

From the 1970s through the 1990s, a major theme in sociological or anthropological studies concerned the struggle between tradition and modernization—Saudi Arabia's struggle to retain its own values in the face of its rapidly expanding cities and changing rural areas. Rural and urban societies changed radically. In the 1960s, the remaining fully pastoralist groups were often impoverished and malnourished and at the same time were gradually being settled. By the early 1980s, oil income had made it possible to settle more of the bedouin, and the expansion of irrigation and importation of workers were changing the rural economy (Altorki and Cole 1989; Fernea 1983 in Fernea and Fernea, eds., 1987, 293–316), and Saudi Arabia shared various problems with its fellow developing nations. Some of the settlements did not take into account the preferences and needs of the rural people, and, in succeeding planning stages, the government contracted anthropologists to survey the bedouin. The results of resettlement were positive in terms of stabilizing income, but some critics noted uninhabited projects in Riyadh that were not designed for large families. Also, in Nassim, some enterprising folks had received land grants and built property that they rented out, thereby avoiding any need to work (Mackey 1987, 220–221). Other kinds of dislocation took place; the male Saudi Arabians were often displaced from their wives and children, as they moved to work in the cities and towns or in the National Guard. Some people had more access to the resources of the country than did others, whose access was limited due to illiteracy, their unfamiliarity with bureaucratic structures, or physical distance (Doumato in Metz, ed., 1993). Social debates over the positive and negative aspects of progress continued and were reflected in literature that had implications for public policy (Abdul Aziz 1994; Fabietti 2000; Finan and al-Haratani 1998). Urbanization was seen as having mixed outcomes, but clearly, at least by 2000, the effects of modern living, employment patterns, and social conceptions were more crucial to the measured success of the government (Akers 2001) than the previous focus on the transition of bedouin communities.

FOREIGN WORKERS

Two approaches to foreign workers or illegal immigrants to Saudi Arabia are common in the literature; one concerns their mistreatment and supposes racism, which may actually be discriminatory behavior arising from disputes due to the legal status of the worker or immigrant. The other trend in the literature supports Saudization policies and seeks to understand why foreign labor continues at high levels. Because both illegal and legal immigration to Saudi Arabia are ongoing, a person's residency and occupational status is very important as well as his or her country of origin. Checkpoints on roads or city streets require drivers to produce legal documents.

URBAN ANNUAL GROWTH RATE IN SAUDI ARABIA

Saudi Arabia's population has moved into cities and towns, making it primarily an urban population. The speed of urbanization has slowed; however, the population continues to increase, and foreign workers live in the urban areas as well. The visual transformation of urban areas has been profound.

Year	Urban Annual Growth Rate (%)
1975–1980	8.04
1980–1985	7.81
1985–1990	5.73
1990–1995	2.85
1995–2000	2.92
2000–2005	2.81
2005–2010	2.51
2010–2015	2.31
2015–2020	2.10 (estimated)

Source: UN Population Division, 2008/2009.

Apparently, the largest group of illegal immigrants are Yemenis, who like the Saudi Arabians are mostly of Arab descent, and Somalis and Eritreans, who usually cross over from Yemen. Other groups from Asia, South Asia, and Africa manage to enter the country as well.

The lowest of the low in the illegal immigrant groups are children who are stolen in their home country and taken over the border to beg in Saudi Arabia, turning over some of their earnings to adults. Some have run away from their smugglers but have no recourse but begging. They are often beaten and may be mutilated. There are thousands of street children in Jeddah, and a smaller number can be found in Riyadh. Some sources claim they are nearly all boys and come from Yemen, Somalia, Chad, India, and Pakistan. However, other sources note that girls are also on the streets and that many of these are Saudi Arabians of poor families. The Yemeni government admitted that about 300 children per month were crossing the border into Saudi Arabia, and a center for rescued children was opened in 2007 at the Harad border crossing (BBC Two, March 27, 2007).

Approximately 240,015 Palestinian refugees live in Saudi Arabia (*CIA World Factbook 2010*). On the one hand, Palestinians have received political support from Saudi Arabia and badly need that support. Nevertheless, some have legitimately complained about their second-class status in the country. They must renew their residence permits every two years for a fee of 2,000 riyals and be sponsored by a

Saudi Arabian citizen in order to work or own a business or property. To change jobs, a Palestinian (like other foreign workers) needs to change sponsors, again for a fee, and receive a release letter. University attendance may or may not be permitted; those admitted cannot choose their own major field of study.

An estimated 1.2 million Egyptians work in Saudi Arabia in a variety of sectors (*al-Masry al-Yom*, May 10, 2010). In 2008 and 2009, labor protests began in Saudi Arabia involving many types and situations of foreign labor. Some disputes have occurred in previous years, and it was often written that Arab labor became less desirable than Asian labor in some sectors due to the political views of the Arab workers, particularly Egyptians and Palestinians. This is not entirely true, as their labor was not completely supplanted. Egyptians have long migrated to Saudi Arabia to work in professional jobs (for example, as engineers and doctors) and also lower-paying positions (as service and hotel workers, construction workers, drivers, salespersons, and agricultural laborers). Egyptian women have also migrated to work as nurses, doctors, teachers, and servants. Egyptians, whether in low- paying or professional jobs, have reported difficulties in changing jobs and problems with certain employers who delay salaries. Some violent incidents have occurred, including attacks on Egyptian doctors and the shooting of two Egyptians, one of whom was a journalist, in July 2010, resulting in their deaths. An Egyptian driver was murdered in August, and there have been other incidents that appear to be the actions of young Saudi Arabians who previously had no acquaintance with their victims.

Pakistanis, Bangladeshis, Indians, Sri Lankans, Nepalese, Indonesians, Filipinos, and other Asian nationalities are also employed in Saudi Arabia. Their status depends on a variety of factors: if they are Muslims or not, if they speak Arabic and are literate, and what type of occupation they are engaged in. Some South Asians or Southeast Asians are longtime or even historic residents of Arabia and have much a higher social status than the foreigners working on temporary contracts.

The fourth-largest group of foreign workers in Saudi Arabia come from the Philippines. Filipinos began immigrating to Saudi Arabia for work in 1973. Evidence of their long presence is reflected in 24 Philippine schools in the country. They work in the health fields as doctors and nurses, in the oil and manufacturing sector, in services, and in homes, as servants. As with the other groups, their status varies considerably based on the nature of their work and their employers. One point of tension for certain Philippine immigrants is their religion and the restrictions on public worship.

Other reports indicate widespread mistreatment, including some horrendous physical abuse, rape, and attempted murder; sometimes nonpayment; and confinement of some domestic workers (migrants who work in domestic service are estimated to number 1.5 million). Kenyans, Indonesians, Nepalese, Sri Lankans, Filipinos, and others have been targeted, because they are vulnerable inside private homes (Human Rights Watch 2008, September 2, 2010), and labor laws had not addressed their situation. In response, the Saudi Arabian government created its own commission for human rights, which includes the minister of social affairs and others.

Western workers and their families number under 100,000 (one estimate in 2004 gave skilled workers at 38,000). Many Americans, Britons, and other Europeans considered their jobs and living conditions in Saudi Arabia to be excellent as most were employed in high-paying skilled positions, enjoyed tax benefits, and had housing and schooling provided by their companies. However, when Westerners were targeted in attacks by Saudi Arabian militants in Riyadh, Khobar, and Yanbu in 2003 and 2004, large numbers of foreigners left, including all 90 employees of ABB-Lummus in Yanbu, after a serious attack killed six (*Christian Science Monitor*, May 4, 2004).

POVERTY

Poverty exists in Saudi Arabia's cities, villages, and rural areas. Official government statistics and reports claimed that nomadic and peasant poverty had been eradicated. These had not kept up with the growth of poverty due to the price increases in the oil boom period and the effects of the first and second oil price drops. Poverty cannot be measured from the appearance of older areas but rather from the specific circumstances of the inhabitants. Those without jobs; those who are no longer in school; the unemployed who are now married, widowed, or divorced; and those with disabilities are the obvious categories to have fallen into poverty, but they are not the only poor groups. Crown Prince 'Abdullah acknowledged the situation in 2002 and made a visit to poor residents in Riyadh. A national strategy to combat poverty was announced early in 2003, in which new poverty guidelines were to be developed. The government issues social security payments to families without breadwinners (men), but this amount is only about $5,000 and ceases under some circumstances. A Saudi Arabian opposition leader in London claimed that the level of poverty was at 25 percent or even 30 percent (*Los Angeles Times*, May 16, 2003). As Saudi Arabians sought to identify the causes of the terrorist attacks in 2003, some thought that the poor and unemployed might be more susceptible to recruitment by Islamist militants. At the very least, the existence of poverty and corruption in Saudi Arabia were grievances exploited by the extremists (since a fully Islamic government should address the needs of the poor).

THE ROYAL FAMILY

The Islamic model of leadership has almost always exceeded the capabilities of rulers; some of these were pious and administratively effective, but others were not. A tribal leader might have the status of *amir* (a prince or ruler; the plural, *umara*, applies to the princes and princesses of the royal family) and was assisted by an *amin*, who collected taxes. The *amir* also had to fulfill the function of a *shaykh* in deliberating over disputes. The leader had noble blood but also a noble character, and he ruled men who considered themselves his peers. He could not task or penalize them without reason, and they were permitted to criticize him and give him counsel.

Today, the al-Sa'ud family is so large that it can be seen as a social class of its own. However, unlike the case of royalty or the aristocracy of England or France in the premodern era, certain egalitarian norms are embedded in Arabian society, partially via religious belief and tribal custom. Special titles are given to the offspring of 'Abd al-'Aziz al-Sa'ud, because they are the ruling clan of the family and the nation, and they are addressed His (or Her) Royal Highness. Other members of the family are simply addressed as Your (or His) Highness or Prince (*amir*). Like other royalty, the al-Sa'ud family has the disadvantage of living life in the public eye; consequently, family members are under greater scrutiny and subject to more familial criticism than other members of society. Any dishonorable behavior is treated seriously. Cohesion and cooperation are expected of family members.

Prince Al-Walid ibn Talal al-Sa'ud is the world's eighth-richest man, with an estimated net worth of $20 billion; however, not all of the royal family are wealthy, and most of the other extremely wealthy Saudi Arabian businessmen are not al-Sa'ud family members. Conspicuous consumption and building have marked Saudi Arabia's wealthy groups since the first oil boom.

The family members of 'Abd al-'Aziz al-Sa'ud were appointed to governmental positions but were expected to demonstrate skill and wisdom in these positions. Their appointment was not so much a matter of nepotism, as critics accused, as a way of meeting the social expectations that the ruler would ensure attention and good governance by the assigning of those closely related to him. Sometimes important duties or an especially delicate or politically troublesome task were assigned by one brother to another, while others were given to the sons of powerful princes. An example might be the personal intervention of the king following the Intifadhat 1400 in the eastern provinces, who assigned the investigation and mediation into the condition of the Shi'a to his son.

In general, the principle of succession follows along seniority and reflects a consensus of the key family members (Kechichian 2001; also see Chapter 2, History, and Chapter 3, Government and Politics). Over time, many nonroyals with professional credentials were also appointed to key governmental posts, a fact adding to the legitimacy of the al-Sa'ud rather than detracting from it.

Acquiring proximity to those in elevated social and political positions is desirable in Saudi Arabia for a variety of reasons. The growing bureaucracy was difficult for ordinary persons to navigate so they might seek or resort to a *wasta* (a connection or intermediary) if a problem or a crime were to occur. Grievances could also be presented personally, but the cultivation of such connections, whether to deal with a grievance or obtain aid, is still considered important, just as it is in other Arab societies today.

REFERENCES

Abdul Aziz, Moudi Mansour. *Settling the Tribes: The Role of the Bedouin in the Formation of the Saudi State*. London: Al Saqi, 1994.

Akers, Deborah S. "The Tribal Concept in Urban Saudi Arabia." PhD diss., Ohio State University, 2001.

Alsanea, Rajaa. *Girls of Riyadh*. Translated by Marilyn Booth. New York: Penguin, 2008.

Altorki, Soraya. "Sisterhood and Stewardship in Sister-Brother Relations in Saudi Arabia." In Nicholas Hopkins, ed. "The New Arab Family." Special issue of *Cairo Papers in Social Science* 24, nos. 1–2 (2003), 180–200.

Altorki, Soraya. "The Concept and Practice of Citizenship in Saudi Arabia." In *Gender and Citizenship in the Middle East*, edited by Suad Joseph. Syracuse, NY: Syracuse University Press, 2000, 215–236.

Altorki, Soraya. "At Home in the Field." In *Arab Women in the Field: Studying Your Own Society*, edited by Soraya Altorki and Camillia Fawzi El-Solh. Syracuse, NY: Syracuse University Press, 1988, 49–68.

Altorki, Soraya. *Women in Saudi Arabia: Ideology and Behavior among the Elite*. New York: Columbia University Press, 1986.

Altorki, Soraya, and Donald P. Cole. *Arabian Oasis City: The Transformation of 'Unayzah*. Austin: University of Texas Press, 1989.

Ansary, Abdullah F. "Combating Extremism: A Brief Overview of Saudi Arabia's Approach." *Middle East Policy* 15, no. 2 (Summer 2008), 111–142.

Arebi, Saddeka. *Women and Words in Saudi Arabia: The Politics of Literary Discourse*. New York: Columbia University Press, 1994.

al-Askar, Abdullah. *al-Yamama in the Early Islamic Era*. Reading, UK: Ithaca, 2002.

Bagader, Abu Bakr A., and Ava Molnar Heinrichsdorff, eds. and trans. *Assassination of Light: Modern Saudi Short Stories*. Washington, DC: Three Continents, 1990.

al-Baz, Rania. *Disfigured: A Saudi Woman's Story of Triumph over Violence*. Translated by Catherine Spencer. Northampton, MA: Interlink, 2008.

BBC Two. "The Child Slaves of Saudi Arabia." This World. BBC. March 27, 2007.

Bell, Gertrude. *The Arabian Diaries, 1913–1914*. Edited by Rosemary O'Brien. Syracuse, NY: Syracuse University Press, 2000.

Birks, J.S., and C.A. Sinclair. *Saudi Arabia into the 90s*. Durham, UK: Mountjoy Research Center, University of Durham, 1988.

Blunt, Anne Noel. *A Pilgrimage to Nejd, the Cradle of the Arab Race, a Visit to the Court of the Emir and "Our" Persian Campaign*. London: Century, 1985. (Originally published in 1881.)

Burckhardt, John Lewis. *Travels in Arabia Comprehending an Account of Those Territories in Hedjaz Which the Mohammedans Regard as Sacred*. London: Henry Colburn, 1829; reprinted, Beirut, Lebanon: Librairie du Liban, 1972.

Burckhardt, John Lewis. *Notes on the Bedouin and the Wahabys*. London: Henry Coburn and Richard Bentley, 1831.

Burton, Richard Francis. *Personal Narrative of a Pilgrimage to Al-Madinah and Meccah*. 2 vols. (Originally written 1855–1856 and first published in 1857.) Memorial Edition 1893; London: George Bell and Sons, 1907.

Cole, Donald P. "Pastoral Nomads in a Rapidly Changing Economy: The Case of Saudi Arabia." In *Social and Economic Development in the Arab Gulf*, edited by Tim Niblock. New York: St. Martin's, 1980, 106–121.

Cole, Donald P. *Nomads of the Nomads: The Al Murrah Bedouin of the Empty Quarter*. Chicago: Aldine, 1975.

Cole, Donald P. "Al Murrah Bedouins: The Pure Ones Roam Arabia's Sands." *Nomads of the World*, edited by Gilbert Grosvenor. Washington, DC: National Geographic Society, Prepared by the Special Publications Division, 1971, 52–71.

Cole, Donald P., and Soraya Altorki. "Production and Trade in North Central Arabia: Change and Development in Unayzah." In *The Transformation of Nomad Society in the Arab East*, edited by Martha Mundy and Basim Musallam. Cambridge: Cambridge University Press, 2000, 145–149.

Dickson, H.R.P. *The Arab of the Desert: Bedouin Life in Kuwait and Saudi Arabia*. London: Allen and Unwin, 1949.

Doughty, Charles M. *Travels in Arabia Deserta*. Abridged by Edward Garnett. Gloucester, MA: Peter Smith, 1968.

Doumato, Eleanor A. *Getting God's Ear: Women, Islam and Healing in Saudi Arabia and the Gulf*. New York: Columbia University Press, 2000.

Doumato, Eleanor A. "Environment" and "Society." In *Saudi Arabia: A Country Study*, edited by Helen Chapin Metz, Federal Research Division, Library of Congress. Washington, DC: Library of Congress, 1993.

Fabietti, Ugo. "State Policies and Bedouin Adaptations in Saudi Arabia, 1900–1980." In *The Transformation of Nomad Society in the Arab East*, edited by Martha Mundy and Basim Musallam. Cambridge: Cambridge University Press, 2000, 82–89.

Fernea, Elizabeth. *In Search of Islamic Feminism: One Woman's Journey*. New York: Doubleday, 1998.

Fernea, Robert. "Hail, Saudi Arabia" and "The Anthropologist in the Field." In *The Arab World: Personal Encounters*, by Elizabeth Warnock Fernea and Robert Fernea. Garden City, NY: Anchor Books, 1987, 293–316.

Finan, Timothy Joseph, and E.R. Al-Haratani. "Modern Bedouins: The Transformation of Traditional Nomad Society in the Al-Taysiyah Region of Saudi Arabia." In *Drylands: Sustainable Use of Rangelands into the Twenty-First Century*, edited by V.R. Squires and A.E. Sidahmed. Rome, Italy: International Fund for Agricultural Development, 1998.

Gordon, Murray. *Slavery in the Arab World*. New York: New Amsterdam Books, 1989.

Hamdan, Amani. "Women and Education in Saudi Arabia: Challenges and Achievements." *International Education Journal* 6, no. 1 (2005), 42–64.

Hegghammer, Thomas. "Terrorist Recruitment and Radicalization in Saudi Arabia." *Middle East Policy* 13, no. 4 (Winter 2006), 39–60.

Hoggarth, David P. *The Penetration of Arabia: A Record of the Development of Western Knowledge Concerning the Arabian Peninsula*. Beirut, Lebanon: Khayats, 1966. (Originally published in 1905.)

Hopper, Mathew S. "Pearls, Globalization and the African Diaspora in the Arabian Gulf in the Age of Empire." Paper presented at the 124th Annual Meeting of the American Historical Association, San Diego, January 9, 2010.

Hopper, Mathew S. "The African Presence in Arabia: Slavery, the World Economy, and the African Diaspora in Eastern Arabia, 1840–1940." PhD diss., University of California, Los Angeles, 2006.

Hopwood, Derek. ed. *The Arabian Peninsula: Society and Politics*. Totowa, NJ: Rowman and Littlefield, 1972.

Human Rights Watch. "Saudi Arabia: Domestic Worker Brutalized." September 2, 2010. http://www.hrw.org/en/news/2010/09/02/saudi-arabia-domestic-worker-brutalized

Human Rights Watch. "As If I Am Not Human." July 7, 2008. http://www.hrw.org/en/reports/2008/07/07/if-i-am-not-human-0

Hume-Griffith, M. E. *Behind the Veil in Persia and Turkish Arabia: An Account of an Englishwoman's Eight Years' Residence amongst the Women of the East.* London: Seeley, 1909.

Hunter, Margaret. "Color and the Changing Racial Landscape." In *Race and Racialization: Essential Readings,* edited by Tania Das Gupta, Carl E. James, Roger C.A. Maaka, Grace-Edward Glabuzi, and Chris Andersen. Toronto: Canadian Scholars Press, 2007, 301–315.

Ingham, Bruce. *Bedouin of Northern Arabia: Traditions of the Al-Dhafir.* London and New York: Kegan Paul, 1986.

Jones, Toby. "Saudi Arabia's Not So New Anti-Shi'ism." *Middle East Report* 242 (Spring 2007).

al-Juhany, Uwaidah M. *Najd before the Salafi Reform Movement: Social, Religious and Political Conditions in the Three Centuries Preceding the Rise of the Saudi State.* Reading, UK: Ithaca, 2002.

Katakura, Motoko. *Bedouin Village.* Tokyo: University of Tokyo Press, 1977.

Keane, John F. *Six Months in the Hejaz: An Account of the Mohammedan Pilgrimages to Meccah and Medinah. Accomplished by an Englishman Professing Mohammedanism.* London: Ward & Downey, 1887.

Kechichian, Joseph. *Succession in Saudi Arabia.* New York: Palgrave, 2001.

Kupershoek, Marcel. *Arabia of the Bedouins.* London: Al Saqi, 2001.

Lacey, Robert. *Inside the Kingdom: Kings, Clerics, Modernists, Terrorists and the Struggle for Saudi Arabia.* New York: Viking Penguin, 2009.

Lancaster, William. *The Rwala Bedouin Today.* Cambridge: Cambridge University Press, 1981.

Lewis, Bernard. *Race and Slavery in the Middle East: An Historical Enquiry.* New York: Oxford University Press, 1990.

Long, David E. *Culture and Customs of Saudi Arabia.* Westport, CT: Greenwood, 2005.

Mabro, Judy. *Veiled Half-Truths: Western Travellers' Perceptions of Middle Eastern Women.* London: I. B. Tauris, 1991.

Mackey, Sandra. *The Saudis: Inside the Desert Kingdom.* New York and Scarborough, ON, Canada: New American Library, 1987.

Malmignati, Countess. *Through Inner Deserts to Medina.* London: Phillip Allan, 1925.

Melman, Billie. *Women's Orients: English Women and the Middle East, 1718–1918.* Ann Arbor: University of Michigan Press, 1992.

Nicholson, Reynard A. *A Literary History of the Arabs.* Cambridge: Cambridge University Press, 1977. (Originally published in 1907.)

Ochsenwald, William. "Muslim European Conflict in the Hijaz: The Slave Trade Controversy 1840–1859." *Middle Eastern Studies* 16, no. 1 (1980), 115–126.

al-Rasheed, Madawi, and Robert Vitalis, eds. *Counternarratives: History, Contemporary Society, and Politics in Saudi Arabia and Yemen.* New York: Palgrave Macmillan, 2004.

Rugh, William. "Emergence of a New Middle Class in Saudi Arabia." *Middle East Journal* 27, no. 1 (Winter 1973), 9–20.

al-Sa'ud, Norah bint Muhammad, al-Jawhara Muhammad al-'Anqari, and Madeha Muhammad al-'Atroush, eds. *Abha, Bilad Asir: Southwestern Region of the Kingdom of Saudi Arabia.* Riyadh, Saudi Arabia: By the editors, 1989.

Shehata, Talaat. "Abolition in Asia." In *Historical Encyclopedia of World Slavery*, edited by Junius P. Rodriguez. Santa Barbara, CA: ABC-CLIO, 1997.

Al-Shetaiwi, Abdullah S. "Factors Affecting the Underutilisation of Qualified Saudi Women in the Saudi Private Sector." PhD diss., Loughborough University, 2002.

Snouck Hurgronje, Christaan. *Mekka in the Latter Part of the Nineteenth Century, 1885–1889.* Translated by James Henry Monahan. Leiden, the Netherlands: Brill, 1931. (Reprinted in 1970.)

2008 Annual Arab Public Opinion Poll. Survey of the Anwar Sadat Chair, University of Maryland with Zogby International. Conducted March 2008 in Egypt, Jordan, Lebanon, Morocco, Saudi Arabia, and the United Arab Emirates.

Vidal, Frederico. *The Oasis of Al-Hasa.* Vol. 2 of *Aramco Reports on Al-Hasa and Oman 1950–1955* by William E. Mulligan, Frederico Vidal, and George S. Rentz. Cambridge: Cambridge Archive Editions, 1990.

Yamani, Maha A. Z. *Polygamy and Law in Saudi Arabia.* Reading, UK: Ithaca, 2008.

Yamani, Mai. *Cradle of Islam: The Hijaz and the Quest for an Arabian Identity.* London: I. B. Tauris, 2004.

Yamani, Mai. *Changed Identities: The Challenge of a New Generation in Saudi Arabia.* London: Royal Institute of International Affairs, 2000.

Yamani, Mai. "Changing the Habits of a Lifetime: The Adaptation of Hejazi Dress to the New Social Order." In *Languages of Dress in the Middle East*, edited by Nancy Lindesfarne-Tapper and Bruce Ingham. Richmond, UK: Curzon, 1997, 55–66.

Yamani, Mai. "Some Observations on Women in Saudi Arabia." In *Feminism and Islam: Legal and Literary Perspectives*, edited by Mai Yamani. Reading, UK: Garnet, 1996, 263–281.

Zain al-Abedin, Sohaila. *Bina' al-usra al-Muslima.* Jeddah, Saudi Arabia: al-Dar Sa'udiyya li-Nashr wa-Tawzi', 1984.

Zain al-Abedin, Sohaila. *Masirat al-mar'a al-Sa'udiyya ila ayna?* Jeddah, Saudi Arabia: al-Dar Sa'udiyya li-Nashr wa-Tawzi', 1982.

Ze'evi, Dror. "Slavery." In *Encyclopedia of the Modern Islamic World*, edited by John Esposito. New York: Oxford University Press, 1995, 79–81.

Zirinsky, Roni. *Ad-Hoc Arabism: Advertising, Culture and Technology in Saudi Arabia.* New York: Peter Lang, 2005.

Zuhur, Sherifa. *Ideological and Motivational Factors in the Defusing of Radical Islamist Violence.* Carlisle, PA, and Cairo: Institute of Middle Eastern, Islamic, and Strategic Studies, 2010.

Zuhur, Sherifa. "Considerations of Honor Crimes, FGM, Kidnapping/Rape and Early Marriage in Selected Arab Nations." Paper prepared for "Good Practices in Legislation to Address Harmful Practices against Women," United Nations Division for the Advancement of Women and United Nations Economic Commission for Africa, Addis Ababa, Ethiopia, May 25–28, 2009.

Women and Marriage

When the Kingdom of Saudi Arabia was proclaimed in 1932, women's roles reflected the Arab cultural ideals of honor and the premodern gendered division of labor. In Arab societies, male honor is linked to women's chastity and modesty. Women may bring shame on their entire family for violating gender norms. Therefore, women's family members socialize them to strict norms and enforce these. Early, arranged, and endogamous marriages were preferred, and marriage is expected for both men and women. Men were active in the economic sphere, and women were responsible for home and family; however, women in bedouin groups still involved in herding, or those in agricultural communities, contributed their labor. Segregation from all men who are not closely related to women (a *mahram*, one a woman cannot marry) is the ideal and the law. This custom was reflected in living patterns, customs, and the organization of work, but it came to be more strictly enforced later in the 20th century.

Saudi Arabia follows Islamic law, in particular, the Hanbali *madhhab*, or school of Islam; a minority follow the Maliki *madhhab*. Also resident in Saudi Arabia are Shi'a and Isma'ili Muslims who follow their own legal teachings. In all four existing schools of Sunni Islam and in Shi'a Islam as well, men's rights and responsibilities differ from women's. Men are the legal guardians of women and may restrict women from numerous activities unless they give permission. Based on custom and also Islamic law, the Basic Law of Saudi Arabia therefore reads: "The family is the basic unit of Saudi society and the guardian (male) should be obeyed" (Article 40). Women also possess rights under Islamic law. They keep their own names and control over any property that is theirs and need not cede or share this with their husbands. They have rights to divorce if men fail to support them economically and under certain other conditions, although they have not always had the ability to pursue their legal rights. Women have spiritual rights equal to men's and religious duties. They are not supposed to be mistreated by their husbands, and they typically resorted to their own relatives to support them in such situations. Unfortunately, these relatives might not be supportive or economically capable of providing a refuge.

Due to the historic alliance of the Sa'udi family and the religious elite, the deeply ingrained cultural ideals of gender, and also a religious revival and official intensification of religious demeanor and rules that began in the 1980s, Saudi Arabian women have not been treated as equal citizens with men. They are not permitted to vote or stand for office. Only in 2009 was a woman appointed in a deputy ministerial post, and they are precluded from working in many occupations. They cannot drive, must cover their bodies and hair in all public places, and cannot mix with unrelated men, with only certain exceptions. Conservatives have sought to restrict women's ability even to approach the Ka'ba at the *hajj*, whereas women had previously been free to walk and pray alongside men while attending that ritual. Women have made strides in certain professional areas, particularly education and health, but due to the system of sex or gender segregation and tensions over women's roles, this progress has not been without obstacles.

The history of women's roles in Arabia is complex. The 19th-century scholar Robertson Smith proposed that the Arabian tribes showed evidence of matrilocal and matrilineal practices (Ahmed 1992, 43). In addition, there were even plural forms of marriage for women as well as men, something that Islam would end. The 20th-century scholar Montgomery Watt suggested that the mercantile lifestyle and seden-tarization of the tribes there had promoted a shift to patrilineality (1956, 272–273). Patrilineality is supported by marriage customs and rules of behavior introduced in the early Islamic community. These customs, such as women's virginity until mar-riage and strict fidelity within it, ensure that offspring are indeed their father's prog-eny and deserve to inherit from them. Polygyny for men was restricted by Islamic rules to four legal wives, and these were to be equally treated and provided for. The men benefited from multiple family alliances and additional offspring.

Women in ancient Arabia were essentially the property of their tribe, could be married without their consent, and had very limited rights in some groups (in oth-ers, they had more power). A school of Western scholarship postulated that the shift to patrilineality and patrilocality had worsened women's situation, as did the shift from a barter to a money economy and economic instability in periods of tribal strife. However, Islam addressed some harmful practices such as the exposure of female infants, forbidding it; Islam also specified that women had to assent to their mar-riages and that society must uphold morality and control unlicensed sexual behavior. Women, who had been treated like chattel, gained particular rights under Islam, even though many contemporary non-Muslims view Islam as the factor impeding wom-en's agency. Segregation of women was adopted by the Prophet apparently under the influence of surrounding societies like Byzantium, where it was practiced. Veiling was not new in Arabia in Muhammad's day but was prevalent only among upper classes; it was required of Muhammad's wives but not necessarily other women. In fact, historian Leila Ahmed points out that "she took the veil" was the phrase used to indicate that a woman had become the Prophet Muhammad's wife in hadith lit-erature (Ahmed 1992, 55).

The system of segregation by sex in Saudi Arabia is enforced by the religious police known as the Committee for the Promotion of Virtue and the Prevention of Vice, or *mutawa'in*. The *mutawa'in* are supposed to punish all visible violations of Islamic law, but in fact they have tended to focus on particular issues such as violations of women's dress code or occasions that men and unrelated women might attend. As a journalist wryly noted, the *mutawa'in* were not knocking on the doors of men who deny economic support to their dependents or who abuse their wives. Until 2006, when a Ministry of the Interior decree was issued, the *mutawa'in* could beat offenders or hold them and interrogate them in their own detention facilities. They might de-mand to see a couple's marriage license and arrest them if they lacked one. A foreign physician described a thwarted *mutawa'in* raid during a mixed dinner organized for international guests of a medical symposium held in 2000 (Ahmad 2008, 227–247). I experienced *mutawa'in* harassment of women entering the Janadiriyya, at a folklore festival in 2005, on the day set for women's attendance. Although the male *mutawa'in* could not enter the festival grounds, they congregated at the entrance to yell at and admonish women they considered improperly dressed, like one of our Western com-panions. When I defended her and promised to buy her a proper covering, the very young *mutawa'* in his short *thobe*, wild hair, and facial expression turned on me and complained in a thundering voice that my long skirt worn under my *abaya* should be an inch longer (my *abaya* and my skirt were ankle-length). At the Kingdom Mall, where a floor is reserved for women, one could observe *mutawa'in* crowding at the escalators on the floors just above and below, to chastise women who had not covered up sufficiently.

During a fire at a girls' school in Mecca in 2002, the *mutawa'in* prevented firefighters from entering as they feared the girls were not wearing their *abaya*s. As a consequence, 14 girls died, and 52 were injured. In an official reaction, the Majlis al-Shura reportedly balked at budget increases requested by the *mutawa'in* and permitted trials to be held in several cases of alleged abuses in 2007.

International criticism of women's status in Saudi Arabia may be met with defensive statements that the country is different from its Arab neighbors or the West. Some Saudi Arabian women observe that the government has given ambiguous messages about the degree of change it wants to promote for women. A longtime observer of the kingdom noted that older women's facilities had not excluded men, whereas, now that separate facilities are created for women, they are certainly unequal to those for men. For example, women's facilities at King Sa'ud University were not equal—the women's library was inconveniently located, communication with male professors occurred via telephone and television connections, and women's prayer facilities were less handsome and not equivalent (Doumato 2000, 24). This has been a rationale for creating private and public universities restricted to women.

Fundamentalism, or neosalafism, has influenced the question of women's roles in several directions. One example is Islamic feminists, who draw on Islamic thought

---

GENDER EQUITY IN SAUDI ARABIA

Women fare poorly in Saudi Arabia as compared to men and women in other nations, ranking 129 out of 134 countries in 2010 (*Gender Gap Index*, 2010). In 2009, Saudi Arabia's gender gap ratio was 130.

The female-to-male ratio in the workforce is 22 women to 82 men. Saudi Arabia is ranked 132 (out of 134) and scored 0.27 on labor participation.

The female-to-male ratio for tertiary education (college) is high (37 women to 23 men). The country ranks first in this area.

Saudi Arabian women rank 65 (out of 134) for healthy life expectancy.

Their rank is 0 in all criteria for political empowerment (but the data have not taken account of the one female deputy minister appointed).

Women receive 10 weeks of maternity leave. Ninety-one percent of births are attended by medical staff. Saudi Arabia received the worst score (1) for paternal versus maternal authority and (lack of) existence of legislation allowing acts of violence against women.

Source: Ricardo Hausmann, Laura D. Tyson, and Saadia Zahidi, The *Global Gender Gap Report.* Geneva: World Economic Forum, 2010, 262–263.

and have created study circles to obtain access to religious knowledge (Mai Yamani 1996, 263–264). Also, many Saudi Arabian women eschew any desire for enhanced rights for women, like driving or additional work opportunities, as they oppose Westernization. These women call for stricter covering, including covering of the face, and enhanced Islamic education (Mai Yamani 1996, 279–280). Some neosalaf-ists favor greater political participation for their male supporters but not for their female sympathizers.

WOMEN AND EDUCATION

Schools for women and girls outside their homes were at first controversial and were opposed by some of the *'ulama* on the grounds that this would lead to Westernization and the abandonment of women's domestic duties. However, women's education was strongly supported by Queen (also known as Princess) Iffat, King Faysal, other moderates in the government, and middle-class men who outspokenly defended women's education (al-Baadi 1982). Queen Iffat, who had first established a model school to educate her own sons at Ta'if, provided land and funds for a girls' school in 1956 as an orphanage, the Dar al-Hanan. Some Jeddah families enrolled their daughters (Lacey 1981, 364–366), and the small school eventually served 1,300 students.

King 'Abdullah ibn 'Abd al-'Aziz al-Sa'ud (center) laws the cornerstone for the Princess Norah bint Abdulrahman University in Riyadh, Saudi Arabia in 2008. This will be the larg-est women's university in the world, able to accomodate 40,000 students. (AP/Wide World Photos)

Queen Iffat opened a teacher-training school in Riyadh to prepare staff for the girls' schools that were established, even though enrollment was very low; in 1960, only 2 percent of girls and 20 percent of boys were enrolled ("Education," in Metz, ed., 1993, 97). Enrollment increased substantially, doubling by 1990 and then doubling again in the next decade. The female literacy rate, which had been only 2 percent, had risen to 48 percent in 1990 (Doumato 1993, 96). The female illiteracy rate is currently about 30 percent (*CIA World Factbook 2009*). For many years, female education was the responsibility of the *'ulama*-controlled Directorate General of Girl's Education rather than under the Ministry of Education, which supervised boys' education. Despite protests by conservatives, women's and girls' education has been restored to the appropriate ministry (the Ministry of Education). Women's matriculation from secondary education outstripped men's. In undergraduate educational settings, boys were able to participate in sports and physical education courses, but girls could not. Girls had fewer opportunities for higher education and currently are not permitted to work in certain fields, such as engineering, law, and journalism, nor are women active in military science, strategic studies, or foreign policy, although they could contribute to research in these fields even with work restrictions.

RESTRICTIONS

The religious leadership had agreed that women could be employed but only in segregated environments. However, other rules were imposed on women even as more attained education and professional standing. The Libyan anthropologist, the late Saddeka Arebi noted that in the 1970s the *'ulama* began to often speak and theorize about women's "deficiencies" on the basis of biology. These *'ulama* included the mufti of Saudi Arabia, 'Abd al-'Aziz ibn Baz (Arebi 1994, 18), who issued a *fatwa* claiming women are deficient in reason and religion. Some of these views are also expressed in *fatawa* by members of the Permanent Council for Scientific Research and Legal Opinions, which claim that a woman invalidates the prayers of men if she passes in front of him or follows the imam at the Grand Mosque in Mecca (issued by Ibn 'Abd al-Rahim al-'Uthaymin). Other *fatawa* state that men may beat their wives (lightly) and that a husband can forbid his wife from visiting her family (Saleh b. Fawzan). Another says women are the majority of those in hell (al-Uthaymim), and yet another expresses doubt that university education is needed for women, as marriage is preferable (see these opinions in Abou El Fadl 2001, 272–297).

New rules to prevent women from traveling abroad or conducting business without a male representative from their family were imposed following the uprising at the Grand Mosque in 1979. Women working as secretaries were fired, recreational areas established different hours for men and women, organizations that had included Saudi Arabians and foreigners were disallowed, Western music was not to be played in shops, women newsreaders stopped appearing on television at that time, and in some places beauty salons were shut down (Doumato 2000, 12–15). Government scholarships for women declined. Even when women could travel abroad for advanced studies, women's families often expected them to agree to marry prior to their departure to protect the family's reputation (Ahmad 2008).

EXPANSION

Following the cessation of Saudi Arabian student travel to the United States following the terrorist attacks of September 11, 2001, it resumed in 2007, and female students are traveling to the United States, the United Kingdom, and other countries for study, although they are supposed to be supervised by a male guardian. The government has opened more colleges for women in the kingdom in the last 20 years. King Sa'ud University created a women's branch and excluded women only from engineering, and King Faisal University and King 'Abd al-'Aziz University admitted women. Universities that offer religious education also enroll women, such as the Imam Muhammad ibn Sa'ud Islamic University and Umm al-Qura University. The newly created King Abdullah University for Science and Technology enrolls men and women. When a religious official objected to this, he was removed from office. In 2011, the largest women-only university, Princess Norah bint Abdulrahman University, was inaugurated and will have space for as many as 40,000 students. If the college offers courses of study in more traditionally male-dominated fields, it will greatly benefit women. For example, other Arab and Middle Eastern women have moved into all areas of engineering, but Saudi Arabian women have not yet been permitted to work in petroleum engineering.

EMPLOYMENT

The separation of the sexes has enabled the fields of education and health care to employ many women; however, in the latter field, foreign nurses outnumbered Saudi Arabian nurses. Saudization, a policy intended to enhance the employment of nationals, is supposed to be addressing this problem, but other policies and practices that shape women's lives are also impeding Saudization. Due to segregation, women's banks operate, which has allowed for an additional employment area (AlMunajjed 1997, 91–121; Doumato 2000, 16).

Saudi Arabia has the lowest female employment rate of any country. The three necessary conditions of need, ability, and opportunity are not met. Although there was a need for workers, large numbers of foreign workers were financed, even though this was recognized as a social and national problem (Hijab 1988, 137).

If women were permitted to participate in politics and in areas of the national government now closed to them, this would open another arena for them in both an economic and a political sense. Women in the past occasionally held political power. Burckhardt, the well-known European traveler to the Middle East, chronicled the role of an older woman, Ghalya, who governed the Begoums (1831, 268–269). Women were also employed in traditional services and arts, for instance, as midwives and healers who read the Qur'an (Doumato 2000) and as women musicians (Campbell in Zuhur, ed., 1998). However, women worked much more widely in the past than is apparent from sources, for example, in the agriculture of 'Unayzah and also as merchants and moneylenders in the *suq al-harim*, or women's area of the market (Altorki and Cole 1989, 142–161).

Likewise, women's wages have become important to families and have influenced social interactions and decision making, and women have greater responsibilities for supporting their families (Altorki and Cole 1989, 202–207). This is so even though segregation permitted women to work only in certain salaried sectors, whereas service positions were largely restricted to men. Officially, the government projected that the female labor rate would increase at a higher rate (6.9 percent) than men's (4.5 percent) as it moved into the Fifth Development Plan (AlMunajjed 1997, 84–85). However, difficulties arise in combining marriage and work. Women have additional costs; for example, they must employ a driver. These factors, in addition to severe limitations on the types of jobs available to women, have impeded progress in expanding women's share of the workforce. In 2009, the Ministry of Foreign Affairs was still closed to women, although it had been publicly announced that women would be allowed to work there; that announcement was followed by the statement that they might at least begin to work there as secretaries. This exclusion means that Saudi Arabia is represented internationally by men, even on United Nations committees concerning women's rights. Women are excluded from employment in the defense sector and in defense or strategic planning, although there are special women guards and police utilized at special women-only events and at the airports.

Aramco has employed women, although only about one-tenth of those employees were Saudi Arabians in the 1990s. Prince Walid, a highly successful businessman, employs women in his own industries in positions they cannot fill elsewhere in Saudi Arabia, including the job of pilot. In his Kingdom Mall, one floor is exclusively for women, and several women-owned businesses are located there. I met there with a group of businesswomen and other professional women in 2005 who spoke of their own pathways to professional success or activism. Many explained that they have had family support. They do not see themselves as exceptional, even though navigation of their tasks and business with government offices is more complicated than for men due to the prevailing rules. Women are also sponsoring training programs and the production of traditional Saudi Arabian arts and crafts (Fernea 1998, 240). However, even the most illogical service positions are held by men, for example, the selling of women's underwear, more than five years after the minister of labor, Dr. Ghazi al-Qusaibi first called for women to be allowed to sell these items to other women. Reem Assad, a college lecturer, has campaigned for women to enter this occupation (*Saudiwoman's Blog*, 2010), and by June 2011 it was announced that they would be able to do so.

RULES AND EXPECTATIONS

Women are expected to be virgins at marriage and obtain a larger *mahr* (bride price) as a virgin. This custom has several effects: It encourages strict control over the sexual and social behavior of young women, and it has led to a certain amount of abuse of women's free consent to marriage, which is supposedly guaranteed in Islam, and to unions with a significant difference in age and power. If a woman were known or rumored to have been sexually active, she could certainly not marry well. If a woman who married later divorced and then wanted to remarry, she would lose custody of her children and also receive a lower *mahr*. Women would object to their sons' marriage to a divorced woman, a foreign woman, and, possibly, an employed woman.

The custom of female circumcision, usually called female genital mutilation (FGM) in the West, has occurred historically and in contemporary Saudi Arabia. It is not clear why some groups practiced it, such as the Manasir, the al-Murrah, Qahtan, Bani Hajir, al-Saar, and 'Ajman, and those in Hasa, according to both historical and more modern sources (Philby 1933, 81–82; Doumato 2000, 190–194). It is also unclear why Saudi Arabian officials deny that it is practiced or claim that only immigrants (Africans) practice it. This custom, *tahara*, is considered to be purifying and to diminish women's sexual urges. Female circumcision has several forms; the more severe version, including infibulation, was described by St. John Philby's interlocutor (1933). Some do not consider form 1, a partial cliterodectomy, to be FGM, calling it instead Islamic or *sunnah* circumcision. A Saudi Arabian pediatric surgeon differentiated this kind of "Islamic circumcision," claiming that it did not hurt women and that he commonly performed it (Akeel 2005). A study of 260 women at King Abdulaziz University Hospital from 2007 to 2008 found that half of the women had been subjected to FGM; however, critics of that study claimed immigrant women were included (Zuhur 2009; *Guardian*, November 13, 2008).

GUARDIANSHIP

Women's social reputations are the concern of their guardians, first their father or other male relative, then their husband, and, if they are widowed, their sons. Various rules and regulations restrict women's access to public procedures, courts, medical treatment, and travel based on the guardian's permission. Women cannot be admitted to a hospital, examined, or provided a surgical procedure, even elective surgery, without the guardian's permission (Mobaraki and Soderfeldt 2010). Women cannot travel without a guardian. A Saudi Arabian feminist, Wajiha al-Huweider, tested this rule, trying to cross into Bahrain weekly (Human Rights Watch 2009). On the other hand, Saudi Arabian women had been going on the *'umrah* pilgrimage without a male guardian since the late 1970s. They are supposed to sacrifice an additional animal as compensation for breaking this rule (Altorki 1986, 45). A guardian's consent is required for issuance of a photo identification card. The lack of these cards was one reason cited for women's exclusion from voting in 2005, but they will vote in 2015.

GUARDIANSHIP AND MARRIAGE

Saudi Arabian women expect to marry, and because of the prevalence of polygamy, they may be willing to become a second wife rather than remain unmarried. When married, they obtain higher social status and usually (but not always) a greater degree of freedom than unmarried women have. Spinsters and bachelors live with and sometimes care for aging parents or other relatives, and they are seen as exceptions. To live alone would ruin a Saudi Arabian woman's reputation.

A woman's guardian is involved in arranging her marriage and represents her in the engagement and marriage ceremonies, in which a contract is signed. Guardianship impacts women's behavior in many ways. A woman's father is her *wali* (guardian), and if he should die, then the responsibility to support her, arrange her marriage, and preserve her honor falls on her brother. Once she is married, her husband assumes rights by which he can restrict her from working, going out of the house, or studying, but she still has responsibilities to her natal family. If her husband dies, leaving her widowed, her son should support her and becomes her guardian. The concept has been protested by external groups such as Human Rights Watch, because it limits women's legal rights, reducing women to the status of minors.

Guardianship also impacts the social structures by which marriages are arranged and women's negotiations to work, study, and visit friends. By the 1970s, social attitudes were already changing. Earlier, women might not have been consulted about their marriage; their family members and the groom, or the groom's family members, would arrange the union. This was the case even though women had a formal right to assent to or reject a husband. Women played an active role in finding husbands for their unmarried daughters. Middle-aged and older men and women deeply disapproved of any potential bride who looked for a husband on her own or who rejected a suitor, even if she was older than the customary age for a bride (Altorki 1986, 86). Marriage usually brought a degree of freedom for the new wife. Altorki described a case where a mother threatened her son with her anger (*ghadab*) and left the house when her son rejected a marriage proposal extended to his 35-year-old sister. Her son wanted his sister to continue assisting in the raising of his own children. Typically, a woman's interests are pursued only by her mother or another married sibling (Altorki 1986, 87), and sometimes by her father.

The system of guardianship might be abused for economic as well as social reasons, because the bride is supposed to receive the marriage payment called a *mahr* (bride price). Retaining that wealth is supposed to be one of the purposes of *bint 'amm* marriage—a man's marriage to his father's brother's daughter or to a second cousin from the father's lineage. For the elite, as Madawi al-Rasheed has shown in her study of her own family, there are other reasons for tribal endogamy: developing political alliances and maintaining hierarchies while healing political divisions (Al-Rasheed 1991, 184–200).

In 2008, a Saudi Arabian man married off his eight-year-old daughter to a 47-year-old man to have his debts forgiven. His wife sought an annulment, which a Saudi Arabian judge refused to grant (*CNN.com*, January 17, 2009). More recently, the girl's mother retracted her case when her husband, who had left her during the dispute, returned to her. The judge's argument was that the girl herself could call for a divorce when she was old enough (18) and that it was legal to marry off a girl who had reached puberty. The Saudi Arabian government responded to the international outcry about the case by saying it may enact a child marriage law.

The financial requirements of marriage can delay marriage for men, who must work and save for the celebration, bride price, dwelling, and gifts. In the past, a couple might not meet each other before their arranged marriage. It has become more acceptable for them to do so today. In Saudi Arabia, the rate of consanguineous marriage (to a close relative, a second cousin or closer, usually a first cousin) is very high, at 57.7 percent nationally (El-Hazmi et al. 1995); and other studies indicate it is 51.2 percent in Riyadh (Al Hussain and Al Bunyan 1997) and 52 percent in Dammam (al-Abdulkareem and Ballal 1998). Consanguinity in marriage is thought to protect women's rights. It may, however, make it more difficult for women to obtain divorces. Men may marry relatives under pressure from their families and then seek a second wife outside the family circle. There are public health consequences, because genetic diseases lead to higher rates of infant mortality (18.5 per 1,000 in 2005). Some 1.5 million Saudi Arabians either have or are carriers of inherited blood disorders; one is the beta-thalassemia trait (Mobaraki and Soderfeldt 2010). Thalassemia is an autosomal recessive blood disease that causes anemia. The beta variant is found in peoples of the Mediterranean. Some Saudi Arabian researchers have disputed the high rates of genetically related diseases, apparently examining different diseases, such as Down's syndrome and type 1 diabetes, but nonetheless admit a higher rate of congenital heart disease among children of consanguineous marriages (El Mouzan et al. 2008).

SOCIAL EQUIVALENCE AND POLYGYNY

It is thought that women should marry men whose level of education and status is equivalent to their own. There are many unmarried women of elite status, including in the royal family. Polygyny (up to four wives for men) is permitted under Islamic law and is often justified by saying that since no relationships can take place outside of marriage, this controls social mores. A Saudi Arabian man who had married six women was arrested and punished. However, it is obvious that polygyny (often referred to as polygamy) impacts women more negatively than men. Some arguments in favor of polygyny are that there are proportionally more women than men, which is untrue; that men whose wives are infertile or ill have a right to another wife to produce offspring; or that men simply view it as a male privilege necessary because men's sex drives are stronger than women's (which is also untrue from a medical and physiological stance). The practice impacts fertility rates and discourages the use of contraception. Women may bear children to preserve their marriages. Then, they may also have a more difficult time in the labor market as employment is more complicated for women caring for larger families. The major argument against polygyny is that Islam requires men to treat their wives equally; however, that is not necessarily possible from a psychological or material standpoint (Maha Yamani 2008).

The United Nations Division for the Advancement of Women opposes polygyny in Saudi Arabia, viewing it as a source of gender inequity. It is believed to be a major reason for divorce in Saudi Arabia. Typically, a first wife divorces her husband for taking a new wife. While Saudi Arabian women may oppose polygyny, some, like the writer Sohaila Zain al-Abedin, support polygyny, because Islam allows it; however, she does oppose the ways men abuse it (Arebi 1994, 240).

Because divorce can bring stigma and become women will likely lose custody of their children or are economically vulnerable, more women agree, willingly or not, to the introduction of a second wife than one might expect. Public writing critical of polygyny has been increasing. Polygyny ensures women's compliancy and is a source of mental anguish or poor emotional health. A Saudi journalist, Nadine al-Badair, recently lampooned the practice in an article about her right to marry four husbands, taking a new one when she tired of the old ones (al-Badair 2009). She could not have published the article in Saudi Arabia, and conservatives in Egypt, where it was published, attacked it.

DIVORCE

Women may divorce men, but the procedure is much more difficult than when men initiate divorce in Saudi Arabia. There is a stigma against divorce for both men and women; it is nearly unthinkable for the older generation, and relatives may try to convince a couple not to divorce. The male-initiated divorce takes place with a verbal formula and does not require a reason, and he can go later and register the divorce. Such a divorce is revocable. A judge must grant women a divorce if they initiate it, and the grounds for divorce are very limited. Women may not obtain alimony under Islamic law, but they do have the right to the deferred portion of their *mahr* (bride price) if the man has initiated the divorce. A man is supposed to pay for his wife's and any young children's maintenance for three months, after which the divorce is final. Thereafter, she is not entitled to any money from him, and he is likely to obtain custody of all but very young children. If a woman has initiated the divorce, she isn't entitled to any property or income that is in his name, and she may have to return the *mahr* and any marriage gifts, no matter how long they were married.

Some think that Muhammad 'Abd al-Wahhab's ideas about women and marriage were no stricter than any other form of classical Islamic thought (Delong-Bas 2004, 159–163). However, others believe they were, as he gained fame when he stoned a woman to death who had admitted illicit relations with a man. However, the only type of divorce that 'Abd al-Wahhab permitted women to initiate was *khul'*, which requires them to give up their *mahr* (Delong-Bas 2004, 184–185). Women typically lose the custody of their children under Hanbali law and the local judicial interpretation when a boy reaches the age of seven and a girl the age of nine or when the girl becomes sexually mature.

Because of the disadvantages women experience in divorce, and the fact that most men will not take a divorced woman as a single wife, a large number of couples choose to separate without divorcing. However, if this happens, the man may take another wife, and yet the separated wife is not free to establish a new life. Divorces have been increasing over the last decade, and some sources report that as many as 30 percent of marriages end in divorce, mostly in the first few years; the most common reason for divorce is that the husband wants to marry an additional wife. In November 2008, a public meeting about the stigma and difficulties of divorce was held in Dammam called the Saudi Divorce Initiative Forum (*American Bedu*, http://americanbedu.com/2009/02/08/saudi-arabia-you-asked-american-bedu-answers/ February 8, 2009).

ABUSE

Physical abuse of women by men in Saudi Arabia is an enormous problem. The subject was rarely broached in public, but in April 2004, the husband of Rania al-Baz, a pretty television announcer on the program *The Kingdom This Morning*, beat her until he thought she was dead and left her outside a hospital. Al-Baz decided to appear onscreen to show her fractured and swollen face and later was able to obtain a divorce from her husband (*Sunday Times*, October 16, 2005) and documented her experience in a book (al-Baz 2009). Women were often treated medically and then sent home since it has been considered acceptable for men to abuse their wives physically and also verbally or emotionally. Because divorce is difficult for women to obtain, it is hard for battered women to find a solution. The government responded to the al-Baz case with Royal Decree No. 11471, which established a National Family Safety Program to provide some services to victims.

RAPE

In 2006, a young woman, referred to as the Girl from Qatif, was raped by a group of men. She had been attempting to reclaim a photograph that a male acquaintance had obtained from her since she had become engaged to a different man. He said he would not give it to her unless she came to meet him. Once in his car, the two of them were captured and raped by a group of men. But the judge sentenced her and her male companion to lashings for defying the law against men and women being alone together. When her lawyer appealed, the judge doubled the sentence against them and rescinded her lawyer's license. After the incident, the rapists tried to blackmail her family and her intended groom. She obtained justice because her groom's uncle took the matter to the governor of the Eastern Province. King 'Abdullah pardoned the girl and the man with her who had also been raped, and her lawyer was given back his license. Sadly, the scandal was too much for the young man to whom she was engaged, whose family pressured him to leave the girl, although he stood by her during the trial (Lacey 2009, 305–315). A similar case involved a woman in Jeddah, who was impregnated during a gang rape. She was convicted of *zina'*, although the sentence was postponed until she gave birth. Then, she was to receive 100 lashes and spend a year in prison. She too had been lured to the location of the rape by getting into a car with a man, and that action alone made her guilty from the judge's perspective. As rapists typically argue that their victims are engaging in consensual sex, gang rape is the preferred scenario for the men involved as conviction for *zina'* requires statements by eyewitnesses.

DRESS

The most ubiquitous symbol of Saudi women's requirement to observe modesty is the black *'abaya*, which must be worn from entry to the country in all public places. The *'abaya* covers a woman's clothing and may be decorated with embroidery, satin, or sequins. It is worn with a black head covering called a *shayla*. Some women wear *hijab* under the *shayla*, and others do not. When women are in a private or segregated space, they may remove the *'abaya*. Women are expected to dress more modestly than in other countries, even under their outer covering, but not all do. Some also cover their hair, legs, forearms, and wear higher necklines and long sleeves, whereas others wear more revealing, or tightly-fitted clothing which cannot be seen in public places.

SERVANTS

Women employ servants or household help more frequently than in the West. Given the domestic expectations of women, this additional source of labor is crucial for working women, but it presents some additional problems. Many servants and household workers are contracted employees from Asian countries but not all of them. People are expected to hire household labor if they can afford to do so. Families should entertain and provide food for guests, and in some cases the extended family is served meals; in other situations there are multiple families living in a home or compound. Public discussion tends to blame women for abandoning their domestic duties; particularly child raising, whether women are actually dedicated parents or not. There are also situations where domestic labor is exploited; international organizations have urged reforms in this area.

Saudi Arabian authors write about the trials of women's condition in an outspoken way, as do reporters, and many people—men and women—have published letters in the newspapers about women's issues. Yet Saudi Arabians do not want to lose the unique and closely woven family ties that buttress their social structure, and authorities have rejected many of the international human rights standards that apply to women. The United Nations special rapporteur on violence against women, Yakin Ertürk, visited Saudi Arabia in February 2008 and urged changes in the kingdom's legal framework to uphold international human rights standards and include a law criminalizing violence against women as well as family law principles that recognize these standards.

REFERENCES

Al-Abdulkareem, A.A., and S.G. Ballal. "Consanguineous Marriages in an Urban Area of Saudi Arabia: Rates and Adverse Health effects on the Offspring." *Journal of Community Health* 23 (1998), 75–83.

Abou El Fadl, Khalid. *Speaking in God's Name: Islamic Law, Authority and Women*. Oxford, UK: Oneworld, 2001.

Ahmad, Qanta. *In the Land of Invisible Women: A Female Doctor's Journey in the Saudi Kingdom*. Naperville, IL: Sourcebooks, 2008.

Ahmed, Leila. *Women and Gender in Islam*. New Haven, CT: Yale University Press, 1992.

Akeel, Mona. "Female Circumcisions: Weight of Tradition Perpetuates a Dangerous Practice." *Arab News*, March 20, 2005.

AlMunajjed, Mona. *Women in Saudi Arabia Today*. Houndmills, UK: Macmillan, 1997.

Altorki, Soraya. "Sisterhood and Stewardship in Sister-Brother Relations in Saudi Arabia." In Nicholas Hopkins, ed. "The New Arab Family." Special issue of *Cairo Papers in Social Science* 24, nos. 1–2 (2003), 180–200.

Altorki, Soraya. *Women in Saudi Arabia: Ideology and Behavior among the Elite*. New York: Columbia University Press, 1986.

Altorki, Soraya, and Donald P. Cole. *Arabian Oasis City: The Transformation of 'Unayzah*. Austin: University of Texas Press, 1989.

American Bedu (Web-blog). "Saudi Arabia: You Asked. American Bedu Answers." February 9, 2009. http://americanbedu.com/2009/02/08/saudi-arabia-you-asked-american-bedu-answers/

Arebi, Saddeka. *Women and Words in Saudi Arabia: The Politics of Literary Discourse*. New York: Columbia University Press, 1994.

Al-Baadi, Hamad Muhammad. "Social Change, Education, and the Roles of Women in Arabia." PhD diss., Stanford University, 1982.

al-Badair, Nadine. "Ana wa Azawaja Arba'ah" [Me and My Four Husbands]. *Masry al-Yom*, November 11, 2009. http://www.almasry-alyoum.com/article2.aspx?ArticleID=236320&IssueID=1616

Bagader, Abu Bakr, Ava M. Heinrichsdorff, and Deborah S. Akers, eds. and trans. *Voices of Change: Short Stories by Saudi Arabian Women Writers*. Boulder, CO: Lynne Rienner, 1998.

al-Baz, Rania. *Disfigured: A Saudi Woman's Story of Triumph over Violence*. Translated by Catherine Spencer. Northampton, MA: Olive Branch, 2009.

Burckhardt, John Lewis. *Notes on the Bedouin and the Wahabys*. London: Henry Coburn and Richard Bentley, 1831.

Campbell, Kay Hardy. "Folk Music and Dance in the Arabian Gulf and Saudi Arabia." In *Images of Enchantment: Visual and Performing Arts of the Middle East.* Cairo and New York: American University in Cairo Press, 1998, 57–70.

Campbell, Matthew. "Interview: Matthew Campbell Meets Rania al-Baz." *Sunday Times*, October 16, 2005. http://www.timesonline.co.uk/tol/news/article578853.ece

Delong-Bas, Natana. *Wahhabi Islam: From Revival and Reform to Global Jihad*. Oxford, UK: Oxford University Press, 2004.

Doumato, Eleanor Abdella. "The Society and Its Environment." In *Saudi Arabia: A Country Study*, edited by Helen Chapin Metz, Federal Research Division, Library of Congress. Washington, DC: Library of Congress, 1993.

Doumato, Eleanor Abdella. *Getting God's Ear: Women, Islam and Healing in Saudi Arabia and the Gulf*. New York: Columbia University Press, 2000.

Al-Ghadeer, Moneera. *Desert Voices: Bedouin Women's Poetry in Saudi Arabia*. London: Tauris Academic Studies, 2009.

Hamdan, Amani. "Women and Education in Saudi Arabia: Challenges and Achievements." *International Education Journal* 6, no. 1 (2005), 42–64.

El-Hazmi, M.A., A.R. Al-Swailem, A.S. Warsy, et al. "Consanguinity among the Saudi Arabian Population." *Medical Genetics* 32 (1995), 623–626.

Hijab, Nadia. *Womanpower: The Arab Debate on Women at Work*. Cambridge: Cambridge University Press, 1988.

Human Rights Watch. "Saudi Arabia: Women's Rights Promises Broken. Evidence Shows Male Permission Still Being Required for Surgery, Travel." July 8, 2009. http://www.hrw.org/en/news/2009/07/08/saudi-arabia-women-s-rights-promises-broken

Al Hussain, M., and M. Al Bunyan. "Consanguineous Marriages in a Saudi Population and the Effect of Inbreeding on Perinatal and Postnatal Mortality." *Annual Review of Tropical Paediatrics* 17 (1997), 155–160.

Lacey, Robert. *Inside the Kingdom: Kings, Clerics, Modernists, Terrorists and the Struggle for Saudi Arabia.* New York: Viking Penguin, 2009.

Lacey, Robert. *The Kingdom.* New York: Harcourt Brace Jovanovich, 1981.

Mobaraki, A.E.H., and B. Soderfeldt. "Gender Inequity in Saudi Arabia and Its Role in Public Health." *Eastern Mediterranean Health Journal* 16, no. 1 (January 2010).

El Mouzan, M. L, A. A. Al Salloum, A. S. Al Herbish, M. M. Qurachi, and A. A. Al Omar. "Consanguinity and Major Genetic Disorders in Saudi Children: A Community-Based Cross-sectional study." *Annual of Saudi Medicine* 228 (2008), 69–73.

Philby, Harry St. John Bridger. *The Empty Quarter: Being a Description of the Great South Desert of Arabia Known as Rub' al Khali.* London: Constable & Company, 1933.

Al-Rasheed, Madawi. *Politics in an Arabian Oasis: The Rashidi Tribal Dynasty.* London: I. B. Tauris, 1991.

el-Sanabary, Najat. "Women and the Nursing Profession in Saudi Arabia." In *Arab Women: Between Defiance and Restraint,* edited by Suha Sabbagh. New York: Olive Branch, 1996, 71–83.

Saudiwoman's Blog. http://saudiwoman.wordpress.com/

Al-Shetaiwi, Abdullah S. "Factors Affecting the Underutilisation of Qualified Saudi Women in the Saudi Private Sector." PhD diss., Loughborough University, 2002.

Watt, W. Montgomery. *Muhammad at Medina.* Oxford, UK: Clarendon, 1956.

Yamani, Maha A. Z. *Polygamy and Law in Saudi Arabia.* Reading, UK: Ithaca, 2008.

Yamani, Mai. "Muslim Women and Human Rights in Saudi Arabia: Aspirations of a New Generation." In *The Rule of Law in the Middle East and the Islamic World: Human Rights and the Judicial Process,* edited by Eugene Cotran and Mai Yamani. London: Tauris, in association with the Centre of Islamic Studies and Middle Eastern Law, SOAS, University of London, 2000.

Yamani, Mai. "Some Observations on Women in Saudi Arabia." In *Feminism and Islam: Legal and Literary Perspectives,* edited by Mai Yamani. Reading, UK: Ithaca, 1996.

Zuhur, Sherifa. "Considerations of Honor Crimes, FGM, Kidnapping/Rape and Early Marriage in Selected Arab Nations." Paper prepared for the Expert Group Meeting on "Good Practices in Legislation to Address Harmful Practices against Women," United Nations Division for the Advancement of Women and United Nations Economic Commission for Africa, Addis Ababa, Ethiopia, May 25–28, 2009.

Education

Education in premodern Arabia took place within the family; in the *kuttab,* or Qur'anic school; and in the *madrasah,* an Islamic academy usually founded through a *waqf* (endowment; see Glossary). Not everyone was literate, yet many memorized part or all of the Qur'an, and a lengthy tradition of oral literature, poetry, storytelling, and oracular display continued into the 20th century. Medina had attracted scholars of Islamic learning for centuries. As the Wahhabi reform movement grew, the fields of Islamic learning were impacted by the transition within the scholarly class, and their concerns also shaped education after the country's unification by Ibn Sa'ud.

No formal separation was thought necessary between the learning of sciences or other nonreligious material and knowledge of religious material. Vocational learning came about through apprenticing and performance. The relationship of education and childhood was also conceived of differently than in our own time. Young children were treated affectionately in Arabian culture; they were valued because they carried on the lineage and brought prestige to their parents. Yet many families desperately needed income, and children had to assist with their livelihood, running errands or working full-time.

Childhood was a period in which to learn values and manners (*adab*). Children learned their own lineage and acquired information about the values supported by the Prophet Muhammad; first among those were respect and kindness for one's parents. Children are taught that the Prophet Muhammad was consistently kind to children, orphans, and animals (Yamani in Fernea, ed., 1995, 121).

OVERVIEW

Saudi Arabia provides free public education through the national system, and private education is also available. Saudi Arabia has largely replaced traditional *madaris* (the plural of *madrasah*, the secondary level of education, or an Islamic academy) with modern schools and universities with an Islamized curriculum. Islamic knowledge is taught at the primary and secondary levels; in universities, courses in Islamic studies are taught over all four years of the program to reinforce the principles already learned. At the Islamic University of Madinah, the subjects are similar to those in the historical *madaris*, but instruction is delivered through modern teaching methods. In the formation of the national educational system, some institutions were intended to focus on modern sciences and knowledge, and preparation for such studies was provided throughout the arts and sciences curriculum, without neglecting the students' religious or moral development.

Boys' education had been established prior to the creation of Saudi Arabia; in 1901, the Falah schools were established by Hajji Abdullah Alireza. These private schools were endowed by Alireza and were tuition-free (Lacey 1981, 188). In the Hijaz, then a province of the Ottoman Empire, there were 78 public elementary schools by 1915. The first governmental school under the authority of the al-Sa'ud was set up in 1925, with schools thereafter multiplying as the demand for education rose; there were 20,000 students by 1949 (Nyrop 1977, 98–99; Dohaish 1978). As education expanded, it served as an equalizer between regions and social groups.

Arguments about girls' education were similar to those launched in the West before the widespread establishment of girls' schools—that it was unnecessary to their future as wives and mothers and that schools would damage their morals. Proponents of women's education argued that Islam encourages the pursuit of knowledge; that women would be better wives, mothers, and members of society if they were educated; and that they, in turn, could teach other women. Princess Iffat al-Thunayan and King Faysal organized the Dar al-Hanan school for girls in 1955; the director was Cecil Roushdie, who remained for many years. Eventually, public schools for girls were established under the authority of the General Presidency for Girl's Education, beginning in 1964, and girls' schools were built throughout the country by the 1990s. Private and public schools had to be coordinated under the General Presidency for Girl's Education, whose senior leadership was the *'ulama* (religious scholars). This was thought to help with criticism by ultraconservatives since the religious scholars would maintain Islamic standards and the separation of the sexes and still provide women an education.

The Supreme Committee for Educational Policy was formed in 1963. The Ministry of Education, the Ministry of Higher Education, and the General Organization for Technical Education and Vocational Training are responsible for the delivery and assessment of education. As of February 28, 2010, Prince Faysal ibn 'Abdullah ibn Muhammad was minister of education, replacing 'Abdullah al-Obaid. On the same date, the first woman deputy minister in Saudi Arabia, Nora bint 'Abdullah al-Fayez, became responsible for girls' affairs in the Ministry of Education, replacing Prince Khalid ibn 'Abdullah ibn Muhammad. The new deputy minister for boys' affairs was Khalid ibn 'Abdullah al-Sabli (Ministry of Education, Saudi Arabia, 2010). Formerly, the General Presidency for Girl's Education was independent of the Ministry of Education and supervised all girls' schools, colleges, teacher-training colleges, women's vocational schools, and literacy training. Control over girls' and women's education was returned to the Ministry of Education in 2003, and the General Presidency for Girls Education was dissolved.

The Ministry of Education indicates that 31,798 schools now instruct 5,019,007 students and have an academic staff of 425,343. (Male students are estimated at 2,522,658 and females at 2,496,349; Ministry of Education, Kingdom of Saudi Arabia. Projected Summary, 1428–1429 h./2010–2011; note that this does not include private schools or the schools administered by the National Guard or armed forces.) By 2006, 14 large public universities were operating, and other new private and public institutions provided educational opportunities. By 2010, 29 universities (some formed from former colleges) were operating. In addition, the 24 colleges and the Faculty of Medicine at King Fahd Medical City, the Institute of Public Administration, and the Prince Sultan Aviation School offer instruction. Some are described later on.

Academic books are free, and health facilities are available in the schools; moreover, unmarried students at the college and university levels are given a stipend allowing them to study exclusively. Students attend kindergarten, six years of elementary school, three years of middle school, and three years of high school, vocational school, or a religious high school. In high schools, which have a curriculum of arts and sciences, students must take comprehensive examinations offered twice a year by the Ministry of Education.

The school year in Saudi Arabia is 153 days, beginning in September and ending in June. Kindergarten is attended by children ages 3 to 5 but is not mandatory for enrollment in primary school. Only 11.1 percent of boys (51,364) and 10.4 percent of girls (49,350) attended kindergarten in 2007 (UNESCO 2005–2007). In the Ten-Year Educational Plan developed by the Ministry of Education, the education of young children (ages 4 to 6) is to be treated as an independent stage of learning with its own syllabi, which suggests that it is recognized as an important period for the development of learning skills and socialization. Many nursery schools and kindergartens grew out of women's centers established in the early 1970s. The first was set up in 1963 in Riyadh by Princess Iffat and King Faysal's daughters. These centers were necessary for women who were employed. They received royal subsidies and also governmental funds; in addition to children's programs, they offered Montessori teacher training, childcare, nutrition, and health classes (Bird in Fernea, ed., 1995, 289). As women's employment expands, pre-primary education may also grow.

Primary schools admit children who are at least 5 years and 9 months of age. The primary school curriculum has consisted of Arabic, geography, history, home economics, art education, mathematics, physical education, science, and Islamic studies. From sixth grade through high school, a course in civics is offered to boys. Students obtain a general elementary school certificate upon completion. The same subjects at a more difficult level are offered in middle school, with the addition of English.

In high school, those students attending an arts and sciences high school have a common curriculum in the first year. If they score 60 percent in all subjects, they may choose between a scientific and a literary stream for the remaining two years. Those scoring under 60 percent enroll in the literary stream. Biology, chemistry, and physics are studied in high school.

The students who choose an Islamic high school study Arabic language and literature, geography, history, Islamic studies, general culture, and English. To all of the above, the government has added computer training. Students can also enroll in a vocational or technical program, a commercial program, or an agricultural program in the vocational and technical schools, which are supervised by the General Organization for Technical Education. The vocational and technical subjects include electrical skills, machine mechanics, auto mechanics, metal mechanics, radio and television, and architectural drawing, as well as Arabic, chemistry, English, and math. The commercial curriculum includes bookkeeping and accounting, economics, financial mathematics, management and secretarial studies, Arabic, English, and religious studies. The agriculture curriculum includes agronomy, animal husbandry, farm management, horticulture, agricultural economics, applied biology, applied chemistry, applied physics, Arabic, English, marketing, and plant nutrition. Students (and adults) may also apply for technical training courses if they have the middle school–leaving certificates. These courses take a year or a year and a half to complete.

Private schools are also supervised by the Ministry of Education. Their students also receive free books and stipends from the government. A few international schools have been in operation for years, attended by children of expatriate workers. These have a completely separate curriculum geared to prepare students for university studies abroad. Some 24 Philippine schools operate in Saudi Arabia as well.

Students who graduate from the general or arts and sciences high schools may attend universities, women's colleges, or teacher-training colleges. In addition, there are certain technical and scientific programs that last two years and offer a technical degree or lead to a bachelor of sciences. It should be understood that there is significant pressure on girls to marry and to do so before attending graduate school; but to get married and successfully complete graduate school is extremely difficult. This social pressure means that it is somewhat easier and more likely for young men to obtain professional or graduate degrees than for young women.

The 10-year strategic plan of the Ministry of Education (2004–2014) is geared to making the Saudi population competitive internationally while retaining their Islamic identity. The plan has many specific goals, which include increasing kindergarten enrollment to 40 percent, making basic education compulsory, improving teacher education and special-needs education, planning girls' technical education, and reducing dropout rates (UNESCO, International Bureau of Education 2010).

UNIVERSITIES

King Sa'ud University was established as Riyadh University in 1956 as the first non-religious institution of higher education. Enrollment was at 52,187 in 2010, including both men and women, and all courses are free. Instruction is in Arabic for all subjects except medicine and engineering, which are taught in English. The university is ranked highly in the Arab world and has 18 libraries and 14 research centers. The faculty have been trained abroad or in Saudi Arabia (or both), and they are expected to produce research and publications in addition to teaching. The university is made up of multiple science colleges, health colleges, humanities colleges, and two community colleges. A branch of the university that opened in Qasim is now independent.

King 'Abd al-'Aziz University, in Jeddah, was founded in 1967 as a private university and became a state university in 1971. Men and women attend, and while it is smaller than King Sa'ud University, it is still a very large institution. By 2001, more than 37,000 undergraduates were enrolled, several thousand graduate students, and 500 doctoral candidates.

King Fahd University of Petroleum and Minerals was proclaimed in 1963 and began operations in 1964 with 67 male students. Enrollment has now expanded to 6,000 with an additional 2,000 in a preparatory year long English-language program. The university is connected to two community colleges. King Fahd University specializes in higher-level training and research in the fields of engineering, science, and management, aimed at the petroleum and mineral industries. The university is located in Dhahran, about seven kilometers (4.349 miles) from al-Khobar, between the Dhahran Air Base and the headquarters of Saudi Aramco. It lies on top of the dome where oil first emerged in large quantities at Dammam Well No. 7, which is located just off campus. King Khalid University is located in Abha, and King Faisal University, established in 1975, has two branches, the main one in al-Hasa and another in Dammam.

King Abdullah University for Science and Technology was founded in 2009 at Thuwal on the Red Sea coast, about one hour from Mecca. It is a graduate-level research university with instruction in English. It is guided by a board of trustees and an international advisory council, and it intends to produce cutting-edge science and research in a number of fields new to the nation. It is coeducational, and a Museum of Science and Technology in Islam has been opened on the campus. King 'Abdullah was personally involved in the planning and creation of this university.

Saudi Arabians have traveled abroad for educational studies for decades. Students began to travel to the United States after World War II and to the United Kingdom for university studies. In addition, some studied in Egypt at the large national Cairo University, other regional universities, and the private American University in Cairo and in Lebanon at the private American University in Beirut.

Following the terrorist attacks of September 11, 2001, student visas (as well as other forms of visas) were restricted. Some Islamic studies educators and others were forced to return to Saudi Arabia from the United States, as Muslim institutions and motives were attacked. Beginning in 2007, visas were reissued to Saudi Arabian students in large numbers (sources indicated 7,000 to 9,000), resuming the educational relationship of the two countries.

Academia in Saudi Arabia differs in some respects from its counterparts in other countries. There is no guaranteed academic freedom per se. Peer governance is less important than rights of seniority, although committee structures are utilized, as are practices like peer review. There is a great deal of self-censorship and caution. Political science, contemporary history, and sociology are new areas of study, but Saudi Arabian academics cannot engage in the kind of stringent criticism that North or Latin American or European academics launch at their own governments. A few exceptions have emerged who are allowed to be somewhat more outspoken as internal reform began and measures were taken against terrorism. But these expressions have limits, depend on the setting, and in turn are limited to particular themes and topics. Also, for some years, academic publication standards, in some cases, were not as stringent as in top Western universities, reflecting a paternalistic approach to education, the fact of English/Western-language imperialism over academic knowledge, and educators' status as national servants. On the other hand, the upper echelons of academia were required to publish outside Saudi Arabia. At top Western research universities, very little teaching is done by top scholars—to the detriment of students, while the Saudi Arabian faculty's energies are also claimed in professional activities and service on government bodies, as well as teaching and research, and it is not clear how that impacts education.

Finally, there has been little innovation in pedagogies; the lecture method in an authoritative style is far more common than cooperative or active learning models. Cheating, grade inflation, and failure and dropout rates are other concerns but probably no more so than in other Arab countries, and these are also common, if not fully disclosed, problems in West. Students are concerned about unemployment, and the uncertain young people Mai Yamani interviewed in the 1990s are now adults (Yamani 1999), so the pathway from education to employment deserves study as well.

SEPARATE GENDER EDUCATION

Rules and customs that separate women and men result in special challenges. The idea of separation by sex is accepted by educators (el-Sanabary 2002; al-Manea 1984; AlMunajjed 1995); external criticism engenders a strong defense of the practice. Wherever possible, girls are educated by women. This has created a great incentive to train Saudi female teachers, although other Arab women (and men) came to teach in Saudi Arabia despite various restrictions. By about 1989, nearly 40 percent of teachers were non-Saudis, mostly Arabs, and nearly half were Egyptians (Doumato in Metz, ed., 1993). In certain subjects in the universities, male professors were viewed by video in adjoining rooms, and their female students could ask questions by telephone (Bird in Fernea, ed., 1995, 286–287). All-female institutions have the advantages of women's colleges in the West: that women tend to perform better without interaction with or competition from male students. Women are said to learn more about their own preferences and abilities in same-sex education. Some disadvantages occurred at institutions where both women and men studied (together but separately) in that laboratory and library resources for women were less adequate than those for men. At the all-female institutions, advanced curricula were restricted by the need for highly qualified female instructors, until these instructors were prepared and hired. On the other hand, women need the advanced training in scientific areas of study that they can receive at King Abdullah University for Science and Technology. This is the reason the government took a senior cleric's criticism of the admittance of women at that new university very seriously and removed him from his position.

Today, girls make up slightly more than 50 percent of all Saudi Arabian students. In 2006, 53 young women graduated from Effat College in Jeddah, a private institution that Princess Iffat (Effat), along with a team of experts, opened with 30 students just prior to her death in 1999. The campus includes part of the grounds of Dar al-Hanan. By 2006, 250 young women were enrolled in the liberal arts curriculum taught in English. Sciences are taught as well, including degrees in electrical and computer engineering, the first time such programs were offered to women in Saudi Arabia (Campbell, January/February 2007). The college transitioned to become Effat University by royal decree in 2009, and it now has colleges of humanities, engineering, and business. Construction on the Princess Norah bint Abd al-Rahman University for Girls began in 2008, and it was inaugurated in 2011. This all-woman institution will offer courses in medicine, pharmacy, languages, and computer sciences.

In 2005, the government had begun to develop programs for gifted students. Physically and mentally handicapped students are offered programs under the Special Education Department of the Ministry of Education. A director of one of the many private schools for the handicapped explained that the ministry programs are, in fact, not automatically available at these schools. Also, due to transportation issues, families may send students to private schools. The official information tells us that the private institutions also receive government subsidies, but this appears not to apply to many smaller schools that need support for needy disabled students (who cannot afford tuition) and can offer no teacher training in special education. The jurisdiction over such a private school for the disabled was disputed, so its director was shuttled between the Ministry of Education and the Ministry of Social Affairs (Interview conducted March 10, 2005, in Zuhur 2005–2008.).

The Ministry of Defense and Aviation and the Ministry of the Interior as well as the National Guard have operated their own schools, and these most probably have never been included in the statistical information from the Ministries of Education and Higher Education.

Education is credited with improving literacy and development. According to the Saudi Arabian government, the literacy rate for men is now 90 percent (however, other sources list 84 percent; *CIA World Factbook 2010*) and just over 70 percent for women. The rate for children under 15 years of age is 89.2 percent for boys and 93.2 percent for girls (Royal Embassy of Saudi Arabia, Washington, DC, 2010).

INTERNATIONAL SCHOOLS

When Western workers first arrived in the kingdom, some sent their children to Beirut, Lebanon, for schooling. One of the earliest international schools in Saudi Arabia was Riyadh International School. Also in Riyadh are the British International School and King Faisal School. Saudi Aramco developed its own schools, and the international schools group in Dhahran and the Dhahran British Grammar School serve foreigners. In Khobar, the British International School of al-Khobar and al-Hussan Academy operate; in Jeddah, the American, British, and Dutch International Schools are accompanied by the Jeddah Preparatory and Grammar, al-Waha International School, and Continental School; and there are International Schools in Jubayl and Yanbu (which was attacked in 2004). These are college-preparatory schools with a significant tuition paid for by the workers' companies, and they were not open to Saudi students. They helped perpetuate cultural enclaves that differed from the rest of the country.

EDUCATION AND ARAMCO

Aramco's labor needs eventually led to the formation of an elite among its Shi'a workers. At the outset, the Shi'a of the eastern region accepted industrial employment and were nonskilled workers in harsh working and living conditions. They protested these circumstances in the 1953 strikes. Aramco's desire for a loyal, well-trained workforce resulted in company-offered training and higher education for some employees, in addition to other benefits (Louër 2008, 42–43). Thousands of Shi'a employees moved into the managerial strata, and their children, in turn, are encouraged to attend university and gain professional status. Some of them work for the company in highly skilled technical specialties.

The strikes and legacy of frustrated trade union efforts led to a current of leftist opposition among some of the Shi'a, and the first political prisoners and exiles, and opposition parties, such as the Communist Party of Saudi Arabia (Al-Rasheed 2002, 100; Louër 2008, 42–44). This trend was offset by the religious revival among the

Shi'a but, more important, by the loyal elite engendered through Aramco's largely benevolent if self-serving policies.

SHI'A HIGHER EDUCATION AND ACTIVISM

Activist Shi'ism likewise reached Saudi Arabia through education. Although the prominence of 'Abd al-Wahhab's reform movement in Saudi Arabia ensured quietist, nonconfrontational stances in Shi'a worship and religious study, some *'ulama* families and others attracted to scholarship left Saudi Arabia to study in Iraq, Iran, and the other Gulf states. Iraq developed two activist strains of Shi'ism, one known as the Shiraziyyin, who represented the *marja'iyya* (Shi'a religious leadership) of Karbalah and whose political party became the Munnazamat al-Amal al-Islami (the Islamic Action Organization) after 1979. The other trend came from the *marja'iyya* of the city of Najaf, and its activist political elements formed al-Da'wah, a party represented in the post-Saddam leadership of Iraq. Saudi Shi'a studied in the 1970s at the Hawza of the Supreme Prophet in Bneid al-Gar, Kuwait, a center of the Shiraziyyin, and political education was offered by Muhammad Taqi al-Mudarissi, whose Message Movement was later known as the Islamic Action Organization. Some of these cadres, also from Kuwait and Bahrain, acquired military training in Lebanon from the Palestine Liberation Organization (Louër 2008, 124–125). The Saudi Shirazi figure Hassan al-Saffar recruited Saudi students to study in Kuwait, and he also created institutions and attracted followers in Oman. All this shows that the political repression of the Shi'a community led to a pattern of Shi'a higher religious education necessarily moving in and out of the country, which activated revolutionary ideas. The figures discussed are atypical of the majority of the Saudi Arabian Shi'a, who acquired religious education as a quiescent minority but who would like to see greater acceptance of their community in Saudi Arabian society.

ISLAMIC EDUCATION

Specialized Sunni Islamic education is provided for all citizens of Saudi Arabia and for many non-Saudi Muslims who travel to the kingdom for this purpose. Religious education begins with families and continues through the entire educational system. At the level of higher education, some important programs are at the Islamic University of Medina, the Umm al-Qura University, Dar al-Hadith al-Khayriyya in Mecca, which specializes in the teaching of *fiqh* (jurisprudence), and the al-Imam Muhammad ibn Sa'ud University in Riyadh, with an enrollment of more than 24,000 students.

The Islamic University of Medina, established in 1961, which enrolls more than 6,000 students, is tuition-free. It offers undergraduate and graduate-level degrees and a certificate program. It also provides a small stipend and a yearly ticket home and return for students from abroad. Married students who cannot live in the dormitory must cover their own costs; consequently, there are Saudi Arabian male students who are married and have families, but there are apparently difficulties for non–Saudi

Arabians to get visas for their wives. The Umm al-Qura University, in Mecca, admits men and also women who can show proof and approval of an accompanying male guardian, *mahram* (see section on Women or the Glossary). It is tuition-free and provides free housing and a ticket home for single students living in the dormitory; married students pay additional costs. Dar al-Hadith provides studies in the *sunnah* and *shari'ah* for graduates of middle school, high school, and college with knowledge of the Qur'an and does not include Arabic courses, so it is not attended by foreign students unless their Arabic is up to the norm. Imam University offers courses for non-Arabic speakers; tuition and housing are free for single students.

A much larger proportion of students in Saudi Arabia specialize in Islamic studies than in other countries, and part of this interest enables the perpetuation of a scholarly class. Historically, this form of knowledge came about when students apprenticed themselves intellectually to a senior scholar, learning whatever they could from him and receiving a *shahadah*, or certificate, for the completion of certain studies, or the right to teach that subject to others. The great medieval academy al-Azhar in Cairo transitioned to a college and then a university, and it taught all four of the Sunni Islamic legal traditions, as well as the Ja'fari *madhhab*. However, not all Sunni scholars, by any means, were educated there, nor did they lack for other senior scholars with whom to study. To some degree, the royal initiative in opening the King Abdullah University of Science and Technology (and other regional universities) is a response to the charge that too many Saudi Arabian students pursue religious studies and too few enter scientific and technological pursuits, which are demanding fields but necessary to the country's future. It is also an aspect of Saudization. In fact, both religious and scientific education are necessary in the special Islamic environment that is the kingdom and to perpetuate Islamic knowledge in the broader Muslim world.

CRITIQUES OF ISLAMIC EDUCATION

Many Western critics of Islamic education targeted Saudi Arabia for fostering "jihadist tendencies" like the al-Qa'ida movement. Reform-minded leaders such as then crown prince 'Abdullah had already initiated some reform of religious textbooks used in the educational system, a part of the 10-year education plan. The critique of the texts shows some antipathy to the overlap between Wahhabist salafism and mainstream Sunni thought and is mostly concerned with preventing exclusivism and exclusion of other religious and Muslim groups. Reviews of these materials in the West have become media tools; the MEMRI Institute in the United States, which employs Israeli researchers, looks for outrageous statements in Muslim-authored publications, media sources, or individual statements and publishes them in translation on its website. The textbook material was also reviewed in more depth by a Western-trained specialist on Saudi Arabia, who faulted certain texts for claiming the unity of Islam and Muslims; this is seen as willful ignorance of Islam's numerous forms or as promotion of uniformity and salafism (Doumato 2008, 154–155). Arguably, to a Muslim reader, promoting the unity of the *ummah* (the Muslim community) is a positive trend, if an ideal. A quotation about limiting the use of the jurist's personal opinion, *ra'y* and *ijtihad* (see Glossary or the section on religion and law in this chapter), is said by the reviewer to be ignoring the legal tradition of jurisprudence (Doumato 2008, 155). This is misleading because while *ra'y* and *ijtihad* were juridical methods in the past, it is also true that jurists argued against their use for specific reasons. The standard position of the Hanbali legal school *is* to avoid *ra'y* but not necessarily *ijtihad*; this passage in the Saudi Arabian textbook appears to call for respect for the learning of the *'ulama* and to not issue, as jihadists do, independent rulings. A history text, *The Life of the Prophet and the History of the Islamic State* (2003), is criticized for constantly warning against idolatry (*shirk*), for portraying enemies to Islam as a constant threat, and for not discussing Turkish, Iranian, or Moghul civilization (Doumato 2008, 158–159). The reviewer's concerns were about textbooks that might promote intolerance to non-Muslims and cause Saudi Arabians to not befriend or employ them and to avoid mimicking them (by celebrating birthdays, practicing fine or performing arts, or engaging in sports) as expressed throughout a 2002 text, *Tawhid*. She found that the reformed 2003 version does not negate the earlier monotheistic traditions and leaves out attacks on non-Muslims (Doumato 2008, 161–165). A civics text is praised for assigning "new" values to Islam, such as inclusiveness and teaching about public service and how to maintain civil harmony (Doumato 2008, 164–166).

LEARNING BY OTHER MEANS

Television exerts an educational influence from preschool years. In the 1970s, a Kuwaiti-based Gulf Cooperation Council (GCC) effort bought the rights to the *Sesame Street* model for nine years and launched *Iftah Ya Simsim*, which introduced the beloved characters of Nu'man, a camel; Yaqut, a female lavender-colored monster; Abla, a cat; and Malsun, a parrot. The show is supposed to be relaunched, to the delight of many who grew up with it, and the characters will also teach a program on safe driving in Saudi Arabia. Children's television is now broadcast from other Gulf countries, and, like adult television, it entertains, shows advertisements, and sometimes shapes opinions.

Books are popular in Saudi Arabia and are published in literature, religious topics, social science, and other subjects. Books from all over the Arab world and the West are available; however, there is quite a bit of censorship. Bookstores such as the al-Jarir chain or older-style book stalls may be found, and book fairs or international book fairs are held in Riyadh, Jeddah, and Medina. Internet learning is also available but is monitored and censored in Saudi Arabia (for other forms of education, see Sports and Leisure in chapter 6).

Military and defense learning takes place in Saudi Arabia in training environments but also through coordination with other militaries. The U.S. Central Command is part of the U.S. Military Training Mission (USMTM), a joint military training mission to assist Saudi Arabia and its defenses. It was established in 1953 and is headquartered in Riyadh. It has a directorate staff and four service divisions: Land and Air Defenses, Naval Forces, U.S. Marine Corp Technical Assistance Field

Team, and the Air Force division; as well as a joint advisory division. Members of Saudi Arabia's armed forces and National Guard (SANG) have also been traveling to the United States for higher-level military and strategic learning for decades. These include short courses at the senior or executive level at the National Defense University or courses for medical defense personnel at the U.S. Army Medical Department Center and School at Fort Sam Houston in San Antonio, Texas, and at other service institutes. Master's degrees in strategic studies may be earned by those who qualify in English at the U.S. senior service colleges; however, with only one representative per some foreign countries, only a tiny number of Saudi Arabian officers have this opportunity each year. That, in turn, was a rationale for the Saudi Arabian government to institute its own War College in 2009, which had been planned for several years and is to be coordinated through the USMTM. Foreign contractors (male) who are graduates of U.S. service colleges or have combat experience were joining the college staff during 2010. The college has been encouraged to add a specialized research facility for strategic studies; since 2006, a civilian university institute has been producing some research on strategic studies.

REFERENCES

al-Attas, Syed Naguib. *Aims and Objectives of Islamic Education* [Findings of the First World Conference on Muslim Education, 1977]. Jeddah, Saudi Arabia, 1979.

Al-Baadi, Hamad Muhammad. "Social Change, Education, and the Roles of Women in Arabia." PhD diss., Stanford University, 1982.

Bird, Jerine. "Revolution for Children in Saudi Arabia." In *Children in the Muslim Middle East*, edited by Elizabeth Warnock Fernea. Austin: University of Texas Press, 1995, 290–294.

Campbell, Kay Hardy. "Effat's New Roses." *Saudi Aramco World*, January/February 2007.

Dohaish, Abdullatif Abdullah. *History of Education in the Hijaz up to 1925: Comparative and Critical Study*. Cairo: Dar al-Fikr al-Arabi, 1978.

Doumato, Eleanor A. "Saudi Arabia: From Wahhabi Roots to Contemporary Revisionism." In *Islam and Textbooks in the Middle East*, edited by Eleanor A. Doumato and Gregory Starrett. Cairo: American University in Cairo Press, 2008, 153–176.

Fernea, Elizabeth W. *In Search of Islamic Feminism: One Woman's Global Journey*. New York: Doubleday, 1998.

Fernea, Elizabeth W., ed. *Children in the Muslim Middle East*. Austin: University of Texas Press, 1995.

General Presidency for Girls' Education, Kingdom of Saudi Arabia. *Tawhid*. Grade 10. General Presidency for Girl's Education, Kingdom of Saudi Arabia, 1996/1997.

Hazaa, Abdulaziz Mohammed al. "Scenario Projections for Women in Saudi Arabia: Their Changing Status, Educational and Employment Opportunities by the Year 2010." PhD diss., University of Minnesota, 1993.

Lacey, Robert. *The Kingdom*. New York: Harcourt Brace Jovanovich, 1981.

Louër, Laurence. *Transnational Shia Politics: Religious and Political Networks in the Gulf*. New York: Columbia University Press, 2008.

al-Manea, Azeezah A. "History and Contemporary Policies of Women's Education in Saudi Arabia." PhD diss., University of Michigan, 1984.

Ministry of Education, Kingdom of Saudi Arabia. *The Life of the Prophet and the History of the Islamic State*. Grade 10. Ministry of Education, Kingdom of Saudi Arabia, 2003.

Ministry of Education, Kingdom of Saudi Arabia. *al-Tarbiyya al-Wataniyya*. Grades 6, 8, and 10, Ministry of Education, Kingdom of Saudi Arabia, 2003.

Ministry of Education, Kingdom of Saudi Arabia. Shaykh Saleh ibn Fawzan ibn Abdullah ibn Fawzan. *Tawhid*. Grade 10. Ministry of Education, Kingdom of Saudi Arabia, 2003.

AlMunajjed, Mona. *Women in Saudi Arabia Today*. Basingstoke, UK: Macmillan, 1995.

Nyrop, Richard F. *Area Handbook for Saudi Arabia*. Washington, DC: U.S. Government Printing Office, 1977.

Al-Rasheed, Madawi. *A History of Saudi Arabia*. Cambridge: Cambridge University Press, 2002.

Roy, D. "Saudi Arabian Education: Development Policy." *Middle Eastern Studies* 28, no. 3 (1992), 477–508.

Royal Embassy of Saudi Arabia. Washington, DC. Information Office. Health and Education. (Information appears to be circa 2007.)

Royal Embassy of Saudi Arabia. "Index of Master's Theses and Doctoral Dissertations of Saudi Graduates from Universities in the United States." Washington, DC: Royal Embassy of Saudi Arabia.

el-Sanabary, Nagat. "The Saudi Arabian Model of Female Education and the Reproduction of Gender Divisions." Working Paper No. 16. G.E. von Grunebaum Center for Near Eastern Studies, University of California, Los Angeles, 2002.

UNESCO, International Bureau of Education. "Saudi Arabia." Profile derived from *World Data on Education*, 7th ed., 2010/2011. UNESCO, IBE, 2011. http://www.ibe.unesco.org/en/services/online-materials/world-data-on-education/seventh-edition-2010-11.html

UNESCO, International Bureau of Education. "Saudi Arabia." *World Data on Education*, 6th ed., 2005–2007. UNESCO, 2007. Updated February 27, 2007. Available at http://www.ibe.unesco.org/fileadmin/user_upload/archive/Countries/WDE/2006/ARAB_STATES/Saudi_Arabia/Saudi_Arabia.htm

Yamani, Mai. *Changed Identities: The Challenges of the New Generation in Saudi Arabia*. London: Royal Institute of International Affairs, 1999.

Yamani, Muhammad Abdo. "Teach Your Children the Love of God's Messenger." Translated by Farha Ghannam in *Children in the Middle East*, edited by Elizabeth Fernea. Austin: University of Texas Press, 1995, 118–123. (An excerpt from Muhammad Abdo Yamani, *Teach Your Children the Love of God's Messenger* [Jeddah, Saudi Arabia: al-Sharika al-Sandiya lil-Abhath wa-l-Taswiq, 1991].)

al-Zaid, Abdulla Mohamad. *Education in Saudi Arabia*. Jeddah, Saudi Arabia: Tihamah, 1981.

CHAPTER 6

Culture

Language

Arabic is the national language of Saudi Arabia. Arabic is also the dominant language from Morocco and Mauritania eastward to Iraq, but it is not spoken in these countries exactly as in Saudi Arabia. What these countries share is a rich tradition of literature, religious and historical texts, and official and media information. The Arabs of the pre-Islamic era had a poetic tradition, yet they were not literate—and had no written literature. Nonetheless, Arabic, the language of a relatively tiny number of people in northern Arabia in the seventh century, is today a mother tongue for an estimated 280 million people and a second language for about 250 million people. Arabic has had an extraordinary influence on the Islamic regions and culture, because it was the medium of conquest and faith and it had the capacity for keen description, eloquence, and use in scholarship. Although a limited dialect at the outset of its new state, Arabic became as significant as Latin in creating an entire intellectual domain through the efforts of its grammarians, poets, literary figures (Badeau in Hayes, ed., 1992, 12), religious scholars, and philosophers, and it became an official language.

Arabic is a diglossic language. *Diglossia* refers to a language that is essentially two languages or occurs in two or more forms. Arabic has a vast vocabulary and complex grammar particular to its historic and modern written, formal forms. It also has a different vocabulary, grammar, and syntax in its oral, colloquial forms, or dialects. The literary, written, and formal Arabic is based on a classical language, *fusha*, the language of the Qur'an. An updated formal Arabic is used in literature, the media, and formal addresses. Also called *fusha* (pronounced fus-Ha) in the Arab world is a form of classical Arabic that is given the name Modern Standard Arabic in the

West; the differences between modern and classical *fusha* primarily lie in vocabulary. Many older Arabic words have become obsolete, and certain loanwords have been introduced. Spoken Arabic, *'ammiyyah* (ordinary language; colloquial), exists as different dialects that vary quite substantially from country to country and also within countries between rural or bedouin and city dwellers' (sedentary) forms. In Saudi Arabia, the dialects correspond to geographic regions: Najdi, Hijazi, Eastern (Gulf) Arabic, and Janubi (from the south), and as just described, whether the speakers are pastoral or formerly pastoral, or city or town residents. This means that literacy may depend on the mastery of two (or three) "languages," for example, Hijazi urban spoken dialect, *fusha* (Qur'anic), and modern *fusha*, or standard Arabic. A Saudi Arabian may also understand Egyptian dialect, because Egypt has dominated the Arab film, television, and music industries. In addition to Arabic, English is taught in schools in Saudi Arabia, and many businessmen speak English; however, English is not spoken in many city neighborhoods and in the countryside. Other languages are in use, such as Urdu, Somali, Bangladeshi, Chinese, Tagalog, and other Arabic dialects spoken by immigrants, refugees, foreign workers, and others. Signs and maps are rendered in Arabic, thus complicating a situation where many drivers from South and East Asian countries do not know how to read the language.

Arabic is a Semitic language, a language family whose origins are disputed. Some scholars held that a proto-Semitic mother language emerged in the Arabian Peninsula, but it is now thought that this location might have been eastern Africa. Arabic and Amharic are the most recent Semitic languages. A South Arabian language existed before the rise of Islam, and various inscriptions may be found in it. The dynasties corresponding to this southern language were the Sabaeans and the Himyarites in today's Yemen (Nicholson 1977). This South Arabian language and Aramaic, to the north and east, became extinct after Mudari, or northern Arabic, spread with Islam in the seventh century. The South Arabian language was written in the epigraphic *musnad*, as were inscriptions in the northern Arabian language dating back to the eighth century BCE in Hasa in eastern Saudi Arabia. However, southern Arabic was more distinct from northern, or Mudari, Arabic, the language of the Quraysh, the Prophet Muhammad's tribe, just as Italian and French are not merely dialects of one another.

The Nabataeans to the north of Arabia were Arabs who spoke Arabic but used Aramaic for their script (see Chapter 2, History). They have left examples of their language and distinctly Arab names in inscriptions. The Lakhmids of southern Iraq, the Kindites in central Arabia, and the Ghassanids in the Syrian areas produced pre-Islamic poetry and inscriptions in Arabic. Among the most famous pre-Islamic poetry were the Mu'allaqat, known as the Golden Odes, composed by different poets, including Imru' al-Qays and the black knight, 'Antarah ibn Shaddad. These poems typically had a preface in the form of a lament and a main subject. This epic poetry was memorized and recited by professionals and transcribed only later. The vocabulary used was rich in verbs and in words that described the environment; however, not all of these words remained in use. The link between this tradition and post-Islamic Arabic was the poetic form known as the *qasidah* (a stanza form of divided lines [hemistiches] in a special meter followed by a brief refrain), which has survived up to the present.

The spread of Arabic was accomplished through the Islamic conquest, which moved through the peninsula up into Mesopotamia, crossed over to North Africa, and also invaded territory to the east, where other Indo-European languages were utilized. The political impetuses to learn Arabic were accompanied by religious motivations. Since the Qur'an was delivered to the Prophet of God, Muhammad, in Arabic, it was recited in Arabic, and all those who became Muslim studied Arabic, if they did not already speak the language, in order to understand the Qur'an and other religious commentaries and teachings.

The oral tradition of Arabic presented a special problem in the transcription and preservation of the Qur'an. Folk literature and even great and well-known epics were sometimes recited with some differences of pronunciation, which might extend to the meaning of words. The early Qur'an reciters were intent on preserving the version of the Qur'an received in oral form by the Prophet Muhammad. But there were some differences in the pronunciations or oral readings of the Qur'an. After a battle in which quite a few Qur'an reciters were killed, the caliph Abu Bakr approved the creation of a single, authorized version. This was later recensed and rearranged by a committee working for the caliph 'Uthman. Importantly, certain verses were withdrawn (including the now-infamous Satanic Verses, the Gharaniq), and particular variant letters were stabilized. All other versions were destroyed, and by the ninth century, the official version was completely vocalized; that is, the vowels, which were normally not written, were added to the text to clarify its meaning. Nonetheless, it is said that the Prophet approved seven different readings of the text, which are performed in *tajwid*, chanting or singing of the text, and these variants exist until now (Murphy and Zuhur in Tucker, ed., 2010). Not even native speakers of Arabic understand all of the language of the Qur'an, or its religious and symbolic meaning. This has been provided in detailed interpretations with commentary, which are called *tafsir*.

Likewise, to comprehend or emulate the poetic traditions inherited from the past, one must be educated in the traditional vocabulary. The ancient Arabs acknowledged their poet (*sha'ir*), who composed in meters; their tribal orator or spokesman (*khatib*), who spoke without being restricted by meter; and their soothsayers (*kahin*), who used rhyming, enigmatic language (Pellat in Lewis, ed., 1970, 141).

The bedouin dialects of the Hijaz, Najd, and Asir, and the related sedentary (town dwellers') dialects of Najd and Asir, are the closest to the classical Arabic of the Qur'an. This is not true of the city dialects (Jeddawi and Makkawi) in the Hijaz. This is explained by reasoning that the former have had less contact with languages like Turkish and Persian as compared to Iraq or other Arab areas, whereas the Hijazi cities have been decidedly influenced by Egypt and the many pilgrims who have settled in these areas. The dialects of Najd and Asir certainly retained grammatical features of *fusha*, although the word endings (nunation) are omitted in oral form, and in Najdi Arabic, the consonant "qaf" is pronounced as a hard "g" sound (as in *garden*). There is a scholarly dispute about the wide differentiation of Arabic, with one group positing that a kind of lingua franca was adopted in some cities but that the bedouin continued speaking dialects closer to the original Mudari Arabic of the Quraysh tribe. Previously, the opposite claim had been asserted—that the bedouin dialects constituted a kind of lingua franca, which is not strictly the case; however, these dialects share certain tendencies. It is a fact that the Muslim armies of the Islamic expansion set up camps that developed into cities; however, the Arabic spoken in these cities differs widely, and not all settlement was accomplished this way, as bedouin moved into rural areas not far from these regions.

LANGUAGE FEATURES

Arabic is written horizontally from right to left, except for numbers, which are written from left to right. Arabic has 28 letters; some were added by the addition of dots above or below the letter to indicate different sounds. The letters have a different appearance depending on whether they are an initial (at the beginning of a word), medial (in the middle of a word), or final letter.

Tables 6.1 and 6.2 show the Arabic script, the names of Arabic letters in Arabic, and the corresponding letter names and transliteration in English. The first line of Table 6.1 shows the Arabic letter beginning on the right and reading to the left. The second line provides the name of the Arabic letter in Arabic. The third line provides its sound (the first letter, 'alif, is simply an aspirated *ah*, which, when voweled, may shift to a *'ih* sound or *'uh* sound). The fourth line provides the transliteration of the Arabic letter in English.

Arabic is usually written as a script. The initial consonant is not connected to the previous word but connects to the medial consonants, and then the final consonant has a different shape; a small space intervenes before the next initial letter (see Table 6.3).

Some Arabic sounds do not exist in English; these include the consonant 'ain, which is like a growl in the middle of the throat carrying a vowel; the letter *ḥa*, with a harsh breath out; the letter *kha*; and the letter *dhad*, which is a *d* but pronounced

TABLE 6.1 Arabic Script

ر	ذ	د	خ	ح	ج	ث	ت	ب	ا
راء	ذال	دال	خاء	حاء	جيم	ثاء	تاء	باء	ألف
rā'	dhāl	dāl	khā'	ḥā'	jīm	thā'	tā'	bā'	'alif
r	dh	d	ḥ	ḥ	j	t'	t	b	'(a)
ف	غ	ع	ظ	ط	ض	ص	ش	س	ز
فاء	غين	عين	ظاء	طاء	ضاد	صاد	شين	سين	زاي
fā'	ghayn	'ayn	ṭhā'	ṭā'	ḍād	ṣād	shin	sīn	zāy
f	gh	'	ṭh	ṭ	ḍ	ṣ	š /sh	s	z
ء	ي	و	ه	ن	م	ل	ك	ق	
همزة	ياء	واو	هاء	نون	ميم	لام	كاف	قاف	
hamza	yā'	wāw	hā'	nūn	mīm	lām	kāf	qāf	
'	y	w	h	n	m	l	k	q	

TABLE 6.2 Vowel Diacritics and Doubled Letter Symbols

لا	بُّ	بِّ	بَّ	بْ	بُ	بُو	بِي	بَا	بُ	بِ	بَ
lā	bbu	bbi	bba	bb	b	bū	bī	bā	bu	bi	ba

TABLE 6.3 Consonants in Different Positions

Final	Medial	Initial	Isolated	Final	Medial	Initial	Isolated	Final	Medial	Initial	Isolated

Source: Adapted from Ager (*Omniglot*, n.d.) and Wehr (1976). In Ager's work, some letters are rendered for a different dialect.

with the tongue in the back of the throat, and the *ṭa*, a hard *t* in the back of the throat. Because the sound of the ض *dhad* is so unique to it, Arabic is sometimes called the language of ض *ḍād*. The letter *ghain* (غ gh) has no counterpart in English but is close to a Parisian *r*. The *hamza*, ء, shown in English by an apostrophe, is a glottal stop and counts as a consonant. It carries a vowel sign and may sit "on the chair" of the letter 'alif. The letters *Ta* ط and *ṣād* ص are pronounced further back into the mouth as compared to the other (softer) *t* letter, the *ta* . ت, and "s" character *sin* س. Likewise, Hebrew possesses a more and less strongly pronounced *t* sound, the *ta* versus the *tal*, and the Hebrew letter *samekh* is similar to the *ṣād*; both languages have specific letters for the *kha* sound and the *'ain*.

Arabic has only three vowels, an *a*, *i*, and *u*, but these may alter, becoming long vowels with the addition of a consonant (then, they are pronounced *aa*, *ee*, and *oo*), and there are two dipthongs, *ai* (or *ay*) and *aw*. Previous forms of transliteration based on French or English sometimes transliterated the *i* as an *e* and the *u* as an *o*; and in some cases, individuals may use these letters, for instance, in the spelling of their own names (for example, I spell my own name Sherifa instead of Sharifa) or of place-names.

NUMBERS

The Arabic numbers are written from left to right on the top line:

٠	١	٢	٣	٤	٥	٦	٧	٨	٩	١٠

sifr wahid ithnayn thalatha 'arba' khamsa sitta sab'a thamanya tis'a 'ashara

0	1	2	3	4	5	6	7	8	9	10

Although numbers are written left to right, after the number 20, they are verbalized starting with the lower numbers and moving to the higher numbers. Thus, in English, one writes *twenty-two* or *22*, whereas in Arabic one writes *22* but reads or says *two and twenty* (*ithnayn wa-'ashrin*). Also, numbers occur in masculine and feminine forms, and special rules apply when they define a noun. The numbers 1 and 2 precede the noun, and specifically for these two numbers the masculine form of the number is used with a masculine noun. *Wahid* is the masculine form of the number one. To make it feminine, you must add a *ta marbuta*, which makes it *wahidah*. "One book" would thus be *kitab wahid* (or, with nunation [a case ending that indicates nominative, genitive, or accusative case], *kitabun wahidun*), and *bintun wahidatun* means "one girl." Arabic has a special dual form that is used for two of anything; hence, *baytayn* means "two houses" (a pair of houses). For the numbers 3 to 10, a masculine noun takes a feminine form of the number and vice versa. *Thalath* (= 3) is the masculine form. Adding the *ta marbuta* produces *thalathah*, the feminine. Also, from 3 to 10, numbers precede the nouns they define. In Arabic, *thalathatu awlad* means "three boys," and *thalath banat* means "three girls." Other rules apply for numbers in the teens and numbers above 20.

FEATURES OF ARABIC

Arabic words are divided into syllables. Syllables always begin with a consonant; even when a word begins with an *'alif* (like *a*), this is considered a consonant. Arabic is a rhythmic language rather than a tonal language like Chinese. Rhythms come from the dynamism of long and short syllables. Syllables are long if they have a long vowel, such as the word *KAA-tib* ("author"), in which the long vowel occurs because of the *'alif* following the *kaf*. Stress normally falls, if there is no syllable with a long vowel, on the penultimate syllable; for example, the second-to-last syllable is stressed in *fa-HIM-tu* (I understood) and in *Dir-'IY-yah* (the first settlement ruled by the al-Sa'ud near Riyadh) where there is a long vowel.

A primary feature that Arabic shares with other Semitic languages is the use of trilateral verbs as the building blocks of the language. Verbs usually consist of three consonants such as the Arabic verb *fa-ha-ma*, which means "he understood." This is called the first form, or Form I, of the verb. Form II consists of a doubled second consonant indicated by a *shadda* over the *'ha*, yielding *fahhama*, with the meaning "he caused (something or someone) to understand." Each form of a verb has a different meaning and sometimes multiple meanings. For example, *kha-ra-ja*, a Form I verb, means "to go out or leave," and along with a preposition, *'ala*, "to rebel." Form IV of *kha-ra-ja* means "to move out," "to exile (someone)," or "to produce (a play)." Form X also means "to move out," or it can mean "to extract, or to discover (from something)." Some verbs have up to 10 forms; others possess only some of these forms. The verbal roots are often similar to those in other Semitic languages (Hebrew or Amharic).

Verbs must indicate singular, plural (or formal), and gender, unlike in English. This is accomplished by adding letters and vowels; one must write *tifhami* for "you (female) understand," or *tifhamu* for "you (plural) understand." The feminine noun ending is often a "tied *ta*" (*ta' marbuta*), which is only pronounced with the voweled ending in classical Arabic, thus, *shajaratun* (nominative case, meaning a tree), *shajaratan* (accusative case), or *shajaratin* (genitive case). Although this letter is pronounced as a *t* in the grammatical construction known as an *idhafa* (a noun plus a noun that indicates possession), it is otherwise pronounced *a* or *ah*, for example, *mudarrisa(t)* for "female teacher" or Makka(t) for "Mecca." Other feminine endings are a final *a* form, called the *'alif maqsura* (the short *'alif*). However, many words have irregular plural forms. These include some words that are singular collectives but stand for the plural.

The 10 possible verbal forms also create verbal nouns, often in regular patterns. For example, *ka-ta-ba* means "he wrote." If one adds a long vowel, the letter *'alif*, following the *kaf*, this becomes *kaatib*, or "author." By prefacing *mim* and the vowel *fatha* before the trilateral root, one creates the noun *maktab* ("office"), and adding a *ta' marbuta* (the feminine ending) to that yields *maktabah* ("library or bookstore"). This form is the verbal noun of place or action.

Sometimes verbs derive from a quadrilateral root, and these are thought to come from Persian or perhaps another language. Verbs with an onomatopoeic quality are quadrilateral, hence *zalzala* (zain, lam, zain, lam), "to quake, as in an earthquake," and *yuwaswisu* and *waswasa* (he whispers and he whispered).

Arab governments set up the Academy of the Arabic Language in Cairo, the Damascus Academy, and the Iraqi Academy, which made an effort to obstruct the rampant borrowing from other languages by creating Arabic terms for neologisms. However, these have not taken hold (Wehr 1976, viii). Many loanwords are employed for technical or recently introduced items, concepts, or actions, for instance, the word *film* and its plural, *aflam* (preceded by the European word *sinima*). Saudi Arabia, with its large number of religious scholars and officials, also tended to counter the use of loanwords or borrowed phrases informally but with little success. As Hans Wehr explains in one of the most widely utilized dictionaries of classical Arabic, Arab authors also tended to include classical words or phrases that had become archaic, and they included explanations of these terms, but writing styles now aim for readability (Wehr 1976, ix).

To a Western person, Arabic is especially difficult to learn because most written materials are printed without vowels. Only the Qur'an, children's written materials, and, in some cases, poetry are printed with vowels. The reader must know what the actual, invisible vowels are in order to comprehend the case and grammar of a sentence, and sometimes vowels differentiate between words with the same consonantal spellings.

Cases are used in Arabic. In the classical language these are indicated through vowels, but many of the ending vowels drop off in dialects. The cases are nominative, accusative, and genitive. Nominative case is usually indicated with the vowel *damma*, which has the sound *u*. Some words and names do not take the nominative case, so it is indicated by a different vowel, but that is the exception. Arabic does not require the verb "to be" as in English. So a simple sentence might include a noun in the nominative case and an adjective in the nominative case with *tanwin*, which grants a definite form. Subtracting *tanwin* makes the phrase indefinite, but adding the article *al-* (the) *alif-lam* makes it definite without implying "is." *Kitabu jamilun* means "the book is beautiful," while *kitabu jamilu* means "a beautiful book," and *al-kitab al-gamil* is "the beautiful book." When the definite article *'alif-lam* (al) is used, the vowel never has *tanwin*; it is never *un* but *u*. The accusative case is indicated with a *fatha*, the sound of a short *a*. It is used for the object of a verb, as in *fa-ta-ha al-baba* ("he opened the door"). The genitive case, indicated by the *kasra*, an *i* sound, is used for all objects of prepositions, for example, *min al-siyyaratin* ("from the car"). It is also used for the *idhafa* construction, which shows possession or ownership, as in *dar al-amiri* ("house of the prince").

The definite article *al* is affected by the next consonant. The Arabic consonants are either *huruf shamsiyya*, sun letters, or *huruf qamariyya*, moon letters; those marked by the sun overrule the *l* of the *al*, and the *l* becomes like the first letter of the word; for instance, the *shin* creates *ash-* in the name ash-Sharif. However, the word is still written with an *'alif lam*; it is only pronounced *ash* as in ash-Sharif. The sun letters are ن , ل , ظ , ط , ض , ص , ش , س , ز , ر , ذ , د , ث , and ت. The other 14 consonants are moon letters and retain their own sound. However, in the written language, the al- is retained no matter how the following letter is pronounced orally, so one writes al-Najd, but it is correct to pronounce the word an-Najd.

Arabic nouns have a different form for the plural and singular (unlike English, which simply adds an *s* to most words) and also a dual noun and verbal form. The dual (like the English word *twain*) is indicated by adding the ending *ayn* to a singular noun, as in *babayn* ("the two houses"), and all of these change with the case. Usually, the plural form is a broken plural, or an irregular form, which can be predicted based on the verb. Otherwise, the plural ending is *un* for males and *aat* for females. The male plural ending changes in the accusative and genitive cases to *in* (pronounced *een*), as in *mujahidin.*

Many special grammatical features occur in both classical and colloquial Arabic. This similarity has given Arabic both consistency and great variety. For example, the vocative form is used and modifies the noun to the accusative case: *Ya amir* ("O prince!"), *Ya laha min arusah jamilah!* (What a beautiful bride she is!), or *Ya latif!* (How beautiful (or wonderful)!). The word *inna* ("in/so that /for . . . such and such") and several similar words referred to as the "sisters of *inna*" (*anna, li'anna, ka'inna, laissa*) can be moved to the beginning of a sentence to emphasize the noun; it places that noun in the accusative case, for example, *innaha raahit ila waladaiha* ("for she went to her parents"). *Laissa* is a negative but converts the noun to accusative case. The usual preferred sentence order in Arabic is verb, subject, object, in contrast with English. In a simple sentence, the word order is noun, adjective (or adjectival phrase). In a verbal sentence, the preferred word order is verb, subject, object which might be followed by an adverb or prepositional phrase. In sedentary dialects the word order may less often conform with this pattern.

In Arabic, unlike English, it is considered beautiful to elaborate, adding adjectives and finding different ways to express the same sentiment several times. Prose may seem flowery to those unfamiliar to the language, but it is considered especially creative to compose novel word images in this way, within stylistic restrictions.

There is a perfect and an imperfect tense. The perfect implies a completed action, and the imperfect is used with the present or preceded by a syllable indicating the future. Classical Arabic has both an active and a passive voice; the passive is indicated with different voweling, but the passive does not occur in colloquial Arabic.

The negative is indicated by the word *ma* ("not"), *la* ("not"), or *lan* ("never," used with the imperfect) preceding the verb, for example, *Ma dhahaba* ("he did not go"), *la yiktibha* ("he isn't writing it"), and *lan tiktibi* ("don't write it," the jussive form). This is also the form used in colloquial speech in Saudi Arabia (in contrast to a split negative employed in Egypt with the syllable *ma* and consonant *sh* flanking the negated word, as in *ma'rafsh* or *mish 'arif* ["I don't know"]). The imperative is formed from the Form I verb, by prefacing the root letters with an *'alif* with an *a* or *a* voweling (but sometimes *u*), for example, *Iktib!* ("write!") and *Iqra'!* ("read!"). The form differs when it derives from a higher form of the verb.

Arabic consists of both a connected, or cursive, script and various styles of block printing where the letters are not connected. Different styles of script have developed; an early form is the Kufic script. Classical and modern standard Arabic is quite elaborate and difficult, but the regularity of the language—even irregular verbs occur in quite regular patterns—is helpful. Due to its difficulty, children do not read or write well until they are in their fourth or fifth year of study. The complexities of grammar are essential to an understanding of the Qur'an, and so grammar was a specialized subject in the *madaris* (academies).

Arabic calligraphy is still practiced; the skilled calligrapher can form designs, objects, or even animal shapes from words. Various scripts have been used historically, for ordinary communication or design as calligraphy. To be literate, individuals must learn a cursive script and the forms of printed Arabic used in books and newspapers, which can vary greatly in painted or graphic signs and titles. A nonnative speaker must usually study for three to four years before gaining some mastery of the classical language or modern standard Arabic, but colloquial forms may be absorbed more quickly.

The transliteration of Arabic varies widely, as the French and British/Indian systems predated a closer Romanization now utilized. For example, the French used Coran, the British wrote Koran, and, more recently, Standard International Transliteration forms used by Middle East scholars render the book's title Qur'an. In Saudi Arabia, it is common for people to use two *o*'s (*oo*) to transliterate the long vowel *damma* with the letter *waw*, as in Mahmood, as in the Indian or British-Indian system of transliterating English; however, it is considered more correct today, with the advent of Standard International Transliteration to use a *u* and write Mahmud.

In Saudi Arabia, Arabic is utilized everywhere; there is less translation or transliteration than in some other countries. Since some other Arabs are not literate in Arabic script (for instance, Lebanese who were educated in French or have a poor grounding in written Arabic), they communicate on the Internet with a transliterated form of Arabic. Quite a few Saudi Arabians use this form too, which incorporates the number 3 to stand for the letter *'ain* and the number 7 for the *Ha*.

In Saudi Arabian dialects, certain letters may be pronounced differently than in classical Arabic; the letter *qaf* is usually pronounced as a hard *g*—*gaf*—and in the eastern region and among some tribes, the *kaf* becomes a *ch* (as in Iraq). In Riyadh, the consonant *tha* is pronounced *za* by some speakers, as in *bi zabt* ("precisely, exactly"). Most dialects have extra, filler words, and in Saudi Arabia, one is *tara*, which means "know" or "let it be known to you," used for emphasis, as in *tara al-sajan harr* ("Make sure you know the plate is hot").

Literature is almost always written in *fusha*; however, some poetry and the majority of sung folk poetry may be written in colloquial Arabic. Numerous performances of oral poetry and music are available, but these, along with storytelling, may

---

COMMON ARABIC PHRASES HEARD IN SAUDI ARABIA

Anyone traveling to Saudi Arabia might do well to learn the following useful phrases. Saudi Arabians are usually very happy to hear someone trying to use their language and will graciously compliment you on your Arabic, even if you are capable of nothing more than such phrases. Try to remember the gender-ending format: nouns or adjectives ending in a consonant = m.(masculine [usually]) and nouns and adjectives that end in an *a* sound or *ah* are feminine. When using a verb, you need the *i* (*ee*) suffix for the feminine form; for the past tense, the ending sound *a* is masculine, and the ending sound *at* is feminine.

Greetings: *Marhaba!* "Welcome" and/or

As-salam ʿalayk (to a man) or *ʿalayki* (to a woman) "Peace be with you" (the standard Muslim greeting)

Wa-ʿalaykum as-salam (to plural) "And peace be upon you!"

Ya hala! "Welcome." *Ya hala fiik!* "Welcome to you!" (to a man) *Ya hala fiiki!* (to a woman)

Hayaak Allah! "God has praised you." *Ya hala wa marhaba!* "Welcome and welcome."

Shlunak (colloquial, to a man) *Shlunik* (to a woman) "How are you?"

Tayyib(a) al-hamdulillah. "Good, thanks to God."

Esh bak? (to a man) *Esh bik?* (to a woman) Makkawi/Jeddawi colloquial. "How are you?"

Naʿam. "Yes." *Eeh naʿam.* "Yes." (in Riyadh)

La. "No." *Min fadhlak.* "Please." *Law samaht . . .* (followed by phrase) "If you would allow . . ." *Law samahti* (to a woman)

Shukran. "Thank you." *Mashkur.* (to a man) *Mashkura.* (to a woman) "You are thanked."

ʿAfwan. "Excuse me." (or) *Law samaht.* "I'm sorry." Or *ʿAsif.* "I'm sorry"

Faynak? Ma hadd yishufak/yishufik. "Where have you been? No one has seen you." (conveys some reproach to one who neglects his visits)

Ma afham al-lughat al-ʿarabiyya. "I do not understand Arabic."

Ma fi mushkila. "No problem." *Mabruk!* "Congratulations."

Atamna lakum kull khayr wa mustagbal mushrag. "I wish you all the very best wishes and a bright future." (said at a celebration or wedding)

Sabah al-khir "Good morning." or *Sabahak Allah bil-khir.* "May God create a good condition for you in the morning."

Sabah in-nur "Good morning" (said in response; literally, "morning of bright light")

Maʿasalaama. "Goodbye" or, literally, "Peace be with you."

Nshufak ʿala khair. "See you later."

Masaʾ al-khir. "Good evening."

nahar/layl "day/night"

mughlaq/maftuh "closed/open" (a door, or a shop)

harr/barid "hot/cold"

qarib/baʿid "near/far"

bakir/mutaʾakhir "early/late"

hishri/hishriyya "nosy or inquisitive"

marbush/marbusha "lacks poise"

ʿAyn ʿalayki barda (followed by a compliment). "May the evil eye not touch you" (literally, "may the eye be cold on you"). Said by women.

be forgotten or altered if not transcribed. To this end, Lamia Baeshen produced a collection of folktales told in differing versions and written in Jeddah's unique dialect (Jeddawi), entitled *al-Tabat wa al-Nabat* (Baker 2007).

REFERENCES

Ager, Simon. "Arabic." Omniglot.com. http://www.omniglot.com/writing/arabic.htm

Badeau, John Stothoff. "The Arab Role in Islamic Culture." In *The Genius of Arab Civilization: Source of Renaissance*, edited by John Hayes. New York: New York University Press, 1992, 5–15.

Baker, Razan. "Tales of Old Jeddah." *Arab News*, January 25, 2007.

Holes, Clive. *Dialect, Culture and Society in Eastern Arabia*. Leiden, the Netherlands: Brill, 2001.

Ingham, Bruce. *Najdi Arabic: Central Arabian*. Amsterdam: John Benjamin, 1994.

Murphy, Keith B., and Sherifa Zuhur. "Qur'an." In *Encyclopedia of U.S. Middle Eastern Wars*, edited by Spencer Tucker. Santa Barbara, CA: ABC-CLIO, 2010, Vol. 3, 1013–1015.

Nicholson, Reynold A. *A Literary History of the Arabs*. Cambridge: Cambridge University Press, 1969, reprinted 1977.

Pellat, Charles. "Jewelers with Words: The Heritage of Arabic Literature." In *Islam and the Arab World: Faith, People, Culture*, edited by Bernard Lewis, New York: Albert Knopf, 1970, 141–160.

Wehr, Hans. *A Dictionary of Modern Written Arabic*. Edited by J. Milton Cowan. 3rd ed. Ithaca, NY: Spoken Language Services, 1976.

Yamani, Mai. *Cradle of Islam: The Hijaz and the Quest for an Arabian Identity*. London: I. B. Tauris, 2004.

Etiquette

Etiquette in Saudi Arabia has evolved from the culture, religion, and lifestyle. Etiquette upholds the values of generosity, courage, and honor. Society attributes these values to kinship groups: families, clans, and tribes. Hospitality expressing generosity is legendary in the country. In the past, it was understood that since anyone might require food or shelter in a harsh desert environment, these should be offered without question. Even enemies should be hosted for several days. The host's duty to protect guests was nearly sacred, and it was shameful if he failed in this regard. This tenet of protecting one's guests may extend to contemporary business dealings, diplomacy, and foreign relations, but at the same time, the host does not anticipate overt criticism from his guests.

Social and linguistic expressions in Arabic are defined by these values of generosity, courage, and honor. Additionally, they are impacted by Islamic values and constantly reflect the fact that the primary social loyalty is to the family unit. Family is the highest priority, not employers, acquaintances, or the government. Respect for elders in general and one's parents in particular is expected, and the latter is a religious requirement. Respect for religious principles and duties is also required and impacts daily etiquette. For instance, it would not be prudent to telephone someone just as the call to prayer is given.

Social hierarchies matter, differentiating those in tribal groups, the intellectual elite, merchants or businesspersons, the royal family, and expatriate workers. The royal family are held in high esteem and have special privileges. A request by a higher-ranking member of the royal family cannot be turned down, at least not easily, by his own family member or a nonroyal. In general, men obtain special prerogatives as compared to women, and there are systems of etiquette emanating from the gender system, as well as the practice of separating the sexes in order to maintain modesty and virtue.

Normally, an older person takes precedence over a younger person, even if the latter has a higher status. The first greeting in a social situation is given to the elder person, who is served food or drinks before others. If a prince or princess of the royal family is present, this general principle may be overlooked, but often the royal person may choose to defer to the older person present. The place of honor is to the host's right or on the right side. It is polite to allow one's host, or another attentive friend, to make introductions to others. Social gatherings may vary when attended by Saudi Arabians exclusively, and between small groups of friends or family and larger gatherings. More formalities may be observed outside of the family circle. When foreigners are present who might not understand the more formal rules of etiquette, these rules might be relaxed for the foreigners.

An older brother or father, or a mother, must be respected and not opposed, at least not directly. Children are supposed to provide their parents *rida* (parental contentment), avoid their anger (*ghadab*), and not mistreat siblings (Altorki 1986, 73–74). While some of the formalities that the younger generation observed toward their elders had relaxed by the 1970s, it was still thought rude for daughters to cross the room with their shoes on when their mothers were seated, to raise their voices toward them in conversations, or to discuss intimate matters, just as sons would not smoke in their father's presence or continue reclining if he entered the room (Altorki 1986, 75–76). This does not mean that youth always agree with their parents or share the same views (Yamani 2000; Long 2005), and they might resort to subterfuge to avoid conflict.

Modesty and chastity are social virtues in Islam; hence, etiquette requires that men do not converse directly with women who are not their relatives, nor do they socialize with them and vice versa. Many believe that men and women should not shake hands at all. It is normal to refrain from even touching a family member of the opposite sex, once a person has completed his or her ablutions, which necessarily precede the prayers that are observed five times daily. Separation of the sexes impacts numerous aspects of public and social life. On social visits, men may meet solely with men, while women entertain each other in a different space. However, social events where foreigners are invited may be attended by men and women, or Saudi Arabian men might attend without their wives. Social visits are reciprocal and, if not carried out, can signal the demise of a relationship. Formal, prearranged visits called *wu'ud* allow women to invite those who owe them a visit to a common appointment, usually ritualized and held in the late afternoon or early evening.

Respect and care for the family have an enormous impact on many aspects of life, from the psychology of families to legal thinking, customs, and the conduct of politics. For instance, the element of consultation that the al-Sa'ud rulers observe helps to invest more family members in the stability of the regime. The appearance of family solidarity has restrained the al-Sa'ud, according to Robert Lacey, from exposing their disputes to outsiders (Lacey 1981, 350). One such incident that we do know about—the forced abdication of King Sa'ud—came about only after the family grouping of senior princes informed Faysal of their intent and convinced Sa'ud to abdicate (Lacey 1981, 356).

Respect for the family and concern for daughters who do not obtain alimony on divorce are among the underlying reasons for arranged marriages and dislike of divorces; parental input into their children's selection of careers and the value of the collective over the individual are acceptable actions and values and impact etiquette. Endogamous marriages were preferred by tribal and clan groups, especially marriage to cousins (a man would marry his father's brother's daughter). This helped to keep property and interests within the family, even though in the Islamic system of marriage, spousal property remains separate. In addition, care for the elderly and the physically and mentally disabled falls on the family. That meant that institutions for the care of the disabled were not prevalent; the justification was that families preferred to handle their care. A major institution dedicated to the care of the disabled is now sponsored by the royal family. Nevertheless, many disabled students are served only by private schools, and, with the fairly high poverty rate in Riyadh, many families lack the income to enroll their children in the existing programs.

Aspects of Islam are firmly woven into the pattern of Saudi Arabian life. During the month of Ramadan, when Muslims fast from dawn to dusk, non-Muslims should also refrain from eating, drinking, or smoking in public and should be conservative in their dress and behavior at this time. Non-Muslims are not required to observe the fast; however, in Saudi Arabia, Islamic law is firmly upheld for Muslims. In the past, the religious police (*mutawa'in*) might actually interfere with, hit, or arrest those who did not conform to the dress code or who otherwise transgressed Islamic norms. They could detain and beat them, and some died in their custody, until they were discouraged from carrying out arrests in 2007. These official or volunteer morals police are still present and continue to verbally confront offenders, particularly women.

Etiquette combined with culture and religion impact visitors to the kingdom in other ways. Visitors may obtain pilgrimage (*hajj*) visas if they are Muslims. Others can obtain business visas, and foreign workers may be contracted through sponsors who obtain visas for them. However, ordinary tourist visas are not forthcoming, and other special categories such as students or scholars require sponsors. It is the etiquette of the *hajj*, and the status of the kingdom and its government as guardians of the Holy Cities of Mecca and Medina, that thus far has restricted tourism. The performance of the *hajj* involves numerous rites which are discussed separately (see Pilgrimage).

Greetings and initial small talk are expected to precede any serious business or social matter. The standard greeting is *As-salam 'alaykum* ("peace be with you"), and the response is *wa 'alaykum as-salam*. On entry to a home or business, guests or customers hear *Ahlan wa sahlan* or *Marhaba* ("welcome"), and the response is *ahlan fik(i)* or *marhabtayn*, followed by polite inquiries. One should not discuss unpleasant topics, and men should not ask about a Saudi Arabian man's wife, nor should a woman ask about another woman's husband.

The Arabic language is revered, so rhetorical eloquence and elegance are esteemed. Often, indirect references or euphemisms are employed to avoid being impolite. Someone may describe himself as being a little tired, which means he has been ill, possibly quite ill. At a social event, attendees may be curious about any foreigners attending and ask personal questions about their age, marriage status, or religion, which are not thought to be rude. One should respond to these questions. It is not polite to say anything negative or rude about one's own family members, because this will be taken as a negative character trait. A foreigner may be addressed as Mr. or Dr. First Name rather than by his last name.

Couples usually start their families early, and the birth of children is an occasion of celebration. The mother and the father may then be addressed by the name of their firstborn son, or that of their firstborn daughter until a son is born. For example, a man named Muhammad Abdullah would be called Abu Hassan (father of Hassan) and his wife, Umm Hassan. Friends or family might address him this way, and the reason is that the birth of a son (Hassan) endows higher status on both a man and a woman.

Men often attend *majlis*es (*majalis*), or meetings with those in authority, or for business, social, or political reasons. In a prince's or other important person's *majlis*, a particular etiquette is observed. Many persons may attend with requests, and in the case of meetings with royals, these are often written and handed to the royals, although the petitioner first orally presents his request. The bedouin and Islamic tradition of allowing a public audience and access to authority means that, verbally and psychologically, there is less obsequiousness or pomp and circumstance surrounding a prince, or even the king, who may be addressed simply by his first name, "Ya 'Abdullah," by the petitioner. The host may curtly dismiss the petitioner or require the petition to be presented in writing so as to save time, but he has a duty to look into the matter. This allows an opportunity to settle conflicts and deal with needs or grievances.

The importance of etiquette in the Arabic language and the nuances of etiquette that the language provides cannot be easily described in brief. To begin with, Arabic defines gender in the verb form, as well as distinguishing between a plural "you" and a singular "you." More formal or classical language, or more colloquial language, can be employed to different purposes. The vocative—"O [you] Name of the Person"—is used in entreaty or praise but also for emphasis. Saying that one will do something in the future tense does not necessarily imply a promise or even an intent; it may imply only desire to take that action.

Westerners who frequently swear or use obscene words in their own language should refrain from doing so, as Saudi Arabians may not understand if this is intended casually and consider it insulting. This includes expressions like "holy crap," "Jeeze," or "bloody so-and-so," expressions not considered extremely obscene in the United States or the United Kingdom that are offensive in Saudi Arabia. For instance, Jesus is considered a prophet and not to be called on in anger, nor should any slurs be made about Muslims or aspects of their faith.

Saudi Arabians greet each other and close non–Saudi Arabian friends with kisses, usually on the right cheek, and then on the left cheek, and sometimes on the nose or forehead following that. The kissing patterns can vary depending on the geographic or tribal origin of the individuals. In the past, kisses could be given to the right shoulder or to the hand of a royal. Often, Saudi Arabians will shake hands with foreigners who are unfamiliar with the kissing patterns, but they might expect a returning friend to greet them with the same kisses on each cheek and hug that they receive. However, Saudi Arabians will not, as already explained, kiss or shake hands with the other sex. Men may hold hands and embrace each other in addition to greetings, which is a sign of friendship and not anything else.

Etiquette at larger public gatherings, *majlis*es (*majlis* literally means "a place for sitting and meeting"; various individuals or princes may host their own *majlis*es whose attendees make requests or present grievances to them), festivals, or funerals is more specific. Generally, guests should not depart too early, but in long, multihour events, some may depart, and at the majlises held to commemorate the dead and convey condolences to their relatives, guests come and go. Specific formal greetings are expressed. If a royal is hosting the event, one may be presented to him or her. If entertainment in the form of poetry recitation, music, or dance is offered, conversation may go on at the same time.

Saudi Arabians are less aloof and give more time to their friendships than some Westerners may be accustomed to. Loyalty is essential, and friendships may well be mixed with business relationships. Privacy is not as important as in the West, and friends are expected to visit and keep in touch. Once a friendship is established, a person might drop in or might telephone and expect to be seen as soon as possible. Conversely, failing to keep in close touch can be perceived as an offense. E-mail and text messaging have become popular and are another way of expressing friendship.

Favors are expected, and this works on both sides of a friendship, which may be based on a business relationship. Westerners might find that Saudi Arabians are unlikely to decline a request, even if they do not, or cannot, follow through and know that at the time of the request. Because of the intense Saudi Arabian desire to maintain pride, it is important not to excessively pressure Saudi Arabians, even (or especially) in business, for while they may give the impression of being amenable to a request, they may have simply not wanted to decline. Therefore, the response of "yes" usually means "perhaps" or "possibly." Praise is essential, and criticism should be offered only in a very indirect manner. In general, Saudi Arabians will attempt to avoid confrontation and want to save face, and the crux of good etiquette is behaving so that this can occur. Saudi Arabians may not admit to doing anything wrong or that any mistakes were made. Because the isolated lifestyle of the Westerner is not the norm, Saudi Arabians expect a great deal of personal interaction with family, friends, and business acquaintances. However, they are usually averse to publicity and any notoriety, for example, of rumored or controversial business deals, especially anything involving or reflecting on the royal family or the government. This has various implications, ranging from traditional suspicions of advertising to withdrawal from major business transactions if any negative aspects of these were to be publicized.

Saudi Arabians may invite a friend or acquaintance without much notice and may not want to commit to a plan too far in advance. A guest could decline such a last-minute invitation a few times but should then accept. It is polite to arrive on time; however, on the other hand, Saudi Arabian guests may be hours late. As Saudi Arabian men socialize separately from women, a dinner invitation might be extended only to men, and it is worth checking in advance whether others are bringing their spouses.

In Saudi Arabia, the first name is often that person's own single name, followed by *ibn* (son of) or *bint* (daughter of), then the father's name, and finally the grandfather's first name. In some areas a lengthier form of descent is represented in the name, whereas in the Hijaz, just the person's, father's, and grandfather's names are used. Sometimes, the last name may indicate the tribe or place of origin, but in other instances, the tribal name may not be used. Also, in some families a boy may be given the first name of Muhammad or Ahmad in addition to his first (given) name, so he may be referred to by these two first names. Saudi Arabians use the same naming system for others, calling their business friends by their first name preceded by Mr. It is polite to do likewise and, as one becomes more familiar with the person, to drop the use of the preceding "Mr." Members of the royal family may be introduced and usually introduce themselves with their first name and then their father's name, but those directly descended from the king's family should be addressed as Your Royal Highness or Your Highness. Other royals may be spoken of as Prince First Name. Other government officials can be addressed as Excellency. Women keep their own father's name after marriage, as in Sarah bint Muhammad.

The traditional style of serving food is on platters served on a *sufra* (circular mat) on the floor; food is eaten with the fingers of the right hand. The fingers should not touch the mouth or tongue when one is eating from a shared plate. The guest might be given special morsels of food, and it is not polite to refuse these. Today, plastic sheeting may be used in place of the circular mat for sitting on the floor. A guest might be entertained in a Western-style seating arrangement at a table with chairs and cutlery. A host will offer large amounts of food, but it is considered polite to leave food half-eaten on the plate. Prior to eating, the words *Bismillah ar-rahman ar-rahim* ("in the name of Allah, the Merciful and Benificent") are said and, after eating, *al-hamdulillah* ("thanks be to Allah"). Guests say *An'am Allah 'alaykum kathir 'ala khirkum* ("May Allah greatly bless you for your goodness"). Following a meal, Saudi Arabians may smoke cigarettes or a water pipe (*arghileh* or *shisha*). Guests do not linger and usually depart after dinner and the burning of incense.

In restaurants, Western-style tables have often replaced traditional seating. One will find restaurants with private rooms, where women can enter without being seen by other restaurant customers. Some restaurants or hotels have women's or family sections for eating.

COFFEE

Saudi Arabians serve coffee as part of the greeting ritual in homes, offices, and at some public events. Coffee preparation is described in more detail in the section on food, but it may be Turkish coffee, which is black, or Arabic coffee, made from roasted green coffee beans with cardamom, which is quite light in color. It is considered polite to accept at least a cup of coffee, using only the right hand; to indicate that no more is wanted, one turns the cup from side to side or covers it with the palm. Dates may be offered with the coffee, and tea, or herbal teas, follows it. Then coffee will be offered again after the tea. Then, Saudi Arabians may burn incense or scented wood called *'ud*, in a censer called a *madkhana*, fanning the smoke to perfume the guests.

GESTURES

Showing the soles of the shoes or placing feet up on a desk is considered very rude, and it is more polite to sit with legs uncrossed. Beckoning someone with one finger is not polite. Saudi Arabians gesture with the fingers together, palm up, moving the hand outward, indicating one should wait a little or be patient. A nod upward and back while raising the eyebrows and tutting the tongue means "no, not at all."

GIFTS

Gifts should not be given on a first meeting of business associates, unless it is a token item, except for certain official exchanges, as with military or governmental officials, when Saudi Arabians will likely bring official presents; similar items should be presented to them on the same occasion. At special occasions, a gift may be given to all attendees or to some. Saudi Arabians may present acquaintances with gifts of value, and it is important, if possible, to accept the gift. You might return a gift of equal value in the future, but it is not expected. Foreign military or government officials bound by ethics rules constraining them to decline gifts (for instance, U.S. government employees are not to receive gifts exceeding $20 in value) should endeavor to gracefully accept such gifts and explain the circumstances to their agencies, as these are not intended as bribes or a breach of ethics. Gifts of dates at Ramadan are common. Gifts to children are welcome, but one should not offer gifts to the wife of a Saudi Arabian. A Saudi Arabian recipient of a gift might not acknowledge or make a fuss over it or might not even open it until the guest has departed. Gift giving takes place at the 'Id al-Fitr (at the end of Ramadan), at 'Id al-Adha, and at weddings and births but not usually on birthdays, although the Western form of birthday celebrations is catching on. Gifts of jewelry from the *arham*, or affinal relations to a new bride, are expected. Many stories circulate in which guests of Saudi Arabians admire something and then the host feels he must present the guest with the admired item. While this is not always the case, one should be aware of this possibility.

CLOTHING

Dress also expresses elements of etiquette as well as indicating urban or rural status or special occasions. Saudi Arabian men wear a white *thob* or long cotton robe, and they may wear darker colors (gray or brown) in the winter, as well as a white headcloth (*ghutra*) or a red-and-white checked cloth (*shmagh*) at all times. It is not polite to ask a Saudi Arabian man to remove his head covering. Most men wear a black *iqal* (a braided cord) to hold the *ghutra* or *shmagh* in place. Very religious men, the *salafiyya* and the *mutawa'in*, may wear a headcloth without the *iqal* and slightly shorter *thobe*s. In the winter, a jacket or a tailored coat called a *diglah* is worn over the *thobe*. For special occasions men wear a *bisht*, which is a wool or camel-hair cloak. Men wear leather sandals or European-style shoes, and they are not supposed to wear gold jewelry. When Saudi Arabian men are overseas, they often wear Western dress. Western businessmen should dress formally for meetings, with jackets and ties, and avoid wearing shorts. Saudi Arabian men may hold prayer beads (*sibha*), and it is acceptable for men attending a *majlis* to ask to borrow *sibha* and then return them. Shoes may be removed, especially when entering a home. Shoes must be removed when entering a mosque. It is considered impolite to point the sole of the shoe toward anyone.

Women are expected to wear the black *'abaya* over their clothing and the *shayla*, or black scarf (or the head covering of the Hijaz, the *tarha*, a long black headscarf),

A Saudi Arabian woman wearing an embroidered 'abaya in the old city of Jiddah, Saudi Arabia, 2007. 'Abayas are routinely black, but some women wear versions decorated with crystals, sequins, gold ribbon, or even some areas of color. (AP/Wide World Photos)

and they may or may not wear the *hijab*, a separate headscarf, under the *shayla*. Additionally, some women fully veil their face with a *burqa*, or face mask, or the modern-style cloth *niqab*, which exposes the eyes. On some occasions, as when one is invited to a private home, women may remove the *'abaya*, and it is returned to the guest when she leaves. When visiting Saudi Arabians where men are present, a woman may continue to wear the *'abaya*, unless the hosts indicate otherwise. At very large public women's events or parties, women may also discard the *'abaya*. If the *'abaya* is to be removed, it is wise to dress more conservatively than in the West, for instance, in dresses with long sleeves, a higher neckline, and a lower hemline than in the West, basically covering all skin, even though Saudi Arabian women may dress in extremely tight and fashion-forward clothing under the *'abaya*. Only in a few public locations in Najd is it permissible to drop the headscarf or open or remove the *'abaya*, as on the women's floor of the Kingdom Mall in Riyadh. In Jeddah, the attitude toward covering and veiling is somewhat more liberal; however, since the pilgrims travel to Jeddah on their way to the Holy Cities of Mecca and Medina, this is also a matter of context.

DEPORTMENT AND SEGREGATION OF THE SEXES

Until 2007–2008, the Committee for the Promotion of Virtue and the Prevention of Vice, known as the HAIA (Hay'at al-Ma'ruf wa al-Nahaya 'an al-Munkar) or *mutawa'in*, patrolled the streets and public places and were especially harsh to women whom they considered improperly clothed. They might verbally berate Saudi Arabians they considered to be breaking Islamic rules, or even beat them or arrest them, but in 2007, they were instructed by the government to cease doing so.

According to the law, men are the guardians of women; therefore, women's guardians (male relatives) are responsible for women's behavior. Many actions that the *mutawa'in* seek to prohibit are against the law or have become customary etiquette. For instance, couples should not publicly embrace or kiss, and they can be challenged as to their relationship; also, no one should be inebriated, and no one should eat, drink, or smoke during the daylight hours of Ramadan. The *mutawa'in* may also object to skirts that show even a little ankle, to the uncovering of a wrist or forearm, or to men wearing shorts. Women employees are completely segregated from men, with the occasional exception of female doctors at their duties.

In Riyadh, most restaurants are closed to women, except on Thursday evenings as of 2008. Some restaurants were open to women on other evenings, but in previous years, they could be subject to raids by the *mutawa'in*. This excludes the women-only areas such as the women's floor of the Kingdom Mall. Certain restaurants maintain a "family area" meant for women (or men who sit with their family members) or have private rooms for groups including females. Readers may be aware that some other Islamic countries are more liberal about such restrictions, whereas in other places, for instance, in urban Syria and urban and rural Pakistan, it is common for restaurants to include a male seating area and a smaller family seating area.

Women are not supposed to travel alone but rather in the company of their *mahram*, or close male relative or guardian. In order to participate in the pilgrimage, women can obtain special letters conferring the *mahram* duty on their tour leader, and most concede that there is no problem with women traveling to the pilgrimage in such a group if the women are over the age of 45. Foreign businessmen or governmental travelers should obtain a *mahram* letter from their embassy, which essentially means that entity acts as their *mahram*; they should be ready to present it if challenged at the airport or elsewhere.

Women are not permitted to drive or to walk in the streets without their *mahram*. Women who like to walk for exercise have in recent years complained that the *mutawa'in* prevent them from doing so, arguing, for instance, in Jeddah, that it is unsafe for them to walk. There have been periods when it was announced in the media that women would soon be permitted to drive, as in 2005 and 2010, so this limitation may someday cease. At present, Saudi Arabian women often employ a personal driver, who is typically not an Arab, and they must know their area well in order to direct their driver. The rule against driving also applies to foreign women. As of 2006, women visitors could hire a taxi from the airport, although officials used to insist that women be met by their *mahram* (male relative) or a business stand-in. Cars with a driver may be hired by women or men at hotels.

Male-female etiquette is extremely complicated, and the government permits or encourages women to obtain only certain types of jobs to prevent further social mixing. There may be separate elevators for men and women, and special sections exist for families and women in restaurants. Women-only banks exist. In addition, women's lines are formed at the airport and other public places, and women's desks, where women can stand in line and receive service, have started to be instituted in ministries. Women who may work within those ministries are separated. Stores that serve women post signs indicating they are for women and that men are forbidden (Yamani 1996; Zuhur, Personal Interviews and Field Notes, 2005–2008). Women are permitted in hotels, but hotel recreation areas like pools and golf courses are reserved for men. Some branches of government and professions exclude women entirely; thus, women may require male intermediaries to interact with male officials there.

BUSINESS

Business is preceded, as is bargaining, with formal greetings, small talk, and possibly conversation about other matters. This is important to Saudi Arabians, who gauge responses as part of their decision making about the business acquaintance. Rushing or impatience is inappropriate. Confidentiality and discretion are expected. When one meets a Saudi Arabian business partner, he may not be very forthcoming about all of his business activities or not even specify what he does. Rather than asking directly, it is better to look at his business card and then make inquiries from others. Likewise, if you are engaged in many different ventures, it is best to give very little information about these.

Government officials may do business in the evening at their homes as well as in the daytime in their offices. All businesses and offices observe the required prayers, as the noon and afternoon prayers fall within business hours. No one should interrupt someone who is praying. Even outside of Saudi Arabia, the person praying will not respond until he or she completes his prayer. In Saudi Arabia, one will encounter people praying in any public place and on airplanes, especially the pilgrims, who are joyful and excited about attending the *hajj*. Business and official matters may slow in August—when the intense heat inspires many Saudi Arabians who can afford it to take their vacations—and during Ramadan. After Ramadan at the 'Id al-Fitr and in the *hajj* season, during which the 'Id al-Adha occurs, businesses will be closed anywhere from four days to two weeks. During Ramadan, business hours may be quite irregular; offices are usually open until about 2:00 p.m., and shops will reopen after the evening meal, called the *iftar*, which breaks the fast, from about 8:30 p.m. to midnight. Important decisions or meetings might be postponed until after the holiday at the end of the month.

Saudi Arabians may fail to attend a meeting without notice, and one should be flexible about rescheduling. This may occur when someone else has dropped in on them and manners required them to receive that person. One should realize when dropping in on a business person without an appointment that it is best to try to schedule and telephone in advance of a meeting at an office. It is polite to offer refreshments during a meeting and to walk one's visitor to the door if a meeting is held at your office. During a business meeting, there may be many interruptions, others may enter, or telephone calls may be taken. It is best not to expect a serious or private matter to be concluded in one meeting.

BARGAINING

Bargaining is expected, although not in the newer supermarkets or stores in the new malls, where set prices are displayed. Bargaining may well be part of the business process. Prior to bargaining, or setting terms of a deal, it is important to start with greetings. Generally, bargainer and seller are expected to compromise. It is best to know something about the relative value of the goods in question and about the different styles of bargaining. Some people may begin with an extremely low offer with the intent of settling higher. Others may begin much closer to the price or terms they want to settle at.

Bargaining is also part of the business process of setting tips or commissions on services and can impact other travelers, for instance, pilgrims. In business deals, one might bargain on prices and also on terms or the scope of a deal, and one might be more flexible in one area, if not in another. A Saudi Arabian may consider a businessman who is unwilling to bargain to be someone who is determined to overcharge them. It is important to avoid hostility or frustration, possibly by using humor or tact in negotiating. When this is not a long-term business association but simply a purchase where bargaining is underway, then one might have to be willing, when necessary, to simply walk away, as the exercise is supposed to be advantageous to both buyer and seller. However, if you walk away and the seller changes the terms to your advantage, it is rude not to reengage with him. At the successful conclusion of bargaining, the seller may present the buyer with a smaller item for free.

PHOTOGRAPHS

One should not take photographs of women or children, or indeed of anyone, without first gesturing intent, and even then one should proceed cautiously. In rural areas, especially in the past, photographs were feared and considered un-Islamic. Photographing certain facilities, such as military or governmental buildings, may be objected to by guards. Certainly, photographs that show any subjects that are embarrassing to Saudi Arabians should be avoided, just as the key to etiquette in the kingdom is to shy away from publicly embarrassing others.

WEDDINGS AND FUNERALS

Marriages are usually arranged by the two families, and there is still a high rate of cousin (usually first cousin) marriage. Minors may be married, but the marriage would not be consummated until the age of majority (puberty); however, recent international news attention to the marriages of several very young girls may result in a new law forbidding, or more closely regulating, child marriages. Elaborate etiquette surrounds the marriage process, beginning with family inquiries made about the bride and groom and proceeding to a contract that is negotiated and then registered with a judge. The contract specifies the amount of dower to be paid by the groom to the bride and other conditions or stipulations. Some time may pass between this premarital contract and the actual signing of the contract by the bride and groom and the wedding parties. Saudi Arabians do not announce engagements or weddings in newspapers, as is done in the West. Wedding parties and dinners are held separately for men and women. So many rules of etiquette govern such events that if one is invited, it may be a good idea to ask the host or hostess what to do or not do. For instance, an entertainer may perform at the women's *majlis*es, for example, female musicians and possibly a singer. At certain points in the evening, the guests may dance or participate in rhythmic clapping to accompany the music. Saudi Arabians may invite visitors to a wedding who are not close friends, and, in that case, a gift is not expected.

There are many disincentives to divorce (see chapter 5, subsection on divorce). It is often financially and socially disadvantageous to women and frowned on by many in society. Divorce is a much easier legal process for a man to initiate than for a woman. A woman is expected to move back in with her own relatives following a divorce. One may meet women as well as men in Saudi Arabia who are separated from each other but still married because of the stigma against divorce. Nevertheless, many more couples divorce than in the past. Polygamy is permitted in Saudi Arabia, and many women fear the taking of a second wife more than divorce, although the official position is that the institution preserves rather than weakens marriages.

Women whose social standing is impeded by their descent, injury, or age, or who are divorced, may seek marriage as a second or additional wife.

Burials should be held as soon as possible after a death. After the burial, a mourning period called the *'azza* begins, which technically lasts for three days; in fact, the mourning period traditionally extended for a longer period and may continue to do so. Men and women separately receive guests who express their condolences in a *majlis*. Women used to receive condolences in the mornings until noon on Sundays, Tuesdays, or Thursdays up to the 40th day after a death and sometimes for up to four months (Altorki 1986, 108). If a woman has a social relationship with another woman whose relative has died, she absolutely must attend to offer condolences. If a Western woman attends an *'azza*, she should wear an *'abaya* and not wear any makeup, especially lipstick. People may give verbal tribute to the deceased, and verses from the Qur'an are recited. Generally, the items belonging to the deceased are given away, and jewelry is melted down rather than being handed down to descendants. It is considered impolite to discuss inheritance soon after the death of a relative, even though, in reality, families do so. (The information in this section is partially derived from personal experience and from other friends and residents in Saudi Arabia, as well as the listed sources.)

REFERENCES

Altorki, Soraya. *Women in Saudi Arabia: Ideology and Behavior among the Elite.* New York: Columbia University Press, 1986.

Campbell, Kay Hardy. "Folk Music and Dance in the Arabian Gulf and Saudi Arabia." In *Images of Enchantment: Visual and Performing Arts of the Middle East*, edited by Sherifa Zuhur. Cairo: American University in Cairo Press, 1998, 57–70.

Cole, Donald P. *Nomads of the Nomads. The Al Murrah Bedouin of the Empty Quarter.* Chicago: Aldine, 1975.

Cuddihy, Kathy. *Saudi Customs and Etiquette.* London: Stacey International, 2002.

Lacey, Robert. *The Kingdom.* New York: Harcourt Brace Jovanovich, 1981.

Long, David E. *Culture and Customs of Saudi Arabia.* Westport, CT: Greenwood, 2005.

Snouck Hurgronje, C. *Mekka in the Later Part of the Nineteenth Century, 1885–1889.* Leiden: E. J. Brill, 1970.

Yamani, Mai. *Changed Identities: The Challenge of a New Generation in Saudi Arabia.* London: Royal Institute of International Affairs, 2000.

Yamani, Mai. "Some Observations on Women in Saudi Arabia." In *Feminism and Islam: Legal and Literary Perspectives*, edited by Mai Yamani. Reading, UK: Garnet, 1996, 263–281.

Zuhur, Sherifa. Personal interviews and Field Notes. Saudi Arabia. 2005–2008.

Literature

The literary tradition of Arabia is reflective of the broader Arabic tradition of letters. This is true because the nation of Saudi Arabia did not exist in a separate fashion before 1932 but also because the Arab troops who conquered and settled so many other parts of the Arabo-Muslim world during the Islamic expansion carried deep social and political ties with them. The current literary scene is a dizzying wealth of styles and messages heavily influenced by cultural tropes, social realism, and moral messages. Many similarities exist between the work of Saudi Arabian writers and that of other Arab writers; nevertheless, some aspects of public writing are unique. The parallels pertain to writing subjects (such as tensions between religiocultural factors and the spirit of science, rational thought or freedom, and the uncovering of social malaise) and to style (such as experiments with stream-of-consciousness expression or surreal and nonchronological elements). As is explained in the section on language, classical Arabic or a modern standard version of it is utilized in literature, drama, and even some television drama; however, conversation and dialogue as well as some other forms of writing have more recently begun to use colloquial Arabic.

The earliest literature of the Arabian Peninsula was oral, and only some of the oral poetic tradition of the pre-Islamic era has been preserved. There probably was a wider poetic tradition with varying forms and meters, but what scholarship has definitely uncovered was a sudden emergence of the *qasidah* (an ode, a special poetic form) tradition in the first half of the sixth century. Besides this special poetic form, the *rajaz* meter with short rhyming lines is thought to have come from *saj*, rhymed prose that was considered to possess magical powers (Gibb 1974, 14), as the poets were believed to be inspired by the *jinn* (supernatural beings). Poets defended the honor of the tribe and perpetuated the tribe's legacy. It was said of the Arabs in the pre-Islamic era that "they used not to wish one another joy but for three things—the birth of a boy, the coming to light of a poet, and the foaling of a noble mare" (Ibn Rashiq, cited in Suyuti's *Muzhir* [Bulaq: 1282h.], as translated by C. J. Lyall [1885] cited in Nicholson 1977, 71). The poet's satire, *hija*, was unleashed against tribal enemies like a magical curse (Nicholson 1977, 73–74). Poets might represent their tribes as emissaries and spokespersons during wartime. Some of the poetic meters used were *kamil*, *basit*, *khafif*, *wafer*, and *tawil*—these utilize the long and short syllables in Arabic.

The *qasidah* was a long poem or ode, extending to 60 or 80 *abyat* (two half lines that rhyme)—always more than 25 and usually not more than 100—written to praise the poet, his tribe, or his patron or to take aim at rivals and criticize their values. It begins with a section called the *nasib*. Here, the poet is leaving his encampment and, often, his beloved. The next section describes his steed and then the chosen subject of the poem. Hundreds of *qasa'id* have been preserved, including the Mu'allaqat (literally, "hanging") or Golden Odes of 10 great poets or troubadours, among them those attributed to Imru' al-Qays and 'Antarah ibn Shaddad known as the Black Knight of the tribe of 'Abs, born of a slave mother. The *qasid* poets might use any form except the elegy, which was established already. Several women poets were well known for their elegies, such as al-Khansa of the Sulaim tribe, who mourned her brothers, Mu'awiyya and Sakhr. Aside from the *qasidah* and the elegy, many other shorter poems and improvised verses were composed (Gibb 1974, 14–22). These poems convey the values of chivalry, loyalty to tribe and family, generosity, hospitality, courage, and self-sacrifice for both men and women (Nicholson 1977, 80–90). A famous 20-day poetry fair used to take place at Ukaz, and the Prophet Muhammad attended, listening to the poets and the Bishop of Najran, Qays bin Said (Nicholson 1977, 135–136). Among the greatest poets were Ziyad ibn Mu'awiyya, known as Nabigha, whose patron was the king of Hira, and Maymun ibn Qays. Nabigha was also known as A'sha ("the weak-sighted"). A'sha composed striking panegyrics (poetry in praise of rulers); a satirist and wine poet (wine drinking was not prohibited in the pre-Islamic era, and a genre of poetry celebrated the inspiration and elevation of mood produced by wine), he played his harp and declaimed throughout Arabia. He decided to travel to visit the Prophet Muhammad and wanted to become a Muslim. People tried to discourage him, for after all the Muslims forbade drinking, but he was willing to forswear wine, fornication, and gambling. Abu Sufyan, a great enemy of the Muslims prior to his conversion, paid A'sha 100 camels to stay at home in al-Yamamah: "O ye Quraysh," cried Abu Sufyan, "this is A'sha and if by God he becomes a follower of Muhammad, he will inflame the Arabs against you by his poetry. Collect, then, a hundred camels for him" (*Kitab Aghani*, viii, 85–86, I, 10, cited in Nicholson 1977, 124). Such was the perceived power of the poet at the time of early Islam.

THE IMPACT OF THE QUR'AN

The Qur'an directly and indirectly influenced Arabic literature and language. As so many non-Arabs were learning the Qur'an and Arabic, the fields of philology and lexicography grew to explain the language of the text. The literature of the *ahadith* (the plural of *hadith*) was produced in order to help Muslims follow and remember the example of the Prophet, and collecting and studying the *ahadith* became a science and specialization of its own.

Meanwhile, the existing poetic tradition at the arrival of Islam seemed to die out. Great poets were known, such as Labid (Gibb 1974, 41), but they ceased composing after their conversion to Islam. Perhaps this was because of the popular belief in the poets' connection to inspiration via the *jinn* (or a familiar *shaytan*, a devil) or their role as propagandists. About 30 years passed, and then the *qasidah* revived. This time, the poets were of bedouin background but from Mesopotamia, such as al-Akhtal, Jarir, and al-Farazdaq (Gibb 1974, 44).

GHAZAL POETRY

A new form of love poem arose in Mecca, called the *ghazal*. The Meccan *ghazal* was exemplified by a member of the Quraysh tribe, 'Umar ibn Abi Rabi'a (d. 720), who wrote:

> Ah for the throes of heart sorely wounded!
> Ah for the eyes that have smit me with madness!
> Gently she moved in the calmness of beauty
> Moved as the bough to the light breeze of morning
> Dazzled my eyes as they gazed, till before me

All as a mist of confusion of figures,
Never had I sought her and never had she sought me
Fated the hour, and the love, and the meeting. (Palgrave 1872, cited in Gibb
1974, 44)

Some criticized the poet for his outspoken passion, and he was exiled more than once.

A form of the *ghazal* developed in Medina as well. In it, the lover is a martyr who suffers through his star-crossed love. Jamil of the tribe of 'Udhra (d. 701) was the first to express in writing what came to be known as 'Udhrite love (*hubb 'udhri*), an unfulfilled passion similar to that of the chivalrous knights of Arthur's court. It is believed that this romantic tradition actually moved from Muslim Andalus (Spain) into Europe with the troubadours' performances. It also moved from Arabia and influenced poets in Iraq and Syria.

FOLK OR VERNACULAR POETRY AND LYRICS

Poetry, verse, and contests in colloquial Arabic remained important into the 20th century. This genre is discussed to some extent in the section on popular culture, but its strong effect on discourse as a whole should be mentioned here, as well as the fact that it is not merely the poetry or expression of illiterate people, or the "popular classes," as the early chroniclers A. Ibn Khamis (1958, 152–174) and Sh. al-Kamali (1963, 283–304) thought. Saad Abdullah Sowayan (1985, 168) has written about literate Nabati poets who probably chose vernacular composition so that their audiences and the objects of their eulogies (panegyrics) would better understand and appreciate their poems. (The word *nabati* originally meant the Nabataean language but came to denote nonclassical or colloquial language.) Their work had a broader regional impact than might be thought, because although they utilized traditional forms, some traveled. Muhammad ibn Li'bun al-Wayali (1790–1831) had memorized the Qur'an and had beautiful handwriting. He later moved to Zubayr (Iraq) and Kuwait due to politics, and his work draws on the bedouin traditions of Najd and the Arabian coast (Booth in Badawi, ed., 1992, 466). Muhammad al-'Abdullah al-Qadi (1809–1868) memorized the Qur'an as a child, studied *fiqh*, and copied the Sahih al-Bukhari (one of the great hadith collections) in his excellent handwriting; and Ibrahim Je'tin (d. 1943) was very familiar with classical literature (Sowayan 1985, 169). Some poetry concerns the action of writing (Sowayan 1985, 171) or is written in complex forms requiring literacy, such as *al-muhmal* and *al-alfiyya*. *Al-muhmal* are the letters without dots in Arabic (the 15 *mu'jam* letters have dots); poetry composed using only the undotted letters is *muhmal*. *Alfiyya* is a poem made of 28 strophes, each beginning with the next letter of the alphabet. This form occurred in classical medieval poetry and the postclassical forms discussed later on (Sowayan 1985, 171). Even more complex forms allow numbers to stand for letters (as in *hisab al-jummal*). In *al-darsi*, paired letters make another kind of code allowing the poet to disguise the name of a lady, for example; and in *al-rihani*, letters can stand for classes of things like fruits (f, *fakha*) or animals (h, *hayawan*), so the author can make hidden allusions to his subject (Sowayan 1985, 171). Numerous other literary devices like the use of one particular sound per line (the "s" or the "j") come from classical verse of the earlier periods or those contemporary to the poets.

At the same time, oral poetry differs from written literature because direct communication with an audience brings it alive and makes it a process. The poet may precede his poem with a lengthy explanation about the circumstances of the poem, and listeners may participate and ask questions. This discourse is spontaneous. The poem is precomposed and declaimed (*hadd* or *hadb*), or it is sung (*dewineh*; see section on music) either a cappella or accompanied by a *rababa* (or other instrument), in which case the poet plays and then stops playing the instrument to sing the next verse. The poet may declaim his own or someone else's poetry (see also Kurpershoek 1994). Women's poetry is performed as well, and in some instances everyone in the audience knows the words and may loudly, even boisterously, sing the refrain with very emotional language (Campbell 1998, 63–64).

EARLY-MODERN ARAB LITERATURE

Early-modern Arab literature bridged the classical era and the present. Part of its inspiration came from the Arab Revolt in the Hijaz, during which some pro-Arab and anti-pan-Turkic intellectuals, such as Fu'ad al-Khatib and 'Umar Shakir, began to publish in the *al-Qibla* newspaper founded in 1916. Muhammad Surur al-Sabban, one of the literary pioneers, edited, funded, and introduced an important book of the Hashemite era, *The Literature of the Hijaz* (1926). These writers were also influenced by literary critics, such as Muhammad Hassan 'Awwad (1902–1908), an admirer of Muhammad al-'Aqqad, the Mahjar (Arab immigrants to the New World, such as Jibran Khalil Jibran and Mikha'il Na'ima), and the Nahda, or Arabic revival movement of Syria, and a new, freer style of poetry (al-Hazimi et al. 2006, 11). As elsewhere in the Arab world, there was also a revival of a more traditional style poetry, as in the work of Ahmad Ibrahim al-Ghazzawi (1901–1980), who wrote poetry praising King 'Abd al-'Aziz and his sons, and that of Muhammad ibn 'Abdullah ibn 'Uthaymin (1854–1944), whose poetry alludes to the ancient *qasa'id* and has been compared to that of the Egyptian poet Mahmud Sami al-Barudi (al-Hazimi et al. 2006, 12). Romanticism was also taken up by Hamza Shihata, Husain Sirhan, Muhammad Hasan Faqi, and others, as it was in Lebanon and Egypt in the same era.

MODERN POETRY, NOVELS, AND SHORT STORIES

A Sampling of Poets

A few lines from 'Abdullah al-Faysal al Saud's "Illumination" express this romanticism:

> Love, do you likewise feel
> the tremors of our exultant love

Answer me, are you a foreign spirit
in the world of people, if you comfort me in my exile? . . .
Speak out, do not fear any accuser
Our love was never sullied with hypocrisy and lies
It is the covenant of two hearts that flourish to loyalty
Rejecting the treachery of the wolf . . .

Fawziyya Abu Khalid (b. 1955) is known primarily as a poet, but she also publishes essays. Her earlier work mostly dealt with social issues; she then moved to political ones. Criticism was raised against her for writing openly about women's bodies and also for appearing in public forums honoring writers. One of her poems concerns her labor giving birth to her daughter, a symbol of the land. Another brings in the Palestinian experience: "An Unannounced Trial of an Overt Act of Love" (Abu Khalid 1985) is both a powerful love poem and a political reflection.

Ghazi al-Ghosaybi (Qusaybi) (1940–2010) was born in Hofuf; educated in Bahrain, Cairo, the United States, and London; and served as minister of industry and electricity (1976–1983), where he notably established the Saudi Basic Industries Company (SABIC). Then he became minister of health (1983–1985), ambassador to Bahrain, and later ambassador to the United Kingdom. He published many collections of poetry and some 20 books, including anthologies on history and literature. His poetry expresses many moods and tones, from the love poem "When I Am with You" to the frightening and surreal "Octopus" to the bold "Silence," in which the poet's social or political mission is alluded to:

When the brave poet is afraid to die
his best poem is silence

(al-Gosaibi 1987, 232)

This followed an incident, in which, unable to communicate with King Fahd, he decided to write a poem to the king, knowing that he read the newspapers every morning. He submitted a poem to the newspaper *al-Jazeera*. The paper published it on the front page, and he was promptly sacked. The poem followed along a bedouin and also medieval tradition of appealing to the ruler and read:

Between you and me, there are 1,000
informers cawing like crows,
So why do I need to continue talking or
singing?
My voice will be lost and you will feel
its echo.
Between you and me there are 1,000
informers who are lying.
You were cheated and you were pleased

with the cheating,
But in the past you were not like this,
admiring false things.

(*Guardian*, August 24, 2010)

Al-Ghosaybi called for modernization. Specifically, later in his life, he lobbied for women's right to drive and the opening of new fields of employment for women and was opposed by conservatives. He caused another international scandal in 2002 while ambassador to the United Kingdom, when his poem eulogizing a young Palestinian suicide bomber outraged the U.S. and Israeli governments. He was subsequently recalled from London to Saudi Arabia. According to the *Guardian*, his writings were not permitted in Saudi Arabia until a month prior to his death in August 2010 (*Guardian*, August 24, 2010).

Modern Novels

Novels and short stories are a new literary form in the Arab world. Novelists and short story writers may also compose poetry or essays or contribute to writing in the media. One is struck by the incisive social criticism of writers in Saudi Arabia, often individuals who hold sensitive university or governmental posts. Beginning in the 1950s, libraries were founded in Saudi Arabia, and the idea of preserving local culture, including popular literature, spread. In 1958 the Najdi poet 'Abdullah ibn Khamis published *Popular Literature in the Arabian Peninsula*, which was in tune with the sentiment toward preserving cultural legacies then extant in much of the Arab world. Some of these themes were explored by writers using classical rather than bedouin language.

The first Saudi Arabian novel *The Twins*, by 'Abd al-Qaddous al-Ansary, was published in Damascus in 1930 and was followed by Mohammad Nour 'Abdullah al-Jawhari's *The Temperamental Revenge* in 1935 and then by Ahmad Rida Houhou's *Mecca's Maiden* (1947) and others who used their novels as a platform for social reform (al-Hazimi et al. 2006, 28). At the same time, the genre of short story writing was developing, which had the advantage of being publishable in periodicals and newspapers. 'Abd al-Qaddous al-Ansary was the editor of the literary magazine *al-Manhal*. In this capacity, he had a formative effect on the writing of his time, as did Houhou, of Algerian background, who was probably influenced by French writers of his era and their themes of positive realism and rationalism. The magazine published translations of different works as well as original writing. Muhammad Alem al-Afghani, another writer of this period, was literate in English and, given his background, might perhaps have read Chekhov and Gogol, who were so influential in the development of the short story in their region.

Hamid Damanhouri wrote *The Price of Sacrifice* about Meccan businessmen in 1959, and Ibrahim al-Nasser's *A Slit in the Night's Attire* was published soon afterward. These two novels are more concerned with the art of writing. Ahmad al-Siba'i's *Abu Zamil* (1954) was the first book written in an autobiographical form. When he republished that work about 20 years later, as *My Days*, he was very critical of some of the traditional aspects of his upbringing and early schooling. Other autobiographies or memoirs were published in the 1950s by Muhammad 'Umar Tawfiq, Hassan Kutubi, and Hasan Naseef. By the early 1980s, more sophisticated autobiographical writing emerged with Hamza Bogary (also referred to as Bogari; 1932–1984), a student of al-Siba'i, in his *Saqifat al-Safa* (*The Sheltered Quarter*, 1984 and 1991), in which he details old customs and belief, the existing pedagogy, and his coming of age, and with 'Aziz Dia''s *My Life with Hunger, Love and War*, which recollects his experiences during World War I. In the 1990s and the first decade of the 21st century, autobiographical works continued to be written, and some have broken other social constraints.

Short Stories

Fouad Abd al-Hamid Anqawi (b. 1936) earned a degree from Cairo University and studied in London. He was the publisher of the first sports newspaper in Saudi Arabia in 1960–1964, and he wrote travel articles and social essays in addition to a novel, *There Is No Shadow beneath the Mountain* (1974), and a collection of short stories, *Haphazard Days* (1982). He presided over the *hajj* section for European and American pilgrims. His short story "Ali, the Teacher" shows that men, as well as women, are oppressed by filial devotion and the customs of arranged marriages (Bagader and Heinrichsdorff 1990, 15–20).

An entirely different, positive relationship between father and daughter is the subject of Ghalib Hamzah Abu al-Faraj's short story "Violets." Here, fate rewards the daughter's desire to devote herself to her career with an unfaithful fiancé; his infidelity means she is freed from this commitment. Her father, instead of pressing her to marry, understands and sympathizes. Abu al-Faraj was the editor in chief of *al-Madinah* newspaper and was a government administrator; he wrote the novels *Unforgettable Memories*, *The Red Devils*, *The Green March*, *Beirut Was Burned*, *Strangers without Home*, *Faces without Makeup*, and *Hearts Fed Up with Traveling* and collections of short stories (Bagader and Heinrichsdorff 1990, 38–43, 77–78). Muhammad Ali Maghribi, a veteran writer (b. 1914), tells a morality tale about a bad-tempered man whose urine indicates he is pregnant. He takes to his bed in despair. His long-suffering wife explains to him that she had broken the container with his urine in it that he was taking to his doctor for testing. In fear of his vile temper, she had replaced it with her own (Bagader and Heinrichsdorff 1990, 12–14, 78).

The next generation of short story writers included Ibrahim al-Nasser, Ghalib Hamza Abu al-Faraj, Sa'id al-Bawaridi, Najat Khayyat, Abdullah al-Jifri, Louqman Yunis, Abdullah Sa'id Jam'an, and others (al-Hazimi et al. 2006, 22). These writers usually had a main theme in their stories, which were chronological and more consciously written as literature. Some are realistic; other story writers like Hamza Bogary Siba'i Uthman, and Najat Khayat additionally invoke symbolism (al-Hazimi et al. 2006, 23).

Folklore is invoked by Umaima al-Khamees in "Salma the Omani": "If a beautiful witch from Oman lived in the trunk of a palm tree, the trunk would become hollow and fly off" (al-Hazimi 2006, 202). Dark tales were told about a monster-like creature named Abu Dostain, who carried off young girls. Salma lives happily with her mother and her sister, herding, but is carried off at night in a combination of these magical and terrifying story lines (al-Hazimi 2006, 202–205).

The role of the storyteller, a wise/mad fool figure, is troubled by the gap between the old and the new Saudi Arabia in Muhammad 'Ali al-Shaykh's "Tell Us a Story, Abu Auf." The storyteller's thoughts and their collision with his listeners' reactions form the rhythm of al-Shaykh's writing style:

—Blood has changed into milk, he murmured. People lack the old vitality. The pearls are still there, in the bottom of the deep sea . . . but . . . Oh, mad! Mad!
—Finish the story of the boy, Abu Auf! (al-Shaykh in Bagader and Heinrichs-dorff, eds., 1990, 71–75)

Al-Shaykh (b. 1946) headed the literary society in Khulays and wrote *Mind Is Not Enough* in 1982.

Najat Khayat writes of a woman plagued by her unhappy marriage who describes her husband as a "grimy worm" eating her flesh. She rises up against him, and, terrified he will destroy her, she moves first, waking up in the hospital only after he has died. That is the day the sun rose, she writes, the day she was actually born (Khayat in al-Hazimi et al. 2006, 207–210).

Najwa Hashim (b. 1960) is from Jaizan in Asir. Like many women writers, she began writing for newspapers and magazines and published *Travel in the Night of Sadness* in 1986. Her style is breathy and mainly dialogue. "Fever in a Hot Night" is an attack on the institution of arranged marriage and its wild expectations and cruel ending (Hashim 1982 in Arebi 1994, 142–152).

Two of the writers producing heartrending stories exposing the vulnerabilities of women are Khayriyya al-Saqqaf and Sharifa al-Shamlan. Al-Saqqaf was the first women editor at *al-Riyadh* newspaper. She was born in Mecca in 1951, but her family moved soon afterward to Riyadh, Her writing was published in newspapers when she was still a child (Arebi 1994, 139; Hanley 2001, 35). Her story "The Assassination of Light at the Rivers Flow" begins like a newscast: "The stage on which action began was at 450 kilometers, where the road is exploded by thorns. The period is between Wednesday 19/5/1401 and Wednesday 26/5/1401. The event is assassination" (Bagader and Heinrichsdorff, eds., 1990, 47). The abrupt beginning shifts to the lyrical prose of a girl happy with her routine of study, friends, and family. But her father and mother expect her to marry, and her mother slaps her, beats her, and pulls her hair out (Bagader and Heinrichsdorff, eds., 1990, 47–51). In "Reflection" al-Saqqaf took up the theme as a more inevitable move of a girl who wants to escape her own home, built on the misery of her mother, but is then trapped with another abusive man (al-Saqqaf 1982, 69–78).

Al-Shamlan was born al-Zubayr in 1946 (some other sources state 1947). Her family lived in Iraq in the 1960s, and she studied journalism at the University of

Baghdad. She moved to Dammam near Dhahran and was an administrator of social services for women (criminal, disabled, and delinquent). Just as Egyptian novelist Nawal al-Sa'adawi, as a physician and administrator of health services, described the core of human oppression that results in women's oppression, so, too, al-Shamlan describes the stories of women she has encountered. There is no resolution in the story "A Life" (*Ukaz*, April 6, 1987), nor in "Secret and a Death," the story of a young woman, Zahra, who becomes pregnant but never reveals her lover's identity and dies of an infection (al-Shamlan 1989, 23–29; Bagader and Heinrichsdorff 1990, 30–33). "Nawal" relates the jumbled delusions of a newly incarcerated woman. Where can her daughter, Nawal, be? Apparently she has killed her (al-Shamlan 1989, 83–87).

Many Saudi Arabian writers' works and poetry can be found in anthologies, magazine or newspaper excerpts, or individual publications; other notable names include Faisal Akram, 'Ali Bafeeqah, Nasir Bouhaimid, Fawzi al-Dahhan, Muhammad Habibi, Hashim al-Jahdali, Khalid Mustafa, Fatima al-Qarni, Husain Suhail, 'Abdullah 'Aalih al-'Uthaymeen, Fawziyya al-Bakr, Maryam al-Ghamidi, 'Ashiq 'Issa al-Hadhal, Hasan al-Nimi, Laila al-Juhani, Thurayya Qabel, Khadija al-'Umary, 'Abdu Khal, Ruqayya al-Shabib, Wafa Attayeb, Fatna Shakr, Juhayer al-Musa'id 'Abdullah abd al-Jabbar, 'Abd al-Fattah Abu Madyan, Khalid ibn Sultan ibn 'Abd al-'Aziz, Sultana al-Sidairi (in *nabati*), and others mentioned later in this chapter.

THEATER AND DRAMA

Saudi Arabia actually permitted theater briefly in the 1960s but then forbade all public theater or cinemas. This has severely inhibited the growth of an entertainment industry like that found in Egypt, Lebanon, or Syria. Drama is written, but for reading, and performances are limited to college settings. 'Ali Ahmed Bakthir had his first play, which called for the general education of Arab women, produced in Egypt.

Raja' al-'Alim is a noted playwright and novelist who began publishing in the 1970s. Her style is reminiscent of Egyptian playwright Yusuf al-Idris's later period when he experimented with surrealism, in the style of Pirandello or Albee. Better known outside of Saudi Arabia than at home, her work is symbolic, not easy; her characters often lack names, and her underlying message is about liberation. In "The Final Death of the Actor" (in 'Alim 1987b), the owner of a doll factory—or the Master of the Dolls—argues with a Scenarist and an Escaped Character about a renegade doll, actually a statue of an Arabian heroine, Zarqa of Yamamah (Zarqa lived in al-Yamamah before Islam). Zarqa was farsighted and able to see an advancing group of attackers who held trees in front of themselves as they moved. She warned her people that she saw trees advancing. They refused to believe there was any danger, and all perished in the attack (Arebi 1994, 316). Zarqa—and all that she represents—is threatening to the Master and to a "normal actor" (Samson's Actor), while the Escaped Character is threatening to the Scenarist.

LATER NOVELS

Raja' al-'Alim also wrote a novel, *The Silk Road*, which moves back and forth through history to include her grandfather and details forgotten folk customs of Mecca. The surreal journey is controlled by Ibn Khaldun and Mansour the Chessplayer in their chess match. Ahmed al-Duwahi's short novel *al-Raihana* is written in a modern style without a clear timeline and set in the south of Saudi Arabia. Laila al-Juhaini's *Wasted Paradise* is told by Saba, who falls in love with Amir and becomes pregnant. After Amir betrays her and leaves her to marry Khalida, she dies from an abortion; Khalida then takes up the story, and finally the author herself speaks (al-Hazimi et al. 2006, 33–34).

One of the greatest modernist Saudi Arabian novelists is 'Abd al-Rahman Munif (1933–2004). Munif was born to a Saudi Arabian father and an Iraqi mother and grew up in Amman, Jordan. He was active in the Ba'th Party, earned a doctorate in oil economics, and had a career as an oil economist, moving first to Iraq, then to France, and finally in 1981 to Syria, where he devoted himself to writing for the rest of his life, producing 30 books. While in Iraq, he wrote a quasifictional novel, *'Alam bi-la khara'it*, with the great Palestinian writer Jabra Ibrahim Jabra in 1982. He was stripped of his Saudi Arabian passport after he published the first of a quintet of novels called *Cities of Salt* (*Mudun al-milh*), which consists of *al-Tih* (1984; translated by Peter Theroux, 1987), *al-Ukhdul* (1985; translated as *The Trench* by Peter Theroux, 1991), *Taqasim al-layl wa-al-nahar* (1989; translated as *Variations on Night and Day* by Peter Theroux, 1993), *al-Munbatt* (1989), and *Badiyat al-zulumat* (1989). Munir insisted these were fiction, but the protagonist of these novels resembles 'Abd al-'Aziz al-Sa'ud and is the monarch of a desert kingdom where tyranny, oil, political Islam, modernization, and Western influence wreak havoc.

A recent novel is *The Girls of Riyadh* by Raja' (spelled Rajaa on the book cover) al-Sanae (b. 1961), published in 2005 in Arabic, in 2008 in Italian, and then in English. The book truly provides a window onto Arabian society, but the author has been criticized for being a lightweight in literary style (writing "chick-lit"), residing in the West, and producing irreverent social commentary. She explores the circumstances of four friends and Saudi Arabian attitudes, including male reluctance to marry a divorced woman. Male novelists under 40 years of age as of 2009 included 'Abdullah Thabit (b. 1973) a poet, journalist, and author of *al-Irhabi 20* (Terrorist number 20); Mohammad Hassan Alwan (b. 1979), author of *Saqf al-Kifaya* (2002), *Sofia* (2004), and *Touq al-Tahara* (2007); and Yahya Amqassim, born in 1971 in Wadi al-Husseini and the author of *The Crow Leg* (2008) and *Stories from Saudi Arabia* (2004). Alwan, Amqassim, and Thabit were chosen as being among the 39 best Arab authors under the age of 39 and invited to attend a literary festival at the 2010 Beirut world capital festivities (*Beirut 39*, 2010) Other recent novels include Layla Giuhni's *The Lost Song* (2007), Siba Al Herz's (a pseudonym) *The Others* (the first novel mentioning lesbians written by a Saudi Arabian, 2008), and Ahmed 'Abodehman's (b. 1949) *La Ceinture* (2009), considered the first Saudi Arabian novel in French. Nimah Isma'il Nawwah, a poet, writes in English and has published *Unfurled* (2004); she also writes essays about Saudi Arabia. Her poem "Gentleness Stirred" depicts a *mutawwa'* confronting a young woman.

Also attracting attention outside of Saudi Arabia was Turki al-Hamad, who was born in 1953 in Jordan to a family from al-Buraydah. This novelist, journalist, and analyst wrote a trilogy about a teenager, Abir (*Atyaf al-Aziqah*, *al-Mahjurah*, and *Phantoms of Deserted Alleys*), which takes place in the 1960s and 1970s (all were banned in Saudi Arabia). He also wrote *Winds of Paradise*, which concerns the events of 9/11 (Halasa 2005).

THEATER IN PRIVATE SPACES

Yamamah College in Riyadh mounted a production of *Wasati bila Wasatiyyah* ("A Moderates without Moderation") in November 2006. The play concerns Saudi Arabia's hijacking by its extremists, those on the right, and Islamic fanatics but admits that those on the left are also full of failings. Outsiders, including *mutawaʻin*, heard the play was against Islam, and on November 27, 2006, they attacked the actors, props, and stage lights; someone fired a weapon, and state security forces stormed the theater. The incident was filmed on camera phones and then broadcast on *al-Jazeera*. Later, *mutawwaʻa* websites called for the resignation of the president of the college, but the governor of Riyadh threw his support to the college, and the play's performances continued to invited audiences only (Slackilometersan 2007; Nicolaides 2007).

This was by no means the only play produced in a college setting. Maisah al-Sobaihi wrote, produced, and performed a treatment of women's situation in today's Saudi Arabia in *Head over Heels*. The play was produced in 2006 and twice in 2010. It is a social commentary in comedic prose presented in English (Frost 2010).

REFERENCES

Abodehman, Ahmed. *La Ceinture*. Paris: Gallimard, 2000.

Abu Khalid, Fawziyya. *Qira'a sirriyya fi tarikh al-sumt al-ʻarabi.* Beirut, Lebanon: Dar al-Adab, 1985.

ʻAlim, Rajaʻ. *Arbaʻa l Sifr (4l0).* Jeddah, Saudi Arabia: al-Nadi al-Thaqafi al-Adabi, 1987b.

ʻAlim, Rajaʻ. *al-Mawt al-akhir li-l-mumaththal* [The final death of the actor]. Beirut, Lebanon: Dar al-Adab, 1987a.

ʻAlim, Rajaʻ. *Thuqub fi al-Dhahr* [Hole in the back]. Beirut, Lebanon: Dar al-Adab, 1987c.

Alsanea, Rajaa. *Girls of Riyadh*. Translated by Marilyn Booth. New York: Penguin, 2008.

Arberry, A.J. *Aspects of Islamic Civilization: As Depicted in the Texts*. Ann Arbor: University of Michigan Press, 1978.

Arebi, Saddeka. *Women and Words in Saudi Arabia: The Politics of Literary Discourse*. New York: Columbia University Press, 1994.

Bagader, Abu Bakr, and Ava Molnar Heinrichsdorff, trans. and eds. *Assassination of Light: Modern Saudi Short Stories*. Washington, DC: Three Continents, 1990.

Bagader, Abou Baker A., and Deborah S. Akers, trans. and eds. *Histoires D'Arabie Saoudite*. Beirut, Lebanon: Centre International pour les Services Culturels, 2007.

Baker, Razan. "Tales of Old Jeddah." *Arab News*, January 25, 2007.

Beirut 39: New Writing from the Arab World. London: Bloomsbury, 2010.

Bogary, Hamza. *The Sheltered Quarter: A Tale of a Boyhood in Mecca*. Translated by Olive Kenney and Jeremy Reed. Austin: Center for Middle Eastern Studies, University of Texas, 1991.

Booth, Marilyn. "Poetry in the Vernacular." In *Modern Arabic Literature*, edited by Muhammad Mustafa Badawi. Cambridge History of Arabic Literature. Cambridge, New York, and Victoria, Australia: Cambridge University Press, 1992, 463–482.

Campbell, Kay Hardy. "Folk Music and Dance in the Arabian Gulf and Saudi Arabia." In *Images of Enchantment: Visual and Performing Arts of the Middle East*, edited by Sherifa Zuhur. Cairo: American University in Cairo Press, 1998, 57–70.

Frost, Bizzie. "Up Close and Personal with Maisah Sobaihi." *Saudi Gazette*, October 11, 2010.

al-Ghadeer, Moneera. *Desert Voices: Bedouin Women's Poetry in Saudi Arabia*. London: Tauris Academic Studies, 2009.

Gibb, H.A.R. *Arabic Literature: An Introduction*. Oxford, UK: Oxford University Press, 1974.

al-Gosaibi (alternate transliteration of al-Qusaibi or al-Ghosaybi), Ghazi. "Octopus," "When I Am With You," and "Silence." Translated by Sherif Elmusa and Charles Doria. In *Modern Arabic Poetry*, edited by Salma Khadra Jayyusi. New York: Columbia University Press, 1987.

Halasa, Malu. "Triumphant Trilogy." *Time Magazine*, January 17, 2005.

Hanley, Delinda C. "Saudi Arabian Women Dispel Myths and Stereotypes." *Washington Report on Middle Eastern Affairs*, May/June 2001, 35.

Hashim, Najwa. *Al-Safar fi Layl al-Ahzan*. Jeddah, Saudi Arabia: Al-Dar al-Sa'udiyya li-Nashr wa-Tawzi', 1986.

al-Hazimi, Mansur Ibrahim, Ezzat Khattab, and Salma al-Jayusi, eds. *Beyond the Dunes: An Anthology of Modern Saudi Writers*. London: I. B. Tauris, 2006.

Herz, Siba Al. *The Others*. New York: Seven Stories, 2009. (Originally published in 2008.)

Ibn Hurayyil, S.H. *Diwan al-Nabat al-hadith*. Beirut, Lebanon: Matabi' al-Wafa, 1374h.

Ibn Khamis, A. *Min ahadith al-samar*. Riyadh, Saudi Arabia: Matabi' Sharikat Hanifah lil-Ofset, 1978.

Ibn Khamis, A. *al-Adab al-sha'bi fi jazirat al-'arab*. Riyadh, Saudi Arabia: Matabi' al-Riyadh, 1958.

Ibn Khamis, A. *Rashid al-Khalawi*. Riyadh, Saudi Arabia: Dar al-Yamamah lil-bahth wa al-tarjuma wa al-nashr, 1972.

Jargy, Simon. "Sung Poetry in the Arabian Peninsula." In *Garland Encyclopedia of World Music*, edited by Virginia Danielson, Scott Marcus, and Dwight Reynolds. New York: Routledge, 2002, vol. 6, 663–669.

Jargy, Simon. "Sung Poetry in the Oral Tradition of the Gulf Region and the Arabian Peninsula." *Oral Tradition* 4, no. 1–2 (1989), 175–187.

al-Jayyusi, Salma Khadra. *The Literature of Modern Arabia: An Anthology*. London: Kegan Paul, 1988.

al-Kamali, Sh. *al-Shi'r 'inda al-badu*. Baghdad: Matba'at al-Irshad, 1964.

Kurpershoek, P. Marcel. *Arabia of the Bedouins*. London: Al Saqi, 2001.

Kurpershoek, P. Marcel. *Oral Poetry and Narratives from Central Arabia*. Vol. 1. Leiden, the Netherlands: E. J. Brill, 1994.

Munif, Abderrahman. *Variations on Night and Day*. Translated by Peter Theroux. New York: Pantheon Books, 1993.

Nawwab, Nimah Ismail. *Unfurled*. Vista, CA: Selwa, 2004.

Nicholson, R. A. *A Literary History of the Arabs*. Cambridge: Cambridge University Press, 1977. (Originally published in 1907.)

Nicolaides, Harry. "Saudi Students Seize the Day." n.d. Archived at Canada-ESL.com, http://www.canada-esl.com/articles1/seizeday.html.

Palgrave, W. G. "The Poet 'Omar'." In *Essays on Eastern Questions*. London, 1872.

al-Qusaibi, Ghazi. *Chosen Poems*. 1980.

al-Qusaibi, Ghazi. *Fever*. 1980.

al-Qusaibi, Ghazi. *You Are My Riyadh*. 1976.

Saqqaf, Khayriyya. *Li-Tobhira nahwa al-abʻad*. Riyadh, Saudi Arabia: Dar al-Ulum, 1982.

Serjeant, Robert B. *Saudi Arabian Poetry and Prose of Hadramawt*. London: Taylor's Foreign Press, 1951.

Shaker, Fatna. *Nabt al-Ardh* [The earth's planet]. Jeddah, Saudi Arabia: Tihamah, 1981.

al-Shamlan, Sharifa. *Muntahal Hudu'*. Riyadh, Saudi Arabia: Nadi al-Qissa al-Saʻudi. al-Jamʻiyya al-ʻarabiyya lil-thaqafa wa-l-funun, 1989.

Slackilometersan, Michael. "The Not So Eagerly Modern Saudi." *New York Times*, May 6, 2007.

Sowayan, Saʻd Abdullah. "Tonight My Gun Is Loaded: Poetic Dueling in Arabia." *Oral Tradition* 4, no. 1–2 (1989), 151–173.

Sowayan, Saʻd Abdullah. *Nabati Poetry: The Oral Poetry of Arabia*. Berkeley and Los Angeles: University of California Press, 1985.

al-Thabit, Abdullah. *al-Irhabi 20*. Damascus, Syria: Dar al-Mada, 2006; In translation, Paris: Actes Sud Sindbad, 2010.

Visual Art and Film

Visual art has always been a part of the Islamic tradition; however, the use of human figures or representations in mosques or sacred spaces was not allowed. This was meant to distinguish Islam from the worship practices of the polytheists and also from the use of icons and representations of Jesus in the Christian tradition. Actually, there were representations of the Prophet Muhammad and his companions, particularly in book illustrations. By the medieval period the Prophet was sometimes represented with his face veiled. Other representations of human, animal, or natural scenes were not problematic in nonreligious settings, but Muslims did want to avoid the practices of Christian art with several exceptions—the arts of the princes, illustrations in books and manuals, and images in all sorts of media in the 12th and

13th centuries and in folk art (Grabar 1992, 126–127). Several unique forms of art emerged as well: calligraphy, arabesque (repetitive design), and the "art of the object" (Grabar 1992, 130–131), beautifully crafted special functional items.

Neither Islamic art nor Islamic visual tradition has been static. In the seventh and eighth centuries, a process of synthesis began between the culture of Medina and Mecca and the artistic legacy of the peoples and lands conquered by the Muslim armies. This synthesis was carried farther both to the east and west through further expansion, into Spain and past Iran. In about the 10th century, the development of smaller states made for greater differences between areas, and the influence of the Ottoman Empire on many Arab lands (but not Saudi Arabia) further distinguished artistic traditions (Grabar 1992, 108–109).

In Saudi Arabia, artistic design is seen in a variety of crafts, ceramics, building decor, murals, jewelry, clothing, decorated weapons, doors, pottery, rugs, and many other items. A few individuals have tried to record, preserve, and catalog what was made in the past (Topham 1981; Colyer Ross 1978, 1981). Some projects aimed at economic development keep traditional design motifs alive, as in the glazed pottery and costumes produced at the al-Nahda Philanthropic Foundation under the sponsorship of Princesses Sarah and Moudy al-Sa'ud in the late 1990s, and other projects since then.

Studio art first arrived in the 1950s as schools were established. The Department of Education in Saudi Arabia introduced drawing, painting, and art lessons. Some promising art students were sent to other Arab countries or the West for their art education. In 1967 an arts society was founded in Saudi Arabia, which helped to arrange exhibitions and support artists (Ali in Nashashibi et al. 1994, 114). The Gulf Cooperation Council (GCC) and Gulf Art Friends have also supported exhibitions. As in other Arab countries, modern-style artists experimented with realism, cubism, impressionism, surrealism, abstract art, neo-Islamic art styles and, more recently, installations or conceptual art. At the same time, the expatriate community in Saudi Arabia included some artists and those with an interest in the visual arts, and they often mounted exhibitions.

The painter Safiyeh Said Binzagr, born in 1940, began her studies in England, returned to Saudi Arabia in 1964, and then embarked on art studies in Egypt. She first exhibited in Saudi Arabia with Mounirah Mosley. She describes her art style, rendered in different media, as primitive, and indeed it is somewhat like the primitive/naïf styles of artists in Egypt who drew on historical themes of the same era. She became one of the leaders in the early arts movement of Saudi Arabia. Among her well-known paintings is *Zabun*, which depicts a woman in the Hijazi dress style called *zabun*. Another is entitled *Zaffat al-Shibshib*, which shows the neighborhood people bringing the bride's belongings to her new household. Binzagr has established an art studio and gallery called the Dar'ah in Jeddah, which also holds monthly lectures (Nawwab 2001, 20–27).

Mounirah Mosley, born in Mecca in 1952, is a painter, graphic designer, and art teacher who also writes about art in several Saudi Arabian newspapers. Her work has been exhibited in Saudi Arabia, Jordan, Iraq, Spain, London, and the United States.

Mohammed Farea, born in 1968 in Saudi Arabia, has professional art training and an attractive style, showing brilliant colors and abstract shapes with some calligraphic use, as well as mysterious figures. He belongs to two artists' societies, and the patronage of the royal family is important to him, as it is to other artists.

Male artists have been painting contemporary murals and wall art for some time in Saudi Arabia. The female artist Shalimar Sharbatly broke their monopoly in Jeddah with a painting on the Corniche and another in front of the Guest Palace, home to foreign visitors. Sharbatly trained in Egypt and had her first show there at age 18 in 1988, and she wishes there were a ministry of arts and culture in Saudi Arabia (Fakkar 2008).

Jeddah hosts an annual art festival; in 2010, the event hosted 300 artists. In Paris, the Saudi Contemporary Art Exhibition at Musée du Montparnasse, ending in July 2010, exposed French audiences to contemporary Saudi Arabian painting. Since 1982, a special art contest has been mounted for children ages 4 to 14 in Saudi Arabia called The Children's Kingdom, in which they depict their own country and culture. The contest is judged by a panel of artists and teachers, and the exhibition was cataloged by Saudi Aramco, because it shows a wealth of images, like the open-air markets, lifestyles, and occupations now fading into the past, like the water-carrier with his goatskin, traditional dances and weddings, and religious rituals (Nawwab 1995, 18–27). It is significant that art education is offered in the schools, because it counters a conservative position that representational art is forbidden in Islam, particularly images of people. The national competition also shows young people that art is respected and has a connection with heritage and history. Besides the religious prejudice, some artists must deal with traditional prejudices about artisans' work.

PHOTOGRAPHY

Photography is a growing field in Saudi Arabia. Displaying photographs or portraits was considered scandalous in most circles in the early 1940s and earlier; in fact, people said the angels would not visit a home so decorated. Yet, today, one of its internationally recognized practitioners is Princess Reem al-Faysal, a granddaughter of King Faysal who has captured some memorable images of the *hajj* (Melis 2004, 48–50). The *hajj* is a favorite photographic and artistic subject for Muslims. Saudi Arabia and its citizens have been a favorite subject of foreign photographers, too, ever since the days of early travelers like Gertrude Bell, an archaeologist, intrepid adventurer, and eventually oriental secretary to the British High Commission in Iraq (see Bell's photographs in Bell 2000).

YOUNG ARTISTS

In September and October 2010, the Saudi Arabian Pavilion at the 2010 Shanghai World Expo featured a contemporary art exhibition curated by Lulwah al-Homoud and J. W. Stella entitled Nabatt (A Sense of Being) which included 130 works of art by more than 23 young artists from Saudi Arabia. Music, poetry, and calligraphy were included as well. The presenters were Bandar al-Rumayh, Jowhara al-Saud (photography), Ayman Yossri Daydban, Reem al-Faysal (photography), Zaman Jassim (painting, sculpture), Fahad al-Hijlan (painting), Lulwah al-Homoud (media installation), Mohammad Farea (painting), Nohal al-Sharif (sculpture), Mustafa al-'Arab, (calligraphy), Di'a 'Aziz Di'a (sculpture), Maha Malluh (photography), Nasser al-Turki (painting), Mohammed al-Gamdi (installation), Mohammad Alajlan (painting), Fahad al-Gelhami (photography/video), Saddiek Mohammad Wasil (sculpture), Farouk Kondakji (painting), Bakr Shaykhun (installation), 'Abdul 'Aziz 'Ashour (mixed media), and Sahdi and Raja 'Alem (installation). Nabatt also traveled to the MENASART Fair in Beirut in 2011, where films, including Saudi Arabian ones were also shown at Video Box.

Many other young artists are experimenting with different media. Several are featured in a collection on graphic design in the region (Wittner, Thoma, and Bourquin 2008); one of the graphic elements in modern Arab art is calligraphy. A traveling exhibit called Edge of Arabia includes several artists of interest. Manal al-Ghobayan of Dhahran displays a black-and-white photograph of a woman in a hard hat and engineer's uniform with her face covered by a tribal burqa, decorated with coins. Another shows a woman's hand, decorated with henna, gripping a steering wheel—the upper part of her face looks at the viewer, forming a circle with a Y shape inside of it (Edge of Arabia, Berlin 2010).

'Abdulnasser Gharem, from Khamis Mushait near Abha, was a major in the army and also a conceptual artist. He photographed a "performance"/event he staged in Abha, "Flora and Fauna," wrapping a special type of tree imported from Australia and planted throughout Abha, *Cornocarpus erectus*, and himself in plastic, surviving from the oxygen produced by the tree. The tree is a symbol of development schemes gone environmentally awry because this type of tree's roots extend horizontally for up to 100 meters (328.08 feet) running into and killing the root-balls of other trees (Hemming, 2008–2009 and Hemming in *Edge of Arabia*, 2009).

FILM

Theaters featuring drama or cinema have been banned in public forums in Saudi Arabia for decades, but films are watched on television thanks to satellite or on DVDs and videos. The first reason given for the ban on films is that representation is frowned on; however, if that were the case, then the ban on television overturned by King Faysal would have continued. An ancillary objection is the ultraconservative (and traditionalist) idea that women who show themselves on the screen (or onstage) in front of men, or allow their pictures to appear in the newspapers, are *mutabarrajat* (those who display their physical charms) and incite sinful behavior or, if in Saudi Arabia, disgrace their families. The same objection has been raised against some of the women writers mentioned in the Literature section, who have been photographed in the local newspapers. Cinemas do exist in other Gulf countries. In 2009, when the Rotana group screened a comedy, *Menahi*, in Jeddah and Ta'if, religious authorities pronounced that films were against Islam, because they distract people from their

Saudi Arabian man watches, Menahi, *the film at a screening in Riyadh, June 6, 2009. Women were not permitted to attend but the screening at a government-run cultural center was considered a daring step. (AP/Wide World Photos)*

work; the head of the religious police, Shaykh Ibrahim al-Ghayth, declared films to be evil. However, he then stated that if they depicted what was lawful and did not violate *shari'ah*, they could be allowed. Perhaps Saudi Arabia will allow the development of an Islamically compliant cinema as in Iran.

Despite the ban, quite a few shorter documentaries and one big-budget film have been produced, directed, and acted in by Saudi Arabians in their country in recent years, and they have directed and produced films abroad as well. The Saudi Arabian–filmed productions include *Dhilal al-Samt* (2004), *Kayf al-Hal* (2006), *Nisa' bila Dhil* (Women without shadows; 2006); *I Don' Wanna* (2008), *Shadow* (2008), *Three Men and a Woman* (2008), *According to Local Time* (2008), *Sunrise/Sunset* (2008), *Last Day* (2008), *Project* (2008), and *Ayesh* (2010). Directors not mentioned in the following include 'Abdullah al-Muhaisin, Muhammad al-Khalif, Muhammad al-Dahri, Hussam Alhulwah, 'Abdulmuhsin al-Dhabaan, and others.

Kayf al-Hal, a big-budget film, was produced by Ayman Halawani, was directed by Izidore Musallam, and starred Hind Muhammad. The screenplay is about a Saudi Arabian family engaged in the struggle of modern life versus the traditions of the past, and how these impact the character Dunya (Hind Muhammad). The film was actually filmed in Dubai in the United Arab Emirates and shown on pay per view through an arrangement with Showtime Arabia. It screened at the Cannes Film Festival, where the director, who is the general manager of film production for the Rotana Group (see the Music section in this chapter), said he hopes to change attitudes toward filmmaking in Saudi Arabia (Dowd, *BBC News*, May 26, 2006).

Cinema 500 Kilometers (2006) was written, directed, produced, and filmed by Abullah al-Eyaf (b. 1976) and starred Tariq al-Husaini. Al-Husaini's character loves movies but, living in Saudi Arabia, has never seen a movie showing. He drives 500 kilometers to Bahrain to see a movie in an actual cinema theater for the first time. The film was shown at the Emirates Film Competition in Abu Dhabi in 2006. Following this project, al-Eyaf completed three short films: *Etaar, Matar*, about a young man about to become blind and a hearing-disabled child, and *'Ayish* (2010), which won the Gulf Film Festival award for best short documentary. *Women without Shadows* (2006) was directed by Haifa Mansour (b. 1974), who previously directed three short films (*Who?*, *Bitter Journey*, and *The Only Way Out*). *Women without Shadows* deals with the issues of the required covering of the *'abaya* and has been shown in at least 17 international film festivals, winning the best documentary award at the Muscat Film Festival.

A number of films address the plight of children and the disabled in society. Entries in the Islamic Film Festival in December 2009 were *Just Words*, directed by Samir Arif; *The Child Task*, directed by Mamdouh Salem; and *Acquitted Dreams*, directed by Bashir al-Muhaishil. *Just Words* concerns a Saudi Arabian child who on returning from residence in the United States has difficulties assimilating to life in his own country. *The Child Task* is about a child whose parents have left him. *Acquitted Dreams* is the story of an orphaned child and his dreams of becoming a photographer (*AlSaudi. Arabia.com*).

Tawfiq al-Zaydi directed *al-Samt*, which concerns deafness; *Aseel*, directed by Faisal Khalid al-Harbi, is about a man with a blind son. These films, and *Matar* (which was already mentioned), *Ahsin*, and *Nanmool Adventures*, were all entries in the Asian Film Festival in Sri Lanka. *Ahsin* was directed by Faisal al-'Utaybi and was set in the Fayfa Mountains in the south of Saudi Arabia, and *Nanmool Adventures* was a cartoon directed by Muhammad al-Obaid. The Beirut International Film Festival 2010 included *Al-Gandarji*, directed by Ahd Kamel, and *'Ayish* of Abdullah al-Eyaf, which was already mentioned.

Filming is permitted for certain educational purposes and for promotion of internal tourism. Camera phones, which were initially banned in Saudi Arabia, have created thousands of amateur filmed sequences, some of which have been posted on the Internet. However, studios and technical crews are lacking. Certain foreign production crews have been permitted to shoot in Saudi Arabia, as in *Malcolm X* (1962) or *Lawrence of Arabia* (1962), or have depicted issues moving into Saudi Arabia, such as *The Slave Trade Today* (*Le Schiave Esistona Accora*) (1964) or *Le Grand Voyage* (2004). Other recent films focusing on terrorism were shot entirely outside of Saudi Arabia at locations thought to resemble Saudi Arabia; these included *The Kingdom*, directed by Peter Berg and shot in Phoenix and Mesa, Arizona, and in Abu Dhabi in the United Arab Emirates. Berg spent two weeks in Saudi Arabia prior to the film. Nevertheless, some details and aspects of the film suffer from clichés and assumptions to be found in media and "expert" treatments of the terrorist movement in the kingdom, although Faris al-Ghazi, the character of a Saudi Arabian state policeman who helps the American investigators, is depicted as a hero (a rarity in Western films).

REFERENCES

Ali, Wijdan. "Modern Painting in the Mashriq." In *Colors of Enchantment: Theater, Dance, Music and Visual Art of the Middle East*, edited by Sherifa Zuhur. Cairo: American University in Cairo, 2001, 363–385.

Ali, Wijdan. *Modern Islamic Art: Development and Continuity*. Gainesville: University Press of Florida, 1997.

Ali, Wijdan. "Modern Arab Art: An Overview." In *Forces of Change: Artists of the Arab World*. Exhibition director and contributing co-author Salwa Mikdadi Nashashibi, Laura Nader, Etel Adnan, Shehira Doss Davezac, Todd B. Porterfield, and Wijdan Ali. Lafayette, CA: International Council for Women in the Arts; Washington, DC: National Museum of Women in the Arts, 1994, 73–119.

The American Film Institute Catalog of Feature Films 1961–1970. Berkeley and Los Angeles: University of California Press, 1976.

Bell, Gertrude. *The Arabian Diaries, 1913–1914*. Edited by Rosemary O'Brien. Syracuse, NY: Syracuse University Press, 2000.

Binzagr, Safeya. *Saudi Arabia, An Artist's View of the Past*. Lausanne, France: Three Continents, 1979.

Colyer Ross, Heather. *The Art of Arabian Costume: A Saudi Arabian Profile*. Fribourg, Switzerland: Arabesque Commercial, 1981.

Colyer Ross, Heather. *Bedouin Jewellery in Saudi Arabia*. London: Stacey International, 1978.

Dowd, Vincent. "First Saudi Feature Film Aims High." *BBC News*, May 26, 2006. http://news.bbc.co.uk/2/hi/middle_east/5019116.stm

Edge of Arabia: Contemporary Art from Saudi Arabia. Exhibition curated by Stephen A. Stapleton, Lulwah Al-Homoud, and Ahmed Mater Al-Ziad Aseer at the 6th Berlin Biennale. Text and interviews by Henry Hemming and Venetia Porter. From 2008–2011. (Berlin, Germany, July 2010; London, 2010.) Exhibition guides available at http://www.edgeofarabia.com

Elgood, Robert. *The Arts and Armour of Arabia*. London: Aldershot and Brookfield, 1994.

Fakkar, Galal. "An Instinctive Arab Painter." *Arab News*, August 26, 2008.

Grabar, Oleg. "Art and Architecture." In *The Genius of Arab Civilization: Source of Rennaisance*, edited by John Hayes. New York: New York University Press, 1992, 107–131.

Harman, Danna. "Middle Eastern Female Filmmakers Give Glimpse of Once-Veiled Worlds." *Christian Science Monitor/Alternet*, March 10, 2008.

Hayes, John R. *The Genius of Arab Civilization: Source of Renaissance*. New York: New York University Press, 1992.

Helb, Aarnout, ed. et al. A. *Ahmed Mater*. Catalogue of Artspace Exhibition. Dubai, United Arab Emirates, 2009.

Hemming, Henry. "Art of Survival: An Interview." Offscreen Education Program, 2008–2009, and in *Edge of Arabia*. Also at http://henryhemming.com/?book=edge-of-arabia

Le Gouic, Jean-Claude. *Mahdi Al Jeraib*. Paris: Fondation Al Monsouria, 2001.

Melis, Wim, curator. *Nazar: Photographs of the Arab World*. Amsterdam: Stichting Aurora Borealis, 2004.

Nashashibi, Salwa Mikdadi. "Gender and Politics in Contemporary Art: Arab Women Empower the Image." In *Images of Enchantment: Visual and Performing Arts of the Middle East*, edited by Sherifa Zuhur. Cairo: American University in Cairo Press, 1998, 165–182.

Nawwab, Ni'mat. "Painting Cultural History." *Aramco World*, January/February 2001, 20–27.

Nawwab, Ni'mat. "The Children's Kingdom." *Aramco World*, November/December 1995, 18–27.

Al-Osaimi, Najah. "Haifa Film Creates a Stir." *Arab News*, April 21, 2005.

Porter, Venetia, Linda Komaroff, Tim Mackintosh Smith, and Ahmed Al-Omran. *Ahmed Mater*. Foreword by Catherine David. London: Booth-Clibborn Editions (BCE), 2010.

Porter, Venetia, ed.; Henry Hemming, ed. and texts. *Edge of Arabia: Contemporary Art from Saudi Arabia*. London: Booth-Clibborn Editions (BCE), 2011.

Topham, John. *Traditional Crafts of Saudi Arabia*. London: Stacey International, 1981.

Wittner, Benn, Sascha Thoma, and Nicolas Bourquin. *Arabesques: Graphic Design from the Arab World and Persia*. Berlin: Die Gestalten, 2008.

Music and Dance

Music is an important aspect of cultural life in Saudi Arabia. Attention is given here to music and dance, due to the many genres of collectively performed folkloric forms that unite music, poetry, and dance in the Arabian tradition, and to vocal aspects of religious music and recitation. Somewhat more information exists on traditional, or folk, music of the area as opposed to "art" or classical Arabic music, or contemporary commercial popular music in the kingdom, in part due to ethnomusicology's focus on rural traditions. Nevertheless, other types of music are popular, including Western pop, jazz, rock, and other genres and classical music. However, these other genres of music are clearly secular and unconnected with the cultural legacy (*turath*). Religious conservatives oppose the playing of music in public (with the exclusion of religious genres), and music might not be considered a desirable profession for a youngster in a conservative family. Likewise, professional, meaning paid, dance is not likely to be pursued by young Saudi Arabian women, although, in recent years, different genres of dance as exercise are presented in sports and exercise clubs exclusively for women.

It is difficult to disaggregate Saudi Arabia's indigenous musical tradition from that in other parts of the peninsula on a purely national basis; certain genres extend beyond borders, and musicians and their unique styles may have traveled to an area. The term *khaliji* (Gulf) in reference to music or dance refers to the United Arab Emirates, Bahrain, Kuwait, and Oman as well as Saudi Arabia. At the same time, each town or village had its own special musical heritage that is related to its poetic and dance output. A final proviso is that many publications allude to the religious distaste for music, particularly instrumental music, mentioning occasional attacks on musicians who nonetheless continue to perform (Urkevich 2001, 325). This can lead to a misunderstanding that bolsters the salafist rejection of entertainment, popular rituals, and, with them, music and dance. Ordinary people tend to consider the music they hear and perform to be sung poetry, which is accepted, rather than simply (musical) "songs" (Campbell in Zuhur, ed., 1998, 60) as performed by popular Arab singing stars of other countries—even though nearly all vocal music is sung poetry. Paradoxically, music, particularly as part of ceremonial gatherings, is acceptable and enjoyed within private settings and also given certain restrictions. Music is an important part of public occasions, as at the end of the Gulf War, to celebrate the homecoming of a king, and it appears on radio and television. State support is important as well, including sponsorship from Saudi Arabia's Society for Culture and the Arts, whose mission is to preserve folkloric heritage. On an annual basis, the Janadiriyyah festival of cultural heritage held near Riyadh features musical, dance, and poetry performances. Parts of the festival grounds are set up to represent different regions of Saudi Arabia with particular handicrafts sold there and performances given in these special settings. In addition, entertainers perform for invited guests in a main performance pavilion. Some never before exposed to their own country's cultural traditions can experience the songs of Abha shepherds, dancers from the Eastern coast, or the warriors' *'ardha* performance (see later on).

Archaeological findings at Najran display images of four lyres, an important early instrument, which may indicate they were played as an ensemble. Frame drums and at least two other drums were played as well, and Arabia seems to have been influenced by the music of its southern shores, Ethiopia, and eastern Africa, perhaps as much as by the musical traditions coming from farther north (Poché 2002). In the Jahiliyya (the time before Islam), the Arabs referred to music and the singing of poetry with a single term, *ghina'*; drawings show dancers, and texts include references to *zafina* (from the Mehri language of southern Yemen), Ethiopians who danced. The term for slave women who sang, *qiyan*, was in use by the seventh century as well (Poché 2002, 361–362). These entertainers sang for travelers and patrons and played stringed instruments. In addition, texts report communal singing at festivals and special occasions, which the Prophet approved of, according to several Prophetic traditions (Campbell 2002, 696; Campbell in Zuhur, ed., 1998, 69).

The Dutch scholar Christiaan Snouck Hurgronje, who wrote about Mecca in the 19th century (Snouck Hurgronje 1931), described the music of wedding ceremonies and a special song for the bride's headdress, *ghuna al-kharit*. He also described the popularity of the *qanun*, a multistringed zither, and the *qanbus*, a southern Arabian (and Yemeni) small pear-shaped lute (Lambert 2002, 654). Thanks to him, some 150 cylinders were recorded in Jeddah by the Dutch legation early in the 20th century, including women's folk music. Commercial recording began in the Gulf area in the late 1920s and 1930s. Commercial recordings from other Arab countries were circulated to the peninsula, despite the Ikhwan's distaste for music and musical rituals. Ibn Sa'ud, the founder of the modern kingdom, reputedly enjoyed musical gatherings.

This opposition does not carry over to religious musical forms, which are differentiated from secular music or not even considered "music" at all. Many sources claim that what is disdained is instrumental music, as vocalists, percussionists, and clappers are often not considered to be playing instruments. In fact, many traditions of instrumental music go far back in history and may be attached to social groups

NATIONAL ANTHEM OF SAUDI ARABIA

The national anthem of Saudi Arabia was adopted in 1950. The lyrics were written by Ibrahim Khafiji and the music by 'Abd al-Rahman al-Khatib in 1947. Earlier lyrics were written by Muhammad Tal'at.

TABLE S6.2

Transliteration	English Translation
Sār'ī la l-majd wa l-'alyā',	Hasten to glory and supremacy,
Majjedī al-khāliq as-samā'!	Glorify the Creator of the heavens!
Wa arfa'ī al-khaffāq akhdar	And raise the green flag
Yahmil an-nūr al-musattar	Carrying the emblem of Light,
Raddedi: Allahu akbar,	Repeating: Allah is the greatest,
Yā mawatanī!	O my country!
Mawtanī, 'ishta fakhr al-muslimīn	My country, Live as the glory of Muslims!
'Āsh al-malik li- l-'alam wa l-watan!	Long live the King for the flag and the country!

of lower status in some areas but not in all, and this prejudice did not seem to attach to the *rababa* (a bowed upright fiddle) in the bedouin tradition (Campbell in Zuhur, ed., 1998, 60).

Women's music, which is enjoyed at schools, universities, and private parties, is to some degree a separate genre, permissible so long as it takes place in segregated venues. Recordings of women's performances are commercially available (Campbell 1998, 66–67). Saudi Arabian women may perform abroad and for each other, but not in public in front of men in the kingdom; however, women of other Gulf nations may appear in public ensembles. Women's days at the Janadiriyyah festival, an annual cultural event organized by the Saudi Arabian National Guard, are attended by women only and feature performance styles from all over Arabia, as well as special poetry and dance spectacles (Zuhur, Field Notes, 2005).

MUSIC: GENERAL FEATURES

Music is performed on large frame drums (*tar*, singular; *tiran*, plural); frame drums with cymbals; double-skinned larger drums (*tabl*); a vase- or goblet-shaped drum (*darbukka*); the *rababa*, a bowed instrument with a rectangular sound box that is played upright; the *'ud*, a short-necked lute; the *tanbura*, or lyre (also called the *simsimiyya*), usually with five strings; and the *mizmar*, a reeded aerophone in which the two reeds are blown together; and also by clapping, or *tasfiq*. Other instruments may be played in larger ensembles such as the *nay* (bamboo flute), the *qanun* (a plucked zither), violins, and sometimes violas or cellos, and the electronic keyboard. Different areas may feature other instruments such as the *tanaka* (a date or olive tin, perforated with holes and hit with the hand), played in Qahtan in the south, or the *surnay* (an instrument similar to the oboe), played in al-Hasa and used in the *liwa* dance.

Saudi Arabian music in its "art" (*fann*) and "traditional" (*sha'bi* forms, like other varieties of Arabic music, is melodically organized around *maqamat*, which are more like modes than scales (because the note pattern differs on the descent; also, the tonalities may vary even more narrowly than a quarter-tone, and they impart a particular mood), and a poet/singer played an integral role in music (Racy in Hayes, ed., 1992, 160–161; also see Racy 1998.) Each of these *maqamat* has a name and a typical melodic pattern, which emphasizes particular dominant notes and features microtonality—in other words, tones narrower than the half pitch between the black and the white notes of the Western piano. These *maqamat* are further subdivided into smaller subsets (often sets of five notes) in traditional forms. Improvisation on these *maqamat* and the use of call-and-response structures are common musical features. Polyphony (the technical term for harmony) is uncommon, with the exception of certain forms of choral singing, as in the pearl divers' music from the Arabian Gulf. Another feature of Arabian music is its strong use of rhythm and multiple rhythms. A typical multiple or polyrhythmic segment could be performed by the *duff* or *daff* (a frame drum) and a goblet-shaped drum, and also by clappers performing *tasfiq* (clapping hands).

Majlis al-Tarab

In cities and towns, music and dance are performed in a *diwan*, or a *majlis al-tarab*, a large salon in a family home. This area is separate from the living quarters and can accommodate a large number of visitors. Whereas in the other Gulf countries, musical evenings or celebrations with music would, in the past, have been performed for mixed audiences, in Saudi Arabia (and today in certain Gulf state settings) the *majlis al-tarab* would include either male or female guests.

Wedding Celebrations

Wedding celebrations are lengthy and do not conclude on a single day. The engagement may first be celebrated. The actual wedding involves parties for the groom and at least one for the bride, which may be the *laylat al-hinna*, an event where her family and friends beautify her with henna decorations on her hands and feet. A musical ensemble consisting of a *mutriba*, a female singer, and percussionists (women) is hired for the event. Music may also take place at the *laylat al-zaffa* (or *zfaff*). The *zaffa* was traditionally a procession, and the key event on this evening is the joining of the bride and groom. Each of these events could be performed in a *majlis al-tarab* in a family residence. *'Ud* (oud; that is, the scented wood, not the musical instrument) will be burned, the best possible, to perfume the entire evening (Hansen 2000), and women will wear their finest clothes, which will be permeated by the smell of the *'ud*.

These events may be recorded and videotaped, and the recordings might be distributed for sale. Numerous examples of such performances can be found on the Internet, and as some of these video clips were recorded years ago, one may view styles of dance and music no longer performed today.

POPULAR MUSIC INDUSTRY

Radio and television were tremendously influential in popularizing the careers of modern Saudi Arabian performers and disseminating the performances of other Arab, and also Western, musicians and vocalists. As well, Saudi Arabian patronage of live musical entertainment in other parts of the Arab world, and the importing of entertainers as well as musicians to the Gulf region, has made for a kind of musical cosmopolitanism in the Gulf that was not originally present. Just as Saudi Arabian musicians and singers are influenced by regional styles, performers from Lebanon to Egypt to Tunisia have incorporated songs into their performances and recordings based on Saudi Arabian and Gulf rhythms and melodic patterns, which are generically termed *khaliji*.

The Saudi Arabian company Rotana Group, founded in 1987, currently exerts an extraordinary influence on Arab music of the Levant, Egypt, Iraq, and the Gulf, and on performers from all over the Arab world. The conglomerate, known simply as Rotana, includes film production, a record label, a magazine, and numerous television and music channels and is owned primarily by Prince al-Walid ibn Talal, with News Corporation as a 9 percent partner. At least 100 Arab artists are signed to Rotana.

TRADITIONAL MUSICAL FORMS

Such performances involve singing, accompanied by the *rababa* in the bedouin tradition, and sometimes also percussion. Such performance can also be performed by two or more singers. Along the eastern coast and into Kuwait or down into the Gulf, in the 1970s, traveling gypsy ensembles used oil canisters as *rababa*, along with a woman singer and dancer (Røvsing Olsen and Wegner 2001, 796), much as the bedouin on the Red Sea coast (as in the Sinai) use oil canisters to make a facsimile of a *tanbura* (lyre) (Zuhur, Field Notes, 1998–1999). The aesthetics of singing vary somewhat by area and genre, but, generally, a nasal quality was admired in the presentation of older forms such as singing of *qasa'id* (strophic poetry). Also, a sweet singing tone is admired in *khaliji* styles, somewhat more so than in other parts of the Arab musical tradition.

Dewinih

Dewinih is one of the bedouin genres; the name refers to a *diwan*, or poetry collection, sung a cappella or with the performer providing his own accompaniment on the *rababa*. The poetry of the *dewinih* is of the type called *nabati*. The melody is often limited to five notes of a *maqam* (Lambert 2002, 652), which is the traditional building block of the *maqam* as well as the basis of bedouin melodies. Variants include the *mashub*, the *barbi*, and the camel herder's or camel rider's (Jargy 2002, 665) song, the *hjeini*.

Other soloists, or soloists accompanied by ensembles, play the *'ud*, the short-necked lute performed all over the Arab world. Many forms of collective performance involve dance and music and feature poetic lyrics. Some are described in the following.

'Ardha

'*Ardha* has become a national dance and song of Najd; it is also performed in other regions of the kingdom, the United Arab Emirates, and Bahrain. It derives from a war singing tradition intended to scare the enemy and prepare for combat (Urkevich 2001, 326). The *hidwa* (lyrics) are antiphonal and syllabic and glorify the tribe, its honor, its leader, and the ruler (Lambert 2002, 654). It was once performed by men and women together and is now performed by men who carry swords. In Najd, the *'ardha* is performed to a six-beat rhythm (*DUM, DUM, tek, DUM, tek, tek*) played on the *tabl* (double-skinned drum) and *daff* or *tar* (single-skinned held frame drum). It is actually a suite of pieces. In Najd, two lines of men dance, wave swords, and also serve as the chorus. The rulers of Saudi Arabia have always danced the *'ardha* publicly, and it may be performed simultaneously with a military spectacle. The *'ardha* is called *'ayala* in the United Arab Emirates. There and in Bahrain, it is often performed with a double chorus on special occasions and two lines of dancers (Røvsing Olsen and Wegner 2001, 795; Awhan 1988). In southwestern Arabia, the dancers may perform with rifles to a faster 4/4 rhythm (Campbell in Zuhur, ed., 1998, 59). In Oman it is called *wahhabiyya* (Lambert 2002, 654).

Galtih (or Riddiyih)

This is a poetic dueling tradition—a war of words, a part of the *nabati* verse tradition. Each poet-singer delivers lines, which are supposed to be original and may be spontaneously composed, and then the ensemble repeats the text. *Tasfiq*, rhythmic hand-clapping, accompanies the performance.

al-Dawsari

Al-Dawsari is a dance and singing style of the Banu Dawasir tribe, who are found to the southwest of Riyadh, and there are many subforms given the same name (Campbell 1998, 58). The rhythm known as *dawsari* is played as follows: tek a, DUM, ess, tek a, DUM ess (tek = light beat on the side of the drum, the upbeat; DUM = a beat on the deeper center of the drum, and, here, it is the downbeat; ess = a rest).

al-Samri

The *samri*, or *samiri*, are a song cycle performed at night (hence the name, which means "of night") to texts of the *nabati* genre about love or beauty (Urkevich 2001, 326; Lambert 2002, 653). As well as being part of the nomadic tradition, they are performed by now-sedentary bedouin near urban areas (Jargy 2002, 665). They are performed at weddings, festivals, and Thursday night gatherings (Thursday evening is the equivalent of the American Saturday night, since businesses may be closed on the following day, Friday). The *samri* have variants called the *shiri*, *khammari*, and *'ashuri* ('Abd al-Hakim 1980, 74). According to Urkevich (2001, 326), the *samri* were played to keep awake a person bitten by a snake until a healer arrived to treat him or her; the *samri*'s nocturnal performance is also explained by other tales from folk tradition (Tayash 1988).

As with many of the performed musical and dance traditions, the *samri* is organized in two lines of people who sing as a double chorus. Individuals playing the *tar* and *tabl* (a larger double-skinned drum) and *tasfiq* (clappers) accompany a main singer and the two choruses. One line may sing, and then the other responds. The *tar* and *tabl* players are often professionals who display the name of their group on their instruments (Lambert 2002, 653).

As the poet-singer gives the verse, he and the drummers stay in their lines, but lines of dancers move their backs in a special rolling, or undulating, motion. Two or three veiled women may dance between the lines of men. The dancers may playfully snatch articles of clothing from the men, which are given back to them later (Adra 2002, 709).

Aghani al-Ghaws and Fijiri

An important genre of *khaliji* music came from the divers and seamen of the pearling industry, an important trade that died out after the early 1930s. The ships' captains retained a *niham* (*nahham*), a lead singer for the *al-ghaws al-kabir*, the six-month diving season between April and September. The *nahham* led the crew and divers (*ghawwas* was the name for a diver) aboard the dhow in singing songs that marked different stages of their work, and they also performed other special songs (song of the whale) and songs of entertainment when they returned after a voyage, when they convened at a *dar* (the word for a home but also a dwelling with a large hall and a lodge for a crew) and sang and danced in different styles. The specialized genres were known as *aghani al-ghaws* (songs of the diving) or *nahma* (voice of the whale), and the songs of entertainment, which include the *al-haddadi* form, are also known generically as *fijiri* (meaning "of dawn"). The special features of this music included songs performed to a deep drone maintained by the singers/divers/crew, called the *hamhama*, which may be meant to imitate the sound of the whale and also a *nahda*, a lament, and a *janda*, an introductory improvisation (Lambert 2002, 651). Accompanying the song are drums, *tar*, cymbals (*twaysat*), coffee mortars (struck with the grinding stick to produce a rhythm), and *tasfiq* (clapping). There were also traditional women's songs performed when the pearl divers returned home, and these were called *guffal* (Campbell 2002, 698).

Before the pearling dhows launched, a dance called *al-sinkini* was performed to sad and lamenting poetry. The forms of *fijiri* involved dancing in group forms with dancers striking the floor with their hands, and a soloist might improvise. Just before the boat's return to shore, the *'ardha al-bahriyya* (the *'ardha* of the sea) was performed onshore by lines of men, drummers, and sword carriers (Adra 2002, 708).

Liwa

The *liwa*, or *leiwah*, is said to come from Kenya or Tanzania and is performed in areas with large populations originally from Africa, in the Eastern Province, in Bahrain, and in Basra. It may include the *shawm* (alternate names are *surnay*, *zurnay*, or *zurna*; this is a double-reeded woodwind instrument bored like an oboe), singers, and percussion instruments (Røvsing Olsen and Wegner 2001, 796; Urkevich 2001, 327). The dance performed by men and women during the *liwa* is a slow walk around a circle with a step forward, then a step back, and then sometimes a complete turn. The texts of the songs are sad and concern separation from loved ones, and some lines have Swahili words (Adra 2002, 710).

Sawt

The *sawt* is the most important form of music developing in traditional urban settings and is often identified as "art" (*fann*) music. It is played in the Eastern Province and in Kuwait and Bahrain, and it includes other instruments in addition to the *'ud* and percussion, such as the *nay* (a flute) and *qanun*. Although it is like classical Arabic music, played in *maqam* Bayati, Rast, Sikka, and Hijaz, the accompanying rhythms make *sawt* unique. (The *maqamat* are musical modes constructed around an ascending and descending scale, with prominent tonalities; each is thought to affect the mood of the listener in a special way. Bayati, for example, would typically move from the dominant tone of *re*, or D, in its first tetrachord, which contains an E half-flat, to a Nahawand second tetrachord with a dominant tone of *sol*, or G, and a B flat. One can modulate from this maqam to an Ajam trichord on the third or the sixth note. Or one may modulate to the Bayati Shuri *maqam*, which has an A flat. Bayati is associated with the desert tradition.) The genre is said to have come from Yemen ('Abduh Ghanim 1986) and was recorded as early as 1927 in Baghdad and 1929 in Cairo by Abd al-Latif al-Kuwaiti (Lambert 2002, 649–650). It used to be performed in houses that belonged communally to groups of musicians or at performances in private homes. The *sawt* featured a singer who accompanied himself on the *'ud*, four performers on the *marawis* (small double-skinned drums), *tasfiq* (hand-clapping), and possibly other instruments. It includes classical Arabic poetry and also Yemeni colloquial poetry. The *sawt* cycle unfolds with an instrumental introduction (the *istihlal*), then a short sung poem (*istima*), followed by the *sawt* section sung to one of the two rhythms, and a final short poem (*tawashih*) in a precomposed melody usually in *maqam* Rast (Lambert 2002, 652; also see Røvsing Olsen and Wegner 2001, 795). The dance that accompanies the *sawt* is called the *zafan*; in it, dancers may suddenly leap or kneel (Adra 2002).

LARGE-ENSEMBLE MUSIC

The majority of early recordings of *khaliji* music were of the *sawt* form. Beginning in the 1950s and 1960s, male singers began to perform with very large orchestras along the lines of the famous Egyptian vocal artist Umm Kulthum. These orchestras contained modern instruments such as violins, violas or cellos, and the keyboard, along with *'ud*ists, and were not limited to the local traditional instruments and percussion. Among the first Saudi Arabian singers to present this new style, typical of the *ughniya* (song) form, were Talal al-Maddah (1939–2000) and Muhammad 'Abduh Othman al-Asiri (1949–). Al-Maddah first came to the public's attention with his song "Wardak, Ya Zira' al-Ward" in the 1950s, while 'Abduh first sang on the radio in 1960. Several of their songs—Maddah's "Maqadir" and 'Abduh's "Ab'ad" and "Ya Sariya"—became hits throughout the Arab world.

When Egypt fell from Arab favor after signing the Camp David peace treaty, tourism from the Arab Gulf fell off there for some years, and the profitable club scene in Cairo gradually went into a decline coinciding with a religious revival. At the same time, Beirut was no longer an attractive magnet for Arab tourists due to the civil war. The Gulf tourist audiences dispersed to other areas, and a musical recording industry based in Dubai and the United Arab Emirates began to flourish. This, in tandem with performing opportunities in the Gulf, attracted non-*khaliji* singing stars who added Gulf-inspired songs to their own repertoire; for instance, Warda al-Jaza'iriyya, the Egyptian star of Algerian origin; the late singer Zikra, originally from the Maghrib as well; and Kadhim al-Sahir, the Iraqi vocalist.

Some of the best-known Saudi Arabian singers include Talal Maddah, who died onstage in 2000 while performing at the annual Abha music festival, and Muhammad 'Abduh, who has recorded more than 100 albums or CDs. He no longer regularly presents concerts but performed in the Arab Music Festival in Cairo in 2005. Others are 'Abbadi Johar (b. 1953), Saleh Khayri, and 'Abd al-Majid 'Abdullah (b. 1963). Leading composers include Tariq 'Abd al-Hakim (b. ca. 1921), Ghazi 'Ali, Muhammad al-Senan, and Muhammad Shafiq Chughtai. Tariq 'Abd al-Hakim (alternately written as al-Hakeem) was the first to introduce military music to Saudi Arabia; he has contributed greatly to the academic study of traditional Saudi Arabian music and maintained the Castle of Cultural Arts at his home in Jeddah from 1990–2005 (*Arab News*, November 25, 2005). Muhammad al-Senan was a violinist and then an *'ud*ist of the al-Khobar Orchestra, known as the Silver Band, under the Iraqi musician Tawfiq Jadd in 1962. He was active in Dammam and Qatif and was imprisoned for political activism; then, after returning from a 10-year hiatus in Kuwait, he began composing, winning competitions. Leading singers perform his music.

Rabih Saqr is in the next generation of singers and is known for a more modern, or "pop" sound. He was introduced, as were many of the other male and female singers, by al-Maddah in 1992. Other singers include Talal Salama (b. 1966) and also Hisham 'Abderrahman (b. 1980), the winner of the Star Academy 2 Awards, a televised contest of Arabic music similar to *American Idol*. Unfortunately, the Saudi Arabian *'ulama* condemned the Star Academy, calling it a crime against Islam, and urged 'Abderrahman to repent. Perhaps the best-known Saudi Arabian female singer is 'Itab. Ibtisam Lutfi is another well-known female singer. Tuha, who composed many songs sung by other singers such as Talal Maddah, sings in the wedding-party circuits and plays the *'ud*. Sara 'Othman is another singer of this genre. Waed (her real name is Hanan Bakri Younes) is a younger female singer; her mother is Iraqi, and her father was one of the founders of Saudi Arabian radio broadcasting at the National Broadcasting Service, which has played an important role in introducing local artists to their Saudi Arabian audience.

STYLES OF HIJAZ AND ASIR

Urban Music

The urban music of the Hijaz was recorded by the Dutch orientalist Snouck Hurgronje. Later recordings were made by Muhammad al-Sindi, who sang, played the *'ud*, and was accompanied by a *mirwas* and a deeper drum. The *qanbus*, or southern Arabian lute, was replaced by the *'ud* over the course of the 20th century. Typically, the music includes an improvised, nonmetered segment called *mawwal* or *majass*, played in the middle of a piece that otherwise features rhythm (Ba Ghaffar 1994, 52). The *maqamat* played are close to Rast and Hijaz; what is special about the style is the syncopation of the percussion (Lambert 2002, 655).

Majrur

The *majrur* is performed in Ta'if and in Asir. The musical text may be an epic lament or a love poem. All of those participating play a treble *tar* except for the lead drummer, who is positioned between two lines of players and plays a low-pitched *tabir* as well as a *tar*. The dancers sing while moving to the center. Participants can leave their place in the performance and then start leading the group in a new rhythm, which might include *majrash* and *shabshar* beats (Urkevich 2001, 326). Campbell describes the *majrur* of Ta'if as involving dancers who move with twirling motions in *thobs* made with circular skirts (Campbell in Zuhur, ed., 1998, 58).

Mizmar

The *mizmar* is a very popular dance of the Hijaz performed in Jeddah, Mecca, and Medina by men. The men hold long wooden canes and pretend to fight each other as in the Egyptian Sa'idi cane dance (*al-'asayya*). The name of the dance refers to the *mizmar*, a double-reeded pipe that is also played in Sa'id and is important to this dance. The melodies are called *zawamil*, and they are accompanied by about six frame drums called *tiran* (*tar* is the singular).

Sahba

Sahba were performed by the fishermen of the Hijaz when they returned home after the voyaging season. These evidence both Egyptian and Yemeni styles. The *sahba* from the area of Medina is a different form, similar to the *muwashshah*, the famous strophic songs of Andalusia and Syria.

Yanbuwiyya

The *yanbuwiyya* is a special musical form coming from Yanbu on the Red Sea. It features the instrument called the *simsimiyya* (and sometimes known as the *tanbura*), a six-stringed lyre that is played on both coasts of the Red Sea (Campbell 1998, 58). The songs were sung by sailors as they carried out set tasks. Another form is known as *al-khobaytiyya*, which involves very complex movements by individual dancers, who also sing.

Zar

A *zar* is a ceremony of exorcism and also a song type performed for those occasions. People are believed to be possessed by spirits, and certain singers and instrumentalists, often including a soloist on the *tanbura*, or *simsimiyya* (lyre), specialize in this genre (Shiloah 2001, 830; also see Tayash 1988). Christian Poché (2002, 319) has suggested that the *zar* shows the connection between the lyre and the *jinn*, who may possess individuals (the lyre was also known in historical texts as the *ma'azif*, and its root, *'azf*, means the voice of the jinn). The *zar* tradition is found in areas along the Red Sea, including Saudi Arabia, Egypt, Sudan, and farther into eastern Africa, and also in the Arabian Gulf area. The *zar* may be danced in Saudi Arabia to *samiri* poetry. Dancers wear goat's hooves on their belts, and when they stamp their feet, these rattle (Adra 2002, 209).

DANCE

Dance is generically called *raqs*, or it might be titled according to the type of poetry that is being performed. Dancers may perform together in a line formation but sometimes also in a circle, a horseshoe, or a square shape. Dancers may also perform in a solo fashion or as a couple improvising as they move. Although some dances feature steps with hops and leg motion, as a general norm the dancing styles do not involve lifting of the legs, as Western ballet does. The dances of the sailors or pearl divers from the Gulf or the Red Sea may involve kneeling positions and movements that simulate tasks aboard a boat. Dances may be segregated by gender, particularly in Saudi Arabia, and in urban settings, recordings exist of mixed-gender performances. In addition, there were some settings where female professional dancers performed for men or women. A special movement in women's dance on the Arabian Peninsula is called *nuwwash*, or *na'ash*, and involves swinging of the hair and head. The oversized, brightly colored *thob* of the Eastern Province may also be swung and moved as part of the dance. Another general characteristic is artful playing with the movement, or variations of the movement but within a restrained repertoire of overall movements. Dance may be an important means of asserting tribal identity, as Najwa Adra has indicated for Yemen (Adra 1982; Adra in Zuhur, ed., 2001).

There are numerous dance traditions that are particular to celebrations or to particular regions. For instance, dancing may be performed by the mother of the bride or of the groom, who dances around incense, spices, and eggs with a tray on her head bearing lit candles. The candles are supposed to remain lit throughout the dance (Adra 2002, 709). At the Janadiriyyah Heritage Festival, I observed a dance from the Hijaz that is similar to the one performed at the *sabu'a*, the seventh-day celebration following the birth of a child. In Asir, women perform a special line dance called *al-khatwah* in which they link their arms and dip to the music while moving in tiny steps (Campbell 1999); also, in women's warlike dance of Mahayil women stamp, wearing anklet bracelets, and hold small daggers. The clothing worn in this dance resembled the white cotton highland styles of Ethiopia (Campbell 1999).

A dance called the *farisa* in the coastal towns of the Gulf region is somewhat like the dance known as the *khil* (horse-imitating), or hobbyhorse dance of Egypt. A dancer wears a cardboard horse form and dances in the middle of a circle of women who play tambourines. Another dancer may lead the horse in its motions (Adra 2002, 209).

Belly dancing is not indigenous to the peninsula, but given its popularity throughout the Middle East, it may be performed informally in private gender-segregated settings or by professional dancers imported for such occasions.

RELIGIOUS MUSIC

Whereas sacred music has played a very strong role in the Western musical tradition, in the Muslim world, religious music and chanting are considered to be completely separate from music (*musiqa*) or secular music. This holds for religious songs that are clearly based on musical forms, not just for *tajwid*, or Qur'anic, recitation. Nevertheless, these forms are discussed here as religious music, because readers desiring further information can search under this rubric.

Adhan

The call to prayer (*adhan*) performed by the *mu'adhdhin* is delivered five times a day according to a schedule that may be printed in the newspapers, published online, or given on television. Muslims then perform *salat*, the prayer cycle. At Medina, where Muslim practices were developed, the decision to deliver the call to prayer with the human voice differentiated Muslim prayers from Jewish, Christian, or polytheistic traditions. The first *mu'adhdhin*, Bilal, was chosen for his fine voice. The position of the *mu'adhdhin* was respected, large mosques employed multiple callers, and the callers had their own guild under the Ottoman Empire (Neubauer and Doubleday 2001, 601). The *adhan* is chanted from the minaret and then inside the mosque just before prayer. It is as follows: "*Allahu Akbar* (Allah is the Greatest) [repeated 4 times or 2 times] *Ashhadu anna la ilaha ilallah*. (I testify there is no god but Allah) [2 times] *Ashhadu anna Muhammada rasulullah* (I testify that Muhammad is the Prophet of Allah) [2 times] *Hayya 'ala salat* (Hasten to the prayer) [2 times] *Hayya 'ala falah* (Hasten to success) [2 times] *As-salatu khayru min an-nawm* (Prayer is better than sleep) [2 times but only at dawn prayer] *Allahu akbar* (Allah is the Greatest) [2 times] *La illaha illallah* (There is no god but Allah) [1 time]."

The text of the *adhan* is set; however, the first phrase *Allahu Akbar* is chanted four times, rather than two times, by those of the Maliki legal school (one of the four Sunni *madhahib*, or legal traditions; it exists in Saudi Arabia, although the Hanbali school predominates). The final phrase *La illaha ilallah* is chanted once by Sunni Muslims and twice by Shi'a Muslims. Muslims repeat the *adhan* to themselves as it is intoned.

The tonal rendition of the *adhan* differs depending on the *mu'adhdhin*. Some render the call close to *maqam Rast* or *maqam Hijaz*, and certain words are sung with melismas. A different, very plain style may be performed on only two notes, and some call this *adhan shar'i*.

Tajwid and Qira'a

Qira'a is the recitation of the Qur'an by a *qar'i*. *Tajwid* is the art or science of reciting the Qur'an and is not considered music as such. It is consistently differentiated from secular music (Faruqi 1985), although under the high caliphal tradition, elaborate performances of *tajwid* were apparently staged (Neubauer and Doubleday 2001, 601). *Tajwid* is also used interchangeably with one of the two forms of recitation, *mujawwad*. However, the recitation follows along the *maqamat* (modal) system, and a great reciter requires all the vocal techniques of a great singer and is well aware of the *maqamat* and the vocal agility required. The reciter is in some ways like the cantor in the Jewish tradition. Like a singer, the reciter must know where to breathe in the text, what weight to give different consonants, what length (of time) is to be given to syllables, and where ornamentation may be performed. Classes are offered in *tajwid*, and contests take place in various parts of the Islamic world. Some consider the following to be great reciters: Ayman Swayd of Jeddah; Hamad al-Bukhari of Medina; Muhammad Sa'id al-Iskandariyya of Alexandria, Egypt; 'Adil Abu Shi'r of Damascus, Syria; 'Adil Al-Sunayd of Riyadh; and Shaykha Rebab Shaqaqi of Jeddah. A popular recorded version of the entire Qur'an is by Mishary Rashid Alafasy of Saudi Arabia, who achieves an effortless, stunning reading.

Inshad and Mada'ih

Inshad (or *anasheed*, the plural of *nashid*) are religious songs and verse, and *mada'ih* are verses of praise, typically praising God or the Prophet Muhammad. *Inshad* may also glorify other venerated Muslim men and women in the Sufi tradition, who reportedly composed and inspired *inshad*. This tradition was notably attacked by the followers of Muhammad ibn 'Abd al-Wahhab in Saudi Arabia. Ironically, perhaps, as the *hajj* gathers Muslims from throughout the world, the *inshad* tradition has been perpetuated in the peninsula. The lead vocalist of the *inshad* is called the *munshid*.

Inshad of the Mawalid

The *inshad* celebrating the *mawalid* (festivals of the holy men and women of Islam) are extremely varied. In one example from Jeddah, the *munshid* leads the audience/chorus in simple, mostly unison versions, on the *mawlid* (alternatively *mulid*; meaning the birthday) of the Prophet Muhammad and heavily ornaments the sections he intones alone (Mawlid Jidda, ca. 2006). A continuing Sufi presence in Saudi Arabia, despite the Wahhabi reform movement, has been documented—the performance of this very *mawlid* led in 1941 to the expulsion of the *shaykh* of the Dandarawi Sufi (Sedgwick 1997, 349).

SONGS OF PILGRIMAGE

The traditions of songs of the pilgrimage are ancient, comprising those played at pilgrims' departure, while on the *hajj*, and upon pilgrims' return. Since the Islamic awakening of the 1970s, many performers of popular music have added religious songs to their repertoire and made programs and films about the *hajj*; some have turned exclusively to religious music. However, the songs of pilgrimage, referred to as *tahlil*, reflect their own national genres. Saudi Arabia has its own songs of pilgrimage, too, as many in the kingdom participate in the annual *hajj*. Historically, military bands, which included a *tabl al-hajj* (drum), might play for departing pilgrims or accompany pilgrims on the *hajj* (Neubauer and Doubleday 2001, 602).

Certain rites involve religious chanting, as in the *takbir*, which is recited at a special morning prayer during the 'Id al-Adha, the feast of the sacrifice on the 10th of the month, Dhu al-Hija, during the *hajj*, which may be simply:

TABLE 6.4

Allāhu akbar, Allāhu akbar, Allāhu akbar	الله أكبر الله أكبر الله أكبر
lā ilāha illā Allāh	لا إله إلا الله
Allāhu akbar, Allāhu akbar	الله أكبر الله أكبر
wa li-illāh il-ḥamd	ولله الحمد

Allah is the Greatest, Allah is the Greatest, Allah is the Greatest. There is no God but Allah. Allah is the Greatest. Allah is the Greatest. And all praises are due to Him.

REFERENCES

'Abd al-Hakim. Tariq. *Ashhar al-fulklurat al-sha'abiya* [The most famous forms of folkore]. Riyadh, Saudi Arabia: al-Jam'iyya al-'Arabiyya al-Sa'udiyyah lil-Thaqafa wa-l-Funun, 1980.

'Abd al-Hakim, Tariq. *Masahhir al-musiqiyin al-'arab* [Famous Arab musicians]. n.d. [ca. 1966].

'Abduh Ghanim, Nizar. "Al-Judhur al-Yamaniyya li-fann al-sawt al-khalij" [The Yemeni roots of the Sawt in the Gulf]. *al-Ma'thurat al-Sha'biyya* 4 (1986), 9–28.

Adra, Najwa. "Dance in the Arabian Peninsula." In *Garland Encyclopedia of World Music*, edited by Virginia Danielson, Scott Marcus, and Dwight Reynolds. New York: Routledge, 2002, vol. 6, 703–712.

Adra, Najwa. "Dance: A Visual Marker of Qabili Identity in Highland Yemen." In *Colors of Enchantment: Theater, Music, Dance, and Visual Arts of the Middle East*, edited by Sherifa Zuhur. Cairo and New York: American University in Cairo Press, 2001, 175–210.

Adra, Najwa. "Qabyala: The Tribal Concept in the Central Highlands of the Yemen Arab Republic." PhD diss., Temple University, 1982.

Akeel, Maha. "Old Songs in Old Nights." *Arab News*, December 25, 2004. http://www.arab-news.com/?page=21&section=0&article=56530&d=25&m=12&y=2004

Awhan, Faruq. "Raqsat al-'ayyala fi-l-'Imara al-'Arabiyya al-Mutahidda" [The 'Ayyala dance of the United Arab Emirates]. *al-Ma'thurat al-Sha'biyyah* 9 (1988).

Ba Ghaffar, Hind. *Al-aghani al-sha'biyya fi-l-Mamlakah al-'Arabiyyah al-Sa'udiyyah* [Folk songs in the Saudi Arabian Kingdom]. Jeddah, Saudi Arabia: Dar al-Qadsiyya li-l-tawzi' wa-l-nashr, 1994.

Campbell, Kay Hardy. "Saudi Folk Music: Alive and Well." *Saudi Aramco World Magazine*, March/April 2007.

Campbell, Kay Hardy. "Music in Performance: A Saudi Women's Wedding Party." In *Garland Encyclopedia of World Music*, edited by Virginia Danielson, Scott Marcus, and Dwight Reynolds. Vol. 6, *The Middle East.* New York: Garland Press, 2002, 696–698.

Campbell, Kay Hardy. "Days of Song and Dance." *Aramco World* 50, no. 1 (1999), 78–87.

Campbell, Kay Hardy. "Folk Music and Dance in the Arabian Gulf and Saudi Arabia." In *Images of Enchantment*, edited by Sherifa Zuhur. Cairo: American University in Cairo Press, 1998, 57–70.

Campbell, Kay Hardy. "Recent Recordings of Traditional Music from the Arabian Gulf and Saudi Arabia." *Middle East Studies Association Bulletin* 30, no. 1 (July 1996), 37–40.

Farmer, Henry George. *A History of Arabian Music to the XIIth Century*. London: Luzac and Co., 1929.

Faruqi, Lamya (Lois) Ibsen. "Music, Musicians and Muslim Law." *Asian Music* 7, no. 1 (1985), 5–36.

Grund, F. "Danses d'ailleures: La mâle danse, ceremonies masculines en Arabie Saoudite." *Danser*, no. 269 (September 1998), 26–28.

Hansen, Eric. "The Hidden History of a Scented Wood." *Saudi Aramco World*, 51, no. 6 (November/December 2000), 2–13.

Hanzal, Falih. *Mu'jam al-qawafi wa-l-alhan fi-l-khalij al-'arabi* [Dictionary of rhymes and melodies in the Arabian Gulf]. Al-Sharja: Ittihad Kuttab wa-Udaba al-'Imarat al-'Arabiyyah al-Mutahhida 1987.

Jargy, Simon. "Sung Poetry in the Arabian Peninsula." In *Garland Encyclopedia of World Music*, edited by Virginia Danielson, Scott Marcus, and Dwight Reynolds. New York: Routledge, 2002, vol. 6, 663–669.

Jargy, Simon. "Sung Poetry in the Oral Tradition of the Gulf Region and the Arabian Peninsula." *Oral Tradition* 4, no. 1–2 (1989), 175–187.

Jargy, Simon. "Comments on the Concept and Characteristics of the Folk Music in the Gulf and Arabian Peninsula." *Ma'thurat al-Sha'biyyah*, January 1, 1986.

Lambert, Jean. "The Arabian Peninsula: An Overview." In *Garland Encyclopedia of World Music*, edited by Virginia Danielson, Scott Marcus, and Dwight Reynolds. New York: Routledge, 2002, vol. 6, 649–661.

Nelson, Kristina. "The Qur'an Recited." In *Garland Encyclopedia of World Music*, edited by Virginia Danielson, Scott Marcus, and Dwight Reynolds. New York: Routledge, 2002, vol. 6, 157–163.

Nelson, Kristina. *The Art of Reciting the Qur'an*. Austin: University of Texas Press, 1985.

Neubauer, Eckard. "Arabic Writings on Music: Eighth to Nineteenth Centuries." In *Garland Encyclopedia of World Music*, edited by Virginia Danielson, Scott Marcus, and Dwight Reynolds. New York: Routledge, 2002, vol. 6, 363–386.

Neubauer, Eckhard, and Veronica Doubleday. "Islamic Religious Music." In *The New Grove Dictionary of Music and Musicians*, edited by Stanley Sadie. New York and London: Macmillan, 2001, 599–610.

Poché, Christian. "Music in Ancient Arabia from Archaeological and Written Sources." In *Garland Encyclopedia of World Music*, edited by Virginia Danielson, Scott Marcus, and Dwight Reynolds. New York: Routledge, 2002, vol. 6, 357–362.

Racy, Ali Jihad. "The Life History of the Lyre (in the Path of the Lyre). The Tanburah of the Gulf Region." *Musike: International Journal of Ethnomusicological Studies* 2, no. 2 (2006).

Racy, Ali Jihad. "Music of the Arabian Desert in the Accounts of Early Western Travelers." Translated by the author as "Musiqa al-Badiyah fi Sijillat al-Rahhalah al- Gharbiyyin." In *al-Ma'thurat al-Sha'biyyah*. Doha, Qatar: The GCC Arab Gulf States Folklore Center, 1998.

Racy, Ali Jihad. "Music." In *The Genius of Arab Civilization: Source of Renaissance*, edited by John R. Hayes. New York: New York University Press, 1992.

Røvsing Olsen, Poul. "La musique africaine dans le Golfe persique." *JIFMC* 19 (1967), 28–36.

Røvsing Olsen, Poul, and Ulrich Wegner. "Arabian Gulf." In *The New Grove Dictionary of Music and Musicians*, edited by Stanley Sadie. New York and London: Macmillan, 2001, vol. 1, 795–797.

al-Sa'id, Labib. *al-Maqari wa-l-qurra'*. Cairo: Matba'at al-Sa'adah, 1976.

al-Samiri, 'Abd al-Jabbar. "Masadar wa maraji fi fulklur al-khalij al-'arabi wa al-jazira: al-raqs al-sha'bi" [Sources and References in the Folklore of the Arabian Gulf and the Peninsula: Folk dance]. *al-Turath al-sha'bi* 9, no. 7, 268–270.

al-Sa'ud, Norah bint Muhammad, al-Jawhara Muhammad al-'Anqari, and Madeha Muhammad al-'Atroush, eds. *Abha, Bilad Asir: Southwestern Region of the Kingdom of Saudi Arabia*. Riyadh, Saudi Arabia: By the editors, 1989.

Sedgwick, Mark. "Saudi Sufis: Compromise in the Hijaz 1925–1940." *Die Welt des Islams* 37, no. 3 (1997), 349–368.

Sells, Michael. "Sound, Spirit and Gender in Surat al-Qadr." *Journal of the American Orientalist Society* 11, no. 2 (1991), 239–259.

Shiloah, Amnon, II. "Folk Music" (section of the article on "Arab Music"). In *The New Grove Dictionary of Music and Musicians*, edited by Stanley Sadie. New York and London: Macmillan, 2001, vol. 1, 824–883.

Snouck Hurgronje, Christaan. *Mekka in the Latter Part of the Nineteenth Century, 1885–1889*. Translated by James Henry Monahan. Leiden, the Netherlands: Brill, 1931.

Tayash, Fahad. "Sameri Tradition and Zar Dance in Saudi Arabia." *al-Ma'thurat al-Sha'biyya* 9 (1988), 23–36.

Urkevich, Lisa A. "Saudi Arabia, Kingdom of." In *The New Grove Dictionary of Music and Musicians*, edited by Stanley Sadie. New York and London: Macmillan, 2001, vol. 22, 324–328.

Zuhur, Sherifa. Personal interviews and field notes, Egypt and Sinai Peninsula 1998–1999, and Riyadh, Jeddah, Dir'iyyah, Khobar, London and Washington DC, 2005–2008.

Selected Recordings

A Musical Anthology of the Arabian Peninsula. Recorded by Simon Jargy and Poul Røvsing Olsen (also cited as: and 'Ali Zakariyya al-'Ansari). 4 vols. 1, Sung Poetry of the Bedouins. 2, Music of the Pearl Divers. 3, *Sawt*: Music from the City. 4, Women's Songs. Geneva: Archives Internationales de Musique Populaire de la Musée d'Éthnographie, 1994 (Field recordings made in the Gulf and the Arabian Peninsula from the early 1970s). Dist. Gary Thal Music Inc.,: 1994, VDE-Gallo CD 758–59–60–61.

Arabie saoudite: Musique de 'Unayzah, Ancienne Cité du Najd. Pierre Bois, dir. Paris: Maison des Cultures du Monde. Inédit. CD W 260087. 1999.

Ettab-Talal Madah. Performed by 'Itab and Talal Madah, Funun al-Jazeera, FJCD 1109.

"Mawlid Jiddah Sharif." Video example of *mada'ih* of the *mawlid al-nabi*. n.d. [ca. 2006]. http://www.youtube.com/watch?v=5n_dikNnsS8

Musique des bédouins. Bhattacharya, Deben, dir. Paris: Bam. Folkore et Musiques de l'univers. LD 5783, LP, disk. n.d. [ca. 1970s].

al-Qur'an al-Karim. Mishary bin Rashid Alafasy (*qari'*). 26 CDs in set. UFI Inc. 2003/1424h..

Rayigh. Performed by A. Abd al-Majid. Rotana. 397 TC ROT, 1997.

Rhythms from an Oasis [instrumental music]. Comp. Dhafer Kohaji and 'Aref al-'Amer. Saudi Aramco, 2003 CD.

Samra: Songs from Saudi Arabia. Produced by Kay Hardy Campbell. Audiocassette, 1985.

Samra II: More Songs from Saudi Arabia. Produced by Kay Hardy Campbell. Audiocassette, 1986.

Sha'biyyat. Vol. 15–16. Performed by Muhammad 'Abdu, Sawt al-Jazira MACD 528 and MADC 529.

Sha'biyyat/Muhammad 'Abduh: Folk Songs. Performed by M. 'Abduh. Sawt El Jezira (same as Sawt al-Jazira). MACD 516 and MACD 517, 1991.

Tanburah; Music of the Gulf. Coll. A. J. Racy (accompanies volume). Arab Gulf States Folklore Center, 1988.

Al-Tawhîd. Comp. by Siraj Omar, lyrics by Prince Khalid al-Faisal. A modern musical epic with vocals by Talâl Maddâh, Muhammad 'Abduh, 'Abd-al Majîd 'Abd Allah, 'Abd Allah Rashâd, and Râshid al-Mâjid. W 260001, Maison des Cultures du Monde, 1994.

The Very Best of Ettab. Performed by 'Itab. Relax-In REL CD 313, 1989.

Food

Food customs and the culinary tradition in Saudi Arabia tend, as in the rest of the Arab world, to feature traditional foods, whether these are specifically local dishes or part of the regional repertoire. These traditional dishes should be prepared with the freshest ingredients possible, although frozen, canned, and pre-prepared foods are now available and used. When preparing traditional dishes, individual cooks may vary them by adding an extra teaspoon or pinch of this or that. Food consumption has changed due to technology, modernization, and shifts in lifestyles, so what is traditional now differs from the past. No great appreciation for radical experimentation exists as in American food, outside of large hotels and business settings, or in demonstration cooking. However, as in *nouvelle cuisine*, lighter versions of traditional dishes are now sometimes available, and measurements are now given in cooking instruction, shows, and books. Cooking shows on satellite or cable television have become popular, and these sometimes glamorize food, instructing on both preparation and presentation.

It is sometimes difficult to distinguish which foods were originally Saudi Arabian and which came from the Levant or Iraq, Syria, or Egypt, because certain foods are linked in a common tradition going back to the Abbasid era, while others have moved into the Arabian Peninsula due to the movement of labor, pilgrims, and scholars. Saudi Arabians consider the breakfast foods of *ful mudammes* (fava beans) and *shakshooka* (eggs cooked with minced meat) to be their national dishes, even though these are regarded as national dishes in other countries (the first dish in Egypt and the second in Tunisia). *Karkadeh*, a tea of hibiscus hips that can be consumed hot or cold, is found in Mecca and Medina and throughout Egypt. Saudi Arabians prepare *sanbusak*, a sort of half moon–shaped ravioli stuffed with a leek filling, which can be served with a yogurt sauce; the same dish, of Ottoman origin, is offered in Syria. One can find *kabsa*, a Saudi Arabian specialty, prepared in takeout kitchens in Damascus, Syria, thanks to the large number of Saudi Arabian tourists.

Culinary historians have studied manuscripts of Abbasid-era cooking. The recipes show a great similarity to modern dishes in the Arab world (Arberry 1939; Roden 1974, 7–17). The cuisine of the Ottoman Empire traveled throughout its holdings, which did not include Saudi Arabia except for a relatively short period that ended the first Sa'udi state (see Chapter 2, History). Yet these foods entered Saudi Arabia as other Arabs settled there following the pilgrimage or as they have worked in the kingdom since the 1930s. The cuisine of the Arabian/Persian Gulf is also a mixture of influences. Throughout the kingdom, South Asian food is also available. Similarities in the traditional Arab regional foods are based on (a) the use of small appetizers and salads called *mezzah* that preface main dishes; (b) the use of many fresh vegetables, garlic, and spices; (c) the balancing of vegetables and protein foods like chicken, lamb, or goat with either rice or cooked wheat, as in other highland areas of the Arab world, and/or bread; (d) sweets based on the Ottoman culinary tradition or servings of fresh fruit; (e) serving of vegetables stuffed with a rice or rice-and-meat filling: peppers, grape leaves, tomatoes, or cabbage; (f) grilling, frying, and baking of meats; (g) use of olive oil or *samnah*, a clarified butter; (h) a special tradition of preparing and serving coffee (and tea) to demonstrate hospitality; (i) the use of syrup-based cold drinks and herbal teas for medicinal purposes; and (j) the observance of Muslim dietary rules.

The word *halal*, "allowed or lawful," comes from the Qur'an and is a category of substances including food that contrast with those that are *haram*, unlawful and forbidden. The Qur'an designates plants and animals that are lawful for Muslims to eat (Qur'an, 80:25–32, 2:168; 2:172, and 16:14), which include goats, sheep, cattle, and camels and also fish and other wild animals so long as they meet the criteria in the law (5:94–96). However, swine, animals that are already dead, and those prepared for sacrifice to deities other than Allah are forbidden (Qur'an 5:3, 6:45; Campo 1995, 375). Muslims must not eat pork or bacon. Other animals are ritually slaughtered and referred to as *halal* meat and are certified as such in Saudi Arabia. The slaughtering consists of saying *"bismallah"* and cutting the animal's throat, although camels were supposed to be killed by a knife or sword to the upper chest. Then the carcasses are hung to drain the blood. The method thus resembles the ritual slaughter practiced by the Jews under their *kashrut*, or kosher, dietary laws.

The ancient Arabs drank wine made from dates (*khamr*), which was forsworn by the Emigrants (those who left Mecca for Medina with the Prophet in the *hijrah*) and the Ansar (those already resident in Medina) and was condemned in the Qur'an (5:90–91). The Hanbali legal school considers *khamr* to pertain to wine made of grapes as well as dates and other intoxicating beverages, and it was outlawed along with all intoxicants in 1929 for Muslims in Saudi Arabia.

Both bedouin and sedentary lifestyles produced different types of foods and influenced trade. The bedouin had grazing animals and therefore access to milk, cheese, and yogurt and, on special occasions, meat. Other traditional foods of the bedouin included dates, lentils, pumpkins, leeks, zucchini (courgettes), eggplant, and occasionally goat, lamb, or camel. Frequently, they grew their own vegetables if they were settled or settled for part of the year, or they traded with sedentary or partially sedentary groups to obtain their other food needs. The Najd and Hasa regions produce wheat, which is very much a part of the cuisine in that area. Government-sponsored programs to subsidize farmers, particularly those growing wheat, were opposed on economic grounds by some Western observers, who thought the massive amounts of water needed were too costly. On the other hand, those countries that have instituted grain imports have become highly dependent on a different type of government subsidization intended to keep down the costs of the finished product.

The rules of hospitality also impact food and its preparation, serving, and reception. The host is expected to prepare more food than is necessary and to use excellent ingredients as a sign of generosity; to serve a guest first and to treat a guest from far away prior to one who is a regular visitor; and to be cheerful and not argue. He or she will expect reciprocity from a close friend or relative, although not necessarily from a stranger (also see the section on etiquette). The phrase *Bismallah* ("in the name of Allah") is pronounced before eating, and eating with one's fingers is considered polite and has its own set of rules as detailed as European table manners.

Coffee first gained popularity in Arabia and Yemen (Roden 1974, 445). It was discovered in Ethiopia, perhaps by Yemenis, or perhaps its fruits (coffee cherries) were known to slaves who came from Sudan to Yemen and Arabia through the port of Mocha (al-Mukha). Some sources claim it may have been cultivated as early as the 13th century. It was certainly being consumed (as was tobacco) in the early 16th century (Bouzigard 2010) and cultivated, mainly in the Ottoman Empire, and made its way to Safavid Iran (Matthee 2005, 144–145) and Europe.

Preparing and offering coffee for guests has been a requirement of Arab hospitality ever since. Coffee preparation was usually the host's task, and it is said of a generous man that "he makes coffee from noon until night" (Mahy 1975). The coffeepots of the bedouin (*dellal*) were carried in a *fatya* (coffee-gear basket) so that they were always at hand, despite the constant packing and unpacking of the nomads described by the traveler Charles Doughty in the 1870s. His host, Zeyd, sometimes pretended to be busy with another matter when men approached his open tent: "He tells them, wellah, his affairs do call him forth, adieu, he must away to the mejlis, go they and seek coffee elsewhere. But were there any sheykh with them, a coffee lord, Zeyd could not honestly choose but abide and serve them with coffee; . . . except he gently protest, 'billah, he would not drink'" (Doughty 1968, 57–58).

What is known as Turkish coffee in much of the Middle East is prepared according to the guest's or customer's taste for additional sugar, and in Lebanon, rose water is usually added. Arabian coffee is served without sugar and with cardamom. In the past, a host would roast the beans and pound them in a *mahbaj* (coffee grinder) and add this *bunn* (finely powdered coffee) to the pot and then cook it in front of the guests. Cardamom pods could be added, and then it was served, as today, in very small cups without a handle. In the past, people ground their own spices as well as coffee. Today, coffee can be bought ground, and cardamom is obtained from spice vendors or available in powdered form in containers in supermarkets. The addition of cardamom and straining of the coffee grounds make the coffee "whiter." Coffee is presented at all formal occasions and meetings and at less formal ones in homes. Middle-class and wealthy Saudi Arabians may frequent coffee restaurants in the modern city malls, which serve lattes, cappuccinos, Nescafé, and more rarely German- or American-style brewed coffee, as well as Arabic coffee. These are important spaces for social exchange as well.

QAHWAH 'ARABIYYAH (ARABIC COFFEE)

3 c water

3 tbsp powdered cardamom

2 tbsp Arabic coffee

¼ tsp saffron (optional)

    Boil the water in a pot. Add the coffee to the water, and bring to a boil over low heat. Remove from the heat for five minutes to allow the coffee to settle. Put the cardamom in the pot (some strain the coffee at this point), and add the saffron. Bring back to boil once and serve. Serves 8 to 10 persons in tiny cups (or 6 in larger glasses).

Whereas the Bedouin had plentiful milk, they could hunger for other food, as they could not afford to kill their animals except for special occasions such as a circumcision, a wedding, or the religious feast days. Today, the change in consumption patterns has affected certain health conditions; obesity and heart disease are on the rise, as in the West. Another important change is the availability of all types of food in different parts of the country and the presence of excellent restaurants; it is no longer true that Saudi Arabian food is available only in homes. Some restaurants specialize solely in Saudi Arabian food, but many also offer grilled and Lebanese or continental dishes, and a sizable business in catering or takeout has developed as well.

A specialty of Najd and the Hasa oasis is the use of wheat in the cuisine (in addition to bread) as in the recipe for *mufallaq* later on. This is Saudi Arabia's answer to the *fariqa* of Syria or Egypt and to North Africa's couscous. Wheat agriculture also makes possible many varieties of bread: the flat loaves of *khubz 'arabi* (Arabic bread), *tamis* (a bigger loaf with more crust, in the east), and *shurayk* (a soft and golden loaf). *Khubz ruqaq*, which is a mixture of flour, water, salt, and date syrup baked on a griddle, is made in Najd throughout the year and in other areas during Ramadan. When little pieces of this bread are filled with egg, they are a child's treat called *hinnuwah* (Mahy 1975).

To the east, rice is the preferred grain, and it is served with fish or shrimp around the Persian Gulf, sometimes flavored with tamarind. The rice might be seasoned with tomato or *muhammara*, and the fish is seasoned with a spice mix called *baharat*.

In the past, a heavier meal at lunchtime was preferred, but a full dinner may also be eaten, quite a bit later in the evening than is common in the West. During Ramadan, people consume a meal sometime before dawn and then fast all day, breaking their fast with an *iftar*. The food of the *iftar* should not be too heavy on the stomach; first, dates and water may be eaten and then a nourishing soup and other dishes. Desserts make up for the daytime decrease in caloric intake during Ramadan.

In Najd, the traditional preference for dessert is fresh fruit such as grapes, pomegranate, or melon. A candy was made of the *utrunj* (sometimes called uglyfruit, it is a type of citrus). The rind of the *utrunj* was marinated in its own juice, water, and

QOUZY *OR* KHARUF MAHSHI (*WHOLE STUFFED KID OR LAMB*)

A feast dish of whole roasted kid (*qouzy*) or milk-fed lamb (*kharuf*) was served on behalf of honored guests or for the feast days. The kid or lamb is stuffed, then roasted outdoors over charcoal, or it can be cooked in an oven.

1 baby lamb (headless and prepared for stuffing), 15 to 18 lb

2 tbsp ground coriander

1 tsp ground ginger

1 tbsp turmeric

2 tbsp lemon juice (optional)

10 garlic cloves

1 tbsp black lime powder

Salt and pepper

Stuffing

6 c long-grained rice (or 5 c rice and 1 c chickpeas)

1 tbsp turmeric

10 cardamom pods, crushed

2 c onion, finely chopped

2 tbsp oil

1 c rose water

2 tbsp lemon juice

1 c chopped walnuts

½ c chopped pistachio nuts

½ c almonds (pine nuts can be substituted for the walnuts)

Mix of ½ c tamarind juice, ½ c rose water, ½ c water, and 2 tbsp *baharat* (mixed spices)

10 cloves garlic, chopped

Hard-boiled eggs (optional), one for each guest

Butter or *samnah* for basting

Salt and pepper

Wash the lamb inside and out, and pat dry. Mix the spices with garlic, lime powder, and salt and pepper, and rub onto the lamb all over outside and inside. (You may also mix the spices with 2 tbsp. lemon juice and then rub the lamb with that mixture, although some prefer to season solely with dry ingredients.) Prepare the stuffing by boiling the rice (and chickpeas) in water with turmeric, cardamom pods, and salt until partially cooked, about 10 minutes. Discard the cardamom pods and the liquid. Fry the onions in oil, and add rose water, lemon juice, nuts, and the tamarind mixture, and cook for about 10 minutes. Add shelled hard-boiled eggs if you wish (if not, you can garnish the serving plate with sliced hard-boiled eggs) and the additional 10 cloves of chopped garlic, stuff the lamb, and sew the cavity closed. Roast for 4 to 6 hours on an open fire (depends on the size of the lamb), basting it with its own juice and butter or *samnah* if desired. If roasting in the oven, preheat to 450°F, then reduce to 350°F. Cover the lamb with foil, and uncover during the last half hour of cooking, basting regularly with butter or *samnah*. This should take about 2 to 2½ hours or longer for a larger lamb. Remove the thread, and empty the stuffing. Serve on a large platter surrounded with the stuffing. May be garnished with parsley and sliced hard-boiled eggs (if you did not add these to the stuffing), or smaller dishes of tomatoes, cooked pumpkin, sliced melon, and apricots can be served along with the main dish (Roden 1974, 210–211; Abdennour 2005, 108–109; Mahy 1975).

BAHARAT

⅓ c black pepper

¼ c ground coriander

Scant ¼ c cinnamon

¼ c ground cloves

¼ c ground cumin

2 tsp ground cardamom

¼ c ground nutmeg

½ c ground paprika

⅓ c curry powder

Scant ¼ c ground dried (black) limes (this is a popular spice of the Gulf and can be bought in larger-size jars)

Mix together and store in a glass jar. Some also add allspice or ginger.

Another spice mix is *Hawaij*:

HAWAIJ

2 tbsp black peppercorns

1 tbsp caraway seed

½ tsp cardamom seeds

1 tsp saffron threads

1 tsp turmeric

Heat peppercorns, caraway seeds, and cardamom seeds in a pan for a few minutes. Pound in a mortar or grind. Add saffron and grind. Pour into a bowl, stir in turmeric, and keep in an airtight container.

Other favorite dishes include the following:

KABSA (*PREPARED WITH CHICKEN*)

1 lb U.S. or basmati rice

2 medium onions, sliced

1 c corn oil (canola oil may be used)

1 frying chicken, cut in pieces

1 can tomato purée (approximately equal to a 6 oz. can)

2 medium tomatoes, chopped

5 cloves garlic, mashed to a pulp in a mortar

3 c hot water

6 cloves (*arumfal*)

6 cardamom pods

4 sticks of cinnamon

Salt and pepper

2 medium carrots, grated

Grated rind of one orange

4 tbsp raisins

4 tbsp almonds, soaked and split

Wash the rice, and cover with water for at least 15 minutes before cooking. Sauté the onion in oil until it is browned. Add the pieces of chicken, tomato puree, chopped tomatoes, and garlic. Stir for about five minutes over low heat. Add hot water, the spices, salt and pepper, grated carrots, and orange rind. Cook 20 to 26 minutes or until the chicken is done. Remove the chicken, and put in the oven to keep warm. Add the rice to the sauce, and cook for 15 minutes. Arrange the chicken atop the rice on a platter or large plate, and decorate with raisins and almonds.

MUFALLAQ

3 c *jarish* (crushed wheat, a favorite of Najd and the Hasa oasis and a substitute for rice)

4½ c water

1 lb lamb cut into large chunks (lamb neck is acceptable too)

1 small can tomato paste

2 onions, chopped

Small amount (2 tbsp) of olive or canola oil. If on a low-fat diet, you can spray the pan with olive-oil spray. For a traditional taste use *samnah.*

Salt and pepper to taste

Wash the wheat, then soak in water for two hours. Brown the meat in oil, add tomato paste, salt and pepper to taste, and 1 cup water. Cook over medium heat until the meat is tender, then spoon the meat out onto a plate and cover. Drain the water off the wheat, then fry the wheat over low heat in oil (or *samnah*, which many now avoid to keep down cholesterol levels) until it browns. Add the meat mixture and 3½ c water to the wheat. Cover and cook until the wheat is dry and fluffy. Fry the onion and place at the center of the wheat. Continue to steam the mixture for another 15 minutes on very low heat. Stir the onion into the wheat, and serve on a platter, topping with the meat pieces.

JARISH BI-LABAN (*CRACKED WHEAT WITH YOGURT*)

With the exception of the yogurt, this dish is almost the same as *harisah*, a dish of the eastern coast of Saudi Arabia, which was similarly pounded and then cooked all day.

4 c yogurt

½ lb margarine

2 tbsp ground cumin

4 red chili peppers

4 c cracked wheat

3 tbsp butter, melted

Salt to taste

Mix yogurt and salt in a pan. Stir over low heat. Combine the margarine, cumin, and chili peppers in a mortar, and grind with the pestle. When the yogurt is almost boiling, add the cumin mixture and mix well. Wash and drain the cracked wheat, and add to the yogurt. Cover and simmer over low heat for three hours. Take off heat and beat with a wooden spoon. Then blend in a food processor (prior to the advent of the food processor, this would have been beaten for at least half an hour). Pour wheat and yogurt mixture into a deep serving dish. Make a depression in the center, pour in the melted butter, and serve.

'AISH BIL-LAHM OR 'AISH ABU LAHM

In the Hijaz this dish is made with *shamar*, *habbah sawda* (black caraway seeds), fennel, and ground lamb.

Dough

1 tbsp yeast

4 c flour

3 eggs

3 tbsp vegetable oil

Salt

½ tsp powdered bread spices (black pepper and cumin); or use 1 tsp *habbah sawda* (black caraway seeds) and 1 tsp fennel seeds

Stuffing

¾ lb ground beef (or ground lamb)

2 onions, finely chopped

2 tsp salt

½ bunch leeks (*kurrash*)

3 tbsp corn oil

6 tbsp *tahina* (sesame paste with oil)

½ tbsp vinegar

4 cloves garlic, pressed or mashed

2 black peppercorns

1 tbsp poppy seeds (or black caraway seeds)

Dissolve yeast in half a cup of warm water, and set aside to soften. Put flour in a large bowl, make a well in center, and add eggs, oil, yeast, salt, and bread spices. Mix well, adding water a little at a time until you have a firm dough. Grease a large baking sheet with oil. Put dough on tray and cover with a damp cloth. Place dough in a warm place for at least two hours.

Put ground beef, onion, and salt in a saucepan with the corn oil. Place over medium heat, stirring until meat is cooked. Set aside to cool. Finely chop leeks, and wash several times in a strainer. Spread leeks on a paper towel to absorb excess water. Add leeks to ground meat. Mix *tahina* with a small amount of vinegar, a little water, garlic, and black pepper. Once this is smooth, add to leek and meat mixture and mix. Once the dough has risen, roll out. Cut into circular shapes, and spread the meat mixture over the dough, leaving the edge uncovered. A different way of making this dish is to roll the dough out and cover a deep pie dish (more typical of the Hijaz) and spread with the meat-leek mixture. Sprinkle with poppy seeds or with black caraway seeds and fennel seeds. Bake at 350°F for half an hour or until bread is baked.

BASAL MAHSHI (STUFFED ONIONS)

Stuffed green peppers, tomatoes, eggplant, grapevine leaves, cabbage, and zucchini are prepared in every other Arab country as well as Saudi Arabia because they apparently come from a shared Abbasid tradition. However, stuffed onions are a type of *mahshi* (stuffed dish) that is unusual elsewhere.

¾ c tamarind paste or frozen tamarind

1 lb large onions

3 tbsp butter or oil

1 tbsp vinegar

About 4 c hot water

Filling

½ c rice

½ lb lean lamb

½ c onion, grated

1 tomato, chopped

4 cloves garlic, pressed or crushed

Salt and black pepper

2 tbsp chopped parsley

½ t ground cinnamon

   Soak the tamarind paste, or defrost frozen tamarind. Peel onions and boil for 15 minutes or until cooked, then drain. Wash the rice, drain it, and mix well with the ground lamb, grated onion, tomato, garlic, salt and pepper, parsley, cinnamon, and 1 tbsp oil or butter. Separate the layers of the onions, and gently remove the central layers. Set these aside. Place the stuffing between the layers of the onions, roll up, and seal by placing them very closely together in a pan. Put the onion hearts on top of the stuffed onions. Strain the tamarind, and add 1 tbsp of vinegar, 2 remaining tbsp of oil, and just enough water to cover the onions with this liquid mixture. Cook over medium heat until done. Eat hot or warm.

Not all Saudi Arabians drink coffee. Tea, soft drinks, fruit juices, and *sharbat*, or fruit syrups mixed with water, are popular. Tea made of mint or other herbs is also enjoyed.

SHARAB AL-NA'NA' (HOT MINT DRINK)

½ c fresh mint, washed well, or 3 tbsp dried mint

Sugar to taste

1 pinch ground saffron

3 c boiling water

Wash the mint carefully and then put in a small teapot or a long-handled metal pot. Next, add sugar, saffron, and boiling water. Bring nearly to a boil, remove from heat, and then serve. Serves 3.

TUMR BI-L-SIMSIM

½ lb blanched almonds (you may also use presliced almonds)

¼ c corn oil (some prefer canola oil)

1 c sesame seeds

2 lb soft dates

1 tbsp ground cardamom

If you cannot obtain blanched or sliced almonds, dip almonds in boiling water, remove the skins, and split in two. Fry almonds in the oil until golden. Drain on paper towels. Brown the sesame seeds without oil until they are golden. Spread the browned sesame seeds onto a tray. Remove all seeds from the dates. Mix with cardamom to form a soft dough. Break off a piece the size of a date, and stuff with a piece of almond. Roll in the sesame seeds, and arrange on a plate. Serves 8 to 10.

---

sugar to make the candy (Mahy 1975). However, today, European-style cakes or Arabian pastries may be offered. During Ramadan, sweets were traditionally prepared throughout the country. *Muhallabiyya* (similar to the Egyptian version) is a rice and milk pudding that can be flavored with orange-blossom or rose water or with mango. *Sagudanah* is a sago pudding, or tapioca. Both may be decorated with almonds and pistachios. At Ramadan in the Hijaz, other poplar sweets are *qatayif* (a type of pancake stuffed with nuts or cheese, fried, and soaked with syrup), *basbusa* (a semolina sweet also drenched in syrup), *luqmat al-qadi* ("morsels of the judge": dough fried in oil and covered in syrup; Mahy 1975), or *kunafah* (a shredded pastry with a layer of cheese or clotted cream and nuts, as in all of the preceding items, that is cooked and then covered with syrup). *Kunafah* is shared with the Levant, and *qatayif* and *basbusa* are also claimed by Egypt. On the occasion of the 'Id al-Fitr, which concludes Ramadan, *ma'mul* (a rich cookie) stuffed with dates are eaten. Other desserts include *ghoraybeh*, a kind of shortbread, *baqlawa*, and custard. Dates are especially prized and come in delicious varieties not available elsewhere. Another delicacy is *tumr bi-l-simsim* (dates with sesame seeds).

A traditional date dish for breakfast in Najd in the wintertime, *hunayni*, was prepared from soft dates, semolina flour or bread, butter, and cardamom.

Food and cooking have become even more popular due to the professionalization of cooking through the hotel and restaurant industries and as a result of cooking shows and contests on television. In 2009, the four-day Salon Culinaire festival, also known as Food Expo and featuring cooking exhibitions and contests was inaugurated during the Food, Hotel and Propac Show. It met again in 2010 and was sponsored by the Saudi Arabian Chefs' Association, a member of the World Association of Chefs' Societies, and also by the al-Harithy Company for Exhibitions at the Jeddah Center for Forums and Events. The chefs competed in 21 categories, mainly continental but also Middle Eastern food and *tapas*. The Saudi Arabian Chefs' Association counted 150 members in 2010 and reported that its Saudi Arabian membership was growing (Ramkumar 2010). It was founded and is headed by Chef Yasser Jad, who began his career as a food-quality controller with Saudi Arabian Airlines and advanced to head the company's food production. The group also founded the Saudi Arabian national cooking team (*What's Up KSA*, what'supksa.net, posted September 2010). Televised cooking shows have been popular for quite some years in the kingdom and include programs on Arabic, Pakistani, Indian, and other channels.

REFERENCES

Abdennour, Samia. *Egyptian Cooking and Other Middle Eastern Recipes*. Cairo: American University in Cairo Press, 2005.

Adib, Naziha, Ferdous Al-Mukhtar, Ban Ismail, and Jala Makhzumi. *Arabian Cuisine: From the Gulf to the Mediterranean*. LAAM Ltd., 1993. (Originally published in Arabic in 1965.)

Alford, Jeffrey, and Naomi Duguid. *Flatbreads and Flavors: A Baker's Atlas*. New York: William Morrow, 1995.

AramcoExpats. "Arab Favorites." *Aramcon Recipes*. http://www.armacoexpts.com

Arberry, A.J. "A Baghdad Cookery-Book." *Islamic Culture*, no. 13 (1939).

Bouzigard, Aimee. "Archaeological Evidence for the Consumption of Tobacco and Coffee in Ottoman Arabia." Master's thesis, Department of Anthropology, East Carolina University, 2010.

Campo, Juan Eduardo. "Dietary Rules." In *Encyclopedia of the Modern Islamic World*, edited by John Esposito. New York: Oxford University Press, 1995, vol. 1, 375–377.

Doughty, Charlies M. *Travels in Arabia Deserta*. Abridged by Edward Garnett. Gloucester, MA: Peter Smith, 1968. (Originally published in 1888).

al-Hamad, Sarah. *Cardamom and Lime: Recipes from the Arabian Gulf*. London: New Holland, 2008.

Long, David. *Culture and Customs of Saudi Arabia*. Westport, CT: Greenwood, 2005.

Mahy, Lyn. "Saudi Aramco World Flavored with Tradition: Food from Saudi Arabia." *Aramco World*, November/December 1975, 32–40.

Matthee, Rudolph P. *The Pursuit of Pleasure: Drugs and Stimulants in Iranian History 1500–1900*. Princeton, NJ: Princeton University Press, 2005.

Nawwab, Nimah Ismail. "Ramadan Recipes: Family Favorites." *Saudi Aramco Week*, October 28, 2004. Archived at http://www.aramcoexpats.com

Ramkumar, K.S. "Top Chef, Art de Table Contests Major Draw at Food Expo." *ArabNews.com*, September 18, 2010.

Riolo, Amy. *Arabian Delights: Recipes and Princely Entertaining Ideas from the Arabian Peninsula*. Herndon, VA: Capitol Books, 2008.

Roden, Claudia. *A Book of Middle Eastern Food*. New York: Vintage Books, 1974.

Tastes of Jubail. http://www.aaljumah.com. (and other websites)

Weiss-Armush, Anne Marie. *The Arabian Delights Cookbook: Mediterranean Cuisines from Mecca to Marrakesh*. Los Angeles and Chicago: Lowell House, 1994.

Weiss-Armush, Anne Marie. *Arabian Cuisine*. Beirut, Lebanon: Dar al-Nafaes, 1993.

Yamani, Mai. "You Are What You Cook: Cuisine and Class in Mecca." In *A Taste of Thyme: Culinary Cultures in the Middle East*, edited by Sami Zubaida and Richard Tapper. London: Tauris Parke, 2000.

Sports and Leisure

SPORTS

Modern and traditional forms of sport, hobbies, and leisure pastimes coexist in Saudi Arabia. The traditional contests of camel racing, horse racing, and poetry added to the prestige of the tribe. Today's promotion of athletics and sports is a matter of national pride and social development. Government planning for sports education and facilities began in the late 1960s and expanded during the 1970s. The government budgeted for and built facilities throughout the country, including large sports arenas and stadiums, and implemented training in schools. However, the idea of individual fitness or exercise for all is still not entirely accepted.

Sports are not forbidden in Islam. Nevertheless, some conservatives oppose the enthusiasm that youth have for sports. A high school educational religious text condemned sports as a poor use of time, because they "cause youth to miss prayers and ignore household obligations" (Doumato 2008, 162). However, in this aspect of social development, governmental support is obvious and legitimates these activities despite the views of some religious scholars.

Women had been excluded from sports at an official level entirely up until 2010, even though segregated sports activities do take place. Private schools have offered physical education, and national schools followed suit despite the concerns about public spectator sports. Beginning in the *Third Development Plan* (1980–1983), the need for facilities for sports in girls' schools was specifically addressed (Bird 1995, 289; Third Development Plan, Ministry of Planning 1985, 375). Women are excluded from attending many sports events. All official athletes of the Olympic team and national leagues are men, as are the trainers and referees. And even though women are not allowed to drive, they cannot exercise by walking in the streets, as this is also frowned on. Most sports and exercise activities take place in private clubs. Certain workplaces have their own health clubs or exercise facilities. Women are excluded from some of these but may participate in others, as in hospitals, which are officially licensed to operate health clubs. Health clubs and exercise facilities at hotels are restricted to men. Without licenses, many clubs have offered exercise classes, physical training, and even yoga classes, because no government agency was willing to issue licenses to women's facilities elsewhere. Several women's health facilities were closed in Jeddah and Dammam in 2009 because of the licensing and registration issue (Alsharif 2009).

Soccer (Football)

Soccer, known as football in Saudi Arabia, is probably the most popular sport, as is also true in the other Gulf states and the Arab world. The Saudi Arabian Football Federation was founded in 1956 and was headed by Prince Sultan bin Fahd ibn 'Abd al-'Aziz. The Saudi Arabian national team is known as the Green Falcons, and they have often qualified to play in the Fédération Internationale de Football Association (FIFA) World Cup since they first entered in 1994 (however, they did not qualify in 2010).

A 12-team national league, the Saudi Professional League, plays regularly. The al-Hilal Saudi Club is probably the most popular soccer team; it is based in Riyadh and plays at the huge 67,000-seat King Fahd Stadium. Al-Hilal belongs to the Asian Football Confederation's Asian Champions as well as the Saudi Professional League. Other Riyadh-based teams are the al-Nasr and al-Shabab football clubs. Al-Ittihad Jeddah ranked ahead of al-Hilal (2.1 to 1.5) in the FIFA rankings in 2010. The al-Ahli Sports club is also based in Jeddah. Al-Ittihad plays at the Prince Abdullah al-Faisal Stadium (27,000 seats), and al-Ahli plays in the Prince Sultan bin Fahd Stadium (24,000 seats). There are football clubs in Abha, Mecca, Dammam, and Tabuk.

In 2008 the Under 17 Gulf Cup of Nations was held in Saudi Arabia, and teenagers from Saudi Arabia, the United Arab Emirates, Oman, and Bahrain took part. Also in 2008, the Under 23 Gulf Cup of Nations was hosted by Saudi Arabia. The Asian Football Confederation (AFC) U-19 Championship was held in Saudi Arabia in 2008. This was the 35th event of this tournament, an activity of the Asian Football Confederation. The A group, which included Saudi Arabia, played seven games, and all four groups played between October 12 and November 14 at the Prince Muhammad ibn Sa'ud Stadium in Dammam; the final game was played at Prince al-Jilawi in Khobar. Both stadiums are in the Eastern Province. The three matches involving the Saudi Arabian team (against Japan, Yemen, and Iran) were all very well attended, with attendance varying from 6,000 to 8,000.

Basketball

The Saudi Arabian Basketball Federation is a member of the Fédération Internationale de Basketball (FIBA) and is located in Riyadh. It had 72 registered teams as of 2010, all of which are male. These include the al-Hilal basketball team in Riyadh and the al-Ittihad team in Jeddah.

Women are playing basketball and soccer but have no officially sponsored teams or clubs. Danaya al-Maeena is the cofounder of the women's Jeddah United Basketball

Team. Her sister Lina was the trainer of the team in 2008 and pointed out that nearly all other Muslim countries are now training women athletes and sending them to the Olympics (Thorold 2008). In basketball, as with all sports, women play fully veiled, in long sleeves and pants, as in other Gulf countries.

Golf

Golf has become popular in Saudi Arabia in recent years. Golf clubs with memberships have been established, and visitors can pay on a daily or short-term basis to enter. Among these are the Arizona Golf Resort in Riyadh and the International Hotel in Riyadh, which has a nine-hole course that is lit at night. Unfortunately, women are not permitted to play golf there or even walk on the course. Golf training is also offered in Saudi Arabia.

Martial Arts

Wrestling, various forms of karate (including *shotokan* and *kyokushin*), tae kwon do, aikido, and judo are taught and practiced in Saudi Arabia. The *'ardha*, or sword dance of Najd, and stick-fighting dances of the Hijaz (see the Music and Dance section in this chapter) allude to the fighting traditions of the premodern period as well.

Olympic Participation

Saudi Arabia joined the International Olympic Committee in 1964. Saudi Arabia's Olympic athletes compete in many sports, first winning medals in track and field and equestrian sports jumping events. In 2000, Hadi Souan al-Somayli won the silver medal at the Olympic Games in the 400-meter hurdles, coming extremely close to winning the gold; his foot crossed the finish line first, but the American competitor's chest was forward, crossing the finish line before al-Somayli's upper body. Al-Somayli continued competing and then directed the sprint team at the Beijing games. Other track-and-field athletes from Saudi Arabia have excelled. In the Youth Olympics of 2010, held in Singapore, a Saudi Arabian female equestrian, Dalma Malhas, received a bronze medal for show jumping, and her participation was praised by the chairman of the International Olympic Committee, Jacques Rogge. He saw this as a breakthrough, even though she was excluded from the official delegation of Saudi Arabian Olympic athletes and had to pay for her own entry to the event (Zoepf 2010).

Islamic Solidarity Games

The Islamic Solidarity Games, an international competition, were held in Mecca in 2005. Fifty-five nations participated with a presence of 6,000 athletes, all male. These featured the categories of aquatics, athletics, basketball, equestrian, fencing, soccer (football), handball, karate, table tennis, tae kwon do, tennis, volleyball, and weightlifting. The Islamic Solidarity Games were scheduled to be held in Iran in 2010. Saudi Arabia withdrew due to an argument about the proper name for the Arabian Gulf, which Iran insists is the Persian Gulf, and the games were cancelled.

Cricket and Baseball

Cricket is popular in Saudi Arabia, particularly in those countries that were culturally influenced by the United Kingdom. The Riyadh Cricket Association and the Jeddah Cricket Association list many teams and their schedules. At a national level, the Saudi Cricket Center is located in Jeddah.

Baseball is also played as a youth sport. A number of Little League teams are in operation and include the members of the Jeddah Youth Baseball League.

Rugby

Rugby is played in Saudi Arabia, and the teams are made up of Saudi Arabian nationals along with expatriates from many countries. The Riyadh Rugby Football Club and the Jeddah Rugby Football Club play regularly.

Horse Racing and Equestrian Sports

The Arabian horse is famous throughout the equestrian world, and clubs and associations exist in the region and in the West linking racing and breeding industries in the northern and southern hemispheres. Amazing relationships between people and these horses link them, Arabia, and the bedouin to aficianados like Carl Reinhard Raswan, who devoted himself to sharing his knowledge of Arabians (Raswan 1955, 1990). Many Saudi Arabians are involved in equestrian and horse racing, breeding, and competitions throughout the world, not only inside the kingdom. King 'Abdullah is himself a sponsor of equestrian sports as president of the Arriyadh Equestrian Club, founder of the Saudi Arabian Equestrian Federation, and patron of the King 'Abd al-'Aziz Arabian Horse Center, at Dirab, which along with the al-Janadiriyyah farm are world-renowned horse-breeding farms. The main national horse racing event is the King's Cup Race and the Crown Prince's Race held in March or February at the King 'Abd al-'Aziz Racetrack at Janadiriyyah. The same tracks offer races from September to April.

The Arabian Horses Festival takes place over 10 days in Riyadh in the winter. Among the events is a long-distance or endurance race of 75 kilometers (46.6 miles). This type of race gained acceptance as an Olympic sport with the sponsorship of racers and riders here and in other Arab countries. The festival also includes show jumping and a horse beauty contest. The long-distance race, sometimes called the race of a million steps, is held at Thumama Park. It is divided into three sections of 25 kilometers (15.5 miles), with a rest of 30 minutes and opportunity for veterinary inspection in between each part.

Khaled al-Eid, Saudi Arabian equestrian champion on Presley Boy, World Equestrian Games, Lexington, Kentucky, 2010. (AP/Wide World Photos)

The Equestrian Federation is located in Riyadh, and clubs are found around the country. In the 1980s show jumping was introduced to the kingdom. Arabian horses were not as well suited to this sport as to racing, so other thoroughbreds began to be imported for jumping. Members of the Olympic show-jumping team, the brothers Khalid and Fayad al-Eid trained in Germany, England, and the United States. Khalid placed 30th in the 1996 Olympics. As part of the Saudi Arabian Olympic jumping team, he trained with Nelson Pessoa, a Brazilian equestrian show jumper based in Belgium. Khalid al-Eid won the bronze medal in 2000 (Harrigan and Mazzawi 2001) and is still competing. In the Alltech World Equestrian Games of 2010, al-Eid at age 41 moved from fifth place to first in a nearly flawless performance on his stallion, Presley Boy, on the third day of the competition. Other important members of the show-jumping team and previous qualifiers for the World Cup are 'Abdullah Shurbatly, Khalid Ba-Hamdan, and Prince 'Abdullah ibn Miteb.

In 2008, Arwa Mutabagani, a woman and the mother of the show jumper Malhas, who won a bronze medal, was appointed a top sports administrator at the Equestrian Federation. She has set up an equestrian center in Jeddah that trains women. In 2008, 50 women participated in equestrian events there. However, they could not compete in the national and international shows, and this type of competition is necessary to produce winners (Thorold 2008).

On July 31, 2010, 'Ali Ahmed of the Institute of Gulf Affairs, a critic of the Kingdom of Saudi Arabia, began a "No Women No Play" campaign to get the International Olympic Committee to ban Saudi Arabia from participation if it did not allow women on its team. His reasoning was that this violated the International Olympic Committee's own policies and was much like South Africa's exclusion of black athletes under apartheid (Zoepf 2010). The International Olympic Committee did not, however, exclude Saudi Arabia. (Only Qatar and Brunei also exclude female athletes from their teams.) Malhas, age 18, participated independently in the Youth Olympics in Singapore in August 2010. Her winning of a bronze medal sparked many recriminations from conservatives in Saudi Arabia. They are the reason that women are not provided sports in schools and are not encouraged to exercise or engage in sports, or must do so at unmarked facilities. A cleric, Shaykh Sa'ud al-Funiasan, said that women in equestrian events are "defiant public violators" of Islamic law and should not be part of national or international equestrian competitions, because this violates the rules of modesty and causes them to mingle with men.

Camel Racing

The Arabian camel is a single-humped dromedary found in a variety of colors and sizes. It has traditionally been ridden and raced in Saudi Arabia. Throughout the winter season, camel races are held on Mondays at the King Fahd International Stadium. In February or March, the Janadiriyyah Cultural Festival is opened with the King's Camel Race. This takes place at Janadiriyyah, not far from Riyadh. Every day of the Janadiriyyah Festival, camel races are held, with about 2,000 camels participating and 20,000 to 30,000 spectators. No gambling is allowed at such games (or anywhere in Saudi Arabia) due to religious prohibitions. Some reports claim that very young children are used as camel jockeys, and although it is illegal to employ them, some races are held outside regular hours, so the practice might be continuing.

Camels are no longer necessary for travel or production, but they are prized as a symbol of times past and are today a multimillion dollar industry in Saudi Arabia. Camel beauty pageants are held throughout the country, and the contestants are judged for their physical qualities, which include large eyes with double rows of curly eyelashes, long necks, and their dressage. Camel markets are held, the largest of which is in Riyadh; these include camels raised for riding, for milk, or for slaughter as food (Zoepf 2008). In the late winter, owners may go on special outings to spend time with their favorite camels.

Auto Racing

Auto racing is held at the Jeddah Raceway, which opened in 2006 and operates a school to train race drivers. Unfortunately, auto racing is somewhat of an undeclared sport on the highways and even in cities, and it is exceedingly dangerous.

Tourism, Camping, Hiking, and Outdoor Recreation

Saudi Arabia maintains many parks and wildlife and game reserves and has plans for expanding them. Tourism within Saudi Arabia is a fairly new endeavor, as most travel to the kingdom is undertaken for the *hajj* and secondarily for business; touristic travel has required a sponsor and specific permission. Saudi Arabians travel within their country primarily for business, the *hajj* or *'umrah*, and visits to family members. Internal tourism as a feature of education is another aspect of the country's development that is being expanded. Saudi Arabian students visit the national museum in Riyadh and Dir'iyyah, the site of the first Sa'udi state and other locations.

The Saudi Commission for Tourism and Antiquities was created in 2000. As of 2010, it was presided over by Prince Sultan ibn Salman (a former Royal Saudi Air Force lieutenant colonel and the first Arab and Muslim to participate in a space mission, mentioned later on again for his interest in traditional-style architecture). Prince Sultan wants to develop internal and external tourism to natural sites and historic monuments and to expand tourism as a means of employing more Saudi Arabian nationals. The Prince Sultan College for Tourist and Hotel Management was opened in 2001 in Sultan City, which is on the road from the Abha regional airport.

Among many nature-touristic sites the government established was the al-Hada resort in Ta'if. This has a 4,200-meter- (about 2.6-mile-) long cable car route that connects al-Hada with the al-Kar touristic village, which is at a lower elevation. Hotels, parks, and playgrounds were built to encourage family tourism.

While this type of development is in tune with modern Saudi Arabians, families and groups also camp in a style closer to the bedouin, now making use of jeeps and sports vehicles. And some families, settled for generations, nevertheless enjoy setting up tent areas on a temporary basis in the right weather and location. Picnics are popular throughout the country; families used to bring radios, then televisions, and now newer electronic viewing devices.

Private international tourism was inaugurated in 2000, and some obstacles to its success reside with national policies and the degree of understanding of tourists and operators. Tourism may allow outsiders to better understand history, gender, and nationality in Saudi Arabia, or it may succeed in further strengthening stereotypes (Okruhlik in Rasheed and Vitalis, eds., 2004, 201–208).

Saudi Arabia offers many other possibilities for hiking, climbing, trekking, spelunking, dune skiing, and diving. The coral reefs off the Red Sea coast offer divers sights of wonderful fish and fauna. Divers should be licensed and experienced. Snorkeling, boating, and other water sports are also available. Dune skiing is an unusual sport particular to the Arabian Peninsula. In the Rub' al-Khali, the sand dunes can be hundreds of meters high, so a skier can glide downward swiftly.

Avid mountain climbers or hikers can enjoy climbing in the Abha region. John Pint, who has written about many natural wonders in Saudi Arabia, also describes the climbing available at the black and white volcanoes of Harrat Khaybar lava field, which lies 190 kilometers (118 miles) north of Jeddah. Not only is there excellent climbing, but the conjunction of the Qidr volcano, which puts out black lava, and the two white volcanoes, Jabal Bayda and Jabal Abyad, is visually stunning. Jabal Bayda is an easier climb than Jabal Abyad. Climbing the Qidr volcano involves moving up the roofs of relatively recent lava tubes.

Pint also writes about access to the desert caves at the Summan Plateau, not far from Riyadh or Dhahran (Pint n.d.). Pint recommends hiking with groups like the Hash House Harriers, an expatriate group that organizes hikes, runs, and outdoor events, and the Natural History Society.

Another reason to hike and walk is to see the many natural phenomena of Saudi Arabia. Expeditions are made to Tuwair in the spring to witness the simultaneous flowering of the iris, which occurs at 1:00 p.m. on a sunny day and a bit later if it is cloudy. Another strange phenomenon is the "desert rose," which can be found in the *sabkha*s, or salt flats. When water moves into these areas in the Eastern Desert and evaporates, gypsum crystals are formed and shaped by the sand into a rosette shape, usually buried under the surface.

Other enjoyable travel destinations are historic sites, which are located throughout the kingdom, such as Mada'in al-Saleh, the ancient city near Medina; the settlement of Dir'iyyah; and various locations in and near Ta'if, which can be cooler and more pleasant. Ta'if possesses three wildlife refuge sites where endangered species have been reestablished. Musma Park will be developed to the east of Ha'il as an ecotourism destination, with a tourist city or village, which means there will be accommodations for families and services.

Hunting and Falconry

Hunting is a popular pursuit in the kingdom as well as in other GCC countries. Several species were hunted to extinction, such as the Arabian wild ass and the Arabian wild ostrich. The Arabian oryx nearly died out, but some were captured and kept in zoos and then reintroduced in wildlife parks under a protected status. Antelope and gazelles were hunted but are also now on the endangered watch list. Birds and lizards are hunted. Hunting used to be carried out on horseback, but now it is done by four-wheel-drive truck. The prized dog of the bedouin, the *saluki*, could be at the center of the hunt, chasing after antelope for its owner.

Falconry is a special form of hunting. The use of falcons and hawks dates far back in history, and training of birds of prey for hunting is mentioned in the Qur'an. The *saqr* (falcon chirrup) is the most popular bird used and is bred in breeding farms and entered in falcon beauty contests. A prize falcon can cost as much as $100,000. To train the bird, the trainer, or falconer, swings a lure around his head and the bird follows it. Once the falcon lands on the lure, it is given a reward of a piece of meat. Jesses are attached to the falcon's leg, and a hood covers its eyes when it is not training so it remains calm. The falconer wears a glove so the bird's sharp talons do not hurt him. Prince Fahd bin Sultan, the governor of Tabuk as of 2007, is known as a great falconer and employed very experienced falcon masters such as Hadi al-Aimi. Members of the royal family have long been associated with the sport; one of King 'Abd al-'Aziz's epithets was al-Saqr al-Jazira (the Falcon of the Peninsula; *New York Times*, June 12, 2007). He was so named for his falconry but also because of his conquest of the area. Some princes of the royal family used to transport their falcons with their personal goods when traveling abroad for study. As with specialty camel and pedigree horse raising, falcons are bred for the sport.

LEISURE AND ENTERTAINMENT

The most pervasive leisure activity in the kingdom is social interaction, mainly participation in family, peer, and business-related visiting networks. People entertain frequently and reciprocate. Social isolation is generally disliked and unusual. Both men and women participate in visiting networks that mark all important events in families' lives from births to deaths. Visiting is therefore the most traditional of activities, and yet it has been changed by the swift growth of cities, traffic, and the movement of families, in some but not all cases, away from extended-family households.

Most of this social interaction takes place in the separate worlds of men or women. Prominent men and princes held and still hold visiting hours, which may take place as a *majlis* (literally, a "sitting"). These are often a mixed encounter of social interaction and business, or petitioners may leave a formal written request after presenting it briefly. Men usually coordinate with their wives unless they have a large waitstaff, so that food and beverages are prepared and so that their wives can attend to their visits with other women on different days.

Weddings and celebrations can be enormously elaborate events; schools also put on ceremonies that include entertainment. The annual Janadiriyyah Festival includes many different types of events and opening ceremonies. A large, special reception is held for invited women guests on the women's days of the festival and is hosted by members of the royal family. At this women-only event, poetry recitations, songs, and dances, including the dances of the eastern provinces in the colorful *thawb nashal* (an outer bright-colored, gold- and sequin-embroidered garment), are performed, often by very young women or schoolgirls. Theatrical entertainment has occasionally been presented in school settings, but religious conservatives have protested this, so there are no national or public theaters as there are in Egypt or Lebanon and no movie theaters. However, there was a theater and small film scene in the 1960s. Sometimes, those who can drive go to Bahrain to view films. It is possible, given statements in 2009 and 2010, that cinema showings, and possibly even regular theaters, might be reintroduced.

Card games are played, as are chess, backgammon, and video games, now on handheld devices. Gambling, and games of chance, however, are not permitted in Islam.

Poetry and calligraphy festivals are held. Poetry remains a popular interest in a way it no longer is in Western societies, but it too has undergone change. In the past, men would gather socially in the evenings, particularly in the summer, and open a cycle of poetry recitation and commentary on poetry by asking if the attendees knew of a certain poem composed by so-and-so and then reciting it. Such events provided a chain of transmitters and perpetuated knowledge about poetry. Beginning in the mid-1980s, the University of Riyadh began sponsoring a three-day poetry festival that was recorded on videotape. Radio and television programs also feature poetry shows, which are very popular with audiences, who might write in or call in concerning a particular poem and its wording (Sowayan 1985, 126–129; also see Literature section in this chapter).

Numerous gatherings and special events are sponsored by cities or business groups, ranging from inaugurations of facilities to special-events concessions with business or industry themes (see section on food in this chapter).

Restrictions

No cinemas or discotheques, dancing clubs, casinos, or, obviously, bars or nightclubs exist in Saudi Arabia. People also meet for social or business purposes in restaurants or large hotels. Women are not able to visit restaurants at all times in Riyadh, but these rules are more relaxed in the large international hotels. Dancing and music are performed at special occasions, parties, and weddings (see Music and Dance section in this chapter) but not in mixed-sex settings. Aerobic dance and some other forms of dance are offered as exercise in women's spas and clubs. Women's gyms have also been set up in this way but have faced licensing problems due to opposition by conservatives.

Shopping

Shopping has become an important pastime. Families shop together, and women or men (separately) may meet for shopping. Family areas are located in the malls, which may also have family-style eating concessions. Just a few are the Kingdom Center, Le Mall, the Faisaliyya, and Riyadh Sahara Mall in Riyadh; the al-Azziziah Hyper Panda, the al-Hasan, and the al-Rashid Mega Mall in Medina; and the Mall of Arabia Sultan Mall, Jareer Mall, al-Hijaz, and Le Mall in Jeddah. Women meet at the women's floor of the Kingdom Center in Riyadh for social purposes or business or may also shop or window-shop. High fashion is at least as popular in Saudi Arabia as in Europe, since many women wear Western fashions under their outer garb of the black *'abaya*. Designer labels from Europe are available and desired, but there are also up-and-coming Saudi Arabian designers such as Wijdan al-Sharyoufi; the transplanted Summer Olayan, operating in Los Angeles; and Siraj Sanad.

Media Entertainment

Without movie theaters or cinemas, the watching of television, videos and DVDs, satellite television, and new media technologies is ever growing in Saudi Arabia. Certain television series acquire almost a cult following; among these were several Turkish series dubbed in Arabic, including *Nur* and *Aški Memu'a* (the Turkish title, or *'Ashqi mamnu'a* in Arabic), which were equally popular elsewhere in the Arab world. Certain satellite channels are blocked on regular services but may be available at other locations in the kingdom, such as international hotels. News is consumed and eagerly discussed in Saudi Arabia. News services in the kingdom are censored, and a complex system is in place to filter out content or influences that are not approved.

Telephone- and computer-based contacts occupy leisure time for many, especially young people. For a time, cell phones with cameras were forbidden, but they have proliferated anyway. Blackberry services began and then were cancelled in August 2010, probably because these are more difficult to monitor; cell phone texting remains popular. Internet use has grown rapidly in Saudi Arabia and has been a source of certain security concerns inasmuch as political opponents, religious militants, and severe critics of the kingdom also post there. Numerous Islamic Internet sites are accessed; some are commissioned by government centers, while others are independent. The Internet is thus educational and a site of conservative knowledge, and not only a liberal connection (Bunt 2009). E-mail is similarly convenient, connective, and often monitored. Blogging has gained in popularity and is subject to some restrictions; it has been used to protest many conditions in Saudi Arabia or has simply been used for social purposes (Cooke and Lawrence 2005). Facebook operates in a similar way and is an interesting site for debates about social or political change, allowing the Saudi Arabian feminists, like Wajiha al-Huweidar, Manal Sharif and others to speak (Khannous 2010; see Chapter 7, Contemporary Issues) and still others to respond.

REFERENCES

"Alltech FEI WEG Jumping: Saudi Arabia's Al Eid Heads Individual Rankings while Germany Heads Team Leaderboard." *Equestrian Times*, October 6, 2010.

Alsharif, Asma. "Saudi Arabia Clamps Down on Unlicensed Female Gyms." *Reuters*, April 30, 2009.

Bird, Jerine. "Revolution for Children in Saudi Arabia." In *Children in the Muslim Middle East*, edited by Elizabeth Warnock Fernea. Austin: University of Texas Press, 1995, 290–294.

al-Bogari, Naima. "Motivation for Domestic Tourism: A Case Study of the Kingdom of Saudi Arabia." In *Consumer Psychology of Tourism, Hospitality and Leisure*, edited by Arch G. Woodside. Oxfordshire, UK: CABI, 2004.

Brock, Paul. "Al-Hurr: Noble One." *Saudi Aramco World*, March/April 1973, 2–5.

Bunt, Gary. *iMuslims: Rewiring the House of Islam*. Chapel Hill: University of North Carolina Press, 2009.

Cooke, Miriam, and Bruce Lawrence, eds. *Muslim Networks from Hajj to Hip Hop (Islamic Civilization and Muslim Networks)*. Chapel Hill: University of North Carolina Press, 2005.

Doumato, Eleanor A. "Saudi Arabia: From Wahhabi Roots to Contemporary Revisionism." In *Islam and Textbooks in the Middle East*, edited by Eleanor A. Doumato and Gregory Starrett. Cairo: American University in Cairo Press, 2008, 153–176. (Also published as *Teaching Islam: Textbooks and Religion in the Middle East*. [Boulder, CO: Lynne Rienner, 2007].)

Eickelman, Dave, and Jon Anderson. *New Media in the Muslim World: The Emerging Public Sphere*. Bloomington: Indiana University Press, 1999; 2nd ed., 2003.

Franklin, Jo., dir. *A Gift from the Desert: The Arabian Horse* [documentary film]. SeaCastle, 2010.

Harrigan, Peter, and Rosalind Mazzawi. "Saudi Arabia's First Olympic Medals." *Saudi-Aramco World*, January/February 2001.

Khannous, Touria. "In Search of an Arab-Muslim Feminism on the Internet." Paper presented at the Conference on Interculturality and Gender, University of Fes (Fez) Morocco, May 29–30, 2010.

Ministry of Planning, Kingdom of Saudi Arabia. *Third Development Plan, 1980–1985*. Riyadh: Ministry of Planning, Kingdom of Saudi Arabia, 1985.

Okruhlik, Gwen. "Struggles over History and Identity: Opening the Gates of the Kingdom to Tourism." In *Counternarratives: History, Contemporary Society, and Politics in Saudi Arabia and Yemen*, edited by Madawi al-Rasheed and Robert Vitalis. New York: Palgrave Macmillan, 2004, 201–228.

Pint, John. "Outdoor Activities in Saudi Arabia." Outdoor Activities in Saudi Arabia: Hiking, Climbing, Dune Skiing and Open-Air Recreation in the Desert. n.d. http://www.suite101.com/content/outdoor-recreational-activies-in-saudi-arabia-a58568#ixzz11hDnUkaB

Raswan, Carl (Reinhard). *The Arab and His Horse*. Oakland, CA: By the author, 1955. (German version: Hildesheim: G. Olms, 1990.)

Raswan, Carl (Reinhard). *In the Land of the Black Tents*. 2nd ed. (German). Hildesheim: G. Olms, 1990.

"Saudi Arabia." Fédération Internationale de Football Association. http://www.FIFA.com

Sowayan, Saad Abdullah. *Nabati Poetry: The Oral Poetry of Arabia*. Berkeley and Los Angeles: University of California Press, 1985.

Thorold, Crespin. "Saudi Women Vie for Olympic Rights. BBC, June 13, 2008.

Wynne, Lisa. "The Romance of Tahliyya Street: Youth Culture, Commodities and the Use of Public Space in Jiddah." *Middle East Report*, no. 204 (July–September 1997), 30–31.

Zoepf, Katherine. "For Saudi Women Biggest Challenge Is Getting to Play." *New York Times*, November 17, 2010.

Zoepf, Katherine. "Camel Beauty Pageants Become Popular Pastime." *Seattle Times*, March 17, 2008.

Popular Culture

Popular culture in Saudi Arabia is usually associated with traditional culture, or folk custom, rather than youth trends. Unlike Egypt, where a juxtaposition of the culture of the common people (*al-sha'b*) versus the elite groups (*al-khassa*) was once clear (Sonbol 2000), Saudi Arabia does not present clear-cut distinctions. Members of the *'umara*, the royal family, or elites may patronize or preserve popular culture and symbols of the Arabian past yet pursue modern interests and consumption patterns. Certain aspects of popular culture are preserved only as *turath* (legacy) at festivals, exhibits, and museums and in publications. It is strongly associated with the nomadic bedouin heritage or specific geographic areas as well.

AMTHAL

A *mathal* (singular form) is a brief proverb or statement reflecting popular belief and custom or attributed to religious tradition. Saudi Arabians use *amthal* in conversation, explanation, and analysis of social situations. Some date back far into the past. As with literature, it is difficult to confine the form to the Arabian Peninsula. Early collections were the *Majma'a al-Amthal* (Cairo, 1310), containing 4,766 proverbs compiled by Ahmad ibn Muhammad al-Maidani. He referred to 50 sources in it that had contained proverbs (Rayyes 1969). Abu al-Qasim al-Zamakhshari compiled some 3,461 proverbs in *al-Mustaqsa fi Amthal al-'Arab* (The sought-after Arabic proverbs) in 1107.

Proverbs may liken humans to animals. This tradition appears in classical Arabic literature, in a famous fable collection, *Kalila wa Dimna*. Some of the proverbs are: "If a camel once gets his nose into a tent, his body will soon follow." "A kind word can attract even the snake from his nest." "Do not seek bones from the flesh of a starved camel" (said of trying to force a person to comply who cannot). "Throw a lucky man in the sea, he will come up with a fish in his mouth." Or based on verses of the renowned medieval poet Abu al-Tayyib Mutanabbi: "If you see the lion's jaws open, do not think he is smiling" (things are not always as they seem). Or, "In seeking honey, expect the sting of bees" (any quest for an object of value will involve some tribulations). Others refer to the values of the tribe: "Assist thy brother, whether he is wrong or right." "God ordains the going out on raids and the returning from raids" (an expression used to explain a change of mind; (Sowayan 1985b, 132).

Many are attributed to the Prophet Muhammad or to principles of religious belief. Two early collectors of such proverbs were Ibn Khallad al-Ramhurmuzi and Abu Hilal al-Askari, who published *Amthal al-Nabi* (Brockelman 1913–1938). "Fear not the man who fears God." "Riches are not from abundance of worldly goods, but from a contented mind." "Let go of the things of which you are in doubt for the things in which there is no doubt" (Rayyes 1969).

Others derive from the Qur'an: "Whatever good you possess is all from God. Whatever evil, all is from yourself." "Allah will not change the condition of men, until they change what is in themselves." "Work for your future as if you are going to live forever, for your afterlife as if you are going to die tomorrow." "Allah is with those who patiently preserve." Others come from *ahadith*: "Feed the hungry, visit the sick and free the captive" (al-Bukhari). "The dearest to me are those who are best in character" (al-Bukhari).

Arabian proverbs may be very close to Western ones: "Love is blind," "Speak of an angel and you hear his wings" (like "the walls have ears" or "speak of the devil") (al-Maidani 57). "A liar must have a good memory" (al-Maidani 49). "To fall between two stools" (al-Maidani 64, similar to "between Scylla and Charybides" or to fall "from the frying pan into the fire"). "Save your white coin for your black day" (save for a rainy day). "Repeated visits cause boredom" (familiarity breeds contempt) (Rayyes 1969).

Others are more unique: "A book is a garden carried in the pocket," "one hand alone cannot clap" (unity is necessary, or it takes two); "the fingers of your hand are not the same" (human beings, even members of a group, are unique); and "a tree without fruit attracts no birds" (to explain attacks or negative reactions to one's effort). A regionwide proverb is "the ship led by two captains will sink" (too many cooks spoil the soup); revised and somewhat mocking of Saudi Arabia, it is: "I am a prince and you are a prince, who will lead the donkeys?" (all chiefs and no Indians).

JOKES, *NAWADIR,* AND SHORT TALES

Jokes may completely overtake conversational exchanges at gatherings. Typically one or two display their memories and talents for comedic timing by relating joke after hilarious joke. Sometimes they are complicated stories that take five minutes or so to relate and can have a reprise form. *Nawadir* are anecdotes or short stories. In modern times, these might be circulated by e-mail. Older children's stories and lullabies forms of popular culture in danger of being forgotten; Lamia Baeshen, who is trying to preserve these genres, published a book of tales from the Hijaz in that dialect in 1997 and a CD including the lullaby "Doha ya Doha" (Baeshen 1997, 201).

SUPERSTITIONS

Many superstitions are reflected in folktales. The *jinn* (literally, "hidden beings") are a broad category of supernatural beings, both harmful and helpful. To become *majnun* (crazy or mad) means to become possessed by jinn. One powerful variety of jinn lives on the open water. An *ifrit* (*afrit*; *afarit* is the plural) is an evil spirit, sometimes blamed for evil events. A capsized ship is said to be overturned by *afarit*. Also, a misbehaving child or a bride who chafes at new restrictions and cries (*hiyya 'ad al-awwil tit'afarit*) are said to be "like afrit" (Holes 2001, 345) A *ghul* is an even more terrifying shape-shifter who lives in the desert, digs up the dead, may prey on children and travelers, and is apparently the origin of the English word *ghoul*. All make appearances in traditional stories. In the story of Sitt Lahab, she is visited by a *ghul*. The *ghul* demands to know what the beautiful girl saw at her teacher's house. She reports she saw him reading the Qur'an. The ghoul threatens her with killing her family's animals and her parents and destroying their home, if she will not say more. She won't, and he does away with all dear to her. She flees and is discovered and married by a prince. The ghoul finds her and threatens to kill the children she conceives, three times, and takes each child, but she refuses to falsely report. Finally, a vision of her old teacher visits her and restores her children, her parents, and all their goods to her; then, finally, the ghoul disappears (Bushnaq 1986, 132–137). People feared certain places due to rumors of evil beings. Reading of shells was a form of fortune-telling to learn about the future, bad or good; and fortune-telling was practiced in various parts of the country even though certain Wahhabist officials considered it sorcery.

GAMES

Card games, video games, and handheld electronic games abound, but any that involve gambling are forbidden. A once-popular game for little girls was *al-saqlah.* The girls sit on the ground where they have made a slight hole filled with some pebbles or shells. One throws a key stone, larger and different from the others, up into the air toward the hole and scoops the pebbles or shells—as many as she can—out while the key stone is in the air and then catches it before it hits the ground. She keeps trying to remove them, so long as she catches the key stone, but if she drops it, she has to return the last pebble/shell or set of pebbles/shells to the hole, and then it is the next girl's turn. The winner is the one who collects the largest number of pebbles/shells.

"The hunter" is played, usually by 5 to 10 boys together, and sometimes by girls, while some remember playing in a mixed group. The hunter counts from 1 to 10, closing his or her eyes while all the other children run and hide. If the hunter finds anyone, he has to tag them. If he can't find them all, he has to tell them to start over. Otherwise, the first one who is caught becomes the next hunter. This is very similar to *al-ghomaid*, which is played in different parts of the Arabian Peninsula.

When a Meccan child carries out his first *hajj*, a party called JoJo is held. Everyone starts singing "Jojo, they have made the pilgrimage (jojo hajjo)!" The mother of the *hajji* child sprinkles candy and money (previously, one-riyal coins) on her child, and all the other children rush to collect as much of the candy and money as they can (Saudi Jawa as interviewed on *American Bedu*, March 4, 2010).

TRIBAL LAW AND MEDIATION

'*Urf*, or tribal law, governed the behavior of the tribes. It stands in contrast to the state-appointed officials, judges, and urban-centered '*ulama*. It is a basic building block of popular culture, because its purpose was to limit violence and restore justice. '*Urf* influenced *shari'ah* in three ways: first, the classification of crimes and their punishments (*qisas*), which require injury in kind (*talion*) or blood payment (*dhiyya*), were integrated into Islamic law; second, the legist tended to draw on '*urf* as a source of *fiqh* (jurisprudence), because it founded *ijma'* (consensus) and the *sunnah* of the members of the early Muslim community at Medina.

Thirdly, to settle a conflict, special men who hold a precedent in certain types of cases act as judges and mediators. In a blood dispute (meaning manslaughter or bodily injury), the judicator came from the Biliy of western Arabia. In a matter of *irdh* (sexual honor), the judicator came from the Masa'id (Stewart in Chatty, ed., 2006, 243). The vengeance group are those who exert revenge against someone who has killed their family member. A blood-money group are all those in the lineage of the killed or injured who could collect the *dhiyya* (blood payment), often a larger group than the vengeance group (Stewart in Chatty, ed., 2006, 257; Hardy 1963). In a dispute, the plaintiff and the defendant agree to two judicators, one for each. The trial takes place at the judicator's house, and he is paid for the proceedings. The parties may also hire a lawyer (*kabir*), who prepares a pleading for the plaintiff. The defendant responds with his own pleading (Stewart in Chatty, ed., 2006, 263).

These cases may present evidence. According to '*urf*, if there was no evidence, each party could take oaths. Also, in the past, they might undergo the *bish'a* (or *ba'a*), such as licking a heated iron object, like a spoon. If the tongue is unscathed, the individual has told the truth. This ordeal was made illegal in some other areas where it was practiced, for example, Palestine. It should be emphasized that *'urf* was not identical in all groups, nor limited to the bedouin or rural regions; being "customary" it extends to tribal descendants in settled, even urban areas.

Tribal-law procedure is part of business contracts, marriages, and marital disputes. Typically, a three-party contract is formed; A who agrees to do/pay something to B, and C, a guarantor must stand up for A and pay back the amount loaned by him, for example, if he defaults. If not, C's face "is blackened with dishonor" (Stewart in Chatty, ed., 2006, 268). So strong were the bonds of honor that this type of contract usually worked well.

Honor was preserved through marriages, and *shari'ah*'s insistence that a woman be represented by her male guardian appears to have come from *'urf* (a tradition that many women and reformers would like to change). The guardian can marry off his female ward and usually did not consult her if she was a virgin. Her husband could beat her but not seriously injure her (Stewart in Chatty, ed., 2006, 259). If he did injure her, then she would usually go to her guardian, or even move back in with him, if divorce were the outcome of such a situation.

The behavioral patterns coming from *'urf* are what leads to honor crimes, that is, killing of female relatives who have violated the sexual code of behavior or are suspected of doing so (Zuhur 2005). While this is a taboo subject, the principle of honor must be respected from the poorest in society to the royal family; the purpose of strict separation of men and women is to preserve honor but also Islamic virtue. Since honor crimes do not represent marriage as idealized in Islam, some in Saudi Arabia will say that honor crimes are not Islamic.

TRIBAL AND TRADITIONAL MEDICINE

Several alternative forms of medicine are practiced alongside modern Western medicine; some of these are new to the area. Others come from the Arabic medicine tradition or from *unani-tibb*, which are, respectively, Greco-Arab and Indo-Arab Muslim; another form is called *tibb nabawi* (medicine of the Prophet), or Islamic medicine.

Ethnobotany, the use of plants, herbs, and flowers by the bedouin and others for medicine, is extant in all areas where bedouin live; sometimes similar treatments in distant areas exist, or local treatments have developed (Abu-Rabia 2005). Similarly, whether among the bedouin farther to the north, or in some areas of Saudi Arabia, women as well as men served as healers (Doumato, 2000).

The following substances are sold by *attarin* (herbalists and sellers of perfumed oils) or used in traditional medical treatments. Alum is an astringent used to staunch bleeding and heal wounds. In the form of *shabba* stone, it is a deodorant. Aniseed is brewed as a tea (*yansun*) for stomach pain, indigestion, and menstrual cramps, and to aid the urinary system (Lebling and Pepperdine 2006a). It appears in historical references to Islamic medicine and other bedouin traditions (Abu-Rabia 2005) and among settled groups to the north. Also sold are asafetida, a sedative, antispasmodic, and circulatory agent; *nigella sativa* (*habba suda* or black seed), also found in cooking (see Food section in this chapter), which treats asthma, colic, and rheumatism; cardamom (*hail*), which treats indigestion and gas; chamomile (*babunaj*) tea, which calms the stomach and promotes sleep; garlic, which is put onto ant and scorpion stings; and myrrh, which is soaked in water, which is then used on burns, boils, or other wounds, as are soaked pomegranates (Lebling and Pepperdine 2006a). *Tarthuth* (*Cynomrium coccineum*, or Maltese mushroom/red thumb) has a long history of use in Islamic medicine and by the Knights Hospitaller of St. John of Jerusalem of Malta. This parasitic plant is eaten and used to make a red dye and, when the stalks are dried, to treat ulcers and colic (Lebling 2003).

Qur'anic medicine refers to healers' practice of chanting Qur'anic verses or writing them in the liquid ink known as China ink and then soaking these in water (or the inscription may be made on earthenware bowels into which water from Zamzam is poured). A patient drinks this *mahw* (the water) to treat illness, bad dreams, or possession by bad spirits. A *shaykh* might recite Surah Ya Sin of the Qur'an (Bogary 1991, 35–101), which is considered important for a cure. While Islam forbids witchcraft, folk belief in spells called for antidotes, and this type of treatments were not prohibited (al-Jaraisy 2001). People wore amulets to protect them from illness or mishap; these amulets were often inscribed with quotations from the Qur'an, or, in traditional forms of jewelry, the inscription might be placed inside. People uttered supplications following prayer to ask for healing. Until the Wahhabi movement forbade it, prayers and supplication were made at the tombs of holy persons; often, special prayers were made to request the improvement of health or fertility.

Possession by spirits is a special form of psychological illness. It was treated in Bahrain, Kuwait, Arabia, Egypt, Sudan, and eastern Africa by holding a *zar*, a ritual of exorcism. The music and prayers of the *zar* would unseat the spirit in question (see also Music and Dance section in this chapter). The *zar* was officiated over by a woman leader for women (and a man for men) and was a sort of cult, in that the spirits demanded the *zar* and sometimes required additional or repeated ceremonies. It was prevalent in Mecca during the Dutch administrator Snouck Hurgronje's stay (1885–1889), from whose writing we obtain a valuable historical chronicle of that city (Snouck Hurgronje 1931, 100) and was apparently revived in the 1970s to the disgust of Wahhabi *shaykhs* (Doumato 2000, 178).

Cautery is another traditional healing method. In years past it was common to see patients with scarring from treatment with hot stones (Ahmad 2008; personal field notes) or cauterization (cautery), which was used to resolve major wounds, internal pain (al-Awamy 2001; al-Bedah 2005; Bogary 1991, 16), and even psychological disorders (Qureshi et al. 1998). The medical studies showed that problems arose with such remedies when patients failed to receive other necessary forms of treatment.

Popular healers for horses and camels have been important to the pastoral culture of Saudi Arabia. They, too, utilize cautery, herbal remedies, bonesetting, and modern medicinal remedies. Their methods in treating camels have been studied, and some admitted that they would no longer use cautery for certain medical problems. Possibly it was effective for tendoarthritis, as the underlying principle resembles the counterirritation process in 19th-century medicine, when inflammation was countered with mercuric and ammonia salts (Abbas, al-Qarawy, and al-Hawas 2002, 377).

POPULAR OCCASIONS

Oral poetry and singing competitions were traditionally held in the summer among the nomads. Sa'd al-'Abdullah Sowayan, a scholar of Saudi Arabia's popular litera-ture, recalled that his own grandfather, who farmed for part of the year, had time to leave and attend these *mzayyan*. His recollections could be compared to the existing tradition Sowayan taped and collected. At the *mzayyan*, men and women celebrated; a young woman, the *hasi*, was chosen to dance. She would unplait her hair (presum-ably to swing it while dancing) and moved between the lines of all those assembled (Sowayan 1985a, 119). Music was played, and poems were recited and prefaced with their *sawalif* (the narratives associated with the poem, which explain it). People re-ferred to the declaimer, or *rawi*, as speaking the "language of real men" (*kalam rijaal*), because the texts referred to heroic deeds of men, and only one with a sophisticated knowledge of *nabati* could really appreciate them. Bedouin life changed with the substitution of the car and truck for the camel, but even modern-day compositions may resemble the opening of the classic *qasidah*. A woman's *nabati* poem declaimed: "Since the day they left in the car / My heart fled but I brought it back" (Ibn Raddas 1972, 48, cited in al-Ghadeer 2006, 1006).

Just as these narrative and musical events were enhanced with audience participa-tion, so, too, were the weddings and parties featuring women's music in urban Saudi Arabia. Their setting was the *majlis al-tarab*, a guest-reception room that should produce ecstasy or enchantment (*tarab*; Campbell 1998). (This should put to rest the idea that all who adhere to Wahhabi beliefs disallow happy occasions, music, and laughter.) The lyrics of women singer-poets (*mutribaat*) were chanted by all and reflect beliefs about fate, retribution, honor, and so on (Campbell 1985).

Feast days also reflected joy and happiness. There are many popular traditions concerning the Mawlid al-Nabi (see Holidays section at the end of the book) and the two 'Id holidays, as well as the *hajj* itself. On the 'Id al-Fitr, either clothes, children's toys, or money are given as gifts called *eidiyya* (*'idiyya*). Children anxiously await to see what they will receive. Muslim servants generally receive a gift of money on the d to help them cover the extra expenses of the holiday.

Families gather on the first morning of the 'Id al-Fitr to give a special prayer called the Salat al-Mashshad (or *salat al-'id*), during which the *takbir* (saying "Allahu Akbar") following the first kneeling is repeated seven times and then five times after the second one. Then they eat a special breakfast together. Holiday foods are served, which in the Hijaz used to include *halawa turki* (Turkish pudding), *shiriyya* (sweet noodles), and *debyaza* (a mixture of apricots, dates, and nuts cooked together). In re-cent years, many young and even middle-aged Saudi Arabians have begun celebrat-ing Valentine's Day and ordering roses for their sweethearts. Some of the *mutawa'a* and *'ulama* publicly denounced this trend and proclaimed it anti-Islamic.

CLOTHING AND HISTORIC COSTUME

Dress styles differed according to wealth, age, gender, geographic area, and tribe prior to the unification of the Kingdom of Saudi Arabia. The decoration of tradi-tional popular dress is really a professional craft or art form now disappearing as

Bride's costume from Medina. (Palms and Pomegranates: Traditional Dress of Saudi Arabia. U.S. Committee for Saudi Arabian Cultural Heritage, c. 1987–1989)

Western-style clothing (off the rack or tailored) is replacing it, but at folk festivals, traditional styles are crucial to the events.

A beautiful example of a Hijazi urban upper-class female dress that has been preserved is a princess-cut ankle-length dress called a *zabun*, made of organdy (a very sheer form of cotton); *sirwal* (pantaloons) in a cream color; a *sidariyya* (a fitted, buttoned underblouse); and, over all, a diaphanous rust-colored (or other colored) rectangular-shaped gauze *thawb* (robe). Instead of a black scarf, this costume had a *mihrama wa mudawara* (light-colored headscarf that was highly embroidered and topped with a diamond brooch). An everyday type of headscarf could be of light-colored voile, sometimes printed with floral designs. Ladies wore red and yellow slippers; in the Ottoman period, urban women were given *qubqab*, a wooden platform shoe decorated with mother-of-pearl. In the past, women wore a *burqa milayya*, meaning a long, white face veil, and a gray-colored silk mantle (Colyer Ross 1981, 90–92).

Near Mecca, Jeddah, and Medina, the dresses of the Harb tribe are typically black cotton with heavily decorated shoulders and upper arms, a yoke designed in seven squares, and hem panels. The embroidery is in red, yellow, and white shirt buttons are added as an integral part of the design (Colyer Ross 1981, 87). In southern

Hijaz, near Asir, the *badu* wore black dresses embroidered in colorful silk thread on a rectangular yoke (chest); or the design included embroidery on the yoke, on bands around the hem, and in a rectangular stripe from shoulder to hem on each side of the front and back. At Ta'if women wore shiny black cotton kaftan dresses with extra inserts of fabric at the sides. In the 1980s tailors made these "Taifi wedding dresses" in black or bright-colored velvets with bright-colored embroidery (Colyer Ross 1981, 96–97). Another highland *mudandash* (long dress) from near Sarawat had a slimmer fit than dresses in the north and was black with red, yellow, and white decorations (Colyer Ross 1981, 99, 115). With the Sarawat outfit a black hood decorated with buttons, embroidery, or beadwork might be worn.

Bedouin embroidery, beading, and textile production are now becoming less common and often cruder. The stitches (open chain, herringbone, feather bone, etc.) tell the origin of a garment, as do the patterns of woven items (Colyer Ross 1981, 133–153; Hilden 2010).

In the highlands, women also wore head circlets (*'asayib*) atop cloths and often a woven palm-frond hat atop that circlet in Asir or Tihamah. Another Asir *durra'ah* (a name for a long dress) is black, blue, and yellow patterned on top of a yellow-striped black skirt; a piece falls over the yoke and back, and a large striped cotton scarf is tied around the hips (*Palms and Pomegranates*, n.d. [ca. 1987], 20). In the Hijazi towns, women often wore a three-piece head covering with decorations showing, or the two pieces of the *shayla* and *gnaa*. Elaborately decorated *burqa*s (face masks) were worn by some groups in the Hijaz (but not all; Colyer Ross 1981, 47). East of Dhahran al-Janub, women wore green dresses and bright yellow headscarves. To the south, the *tawb aswad* (colloquial term for *thawb aswad*, or black dress) of Najran is black with very long pointed sleeves (Colyer Ross 1981, 101). Sandals made of camel hide were eventually replaced with Indian cow-hide imports, and palm-frond sandals were made in the West.

The Bedouin dress of the northern region used to be a patterned *fustan* (dress) with shoulder patches of brilliant pink and orange; another dress of a tribe to the west and south of the northern region is wide cut and of a unique burgundy color trimmed with pink and orange embroidery. Sometimes the dress is green, possibly because that color was worn by widows and women pilgrims (Colyer Ross 1981, 79). The Najdi Bani Tamim *thob* is very dramatic—black with wide stripes of pink, turquoise, yellow, and some red down each shoulder and side panel (Colyer Ross 1981, 70; *Palms and Pomegranates*, n.d. [circa 1987] 12). The *thawb magassab* is also Najdi, made in silk; it is purple or in other colors, with heavy gold-sequined trim and gold and turquoise neckline buttons.

The *thob nashal* of the eastern regions is a very sheer, very large rectangle with a neck opening, decorated with sequined embroidery and worn over a *fustan* or *dharrah* (gown). The wide sleeves of the *thob* can be drawn up over the back to cover the head. Most are now machine made and imported from India (Colyer Ross 1981, 72). They are now worn throughout Saudi Arabia, although they are Eastern dress. For weddings, a cherry-colored dharrah (dhurra'ah), known as an *omasa*, was worn or a cerise-colored *thob nashal*, red being a favorite color for weddings (Colyer Ross 1981, 56–57). A fitted kaftan with a back zipper, made in similar bright-colored

Banu Tamim thawb. (Palms and Pomegranates: Traditional Dress of Saudi Arabia. U.S. Committee for Saudi Arabian Cultural Heritage, c. 1987–1989)

material and a lavishly decorated (in India) front panel, including crossed swords, was the Sa'ud-era dress of the 1940s and 1950s (Colyer Ross 1981, 55). In Najd, a type of black *thawb* made of tulle or fine lace is worn for special occasions, decorated with gold or silver at the yoke and along the sleeve bands.

Henna

Women also decorate their hands and feet with henna, in either red or black. Henna is often used to color the hair as well. Elaborate patterns are made and self-applied or applied by a friend or a professional *hinnawah*. Henna used to be applied at the 'Id al-Fitr holiday and at the *laylat al-hinna* or *ghumra*, a bride's party prior to her wedding. This party was followed by the *zaffat al-shibshib*, which was a festive procession held in Jeddah to bring the bride's belongings to her new home.

Some, but not all, tribes used tattoos for decoration, which were generally small and on the face; these are seen now solely on the very elderly. However, Western-style tattoos are popularly said to be un-Islamic with no explanation of the previous tradition.

Kohl, made from antimony, is a traditional eyeliner and sometimes brow enhancer. In the past, men as well as women wore it. Doughty (1921) reported that Muhammad ibn Rashid "had his bird-like eyes painted." Public health researchers have long warned that kohl contains lead (al-Ashban, Aslam, and Shah 2004) and recommend lead-free varieties. Other premodern cosmetics like *zerkoun* were applied to the lips and cheeks. Scent, often made from local flowers or musk, henna, or amber, was applied. Elaborate hairstyles, often with braided sections and hair decorations, were worn. A bedouin woman's jewelry was usually part of her *mahr* (groom's payment to the bride). The contemporary urban woman will collect gold jewelry, some made abroad, and wear *au courant* Western cosmetics and hairstyles (although long hair is still preferred); some adult women and younger girls do not wear makeup at all, but other women may apply makeup heavily.

The Modern Niqab and Covering

For the last two decades, more and more women have been wearing more concealing clothing and a black face veil (*niqab*); the favorite style has a thin divider on the nose. The more conservative add gloves. Covering of the face is a point of contention between conservatives and salafists, on the one hand, and those who are just as pious but are traditionalists or liberals, on the other hand (Zuhur, Personal Interviews, 2005–2008). The *'abaya* is required on top of the clothing for older girls and women, and it must be black. Many women wear a *shayla*, a long black, sometimes decorated scarf over their head, but some also wear a *hijab* (headscarf) under the *shayla*. No part of the leg or arms should be revealed. Under the *'abaya*, all Western styles, including tight trousers or jeans, may be worn.

Children and Men

Children's clothes were once handmade from gauze. They wore a *gub* (hood) on their heads, which was black (to deflect the evil eye); it was replaced at age eight with a *kuffiya* (skullcap) for boys or with a *bukhnug* (hood) and later a *tarha* (headscarf) and *'abaya* for girls. School uniforms and other Western dress or versions of adult clothing are worn today.

Men dress in a white or cream cotton *thob* (*thawb* is the classical word) of cotton or a synthetic/silk mixture. It may be decorated with braiding, a tassel at the neck, or a decorated or buttoned collar; studs and cufflinks may be worn. In the winter, a *thob* of a heavier fabric in gray or light brown might be worn. The ultraconservatives insist that a *thob* must be worn short, above the ankles, but other men protest tailors' efforts to follow the ultraconservatives (al-Dahkil in Craze and Huband, eds., 2009, 198–199). An outer cape or mantle (*bisht*) might be worn for formal occasions. In the past, men wore *sirwal* (long pantaloons) and, until the 1940s, a body shirt, called a *shillahat* or *merodan*, which had long, pointed sleeves; over that an ankle-length robe or coat was worn, and on top of that, a jacket. Embroidered jackets (*kote, damir, furmaliyya*) are imported from Damascus and worn for special occasions like the dancing of the *ardha* (sword dance; Colyer Ross 1981, illustr. 42, 40–43). Previously, daggers, swords, and rifles were worn in belts and bandoliers, some of which were decorated with silver and semiprecious stones. Men also carried a stick and a leather bag (*mizuda*). In some tribes in the south and to the southwest men also wore a *fouta*, fabric wrapped around the waist and then brought back to the front between the legs to be tucked up in front, and a shirt. Some groups wore this under a *thawb* and wore the *fouta* alone, without a *thawb*, exclusively when in their own homes.

A man's headgear includes the *kufiyya* (skullcap), which is often white but sometimes in other colors and may be embroidered. Over that, the white *ghutra* (headcloth) or the *shmagh*, in a red-and-white checkered pattern, is worn. The *iqal* (head circlet) holds the cloth onto the head. A man may toss one or both of the side ends of the *ghutra* or *shmagh* back over his head. This headgear of Najd replaced the muslin or cotton turban worn in the Hijaz. In some rural areas, the turban is still worn (Ingham 1997, 40–53). The ultraconservatives prefer to wear a head covering without an *iqal*.

Practical Weaving

Bedouin women weavers made, and still make, the *khayma*, or *bayt sha'r* (tent), from the hair and wool of sheep and goats, and the tents belong to them. The *maghzal* or *mubrah* (spindle) is used to make the warp yarn, and the weft yarn is carded, made into ribbon, usually dyed, and then spun (Kay 1978; Colyer Ross 1981, 125–127; Alruways 1998). Their hand looms (*matarih*) were long and narrow, and they sat on the ground to weave *g(q)ummash* (material), using a *misha* (stick/shuttle) as a shuttle, then pressing it with a *natha* (a rod) and a *middrah* (pick) of gazelle horn. The back curtain is usually plain colored; the internal dividing curtains were woven with patterns particular to the tribe. They also wove handbags, camel bags, and rugs.

REFERENCES

Abbas, B., A. A. al-Qarawy, and A. al-Hawas. "The Ethnoveterinary Knowledge of Traditional Healers in Qassim Region, Saudi Arabia." *Journal of Arid Environments* 50 (2002), 367–379.

Abu-Rabia, Aref. "Urinary Diseases and Ethnobotany among Pastoral Nomads in the Middle East. *Journal of Ethnobiology and Ethnomedicine* 1, no. 4 (2005). http://www.ethnobiomed.com/content/1/1/4

Ahmad, Qanta. *In the Land of Invisible Women: A Female Doctor's Journey in the Saudi Kingdom.* Naperville, IL: Sourcebooks, 2008.

Alruways, Bader. "The Tent and Its Contents: A Study of the Traditional Arts of Weaving by the Otaiba Tribe in Saudi Arabia." PhD diss., University of North Texas, 1998.

Al-Ashban, R. M., M. Aslam, and A. H. Shah. "Kohl (Surma): A Toxic Traditional Eye Cosmetic Study in Saudi Arabia." *Public Health* 188, no. 4 (June 2004), 292–298.

al-Awamy, Dr. Baker H., Dr. Fakhry, and Department of Pediatrics, al-Muhawis Hospital, Dammam. "Evaluation of Commonly Used Tribal and Traditional Remedies in Saudi Arabia." *Saudi Medical Journal* 12, no. 22 (December 2001), 1065–1068.

Baeshen, Lamia. *Youssef et le palais des chagrins: Contes d'Arabie saoudite*. Translated by Kadria Awad. Paris: L'Harmattan, 2010. (Originally published as *al-Tabat wa al-Nabat* in 1997.)

Ba Ghaffar, Hind. *Al-aghani al-sha'biyya fi-l-Mamlaka al-'Arabiyyah al-Sa'udiyyah* [Folk songs in the Saudi Arabian Kingdom]. Jeddah, Saudi Arabia: Dar al-Qadsiyya li-l-tawzi' wa-l-nashr, 1994.

al-Bassam, Laila. "Traditional Costumes of Asir." *al-Ma'thurat al-sha'biyya* 67 (2003), 8–29.

al-Bedah, Abdullah M.N. "Kingdom of Saudi Arabia." In *World Health Organization Global Atlas of Traditional, Complementary and Alternative Medicine*, vol. 1, edited by G. Bodeker, C.K. Ong, C. Grundy, G. Burford, and K. Shein. Kobe, Japan: World Health Organization, 2005.

Bogary, Hamza. *Sheltered Quarter: A Tale of a Boyhood in Mecca*. Translated by O. Kenny and J. Reed. Austin: Center for Middle Eastern Studies, University of Texas, Austin, 1991.

Brockelman, C. "Mathal." In *First Encyclopaedia of Islam*, edited by Martijn Theodoor Houtsma. Leiden, the Netherlands: E.J. Brill and Luzac, 1913–1938, vol. 3, 407–410.

Bushnaq, Inea, ed. and trans. *Arab Folktales*. New York: Pantheon, 1986.

Campbell, Kay Hardy. "Folk Music and Dance in the Arabian Gulf and Saudi Arabia." In *Images of Enchantment*, edited by Sherifa Zuhur. Cairo: American University in Cairo Press, 1998, 57–70.

Campbell, Kay Hardy, producer. *Samra: Songs from Saudi Arabia*. Audiocassette, 1985.

Chatty, Dawn. *Nomadic Societies in the Middle East and North Africa: Entering the 21st Century*. Leiden, the Netherlands: Brill, 2006.

Colyer Ross, Heather. *The Art of Arabian Costume: A Saudi Arabian Profile*. Fribourg, Switzerland: Arabesque Commercial, 1981.

Cuddihy, Kathy. *Saudi Customs and Etiquette*. London: Stacey International, 2002.

al-Dakhil, Khalid. "Saudis Resist Efforts by Clerical 'Class' to Create Nation of Fashion Slaves." In *The Kingdom: Saudi Arabia and the Challenge of 21st Century*, edited by Joshua Craze and Mark Huband. New York: Columbia University Press, 2009.

Doughty, Charles M. *Arabia Deserta*. Vols. 1 and 2. Philip Lee Warner for Medici Society Limited; London and Boston: Jonathan Cape, 1921.

Doumato, Eleanor. *Getting God's Ear: Women, Islam and Healing in Saudi Arabia and the Gulf*. New York: Columbia University Press, 2000.

al-Fuhayd, Mandil. *Min adabina al-sha'biyya*. Riyadh, Saudi Arabia: Dar al-Yamamah li-l-bahth wa tarjumah wa nashr, 1978.

Al-Ghadeer, Moneera. *Desert Voices: Bedouin Women's Poetry in Saudi Arabia*. London: Tauris Academic Studies, 2009.

Al-Ghadeer, Moneera. "The Inappropriate Voice: Introducing Bedouin Women's Oral Poetry from the Arabian Peninsula." In *Nomadic Societies in the Middle East and North Africa: Entering the 21st Century*, edited by Dawn Chatty. Leiden, the Netherlands: Brill, 2006, 994–1012.

al-Ghamdi, Hayat. "Traditional Women [sic] Clothes on Display in Abha Summer Fest." *Arab.News.com*, July 30, 2010.

Ghazanfar, Shahina. *Handbook of Arabian Medicinal Plants*. London: CRC Press, 1994.

al-Hadhdhal, A. I. *Mukhtarat min al-shi'r al-nabati al-mu'asir*. Riyadh, Saudi Arabia: Matabi' al-shihri, 1392h.

Hardy, M.J.L. *Blood Feuds and the Payment of Blood Money in the Middle East*. Leiden, the Netherlands: E. J. Brill, 1963.

Hawling, G.R. "The Development of the Biography of al-Harith ibn Kalada and the Relationship between Medicine and Islam." In *The Islamic World, from Classical to Modern Times*, edited by C.E. Bosworth, Charles Issawi, Roger Savory, and A.L. Udovitch. Princeton, NJ: Darwin, 1989, 127–137.

Hilden, Joy Totah. *Bedouin Weaving of Saudi Arabia and Other Countries*. London: Arabian Publishing; Oakfield, CT: David Brown, 2010.

Holes, Clive. *Dialect, Culture and Society in Eastern Arabia: A Glossary*. Leiden, the Netherlands: Brill, 2001.

Ibn Khamis, A. *Min ahadith al-samar*. Riyadh, Saudi Arabia: Matabi' sharikat Hanifah lil-Ofset, 1978.

Ibn Khamis, A. *Rashid al-Khalawi*. Riyadh, Saudi Arabia: Dar al-Yamamah lil-bahth wa al-tarjuma wa al-nashr, 1972.

Ibn Khamis, A. *al-Adab al-sha'bi fi jazirat al-'arab*. Riyadh, Saudi Arabia: Matabi' al-Riyadh, 1958.

Ingham, Bruce. "Men's Dress in the Arabian Peninsula: Historical and Present Perspectives." In *Languages of Dress in the Middle East*, edited by Nancy Lindisfarne-Tapper and Bruce Ingham. Richmond, UK: Curzon, 1997.

Al-Jaraisy, Khaled, comp. and ed. *Selected Fatwas on Faith Healing and Witchcraft*. Translated by Mohammed Atif Mogahed Mohammed. Riyadh, Saudi Arabia: al-Jaraisy Establishment, 2001 (1422h.).

Jargy, Simon. "Sung Poetry in the Arabian Peninsula." In *Garland Encyclopedia of World Music*, edited by Virginia Danielson, Scott Marcus, and Dwight Reynolds. New York: Routledge, 2002, vol. 6, 663–669.

Jargy, Simon. "Sung Poetry in the Oral Tradition of the Gulf Region and the Arabian Peninsula." *Oral Tradition* 4, no. 1–2 (1989), 175–187.

Katakura, Motoko. *Bedouin Village*. Tokyo: University of Tokyo Press, 1977.

Kay, Shirley. *The Bedouin*. North Vancouver, BC, Canada: Douglas David and Charles, 1978.

Kurpershoek, P. Marcel. *Arabia of the Bedouins*. London: Al Saqi, 2001.

Kurpershoek, P. Marcel. *Oral Poetry and Narratives from Central Arabia*. Vol. 1. Leiden, the Netherlands: E.J. Brill, 1994.

Lebling, Robert W., Jr. "The Treasure of Tarthuth." *Saudi Aramco World*, March/April 2003.

Lebling, Robert W., and Donna Pepperdine. "Natural Remedies of Arabia." *Saudi Aramco World*, September/October 2006a.

Lebling, Robert W., and Donna Pepperdine. *Natural Remedies of Arabia*. London: Al-Turath/Stacey International, 2006b.

Long, David E. *Culture and Customs of Saudi Arabia*. Westport, CT: Greenwood, 2005.

Murad, Amnah. *Lamhat min tarikh al-tibb al-qadim*. Cairo: Maktabat al-Nasr al-Hadith, 1966, 1–32.

"Palms and Pomegranates: Traditional Dress of Saudi Arabia." Exhibit 1987–1989 that toured the United States in 1989 including display at the American Museum of Natural History in New York. Curated by Johara Alatas.

Palms and Pomegranates: Traditional Dress of Saudi Arabia. Exhibition catalog. Washington, DC: The U.S. Committee for Saudi Arabian Cultural Heritage, n.d. [ca. 1987].

Qureshi, Naseem Akhtar, Aladin Hadi al-Amri, Muzamil Hasan Abdelgadir, and Ahmed El-Haraka. "Traditional Cautery among Psychiatric Patients in Saudi Arabia." *Transcultural Psychiatry* 35, no. 1 (March 1998).

Rayyes, Fuad. "The Cream of Wisdom." *Saudi Aramco World* 20, no. 1 (January/February 1969).

Al-Said, Mansour Solyman. "Medicine in Islam." In *Encyclopedia of the History of Science, Technology, and Medicine in Non-Western Cultures*, edited by Helaine Selin. Dordrecht, the Netherlands: Kluwer Academic, 1997, 695–698.

al-Sa'ud, Norah bint Muhammad, al-Jawhara Muhammad al-'Anqari, and Madeha Muhammad al-'Atroush, eds. *Abha, Bilad Asir: Southwestern Region of the Kingdom of Saudi Arabia.* Riyadh, Saudi Arabia: By the editors, 1989.

al-Shatti, Ahmad. *al-'Arab wa al-tibb.* Damascus, Syria: Manshurat Wizarat al-Thaqafa, 1970.

Snouck Hurgronje, Christaan. *Mekka in the Latter Part of the Nineteenth Century, 1885–1889.* Translated by James Henry Monahan. Leiden, the Netherlands: Brill, 1931.

Sonbol, Amira. *The New Mamluks: Egyptian Society and Modern Feudalism.* Syracuse, NY: Syracuse University Press, 2000.

al-Sowayan, Sa'd al-'Abdullah. *al-Shi'r al-sha'bi fi al-mamlakah al-'arabiyyah al-sa'udiyyah.* Doha, Qatar: Arab Gulf States Folklore Center, 1985a.

Sowayan, Sa'd Abdullah. *Nabati Poetry: The Oral Poetry of Arabia.* Berkeley and Los Angeles: University of California Press, 1985b.

Sowayan, Sa'd Abdullah. "Tonight My Gun Is Loaded: Poetic Dueling in Arabia." *Oral Tradition* 4, no. 1–2 (1989), 151–173.

Stewart, Frank H. "Customary Law among the Bedouin of the Middle East and North Africa." In *Nomadic Societies in the Middle East and North Africa: Entering the 21st Century*, edited by Dawn Chatty. Leiden, the Netherlands: Brill, 2006, 239–279.

Topham, John. *Traditional Crafts of Saudi Arabia.* London: Stacey International, 1981.

Yamani, Mai. *Changed Identities: The Challenge of a New Generation in Saudi Arabia.* London: Royal Institute of International Affairs, 2000.

Zuhur, Sherifa. Personal interviews. Riyadh and Jeddah, 2005–2008.

Zuhur, Sherifa. *Gender, Sexuality and the Criminal Laws in the Middle East and North Africa: A Comparative Study.* Istanbul, Turkey: WWHR (Women for Women's Human Rights)-New Ways, 2005.

Architecture

Architecture encompasses every aspect of the built environment. To focus on what is quintessentially Muslim and Saudi Arabian glosses over shared features of Gulf-state traditions and Persian, Ottoman, and modern global architectural influences.

Premodern Saudi Arabia reflected the needs of the tribes, communities, and their environments. The tents of the nomadic community (see Popular Culture section in this chapter) could be disassembled and carried. They were divided according to the gender of the group, with the "male" or public side flapped up for visits. Each tribe had its own *dira* (pattern of travel) and its own grazing areas (see Chapter 4, Economy, section on agriculture), and those who were partially sedenterized also lived in homes near their farming areas. When loans became easily available, a building boom also took place, with a shift into new housing. This took place in cities as well, where the availability of funding, and some degree of peer example, led elite families to leave their older homes in cities like Jeddah, They moved into single-family villas set in gardens, very different from the historic homes (Altorki 1986, 29–30). People first settled al-Raghbah in Najd in 1668, moving from a disputed original site to al-Bilad al-Sufla, and from there to two neighborhoods, al-Hazm and al-Nab'a, in about 1695; then they moved to al-Jaw al-Zahiri until the construction boom. Two floods in 1979 and 1985 damaged homes, which encouraged all others to move to new homes. Thus, they left behind the old quarters that illustrate living styles of the past (al-Jeraisy 1999, 92–95).

Historians and architectural specialists sometimes speak about the Islamic nature of cities and towns, which, in addition to their relationship to production, impacted their building patterns and appearance. In the premodern era, villages and towns included public markets, mosques and other places of prayer, shopping areas (often organized by product), areas for any unclean work (tanneries), fountains or wells, and homes. Private, inner spaces differed from public-facing facades; often, in parts of Arabia, the lower floors had no windows for reasons of security. The use of the home oriented inward, and some included an area, or manger, for animals. Elite homes reflected the gender division with a salon for men and another family or female-only living space. In certain areas, such as Najd, due to battles between different groups, the older buildings date back to about the 18th or at the earliest the 17th century. Historical works describe the older settlements; in some cases their ruins lie nearby (as in Dir'iyyah or Raghbah) or were built over (Ministry of Education [ca. 2001]). Most of the older homes have been abandoned for new housing. The homes of middle- and lower-class residents were often built in adjoining fashion, with common walls, and there were narrow walkways in between blocks of homes. Depending on the area, some homes had roofed-over portions, as well as open-roofed sections, and might be multilevel. Families could incorporate new members when their sons married. In Mecca, large numbers of families used to rent out sections of their homes during the *hajj* season and retreated to alternate rooms. Throughout the peninsula common building material was mud brick, and in some places stones are incorporated into the architecture.

THE MOSQUE

The mosque was the first specifically Muslim structure; it may be called a *masjid* (place of bowing), a *musallah* (place of praying), or a *jami'*, a congregational mosque meant for Friday communal worship. The first mosque was established by the Prophet

Ruins of the city of Dir'iyyah, Saudi Arabia, site of the First Saudi Arabian state. (Saudi Aramco World/SAWDIA)

Muhammad leading his community in prayer at Medina. The Prophet ascended a stone platform to give his sermon (*khutbah*) and leaned, according to hadith, on a palm trunk. Since 750 CE, the *minbar*, a set of stairs leading to a short platform, are used for the *khutbah* and stand next to the *mihrab*, a niche in the *qiblah* (direction of prayer) wall facing Mecca. It is thought that the *mihrab* used to contain a hanging lantern, but today's are normally empty (Ettinghausen 1976). The *qiblah*, or directional orientation of prayer, originally faced Jerusalem but was altered to face Mecca in 629 CE. The *qiblah* was indicated by a spear thrust into the sand for those praying out in the open desert or with a piece of rock, as in the Prophet's house, which like other houses was made of mud brick. His house had a large courtyard surrounded by brick walls with a row of sheltered areas against two walls. Historians agree that the early mosques built in and outside of Arabia, in Iraq up to 650 or so, were based on the Prophet's house in Medina (Kuran 1995, 135).

The Islamic expansion moved into Mesopotamia, and the Basra and Kufa mosques, which had been based on this plan, were renovated in 665 and 670 CE, thereafter featuring a *haram* (prayer hall) and a *sahn* (court) with double rows of *riwaq*s (porticos) surrounding it. Large mosques in other areas of the Muslim empire incorporated the use of aisled *haram*s with supporting pillars and porticos surrounding a court. The mosques of Samarra, Abu Dulaf, and Ibn Tulun at Fustat were all surrounded by a *ziyadah* with walls. The *ziyadah* was an open space converted to a

Riyadh Mosque, Riyadh, Saudi Arabia. (Saudi Aramco World/SAWDIA)

prayer area when very large crowds attended (Kuran 1995, 136–137). A minaret from which the *mu'adhdhin* (muezzin) delivered the call to prayer was built; at Medina, the *mu'adhdhin* Bilal had simply climbed atop a wall. Minaret styles have developed in each geographic area. Another design feature incorporated as Muslim rule expanded was the use of mosaic tile as decoration, typically on interior walls or on exterior walls and even domes. All of these styles and features eventually moved back again to larger mosques built on the Arabian Peninsula.

The minarets of the old Imam Turki bin 'Abdullah (Grand Mosque) in Riyadh were a mix of Ottoman and Egyptian styles, with two rectangular sections topped by three rounded sections and a top section coming to a point with round shapes atop it; the courtyard porticos rose in a triangular point with decor above. The minarets were rebuilt in rectangular neo-Najdi shapes, the courtyard was completely resurfaced, and the porticos are now a modernized version of their former shape (High Commission for the Development of Arriyadh, Kingdom of Saudi Arabia al-Riyadh, 1424h., 9–10).

MARKETS

In the older cities of the Muslim world, markets (*suq* s. or *aswaq.* pl.) were located near large or important mosques. Women could shop in their own areas of larger markets (*suq al-harim*). The Haraj, or Auction market, was next to the Grand Mosque in the 1940s. It remains as a partially open discount market with booths roofed in red and white (High Commission for the Development of Arriyadh, Kingdom of Saudi Arabia, al-Riyadh 1424h., 7–8). Shops were housed in permanent buildings for heavier items or those requiring equipment. Vendors of clothing were grouped near each other, housewares in their own section, and so on. Malls and shopping centers have begun to displace older shops, although certain planned communities retain their shopping areas. Much of this new construction is cement-block, although some of the larger malls have attractive, modernist exteriors.

GENERAL FEATURES OF THE HIJAZ

The cities of the Hijaz feature multistoried traditional houses up to seven stories tall. Most houses are not more than 200 years old; the climate varies from the cooler areas in the highlands to the extreme heat of the valley where Mecca is located (the Batn), and houses deteriorate from the heat. Architecture in Jeddah and Mecca was influenced in some ways by the Ottomans and by the availability of wood imported from India. Elaborately carved doors and balconies from this wood can be seen on older buildings. Also typical is the use of *mashrabiyya* or *rushan* (also given as *rawshan*); these are carved screens put over the windows or balconies to maintain the privacy of women inside. The women's quarters were often in the upper stories of the houses; the *rushan* are located over these windows.

Mecca's jewel is the Masjid al-Haram, or Holy Mosque, which contains the Ka'ba, a tall rectangular structure in a courtyard at the center of the mosque. The Ka'ba is pre-Islamic in origin but was cleansed of its idols and reestablished as an object of pilgrimage after the conquest of Mecca in 628. The pilgrims walk around the Ka'ba in the *tawwaf* (circumambulation). The area around the Ka'ba was first enclosed by a wall in 638 to provide space for the *tawwaf*, and that area was enlarged in 646 when a new enclosure wall with arcades was built. The mosque was again enlarged in 684 under the rule of 'Abdullah ibn al-Zubayr and beautified with marble and mosaic decoration.

Caliph al-Walid covered the arcades of the mosque in 709 with a teak roof resting on marble columns. Caliph al-Mansur enlarged the mosque from 754 and 757, and its first minaret was built. In 1564, the Ottoman sultan Sulayman the Magnificent ordered rebuilding, and the flat roofs of the arcades were given stone domes, and the minarets were rebuilt. Further renovation took place under the al-Sa'ud; the mosque is now the largest in the world and has two-story arcades around a larger courtyard and seven minarets.

The well of Zamzam is also located here and had been covered with a roof in the ninth century. From the Ottoman period, this Maqam ("place or area of") Zamzam was used as a teaching area for jurisprudence, with each *madhhab* (legal school) possessing its own *maqam* in the courtyard. The Saudi Arabian renovation removed these areas to make more room for the growing number of pilgrims. Two underground rooms for ablutions performed prior to prayer were built and fed by the well of Zamzam. Another feature, the Maqam Ibrahim, was a building with a stone with footprints said to be those of Ibrahim (Abraham) the Prophet, and this was restored in the 1950s.

Mecca grew with pilgrim settlement; many built their homes on hills to avoid the seasonal floods. As there were no hotels and many made an income from providing lodging, food, or guide services to pilgrims, homes were built to accommodate families and visitors. The roofs were flat and, in the hottest season, could be used for sleeping. The architecture was influenced by the Ottoman era and also by the need for privacy. In traditional homes, a heavy and elaborate door in a brick-decorated facade led to the first-floor hall, or salon, which was reserved for men and visitors and had built-in benches for seating. Another room on this floor, a *maq'ad*, was for entertaining close friends. A winding enclosed staircase led upstairs; the upper floor was reserved for women and the men of that family and contained the bedrooms, bathrooms, kitchen, and an additional salon area. Additional areas and bedrooms might be roofed or not, and mosquito nets could be hung to cover those sleeping under the stars. The *rawshan*, or *mashrabiyya*, screens lent charm and status to the buildings (Bogary 1991, 57, 66–67; Uluengin and Uluengin 1993, 22–29). Today, contemporary housing has been built in much of Mecca and is, according to many Meccan natives, so expensive as to force them to move to the suburbs or live in Jeddah. For a view of the Grand Mosque, one pays triple the price, and many residences are used solely during the pilgrimage season. Special objections to this commercialization of the holy city have been expressed with respect to the Royal Mecca Clock Tower, a gigantic complex housing 800 hotel rooms, a mall, and prayer halls and topped by an Arabicized Big Ben (*New York Times*, November 29, 2010).

Medina is the second holy site in Islam. Located to the north of Mecca and about 110 miles from the Red Sea, the city is built on an ancient oasis. Here, the Prophet Muhammad's home and grave are located. The Prophet died in his wife's apartment, and he is buried just off the courtyard of his house, used as the first mosque. His sarcophagus is within a draped, and fenced, area, the Qubbat al-Nabi (Dome of the Prophet), within the enlarged Masjid al-Nabawi.

Medina is surrounded by walls, and nine gates permit access to and from the city. Travel from Mecca to Medina used to be undertaken by camel, and pilgrims might hire a *muzahhid*, who sang to inspire people to abandon their normal life and go to visit Medina (a practice later frowned on; Bogary 1991, 18–19). The original area of prayer was a rectangular space of about 98 by 114 feet, with mud walls reinforced with palm trunks and three entrances. In 629, the mosque was expanded. In 707, Caliph al-Walid ibn 'Abd al-Malik replaced the structure with a larger one about 276 by 330 feet, with a teak roof supported on stone columns. Mosaics decorated the walls. Caliph al-Mahdi enlarged the mosque further between the years 778 and 781 and added 20 doors. A dome was erected over the Prophet's tomb during the reign of the Mamluk sultan Qalawun, and a fountain was built outside the Bab al-Salam, one of the entrances. The surrounding mosque complex was expanded, rebuilt, and gained additional minarets of an Ottoman style under Qaitbay and Sulayman the Magnificent. Also, a new dome atop Muhammad's tomb was painted green. The Ikhwan were averse to tomb mosques in general, because they disapproved of Muslims'

Dome of the Prophet Muhammad's mosque in Medina. (Ali Jarekji/Reuters/Corbis)

visits and rituals there in pursuit of intercession by these holy figures; however, the Prophet's tomb is an exception. Under Sultan Abdulmejid's reign in the 1840s and 1850s, more expansion occurred; the mosque's domes were decorated with poetry, and calligraphic tiles were added to the *qiblah* wall. Further changes were made under King Faysal and King Fahd to a now-vast, air-conditioned structure with seven minarets, encircled with a wall (King 1986; Pierpaoli and Zuhur 2008).

Jeddah has a population of at least 2,110,000, which swells in the pilgrimage season and during Ramadan. Being built along the sea gives the city a unique character. Its Corniche, a boulevard along the sea, is full of hotels. The traditional architecture of Jeddah shares some similarities with that in Mecca, in its Ottoman influences. In the old city, limestone was used, and the balustrades of balconies, the decor, and *rawshan* are in white or light colors (Pesce 1976). As already noted, however, many people originally from Jeddah have moved out of these older areas, which are now owned or rented by more recent settlers from other areas in Saudi Arabia and by immigrants. A noted example of older architecture is the Aseef House; the *rawshan* and decor are darker wood, and the top of the house is an ornate square. Jeddah is also home to at least 40 skyscrapers, with others under construction. Some noted buildings include the National Commerce (Commercial) Bank, shaped like a giant isosceles triangle; the Islamic Development Bank; Abraj al-Farsi, the 30-floor mainly residential Farsi Towers; and several hotels, including the Westin, along the Corniche. The Jeddah Port Control Tower, completed in 1990, has a unique shape and an observation deck. It is lit at night, as is the King Fahd Fountain, the tallest in the world at 1,024 feet.

ASIR AND ABHA

Abha is located in the Asir Mountains of southwestern Saudi Arabia at about 7,300 feet above sea level. It has a population of more than 200,000 drawn from the Zamir, Qahtan, Asir, and Ghamid tribes. The traditional architecture of Abha and Bahah is built of stone and mud brick, which is painted in bright colors. Specialists come to paint the houses according to the taste of their residents, and the designs are bold, in brilliant colors, and geometric (Mauger 1996). The typical building type is a tall, multistory house, as in other parts of the western Arabian Peninsula. However, on the Tihamah Plateau, a conical type of hut (*usba*) used to be constructed out of reeds and fronds of the palm tree. Dwellings in Khaybar, in Charles Doughty's time were built with an upper room, *suffa*, whereas the area below was used as a stable with a palm ladder. Doughty was surprised by the black residents, the volcanic soil, and the houses and wrote, "Kheybar is as it were an African village in the Hejaz" (Doughty 1968, 227).

NAJD

In Najd, buildings were primarily made from mud brick, with tree trunks and palm fronds for roofs. Towers, turrets, and walls were built for fortification in the various wars carried out between the leading groups in the region. These wars and the shifts in allegiances to the al-Sa'ud and the *da'wah* of Muhammad ibn 'Abd al-Wahhab, and then the Ottoman incursion and next set of wars, changed settlement patterns as well. Parts of the al-Sa'ud family's buildings and guesthouse at Turayf at the Dir'iyyah oasis and some of the main oasis walls have been restored (Muhammad al-'became the ruler of Dir'iyyah in 1726). Life there was complicated by droughts and by conflicts within tribes, with the *ashraf*, and then with groups resisting the political and religious movement of Ibn 'Abd al-Wahhab and the al-Sa'ud rulers. Ibrahim Pasha's forces blockaded it for six months, and the town fell in 1818. The ruins show the skeletons of large and small dwellings, fortifying walls with narrow openings, and also large dwellings and a large walled bathhouse combined with a guesthouse for visitors (Ministry of Education 1419–1420h.; Facey 1997, 48–53). Most walls and roofs showed a unique triangular shape making a zig-zag design.

The storming of the Musmak fortress in Riyadh in 1902 was the symbolic beginning of 'Abd al-'Aziz al-Sa'ud's efforts to conquer and unite the country. Qasr (fortress) al-Musmak was built in 1895. It had a large wood door with a smaller door inside and is built around four small courtyards, with a watchtower at each end and a well inside one room. It is used as a museum, housing photographs, weapons, and historical information (Ministry of Education 1999).

Characteristic mud-brick shapes with small geometric designs are seen elsewhere in Najd. Raghbah had joined the *daʿwah* of Ibn ʿAbd al-Wahhab and withstood a siege in 1751 by enemies of the al-Saʿud. Al-Jeraisy's son supported ʿAbdullah ibn Saʿud. Therefore, the Ottomans destroyed al-Uqdat, the castle of Shaykh ʿAli al-Jeraisy. Its ruins have been studied and preserved. The castle was a square fortress with four rounded watchtowers (al-Jeraisy 1999, 42–43). In the middle of its courtyard was a well; a *diwan* (entertaining area) was at one end, and a mosque at the other (al-Jeraisy 1999, 121). Another interesting ruin is the al-Marqab Tower, a tall observation tower built in the 1840s of mud and bricks with stone tiles. Inside is a cylindrical staircase (al-Jeraisy 1999, 124–129). Mud-brick building required the digging of a shallow foundation and then partial construction of a stone foundation and walls (if the builder could afford it) and then atop it mud brick. Mud, straw, and water were used to form blocks; a chiseler evened out the walls and added more mud and straw to smooth them (al-Jeraisy 1999, 115).

This is quite similar to the building methods found in Nubia and the old American southwest, and it is promoted by the Egyptian architect Hassan Fahmy. The older

The Kenyan Embassy in Riyadh shows the architectural detail, especially on the roofline, of the Najd region. (Saudi Aramco World/SAWDIA)

homes have nearly all been abandoned; one, built by Yahya al-Hameedi, is divided into two sections, one for men and one for women, each with its own entrance and courtyard, and two staircases at each end of the house. There are no windows or openings in the first-level walls, but an elevation at the front of the house has three windows, each with wooden screens. The other house has windows on each wall of the lower floor and surrounds a courtyard. A loggia, held up with pillars, surrounds the courtyard. In addition to its use as a diwan, for sitting and entertaining, the roof could be used for sleeping at night in the hot weather (al-Jeraisy 1999, 106–113). These older homes contrast with typical two-story modern villas in Raghbah with a staircase at one end, sitting rooms, a kitchen, and a dining room on the ground floor and another hall and bedrooms on the first floor (al-Jeraisy 1999, 134–135).

At 'Udhaibat, another town that has undergone a complete shift in housing from the old to the new, a very elegant remodeling of an older farmhouse was undertaken by Prince Sultan ibn Salman al-Sa'ud. As elsewhere in Najd, the very thick walls help to keep the building cool. Traditional-style built-in seating and wood in the roofs have been used. With so many people moving into housing developments with little character, Prince Sultan ibn Salman hopes to encourage the preservation and appreciation of unique indigenous architecture (Facey 1997, 1999, 32–46).

At Ha'il to the north, stone was used as well as mud brick. In his approach to the city, Charles M. Doughty wrote, "We saw afterward some high buildings with battled towers. These well-built and stately Najd turrets of clay-brick are shaped like our lighthouses." Of the Amir Rashid's summer house, he wrote, "As we approached Hayil I saw that the walls extended backward, making of the town a vast enclosure of palms, closed by high walls. Now it appeared as it were suspended above the town, the whitened donjon of the Kasr,—such clay buildings they whiten with jiss" (Doughty 1968, 149–150).

Riyadh, the capital, has expanded in an amazing and startling fashion, not all of it beautiful. Efforts have been made to create aesthetically pleasing spaces, and in addition to many ordinary skyscrapers, the Faisaliyyah Tower, with its unique triangular shape, and the Kingdom Tower, constructed like a curving rectangle with a cutout circular shape at the upper floors, stand out. Official buildings such as the Ministry of the Interior and the design of the gate at the King Khalid International Airport at Riyadh are striking. Since the 1960s, roundabouts have been built as well as major thoroughfares, now quite crowded. Some more traditional shopping areas persist; the al-Migaybrah Market is today's al-Zal market, known as *al-mashaleh*, which sells carpets, *'ud*, and clothing. The al-Dokhnah Gate has been renovated but is now dwarfed by other architecture. The Diplomatic Quarter, primarily a residential area with greenery, has been built on an area that was barren prior to the 1980s. Land is quite expensive there; villas are built with walls, and the newer styles are multifloored with large reception areas. Security guards check automobiles entering certain areas.

EASTERN PROVINCE

The traditional architecture of the Eastern Province exhibits some Ottoman and Persian influence. Buildings may be built from coral brick, stone, mud brick, limestone, or other types of stone and wood and are plastered or stuccoed. A pointed arch was often used in the designs of buildings, and openings were constructed in the flat roofs that catch the breezes and carry them into the house, like a natural form of air-conditioning. These are called *barajil*. At one time, huts were built of palm fronds called *barasti*.

The Eastern Province is Saudi Aramco's base, and the originally American company has strongly influenced the built environment. The housing of Arab workers was far inferior to that for the American and Western workers, but the company sponsored land for its workers, giving rise to several waves of building. The eastern cities still provide services for traveling businessmen related to the petroleum industry and to their own. Today, the city of Khobar has at least 22 hotels, including high-rises, and many housing complexes. The city of Dammam has a popular Corniche along the sea featuring large-scale art installations and many clubs for sports and recreation on the way to Khobar. Half Moon Bay is a popular beach area to the south of Dammam with two amusement parks.

The construction boom in Saudi Arabia has provided many opportunities for those in engineering and architecture, as well investments in real estate. The changes in the built environment, whether in the cities or in the rural areas, are widespread. One may hope for preservation of and interest in the traditional architecture and that designs of the future will continue to reflect a sense of Saudi Arabia's unique culture.

REFERENCES

Altorki, Soraya. *Women in Saudi Arabia: Ideology and Behavior among the Elite*. New York: Columbia University Press, 1986.

Arab Urban Development Institute. *Riyadh: City of the Future*. Riyadh, Saudi Arabia: al-Ma'ahad al-'arabi li-inma al-mudun, 1984.

Ba-Ubaid, Ali Yeslam. "Environment, Ethics, and Design: An Inquiry into the Ethical Underpinnings for a Contemporary Muslim Environmentalism and Its Environmental Design Implications." PhD diss., University of Pennsylvania, 1999.

Bogary, Hamza. *The Sheltered Quarter: A Tale of a Boyhood in Mecca*. Translated by Olive Kenney and Jeremy Reed. Austin: Center for Middle Eastern Studies, University of Texas, 1991.

Doughty, Charles M. *Travels in Arabia Deserta*. Abridged by Edward Garnett. Gloucester, MA: Peter Smith, 1968. (Abridgement first published in 1931. Doughty originally wrote *Travels* in 1879, and it was published in 1888.)

al-Doussari, Mohammed Hasan. *Evolution of the Urban System in the Eastern Province of Saudi Arabia 1900–1970*. Al-Ahsa, Saudi Arabia: King Faisal University, 1999.

Ettinghausen, Richard. "The Man-Made Setting." In *Islam and the Arab World*, edited by Bernard Lewis. London: Thames and Hudson, 1976, 57–72.

Facey, William. "Al-'Udhaibat: Building on the Past." *Aramco World* 50, no. 3 (July/August 1999), 32–46.

Facey, William. *Back to Earth: Adobe Building in Saudi Arabia*. Riyadh, Saudi Arabia: Al Turath and St. Martin's, 1997.

Facey, William. *The Story of the Eastern Province of Saudi Arabia*. London: Stacey International, 1994.

Facey, William. *Riyadh: The Old City from Its Origins until the 1950s*. London: Immel, 1992.

Grabar, Oleg. "Art and Architecture." In *The Genius of Arab Civilization: Source of Renaissance*, edited by John Hayes. New York: New York University Press, 1992, 107–130.

al-Harbi, Abdullah. "The Impact of New Towns in Saudi Arabia: A Case Study of Yanbu." PhD diss., University of Lancaster, 1991.

al-Hathloul, Saleh Ali, and Narayanan Edadan. *Urban Development in Saudi Arabia*. Riyadh, Saudi Arabia: Dar al-Sahan, 1995.

Hattstein, Markus, and Peter Delius. *Islam kunst en architectuur*. Amsterdam: Könemann, 2006.

High Commission for the Development of Arriyadh, Kingdom of Saudi Arabia. *Al-Riyadh: Abq al-'Asala wa Rawnaq al-Hadith* [Riyadh: The Redolence of the Original (City) and the Beauty of the Modern]. Riyadh, Saudi Arabia: High Commission for the Development of al-Riyadh, 1424h. (2003).

Hillenbrand, Robert. "Traditional Architecture of the Arabian Peninsula." *Bulletin of the British Society of Middle Eastern Studies* 16, no. 2 (1989), 186–192.

Ismail, Muhammad Kamal, and Committee Members. *The Architecture of the Holy Mosque, Makkah*. London: Hazar, 1998.

Al-Jeraisy, Khaled Abd al-Rahman. *Raghbah*. Raghbah and Riyadh, Saudi Arabia: Khaled al-Jeraisy, 1420h. (1999/2000).

Kay, Shirley, and Darius Zandi. *Architectural Heritage of the Gulf*. Dubai, United Arab Emirates: Motivate, 1991.

King, Geoffrey. *The Traditional Architecture of Saudi Arabia*. London: I. B. Tauris, 1998.

King, Geoffrey. *The Historical Mosques of Saudi Arabia*. New York: Longman, 1986.

King, Geoffrey. "Some Notes on Mosques in Eastern and Western Saudi Arabia." *Bulletin of the School of Oriental and African Studies* 42, no. 2 (1980), 251–276.

King, Geoffrey. "Traditional Najdi Mosques." *Bulletin of the School of Oriental and African Studies* 41, no. 3 (1978), 464–498.

Kuran, Aftullah. "Mosque Architecture." In *Encyclopedia of the Modern Islamic World*, edited by John Esposito. New York: Oxford University, 1995, 135–140.

Mauger, Thierry. *Impressions of Arabia, Architecture and Frescoes of the Asir Region*. Paris: Flammarion-Pere Casto, 1996.

Ministry of Information and Deputy Ministry of Tourism, Kingdom of Saudi Arabia. Information posted in Dir'iyyah, the Al-Sa'ud's original capital. Some is circa 2001; other displays are older. Sighted and recorded, 2005.

Ministry of Education, Deputy Ministry of Antiquities and Museums, Kingdom of Saudi Arabia. *al-Musmak Museum Guide*. Riyadh: Deputy Ministry of Antiquities and Museums, Ministry of Education, Kingdom of Saudi Arabia, 1419h. (1999).

Ministry of Information and Deputy Ministry of Tourism, Kingdom of Saudi Arabia. *Hamam al-Turayf wa qasr al-dhiyafah*. Riyadh, 1419–1420h.

Mogassabi, Khalil S. "Modernity and Tradition in the Design of New Towns: Sadat City, Egypt and Yanbu, Saudi Arabia." Master's thesis, Massachusetts Institute of Technology, 1990.

Nawwab, Ni'mah Ismail. "The Suqs of Asir." *Saudi Aramco World* 49, no. 4 (1998), 2–9.

Nomachi, Ali Kazuyoshi, and Sayed Hossein Nasr. *Mecca, the Blessed, Medina, the Radiant: The Holiest Cities of Islam*. New York: Aperture, 1997.

Pampanini, Andrea H. *Cities from the Arabian Desert: The Building of Jubail and Yanbu in Saudi Arabia*. Westport, CT: Praeger, 1997.

Pesce, Angelo. *Jiddah—Portrait of an Arabian City*. Cambridge, UK: Falcon, 1976.

Pesce, Angelo, and Khalid Khidr. *Taif: The Summer Capital of Saudi Arabia*. Jeddah, Saudi Arabia: Immel, 1984.

Peters, Francis E. *The Hajj: The Muslim Pilgrimage to Mecca and the Holy Places*. Princeton, NJ: Princeton University Press, 1996.

Peters, Francis E. *Mecca: A Literary History of the Muslim Holy Land*. Princeton, NJ: Princeton University, Press, 1994.

Pierpaoli, Paul G., and Sherifa Zuhur. "Medina." In *Encyclopedia of the Arab-Israeli Wars*, edited by Spencer Tucker. Santa Barbara, CA: ABC-CLIO, 2008, 673.

al-Qarney, Mohsin ibn Farhan. *al-Qura al-taqlidiyya bi al-mantaqah al-janubiyah* (Traditional Villages in the Southern Region). King Saud University, 1414h.

al-Shayeb, Abdullah A. *Al-Jubail: Saudi Village (Architectural Survey)*. Doha, Qatar: Arab Gulf States Folklore Center, 1985.

Tarabulsi, Mohammed Yusuf (given Yusof). *Jeddah: A Story of a City*. Riyadh, Saudi Arabia: King Fahd National Library, 2006.

Uluengin, Bülent, and Nihal Uluengin. "Homes of Old Makkah." *Aramco World* 44, no. 4 (July/August 1993), 20–29.

Wheeler, Brannon. *Mecca and Eden: Ritual, Relics and Territory in Islam*. Chicago: University of Chicago Press, 2006.

Wolfe, Michael. *One Thousand Roads to Mecca: Ten Centuries of Travelers Writing about the Muslim Pilgrimage*. New York: Grove, 1997.

CHAPTER 7

Contemporary Issues

Many contemporary issues concern Saudi Arabia's ability to provide security and justice to a wider constituency (including women) while adapting to globalization. Contemporary issues are hotly debated within Saudi Arabia and are not extricable from the political interests of its ally, the United States, and the forces that nation confronts in the Middle East. At the same time, Saudi Arabia's national interests and concerns are quite distinct from those of the United States, which, in regard to Saudi Arabia, chiefly reflect concerns about the petroleum supply and securing stable political conditions to protect that vital interest.

DEFENSE

Saudi Arabia's defense sector is made up of the Royal Saudi Air Defense, Royal Saudi Navy, Royal Saudi Land Forces (RSLF), the Saudi Arabian National Guard (SANG), the Saudi Royal Guard, and the Emergency Forces, totaling 250,000 (some other sources give higher estimates of 260,000 and lower ones). That number could be slightly inflated and includes reserve and militia forces. The Ministry of Defense and Aviation (MODA), which is also responsible for all meteorological operations and civilian airports, commands these services, although SANG has been separate. For decades, it had been under the authority of King 'Abdullah, until November 2010. At that time, he stepped down and assigned the leadership of the SANG to his son Prince Mitab. The minister of defense and aviation was Crown Prince Sultan ibn 'Abd al-'Aziz, whose health was failing in 2010–11, and upon his death on October 22, 2011, a new defense minister will be named. The vice minister is his brother

Prince 'Abdulrahman. Sultan's eldest son, Khalid ibn Sultan, is assistant minister of defense for military affairs. Other al-Sa'ud princes are represented within the armed forces as well.

U.S. military advisory and training missions established a program in 1952 that was intended to create an army of three to five regiments over three years, but that goal was not achieved even after 10 years. Among the reasons were the shifts in Saudi Arabian foreign policy, which oriented the country first away from cooperation with the United States and then back again (as described in Chapter 2, History). Saudi Arabia gave special attention to building up its air forces because of the country's lack of road infrastructure and great distances. With regard to aircraft, up to 1958, Saudi Arabia received 9 Douglas B-26 Invader bombers, 10 Lockheed T-33A trainers plus some Beech A-45s, 6 C-123 Provider transports, and 12 F-86 Sabre fighter aircraft.

The Royal Saudi Land Forces, or Army, commanded 100,000 troops as of 2003 (Cordesman 2003a) and is now estimated at 150,000 troops (Center for Strategic and International Studies 2005); in contrast, Willbanks (2008, 894; 2010, 1075) gives a figure of 75,000. (For comparative purposes, Iran's Army was then estimated at 350,000, its Revolutionary Guard at 125,000, its Navy at 38,000, its Air Defense at 15,000, and its Air Force at 52,000, for a total force of 580,000. Iraq's Army was in the process of expanding to 375,000 troops, not all operational at the time these statistics were drawn up by *Military Balance*.) The Saudi Arabian Army has 4 armored brigades, 17 mechanized infantry brigades, 3 light motorized rifle brigades, 1 airborne brigade, and 5 independent artillery brigades and an aviation command. The main point of interest is that the Army has equipment for a force perhaps one and a half times its actual size.

Members of the Saudi Arabian National Guard (SANG) in 1980. (AP/Wide World Photos)

THE SAUDI ARABIAN NATIONAL GUARD (SANG)

The Saudi Arabia National Guard (SANG) is a regular, professional force of an estimated 125,000 troops. Unlike the National Guard in the United States, which has been considered a paramilitary ancillary force (until the manpower needs of the engagements in Iraq and Afghanistan), the SANG was sometimes said by foreign analysts to be even more effective, and possibly more loyal, to the al-Sa'ud than the regular army. One segment, an estimated 25,000 troops, is a militia. SANG is, however, like the U.S. National Guard in that it meets internal challenges to security, including counterterrorist campaigns, and it also proved itself in the Gulf War. The Ikhwan of King 'Abd al-'Aziz formed the basis of SANG, and its tribal structure and loyalties have been important. King 'Abdullah served as the commander of SANG from 1962 to 2010. Until 2005 (when he became king) he was also the crown prince. He reported directly to the king, rather than through the Ministry of Defense and Aviation. In 2010 King 'Abdullah handed over command of SANG to his son Prince Mitab ibn 'Abdullah (*Saudi News Agency* and *Washington Post*, November 17, 2010). National Guard military schools, regional training centers, the SANG Signal School, the Allied Health Science Military School, and the King Khalid Military College provide education and training functions for SANG. SANG was modernized and then expanded following the Gulf War and is now again undergoing modernization.

It possesses 1,055 main battle tanks (315 M-1A2s, 450 M-60A-3s, and 290 AMX-30s)—about half of these have been in storage—and 300 tank transporters. Information from 2007–2008 showed there were 1,000 tanks, 3,000 other armored vehicles, and 500 important artillery pieces, according to (Willbanks 2008; 2010, 1075). Not all the tanks were operational when reviewed due to conversion issues. Saudi Arabia has about 2,600 other armored vehicles; enough of these are of American make as to afford multioperationality. The RSLF is complemented by the SANG; and during the Gulf War, forces of 500,000 were stationed in Saudi Arabia. In much recent literature on the military, the underlying presumption is one of coalition readiness and that U.S. forces would presumably be involved in a defense of Saudi Arabia. This presumption underlies Cordesman's main critique of the Saudi Arabian armed forces: that they possess more equipment than they can reasonably deploy on their own. Their overarmament for their troops makes sense so long as the Saudi Arabian–American alliance is strong, but it has engendered strong critiques from the Islamist strand of opposition in the country from the Gulf War on. This obvious dependence on Western military support sparked Osama Bin Laden to argue that his forces should protect the land of the Two Holy Places (Saudi Arabia) rather than the foreign alliance that promotes political stances alien to Saudi Arabia's best interests.

SANG is a regular, professional force of more than 125,000 troops. The SANG is a mechanized infantry and a light infantry known for its mobility and rapid firepower, providing a balance to the more heavily armed RSLF. One segment, an

Royal Saudi Air Force troops pose in front of a Mirage F1 during Operation Desert Shield in 1990. (Department of Defense)

estimated 25,000 troops (in 2008) is a militia. As the Ikhwan of King 'Abd al-'Aziz formed the basis of SANG, the large numbers of tribal members with special loyalties to the al-Sa'ud have been important. King 'Abdullah served as the commander of SANG from 1962 to 2010 and reported directly to the king, rather than taking his direction through the MODA. His handoff of the SANG to his son is thought to be foresight. It was necessary in light of his increased responsibilities as king and due to his back problems in 2010. SANG's headquarters are in Riyadh, and it has two regional command centers, at Dammam and Jeddah.

The Saudi Royal Air Force has 11 wings stationed in different parts of the country, and one estimate is of 20,000 men organized into six wings (Willbanks 2010, 1076). Its most important aircraft are probably the Panavia Tornados and Boeing F-15 Eagles, and it should be receiving 72 Eurofighter Typhoons under an agreement with BAE (British Aerospace Systems). The Air Force performed well in the Gulf War, flying 6,582 sorties between January 17 and February 28, 1991 (Willbanks 2010, 1076). About 50,000 Saudi Arabian ground forces fought along with other Arab and national forces under Prince Khalid ibn Sultan's command during the Gulf War.

That war was a major cause of the next phase of expansion and modernization of the defense forces. With the end of Saddam Hussein's Iraq, Saudi Arabia considers Iran with its large armed forces a potential threat (and other than Iran, the Israeli Defense Forces would be the main strategic threat to Saudi Arabia). The revelation of U.S. diplomatic documents in November 2010 by Wikileaks showed that at least two strands of opinion existed, with the king and the ambassador to the United States arguing that the United States should strike Iran and the Saudi Foreign Ministry tending to call for caution and restraint with respect to Iran.

The Israeli Defense Forces are the most skilled and largest threat in the region and possess nuclear weapons. As well, if the new Iraqi government were ever to become hostile to Saudi Arabia, its newly constituted armed forces would far outnumber the Saudi Arabian services. However, Iran's forces are larger than either Iraq's or Saudi Arabia's.

The Saudi Navy consists of 15,500 men with 3,000 Marines. There is also a 7,500-man Coast Guard based at Azizam, whose primary function is to deter smuggling. The Navy's Gulf-based force at King 'Abdul 'Aziz Naval Base in Jubayl has the capacity to fight wars, but its Red Sea force does not, according to military sources. However, the Navy had not been part of joint war-fighting operations. Its equipment includes three al-Riyadh-class (modified La Fayette–class, F3000S) frigates armed with eight MBDA Exocet 40 Block II surface-to-surface missiles, launch systems for the Eurosam Aster 15 surface-to-air missiles, four torpedo tubes for the DNS 517 (heavyweight antisubmarine torpedo), and a single helicopter landing spot. It has four al-Madina-class (F-2000) frigates based on the Red Sea, armed with one 8-cell surface-to-air missile (SAM) and torpedo tubes. It also has four Badr-class missile corvettes (in the Gulf), nine al-Siddiq-class guided-missile craft, three Dammam-class (German Jaguar) torpedo boats, other fast craft and patrol craft, and three Sandown-class minehunter ships. The U.S. assessment of Saudi Arabian naval capacity mostly concerns scenarios of Iranian Navy attacks or other defense of oil facilities.

The King Khalid Military City was designed by the United States and financed by Saudi Arabia; it was the largest project ever undertaken by the U.S. Army Corps of Engineers. The base hosted U.S. and Coalition troops during Operation Desert Storm and Operation Desert Shield. Construction of this military base approximately two hours from the Kuwaiti border began in 1974. It can accommodate an army division of three brigades, approximately 65,000 persons, and includes some 3,398 family housing units. The city has its own airfield, which by itself cost some $700 million, and five mosques. The U.S. Military Training Mission was stationed at the King Khalid Military City from the late 1980s until 2005, when the mission was reduced. There are now fewer than 50 U.S. personnel there. The base was crucial to the war effort against Iraq; it was fired on by Iraqi scud missiles, but it was protected by Patriot missiles that surround the base. After 1995, most American equipment was moved from the base, and additional living quarters and a presidential complex were added (Pierpaoli in Tucker, ed., 2010; Bronson 2008).

In general, most critique of the defense services concerns their need for jointness (joint training with other services and other militaries) and peacetime. SANG, once the Ikhwan or White Army, was trained for many years by the Vinelli Corporation, and hence the attack on it, mentioned later, calls into question the continuing practice of Western firms hiring and training defense personnel. That practice, which is also the case in Iraq and Afghanistan, has become routinized, even as the United States withdrew most of its personnel from Saudi Arabia and has operated from Kuwait, Doha, Qatar, and Bahrain, where the U.S. Fifth Fleet has been stationed.

According to some other expert analyses of Saudi Arabia's strategic readiness, it may not possess sufficient defenses against attacks by air—its CSS-2 missiles are a deterrent of sorts but not a sufficient one against Iranian CBRNs. The United States is scheduled to commit to a major arms sale to Saudi Arabia under the philosophy that, given Iranian movement toward (what they believe is probable) offensive nuclear capability, bolstering Saudi Arabia's conventional weapons makes more sense than denying it those weapons and thereby encouraging nuclear proliferation in the region. The sale, yet to be approved at the time of writing by the U.S. Congress, would include 84 Boeing F-15 fighter jets and 72 UH-60 Black Hawk helicopters, as well as refurbishing of 70 Saudi Arabian F-15s (*Bloomberg*, October 24, 2010).

The Gulf War of 1991 was a turning point for Saudi Arabia's defense sector and foreign policy, and it sparked opposition to the country's alliance with Western forces (see Chapter 2, History). The RSLF, Air Force, and SANG all performed well, but it was fairly clear to observers that the Gulf Cooperation Council (GCC) forces could not have overcome the Iraqis, even if they fought together in a well-coordinated manner. How could they combat the much larger Iranian or the current Iraqi forces (should that nation oppose them for some reason)? Perhaps it is unnecessary to ask what might happen if they were drawn into conflict with Israeli forces, which are believed to be the strongest, if not the largest, in the region.

Continued alliances with Western militaries are likely for the foreseeable future. To foster this and advance the higher-level training and strategic understanding of the armed forces, the War College has been established, and a strategic studies institute is to be established within it along the lines of the specialized Strategic Studies Institute of the U.S. Army. Strategic studies has already been developed as a program within the Institute of Diplomatic Studies. Unfortunately, no women are involved in any of this, although they might well play an important role in the brainpower of the military. Some women are employed by the SANG and utilized at women-only events as guards.

The questions about Iran's nuclear capabilities, given the discovery of nuclear sites in that country, opened parallel queries about Saudi Arabia's air defenses, possible development of nuclear forces, and, most certainly, nuclear energy capabilities. In 2010, U.S. embassy cable correspondence was leaked to the world press; it showed that Saudi Arabia was unwilling to reopen its embassy in Iraq in 2008 but supported U.S. views that Iran was increasing its power in that country. The Saudi Arabian ambassador to the United States indicated in a meeting between Saudi Arabian and American officials, including General David Petraeus, that King 'Abdullah had urged the bombing of Iran to "cut off the head of the snake" (Cable U.S. Embassy in Riyadh, April 20, 2008). Further notes by the deputy chief of mission (DCM) at the cable U.S. embassy in Riyadh, Michael Gfoeller, who had then been in Riyadh for somewhat more than three years and had previously been posted in Iraq, alluded to frequent bellicose statements by certain royals. These were contrasted to Saudi Arabian Foreign Ministry representatives, who urged prudence, caution, and use of other means to discourage Iranian ambitions, just a few months after the "cut off the snake's head" incident (U.S. Embassy in Riyadh, July 22, 2008). A variety of Saudi Arabian views on the threat represented by Iran were obvious in the summer of 2008 (Zuhur 2008), but it is interesting that the more hawkish views were expressed by leadership in private high-level meetings.

Other matters that appeared in the leaked documents were Israeli officials' opposition to Saudi Arabia's receipt of F-15 aircraft and their own intentions regarding Iran (U.S. Embassy, Tel Aviv, November 18, 2009); however, Israeli opposition to Saudi Arabian military upgrading was no secret. More surprising were revelations that the United States and Yemen's foreign minister agreed to go on falsifying the American role in bombings in that country, where Saudi Arabia has also been involved in attacking the Houthi rebellion and, more recently, al-Qa'ida. Yemen was wracked by attacks by a separatist movement and six months of huge popular demonstrations against President Saleh, who, wounded, left the country in early June 2011. Saudi Arabia's military activity in Yemen will depend on its political restabilization. Since the fall of Saddam Hussein's government in Iraq, the greatest security threat in Saudi Arabia has been internal opposition—violent attacks by salafist militants. Although various sources claimed that this terrorist threat had been dealt with by 2006, the media continue to report attempted plots and incidents, including one as recently as late November 2010, when 149 were arrested, including 124 Saudi Arabian nationals alleged to be members of al-Qa'ida (*CNN.com*, November 26, 2010). Most of the focus on al-Qa'ida has moved to Yemen, where the organization was able to take over in Zinjibar, although the Yemeni forces continued to fight them. However, the organization is still believed to be active in Saudi Arabia as well. In addition, other groups who are part of the *sahwa* (islamic Awakening) are possibly a larger entity that might oppose very liberal reforms. Since the Arab Spring of 2011, the Saudi Arabian government has been concerned about opposition to its tenure from sources other than Islamic radicals as well, facing protests in the Eastern province.

ISLAMIST OPPOSITION AND TERRORISM

Saudi Arabian security and intelligence services have been confronting a violent opposition movement since 2003 and operating since about 2001. Many Western and some Middle Eastern sources treat this threat as al-Qa'ida's "third front" (Riedel and Saab 2008), but the operations of various cells appear to be independent of direction from al-Qa'ida in Pakistan and Afghanistan.. Its origins are a mixture of external and internal influences, including the following:

- The indirect effect of policies established in the wake of the 1979 takeover of the Grand Mosque in Mecca by Juhayman al-'Utaybi and his brother-in-law Muhammad ibn 'Abdullah al-Qahtani (Zuhur 2005b, 21–22; Trofimov 2007).
- Causes and stances raised by the internal *sahwa* (Islamic Awakening) movement, which emerged in 1992.
- Saudi Arabians who went to fight in Afghanistan, Bosnia, or Chechnya on behalf of Muslims and were trained by or had contact with Osama Bin Laden or the charity and movement of 'Abdullah 'Azzam, and the impact their experience had on their personal networks (Hegghammer 2010, 38–43, 45).

- Saudi Arabians who fought or were active in Iraq in militant Islamist groups fighting the Coalition forces, the new Iraqi army, and Shi'a organizations and civilians, although many of these were detained upon reentry into Saudi Arabia (Zuhur 2010b).

- Saudi Arabians and others who had no external militant training but were recruited within Saudi Arabia to engage in actions against Westerners, oil facilities, or the government.

- The deaths of senior conservative '*ulama* and imprisonment of the *Sahwa* preachers, leaving the ideological field open to the influence of the militant al-Shu'aybi network.

- Jihadists' revenge and despair over the brutality toward, torture, and murder of prisoners prior to 1999 (Hegghammer 2010, 76–77) and hardnosed police tactics in 2002 (by which time it was too late to eradicate the movement).

The 'Utaybi uprising of 1979 with its millenarian claims and direct challenge to the Grand Mosque in Mecca and the royal family (see Chapter 2, History) was quite different from the contemporary opposition movement. However, the government's response to that incident, in attempting to preempt conservative and Islamic objections, increasing funding for religious endeavors, and heightening support for threatened Muslims overseas (1979 was also the year of the Soviet invasion of Afghanistan), was significant. Some observers trace the enlarging ultraconservative population to this period and its policies (Yamani 2001, 2005).

Given the impact of 9/11 on scrutiny of Saudi Arabia's "Islamic" foreign policy and its links to the transnationalism of Islamic radicalism, extricating sound analysis from a muddle of prejudice is very difficult. In Chapter 3, Government and Politics, we summarized the evolution of Saudi Arabia's Islamic policies as a counterweight to the radical Arab nationalism operative in King Faysal's era. Islamized foreign policies have also been pursued at times by Pakistan, Malaysia, and Indonesia—and these need not automatically lead to global terrorism.

Events in the 1990s were also important. During the Gulf War, the *Sahwa* (Islamic awakening) preachers arose in Saudi Arabia. Safar al-Hawali and Salman al-'Awda argued strongly against the United States' penetration of Saudi Arabia and the regime's alliance with the United States, American support for Israel, and corruption and socioeconomic ills within Saudi Arabia (Hawali 1991; Fandy 1999, 61–133; International Crisis Group, September 21, 2004; Zuhur 2005b, 25–26). Audiocassettes of their sermons circulated through the country, as did those of preachers refuting or agreeing with them. Two groups called for reforms and publicly presented their demands to the Saudi Arabian government. One was mainly composed of progressive reformers calling for the consultative council (which was eventually created), women's rights, educational reform, and judicial independence; the second group in 1992 called for ending relations with Western powers, cessation of corruption, and a return to *shari'ah*. The second group was condemned; the *sahwa* clerics were imprisoned, and some members of the Islamic opposition fled the country (Zuhur 2005b, 26–27).

The *mujahidin* movement in Afghanistan attracted young Muslims from throughout the world, including Osama Bin Laden. The anti-Soviet movement was supported by various Muslim governments and aid societies. It was here that Bin Laden and his colleagues developed ideas about jihad, the need to resist anti-Muslim forces. And yet it was the Gulf War that proved a catalyst for Bin Laden's opposition to King Fahd's leadership in Saudi Arabia.

When the Saudi Arabians who participated in jihad in Afghanistan returned in 1992, they were interested in the *Sahwa* preachers' complaints and the salafist opposition, some of whom were being detained in prison. On November 11, 1994, Abdullah Hudayf threw sulfuric acid at the face of a Riyadh policeman. His father, brother, and friends were being held by the police; Hudayf believed they were being tortured. Hudayf was part of a network of extreme radicals who knew and admired the *Sahwa* preachers but were not closely connected to them. Hudayf was detained and apparently executed on August 11, 1995. The November 13, 1995, bombing attack outside the Vinelli Corporation (see the Timeline in Chapter 2) was carried out in response by three Afghan veterans and a fourth who was a friend of the Jordanian preacher Abu Muhammad al-Maqdisi (Hegghammer 2010, 71–72), Following this bombing, the Saudi Arabian government proceeded to arrest and interrogate large numbers of former jihadists who had gone to Afghanistan and Bosnia. After the 2006 Khobar bombing, unrelated to the preceding group, several more waves of arrests took place, along with torture and accusations by prison officials that the militants were "*takfir*ists"—that they denied the Muslim nature of their own rulers. These brutal tactics led to revenge operations (Hegghammer 2010, 75–76). In 1999, prison reforms took place, but the internal opposition movement grew.

Bin Laden's statements and actions garnered some sympathy in Saudi Arabia, particularly from the growing numbers of neosalafists. His reproaches to the Saudi Arabian government in 1995 mostly concerned the alliance with the West. He said, "Your kingdom is nothing but an American protectorate, and you are under Washington's heel" (Jacquard, ed., 2002, 174). He, stripped of his citizenship, had relocated to the Sudan and then again to Afghanistan. In 1994, Bin Laden was deeply disturbed by the arrests of Shaykh Salman al-Awdah and Shaykh Safar al-Hawali. He is reported to have said that he would not have raised his voice but for their arrests and silencing by the government (Bergen 2006, 149). His mother and other family members made numerous visits to Khartoum to request his return to Saudi Arabia to apologize to King Fahd, which he refused to do (Bergen 2006, 151–152), and the Saudi Arabian authorities again sent the same request to Kandahar (Bergen 2006, 239). By 1996, Bin Laden had started a network in Saudi Arabia, but it encountered many difficulties due to its visibility to authorities and the ongoing investigations of the Khobar bombings in that year, which had been carried out by a separate group, Hizballah. Some evidence suggests that Bin Laden imposed a moratorium on al-Qa'ida attacks in Saudi Arabia after an abortive effort in 1998. Saudi Arabian recruits continued moving to Afghanistan up to 2001. 'Abd al-Rahim al-Nashiri (a pseudonym used by 'Abdul-Rahim Husayn Muhammad 'Abdu, also known as Abu Bilal) was recruited in 1997 and organized the USS *Cole* attack and other operations until 2002, when he was captured. He was water-boarded at Guantanamo, subjected to a false execution, and forced to make various confessions, including that Bin Laden had a nuclear bomb. Al-Nashiri, however, did not organize the movement that was to erupt in Saudi Arabia.

During the late 1990s and early 2000s, the opposition movement (not in direct contact with Bin Laden) was galvanized by the Chechnya conflict, the Western antipathy to the Taliban, and the second Palestinian (al-Aqsa) *intifadhah*. Many unexplained bombings and attacks on Westerners occurred in these years, and bombings attributed to alcohol traders were all probably activities of the militant opposition (Hegghammer 2010, 81–83). Also, five *'ulama* of varying statures became more visible, issued increasing numbers of *fatawa*, and supported extreme positions (Hamid ibn Uqla al-Shu'aybi, Nasir al-Fahd al-Humayyin, 'Abd al-'Aziz al-Jarbu, 'Ali al-Khudayr, and Sulayman al-Ulwan).

In late 2002, Saudi Arabian police arrested about 100 people with alleged links to terrorism. The first gunfights broke out with police. The United States was pressing for action, and the security forces had discovered plots against the Prince Sultan Airbase and Ra's Tanura in the spring of 2002. The 'Uyayri network of al-Qa'ida in the Arabian Peninsula was by then avidly organizing, but the police arrested about 400 other people with terrorism links and certain religious scholars. The Saudi Arabian police realized that there was a threat of suicide operations in the kingdom by May 6, 2003, when they discovered explosives and the testimonies of "martyrs"; however,

Saudi Arabian police and seized weapons and ammunition captured at al-Rass on April 6, 2005 where a shoot-out between security forces and suspected militant extremists killed 14 of the extremists. (AP/Wide World Photos)

they lacked the security intelligence necessary to prevent the May 12 attacks by suicide bombers, who successfully launched three bombs (Zuhur 2005b). Al-Nashiri had been operating independently of Yusuf al-'Uyayri, known only as the Sabre (*battar*), and his recruits, who were mainly responsible for the growth of al-Qa'ida on the Arabian Peninsula (Hegghammer 2010, 171). 'Abd al-'Aziz al-Muqrin was a key recruiter, primarily from former Saudi Afghan fighters. The militants tried, through extensive Internet postings and publications, to make the organization look larger than it was. Numerous attacks against Westerners shook the expatriate community's confidence, and quite a number left Saudi Arabia after many years there. Perhaps most shocking to this community was the beheading of Paul Marshall Johnson Jr., an American helicopter engineer who worked for Lockheed Martin. He was kidnapped at a fake checkpoint on June 12, 2004, and beheaded several days later by an al-Qa'ida fi Jazirat al-'Arabiyyah cell.

Two networks in Riyadh and one in the Hijaz continued to mount attacks, but nearly all of the original leaders were killed off by 2006, when an attack on the Abqaiq oil facility failed. Probably, most significantly, Donald Rumsfeld, the U.S. defense secretary, announced that all U.S. forces would be exiting from Saudi Arabia except a small number attached to the U.S. Military Training Mission. Many Americans took this as a sign that Saudi Arabia was hostile to the United States or too unsafe to host its military personnel; this U.S. withdrawal met one of the terrorists' aims—decreasing Western presence but without increasing their influence. That was not the end of terrorist efforts, however. The Saudi Arabian government responded to the 9/11 Commission's report and took hundreds of legal, regulatory, and security actions to address to international and local terrorism, including establishing a Financial Intelligence Unit to combat the transfer of funds to terrorists (Cordesman 2003b). Terrorist actions and gun battles with security forces continued from 2003 until 2007 with frequency. Thereafter, many attempted incidents were not widely reported in the international media, but efforts to destabilize the regime continued. The government detained thousands of individuals in Saudi Arabia and tried 330 persons for terrorist crimes in 2009. About 991 suspected militants were charged for participation in terrorist attacks between 2004 and 2009, and more have been charged since.

A successful attack killed four French tourists at the Mada'in al-Saleh archaeological site on February 27, 2007. This attack was carried out by a cell based in Medina, whose members were then hunted down (Hegghammer 2010, 216). Security services foiled an attack involving seven cells at the end of April 2007, and some 172 persons were arrested (Associated Press, April 28, 2007). Then, a plot meant to take place during the *hajj* was interrupted at the end of 2007. Almost every year there were announcements that a plot had targeted the *hajj*, so it is difficult to know if this was a fact or part of the antiterrorism strategic communication campaign. More detentions and arrests took place in 2008 (Zuhur 2009b). Several key al-Qa'ida in the Arabian Peninsula operatives escaped, and a new coalition between the Saudi Arabian based al-Qa'ida fi Jazirat al-'Arabiyyah and two Yemeni jihadist organizations was announced in 2009—again under the name of al-Qa'ida fi Jazirat al-'Arabiyyah. On August 27, 2009, a suicide bomber and intended assassin, 'Abdullah Hassan al-Asiri, went to meet the deputy minister of the interior on the pretext of seeking amnesty.

He detonated his bomb, killing himself but only wounding Prince Muhammad, the deputy minister. Two terrorists and one policeman were killed and one terrorist was arrested in an incident at a checkpoint in Jazan on October 13, 2009. Saudi Arabia mounted aerial attacks on Yemen in early 2010, actually aimed at the Houthi rebellion, but these were justified as attacks on the al-Qa'ida operatives now active in Yemen. In October 2010 a warning was issued to Americans in Qasim, although this would most likely have involved a cell of militants unconnected to the al-Qa'ida in the Arabian Peninsula cells in Yemen.

The Saudi Arabian government has taken very seriously the issue of a broader militant salafist recruiting base utilizing particular religious ideas. It mounted a propaganda campaign against the movement in the press, depicting it as revolutionary and violent and showing its Muslim victims on billboards and in news photographs. The government also began the Sakinah campaign, an effort to counter the movement and its influence on the Internet, by monitoring transmissions and also arguing with the ideas of Ayman al-Zawahiri and other theorists of al-Qa'ida. Third, efforts were made to get prisoners who were guilty only of association with militant elements to recant. Saudi Arabian government officials acknowledged that political disaffection with U.S. policy in the region was a factor in recruitment of would-be jihad fighters. Nonetheless, the government's response and prison-based deradicalization program primarily address the religious justifications for violence or extremism. It has been using leaders formerly involved in violent opposition to appeal to possible recruits and to teach them moderation (*wasatiyya*) and encourage them relinquish extreme views as part of what is called a "reeducation" (counseling) process (Boucek 2009; Zuhur 2009a, 2010a). Those detainees who had not engaged in proven acts of violence, as well as others, were eligible to volunteer for this Counseling program established in 2004 (those who had engaged in violence could enroll, according to my sources, but would not be released). Also, a group of about 10 to 15 percent of these prisoners refused to participate or listen to the authorities leading the rehabilitation efforts (Zuhur 2010a).

A large group of religious specialists, psychiatrists, and counselors devised the program. It consisted of a review of each individual enrollee and then what could be called a deradicalization course of study. Different subjects were addressed, such as the improper rationale for jihad, that is, following an illicit Muslim authority instead of one allowed to lead the jihad; the wrong use of *takfir*, infidelizing fellow Muslims who do not meet the salafists' religious standards; the need for moderation in religion; and relations between Muslims and Peoples of the Book (Jews and Christians; Ansary 2008, Boucek 2008; Zuhur 2009a, 2010a). The program issued carefully positive media statements, and journalists were permitted to see the facilities, among the seven new prisons built in Saudi Arabia, and meet with the Ministry of the Interior's spokespersons. A similar program was established in the formerly American-run prisons in Iraq, and more than 21 Islamist-generated books of recantation or "self-correction" issued by incarcerated Egyptian and Libyan militants mirror some of the same ideological principles (Zuhur 2010a). It is not clear the original branch of al-Qa'ida fi Jazirat al-'Arabiyyah (the branch in Saudi Arabia, as opposed to the 2009 consortium of Yemeni and Saudi Arabian organizations formed in Yemen) has been fully defeated, because every few months there are reports of new arrests. In late November 2010, the spokesman of the Ministry of the Interior, General Mansour al-Turki, said that the 149 persons arrested (Saudi Arabians as well as Egyptians and other Arabs) were al-Qa'ida members who planned to kill government officials, security forces, and media employees; that they had been part of 19 different cells; and that 2.24 million riyals (about $600,000) had been seized (*CNN.com*, November 26, 2010). Saudi Arabia has previously hinted at the involvement of Yemen and Somalia as training grounds for al-Qa'ida, but it appears more likely that recruitment and training had been going on within Saudi Arabia, with foreigners traveling into the country. Shifting the media and policy focus on al-Qa'ida to Yemen was somewhat natural because the levels of violence there have risen (particularly in May and June 2011). In January 2011 the Saudi Arabian government acknowledged the fluidity of the terrorist networks and had identified and given information and photographs to Interpol about 47 Saudi Arabians operating abroad who were "part of the deviant ideology," dangerous, and likely to form activist cells (*Mail Online*, January 13, 2011).

The larger dilemma for the Saudi Arabian government is that resistance from its Islamist-oriented opposition is likely to arise again in the future from within the country even if al-Qa'ida is contained via a combination of security measures, truces, and deprivation of operating space. To the degree that the reform agenda of King 'Abdullah is successful, resistance could continue to arise from both the salafist opposition and conservatives.

Many critics of Saudi Arabia charged it with either direct or indirect funding to al-Qa'ida, the mother organization that had surrounded Osama Bin Laden and similarly extremist groups, but many Saudi Arabians strongly disagree. At issue is the role of funding for religious materials, propagation of Islam (*da'wah*), and activities by charitable institutions. To Muslims, this is a completely valid form of *zakat*, one of the requirements of all Muslims. But critics charged that the funding for *salafi*, or radical preachers, or those with a connection to Saudi Arabia, and those who teach Qur'an memorization in the United States, Asia, Europe and elsewhere tended to increase support for Wahhabism, and salafism, and thus for extremism. In 1985 alone, funding for such persons in the United States amounted to 2,477,000 Saudi riyals, and in 1983 worldwide support was 25,655,000 SR (AbuKhalil 2004, 142–143). AbuKhalil is not convinced that those in the Wahhabiyya can be moderate (AngryArab.blogspot.com). Nor are many other Saudi-phobic and Islamophobic forces (AbuKhalil is not of this latter group, and he opposes the rulers, not the Saudi Araiban populace) in the United States which forced the closure of several Islamic educational endeavors in the United States, charging that they had terrorist Saudi Arabian links. The Saudi Arabian rulers can hardly separate themselves from the beliefs of their esteemed teacher, Muhammad ibn 'Abd al-Wahhab, and are instead allowing a certain amount of external publication that is either critical of extremism in his thought or suggests he has been misinterpreted. Supporters of the Saudi Arabian rulers point to the fact that King 'Abdullah launched a major effort to condemn militant preaching and reeducate preachers and that a major social discussion has been carried out about the dangers of militance. It is safe to predict that Wahhabist thought will remain important in the large community of Islamic studies in Saudi Arabia, which had passed on and amplified its core puritanism, and that the government must continue to address the root causes of politicized opposition.

HEALTH

Public health in Saudi Arabia has improved vastly since the first half of the 20th century due to increases in income, inoculations, better water supplies, dissemination of health-related information, and the availability of clinics, hospitals and medical personnel. Spending on health care is relatively high in comparison to other countries. According to United Nations (UN) statistics ("Prospects 2010"), Saudi Arabia ranks 86th in the world (among countries with populations over 100,000) for life expectancy, which is at 72.8 years (70.9 years for males and 75.3 years for females). This compares with the average life expectancy in the United Kingdom, ranked 22nd at 79.4 years, and in the United States, ranked 38th at 78.2 years. These figures are lower than those provided in the *CIA World Factbook* (2010) statistics, which show Saudi Arabia ranked 69th in the world with an average life expectancy of 76.3 years (74.23 years for males and 78.28 years for females).

Some particular problems come from traditions and cultural practices, aspects of traditional or modern lifestyles, and women's subordinate status. Others arise from a health-care situation in which many non–Saudi Arabians are cycled in and out of the

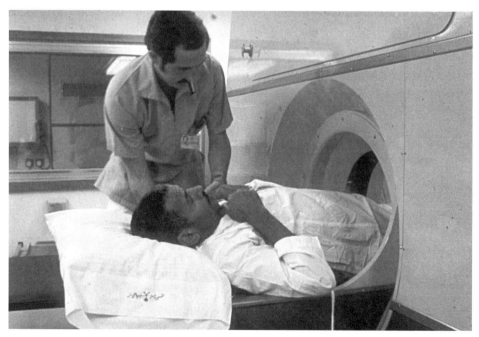

Medical technician adjusts a patient's position in an MRI scanner at the King Faisal Specialist Hospital in Riyadh. (Saudi Aramco World/SAWDIA)

nursing and physician pool, while Saudi Arabians have been reluctant to enter nursing in particular because of its low status and because of accusations of an immoral atmosphere, as women and men must work together. Despite this, some dynamic Saudi Arabian women have promoted nursing, specialist training, and master's-level nursing programs and are determined to improve the profession (El-Sanabary 1996, 71–83; Personal Interviews, 2005).

Resorting to traditional medicine when modern medicine could provide relief is an issue dependent on intervention and education. Some of the traditional methods include herbal treatments, cupping, cautery, and Islamic medicine (see Popular Culture). Public health personnel and journalists only began to mention female circumcision in the country in about 2006. A serious study was discounted because the population it studied included African immigrants and others impacted by a different, more severe form of female genital mutilation (FGM) (FGM is now classified into types I, II, and III; certain African countries practice type III (sometimes called "Pharaonic") FGM with removal of the outer labia as well as the clitoris and infibulation) and not the "*sunnah*" version of FGM inflicted on little girls by physicians as well as parents or grandparents in Saudi Arabia. In this form, the clitoris is fully

---

NURSING IN SAUDI ARABIA

Nursing is not yet a fully respected profession for women in Saudi Arabia, because doctors and nurses work with the opposite sex. A pioneer for female education and health facilities and inoculations for women and children was Lutfiyya al-Khateeb, dubbed Saudi Arabia's Florence Nightingale, who earned her nursing diploma in 1941 in Cairo (El-Sanabary in Sabbagh, ed., 1996). Large numbers of nurses have been expatriates working on contract; however, Saudi Arabian nurses have grown from 9 percent of the nursing workforce in 1996 to 18 percent in 2003. A regulatory Nursing Board was established in 2002. By this time, nurses could obtain a three-year diploma of nursing or a five-year bachelor of science in nursing. The first class of 12 nurses with bachelors of science graduated from the College of Nursing and Allied Health Sciences at King 'Abd al-'Aziz Medical City in 2004. By then, an advanced diploma and several diplomas of specialization were available (Rosser et al. 2006). International bridging groups have been created between Western and Saudi Arabian professional nurses. In 2009, an international symposium on nursing was held at King Faisal Specialist Hospital and a conference at the College of Nursing at al-Hasa, where Dr. Elham Al Ateeq, who obtained a doctorate in nursing, is associate dean.

Sources: Miller-Rosser, Kolleen, Chapman, Ysanne and Francis, Karen. "Historical, Cultural, and Contemporary Influences on the Status of Women in Nursing in Saudi Arabia." *Online Journal of Issues in Nursing* 11, no. 3 (2006); El-Sanabary, Najat. "Women and the Nursing Profession in Saudi Arabia." In *Arab Women: Between Defiance and Restraint*, edited by Suha Sabbagh. New York: Olive Branch, 1996, 71–83.

or partially removed. It cannot be accurately claimed to be "*sunnah*" because the Prophet Muhammad prescribed circumcision for men, not women, although he was aware that it was practiced on females during his lifetime. Sexual satisfaction of women is considered important in Islam, and the procedure can interfere with that; it is primarily practiced due to a belief that it will inhibit sexual desire. Hopefully, this stage of denial (even some physicians claim there is nothing wrong with lesser forms of FGM) will abate so that families can be educated about the negative impact of all forms of the practice. (Zuhur 2009b; Akeel 2005).

The cultural preference for endogamy, particularly cousin marriage, has put Saudi Arabians at risk for various genetic-linked disorders, such as sickle-cell disorder, hemoglobin deficiencies, and other problems, such as a higher rate of congenital heart failure (El Mouzan et al. 2008). Some medical research appears to address the issue defensively, asserting lesser risks for consanguinity than is claimed in Western research, but hopefully neutral and objective scientific research on such issues will continue. Some suggestions have included counseling for couples as well as genetic testing.

Maternal mortality and medical problems because of childbearing by teenagers have been problematic in the past, as in other developing countries. Cultural pressure to bear children, easy divorce for men, and polygamy have separately and together subjected women to great stress, complicated by divorce, life as or with a second wife, and accompanying depression and insecurity. Interest in medically assisted fertility procedures is also high.

A fairly high percentage of children are malnourished: About 14 percent of children under age five are underweight, 20 percent are stunted, and 11 percent suffer acute malnourishment. The causes are neglect, poverty, lack of dietary information, and insecure circumstances due to a parent's remarriage or relocation for children. At the same time, more Saudi Arabians are becoming obese, about 25 percent of women and 15 percent of men (Ministry of Health 2006). Obesity is considered a lifestyle and dietary issue. It is not helpful that women cannot walk or exercise outside of fee-based clubs (to which they must be driven). Also, smoking of cigarettes is extremely prevalent, and most people do not recognize the connection to cancer and risk for strokes or heart attacks.

The belief that families must care for their own ill members, elderly, or mentally or psychologically challenged can lead to abuse or neglect and to improper treatment due to lack of skills, resources or training, or home health care. On the other hand, it is more affordable to hire nonspecialist home care than in the West, allowing more people to remain in their homes and alleviating the pressures on family caregivers.

It is my understanding that relatively few clinics providing physical rehabilitation services existed as of 2006, at least in the western part of the country. These are needed due to stress injuries, automobile accidents, and other problems. Automobile accidents are a major cause of injury and death (Ahmad 2008). The high incidence can be reduced only by increasing penalties on poor drivers. Alcohol poisoning and drug use are other difficult issues to address in Saudi Arabia; the heavy penalties are not sufficient to deter everyone from illegal pursuits, as is usually claimed (al-Menaa 1995). Finally, AIDS, HIV, and pandemic diseases pose threats to the population.

The Saudi Arabian government took measures to contain the H1N1 version of the flu, which hit many of the pilgrims in 2009.

Some health threats exist due to cultural factors. For instance, breast cancer, as in other developing countries, is often discovered by medical personnel at too advanced a stage to help women. Princess Reema Bandar ibn Sultan has led a breast cancer awareness initiative called the Zahra Breast Cancer Association, providing education about the disease and support to those afflicted by it. According to her, 10,513 cases of all types of cancer were reported to the Saudi Cancer Registry in 2005. Of these, 948 were breast cancer. Other important health problems arise from consanguinity. Couples can receive counseling, but abortion is not an option in Saudi Arabia; strong cultural pressure to marry endogamously still exists, and, until that changes, risk factors will remain high.

Medicine is an important area for women's employment. Yet there is a strong cultural bias against working in medicine whether as physicians or as nurses (nursing is less prestigious and less respected). This is due to the cultural, religious, and social restrictions on mixing of men and women in the workplace or anywhere else. In other Muslim countries, women educators and medical practitioners have been at the forefront of social transformation. Working with men has become a norm; they have proven their abilities, and they have been accepted by the public in these fields. In Saudi Arabia, the continued pressures for sex segregation cause the women who work in a mixed environment to be regarded with suspicion.

HEALTH INDICATORS

Saudi Arabia's health-care system is among the government sectors that had to be created from scratch. Whereas many foreign physicians were, and continue to be, hired to work in Saudi Arabia, the numbers of Saudi Arabian physicians have increased.

Provision	Number
Hospitals	386
Beds	54,724
Doctors	40,183
Dentists	5,406
Pharmacists	8,546
Nurses	83,868
Assistant health personnel	49,139

Source: Healthcare Provision Statistics, Ministry of Health, Kingdom of Saudi Arabia, 2006 (SAMIRAD, 2010).

WOMEN AND SOCIAL TRANSFORMATION

Women and the degree to which their lives should change, particularly with regard to their political rights and driving, are the subject of many contemporary media articles and letters to the editor in the Saudi Arabian press. To some degree, the social turmoil over women's status is an acceptable debate, whereas strongly worded political criticisms were not, at least prior to the Arab revolutions of 2011. A good deal of information has been given about these issues already (see the section on women and marriage in Chapter 5); however, the degree of women's activism may have been understated, as well as the nuances of various debates about gender relations and the way that employment and economic concerns fit into them. For instance, large numbers of foreign workers are a feature of life in all Gulf countries today, not only in Saudi Arabia. Altering this trend requires job creation for Saudi Arabian nationals, but some believe this means job creation for men. Conservatives and neosalafists want women to remain at home or operate in completely segregated work circumstances. Various trends in the population are also critical of the large role played by domestic servants in childrearing.

Also, the divorce rate is climbing in Saudi Arabia, and, in some instances, divorced women find themselves in quite difficult and trying economic circumstances since there are so many unemployed female college graduates. This describes middle-class women, but at the bottom end of the scale, large numbers of children are seen begging in the streets, and their mothers often accompany them. These women are quite often divorced or without resources, as second wives who have been replaced by a younger woman (*Gulf News*, April 6, 2007). Thus, poverty, debates over women's visibility and role in society, the rise in women's educational levels, immigration, family law, and Saudization are not separate issues but a set of interacting circumstances.

The summarized history of Saudi Arabia presented in this volume is, due to the exclusion of women from political power, a very male-dominated history (as in the United States prior to the 1970s). If a female history of Saudi Arabia develops, it will probably begin with an elite closely connected to powerful men. Princess Iffat's name already arose in connection with the promotion of female education, and she was a powerful figure in that endeavor. Nora bint 'Abdulrahman al-Sa'ud (1875–1950), the sister of King 'Abd al-'Aziz, who was known to be a great supporter of her brother, and he sought her advice on numerous occasions. She was known as a poet, a charismatic personality, and a supporter of progress. There is only space to list a few women of the al-Sa'ud family and other elite women involved in philanthropy: Princess Hussah, wife of King 'Abdullah, was the founder and chief benefactor of the National Charitable Institute for Home Health Care; Princess Moodi bint 'Abd al-'Aziz was long involved in projects for women, including arts preservation; Princess Loulwa bint Faysal ibn 'Abd al-'Aziz was involved in directing the Dar al-Hanan school and the Effat College projects, supporting Kuwaiti families in the Gulf War School, and supporting the al-Nahda Philanthropic Society; Princess Nouf bint Sultan was a benefactress of the Prince Sultan University; Princess Amira al-Taweel, wife of Prince Walid ibn Talal, is vice chairperson of the al-Walid ibn Talal Foundation (Arabian.Business.com, November 1, 2010); and Princess Nouf bint Bandar

Saudi Arabian women visit an art exhibition of seven Saudi Arabian women artists at the French Embassy in Riyadh in 2008. (AP/Wide World Photos)

al-Saʻud is a physician and artist who recently promoted an art exhibition for 25 Saudi Arabian women artists.

Some Saudi Arabian women are more outspoken than others in calling for change. Certain clerics continue to lambast those women who allow their photographs to appear in the newspaper—these include women with considerable achievements in the country as well as activists. It is true that a considerable conservative male and female audience does not want anything resembling Western feminism to influence their society. Meanwhile, those in favor of social transformation resort to a discourse of universal rights.

Princess Sarah bint Talal ibn ʻAbd al-ʻAziz has called for women's rights in business and education and also for equality in divorce and politics. Saudi Arabian women have been able to attain positions outside of their homeland but not within it. Dr. Thoraya Ahmad has been the executive director of the United Nations Population Fund (UNFPA), but Saudi Arabia is represented by men at UN meetings, including the 2010-established UN Board on Women, and in all ministries except for one deputy minister. Women's calls for rights typically invoke their claim to equality under *shariʻah*); they do not reject *shariʻah* but rather suggest it has been misinterpreted in the present circumstances.

Ahmad and many other women I was able to interview pointed out that Saudi Arabian women should not be stereotyped. Yet in every conversation about women, someone will state that Saudi Arabian women should not emulate other Arab women or proceed to modernize at the same pace, as they are unique. This *khususiyya*, or cultural specificity, provides constant excuses for failure to change and reform, according to the folklorist Sowayan (Sowayan in Craze and Huband, eds., 2009). In 2009, Wajiha al-Huwaidar and other women began a campaign against men's legal guardianship of women in *shari'ah*, using the Internet to their advantage. Al-Huwaidar also posted a video of herself driving in 2008 to protest the continuing ban on women's driving. Another Saudi Arabian woman decided to do this in 2011, and by then the authorities were much more nervous about the wildfire effect of YouTube-mounted videos on the Internet and arrested her. People have been commenting on or protesting women's inability to drive in editorials and through letters to the editor in the press for the last decade.

MEDIA, FREEDOM OF SPEECH, AND CENSORSHIP

Some of the most stringent critiques of Saudi Arabia have come from neoconservatives and Islamophobes in the United States since September 11, 2001. Other stinging indictments come from anti–Saudi Arabian or anti-Wahhabi voices in or of the Arab world. Some credible arguments are made concerning human rights and tight control over the media, even though the critics speak from a history of Saudi Arabia's suppression of various forces. In recent years, some new challenges have arisen to the large number of Saudi Arabian media instruments, chiefly from *al-Jazeera*, based in Qatar, and from *al-Manar*, Hizbullah's outlet in Lebanon. Typically, the Saudi Arabian media or others fire back, as when Muhammad Hassenein Heikal, journalist and confidante to President Gamal Abd al-Nasser, challenged Saudi Arabia's narrative of regional politics in a retrospective entitled "Ma'a Heikal" in *al-Jazeera*. *Al-Arabiyya*, a Saudi Arabian television and news outlet, then launched a series called "al-Sayyid al-'Arabi." Heikal then gave interviews critical of (Ambassador to the United States) Prince Bandar ibn Sultan's policies vis-à-vis Iran and the lightweight efforts to heal the Arab-Israeli conflict. Turki al-Sudayri, the editor of *al-Riyadh*, retorted that Heikal was nothing but a hired pen of a hired pen. Other attacks came from Mamoun Fandy, an Egyptian critic of Saudi Arabia turned supporter, and Lebanese journalist Samir Atallah, in the newspaper *al-Sharq al-Awsat* (Hammond 2007). What was at stake was a particular version of history, something the Saudi Arabian government considers crucial to influence. Whereas Lebanon and Egypt are far from having perfectly free intellectual environments, it is difficult to see how Saudi Arabia can develop freedom of speech without allowing for at least an equivalent amount of discord and divergence.

The political atmosphere has shaped information. Andrew Hammond explains that in the wake of the Gulf War, the Middle East Broadcasting Corporation (MBC) was set up by Walid al-Ibrahim, a brother-in-law of King Fahd. Also, when Prince Khalid ibn Sultan, the former commander in the Gulf War, retreated into life as a businessman, he gained control over the London-based newspaper *al-Hayat*, the largest Arabic daily. Meanwhile, the sons of Prince Salman, governor of Riyadh, took over *al-Sharq al-Awsat*, previously *al-Hayat*'s competition.

Saudi Arabian control of television, entertainment, and news proceeded as well. Orbit TV was set up in 1994, and ART (the Arab Radio and Television network) was

Producers and technicians oversee the broadcast of "Good Morning Saudi Arabia," a television show hosted by Wafà Younis at Riyadh Television. (Saudi Aramco World/SAWDIA)

established by Prince al-Walid ibn Talal and Saleh Kamel in 1994 as well (Hammond 2007). MBC, Orbit, and ART broadcast entertainment—mainly soap operas (*musalsilat*), Western movies, and talk show formats—throughout the Arab world. These formats have increased with satellite expansion in Saudi Arabia and subscriptions by Arab viewers in the West, leaving most television devoid of any serious political content but for an hour here or there on cable networks and satellite television from other Arab countries. Hammond's point is that the Saudization of television (and the media), which incorporated a lot of "soft" entertainment rather than sharp debate or news, had pacified the public (with bread and circuses rather than calls to mobilize à la Nasser (Hammond 2007).

As of the spring of 2011, this situation has changed again. The Arabic news channels remain dominated by Saudi Arabia and Egypt (and to some degree Lebanon). *Al-Jazeera* proved a powerful counterweight to official denial of the ongoing revolutions in Tunisia and Egypt on the other channels and news sources. It continued its coverage as protests moved to Yemen, Libya, Bahrain, Syria, and even Saudi Arabia, opening up the prospect of swift political change to the Arab mass public. The only strategy that could be employed in Saudi Arabia was to block some transmissions and limit its citizens' access to Facebook.

Telecommunications in Saudi Arabia and official monitoring and filtering of the Internet manage to block many types of transmissions from the outside world. The main justification is to prevent any access to pornography or illegal mixing of men and women, as well as anything relating to homosexuality. Actually, censorship through filtering addresses political, social, and religious content and also selectively blocks presumed terrorist or jihadist content. The filtering was accomplished by the Internet Services Unit (ISU) of the King 'Abdulaziz City for Science and Technology (KACST), which is the country's national science agency with its national laboratories. The ISU explains that 25 licensed service providers connect the users to the national network, and it admits its filtering activities, which are aided by citizens who call in with information about unfiltered sites that the ISU is unaware of. The Communications and Information Technology Commission, previously called the Saudi Communications Commission, then took over the services managed by KACST. Foreign news services are sometimes blocked, for instance, the site of the Israeli newspaper *Haaretz*, which has an English-language edition. Others have been blocked and then were opened, various sites dealing with human and political rights among them, such as the Voice of Saudi Women (http://www. saudiwomen.net) ("Saudi Arabia." *Open Net Initiative*, 2009).

Some bloggers have been arrested, such as Ahmad Fouad al-Farhan, who was imprisoned and whose blog was blocked. Others were able to operate for quite some time, providing a window into the country, as in the famous blog known as *Saudigirl.blog*, whose author eventually revealed himself to be a man. Other blogs protest the actions of the *mutawa'in* (religious police) or call for other reforms. In addition, foreign-based blogs about Saudi Arabia have operated. In November 2010, Facebook was blocked. However, people are able to send group e-mails, and they continue to blog—despite avid monitoring—and communicate in a variety of ways, via cell phones, texting, and other services. Also, quite a number of Saudi Arabians reside part of the time (or full-time) outside of the country, for instance, in Bahrain or Dubai, where Facebook is not blocked.

HUMAN RIGHTS

Human rights are a hot-button topic interpreted differently by various sources. One deep-seated complaint is the presence of poverty and misery in the kingdom, despite the Islamic values and great wealth amassed through the petrochemical sector. There is a false perception that much, or most, of this poverty is suffered by immigrants and not Saudi Arabians, and this theme continues to some degree in reports of the thousands of homeless people. In Jeddah, they live under the cities' many bridges. Some are drug users despite the harsh penalties for drug use; others are simply poor, and still others have some work but nowhere to live (*Saudi Gazette*, November 23, 2010). Children are also homeless, or must beg, or are part of criminal rings in the country. The media had mostly focused on foreign children brought criminally into the country (see Chapter 5, Society). However, even more are Saudi Arabian, according to a 2007 study by 'Abdullah ibn 'Abdul 'Aziz Al Yousuf of the Imam Mohammad Bin Saud Islamic University, which states that some 83,000 children are homeless. Some were smuggled into the country, some are selling low-priced goods, and others are the prey of criminal gangs. This study states that, contrary to the press's assumptions that most of these children are Yemeni or of other nationalities, some 69 percent are Saudi Arabian, a majority of which are girls. It confirms a 2002 International Labor Organization report that many children who were begging were girls with disabilities and that their mothers were begging beside them (*Gulf News*, April 9, 2007).

CAPITAL PUNISHMENT

In Saudi Arabia, 69 persons were put to death in 2009 (*Amnesty*, March 30, 2010). Capital punishment is opposed by many but not all nations today. What human rights observers protest in Saudi Arabia is that habeus corpus is not granted; torture, beatings, and other prohibited actions are used; and prisoners may be tried privately and then sentenced and executed, as occurred with some of the detainees imprisoned in response to violent actions against the government since 2003 (Amnesty International 2009). In early July 2009, the Saudi Arabian government announced that trials of 330 persons, which had begun in March, had now ended. Perhaps an effort could have been made to allow human rights observers, but the Saudi Arabian government's stance is that this a national or internal matter. One defendant was sentenced to death, and 323 were given prison sentences of a few months up to 30 years, in addition to fines. In total, more than 1,000 persons have been charged with particular crimes, but that means that many others were detained without charge or had not yet been charged, and these detentions are lengthy. At the time of this writing, Amnesty International has not yet produced additional commentary or a follow-up report. What Saudi Arabian officials reported was that they had to take more time than they might have liked because it was important to have a fully legitimate process of trial and punishment in place and that many of the most violent offenders had already been killed by the police. They expected some response and outcry from within the

---

CAPITAL PUNISHMENT

Capital punishment is carried out in Saudi Arabia. Executions may involve beheading, stoning to death (for adulterers), being shot by a firing squad, or other means. In May 2009 Ahmed bin 'Adhaib ibn 'Askar al-Shamlani al-'Anzi was beheaded and then crucified in Riyadh (*Amnesty International*, May 31, 2009). In addition to its concerns over punishments that constitute torture, Amnesty International (AI) and other organizations, such as the United Nations Organisation Contre La Torture, oppose the practice of capital punishment in Saudi Arabia. AI believes that the secret and summary nature of the procedures obstructs justice for those charged and that judges' discretionary powers are excessive.

AI notes that whereas executions have declined in all other parts of the world (except for China and Iran), they have increased in Saudi Arabia. Despite a decrease in incidences after 2001, executions increased again after 2007: In 2006, 38 persons were executed, but in 2007, 158 persons were executed (*New York Times*, October 14, 2008). In 2009, 69 persons were executed.

AI and other agencies, such as Human Rights Watch, object to the lack of information given to the defendants, their families, and the public, the lack of clarity regarding the charges, the use of coercion and torture to force confessions, failures in due process, and what appears to be geographic or judicial variations in allowing for appeals or acceptance of *dhiyya* (blood price) compensation in lieu of *talion* (killing or injury to the extent originally committed).

AI is concerned by the fact that capital punishment is ordered for those who have not committed murder. From 1986 to 2008, 748 persons were executed for nonlethal crimes, and 621 had been charged with murder. The nonlethal charges included 503 cases that were drug related and 245 charges that included witchcraft, assaults, robberies, and sexual offences. In today's international legal environment, it seems wrong to execute persons for sexual offenses, claims of witchcraft or sorcery, or mistreatment of the Qur'an as has occurred for some charged with these offenses.

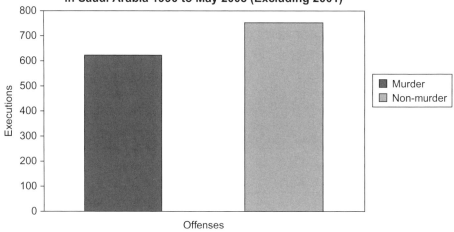

Rates of Executions for Murders and Non-murder Offenses in Saudi Arabia 1990 to May 2008 (Excluding 2001)

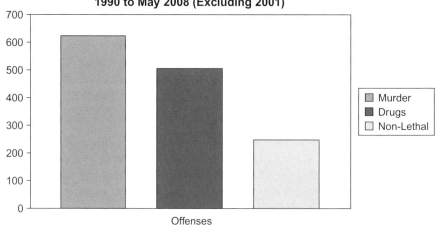

Distribution of Executions in Saudi Arabia by Offense 1990 to May 2008 (Excluding 2001)

AI is also disturbed by the high proportion of foreigners who are executed as compared to Saudi Arabian nationals, as they should not be subjected to lesser standards of justice and to mistreatment or torture by police (Amnesty International, *Affront to Justice: Death Penalty in Saudi Arabia* [London: Amnesty International, 2008]). Juvenile offenders have been executed because, under *shari'ah*, they are considered adults at puberty. As with men, more foreign women than Saudi Arabian women have been executed, and a number of them were either domestic workers or married to Saudi Arabian citizens.

kingdom at the time of the trial (Zuhur, Personal interviews, 2008). Responses from within the kingdom were largely invisible to the outside world but not to Saudi Arabian security forces. Responses regarding the legality of the proceedings on the basis of international law and human rights come from such organizations as Amnesty International and Human Rights Watch.

Not only are some terrorism suspects dealt with harshly, as in the beatings and extreme conditions experienced by one who conducted a hunger strike, but prior detainees also met with harsh sentences. These included protestors against the government who had responded to Sa'd al-Faqih's call for demonstrations on December 16, 2004; they were sentenced to months in prison and 100 to 250 strokes in floggings.

Sa'd al-Faqih, leader of Saudi Arabian opposition group, MIRA in 2011. (Courtesy of Mahan Abedin)

Twenty-one persons including two foreign nationals were arrested and charged. International human rights agencies and groups oppose the use of torture as punishment (Human Rights Watch, January 16, 2005). In the Qatif Girl case (see Chapter 6, Culture, section on women), the victim was sentenced to a flogging for being alone with a man in a vehicle, and that sentence was overturned only by intervention from the highest level.

The same international human rights organizations oppose *shari'ah* punishments for capital crimes because these involve torture and death (see sidebar on capital punishment). And they believe that not enough has been done in the last few years to address violations of workers' rights in Saudi Arabia (some measures are mentioned in Chapter 4, Economy). The process of raising objections on these issues and women's rights appears in some ways to have benefited from the fact that the overall political climate tended to favor reform and demonstrate action following the terrorist attacks in Saudi Arabia since 2003, as described earlier. It's quite possible that without Human Rights Watch, intervention and commentaries suggesting modern-day slavery of foreign workers, and expression of other concerns by demonstrators and activists, the Saudi Arabian human rights response organizations would not have been established. However, these organizations may raise concerns but not necessarily address them, and as already seen, the counterterrorist response continues to involve legal processes that ignore general standards of justice for prisoners.

In 2011, the King of Saudi Arabia announced a package of reforms, cash and loans and other benefits for Saudi Arabians in an effort to stave off political discontent of the sort that has been churning through the Arab Middle East. Political dissent and calls for enhanced popular political participation may well continue, just as it is likely that Islamist (including the *sahwa*) voices will oppose policies of the rulers. Consequently, it is not unfair to end this book with the hope that justice and human rights will be enhanced in Saudi Arabia in the future, and to wish this fascinating country and its people well. Peace be with you!

REFERENCES

al-Abdulkareem, A. A., and S. G. Ballal. "Consanguineous Marriages in an Urban Area of Saudi Arabia: Rates and Adverse Health Effects on the Offspring." *Journal of Community Health* 23 (1998), 75–83.

Ahmad, Qanta. *In the Land of Invisible Women: A Female Doctor's Journey in the Saudi Kingdom*. Naperville, IL: Sourcebooks, 2008.

Akeel, Mona. "Female Circumcisions: Weight of Tradition Perpetuates a Dangerous Practice." *Arab News*, March 20, 2005.

Amnesty International. "Amnesty Releases Death Penalty Statistics." *Amnesty International*. March 30, 2010. http://www.amnesty.org

Amnesty International. "Countering Terrorism with Repression." *Amnesty International*. September 10, 2009.

Ansary, Abdullah F. "Combating Extremism: A Brief Overview of Saudi Arabia's Approach." *Middle East Policy* 15, no. 2 (Summer 2008, 111–142).

Ayoob, Mohammed, and Hasan Kosebalaban, eds. *Religion and Politics in Saudi Arabia: Wahhabism and the State*. Boulder, CO: Lynne Rienner, 2009.

BBC Two. "The Child Slaves of Saudi Arabia." This World. Directed by Rageh Omaar. *BBC*. March 27, 2007. http://news.bbc.co.uk/2/hi/programmes/this_world/6431957.stm

Bergen, Peter I. *The Osama Bin Laden I Know: An Oral History of al Qa'ida's Leader*. New York: Free Press, 2006.

Blackwell, Amy Hackney, and Sherifa Zuhur. "Suicide Bombings." In *The Encyclopedia of U.S. Middle East Wars*, edited by Spencer Tucker. Santa Barbara, CA, and Oxford: ABC-CLIO, 2010, vol. 3, 1172–1174.

Boucek, Christopher. "Jailing Jihadis: Special Terrorist Prisons." *Terrorism Monitor* 6, no. 2 (January 24, 2008). http://www.jamestown.org/programs/gta/single/?tx_ttnews%5Btt_news%5D=4682&tx_ttnews%5BbackPid%5D=167&no_cache=1

Boucek, Christopher. "Extremist Reeducation and Rehabilitation." In *Leaving Terrorism Behind: Individual and Collective Disengagement*, edited by Tore Bjrøgo and John Horgan. New York: Routledge, 2009, 212–224.

Bronson, Rachel. *Thicker Than Oil: America's Uneasy Partnership with Saudi Arabia*. New York: Oxford University Press, 2008.

Center for Strategic and International Studies (CSIS). "The Middle East Military Balance." 2005.

Congressional Research Service (CRS) and Library of Congress. "Saudi Arabia: Current Issues and U.S. Relations." *CRS Issue Brief.* Alfred B. Prados. Washington, DC: Congressional Research Service and Library of Congress. Updated February 24, 2006.

Cordesman, Anthony H. *Saudi Arabia Enters the Twenty-First Century: The Political, Foreign Policy, Economic, and Energy Dimensions*. London: Center for Strategic and International Studies; Westport, CT: Praeger, 2003a.

Cordesman, Anthony H. *Saudi Arabia and the Challenge of Terrorism: Reacting to the "9/11 Report."* Washington, DC: Center for Strategic and International Studies, 2003b.

Cordesman, Anthony H., and Nawaf Obaid. *Saudi Internal Security: A Risk Assessment. Terrorism and the Security Services—Challenges and Developments.* Washington, DC: Center for Strategic and International Studies, 2004.

Cordesman, Anthony H., and Nawaf Obaid. *Saudi National Security: Military and Security Services—Challenges and Developments*. Full Report. Washington, DC: Center for Strategic and International Studies, Draft, September 29, 2004.

Craze, Joshua, and Mark Huband, eds. *The Kingdom: Saudi Arabia and the Challenge of 21st Century*. New York: Columbia University Press, 2009.

Delong-Bas, Natana. *Jihad for Islam: The Struggle for the Future of Saudi Arabia*. New York: Oxford University Press, 2009.

Doumato, Eleanor A. "The Ambiguity of Shari'a and the Politics of 'Rights' in Saudi Arabia." In *Faith and Freedom: Women's Human Rights in the Muslim World*, edited by Mahnaz Afkhami. New York: I. B. Tauris, 1995, 135–160.

Fandy, Mamoun. *Saudi Arabia and the Politics of Dissent*. New York: St. Martin's, 1999.

Hammond, Andrew. "Saudi Arabia's Media Empire: Keeping the Masses at Home." *Arab Media and Society*, issue 3 (Fall 2007).

Hawali, Safar. *Haqa'iq hawla 'azmat al-khalij*. Cairo: Dar Makka al-Mukarama, 1991.

El-Hazmi, M.A., A.R. al-Swailem, A.S. Warsy, A.M. al-Swailem, R. Sulaimani, and A.A. al-Meshari. "Consanguinity among the Saudi Arabian Population." *Medical Genetics* 32 (1995), 623–626.

Hegghammer, Thomas. *Jihad in Saudi Arabia: Violence and Pan-Islamism since 1979*. Cambridge: Cambridge University Press, 2010.

Hegghammer, Thomas. "Terrorist Recruitment and Radicalization in Saudi Arabia." *Middle East Policy* 13, no. 4 (Winter 2006), 39–60.

Hegghammer, Thomas, and Stéphane Lacroix. "Rejectionist Islamism in Saudi Arabia: The Case of Juhayman al-Utaybi Revisited." *International Journal of Middle East Studies* 39, no. 1 (2007), 103–122.

Al Hussain, M., and M. Al Bunyan. "Consanguineous Marriages in a Saudi Population and the Effect of Inbreeding on Perinatal and Postnatal Mortality." *Annual Tropical Paediatrics* 17 (1997), 155–160.

International Crisis Group. "Can Saudi Arabia Reform Itself?" *ICG Middle East Report,* no. 28, (July 14, 2004).

International Crisis Group. "Saudi Arabia Backgrounder: Who Are the Islamists?" *Middle East Report*, September 21, 2004.

Jacquard, Roland. ed. *In the Name of Osama Bin Laden: Global Terrorism and the Bin Laden Brotherhood*. Durham, NC, and London:: Duke University Press, 2002.

Kiely, Robert S. and Sherifa Zuhur. "Saudi Arabia." In *Encyclopedia of Middle East Wars*. Santa Barbara, CA, Denver, and Oxford: ABC-Clio, 2010, 1072–1074.

Lacroix, Stéphane. "Between Islamists and Liberals: Saudi Arabia's New 'Islamo-Liberal' Reformists." *Middle East Journal* 58, no. 3 (Summer 2004).

Ma'ahad al-Dirasat al-Diblumasiyyah. *Al-Arshif al-Alaktruniyya li-Isdarat al-Ma'ahad. 1400–1424 (1980–2004)*. Riyadh: Diplomatic Institute, Ministry of Foreign Affairs, Saudi Arabia, 2005.

Matthiesen, Toby. "The Shi'a of Saudi Arabia at a Crossroads." *Middle East Report Online*, May 6, 2009.

al-Menaa, Fahad Nasser. "The Causes of Drug Usage, Distribution and Smuggling in Saudi Arabia." PhD diss., Washington State University, 1995.

Ministry of Health. Kingdom of Saudi Arabia. Statistics. 2006.

El Mouzan, M.L., A.A. Al Salloum, A.S. Al Herbish, M.M. Qurachi, and A.A. Al Omar. "Consanguinity and Major Genetic Disorders in Saudi Children: A Community-Based Cross-sectional study." *Annual of Saudi Medicine* 228 (2008), 69–73.

Mufti, Muhammad H. *Health Care Development Strategies in the Kingdom of Saudi Arabia*. New York: Kluwer, 2000.

Pierpaoli, Paul G. "King Khalid Military City." In *The Encyclopedia of Middle East Wars*: *The United States in the Persian Gulf, Afghanistan, and Iraq Conflicts*, edited by Spencer Tucker. Santa Barbara, CA: ABC-CLIO, 2010, vol. 2, 691–692.

Al-Rasheed, Madawi, ed. *Kingdom without Borders: Saudi Political, Religious and Media Frontiers*. New York: Columbia University Press, 2008.

Riedel, Bruce, and Bilal Y. Saab. "Al Qa'ida's Third Front." *Washington Quarterly* 31, no. 2 (Spring 2008), 33–46.

Rougier, Bernard, ed. *Qu'est-ce Que le Salafisme?* Paris: Presses Universitaires de France, 2008.

Rugh, William. *Arab Mass Media: Newspapers, Radio and Television in Arab Politics.* Westport, CT: Praeger, 2004.

al-Sahaymi, Abd al-Salam. *The Ideology of Terrorism and Violence in the Kingdom of Saudi Arabia: Origins, Causes for Its Spread and the Solution.* Cairo: Dar al-Minhaj, 2006.

el-Sanabary, Najat. "Women and the Nursing Profession in Saudi Arabia." In *Arab Women: Between Defiance and Restraint*, edited by Suha Sabbagh. New York: Olive Branch, 1996, 71–83.

"Saudi Arabia." *Open Net Initiative.* August 6, 2009. http://opennet.net/research/profiles/saudi-arabia

Scheuer, Michael, Stephen Ulph, and John C.K. Daly. *Saudi Arabian Oil Facilities: The Achilles Heel of the Western Economy.* Washington, DC: Jamestown Foundation, May 2006.

al-Tayer, Abdullah bin Musa. *Amrika allati qad ta'ud.* Riyadh, Saudi Arabia: by the author, 2005 (1426h.)

Teitelbaum, Joshua. *Holier Than Thou: Saudi Arabia's Islamic Opposition.* Washington, DC: Washington Institute for Near East Policy, 2000.

al-Thabit, Abdullah. *al-Irhabi 20.* Damascus: Dar al-Mada, 2006. (Available in translation as *Terroriste no. 20*, translated by Françoise Neyrod [Paris: Actes Sud Sindbad, 2010].)

Trofimov, Yaroslav. *The Siege of Mecca: The Forgotten Uprising in Islam's Holiest Shrine and the Birth of Al Qa'ida.* New York: Random House, 2007.

United Nations. Health Data. "Prospects 2005–2010."

U.S. Embassy in Riyadh. Secret (Cable) Riyadh 001134. SIPDIS. To ISN/RA R. Mangiello and R. Nephew and NEA/ARP B. Mcgrath. Tuesday, July 22, 2008. Obtained from http://www.guardian.co.uk/world/us-embassy-cables-documents/162960?intcmp=239

U.S. Embassy in Riyadh. Cables. Secret. SIPDIS. White House for OVP, Department for NEA/ARP and S/I. Satterfield. Sunday, April 20, 2008 (sent by Gfoeller). Obtained from http://www.guardian.co.uk/world/us-embassy-cables-documents/150519

U.S. Embassy, Tel Aviv. Secret. SIPDIS. 40th Joint Political-Military Group: Executive. Part 1 of 4. November 18, 2009. Obtained from http://www.guardian.co.uk/world/us-embassy-cables-documents/235359?intcmp=239

Wardak, Ali. "Crime and Social Control in Saudi Arabia." In *Transnational and Comparative Criminology*, edited by James Sheptycki and Ali Wardak. London: Glasshouse, 2005, 91–116.

Wehry, Frederick, Theodore W. Karasik, Alireza Nader, Jeremy Ghez, Lydia Hansell, and Robert A. Guffey. *Saudi-Iranian Relations since the Fall of Saddam: Rivalry, Cooperation and Implications for U.S. Policy.* Washington, DC: Rand Corporation (National Security Research Division), 2009.

Willbanks, James H. "Saudi Arabia, Armed Forces." In *The Encyclopedia of Middle East Wars: The United States in the Persian Gulf, Afghanistan and Iraq Conflicts*, edited by Spencer Tucker. Santa Barbara, CA: ABC-CLIO, 2010, vol. 3, 1075–1076.

Yamani, Mai. "Muslim Women and Human Rights in Saudi Arabia: Aspirations of a New Generation." In *The Rule of Law in the Middle East and the Islamic World: Human Rights and the Judicial Process*, edited by Eugene Cotran and Mai Yamani. London: Tauris and the Centre of Islamic Studies and Middle Eastern Law, School of Oriental and African Studies, University of London, 2000.

Yamani, Mai. "The New Generation in Saudi Arabia: Cultural Change, Political Identity and Regime Security." In *Security in the Persian Gulf: Origins, Obstacles and the Search for Consensus*, edited by Lawrence G. Potter and Gary G. Sick. New York: Palgrave, 2001, 189–205.

Yamani, Mai. "The Challenge of Globalization in Saudi Arabia." In *On Shifting Ground: Muslim Women in the Global Era*, edited by Fereshteh Norahie-Simone. New York: Feminist Press, 2005.

Zuhur, Sherifa. *Ideological and Motivational Factors in the Defusing of Radical Islamist Violence.* Carlisle, PA, and Cairo: Institute of Middle Eastern, Islamic, and Strategic Studies, 2010a.

Zuhur, Sherifa. "Sa'ud, Khalid ibn Sultan ibn 'Abd al-'Aziz al-." In *The Encyclopedia of U.S. Middle East Wars*, edited by Spencer Tucker. Santa Barbara, CA: ABC-CLIO, 2010b, 1071–1072.

Zuhur, Sherifa. "Decreasing Violence in Saudi Arabia and Beyond." In *Home-Grown Terrorism: Understanding and Addressing the Root Causes of Radicalisation among Groups with an Immigrant Heritage in Europe*, edited by Thomas M. Pick, Anne Speckhard, and Beatrice Jacuch. Amsterdam: IOS Press, 2009a, 74–98.

Zuhur, Sherifa. Personal interviews, Riyadh, Jeddah, London, Washington D.C. 2005–2008.

Zuhur, Sherifa. "Considerations of Honor Crimes, FGM, Kidnapping/Rape and Early Marriage in Selected Arab Nations." Paper presented at "Good Practices in Legislation to Address Harmful Practices against Women," United Nations Division for the Advancement of Women and UN Economic Commission for Africa, Addis Ababa, May 25–28, 2009b.

Zuhur, Sherifa. "Military Perspectives on the U.S.-Saudi Arabian Relationship and Future of the Global War on Terror" [in Arabic]. Riyadh, Saudi Arabia: Institute of Diplomatic Studies, Ministry of Foreign Affairs, 2005a.

Zuhur, Sherifa. *Saudi Arabia: Islamism, Political Reform and the Global War on Terror*. Carlisle, PA: Strategic Studies Institute, 2005b.

Glossary

'Abaya ('Aba')—A black cloak worn by women in Saudi Arabia that covers the entire body and the clothing worn underneath.

Abu Bakr—The first caliph who led the Muslim community after the Prophet Muhammad's death.

Abu Sufyan—Originally an enemy of the Prophet Muhammad in Mecca; killed many early Muslims but converted to Islam following the capture of Mecca in 630. Abu Sufyan's descendants would become the Ummayyad dynasty of 661–750 CE.

Adhan—Call to prayer, intoned publicly five times a day.

Ahl—Family; a bilateral kin group.

Ahl al-balad—A Hijazi term, literally meaning "people of the country." Used by Hijazis to indicate they are not foreigners, nor recent immigrants, nor from the bedouin tribes (although many may originally derive from tribal groups).

Ahl al-kitab—Literally, "Peoples of the Book." Non-Muslims with a scriptural tradition recognized by Islam: Jews, Christians, Samaritans, and the Sabeans.

Alfiyya—A poem in which each set of hemistiches begins with the successive letter of the Arabic alphabet.

'Alim (singular form of 'ulama)—A religious scholar.

Apostate—Apostasy is the act of denying Islam by a Muslim; and one of the most serious crimes according to Islamic law.

'Arafat—The wide plain approximately 12 miles east of Mecca, where all pilgrims gather on the ninth day of Dhu al Hijah, the 12th month of the Islamic calendar. Pilgrims believe that their prayers uttered here will be heard by Allah directly.

'Ardha—Ceremonial dance performed by men with swords. Also known as *razif* or *galata* in Saudi Arabia and by other names in other countries, such as *al-'ayyala* in the United Arab Emirates.

'Ardh baydha—Uncultivated land.

Arham—Affinal relatives married into one's family or one's spouse's family.

'Asayib—A head circlet, sometimes with tassels, worn by men or women.

Ashraf—Those who claim descent from the Prophet (singular, *sharif*). *Ashraf* families became a local dynasty ruling the Hijaz in the early 20th century and were the custodians of the two holy cities of Mecca and Medina.

'Ashura—The day commemorating the death of Husayn ibn 'Ali at Karbala in the early Islamic era. Ritual parades, self-flagellation, and wounding to the point of bloodletting are traditional in the Shi'a community.

Awqaf—Religious endowments.

Ayat—A verse of the Qur'an. Literally means a sign, symbol, or mirror of God.

'Ayb—Shame.

Badu (singular, badawi)—Bedouin.

Banu Hanifa—One of the major tribes of al-Yamamah in Saudi Arabia.

Banu Nadir—One of three Jewish tribes living in Medina at the time of the Muslim emigration there.

Banu Qaynuqah—One of three Jewish tribes living in Medina in the early Muslim era.

Banu Qurayzah (Quraydhah)—One of three Jewish tribes living in Medina in the early Muslim era.

Bashkat—A group of close friends who meet regularly.

Bay'ah—The oath of allegiance Muslims make to their rulers; in Saudi Arabia, the king receives the *bay'ah*.

Bid'ah—An innovation in Muslim practice. Something not indigenous to Islam or the Islamic way of life. Such an innovation is regarded negatively.

Bint 'amm marriage—Marriage to the father's brother's daughter, a preferred marriage partner. A form of consanguineous marriage.

Bisht—A cloak or mantle worn by men.

Black Stone—A small stone believed to be from heaven (possibly a meteorite) in the southeastern corner of the Ka'ba. The pilgrims salute the stone as they perform the *tawwaf*, or circumambulation of the Ka'ba, and attempt to touch or kiss it.

Bukhur—Frankincense or other incense.

Burqa—A mask, sometimes decorated, worn by women over the face.

Caliph—A political office used to govern urban areas of pre-Islamic Arabia and chosen by the consensus of tribal elders. The term *khalifa* in Arabic means "successor." The first four caliphs were Abu Bakr, 'Umar, 'Uthman, and 'Ali.

Committee for the Defense of Legitimate Rights (CDLR)—Group founded in Riyadh by six scholars to support the Islamic opposition in Saudi Arabia. Its spokesman was Muhammad al-Masari. After arrests, its members left Saudi Arabia and/or went underground. Al-Masari and Sa'ad al-Faqih then set up the CDLR in London in 1994. The UK government allowed the opposition group to operate even in spite of strong pressure by the Saudi Arabian government. The U.S. government did not support the CDLR because of its vocal support of the 1995 and 1996 bombings in Saudi Arabia. Al-Faqih and al-Masari split in 1996.

Communist Party in Saudi Arabia—Formed by communists from within the National Liberation Front in 1975. This party was always illegal (and political parties are still currently illegal). Its youth wing was the Union of Democratic Youth of Saudi Arabia with an office in Damascus. The party was renamed the Democratic Unification in Saudi Arabia in the early 1990s but disbanded as part of a deal with the government whereby political prisoners from this party were released.

Dandana—Singing with the *'ud* (lute) and *tabla* (drum) (Hijaz).

Dar al-harb—Territory that is not controlled by Muslims; literally means "house or domain of war."

Dar al-Islam—Territories or countries governed by Muslims where Islamic law is observed.

Da'wah—The mission to spread Islam in the world and to Islamize, or remake Muslim society in a more authentic manner.

Dewinih—A bedouin genre of poetry and song.

Dhiyya—Blood payment offered to the kin of one killed or injured according to *'urf* and *shari'ah.*

Dhurra'ah—A long dress; term used in Najd and other areas.

Dhu al-Hija—The 12th month of the Islamic calendar. The greater pilgrimage, the *hajj*, must be performed in this month.

Dira—A tribe's normal route of travel through lands where it has grazing and water rights.

Fahd—The spotted and brindled wild cat. Also a man's name.

Fallah (plural, fallalih)—Farmer or peasant.

Fatwa—A legal opinion or responsa issued by an Islamic jurist that resolves a question about the lawfulness of a particular topic or action. In Sunni Islam, jurists may draw on the Qur'an, hadith, legal analogy, and consensus to construct a *fatawa*, while Shi'i jurists may also use a methodology known as *ijtihad.*

Fijri—Pearl-divers' music, once performed as part of the trade in the Eastern Province of Saudi Arabia, Kuwait, Bahrain, and the United Arab Emirates and now as part of their musical legacy. It was performed at night, and the name *fijri* refers to the dawn, *fajr.*

Firman—An edict of an Ottoman ruler.

Fitnah—Means sedition, or schism between Muslims, and also to mislead and to guide in error.

Fouta—A length of fabric wrapped around as a skirt and worn by men.

Free Men of al-Qatif (Ahrar al-Qatif)—A Shi'a militant group that issued a statement condemning the HAIA's (the Committee for the Promotion of Virtue and Prevention of Vice) attacks on Shi'a in Medina in the events known as the Intifadha of 1430. It released a statement harshly condemning the religious police and sardonically shortening its name. The group called for demonstrations by other Shi'a in the country and for the support of their "fighting people" in Najran, Medina, al-Hasa, and al-Qatif.

Fusha—(Pronounced *fus-Ha*.) The classical Arabic language.

Ghadab—Anger.

Ghazal—The wild gazelle.

Ghazl—A form of love poetry that developed in Mecca.

Ghul—A ghoul, a terrifying supernatural shapeshifting being.

Ghumrah—A pre-marriage party for women when henna is applied to the bride's skin.

Ghutra—A man's headcloth.

Hadhar—Settled folk in towns or oases, as opposed to *badiya* or *badu* (pastoralists).

Hadith—A form of religious literature that recorded the *sunnah*, or Way of the Prophet. The hadith are short texts about the sayings and actions of the Prophet Muhammad or his Companions, preceded by an *isnad*, or chain of transmitters. Six compilations of hadith are considered to be sound, or reliable, by the majority of Muslims: Al-Bukhari, Al-Tirmidhi, Muslim, Abu Da'ud, Al-Nisa'i, Al-Nawawi, and Ibn Majah.

Hajj—The pilgrimage to Mecca. One who has completed the pilgrimage is a *hajji* (male) or *hajja* (female).

Halal—That which is permitted by Allah. A category of permitted substances (including food) and actions in Islamic law.

Hanbali School—The legal tradition of the jurist Ahmad ibn Hanbal, which is followed in Saudi Arabia. It is often considered the strictest of the four Sunni legal schools (*madhdhahib*).

Haram—(Pronounced HA-ram.) Sanctuary. Implies safety from violence and temporal control. It also means the space used for prayer, or prayer hall of a mosque, and also refers to the entire mosque complex. The dual form, *Haramayn*, refers to the two Holy Cities of Mecca and Medina, while the Grand Mosque in Mecca is al-Masjid al-Haram.

Haram—(Pronounced *Ha-RAAM*.) Taboo. Not permitted Islamically.

Haramayn Brigades—A cell of the militant group al-Qa'ida on the Arabian Peninsula, operative in 2003–2004.

Harrah—(Pronounced *harrat* in construction (*idhafa*) with another definite noun.) Basaltic lava formations.

Hashemite—The descendants of Sharif Husayn of Mecca and Medina, who governed the holy cities prior to their conquest by 'Abd al-'Aziz ibn Sa'ud. Husayn's sons led the Arab Revolt against the Ottomans; his son 'Abdullah became the ruler of Jordan, and his son Faysal became the ruler of Iraq.

Hijaz—The western province of Saudi Arabia. The holy cities of Mecca and Medina are located here, and the Hashemite family, formerly the authorities of the holy cities, came from the Hijaz.

Hijrah—Refers to the migration of Prophet Muhammad and the Muslims from Mecca to Medina, escaping the genocide against Muslims in Mecca around 622 CE.

Hima—A preserve system of collectively used grazing land allocated solely to people of a certain area, or town. Abolished in 1953 and revived in some places in the late 1980s.

Hinnawah—A female professional who applies henna designs on women's feet and hands.

Hizbullah al-Hijaz—A militant oppositionist group believed to be sponsored by Iran and blamed for attacks in the late 1980s and 1990s, including the Khobar Towers bombing of 1996. Most of the group's members were arrested or fled in 1996. The group does not believe in accommodation with the Saudi Arabian government and still advocates armed struggle. It was most recently vocal following the Intifadhah of 1430 in Medina.

Hudud—The most severe and fixed penalties under Islamic law for the most serious crimes such as adultery and fornication (*zina'*), brigandry or highway robbery, theft, false accusations of *zina'* (*qadhf*), apostasy, and wine drinking. Sedition or rebellion comes under the *ahkam al-bughat* and is considered a capital crime by some jurists but not others.

Ibn 'Abd al-Wahhab, Muhammad—A preacher and cleric of the mid-18th century who sought to cleanse Islamic practice in Arabia from innovations. His strict brand of Islam and mission was adopted by Muhammad Ibn Sa'ud and his followers and is referred to in the West as Wahhabism.

Ibn Taymiyyah—A 13th-century Islamic jurist who called for jihad and *takfir* to address the un-Islamic practices of the Mongols, who had invaded the area and influenced local rulers in his era.

Ibrahim—(Abraham) The founder of monotheism and father of Isma'il from his slave, Hajar (Hagar). Also the father of Isaac according to the Bible, Ibrahim destroyed the idols of the polytheists and rebuilt the Ka'bah.

'Id (Eid) al-Adha—The Greater Feast (in contrast with the Lesser Feast, the 'Id al-Fitr). On this day Muslims everywhere, including the pilgrims in Mina on the *hajj*, sacrifice an animal and distribute a portion to the poor. A major holiday in Saudi Arabia.

'Id (Eid) al-Fitr—The feast following the month of Ramadan. It is a major holiday in Saudi Arabia celebrated for at least a few days.

Ifta'—The process of crafting responsa (*fatawa*) to questions of Islamic law or practice.

Iftar—Breakfast. Eaten after sundown during the month of Ramadan.

Ihram—The state of ritual purity that pilgrims must enter and maintain during the *hajj*. It also pertains to the clothing worn by the pilgrims: for men, two white seamless garments wrapped around their waist and across the torso and, for women, modest, loose-fitting garments.

Ihya—Legal acquisition of land through cultivation of barren fields.

Ijma'—Consensus, a principle of Islamic jurisprudence.

Ijtihad—A legal methodology of constructing an independent response to a theological issue that can be performed only by a *mujtahid* (a scholar who is trained and licensed to issue *ijtihad*; literally, "one who makes *ijtihad*"). The Hanbali *madhhab* (tradition or school of Islamic jurisprudence [*fiqh*] deriving from Ahmad ibn Hanbal) school allowed for *ijtihad*, but the other Sunni *madhahib* (schools) ceased doing so.

Ikhwan—Brethren, brotherhood. Refers to the Wahhabi warriors, the group who fought to expand the authority of the al-Sa'ud and the reform movement of Ibn 'Abd al-Wahhab. (A different group, the Muslim Brotherhood, are also called Ikhwan and were established in 1929 in Isma'iliyya, Egypt.)

Imam—An imam may be (1) a leader of an Islamic entity or the *ummah* (community) or (2) simply a prayer leader. Some imams may also be *khatib*s, preachers who deliver the Friday sermon.

Imamate—In Shi'a Islam, the imamate, or *a'ima*, is a chain of Islamic leaders appointed by God to lead the Muslims; the first *imam* was 'Ali ibn Abi Talib. The followers of Sunni *madhahib* do not recognize the institution of the *a'ima*.

Intifadhah—Uprising, literally means "shaking off."

Iqa'—Rhythm.

Iqal— Pronounced igal. The black cord circlet holding a man's headcloth (*ghutra* or *shmagh*) in place.

Iqta—A land grant made by a ruler; granted in the former Ottoman territories.

Islahiyyun—Reformers. Liberal reformers in today's Saudi Arabia.

Istiqamah—Proper social and religious behavior.

al-Jama'ah al-Salafiyyah al-Muhtasibah—The *salafiyya* (salafist) movement in contemporary times. The followers of the movement included Juhayman al-'Utaybi, who led the takeover of the Grand Mosque in Mecca in 1979.

Jammal (plural, jamamil, or jammalun)—One who raised camels and transported them for sale.

Jarish—Crushed wheat used in cooking.

Jihad—Struggle through defensive or offensive warfare, or struggle for Islam. Muslims distinguish between the greater jihad, the daily struggle to fulfill the requirements and ideals of Islam, and the lesser jihad, fighting for the faith.

Jizyah—A tax, similar to the Roman poll tax, levied on the Jews and Christians, who, unlike Muslims, are not subject to payment of *zakat* (the required portion of a Muslim's income and property given as charity or to support Islam).

Ka'ba—A cube-shaped building in the center of the Grand Mosque in Mecca, considered Allah's house on earth. The spiritual center of Islam.

Kabsa—A dish cooked with chicken (or lamb) and rice.

Kaffir—A polytheist or infidel. Some sources, both Muslim and non-Muslim, use *kaffir* to mean any non-Muslim, but its earliest application was to Meccans and their allies, who were polytheists.

Khalas (Deliverance) Movement—A Shi'a political opposition movement launched in 2009.

Khaliji—Of the Arabian Gulf; from Saudi Arabia or the other nations along the Gulf.

Khamr—Wine or any form of alcohol. Forbidden to Muslims and in Saudi Arabia as a whole.

Khariji (plural, Khawarij)—A movement of devout Muslims who seceded from the early Muslim state because they feared that Islamic principles were being degraded. One of the Khawarij killed an early caliph, 'Ali, objecting to his assent to arbitration with the Ummayyads.

Kharuf—Lamb, sheep.

Khatib—Preacher, tribal orator, or spokesman.

Khayma (khaymah)—Tent; also called *bayt al-sha'r* by the bedouin.

Khutbah—Sermon.

Kiswah—A large black cloth embroidered in golden thread with Qur'anic verses that is draped over the Ka'ba. Each year a new *kiswah* is presented, and the previous year's is cut into pieces that are given to pilgrims.

Kuffiya—Mens' or boys' skullcap, also known as a taqiyyah. In Mecca the white skullcap is called a *kuffiya baladi*.

Kuttab—School for teaching the Qur'an.

Laylat al-hinna—A nighttime prewedding celebration when the bride's friends gather to decorate her hands and feet with henna, and sometimes their own as well.

Laylat al-qadr—The night of power, during Ramadan, when the Qur'an was first revealed to the prophet Muhammad.

Laylat al-zaffaf—An all-night party during the wedding celebrations when the bride and groom consummate the marriage.

Mabkharah—Incense burner.

Madhhab—Refers to a system or tradition of lawmaking or jurisprudence (*fiqh*). Often termed a legal school (of thought).

Madrasah—An Islamic academy.

Mahdi—A special figure, the Guided One, who will restore Islam prior to the Day of Judgment. According to tradition, he will descend from the Prophet's lineage.

Mahmal—A ceremonial gift made of silks, jewels, and usually a Qur'an, carried atop a camel and presented by a ruler to the people of Mecca at the outset of the *hajj*. Certain rulers claimed an exclusive right to present the *mahmal*.

Mahr—A payment made by the groom to his bride upon their marriage.

Mahram (plural, maharim)—A male relative whom a woman cannot marry as she is closely related to him. A woman's guardian, *wali*, is from her *maharim*.

Majlis—A meeting or council. In Saudi Arabia a *majlis* is both an occasion (a party or seating when guests are entertained) and also the hall in which the *majlis* takes place.

Maqam—Place; may refer to a structure like the Maqam Ibrahim or a musical mode.

Maqamat (singular, maqam)—Musical structures like modes, featuring microtonalities.

Marja'iyya—Scholarly *'ulama* leadership of the Shi'a. The Shi'a take a cleric as a source (*marja'*) and follow his teachings.

Masjid—Mosque; literally, "place of bowing."

Matarih—Hand loom used by bedouin women.

Mathal (plural, amthal)—A short saying or proverb.

Mawalid—Children of slaves and nonslaves.

Mawlid al-nabi—The birthday of the Prophet Muhammad, celebrated by the majority group on the 12th day of the month of Rabi'a al-Awwal.

Mecca (Makkah)—The birthplace of the Prophet Muhammad and a city sacred to Muslims because it is home to the Ka'ba, a cubelike structure that is considered the first house for monotheistic worship, built by Adam and rebuilt by Ibrahim (Abraham) and his son Isma'il (Ishmael).

Medina—The Prophet's city and the place to which Muhammad and his followers migrated to escape religious persecution by the Meccans and to establish an Islamic society. Medina is also where the Prophet Muhammad and the caliphs Abu Bakr, and 'Umar are buried. Medina is the second-holiest site in Islam.

Mezzah—Small dish or appetizer.

Mina—The sprawling tent city between Mecca and 'Arafat, where pilgrims camped before and after the Day of Standing, and where they perform the animal sacrifice on the 10th day of Dhu al-Hija.

Minaret—A tower of a mosque, from which the call to prayer is chanted.

Mizmar—A men's dance of the western region that simulates combat with canes. Also means a musical pipe; the musician utilizes circular breathing to play it.

Movement for Islamic Reform (MIRA)—An opposition group based in the United Kingdom and headed by Dr. Sa'ad al-Faqih since his 1996 break with the Committee for the Defense of Legitimate Rights (CDLR). Al-Faqih (b. 1957) was one of the organizers of the 1991 Letter of Demands and the 1992 Memorandum of Advice presented to King Fahd. Al-Faqih had served as a physician to the *mujahidin* and issued insights on the jihadists from 2003 to 2006. MIRA launched a satellite radio station, Sawt al-Islah, and a television program and called for demonstrations in Saudi Arabia in 2003 and 2004, requiring police intervention. MIRA's assets were frozen in 2004 after the U.S. Treasury Department had al-Faqih designated a special terrorist by the United Nations.

Mu'adhdhin—The person who issues the call to prayer (*adhan*) in a strong, pleasing voice.

Mudandash—A dress.

Mufti—Issuer of legal opinions (*fatawa*).

Muhammad ibn 'Abdullah—Prophet of Islam who lived from 570 to 632 CE.

Muhmal—The undotted Arabic letters; also, poetry using only the undotted letters.

Muhtasib—A state official who upheld the Islamic command known as the *hisba*, commanding the good and forbidding the evil. This official also ensured fair prices and practices in the markets.

Mulk hurr—Freehold landownership obtained by cultivating previously barren or unused land.

Musalla—A smaller mosque or prayer room. Literally, "place of prayer."

Mutawa'in—Also known in Saudi Arabia as the Organization or Committee for the Promotion of Virtue and Prevention of Vice, as the HAIA, or as the religious police, who enforce a strict interpretation of religious duties and separation of the sexes. The more general Arabic meaning of *mutawa'a* is one who is a very pious or conservative person, a "volunteer" to extra duties in Islam, who chooses to perform supernumerary prayers, additional fasting, and charity in addition to *zakat*.

Mutawwif—An agent specializing in pilgrims.

Mutrib/Mutriba—Male or female singer who leads a musical group. Literally, "one who possesses *tarab* (the ability to enchant or quality of enchantment)."

Muwahhidun—Wahhabis. Literally, means "those who support monotheism (*tawhid*)."

Muzahhid—A man who sang songs to inspire people to leave their affairs and go to visit the Prophet's mosque in Medina.

Mzayyan—A song and poetry competition held by nomadic groups at night, often at the end of the summer.

Nabati—Nonclassical, colloquial, or vernacular language, especially that of Najd; and poetry composed in that language.

Nawadir—Anecdotes, usually humorous.

Niqab—A black mask worn over the face; a face veil.

Nuktah—Joke.

Nuwwash—Swinging of the hair and head while dancing.

Panegyrics—Poetry composed to praise or honor a ruler or another person.

Polygyny—Marriage to more than one woman.

Qabilah—Tribe.

Qabyala—Idea of tribal identity.

Qadi—A judge of Islamic law.

al-Qa'ida on the Arabian Peninsula (AQAP)—Known in Arabic as Tanzim al-Qa'ida fi Jazirat al-'Arabiyyah, which means al-Qa'ida on the Arabian Peninsula. It was formed in 2001–2002. Some members of this group merged with two Yemeni ji-hadist organizations in 2008. AQAP formed in Saudi Arabia under the command of Yusuf al-'Uyayri, who unleashed suicide bombing attacks in May 2003, followed by a large-scale attack in Riyadh, killings of individual foreigners, and then major attacks in Yanbu and at Khobar. The group attacked the U.S. consulate in Jeddah, mounted a failed attack at Abqaiq, and the security forces have foiled other attacks. Most of AQAP's leadership has been killed or imprisoned. Some militants fled to Yemen, where three different organizations reassembled under the name of AQAP. The earlier organization has not been totally eradicated in Saudi Arabia.

Qahwah—Coffee.

Qasidah—A form of poetry with double stanzas and a refrain.

Qiblah —Muslims face Mecca when praying. That orientation is called and indicated by the *qiblah*.

Qisas—The second-most serious level of criminal punishments in Islamic law. These pertain to murder, manslaughter, or bodily injury.

Qital—Fighting or killing, and a term for military activity used in the Qur'an.

Qiyan (singular, qayna)—Women entertainers, singers, reciters of poetry, and instrumentalists.

Qiyas—Reasoning of a judge using legal analogy.

Qur'an—Islamic book of divine revelation. The Qur'an is divided into 114 *surah*s, or chapters, with 6,219 *ayat*, or verses.

Rababah—A bowed, upright stringed instrument with a squarish or rectangular shape.

Ramadan—The holy month of fasting during the daylight hours.

Rami—Gifts of gold or jewelry given at childbirth.

Rawi—One who recited poetry or texts.

Rawshan—Wooden screens used on buildings in the Hijaz; covered windows and balconies so those inside could see out but no one could see in; these may be decorative screens like the *mashrabiyya* (screens of hand-turned wood) used in Egypt.

Ridha—Parental contentment.

Sabkhah—Salt flat; swampy sand formed where the tide meets land.

Sadaqah—Charity.

Safqa (or tasfiq)—Group hand-clapping that accompanies music, providing part of the percussion or counterpercussion.

Sahwah Islamiyya—A religious revival beginning in the 1970s, which Muslims refer to as the Islamic awakening.

Saj—Rhymed prose.

Salafi—An adherent of the *salafiyya* movement. This refers to historic and modern movements for the purification of Islamic practice by followers of Muhammad ibn 'Abd al-Wahhab and other modern *shaykhs* (not the *islah* movement for Islamic reform and modernization of thought led by Muhammad 'Abduh).

Salat—Prayer in Islam.

Saluki—A hunting dog favored by the bedouin.

Samnah—Clarified butter used in cooking.

Saqr—A type of falcon

Al-Sa'ud, King 'Abd al-'Aziz al-Rahman—The founder of the modern state of Saudi Arabia and its first king. He was also known as Ibn Sa'ud.

Al-Sa'ud, King 'Abdullah ibn 'Abd al-'Aziz—King of Saudi Arabia since 2005.

Al-Sa'ud, King Fahd ibn 'Abd al-'Aziz—King Fahd was debilitated by a stroke; many of his state duties were performed by then crown prince 'Abdullah.

Al-Sa'ud, King Faysal ibn 'Abd al-'Aziz—A modernizing king who was assassinated in 1975 by a nephew.

Al-Sa'ud, Prince Bandar ibn Sultan ibn 'Abd al-'Aziz—Former ambassador of Saudi Arabia to the United States.

Al-Sa'ud, Prince Nayif ibn 'Abd al-'Aziz—Crown prince and deputy prime minister. Minister of the interior for many years.

Al-Sa'ud, Prince Sultan ibn 'Abd al-'Aziz—Was crown prince at the time of his death, and first deputy prime minister, and minister of defense and aviation.

Al-Sa'ud, Prince Turki al-Faysal—Previously headed the General Intelligence Directorate until 2001. Ambassador to the United States in 2006–2007.

Sawalif—The prose prefaces to oral poetry.

Sawm—Fasting. Muslims are required to fast during the daylight hours of the month of Ramadan.

Shahadah—Statement or testimony of belief in Islam; also means witness.

Shahid—One who is martyred for the cause of Islam.

Sha'ir—Poet.

Shari'ah—Islamic law, which is based on the Qur'an, the hadith, *qiyas* (analogy), and *ijma'* (consensus).

Shayla (Shaylah)—Woman's black scarf.

Shiraziyyin—Political trend of activist Shi'a claiming authority as leaders in Karbala', Iraq, who taught and influenced Saudi Arabian Shi'a as well as Bahrainis and Lutis in Oman.

Shirk—Belief in many gods, or "sharing" of God with other entities; idolatrous practice, associating someone other than Allah with divinity.

Shmagh—Man's headcloth with a red houndstooth check pattern.

Shuhadah—Martyrdom. Those who participate in jihad and are not seeking self-glory may be considered martyrs (*shuhada'*).

Shura—Consultation with the rulers, a principle of Islamic governance. The Sa'udi rulers may consult with their advisers and inner circles or hold open *majlis*es (councils) to allow for questions, petitions, and grievances.

Sirwal—Long, baggy pants or pantaloons traditionally worn under other clothing.

Subrah—A lease of land through a contract.

Sudqan—Close friends.

Sufi—A Muslim mystic, follower of a mystical order.

Sunnah—Traditions and practices, both in general and specifically the customs and practice of the Prophet Muhammad.

Suq—Traditional marketplace.

Suq al-harim—Area of the traditional marketplace where women sell goods.

Tafisir—Commentary or interpretation of the Qur'an.

Takfir—The action of declaring a Muslim, to be an infidel or *kaffir* on account of their sins.

Talbiyyah—A greeting to Allah that pilgrims chant in unison on the way to Mecca. It begins in a low, speaking tone and rises in volume.

Tanbura—A lyre, also known as the *simsimiyya*.

Tanzim al-Qa'ida fi Jazirat al-'Arabiyyah—al-Qa'ida organization on the Arabian Peninsula.

Taqlid—Blind imitation in matters of religious doctrine.

Tar—A frame drum, or *daff*.

Tasfiq—Rhythmic clapping performed as a type of percussion and counterrhythm.

Tawhid—The absolute oneness and unicity of God. Monotheism in Islam.

Tawhid al-asma' wa al-sifat—The belief that God's multiple names or attributes (such as the Generous or the Beneficent) that may be found in the Qur'an apply solely to God and no one or nothing else.

Tawhid al-'ibadah—Unicity, or absolute monotheism in worship or religious practice.

Tawhid al-rububiyyah—Allah's unique attribute of being the creator of the world and holding dominion over it.

Tawwaf—Circumambulation of the Ka'ba at Mecca.

Ta'zir—A penalty for crimes less serious than capital offenses or those punishable by *qisas*.

Thawb (thob)—A full-length, long-sleeved, high-necked robe worn by men. These are usually white in the summer and white or possibly gray or brown in the winter months. Certain women's garments, long robes, may also be called a *thawb*.

Thawb magassab—A festive or formal decorated dress worn by women.

Thawb nashal—A festive gauzy overdress decorated with gold metallic thread and sequins, worn by women of the Eastern Province.

Tibb—Medicine.

Tibb Nabawi—Prophetic medicine, based on recitations of Qur'anic verses or drinking the water in which written verses have been soaked.

Tufrah—Literally, "jump"; word used to describe the first oil boom and great influx of oil income.

Turath—Islamic or Arab legacy or historical precedent; cultural heritage.

'Ubudiyya—Slavery (*'abd* means one slave).

Ud—(Pronounced *ood*.) Fragrant resin-infused aloeswood that is burned as incense.

'Ud—Musical instrument. A lute with a deep belly and short, back-bent neck.

'Udhrite love (hubb 'udhri)—Unrequited and usually undeclared love.

'Ulama—Religious scholars or clerics. May refer to the scholars as a class or force in society.

'Umara—The princes and princesses of the Sa'udi royal family.

Ummah—The worldwide community of Muslim believers; transcends national, ethnic, racial, or linguistic divisions.

'Umrah—The lesser pilgrimage, made up of the *tawwaf*, circumambulating the Ka'ba at Mecca, and the *sa'y*, running seven times between the two hills of al-Safa and al-Marwa to remember Hajar's search for water and the discovery of Zamzam.

'Uqayli (plural, 'uqaylat)—A long-distance trader, who might have worked also as a labor migrant or a mercenary soldier in the past.

'Urf—Tribal or customary law.

al-'Utaybi, Juhayman—The man who led the 1979 attack on the Grand Mosque in Mecca.

al-'Utaybi, Sa'ud ibn Hammud—A leader of the al-Qa'ida movement in Saudi Arabia who was killed by Saudi Arabian forces.

Wadi—A valley or narrow gulf that may flood with rainwater.

Wafa'—The pattern of social visits by Saudi Arabian women and mutual support and assistance networks. Also refers to the gifts and favors they extend each other.

Wahhabism—Refers to the interpretation of Islam developed by Muhammad ibn 'Abd al-Wahhab. The Arabic term used (usually) by non–Saudi Arabians is *al-wahabiyya*. However, 'Abd al-Wahhab's followers called themselves *muwahhidun* (monotheists).

Wakil—Deputy or guardian.

Waqf (plural, awqaf)—An endowment made in perpetuity under Islamic law; similar to mortmain; a legal status given to land or property by its owner that preserves its upkeep and dedicates the income generated to some public or charitable purpose.

Wasta—An intermediary or connection. Sometimes means someone who must be contacted to obtain a favor, influence an outcome, act as a go-between, or grant some request.

Wudu'—Ablutions, ritual washing prior to Muslim prayers. The hands and forearms, face, ears, head, and feet are washed.

Wufyan—Formal friends. Might include foreigners.

Wu'ud—Formal visits by friends made by appointment.

Zakat—Charity. A voluntary tax on Muslims that is one of the basic requirements of Islam.

Zar—An exorcism ceremony, accompanied by music. Also the name of a musical genre.

Zina' — The sin of illicit sexual relations; when involving married persons, it means adultery.

Ziyadah—An open space adjoining the main area of a mosque that is converted to a prayer area if large numbers attend prayer.

Facts and Figures

The following tables present facts and figures about contemporary Saudi Arabia. These statistics begin with basic facts about the country and continue with the country's demographics (including population, ethnicity, and religion), geography, economy, communications and transportation, military, and education. Following these basic facts and figures, more detailed data of interest are presented as a series of tables, charts, and graphs.

TABLE A.1   Basic Facts and Figures

Country Info	
Location	Occupies most of the Arabian Peninsula in Southwest Asia, bounded by Jordan, Iraq, and Kuwait to the north; the Persian Gulf, Qatar, the United Arab Emirates, and Oman to the east and south; Yemen to the south; and the Red Sea to the west
Official Name	al-Mamlakah al-'Arabiyyah al-Sa'udiyyah (Kingdom of Saudi Arabia)
Government	Monarchy
Capital	Riyadh
Weights and Measures	Metric system
Time Zone	8 hours ahead of U.S. Eastern Standard

(continued)

399

TABLE A.1 Basic Facts and Figures (*continued*)

Country Info	
Currency	Saudi riyal
Head of State	King 'Abdullah ibn 'Abd al-'Aziz al-Sa'ud
Head of Government	King 'Abdullah ibn 'Abd al-'Aziz al-Sa'ud
Legislature	Majlis al-Shura (Consultative Council), appointed by the king
Major Political Parties	None

Sources: ABC-CLIO World Geography database; CIA World Factbook (https://www.cia.gov/library/publications/the-world-factbook)

DEMOGRAPHICS

The following table features information about the people of Saudi Arabia, including statistics on population, religion, and language.

TABLE A.2 Basic Facts and Figures

Demographics	
Population:	29,207,277 (2010 est.)
Population by age	(2010 est.)
0–14	38%
15–64	59.50%
65+	2.50%
Median Age	(2010 est.)
Total	24.9 years
Males	26 years
Females	23.4 years
Population Growth Rate	1.548% (2010 est.)
Population Density	34 people per sq. mile (2010 est.)
Infant Mortality Rate	16.7 deaths per 1,000 live births (2010 est.)
Ethnic Groups	Arab (90%), Afro-Asian (10%)
Religions	Muslim (100%)
Majority Language	Arabic
Other Languages	Urdu, Tagalog, English, Pashto, Bahasa
Life Expectancy (Average)	73.9 years (2010 est.)
Fertility Rate	2.4 children per woman (2010 est.)

Sources: ABC-CLIO World Geography database; CIA World Factbook (https://www.cia.gov/library/publications/the-world-factbook)

GEOGRAPHY

The following table provides general facts and figures on the geography of Saudi Arabia.

TABLE A.3 Basic Facts and Figures

Geography	
Land Area	864,869 sq. miles
Irrigated Land	6,255 sq.miles (2003)
Coastline	1,640 miles
Natural Hazards	sand and dust storms
Environmental Problems	Desertification, water scarcity, coastal pollution from oil spills
Major Agricultural Products	Wheat, dates, barley, watermelon, vegetables, sheep, goats, poultry
Natural Resources	Oil, natural gas, iron, gold, copper
Climate	Arid with extreme temperature variation except for the coastal regions where it is humid.

Sources: ABC-CLIO World Geography database; CIA World Factbook (https://www.cia.gov/library/publications/the-world-factbook)

ECONOMY

The following table offers basic economic information for Saudi Arabia, including financial, labor, trade, and industrial statistics.

TABLE A.4 Basic Facts and Figures

Economy	
GDP	$434.4 billion (2009 est.)
GDP per capita	$14,873 (2010 est.)
GDP by sector	Agriculture, 2.7%; industry, 61.9%; services, 35.4% (2009 est.)
Exchange rate	3.75 riyals = US $1 (2010)
Labor force	Agriculture, 6.7%; industry, 21.4%; services, 71.9% (2006 est.)
Unemployment	10.8% (2010 est.)

(*continued*)

TABLE A.4   Basic Facts and Figures (*continued*)

Economy	
Major industries	Crude oil extraction, natural gas extraction, petroleum refining and processing, petrochemical products, cement, ship repair, aircraft repair, construction
Leading companies	Saudi Basic Industries Corporation, Dallah al-Baraka, Saudi Arabian Airlines, Saudi Aramco Mobil Refinery Company, Arabian Oil Company, Consolidated Contractors International, National Commercial Bank, Saudi American Bank, Riyadh Bank, Saudi Consolidated Electric Company, Al-Rajhi Banking and Investment Group, Al-Faisalia Group
Electricity production	179.1 billion kWh (2007 est.)
Electricity consumption	165.1 billion kWh (2007 est.)
Value of exports	$235.3 billion (2010 est.)
Goods exported	Petroleum, petroleum products
Value of imports	$99.2 billion (2010 est.)
Goods imported	Machinery and equipment, food, chemicals, textiles, motor vehicles
Current account balance	$52.0 billion (2010 est.)

Sources: ABC-CLIO World Geography database; CIA World Factbook (https://www.cia.gov/library/publications/the-world-factbook)

COMMUNICATIONS AND TRANSPORTATION

The following table features facts and figures on Saudi Arabia's communications networks and transportation.

TABLE A-5   Basic Facts and Figures

Communications and Transportation	
Telephone lines	4.2 million (2009)
Mobile phones	44.9 million (2009)
Internet users	9.77 million (2009)
Roads	137,554 miles (2006)
Railroads	865 miles (2008)
Airports	217 (2010)

Sources: ABC-CLIO World Geography database; CIA World Factbook (https://www.cia.gov/library/publications/the-world-factbook)

MILITARY

The following table outlines basic statistics about the Saudi Arabian military.

TABLE A.6   Basic Facts and Figures

Military	
Defense spending	10% of GDP (2005)
Active armed forces	233,500 (2010)
Manpower fit for military service	7,560,216 men (2010 est.)
Military service	Voluntary, age 18 or older

Sources: ABC-CLIO World Geography database; CIA World Factbook (https://www.cia.gov/library/publications/the-world-factbook)

EDUCATION

The following table presents basic information about education in Saudi Arabia.

TABLE A.7   Basic Facts and Figures

Education	
School system	Primary education begins at the age of six and lasts for six years. Students then attend three years of early secondary education, followed by three years of either academic or technical upper secondary education.
Education expenditures	5.7% of GDP (2008)
Average years spent in school	13.5 (2008)
Students per teacher, primary school	10.8 (2008)
Students per teacher, secondary school	11 (2008)
Primary school–age children enrolled in primary school	3,211,387 (2008)
Secondary school–age children enrolled in secondary school	2,788,094 (2008)
Enrollment in tertiary education	666,662 (2008)
Literacy	79.0% (2005)

Sources: ABC-CLIO World Geography database; CIA World Factbook (https://www.cia.gov/library/publications/the-world-factbook)

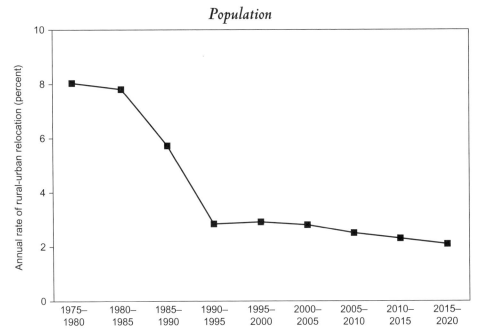

CHART B   Saudi Arabia's Rural-Urban Relocation Rate

TABLE C-1   Urban versus Rural Population

Indicator	1990	1995	2000	2005	2010
Rural population (thousands)	3,807	3,893	4,193	4,492	4,735
Urban population (thousands)	12,449	14,358	16,614	19,120	21,681
Percentage urban (%)	76.6	78.7	79.8	81.0	82.1

TABLE C-2   Urban versus Rural Population

Indicator	1990–1995	1995–2000	2000–2005	2005–2010
Rural annual growth rate (%)	0.45	1.49	1.38	1.05
Urban annual growth rate (%)	2.85	2.92	2.81	2.51

The population of Riyadh has increased steadily during the last 20 years, as have those of the other major cities.

TABLE D   Population Growth of Saudi Arabian Cities

Population of capital city (millions)				
Capital city	1995	2005	2007	2010
Al-Riyadh (Riyadh)	2.576	4.26	4.465	7 (est.)
Populations of other Saudi Arabian cities (thousands)				
City	1990	1995	2000	2005	2010
Al-Dammam	409	533	639	766	903
Medina	529	669	795	944	1,105
Jeddah	1,742	2,200	2,509	2,860	3,239
Mecca	856	1,033	1,168	1,319	1,486

Saudi Arabia is an increasingly urbanized society, although, outside its borders, it is imagined as an undeveloped land of desert dwellers. In 2008, the urban population was 82 percent of the total population of Saudi Arabia (*CIA World Factbook*, Saudi Arabia, 2010). The following table gives an idea of how urbanization has proceeded in different regions of the country.

TABLE E   Urbanization

Urban Population, Agglomerations, and Percentage of Total Urban Population					
Size class	1990	1995	2000	2005	2010
1 to 5 million					
Number of agglomerations	2	3	3	3	4
Population	4,068	6,268	7,244	8,373	10,686
Percentage of urban population	33	44	44	44	49
500,000 to 1 million					
Number of agglomerations	2	2	2	3	3
Population	1,385	1,202	1,434	2,239	2,019
Percentage of urban population	11	8	9	12	9
Fewer than 500,000					
Population	6,996	6,888	7,936	8,508	8,976
Percentage of urban population	56	48	48	44	41

Saudi Arabia's society has a significant stratum of poor and near-poor. In addition to these data, it should be borne in mind that many cannot afford to buy homes because of the high price of land and therefore they rent.

TABLE F   Year-by-Year Economic Data and Some Poverty Indicators

Economic Indicators	2004	2005	2006	2007
GDP (in millions of $)	250,338.9	315,580	356,630.4	383,586.7
Growth of GDP (%)	5.3	5.6	3.2	3.4
Inflation (CPI)	0.3	0.7	2.2	4.2
Unemployment (%)	–	–	6.3	5.6*
Extreme poverty (%)	1.25			
Underweight children under 5 years (%)	–	6.4**		
Foreign direct investment (% of GDP)	−0.1	0.1	0.2	−2.1
Current account balance (millions of $)	51,926.0	90,060.2	99,066.1	95,080.2
Government consumption	23.6	22.2	23.3	22.4
Government expenditure on education (% of GDP)	–	–	–	–
Government expenditure on health (% of GDP)	2.6	2.6	2.5	
Government expenditure on military (% of GDP	8.4	8.0	8.3	9.2

Sources: Bertelsmann Stiftung, *BTI 2010—Saudi Arabia Country Report* (Gütersloh, Germany: Bertelsmann Stiftung, 2009) and UNDP Saudi Arabia Data. *BTI 2010* is based on the World Bank's World Development Indicators 2009; the UNESCO Institute for Statistics; the International Labour Organization's Key Indicators of the Labour Market Database; and the Stockholm International Peace Research Institute (SIPRI)'s Yearbook: Armaments, Disarmament and International Security.

*An extremely low estimate as most text and interview sources suggested rates as high as 20 to 25 percent; also it is not clear if this reflects male unemployment or both female and male unemployment.

**14 percent was estimated based on figures inclusive of 2000–2006 in the UN Human Development Report, 2009. UNDP Human Development Reports 1990–2001. http://hdr.undp.org/en/reports/global/hdr2009/

Oil Production

TABLE G   Top 10 Oil Producers, 2009–2010 (by Total Oil Produced in Barrels per Day)

Rank	Country	Barrels/Day
1	Russia	10,120,000
2	Saudi Arabia	9,764,000
3	United States	9,056,000
4	Iran	4,172,000
5	China	3,991,000
6	Canada	3,289,000

TABLE G   Top 10 Oil Producers, 2009–2010 (by Total Oil
Produced in Barrels per Day) (*continued*)

Rank	Country	Barrels/Day
7	Mexico	3,001,000
8	United Arab Emirates	2,798,000
9	Brazil	2,572,000
10	Kuwait	2,494,000

Source: CIA World Factbook, https://www.cia.gov/library/
publications/the-world-factbook/rankorder/2173rank.html

The following pie charts show the percentage of Saudi Arabia's most important
exports reaching various global destinations. KSA exported 1 million barrels a day
to the United States in 2009; it was the fourth-highest oil exporter to the United
States after Canada, Mexico, and Venezuela. Saudi Arabia exported approximately
55 percent of its crude oil to Asia.

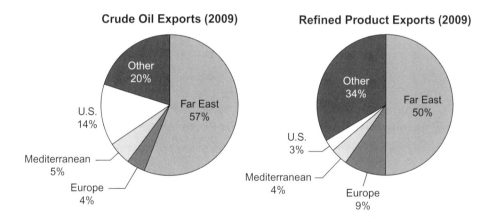

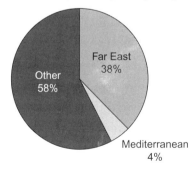

CHART G   Saudi Arabia's Oil, NGL, and Petroleum Product Exports (2009)

Source: Saudi Aramco, 2009 Annual Review.

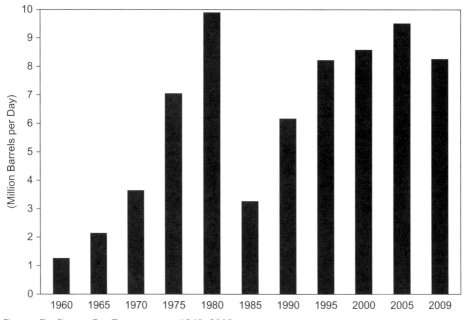

CHART GA CRUDE OIL PRODUCTION, 1960–2009

Source: http://www.eia.doe.gov/aer/txt/ptb1105.html

During the past 50 years, Saudi Arabia's oil production has gradually risen, to a peak of 9.55 million barrels per day in 2009. In 2009, only Russia—at 9.50 million barrels per day—produced more oil per day than Saudi Arabia.

In the late 1980s I studied intraregional trade as a predictor of in-region or global political relations. Despite calls for regional trade and currency zones, all Arab countries traded more heavily with nations outside the Arab world than with each other. This affects the countries' ability to invest in other areas of their economy because their imports often cost more than the value of their exports. Sometimes, intraregional trade helped explain political alliances (like Jordan and Iraq's). Saudi Arabia

TABLE H Saudi Arabia's Leading Regional Trading Partners in the Years of the Oil Boom (1974 to 1982)

Exports			Imports		
Rank	**Country**	**No.**	**Rank**	**Country**	**No.**
1	Jordan	223.5	1	Lebanon	341.2
2	Lebanon	203.0	2	Kuwait	304.85
3	Morocco	185.0	3	Syria	221.8
4	Sudan	116.5	4	Jordan	110.4
5	Syria	112.4	5	Sudan	82.57

TABLE H   Saudi Arabia's Leading Regional Trading Partners in the Years of the Oil Boom
(1974 to 1982) (*Continued*)

Exports			Imports		
Rank	**Country**	**No.**	**Rank**	**Country**	**No.**
6	Tunisia	88.0	6	Egypt	50.7
7	Egypt	79.7	7	Morocco	15.5
8	Kuwait	47.28	8	Iraq	4.0
9	Libya	16.0	9	Libya	.85
10	Iraq	15.8	10	Tunisia	.85
11	Algeria	3.5	11	Algeria	.45

Sources: Quarterly Economic Review (various country editions, 1982–1983); Zuhur, "A View
of Intraregional Trade in the Middle East," 1986.

was far more important as an exporter or importer to other Arab countries than were
they to Saudi Arabia itself, however, its economic relationships with other world
powers are far more significant to its own economic profile than any Arab partners.

The following data show the greater significance of Saudi Arabia's trade with
nations outside of the region, even though its trade (and aid) are important to other
Arab nations.

Trade

TABLE I   Percentage of Saudi Arabia's World Trade That Is Intraregional (IR)

Exports		Imports		Total Value of Trade	
IR total =	9,491	IR total =	9,795	IR total =	19,286
World total =	533,425	World total =	181,828	World total =	715,243
IR portion =	1.77%	IR portion =	5.385%	IR portion =	2.69%
Industrial Countries' Percentage of Total Trade with Saudi Arabia for 1982					
Exports = US$ 64.5 million		Imports = US$82.4 million			

By 2008, the low rate of intraregional trade had not changed. But the world had, as
Asian countries have grown in importance. Saudi Arabia's most important trading
partners were the United States, China, Japan, South Korea, India, and Germany.

TABLE J   Saudi Arabia's Exports and Imports

Saudi Arabia's Exports: Highest Percentages	
To: United States	17.1%
Japan	15.2%
South Korea	10.1%
China	9.3%
India	7.0%
Saudi Arabia's Imports: Highest Percentages	
From: United States	12.2%
China	10.5%
Japan	7.7%
Germany	7.4%
South Korea	5.1%

TABLE K Selected Arab Countries' Trade with Saudi Arabia in 2010

Jordan		Syria		Sudan	Lebanon	Yemen	Egypt
Exports (% of total)	Imports (% of total)	Exports (% of total)	Imports (% of total)	Imports (% of total)	Exports (% of total)	Exports (% of total)	Imports (% of total)
10.56	17.3	5.04	10.1	7.22	7.0	5.8	5.53

Source: CIA World Factbook 2010.

Employment

The data below show that a significant percentage of the employed population had a secondary school education or less. Saudization depends on increasing the educational readiness of the labor force and also supplying targeted training. Of the Saudi Arabian women who work, many have a university education; here, more and varied jobs are necessary.

TABLE L   Distribution of Employed Saudi Arabians by Educational Level and Gender

Educational Level	Male (No.)	Male (%)	Female (No.)	Female (%)	Total (No.)	Total (%)
Illiterate	131,325	4.01	9,945	2.06	141,270	3.76
Literate	111,058	3.39	3,759	0.78	114,817	3.06
Primary	446,288	13.63	7,613	1.58	453,901	12.08
Intermediate	626,781	19.14	11,761	2.44	638,542	17.00
Secondary or equivalent	1,010,102	30.85	54,551	11.31	1,064,653	28.34
Diploma	264,103	8.07	86,327	17.90	350,430	9.33
University	633,777	19.36	298,454	61.88	932,231	24.82
Postgraduate	35,149	1.07	4,323	0.90	39,472	1.05
PhD	15,773	0.48	5,580	1.16	21,353	0.57
Total	3,274,356	100.00	482,313	100.00	3,756,669	100.00

Source: United Nations Development Program and Kingdom of Saudi Arabia, Ministry of Economy and Planning, *Millennium Development Goals* 2009 G./1430 H., p. 34.

The rate of enrollment in school indicates that Saudi Arabia will likely meet its millennium goals of bridging the gender gap in enrollment. However, matriculation rates are even more important.

TABLE M   Youth and Educational Data

Current GDP per capita	**US$14,871**
Youth proportion of population (ages 15–24)	19%
(ages 15–29)	28%
Youth unemployment rate (ages 15–24)	
Total	16.3%
Male	12.2%
Female	15.8%
Net enrollment rate, primary (2008)	
Total	85%
Male	85%
Female	84%
Net enrollment rate, secondary (2007)	
Total (national estimate)	73%

TABLE M   Youth and Educational Data *(Continued)*

Current GDP per capita	US$ 14, 871
Male (UIS estimate)	70%
Female (UIS estimate)	76%
Gross enrollment rate, tertiary (2006)	
Total	30%
Male	25%
Female	36%
Public expenditure on education (2004)	
Percentage of GDP	6.8%
Percentage of total government expenditure	27.6%
Pupil-teacher ratio (2008)	
Primary (national estimate)	11
Secondary (national estimate)	*11

*If correct, this is very low.

Sources: Brookings Institute, "Taking Stock of the Youth Challenge to the Middle East," 2010, http://www.brookings.edu/articles/2010/06_middle_east_youth.aspx?sc_lang=en. Country data and UIS, 2009. United Nations (UNESCO) Institute for Statistics (2009).

Outdoor Recreation

TABLE N   Saudi Arabia's Reserves, Parks, and Wildlife Sanctuaries

al-Jandaliyya	Mahazat al-Sayd
al-Khunfah	Majami' al-Hadb
al-Tubayq	Nafud al-Urayq
al-Taysiyah	Raydah
Farasan Islands	Saja Umm al-Rimth
Harrat al-Harrah	Umm al-Qamari
Ibex Reserve	'Uruq Bani Ma'arid

Major Saudi Arabian Holidays

OFFICIAL HOLIDAYS

Official holidays in Saudi Arabia are the 'Id al-Fitr, the 'Id al-Adha, and Saudi National Day. Ramadan is the month of fasting preceding the 'Id al-Fitr, and businesses and schools typically hold reduced Ramadan hours. The Laylat al-Qadr, the Night of Power, is believed to take place during the final 10 days of Ramadan. On this night, the Qur'an was first revealed. However, it is not known exactly when the Night of Power will fall.

The 'Id al-Fitr and 'Id al-Adha

The 'Id al-Fitr ends the fast of Ramadan. This 'Id is celebrated for several days (up to a week) in Saudi Arabia. The 'Id al-Adha, the feast of the sacrifice, commemorates Ibrahim's sacrificing of a ram in place of his son Isma'il, and occurs on the 10th day of Dhu al-Hija.

The dates given for 2011–2013 might vary by a day or two because the beginning of Ramadan depends on the sighting of the moon or a special arrangement if the moon cannot be seen.

- 1st day of Ramadan, August 1, 2011
- Laylat al-Qadr (Night of Power): Estimated August 26, 2011
- 'Id al-Fitr (end of Ramadan): August 30, 2011
- 'Id al-Adha (10th day of Dhu al-Hija): November 6, 2011

Saudi National Day

Saudi National Day is held on September 23 of the Western calendar every year to mark the establishment of the Kingdom of Saudi Arabia in 1932.

OTHER HOLIDAYS

Other holidays include the Prophet Muhammad's birthday, the Islamic New Year, and the 'Ashura holiday.

Islamic New Year

The Islamic New Year is the first day of the first month, Muharram. It is not an official but rather a religious holiday in Saudi Arabia.

1433 AH	The New Year should occur on November 26, 2011
1434 AH	The New Year should occur on November 15, 2012
1435 AH	The New Year should occur on November 4, 2013

Mawlid al-Nabi

Similarly, the Prophet's Birthday, the Mawlid al-Nabi, is not an official holiday, although it is in other Muslim countries. The dates of this holiday differ. Sunni Muslims, the majority group in Saudi Arabia, celebrate it on the 12th day of Rabi'a al-Awwal, and the Shi'a Muslims, celebrate it on the 17th day of that month to coincide with the birthday of Ja'far al-Sadiq, their sixth imam.

	12th of Rabi'a al-Awwal	17th day of Rabi'a al-Awwal
2011	February 15	February 20
2012	February 4	February 9
2013	January 24	January 29

'Ashura

'Ashura is celebrated by the Saudi Arabian Shi'a as a day of mourning for Imam Husayn. For the majority Sunni group, it is a holiday but not of such magnitude. It is held on the 10th day of the month of Muharram, which should arrive on

1433	December 5, 2011
1434	November 24, 2012
1435	November 13, 2013

Isra'

The Isra' and the Mi'raj were two parts of the Prophet Muhammad's miraculous Night Journey and they are commemorated on the Laylat al-Mi'raj which took place on June 28 in 2011 and is estimated for June 16 in 2012.

Weekly Holiday

The day of communal prayer is Friday. Official businesses are closed on Friday. Some are closed on Friday and Saturday; however, others are closed only on Friday mornings until the ending of the afternoon prayer.

Country-Related Organizations

BUSINESS AND ECONOMIC RESOURCES

Chambers of commerce and industry exist in all of the main cities of Saudi Arabia—Abha, al-Ahsa, Arar, al-Bahah, Bishah, Dammam, Hafr al-Baten, Ha'il, al-Jawf, Jeddah, Jizan, al-Majma'ah, Mecca, Medina, Najran, Qasim, Riyadh, Tabuk, Ta'if, and Yanbu.

Chambers of Commerce

A point of contact is the Council of Chambers:
http://www.saudichambers.org.sa/index_en.htm
or http://www.saudinf.com/main/p2.htm

JEDDAH CHAMBER OF COMMERCE AND INDUSTRY

King Khalid St., Ghurfa Bldg.
P.O. Box 9549
Jeddah 21423
Tel: (2) 642-3535/647-1100
Fax: (2) 651-7373
Website: http://www.jcci.org.sa/jcci/

RIYADH CHAMBER OF COMMERCE AND INDUSTRY

Dhabab St., al-Murabba'
P.O. Box 596
Riyadh 11421
Tel: 966 (1) 404-0044/404-0300/404-2700
Fax: 966 (1) 401-1103
Website: http://www.riyadhchamber.com/index.php

For other addresses, see http://www.saudia-online.com/chamber.htm.

The chambers are headed by the Council of Saudi Chambers of Commerce and Industry in Riyadh, Chamber of Commerce and Industry Building, P.O. Box 16683, Riyadh 11474. Tel. (1) 405-3200/405-7502. Fax: (1) 402-4747. Certain chambers have elected women representatives, and three women stood for election to the Riyadh chamber in 2010.

Kingdom Holding Company

P.O. Box 1
Riyadh 11321
Kingdom of Saudi Arabia
Tel: +966 1 211 1111
Fax: +966 1 211 1112
E-mail: Investor.relations@kingdom.com.sa
Website: http://www.kingdom.com.sa/en/

A public holding company controlled by Prince al-Walid ibn Talal ibn 'Abd al-'Aziz with headquarters in Riyadh. Only 6 percent of the company's shares are public. Its international investments have included Amazon, Citigroup, Fox News Channel, PepsiCo, Motorola, Walt Disney Company, the Lebanese Broadcasting Corporation International, and the Rotana Group (see Music).

Saudi Arabian Market Information Resources (SAMIRAD)

For directory entry or book advertising,
Postal address: SAMIRAD, Littebrook Estate, Poulner Hill, Ringwood, England BH24 3HR
Tel: 00 44 (0) 1425 489901
Fax: 00 44 (0) 1425 461200
E-mail: samirad@saudinf.com
Website: http://www.saudinf.com/

Saudi Arabian Market Information Resources (SAMIRAD) is a business-oriented governmental organization with a website with information on Saudi Arabia organized into a country profile, a current news section, and advertising sections for businesses.

Saudi-U.S. Relations Information Service (SUSRIS)

Patrick Ryan, Editor
Saudi-US Relations Information Service (SUSRIS)
c/o P.O. Box 2931
Cookeville, TN 38502-2931
Tel: (931) 230-5732
Website: http://www.susris.com

Saudi-U.S. Relations Information Service (SUSRIS) is a private-sector informational organization that offers a wide array of articles, interviews, and information on Saudi Arabia and U.S.–Saudi Arabian relations with a website, related blogs, an e-newsletter, and links to National Council of U.S.-Arab Relations.

U.S.-Saudi Arabian Business Council (USSABC)

U.S. Office
8081 Wolftrap Road, Suite 300
Vienna, VA 22182
Tel: (703) 962-9300 or 888-638-1212
Fax: (703) 204-0332
E-mail: ussaudi@us-sabc.org

Saudi Arabian Office
Al Ahsa Street, Al-Malaz
P.O. Box 27582
Riyadh 11427
Kingdom of Saudi Arabia
Tel: 966-1-474-2555/3555 or 966-1-476-7913
Fax: 966-1-476-7167/2697
E-mail: ussaudibc@us-sabc.org

U.S.-Saudi Arabian Business Council (USSABC), formed in 1993, is a bilateral organization of business leaders that aims to promote better mutual understanding and provide information on business opportunities. It has offices in Washington, D.C., and Riyadh. The council is co-chaired by Abdulaziz al-Quraishi, former governor of the Saudi Arabian Monetary Agency and CEO of A.Z. Al-Quraishi & Brothers Co., and Peter Robertson, former vice chairman of Chevron Corporation.

BUSINESS/GOVERNMENTAL

Capital Market Authority

Faisaliyyah
King Fahad Road, C

Tel: (800) 245-1111
E-mail: info@cma.org.sa
Website: http://www.cma.org.sa/

Capital Market Authority (CMA) is responsible for regulating Saudi Arabian capital markets, developing them, regulating the Saudi Arabian Stock Exchange (Tadawul), and creating the necessary regulations. The CMA was formed by royal decree in 2004 (although it has existed unofficially since the 1950s) and is headed in 2010 by a five-person board including Dr. Abdulrahman A. Al-Tuwaijri (chairman), Mr. Abdulrahman Al-Rashed (vice chairman), Mr. Mohammed Al-Sumrani (member), Mazin A. Al-Rmaih (member), and Abdulrahman M. Al-Arrak (member).

Saudi Basic Industries Corporation (SABIC)

P.O. Box 5101
Riyadh 11422
Tel: 1-401-2033/1-401-2361
Fax: 1-401-3831
E-mail: malkusayer@sabic.com
Website: http://www.sabic.com/

Saudi Basic Industries Corporation (SABIC) is a public company manufacturing fertilizers, chemicals, plastics, and metals.

CULTURAL/YOUTH

General Presidency for Youth Welfare (GPYW)

P.O. Box 965
Riyadh 11421
Tel: 401 4576
Fax: 401 0376

General Presidency for Youth Welfare (GPYW) sponsored many cultural programs including classes in folklore, arts and crafts, literary and drama clubs, and also science projects. Nine literary clubs arrange lectures and symposiums and try to encourage young writers through poetry- and essay-writing competitions. The GPYW also sponsors exhibits of calligraphy and visual arts and sponsors Saudi Arabians to participate in international arts events. From 2003 on, the Ministry of Culture and Information took over many of the activities and centers previously affiliated with the GPYW, including the King Fahd Cultural Center.

Mansoojat Foundation

London: +44 (0)78 8692 0254
Saudi Arabia: +966 5 0667 3765

E-mail: info@mansoojat.org
Website: http://www.mansoojat.org
And on Facebook

The Mansoojat Foundation is a nonprofit charity registered in the United Kingdom by a group of Saudi Arabian women who want to revive and preserve the traditional costumes and designs of the different regions of Saudi Arabia. They mounted the Arabia 3D exhibit at IMAX London in 2010.

Saudi Arabian Boy Scouts Association (SABSA)

Website: http://www.scouts.org.sa/a

SABSA is the official national scouting organization of Saudi Arabia and had 19,269 members in 2010. It was formally established in 1961, but scouting activities were available for many years prior to that. Saudi Arabia is a member of the World Organization of the Scout Movement. A scout is called a *kashaf* in Arabic, and the scouting motto "be prepared" translates to *kun musta'idan*.

Saudi Arabian Society for Culture and Arts

The society was formed in 1972 and is affiliated with the General Presidency for Youth Welfare (GPYW; see its entry). It consists of committees for culture, theater, music and vocal arts, folklore, arts, information, and publishing. It has been studying and recording Saudi Arabian folk music and dance since the 1980s, and at least 50 folk groups perform around the country. The society has produced a television program called *Folk Arts*. It sponsors Saudi Arabian artists and established a library, an information center, and a cultural center in Riyadh.

World Assembly of Muslim Youth

Mail Address: Riyadh 11443
or P.O. Box 10845
Tel: (966) 1/4641669
Fax: (966) 1/4641710
E-mail: info@wamy.org
Website: http://www.wamy.org
Facebook: http://www.facebook.com/pages/
WORLD-ASSEMBLY-OF-MUSLIM-YOUTH-WAMY/79897795475

The World Assembly of Muslim Youth was founded in Saudi Arabia in 1972. It is an international organization devoted to promoting knowledge of Islam and Islamic *da'wah* to young adults. Its activities range from organizing soccer (football) tournaments to providing youth camps and scholarship programs. It has been accused in Europe of promoting Wahhabism, or the Muslim Brotherhood, and both trends have been represented in the organization despite their marked differences.

EDUCATIONAL/SCHOLARLY

British Society for Middle East Studies (BRISMES)

BRISMES Administrative Office
Institute for Middle Eastern and Islamic Studies
University of Durham
Elvet Hill Road
Durham DH13TU United Kingdom
Tel: 0191 33 45179
Fax: 0191 33 45661
E-mail: a.l.haysey@dur.ac.uk
Website: http://www.brismes.ac.uk/

The British Society for Middle East Studies (BRISMES), founded in 1973, is a professional society for professors, students, and those with an interest in the Middle East. As for the Middle East Studies Association of North America (MESA; see its entry), some members specialize in Saudi Arabia, and the organization holds an annual conference.

Gulf2000 Project

Email: lgpS@columbia.edu
Website: http://gulf2000.columbia.edu/

The Gulf2000 Project was established in 1993 for scholars, officials, journalists, businesspersons, and others with a professional interest in the Gulf region or studies of that region. The executive director is Gary Sick, and the project is affiliated with Columbia University's School of International and Public Affairs, with funding from the Ford Foundation, Carnegie Corporation, the Open Society Institute, and Exxon-Mobil Foundation; it has an electronic library.

Institute of Diplomatic Studies (IDS) Ma'ahad al-Dirasat al-Diblumasiyya

Director Amb. Dr. Saad bin Abdelrahman al-Ammar
Ministry of Foreign Affairs, Diplomatic Institute
P.O. Box 51988 11553
Riyadh, Kingdom of Saudi Arabia
Tel: +966 1 2011184
Fax: +966 1 2011194
E-mail: alammar1@hotmail.com

Website: http://www.ids.gov.sa/vEnglish/default.asp
or: http://www.ids.gov.sa/en/

The Institute of Diplomatic Studies (IDS) is an educational organization of the Saudi Arabian Ministry of Foreign Affairs headed by a board of directors and reporting to the minister. It was established in 1983 in Jeddah and moved to Riyadh in 1984. In 2007, the IDS was recognized as the main training institute for diplomatic and foreign affairs. It hosts scholars and experts who lecture to the members, produces publications, and since 2007 has established the Center for Strategic Studies, the Center for European Studies, the Center for American Studies, and the Center for Asian Studies.

Institute for Gulf Affairs

1900 L Street N.W., Suite 309
Washington, DC 20036
Tel. (202) 466–9500
Website: http://www.gulfinstitute.org/ali_alahmed.htm

The Institute for Gulf Affairs is an American-based organization, formerly called the Saudi Institute, that has been highly critical of Saudi Arabia. It was organized by 'Ali al-Ahmed. He has now been joined by five others who specialize in Gulf affairs. Al-Ahmed has mainly focused on religious discrimination in Saudi Arabia. The institute's funding source is not indicated. It is included here in the interest of free and open information.

International Organization for Quran Memorization

International Organization for Quran Memorization is dedicated to the teaching of *tahfiz* (Qur'an memorization). It held an international conference in June 2010. This is to be differentiated from the national Charitable Society for the Memorization of the Holy Quran, which was ordered to fire all of its non–Saudi Arabian teachers (1,230 teachers) in November 2010, perhaps as part of the Saudization strategy (*Arab News*, November 3, 2010). It has offices in different countries as well as Saudi Arabia. It is associated with the website http://www.islam.com. To understand the popularity of Qur'an memorization, readers might watch *Koran by Heart*, directed by Greg Barker, to be shown on HBO during Ramadan 2011. The film covers the annual contest held in Cairo, following three winners back to their home countries.

King Abdulaziz Historical Centre

King Abdulaziz Historical Centre is a complex in Riyadh encompassing the al-Murabba' Palace, a park with a palm grove, the Darat King Abdulaziz (King

Abdulaziz Centre for Information and Research), the King Abdulaziz Mosque, the National Museum, the Department of Antiquities and Museums, the King Abdulaziz Public Library, the Lecture Hall, and the Riyadh Water Tower.

King Abdulaziz Public Library

Tel: 966 14911300
Fax: 966 14911949
Website: http://www.kapl.org.sa/

The branch of the library in the Murabba' area of Riyadh within the historical centre complex has a men's, a women's, and a children's library. The library has important holdings in Arabic and Islamic studies, including rare European and Arabic books, and acquired the impressive private libraries of George Rentz and Hamza Bu Bakr as well as holdings from other sources. It also has a photographic archive of more than 5,400 photos, including the collections of Abbas Pasha Hilmi (and displayed the photographs of Princess Alice, a granddaughter of Queen Victoria, taken during her visit to the kingdom), Humberto da Silveira, Col. Muhammad Sadiq Pasha, and the Mirza collection, and also collections of documents, maps, and coins.

King Fahd National Library

Website: http://www.kfupm.edu.sa/library/

This library is located in a modernistic building in Riyadh. It is a research facility and holds a large collection of rare manuscripts of Arabic and Islamic literature. Its holdings of 1,300,000 items and 2,000,000 documents are in at least 10 languages, and it has the largest collection of information about Saudi Arabia (Kingdom Information Center). It houses the Saudi National Bibliography with an author, subject, and title index, an index for Saudi periodicals, and a national archive for historic photographs and audiovisual records. Its information center has 3,000 paintings by Saudi Arabian artists. Its website includes an online catalog, contacts for librarians, and hours for men and women.

King Faisal Foundation

P.O. Box 352
Riyadh 11411
Fax: 1-465-6524
E-mail: info@kff.com
Website: http://www.kff.com/

The King Faisal Foundation is a philanthropic and scholarly organization established by his heirs. In 2010, the chairman of the board of trustees was Prince

Muhammad al-Faisal, and the managing director was Prince Khalid al-Faisal. It aids the al-Faisal University, the King Faisal School, and Effat National College, and it provides research grants, hosts scholars, offers a university preparatory program, and has certain commercial interests. The foundation awards the King Faisal International Prize to individuals who have promoted literature. It operates the King Faisal Center for Research and Islamic Studies (KFCRIS, http://www.kfcris.com/). The chairman of the board of directors of the KFCRIS in 2010 was Prince Turki al-Faisal. KFCRIS publishes the magazine *Islamic Civilization*.

Middle East Policy Council

1730 M Street NW, Suite 512
Washington, DC 20036
Tel: (202) 296-6767
Fax: (202) 296-5791
E-mail: info@mepc.org
Website: http://www.mepc.org
Facebook: http://www.facebook.com/pages/
Middle-East-Policy-Council/312133357360

The Middle East Policy Council is a nonprofit educational organization located in Washington, D.C., whose president and CEO as of 2011 is Frank Anderson. It publishes the *Middle East Policy* journal and offers special sessions open to members of the U.S. Congress as well as workshops for educators. Its website offers timely information on Saudi Arabia.

Middle East Studies Association of North America (MESA)

Website: http://www.mesa.arizona.edu

The Middle East Studies Association of North America (MESA) is a professional scholarly association devoted to the study of the Middle East. It has about 3,000 members. At MESA's annual meetings, panels or individual research papers address Saudi Arabian topics, and publications are displayed on every aspect of the Middle East. MESA publishes two journals, the *International Journal of Middle East Studies* and the *Review of Middle East Studies*, both of which include scholarly publications on Saudi Arabia and reviews of books on Saudi Arabia.

National Council on U.S. Arab Relations (NCUSAR)

1730 M St., NW, Suite 503
Washington, DC 20036
Tel: 1-202-293-6466
Fax: 1-202-293-7770
Website: http://ncusar.org/

The National Council on U.S. Arab Relations (NCUSAR) is a U.S. nonprofit educational organization that promotes good relations between the United States and the Gulf nations, including Saudi Arabia. The organization was founded in 1983, and its president and director as of 2011 was Dr. John Duke Anthony. It offers public briefings, an annual conference, internships, resources, and study trips to countries of the Arabian Peninsula.

Saudi-British Society

Mrs. Ionis Thompson
Honorary Secretary
The Saudi-British Society
1 Gough Square
London EC4A 3DE United Kingdom
Tel: 44 (0) 1372 842788
E-mail: secretary@saudibritishsociety.org.uk
Website: http://www.saudibritishsociety.org.uk/

The Saudi-British Society was formed in 1986 to promote a greater understanding between the peoples of Saudi Arabia and the United Kingdom. It offers lectures on subjects concerning Saudi Arabia; provides sponsorships, grants, and awards; and promotes publications on Saudi Arabia. The president is always the Saudi Arabian ambassador to the United Kingdom, currently Prince Mohammed bin Nawaf al-Sa'ud, ambassador to the Court of St. James's.

FINANCIAL

Islamic Development Bank (ISDB)

P.O. Box 5925
Jeddah 21432
Tel: 2-636-0011/2-636-0054
Fax: 2-637-1334
Website: http://www.isdb.org/irj/portal/anonymous?guest_user=idb_en

The Islamic Development Bank (IDB) is a multinational financial institution with headquarters in Jeddah, Saudi Arabia. It was founded by the finance ministers of the Organization of the Islamic Conference in 1973 and began operations in 1975. It is not a Saudi Arabian organization, but Saudi Arabia is a member along with 53 other member states who are shareholders. The largest shareholders in the IDB are from Saudi Arabia, Sudan, Kuwait, Libya, Turkey, the United Arab Emirates, Iran, Egypt, Indonesia, and Pakistan. The bank's purposes are to promote economic and social development for its members and for Muslim communities in non-member countries, to provide interest-free loans for projects including those creating infrastructure, and to offer technical assistance and training facilities for development purposes.

Saudi Arabian Monetary Agency (SAMA)

Saudi Arabian Monetary Agency
Al-Ma'ather Street
P.O. Box 2992
Riyadh 11169
Saudi Arabia
Tel: +966-1-463-3000
Fax: +966-1-466-2936/466-2966
Cable: MARKAZI
E-mail: info@sama.gov.sa
Website: http://www.sama.gov.sa/sites/samaen/Pages/Home.aspx

The Saudi Arabian Monetary Agency (SAMA), established in 1952, serves as Saudi Arabia's central bank. It issues the national currency, supervises all commercial banks, helps maintain price stability, operates financial systems, and supervises foreign-exchange reserves. SAMA's governor is Dr. Muhammad al-Jasser, who was appointed in 2009.

Supreme Economic Council

Secretariat General, Supreme Economic Council of Saudi Arabia
P.O. Box 94737
Riyadh 11614
Tel: 4803744
Fax: 4834035
E-mail: info@sec.gov.sa
Website: http://www.sec.gov.sa/Home.aspx

The Supreme Economic Council was formed in 1999, chaired then by then-crown prince 'Abdullah ibn 'Abd al-'Aziz. The council aimed to broaden the economic policy–making process, and its goals were to benefit society, provide jobs, control public debt, distribute national income fairly, diversify the economy, increase savings and investments, and aid privatization (*SAMIRAD*, 2010). In 2009, the council was reorganized by a royal decree, to include Prince Sa'ud Al-Faisal (chairman), Prince Mohammed ibn Nayef ibn 'Abdulaziz, Dr. 'Abdulaziz ibn 'Abdullah Al-Khuwaiter, Dr. Mutlab ibn 'Abdullah Al-Nafisah, the minister of commerce and industry, the minister of petroleum and mineral resources, the minister of finance, the minister of economy and planning, the minister of water and electricity, the governor of the Saudi Arabian Monetary Agency, and the secretary-general of the Supreme Economic Council.

Tadawul (Saudi Stock Exchange)

NCCI Building, North Tower
King Fahd Rd.
P.O. Box 60612
Riyadh 11555
Kingdom of Saudi Arabia
Tel.: +966 1 218-9999 (main number)
Tel.: +966 1 218-9090 (customer service)
E-mail: webinfo@tadawul.com.sa
Website: http://www.tadawul.com.sa/wps/portal/!ut/p/c0/04_
SB8K8xLLM9MSSzPy8xBz9CP0os3g_A-ewIE8TIwP3gDBTA08Tn2C-
j4AAvY_dQA_3gxCL9gmxHRQB0Zc_U/

The Tadawul is the Saudi Arabian Stock Exchange and is supervised by the Saudi Arabian Capital Market Authority. The Tadawul All-Share Index's (TASI) end-of-the-year value of shares traded for 2010 was 759.18 billion Saudi riyals or US$ 202.45 billion.

GOVERNMENTAL

Embassy and Consulates

Royal Embassy of Saudi Arabia

601 New Hampshire Avenue, NW
Washington, DC 20037
Tel: (202) 342-3800
E-mail: info@saudiembassy.net

Saudi Arabian Consulate General—New York

866 Second Ave., 5th Floor
New York, NY 10017
Tel: (212) 752-2740

Saudi Arabian Consulate General—Los Angeles

2045 Sawtelle Blvd.
Los Angeles, CA 90025
Tel: (310) 479-6000

Saudi Arabian Consulate General—Houston

5718 Westheimer, Suite 1500
Houston, TX 77057
Tel: (713) 785-5577

Governmental agencies and ministries are listed on the websites of Saudi Arabia's embassies. Only a few are listed here; others are discussed within the book.

General Intelligence Directorate (GID)

P.O. Box 2933
Riyadh 11134
Tel: 1-401-1944
Fax: 1-403-1185
Jeddah office Tel: 2-687-232

Saudi Arabia's largest intelligence agency is responsible for intelligence collection and analysis, security, antiterrorism, and foreign liaisons. The General Intelligence Directorate (GID) was charged by certain Americans in the investigation of the Khobar bombing; however, foreign agencies (from the United States, United Kingdom, and other countries) have also not cooperated with Saudi Arabia's GID with reference to members of opposition groups. Prince Turki al-Faisal resigned as director-general of the General Intelligence Presidency (GIP) which heads the GID, on August 31, 2001, and was replaced by Prince Nawaf ibn 'Abd al-'Aziz, King 'Abdullah's half brother (Cordesman 2002, 263–265), but then Prince Nawaf suffered a stroke. Prince Muqrin ibn 'Abd al-'Aziz has been director-general of the GIP since 2005. Cooperation with the United States on counterterrorism has increased markedly since 2001. The GID is within the Ministry of the Interior.

General Organization for Social Insurance (GOSI)

P.O. Box 2963
Riyadh 11461
Tel: 1-477-7735
Fax: 1- 477-9958
Website: http://www.gosi.gov.sa/index.php

The General Organization for Social Insurance (GOSI) is a governmental agency that regulates social insurance regulations, collects employer contributions, and pays benefits to Saudi Arabian citizens and noncitizens if they are insured in Saudi Arabia. It is supervised by a board of 11 directors.

HAIA or CPVPV (Committee for the Promotion of Virtue and the Prevention of Vice)

Tel: 038602687
Fax: 038602688
E-mail: hisbah@hisbah.gov.sa
Website: http://www.hisbah.gov.sa/ (*This website was down in early summer of 2011.)

HAIA (the Committee for the Promotion of Virtue and the Prevention of Vice) is a division of the Saudi Arabian government that employs the *mutawa'in*, or religious police. They carry out the *hisba*, which is the religious command to promote virtue and do away with sinful behavior, which they interpret as violations of dress codes, any mixing of unrelated men and women, the requirement that businesses close at prayer times, and observance of prayers. It has about 3,500 members but also many volunteers. Since 2007 the HAIA's powers and funding have been more restricted than in the past.

National Commission for Wildlife Conservation and Development

Saudi Wildlife Commission
P.O. Box 61681
Riyadh 11575
Tel: +966 144 18700
Website: http://www.ncwcd.gov.sa/

The National Commission for Wildlife Conservation and Development, created in 1986, is devoted to the preservation of native species, or their reintroduction, and their habitats, and to education about wildlife in Saudi Arabia.

National Human Rights Commission

King Fahd Road, Building No. 373
Riyadh, Kingdom of Saudi Arabia
Tel: 014628071/014655317/014628210
Fax: 014612061
Mailing address:
P.O. Box 58889
Riyadh 11515
Kingdom of Saudi Arabia
Website: http://www.haq-ksa.org/

The commission was created in 2005. It offers a website-based complaint form, and Human Rights Watch has written and posted letters of concern to the commission regarding egregious cases, several involving extreme abuse of women. The commission opened a women's office in 2008. It was tasked to set up a review committee to enable the formation of civil society organizations that are not strictly charities, but it has not actually done so. It has a Western Region office in Jeddah and an Eastern Region office in Dammam.

Royal Saudi Air Defense Force

Ministry of Defense and Aviation (MODA)
Airport Road

Riyadh 11165
Tel: 1 478 5900/1 477 7313
Jeddah tel: 2 665 2400
Website: http://www.moda.gov.sa/detail.asp?InServiceID=214&intemplatekey=
MainPage

The Royal Saudi Air Defense Force is the fourth branch of the Saudi Arabian armed forces. It was part of the Royal Saudi Land Forces until 1981. It is headquartered in Riyadh and has an extensive underground command facility that monitors Saudi Arabia's radar and air defense system, known as the Peace Shield.

Royal Saudi Air Force

Ministry of Defense and Aviation (MODA)
Airport Road
Riyadh 11165
Tel: 1 478 5900/1 477 7313
Jeddah tel: 2 665 2400
Websites: http://www.moda.gov.sa/detail.asp?InServiceID=214&intemplatekey=M
ainPage http://www.moda.gov.sa/Detail.asp?InSectionID=86&InNewsItemID=145

Royal Saudi Air Force (*al-Quwwat al-jawiyyah al-malakiyyya al-sa'udiyya*) is the main air force of the Saudi Arabian military. It possesses an offensive capability with a fleet of F-15 and Tornado aircraft. The minister of defense and aviation is Crown Prince Sultan ibn 'Abd al-'Aziz.

Royal Saudi Land Forces (RSLF, or Saudi Arabian Army)

Tel: +966 (1) 4777777, ext. 7862
Fax: +966 (1) 4777777, ext. 6380
Website: http://WWW.RSLF.GOV.SA/English/pages/default.aspx
Or contact via the Ministry of Defense and Aviation (MODA) as listed in the preceding entry

The Royal Saudi Land Forces (RSLF), estimated at 150,000 troops and headed in 2010 by chief of the general staff, Field Marshal Saleh al-Muhaya. The army of 'Abd al-'Aziz al-Sa'ud was a force of 63 men at the time of the conquest of Riyadh. The army has been expanded and modernized in various stages, and it played an important role in the Gulf War (1990–1991). The RSLF publishes a quarterly magazine, *al-Bariyyah*.

Royal Saudi Naval Forces (RSNF)

Contact via Ministry of Defense and Aviation (MODA) as described in preceding entries

The Royal Saudi Naval Forces (RSNF, or the Royal Saudi Navy) is the naval force of the Saudi Arabian military, founded in 1960. The RSNF has about 15,000 members, including 3,000 marines. Its headquarters are in Riyadh. The Western fleet is located in the Red Sea with a base at Jeddah, and the Eastern fleet is in the Arabian Gulf with its base at Jubail. Additional bases are located in Yanbu, Ras al-Mishab, and Dammam.

Saudi Arabian General Investment Authority (SAGIA)

Riyadh SAGIA Headquarters
Imam Saud Bin Abdulaziz Road (University Road)
P.O. Box 5927
Riyadh 11432
Kingdom of Saudi Arabia
Tel: +966 1 203 5555
Fax: +966 1 263 2894
(SAGIA has eight other offices in other cities of Saudi Arabia)
E-mail: Info@sagia.gov.sa
Website: http://www.sagia.gov.sa/

The Saudi Arabian General Investment Authority (SAGIA) was established April 10, 2000, as part of Saudi Arabia's process of development, growth, and liberalization. It is intended to promote investment in energy, ICT, transportation and other industries. Its 10 x 10 plan aimed to make Saudi Arabia one of the top 10 countries in the world by 2010. It is headed by a governor and chairman, Amr al-Dabbagh, who has the rank of minister.

Saudi Arabian National Guard (SANG)

National Guard
P.O. Box 9799
Riyadh 11423
Tel: 1-491-2400
Fax: 1-491-2824
Website: http://www.sang.gov.sa

The Saudi Arabian National Guard (SANG) is an active-duty armed force of 260,000 that was headed for many decades (1962–2010) by King 'Abdullah ibn 'Abd al-'Aziz al-Sa'ud. It is now commanded by his son, Prince Mitab. SANG was involved in the liberation of Kuwait during the Gulf War. American Vietnam veterans and others conducted a training mission called OPM-SANG by the Vinnell Corporation, and SANG has been undergoing a large-scale modernization process in recent years.

Saudi Arabian Standards Organization (SASO)

P.O. Box 3437
Riyadh 11471
Tel: 1-479-3332
Fax: 1-479-3063
E-mail: sasoinfo@saso.org.sa
Website: http://www.saso.org.sa

The Saudi Arabian Standards Organization (SASO) was established in 1972 and is responsible for creating and enforcing standards for service, products, and utilities.

Saudi Aramco

Media Relations Contact Information
Public Relations Department R-2212
East Administration Building
P.O. Box 5000
Dhahran 31311Saudi Arabia
Fax: 966-3-873-8490
E-mail: international.media@aramco.com

General Inquiries
Saudi Aramco New Business Development
North Park 2, Bldg. 3301
Dhahran 31311
Tel: +966 3872 0115
Fax: +966 3874 1737
Website: http://www.saudiaramco.com/irj/portal/anonymous

Saudi Aramco is the national oil company of Saudi Arabia and is the largest oil corporation in the world, with headquarters in Dhahran. It also operates the Master Gas System. It was known as Aramco (Arabian American Oil Company) from 1933 to 1988. It owns 12 subsidiaries or associated companies, including Aramco Services Company in Houston, Texas, which publishes the bimonthly *Saudi-Aramco World* in English. (See chapter 4)

The Saudi Geological Survey (SGS)

Saudi Geological Survey
P.O. Box 54141
Jeddah 21514
Saudi Arabia
Tel: +966 261 9 5000

Fax: +966 2 619 6000
E-mail: sgs@sgs.org.sa
Website: http://www.sgs.orgs.sa

The Saudi Geological Survey (SGS) is the national geologic survey organization of Saudi Arabia. It is attached to the Ministry of Petroleum and Mineral Resources but is independent. It evolved from the Directorate General for Mineral Resources, the U.S. Geological Survey mission from 1963 to 1999, and the Bureau de Recherche et Geologique mission that was carried out from 1972 to 1999. SGS is based in Jeddah, and it also has a branch office in Riyadh. It is responsible for hydrogeology, mining exploration and development, geological (and topographical) mapping, environmental geology, and the determination of environmental geohazards.

Saudi Press Agency

E-mail: wass@spa.gov.sa
Website: http://www.spa.gov.sa or http://www.spa.gov.sa/english/

The Saudi Press Agency, the national news agency, was set up in 1971. Today, it also operates a website with news of the kingdom in Arabic and English. It can be contacted in the United States at the Saudi Arabian Ministry of Information, 601 New Hampshire Ave. NW, Washington, DC 20037-2405 (at the embassy); tel: (202) 944-3890.

Saudi Railway Authority

Dhahran Airport Street
P.O. Box 92
Dammam 31411
Tel: 3-871-4113
Website: http://www.saudirailways.org

The Saudi Railway Authority, now referred to as the Saudi Railways Organization, was set up to manage the nation's railways. The first line was developed in the 1960s between Riyadh and Dammam. The Meshair railway system opened in 2010 to help reduce overcrowding during the *hajj* and goes to Mina, Muzdalifa, and Arafat. A week *hajj* ticket costs a little less than $70 and was available only to Saudi Arabians and other Gulf nationals in the first season.

Saudi Telecom Company (STC)

E-mail: Contactus@stc.com.sa
Website: http://www.stc.com.sa

Saudi Telecom Company (STC) was initially the sole provider of telecom services until 2002 when that sector was opened to competition. STC began installing IP-VPN service at different speeds and also a home fiber-optic service providing fast Internet service. An advanced system filters sites; the usual claim is that this protects citizens from the mixing of men and women or pornography. The process has been carried out through the Internet Services Unit of the King Abdulaziz City for Science and Technology, and then through the Communications and Information Technology Commission. Blockage of sites like Human Rights Watch is due to its criticism of the kingdom, and given legal arguments put forth by the National Committee on Human Rights, this information may be releasable.

HUMANITARIAN AND DEVELOPMENTAL

Arab Gulf Program for United Nations Development Organizations (AGFUND)

E-mail: info@agfund.org
Website: http://www.agfund.org/

The Arab Gulf Program for United Nations Development Organizations (AG-FUND) is an organization established in 1981 to support United Nations development and humanitarian programs. Saudi Arabia contributes about 78 percent of this program's resources. The program gives about 40 percent of its total resources to UNICEF and also benefits the World Food and Agriculture Organization, the World Health Organization, the World Labor Organization, UNESCO, the World Food Program and its flagship programs, the Arab Open University, Banks for the Poor, and Early Childhood Development. The president is Prince Talal ibn 'Abd al-'Aziz.

Ibn Baz Foundation (Mu'assasat 'Abd al-'Aziz bin Baz)

Website: http://www.binbazfoundation.org/

The Ibn Baz foundation is a charitable organization that offers social and humanitarian aid in Saudi Arabia.

Disabled Children's Association

Tel: 01 454 3913 or (toll free) 1800 124 1118
Website: http://www.dca.org.sa/

The Disabled Children's Association operates centers in different Saudi Arabian cities for disabled children (but not the blind or deaf) and the Prince Salman Disability Research Center.

Ensan (Insan)

Website: http://www.ensan.org.sa/home/

Ensan is a charitable group offering aid to orphans in Saudi Arabia.

Gulf Kids Foundation (Atfal al-Khalij)

Website: http://www.gulfkids.com

The Gulf Kids Foundation is a charitable organization to help children of the Gulf region.

Al-Haramayn Islamic Foundation

A charity and *da'wah* organization based in Saudi Arabia that has had branches or derivatives in Afghanistan, Albania, Bangladesh, Bosnia, Comoros, Ethiopia, Indonesia, Kenya, the Netherlands, Nigeria, Pakistan, Somalia, Tanzania, and the United States. Overseas branches were accused of being a terrorist organization by the U.S. Department of the Treasury in 2004 for allegedly having direct connections to Osama bin Laden and his organization, and the foundation was banned by the United Nations Security Council Committee. For instance, the Comoros branch was accused of sending funds to rebels in Chechnya. The Saudi government and the U.S. Treasury Department blocked the accounts of the Bosnian and Somali branches of the charity in 2002, and the Saudi Arabian government established a high commission for oversight of all charities, contributions, and donations.

Human Rights First Saudi Arabia

Human Rights First Society
P.O. Box 3508
al-Khobar 31952
E-mail: HRFSUS@gmail.com

Human Rights First Society
P.O. Box 3734
Minneapolis, MN 55403-9998
United States
Website: http://hrfssaudiarabia.org/

Human Rights First Saudi Arabia is a nongovernmental organization critical of the human rights situation in Saudi Arabia. It is not legal; only the semigovernmental National Society for Human Rights (NSHR; see its entry in the following) has been granted permission to register. It was founded by Ibrahim al-Mugaiteeb who faced interference in his human rights activities in 2005.

National Society for Human Rights (NSHR)

E-mail: info@nshr.org.sa
Website: http://nshr.org.sa/english/adefault.aspx

The National Society for Human Rights (NSHR; sometimes appearing as the National Human Rights Association) was organized in 2003, with 41 members. It claims to be a nongovernmental organization but is in fact semigovernmental. It is supposed to respond to international human rights organizations, issue periodic reports, help implement human rights charters signed by Saudi Arabia, and monitor violations of women's rights. The group has countered U.S. reports on abuse of labor (*Sharq al-Awsat*, June 17, 2007), claiming these are politically motivated. The website has a contact and complaint submission form.

Prince Sultan bin Abdul Aziz Foundation

P.O. Box 64400
Riyadh 11536
Kingdom of Saudi Arabia
Tel: +966-1-482-7663
E-mail: question@sultanfoundation.org
Website: http://www.sultanfoundation.com

This foundation is headed by Prince Sultan ibn 'Abd al-'Aziz and supports educational, scientific, and charitable endeavors, including programs at the University of California, Berkeley; the Arabian Gulf University; and the University of Bologna, Italy, as well as comprehensive national research on Alzheimer's disease in Saudi Arabia, the Sultan bin Abdul Aziz Humanitarian City (with a hospital, medical center, and various projects), the Foundation for Charitable Housing, MEDUNET, and the Science and Technology Center.

Prince Sultan bin Abdulaziz Fund

The fund was begun in 2007 and is based in Dammam. It helps establish women's small businesses. It is currently headed by Hana al-Zuhair.

Saudi Red Crescent Authority

These contacts were provided per international recruitment and may or may not be accurate:
Assma Altuwajri: atuwajri@srca.com.sa
Sara Alhumaid: salhumaid@srca.com.sa
Rasha Alaftan: ralaftan@srca.com.sa
Fahd Aljuraid: faljuraid@srca.com.sa
Website: http://www.srcs.org.sa/

The Saudi Red Crescent Authority provides medical services to those in need and collects donations. Within Saudi Arabia, it is equivalent to the Red Cross.

Saudi Society for Labor

The Saudi Society for Labor is an illegal society that has sought registration from the Ministry of Labor since 2007 and from the National Committee for Human Rights (NCHR), which has taken no action to enable the formation of civil society organizations that are not charities. It represents workers, has a membership of about 4,000, and was headed by Anice Alansari.

INTERNATIONAL

Gulf Cooperation Council (Cooperation Council for the Arab States of the Gulf)

Website: http://www.gcc-sg.org/eng/

The council is a political and economic union of six Arab Gulf states: Bahrain, Kuwait, Oman, Qatar, Saudi Arabia, and the United Arab Emirates. It holds considerable political weight in the region, and was designed to further the interests of its member states.

Muslim World League (MWL)

Website: http://www.muslimworldleague.org/mwlwbsite_eng/index.htm

The Muslim World League (MWL) was founded in Mecca, Saudi Arabia, in 1962. It aims to enhance Muslim solidarity and to promote Islamic *da'wah* by issuing publications and promoting preachers, Arabic language programs, and Islamic centers. The MWL has been accused by opponents of Saudi Arabia of promoting the Wahhabist current, but the Muslim Brotherhood (who are not Wahhabists) and many other types of Muslim representatives have also been involved in the organization.

Organization of Arab Petroleum Exporting Countries (OAPEC)

Website: http://www.oapecorg.org/

The Organization of Arab Petroleum Exporting Countries (OAPEC) is an organization that coordinates energy policies among Arab countries that derive income from petroleum. Its headquarters are in Kuwait. Kuwait, Libya, and Saudi Arabia agreed to establish OAPEC in 1968. The members of OAPEC are Algeria, Bahrain, Egypt, Iraq, Kuwait, Libya, Qatar, Saudi Arabia, Syria, Tunisia, and the United Arab Emirates. The organization issues statistics and various publications.

Organization of the Islamic Conference (OIC)

P.O. Box 178
Jeddah 21411
Kingdom of Saudi Arabia
Tel: +966 2 65 15 222
Fax: +966 2 651 22 88
Website: http://www.oic-oci.org/

The Organization of the Islamic Conference (OIC) is an intergovernmental organization of Muslim nations established after the Islamic Summit in Rabat in 1969. The precipitant cause was the arson of the al-Aqsa mosque. The OIC deals with pan-Islamic issues and acts to promote Muslim solidarity. With a membership of 57 nations, it is the second-largest international organization following the United Nations. Its 10-year program that started in 2008 aims to promote moderation and modernization.

Organization of Petroleum Exporting Countries (OPEC)

Website: http://www.opec.org/opec_web/en/

The Organization of Petroleum Exporting Countries (OPEC) is a bloc or cartel of oil-producing developing countries including Algeria, Angola, Ecuador, Iran, Iraq, Kuwait, Libya, Nigeria, Qatar, Saudi Arabia, the United Arab Emirates, and Venezuela. OPEC's secretariat was originally in Geneva and was then moved to Vienna, Austria. OPEC tries to stabilize prices and protect the interests of the member nations. Prior to the establishment of OPEC, oil-producing developing nations had very little control over the prices or policies of the large oil companies.

PROFESSIONAL

Association of Language Teachers of Saudi Arabia

Website: http://www.saudiarabianksaalt.org/

Unions are not legal in Saudi Arabia; however, a wide variety of professional associations and groups exist, a few of which have been mentioned in this book. The members of the Association of Language Teachers are primarily teachers of English; the organization mounts an annual conference.

Saudi Arabian Chefs Society (SARCA)

E-mail: saudichefs@gmail.com
Website: http://www.sarca.surge8.com/

The society is a member of the World Association of Chefs' Societies.

Saudi Ophthalmological Society

Website: http://213.230.15.195/sosnew/english/

The society promotes scientific thinking in ophthalmology in Saudi Arabia.

Saudi Organization for Certified Public Accountants (SOCPA)

Website: http://www.socpa.org.sa/

Saudi Pediatric Society

Faculty of Medicine
(P.O. Box 80205
Jeddah 21589
Bldg (1) First floor
Mr. Hisham Hamdi
Tel: 640 1000, ext. 21221
Fax: 6408347)

The Saudi Pediatric Society was a professional society for pediatricians. The Saudi Pediatric Surgery Society now exists at King Abdulaziz University and also links to this name at http://sps.kau.edu.sa/Default.aspx?Site_ID=75706&lng=EN. Another group is the Saudi Society of Pediatric Gastroenterology, Hepatology, and Nutrition http://www.saspghan.org/english/index.php.

SPORTS

Arab Sports Federation

P.O. Box 6040
Riyadh

The Arab Sports Federation was established in 1976 to encourage and develop regional events and ties in various sports. It is based in Riyadh.

The Equestrian Club

P.O. Box 26323
Riyadh 11486
Kingdom of Saudi Arabia
Tel: +9661 25 40 222

The Equestrian Club is a private equestrian organization that organizes events and promotes the sport.

Islamic Solidarity Games Federation

The federation includes the 57 nations of the Organization of the Islamic Conference, and it organizes multisports competitions in various age categories, which are hosted by different member countries. The 2013 games will be held in Indonesia. A website is constructed for the specific meetings.

Saudi Arabian Equestrian Foundation

P.O. Box 60602
Al Maathar Olympic Complex 11555
Riyadh 11555
Kingdom of Saudi Arabia
Tel: (966 1) 482 38 37
Website: http://saef.gov.sa/english/adefault.aspx

The Saudi Arabian Equestrian Foundation is a national organization intended to promote equestrian sports and Saudi Arabian representation in international equestrian events. (See Chapter 6, section on sports.) Horses require passports to come to Saudi Arabia, and the application form is available through the foundation.

Saudi Arabian Football Federation

Al-Mather Quarter
Prince Sultan bin Fahd Street
P.O. Box 5844
Riyadh
Tel: +966-1/482 2240
Fax: +966-1/482 1215
The federation is presided over by Prince Sultan ibn Fahd ibn 'Abd al-'Aziz.

REFERENCES

Cordesmann, Anthony. *Saudi Arabia Enters the Twenty-First Century: The Military and International Security Dimensions.* Westport, CT: Praeger, 2003.

Matthiesen, Toby. "The Shi'a of Saudi Arabia at a Crossroads." *Middle East Report Online,* May 6, 2009. http://www.middleeastdesk.org/article.php?id=2765 Country-Related Organizations.

Annotated Bibliography

Aarts, Paul, and Gerd Nonneman, eds. *Saudi Arabia in the Balance: Political Economy, Society, Foreign Affairs*. New York: New York University Press, 2006.

A post-9/11 consideration of Saudi Arabia's development, capacity for reform, and relationship with extremist Islam.

Abbas, B., A. A. al-Qarawy, and A. al-Hawas. "The Ethnoveterinary Knowledge of Traditional Healers in Qassim Region, Saudi Arabia." *Journal of Arid Environments* 50 (2002), 367–379.

This article describes the treatment of animals in the Qasim region and the healers' own assessments of the efficacy of such traditional procedures as cautery.

'Abd al-Hakim, Tariq. *Masahhir al-musiqiyin al-'arab* [Famous Arab musicians]. n.d. [ca. 1965].

A work on the great Arab musicians by one of the greatest of Saudi Arabia's musicians and composers, known as the Father of Saudi Arabian music, who focused on the formal teaching of Arabic music.

'Abd al-Hakim, Tariq. *Ashhar al-fulklurat al-sha'abiyah* [The most famous forms of folkore]. Riyadh, Saudi Arabia: al-Jam'iyyah al-'Arabiyyah al-Sa'udiyyah lil-Thaqafah wa-l-Funun, n.d. [ca. 1980].

Explains the specific forms or genres of popular music in Saudi Arabia.

'Abd al-Wahhab, Muhammad ibn. "Kitab al-Kaba'ir." In *Mu'allafat al-Shaykh al-Imam Muhammad ibn 'Abd al-Wahhab*. Vol. 1. Riyadh, Saudi Arabia: Jami'at al-Imam Muhammad ibn Sa'ud Islamiyyah, 1398h.

An elaboration of the major sins in Ibn 'Abd al-Wahhab's view, which degrade monotheism, as well as behaviors that governments should avoid.

'Abd al-Wahhab, Muhammad ibn. "Kitab al-Jihad." In *Mu'allafat al-Shaykh al-Imam Muhammad ibn 'Abd al-Wahhab: al-Fiqh.* Vol. 2. Riyadh, Saudi Arabia: Jami'at al-Imam Muhammad ibn Sa'ud Islamiyyah, 1398h. (equivalent to 1977 or 1978).

An essay on jihad as interpreted by the reformist scholar whose ideas were taken up by the al-Sa'ud and their forces.

'Abd al-Wahhab, Muhammad ibn. "Kitab al-Nikah." In *Mu'allafat al-Shaykh al-Imam Muhammad ibn 'Abd al-Wahhab.* Vol. 2. Riyadh, Saudi Arabia: Jami'at al-Imam Muhammad ibn Sa'ud Islamiyyah, 1398h.

An essay on the importance of marriage, the rights and responsibilities of women and men, and interpretations of *shari'ah* as it applies to women and matters of personal status.

'Abd al-Wahhab, Muhammad ibn. "Kitab al-Tawhid." In *Mu'allafat al-Shaykh al-Imam Muhammad ibn Abd al-Wahhab.* Vol. 1. Riyadh, Saudi Arabia: Jami'at al-Imam Muhammad bin Sa'ud Islamiyyah, 1977 (1398h.).

An essay on monotheism or absolute unicity in Islam.

'Abd al-Wahhab, Muhammad ibn. "Kitab al-Tawhid." Translated by Ismail al-Faruqi. Kuwait City: al-Faisal, 1986.

The same essay as in the preceding entry, translated by a leading scholar who promoted *da'wah* in the West.

Abdul Ghafour, P. K. "Mishaal Named Allegiance Commission Chairman." *Arab News,* December 11, 2007.

Article provides the initial membership of the Allegiance (Bay'ah) Commission and explains its role.

al-Abdulkareem, A. A., and S. G. Ballal. "Consanguineous Marriages in an Urban Area of Saudi Arabia: Rates and Adverse Health Effects on the Offspring." *Journal of Community Health* 23 (1998), 75–83.

A scientific study of close relatives' marriages and accompanying health problems.

Abodehman, Ahmed. *La Ceinture.* Paris: Gallimard, 2000.

The first novel written in French by a Saudi Arabian author.

Abou El Fadl, Khalid. *Speaking in God's Name: Islamic Law, Authority and Women.* Oxford, UK: Oneworld, 2001.

A detailed study of the *'ulama*'s acquisition of false authority in Islam and *fatawa* (legal response or responses) that are misogynistic or limit women's rights as issued by the CRLO of Saudi Arabia.

Aboul-Enein, Youssef, and Sherifa Zuhur. *Islamic Rulings on Warfare.* Carlisle, PA: Strategic Studies Institute, 2004.

A study of Qur'anic, hadith, and *siyar* (the laws of nations, or a form of international law in Islam) literature on jihad showing that unlawful treatment of prisoners was not permitted and explaining divergences in interpretations of jihad.

Abu 'Aliyya, Abulfatah. *al-Mamlakah al-'Arabiyyah al-Sa'udiyyah wa Qadiyat Filistin.* Riyadh, Saudi Arabia: al-Dara (King Abdulaziz Foundation for Research and Archives), 1999.

The history of Saudi Arabia's involvement with the Palestinian cause from an official perspective.

Abu Khalid, Fawziyya. *Qira'a sirriyya fi tarikh al-sumt al-'arabi*. Beirut, Lebanon: Dar al-Adab, 1985.

The title translates as "Secret Reading of the History of the Arab Silence." This is a poetry collection by one of the most prominent women poets and essayists.

AbuKhalil, As'ad. *The Battle for Saudi Arabia: Royalty, Fundamentalism and Global Power*. New York: Seven Stories, 2004.

A book that is highly critical of the Saudi Arabian government and its role in Middle Eastern politics. It explores the Sa'udi royal family's influence via religious institutions as well as via their publishing domain.

Adams, Michael, ed. *The Middle East*. New York: Facts on File, 1988.

A survey of the Middle East, its politics, and its economics to the mid-1980s.

Adra, Najwa. "Dance in the Arabian Peninsula." In *Garland Encyclopedia of World Music*, edited by Virginia Danielson, Scott Marcus, and Dwight Reynolds,. New York: Routledge, 2002, vol. 6, 703–712.

An excellent overview of popular or folk dance in Saudi Arabia, Yemen, and the Gulf states.

Ahmad, Qanta. *In the Land of Invisible Women: A Female Doctor's Journey in the Saudi Kingdom*. Naperville, IL: Sourcebooks, 2008.

A rather negative view of the kingdom and its citizens focused on women's issues and written by a Pakistani-British physician.

Akeel, Maha. "Old Songs in Old Nights." *Arab News*, December 25, 2004. http://www.arabnews.com/?page=December 25, 2004. http://www.arabnews.com/?

Information about the Saudi Arabian singer Tuha.

Akeel, Mona. "Female Circumcisions: Weight of Tradition Perpetuates a Dangerous Practice." *Arab News*, March 20, 2005.

One of the first news articles concerning circumcision of women in the kingdom.

'Alim, Raja'. *al-Mawt al-akhir li-l-mumaththal* [The final death of the actor]. Beirut, Lebanon: Dar al-Adab, 1987a.

A play by a noted playwright and novelist.

'Alim, Raja'. *Arba'a/Sifr (4/0)*. Jeddah, Saudi Arabia: al-Nadi al-Thaqafi al-Adabi, 1987b.

Another play in a unique, symbolic style.

'Alim, Raja. *Thuqub fi al-Dhahr* [Hole in the back]. Beirut, Lebanon: Dar al-Adab, 1987c.

Another of 'Alim's plays in her challenging style. All three were meant to be read as well as performed.

Alsanea, Rajaa. *Girls of Riyadh*. Translated by Marilyn Booth. New York: Penguin, 2008.

A chronicle of a young Saudi American woman and her friends.

Altorki, Soraya. "Sisterhood and Stewardship in Sister-Brother Relations in Saudi Arabia." In Nicholas Hopkins, ed., "The New Arab Family." Special issue, *Cairo Papers in Social Science* 24, nos. 1–2 (2003), 180–200.

This paper focuses on the dyadic sibling relationship. It challenges some stereotypes and may idealize the brother's role.

Altorki, Soraya. "The Concept and Practice of Citizenship in Saudi Arabia." In *Gender and Citizenship in the Middle East*, edited by Suad Joseph. Syracuse, NY: Syracuse University Press, 2000, 215–236.

This essay proposes that the universal concept of citizenship is actually Western and does not fit Saudi Arabia, where preservation/retention of the family is the central social concept.

Altorki, Soraya. "At Home in the Field." In *Arab Women in the Field: Studying Your Own Society*, edited by Soraya Altorki and Camillia Fawzi El-Solh. Syracuse, NY: Syracuse University Press, 1988, 49–68.

As part of a volume that examines the role of the researcher in the context of anthroplogy's debate about the emic-etic dynamic, Altorki reflects on her experience studying women in Jeddah. She is both an insider and an outsider due to long years of residence abroad.

Altorki, Soraya. *Women in Saudi Arabia: Ideology and Behavior among the Elite*. New York: Columbia University Press, 1986.

An ethnographic study of three generations of elite Jeddah families conducted in the early to mid-1970s. It highlights aspects of continuity or change in social relations and challenges the then-dominant feminist interpretations.

Altorki, Soraya, and Donald P. Cole. *Arabian Oasis City: The Transformation of 'Unayzah*. Austin: University of Texas Press, 1989.

An ethnographic study of 'Unayzah and its social life during its development from an agricultural and market center in the first oil boom. It also draws on historical descriptions.

al-Ansary, A. R. *Qaryat al-Fau: A Portrait of Pre-Islamic Civilization in Saudi Arabia*. Riyadh, Saudi Arabia, 1982.

This book concerns the excavations at Qaryat al-Fau, an oasis in central Saudi Arabia, which the author believes to be the ancient site of Gerrha as mentioned by Pliny.

Ansary, Abdullah F. "Combating Extremism: A Brief Overview of Saudi Arabia's Approach." *Middle East Policy* 15, no. 2 (Summer 2008), 111–143.

This overview describes the Saudi Arabian government's prison-based counseling program and releasable information concerning the detainees/prisoners charged with terrorism.

Anscombe, Frederick. *The Ottoman Gulf: The Creation of Kuwait, Saudi Arabia and Qatar*. New York: Columbia University Press, 1997.

This book examines the Ottoman Empire's lost opportunities to effectively govern Arabia, due in part to their fears that Great Britain had a larger influence than it truly possessed.

Arab Urban Development Institute. *Riyadh: City of the Future*. Riyadh, Saudi Arabia: al-Ma'ahad al-'arabi li-inma al-mudun, 1984.

Information about Riyadh as it was expanding in the period after the first oil boom.

Arberry, A. J. *Aspects of Islamic Civilization: As Depicted in the Original Texts*. Ann Arbor: University of Michigan Press, 1978.

An important analysis of original texts in translation that provide insight into cultural values.

Arebi, Saddeka. *Women and Words in Saudi Arabia: The Politics of Literary Discourse*. New York: Columbia University Press, 1994.

A study of Saudi Arabian women writers of various types of literature and differing social views. The author discusses these writers' social role in examining and questioning ideas of gender and women's issues, although their writing is creative as well as expository.

Armstrong, H. C. *Lord of Arabia*. London: Arthur Barker, 1934.

A biography of Ibn Sa'ud, the founder of modern Saudi Arabia, and his career.

Al-Ashban, R. M., M. Aslam, and A. H. Shah. "Kohl (Surma): A Toxic Traditional Eye Cosmetic Study in Saudi Arabia." *Public Health* 188, no. 4 (June 2004), 292–298.

The cosmetic use of *kohl* (antimony) to beautify the eyes has health risks because of its lead content.

al-Askar, Abdullah. *Al-Yamama in the Early Islamic Era*. Reading, UK: Ithaca, in association with the King 'Abdul 'Aziz Foundation for Research and Archives, Riyadh, Saudi Arabia, 2002.

A detailed study of the region of al-Yamamah. The sedentary Banu Hanifa and the nomadic Banu Tamim tribes are discussed in tandem with their political allegiances before and after the establishment of Islam.

al-Attas, Syed Naguib. *Aims and Objectives of Islamic Education*. Jeddah, Saudi Arabia, 1979.

Findings of the First World Conference on Muslim Education, held in 1977.

al-Awamy, Dr. Baker H., Dr. Fakhry, and Department of Pediatrics, al-Muhawis Hospital, Dammam. "Evaluation of Commonly Used Tribal and Traditional Remedies in Saudi Arabia." *Saudi Medical Journal* 12, no. 22 (December 2001), 1065–1068.

A useful summary of remedies from herbal medicines to cautery.

Ayoob, Mohammed, and Hasan Kosebalaban, eds. *Religion and Politics in Saudi Arabia: Wahhabism and the State*. Boulder, CO: Lynne Rienner, 2009.

A collection of essays on Wahhabism, Saudi Arabia, and U.S.–Saudi Arabian relations that outlines broad themes and contrasting positions, mostly critical of the Saudi Arabian government or the royal family, and responding to post-9/11 literature.

Al-Baadi, Hamad Muhammad. "Social Change, Education, and the Roles of Women in Arabia." PhD diss., Stanford University, 1982.

A consideration of women's changing roles, particularly with the advent of education.

Badeeb, Saeed M. *The Saudi-Egyptian Conflict over North Yemen, 1962–1970*. Boulder, CO: Westview, 1986.

A study of the conflict or proxy war fought in Yemen.

al-Badi, Awadh. "Institutionalizing Hereditary Succession in Saudi Arabia's Political Governance System: The Allegiance Commission." *Arab Reform Initiative*, February 14, 2008.

A study that gives details of the new Allegiance (*Bay'ah*) Commission.

Baeshen, Lamia. *Youssef et le palais des chagrins: Contes d'Arabie saoudite*. Translated by Kadria Awad. Paris: L'Harmattan, 2010. (Originally published as *al-Tabat wa al-Nabat* in 1997.)

Folktales as they were told to children in the Hijazi dialect in the past.

Bagader, Abu Bakr A., and Ava Molnar Heinrichsdorff, eds. and trans. *Assassination of Light: Modern Saudi Short Stories*. Washington, DC: Three Continents, 1990.

A collection of short stories by well-known Saudi Arabian writers addressing social issues and problems of modernization.

Bagader, Abu Bakr, Ava M. Heinrichsdorff, and Deborah S. Akers. *Voices of Change: Short Stories by Saudi Arabian Women Writers*. Boulder, CO: Lynne Rienner, 1998.

A collection of short stories by noted Saudi Arabian women writers.

Bagader, Abou Baker A., and Deborah S. Akers, eds. and trans. *Histoires D'Arabie Saoudite*. Beirut, Lebanon: Centre International pour les Services Culturels, 2007.

A collection of short stories of Saudi Arabia.

Ba Ghaffar, Hind. *Al-aghani al-sha'biyya fi-l-Mamlakah al-'Arabiyyah al-Sa'udiyyah* [Folk songs in the Saudi Arabian kingdom]. Jeddah, Saudi Arabia: Dar al-Qadsiyya li-l-tawzi' wa-l-nashr, 1994.

Explanations of popular lyrics in verse from Saudi Arabia.

Bahgat, Gawdat. "Foreign Investment in Saudi Arabia's Energy Sector." *Middle East Economic Survey* 47, no. 34 (2004).

Explains Saudi Arabia's interest in international investment in its energy sector in the context of Saudi Arabian economic reform.

Baker, Razan. "Tales of Old Jeddah." *Arab News*, January 25, 2007.

Introduces the tradition of storytelling in Jeddah and Lamia Baeshan's project to preserve folktales in the original Jeddawi dialect.

al-Baz, Rania. *Disfigured: A Saudi Woman's Story of Triumph over Violence*. Translated by Catherine Spencer. Northampton, MA: Interlink, 2008.

The true story of a Saudi Arabian television journalist who was battered by her husband.

BBC Two. "The Child Slaves of Saudi Arabia." This World. Directed by Rageh Omaar. *BBC*. March 27, 2007. http://news.bbc.co.uk/2/hi/programmes/this_world/6431957.stm

Investigative report and program looking into the reasons children come illegally into Saudi Arabia and are forced to beg, remitting money to adults.

al-Bedah, Abdullah M. N. "Kingdom of Saudi Arabia." In *World Health Organization Global Atlas of Traditional, Complementary and Alternative Medicine*, edited by G. Bodeker, C. K. Ong, C. Grundy, and K. Shein. Kobe, Japan: World Health Organization, Centre for Health Development, 2005, vol. 1, 171–174.

A review of the traditional healing practices as well as the entry of external alternative medical treatments into Saudi Arabia.

Beling, William A., ed. *King Faisal and the Modernization of Saudi Arabia*. Boulder, CO: Westview, 1980.

An edited collection on King Faysal's rule and many aspects of modernization, development, oil policy, foreign policy, treatment of the law, and the media at that time.

Bell, Gertrude. *The Arabian Diaries, 1913–1914*. Edited by Rosemary O'Brien. Syracuse, NY: Syracuse University Press, 2000.

Bell, an archaeologist, and later an important political figure in Britain's Middle East foreign policy, set out at age 45 across the Arabian Desert intending to meet the Amir

Rashid and Ibn Sa'ud and move on to Baghdad, recording her impressions in her diaries and photographs.

Benoist-Méchin, Jacque. *Fayçal, roi d'Arabie: L'homme, le souverain, sa place dans le monde 1906–1975*. Paris, 1975.

An insider's view of King Faysal and his importance to Saudi Arabia.

Bergen, Peter I. *The Osama bin Laden I Know: An Oral History of al Qa'ida's Leader*. New York: Free Press, 2006.

A journalist's version of Osama bin Laden's life and goals told through interviews and direct quotations from various sources close to bin Laden.

Bianchi, Robert. *Guests of God: Pilgrimage and Politics in the Islamic World*. Oxford, UK: Oxford University Press, 2004.

A study of the *hajj,* its institutions and its impact, not only on Saudi Arabia but also on selected countries that send large numbers of pilgrims, such as Malaysia, Pakistan, Indonesia, Nigeria, and Turkey.

Bin Laden, Carmen. *Inside the Kingdom: My Life in Saudi Arabia*. New York: Warner Books, 2004.

This title chronicles Carmen bin Laden's marriage to a brother of Osama bin Laden and the difficulties she experienced in the kingdom and in her marriage.

Bird, Jerine. "Revolution for Children in Saudi Arabia." In *Children in the Muslim Middle East*, edited by Elizabeth Warnock Fernea. Austin: University of Texas Press, 1995, 290–294.

A summary of the great changes in children's education in Saudi Arabia.

Birks, J. S., and C. A. Sinclair. *Saudi Arabia into the 90s*. Durham, UK: Mountjoy Research Center, University of Durham, 1988.

A book about social and political change in Saudi Arabia through the 1990s.

Bjurstrom, Eric. "Dreaming of Farasan." *Aramco World* 51, no. 1 (January/February 2000), 18–26.

An illustrated article of the reefs surrounding the Farasan Islands in the Red Sea.

Bjurstrom, Eric. "Diving in the Desert." *Aramco World*, July/August 1997.

Exploration and photographs of limestone sinkholes forming caverns with pools at Dahl al-Hit near Ma'qalah.

Bligh, Alexander. *From Prince to King: Royal Succession in the House of Saud in the Twentieth Century*. New York: New York University Press, 1984.

A study of the royal family's politics, written about the same time as Gary Samore's Harvard University doctoral dissertation (1983) on the topic; it has been updated by Joseph Kechichian's 2001 book on the same topic.

Blunt, Anne Noel. *A Pilgrimage to Nejd, the Cradle of the Arab Race, a Visit to the Court of the Emir and "Our" Persian Campaign*. London: Century, 1985. (Originally published in 1881.)

Lady Annabella King-Noel Blunt traveled through the Middle East with her husband, Wilfred, from 1875 to 1882. Her diaries, field notes, and writing are the basis of the books they coauthored.

al-Bogari, Naima, Geoff Crowther, and Norman Marr. "Motivation for Domestic Tourism: A Case Study of the Kingdom of Saudi Arabia." In *Consumer Psychology of Tourism, Hospitality and Leisure*, edited by Arch G. Woodside. Wallingford, Oxfordshire, UK: CABI, 2004, 51–64.

The motivations for travel in one's own country differ culturally and are important in understanding consumer patterns.

Bogary, Hamza. *The Sheltered Quarter: A Tale of a Boyhood in Mecca*. Translated by Olive Kenney and Jeremy Reed. Austin: Center for Middle Eastern Studies, University of Texas, 1991.

An autographical novel about a young student who becomes a teacher; it includes a vibrant, detailed description of Mecca and its customs during his lifetime.

Boucek, Chris. "Counter-Radicalization and Extremism Disengagement in Saudi Arabia." In *Protecting the Homeland from International and Domestic Terrorism Threats: Multi-Disciplinary Perspectives on Root Causes, the Role of Ideology, and Programs for Counter-radicalization and Disengagement*, edited by Laurie Fenstermacher, Larry Kuznar, Tom Rieger, and Anne Speckhard. Multi-Agency and U.S. Air Research Laboratory, January 2010.

This essay is on the prison-based program in Saudi Arabia that corrects extremist views held by those accused of association with al-Qa'ida fi Jazirat al-'Arabiyyah or similar cells.

Bouzigard, Aimee. "Archaeological Evidence for the Consumption of Tobacco and Coffee in Ottoman Arabia." Master's thesis, East Carolina University, 2010.

A study of material objects and their provenance and similarity to other objects (such as coffee cups produced elsewhere). Provides proof of substance use in the Ottoman period.

Bowersock, G. W. "The Arabs before Islam." In *The Genius of Arab Civilization: Source of Renaissance*, edited by John Hayes. New York: New York University Press, 1992, 17–24.

A summary of scholarship about the pre-Islamic Arabs of the peninsula.

Brand, Laurie A. *Jordan's Inter-Arab Relations: The Political Economy of Alliance-Making*. New York: Columbia University Press, 1994.

This book includes important information about Jordanian–Saudi Arabian relations.

Brock, Paul. "Al-Hurr: Noble One." *Saudi Aramco World*, March/April 1973, 2–5.

An article on the prized falcon of Saudi Arabia.

Brockelman, C. "Mathal." In *Encyclopaedia of Islam*, edited by Martijn Theodoor Houtsma. Vol. 3, edited by M. Th. Houtsma, A. J. Wensinck, and E. Levi-Provençal. 1st ed. Leiden, the Netherlands: E. J. Brill and Luzac, 1913–1938 (vol. 3, 1934), 407–410.

A definitive entry in the most detailed English-language reference that typifies and provides citations to medieval collections of proverbs.

Bronson, Rachel. *Thicker Than Oil: America's Uneasy Partnership with Saudi Arabia*. New York: Oxford University Press, 2008.

A retelling of American–Saudi Arabian relations following the crisis of September 11, 2001.

Brown, Anthony Cave. *Oil, God, and Gold: The Story of Aramco and the Saudi Kings*. New York: Houghton-Mifflin, 1999.

A detailed history of the oil companies' early days in Saudi Arabia, Aramco's expansion, and the changes in the industry.

Bunt, Gary. *iMuslims: Rewiring the House of Islam*. Chapel Hill: University of North Carolina Press, 2009.

An exploration of Islamic websites and uses of the Internet, including institutions and oppositionists in Saudi Arabia.

Burckhardt, John Lewis. *Travels in Arabia Comprehending an Account of Those Territories in Hedjaz Which the Mohammedans Regard as Sacred*. Beirut, Lebanon: Librairie du Liban, 1972. (Originally published in 1829.)

The earlier travels of the adventurer Burckhardt.

Burckhardt, John Lewis. *Notes on the Bedouin and the Wahabys*. London: Henry Coburn and Richard Bentley, 1831.

The observations of a noted European traveler on the tribes, their lifestyles, the Wahhabi-Turkish hostilities, and Islamic and Arabian customs of the time.

Burdett, A. L. P., ed. *King Abdul Aziz: Diplomacy and Statecraft 1902–1953*. 4 vols. Cambridge: Cambridge University Press, 1999.

Primary documents from official British sources detailing the rise of King 'Abd al-'Aziz, Saudi Arabian domestic issues, and the country's relations with other Arab states and foreign nations, including the United Kingdom.

Campagna, Joe. "Saudi Arabia Report: Princes, Clerics, and Censors." Committee to Protect Journalists, May 8, 2006. http://cpj.org/reports/2006/05/saudi-06.php

Saudi Arabian journalists, professors, and activists are censored, or, worse, brought to court, for writing critically about issues in the country, especially when international attention centers on their reports. A few key cases are described here.

Campbell, Kay Hardy. "A Caravan of Brides." Unpublished manuscript.

A fictional treatment of the life of Princess Effat of Saudi Arabia, the wife of King Faysal.

Campbell, Kay Hardy. "Saudi Folk Music: Alive and Well." *Saudi Aramco World*, March/April 2007.

A detailed, brief, illustrated description of Saudi Arabian folk music from various parts of the kingdom.

Campbell, Kay Hardy. "Effat's New Roses." *Saudi Aramco World*, January/February 2007.

A description of Effat College and Princess Effat herself.

Campbell, Kay Hardy. "Days of Song and Dance." *Aramco World* 50, no. 1 (1999): 78–87.

Description of Saudi Arabian music as played in wedding celebrations.

Campbell, Kay Hardy. "Folk Music and Dance in the Arabian Gulf and Saudi Arabia." In *Images of Enchantment*, edited by Sherifa Zuhur. Cairo: American University in Cairo Press, 1998, 57–70.

A description of women's folk music and dance events in Saudi Arabia and the Gulf States.

Campbell, Kay Hardy. "Recent Recordings of Traditional Music from the Arabian Gulf and Saudi Arabia." *Middle East Studies Association Bulletin* 30, no. 1 (July 1996), 37–40.

Descriptions of traditional, or folkloric (as opposed to pop), recordings of voice and ensemble.

Carnegie Endowment for International Peace and Fundacion par las Relaciones Internacionales y el Dialogio Exterior (FRIDE). *Arab Political Systems: Baseline Information and Reforms—Saudi Arabia*. Carnegie Endowment for International Peace and FRIDE, n.d. [ca. 2007].

Comprehensive information about the Saudi Arabian political system apparently drawn from Hooglund (in Metz, ed., 1993, which is not copyrighted and is thus replicated in other sources), updated with more recent official and media reports.

Carter, Robert. "The History and Prehistory of Pearling in the Persian Gulf." *Journal of the Economic and Social History of the Orient* 48, no. 2 (2005), 139–209.

This article provides a history of the pearl-diving industry in the Persian Gulf region from earliest times to the middle of the 20th century as well as archaelogical data from the 6th millenium BCE.

Chatty, Dawn. *Nomadic Societies in the Middle East and North Africa: Entering the 21st Century*. Leiden, the Netherlands: Brill, 2006.

This title includes chapters on Saudi Arabian bedouin and on other nomadic groups, illustrating some of their shared practices and concerns.

Chaudhry, Kiren Aziz. *The Price of Wealth: Economies and Institutions in the Middle East*. Ithaca, NY: Cornell University Press, 1997.

This title examines the Saudi Arabian oil boom period of the 1970s and the development of the Saudi Arabian and Yemeni economies.

Childs, J. Rives. *Foreign Service Farewell: My Years in the Near East*. Charlottesville: University of Virginia, 1969.

The memoirs of the first U.S. ambassador to Saudi Arabia.

Chubin, Shahram, and Charles Tripp. *Iran-Saudi Arabia Relations and Regional Order*. Adelphi Paper 304. First published by International Institute for Strategic Studies, 1996. Reprinted New York: Routledge, 2005.

A paper by one of the leading experts on Iran's strategic aims together with an expert on the Arab world. The republication and revision of the study reflected the diplomatic impasse in Europe toward Iran at that time.

Ciorciari, John D. "Saudi-U.S. Alignment after the Six Day War." *Middle East Review of International Affairs* 9, no. 2 (June 2005). http://meria.idc.ac.il/journal/2005/issue2/jv9no2a1.html

Saudi Arabia's regional and international uncertainties after the Six-Day War served to preserve the Saudi Arabian–U.S. alliance, strained though it was by the 1967 war.

Citino, Nathan J. *From Arab Nationalism to OPEC: Eisenhower, King Sa'ud, and the Making of U.S.-Saudi Relations*. Bloomington: Indiana University Press, 2002.

U.S. officials planned to preserve Britain's access to "sterling oil" in order to safeguard British economic prospects in the postwar era. Eisenhower's government also acted to contain Arab nationalism.

Clark, Arthur. "Samphire: From Sea to Shining Seed." *Aramco World* 45, no. 6 (November/December 1994), 29.

This article describes the agricultural project at Ras Zawr to grow samphire, which can be used as a a salad green, an oil, and a source of animal feed and is irrigated with seawater.

Clark, Arthur C., ed. *Saudi Aramco and Its World: Arabia and the Middle East*. Rev. ed. Houston, TX: Aramco Services, 1995.

A history and account of Saudi Aramco's origins and role in Saudi Arabia and coverage of Arabia. Predates the 2006 version.

Clark, Arthur C., and Muhammad Tahlawy, eds. *A Land Transformed: The Arabian Peninsula, Saudi Arabia and Saudi Aramco*. Dhahran, Saudi Arabia, and Houston, TX: Aramco Services, 2006.

This is a very large volume with encyclopedia-type coverage of many subjects concerning the Arabian Peninsula as well as Aramco's role in the life of Saudi Arabia.

Cole, Donald P. "Pastoral Nomads in a Rapidly Changing Economy: The Case of Saudi Arabia." In *Social and Economic Development in the Arab Gulf*, edited by Tim Niblock. New York: St. Martin's Press, 1980, 106–121.

An analysis of the al-Murrah bedouin as their lifestyle changed after the oil boom.

Cole, Donald P. *Nomads of the Nomads: The Al Murrah Bedouin of the Empty Quarter*. Chicago: Aldine, 1975.

A full study of the al-Murrah bedouin based on Cole's fieldwork in 1968 and 1969.

Cole, Donald P. "Al Murrah Bedouins: The Pure Ones Roam Arabia's Sands." In *Nomads of the World*. Washington, DC: National Geographic Society, 1971, 52–71.

A chapter-length description of the al-Murrah lifestyle in 1968–1969.

Colyer Ross, Heather. *The Art of Arabian Costume: A Saudi Arabian Profile*. Fribourg, Switzerland: Arabesque Commercial, 1981.

A detailed illustrated presentation of contemporary and historic women's and men's traditional garments and jewelry, arts, and crafts of the Arabian Peninsula. These provide some of the best examples of the historic costumes that are described in this book in the segment on popular dress.

Colyer Ross, Heather. *Bedouin Jewellery in Saudi Arabia*. London: Stacey International, 1978.

An illustrated work on the handcrafted jewelry of the bedouin in various styles.

Commins, David Dean. *The Wahhabi Mission and Saudi Arabia*. London: I. B. Tauris, 2006.

A study of the initial Wahhabi reform movement as a challenge by second-strata '*ulama* who subsequently were challenged by other clerics. It is essentially critical of Muhammad ibn 'Abd al-Wahhab's intellectual import and legitimacy, at least as expanded on by his students.

Congressional Research Service (CRS) and Library of Congress. "Saudi Arabia: Current Issues and U.S. Relations." *CRS Issue Brief* Alfred B. Prados. February 24, 2006. http://www.fas.org/sgp/crs/mideast/IB93113.pdf

A useful and important review of matters in Saudi Arabia deemed crucial by the members of the U.S. Congress or their staff members from a U.S.-centered policy perspective.

Cook, Michael. "The Expansion of the First Saudi State: The Case of Washm." In *The Islamic World from Classical to Modern Times: Essays in Honor of Bernard Lewis*, edited by C. E. Bosworth, Charles Issawi, Roger Savory, and A. L. Udovitch. Princeton, NJ: Darwin, 1989, 661–699.

Islamic studies scholar Michael Cook looks at the ideas in the expansion of the first Sa'udi state.

Cordesman, Anthony H. *Saudi Arabia Enters the Twenty-First Century: The Political, Foreign Policy, Economic, and Energy Dimensions*. London: Center for Strategic and International Studies; Westport, CT: Praeger, 2003.

A security-oriented study of Saudi Arabia and its government, oil industry, and strategic interests.

Cordesman, Anthony H. *Saudi Arabia and the Challenge of Terrorism: Reacting to the "9/11 Report."* Washington, DC: Center for Strategic and International Studies, 2003.

A study of Saudi Arabia's responses to the terrorist threats in and from the kingdom.

Cordesman, Anthony H., and Nawaf Obaid. *Saudi National Security: Military and Security Services—Challenges and Developments*. Full Report. Washington, DC: Center for Strategic and International Studies, Draft, September 29, 2004.

This piece is a military balance survey considering transformation as well as capacity.

Cordesman, Anthony H., and Nawaf Obaid. *Saudi Internal Security: A Risk Assessment. Terrorism and the Security Services—Challenges and Developments*. Washington, DC: Center for Strategic and International Studies, May 30, 2004.

This piece updates the main author's assessment following a year of terrorist and counter-terrorist activities in the kingdom.

Cordesman, Anthony H., and Khalid R. Al-Rodhan. *The Changing Dynamics of Energy in the Middle East*. 2 vols. Westport, CT: Praeger Security International, 2006.

This book includes a useful chapter on Saudi Arabia and reflects the lead author's interests in security dynamics.

Cordesman, Anthony H., and Abraham R. Wagner. *The Lessons of Modern War*. Vol. 4, *The Gulf War*. Boulder, CO: Westview, 1996.

This title considers the Gulf War, the underlying military balance, the strategies employed in the war, and its outcomes.

Craze, Joshua, and Mark Huband, eds. *The Kingdom: Saudi Arabia and the Challenge of 21st Century*. New York: Columbia University Press, 2009.

This title is compiled from articles posted at SaudiDebate.com from April 2006 to June 2007; some are reprinted, and all promote an agenda of change. The writers include some of Saudi Arabia's better-known liberal figures.

Crone, Patricia. *Meccan Trade and the Rise of Islam*. Piscataway, NJ: Gorgias, 2004.

A classic study of the rise of trade that benefited Mecca and was directly related to spread of Islam. The author's controversial thesis about Hagarism has divided historians of the early Islamic period.

Cuddihy, Kathy. *Saudi Customs and Etiquette*. London: Stacey International, 2002.

This is a guide to Saudi Arabian manners and customs chiefly for a foreigner doing business in Saudi Arabia.

al-Dakhil, Khalid. *Social Origins of the Wahhabi Movement*. Los Angeles: University of California Press, 1998.

A view of Saudi Arabian society at the time of Muhammad ibn 'Abd al-Wahhab's reform movement. Counters the standard characterization of the movement as a reactive rather than expansionist one.

de Corancez, Louis Alexandre Olivier. *The History of the Wahabis from Their Origin until the End of 1809*. Translated by Eric Tabet. Reading, UK: Garnet, 1995.

Translated from the French, this firsthand account relates the Wahhabi campaigns against the Egyptian forces and their negotiations, and it tells of piracy against English ships.

De Gaury, Gerald. *Faisal: Biography of a King*. New York: Praeger, 1967.

A biography of King Faysal.

Delong-Bas, Natana. *Jihad for Islam: The Struggle for the Future of Saudi Arabia*. New York: Oxford University Press, 2009.

This title postulates that reform and reclamation of Wahhabist principles will save Saudi Arabia from its Islamic opposition.

DeLong-Bas, Natana. *Wahhabi Islam: From Revival and Reform to Global Jihad*. Oxford, UK: Oxford University Press, 2004.

A thorough study of Muhammad ibn 'Abd al-Wahhab's theological and juridical ideas that debunks various claims of his extremism and tells his personal history.

Deputy Ministry of Antiquities and Museums, Ministry of Education, Kingdom of Saudi Arabia. *al-Musmak Museum Guide*. Deputy Ministry of Antiquities and Museums, Ministry of Education, Kingdom of Saudi Arabia, 1999.

This guide provides information on the photographs and exhibits contained within the al-Musmak fort in Riyadh.

Dickson, H R.P. *The Arab of the Desert: Bedouin Life in Kuwait and Saudi Arabia*. London: Allen and Unwin, 1949.

A classic description of bedouin life and customs.

Dohaish, Abdullatif Abdullah. "A Critical and Comparative Study of the History of Education in the Hijaz during the periods of Ottoman and Sharifian Rule, 1869–1925." PhD diss., University of Leeds, 1974.

A study of the various forms of education in the Hijaz from 1869 up to 1925.

Dohaish, Abdullatif Abdullah. *History of Education in the Hijaz up to 1925: Comparative and Critical Study*. Cairo: Dar al-Fikr al-Arabi, 1978.

This title describes education in the Hijaz prior to its annexation to Saudi Arabia.

Doran, Michael Scott. "The Saudi Paradox." *Foreign Affairs*, January/February 2004, 35–51.

This essay relates the Wahhabi concept of *tawhid* (absolute monotheism) to a traditionalist battle for uniformity and claims this principle is ever-present in the kingdom, personified in Prince Nayif as opposed to the reform-minded 'Abdullah.

al-Dosary, Adel S., and Syed M. Rahman. "Saudization—Localization: A Critical Review." *Human Resource Development International* 8, no. 4 (2005), 495–502.

This piece discusses and critiques the fact that Saudization targets have not been reached.

Doughty, Charles M. *Travels in Arabia Deserta*. Abridged by Edward Garnett. Gloucester, MA: Peter Smith, 1931 and 1968.

This is based on the author's 1888 work (published by Clarendon in Cambridge), which has been reprinted in two volumes by Philip Lee Warner for Medici Society Limited and London and Boston: Jonathan Cape, 1921. It was also published in one volume by Random House in New York in 1926; and in two volumes by Dover Press in 1979. The Garnett abridgement includes the author's travels to visit Ha'il, his sojourn with the bedouin, and his time on the *hajj* caravan, the Syrian Darb al-Hajj, from Damascus.

Doumato, Eleanor Abdella. "Saudi Arabia: From Wahhabi Roots to Contemporary Revisionism." In *Islam and Textbooks in the Middle East*, edited by Eleanor A. Doumato and Gregory Starrett. Cairo: American University in Cairo Press, 2008, 153–176. (Also published under the title *Teaching Islam: Textbooks and Religion in the Middle East*. Boulder, CO: Lynne Rienner, 2007.)

An assessment and analysis of changes made to certain textbooks used in the Saudi Arabian national curriculum. The authors of the book believe these changes illustrate greater tolerance, attention to civic identity, and a less extreme attitude.

Doumato, Eleanor Abdella. *Getting God's Ear: Women, Islam and Healing in Saudi Arabia and the Gulf*. New York: Columbia University Press, 2000.

Uses travelers' documents and missionary accounts of life in Arabia to explore women's status before and outside of the Wahhabi realm of influence.

Doumato, Eleanor Abdella. "The Ambiguity of Shari'a and the Politics of 'Rights' in Saudi Arabia." In *Faith and Freedom: Women's Human Rights in the Muslim World*, edited by Mahnaz Afkhami. New York: I. B. Tauris, 1995, 135–160.

The flexibility of *shari'ah* could help women's rights but is not doing so, because the liberal and Shi'a opposition pursue their own interests first, deeming the difficult women's issue as cultural.

Doumato, Eleanor Abdella "Arabian Women: Religion, Work and Cultural Ideology in the Arabian Peninsula from the 19th Century through the Age of Abd al-Aziz." PhD diss., Columbia University, 1989.

This dissertation explores views and activities of Arabian women based on the documents and correspondence of the Arabian mission of the Reformed Church in America and other Western travel accounts of life, mostly at the beginning of the 20th century.

ExxonMobil Corporation. *2007 Summary Annual Report*. Irving, TX: ExxonMobil Corporation, 2008.

The company's annual report for 2007.

Fabietti, Ugo. "State Policies and Bedouin Adaptations in Saudi Arabia, 1900–1980." In *The Transformation of Nomad Society in the Arab East*, edited by Martha Mundy and Basim Musallam. Cambridge: Cambridge University Press, 2000, 82–89.

This is an account of the social adaptations made to governmental development policies that focused on sedentarization and detribalization of the bedouin.

Eyre, Banning. Interview of Joseph Braude in the program "African Slaves in Islamic Lands," May 2006, and "African Slaves in Islamic Lands," February 2007, both cited in

"Africans in the Arabian Peninsula," *Afropop Worldwide*, http://www.afropop.org/multi/feature/ID/692

Discusses the musical traditions derived from former African slaves in the Gulf region.

Facey, William. "Al-'Udhaibat: Building on the Past." *Aramco World* 50, no. 3 (July/August 1999), 32–46.

An illustrated article on the restoration of a home in al-'Udhaibat.

Facey, William. *Back to Earth: Adobe Building in Saudi Arabia.* Riyadh, Saudi Arabia: Al Turath and St. Martin's, 1997.

Describes the art of building with adobe in local design and the process of restoring an old farmhouse at al-'Udhaibat for Prince Sultan ibn Salman al-Sa'ud, who supports Islamic and indigenous design.

Facey, William. *Dir'iyyah and the First Saudi State.* London: Stacey International, 1997.

An illustrated work on Dir'iyyah and the al-Sa'ud conquest of the area, as well as the alliance with Muhammad ibn 'Abd al-Wahhab.

Facey, William. *The Story of the Eastern Province of Saudi Arabia.* London: Stacey International, 1994.

History and description of settlements and architecture in Sharqiyyah, the Eastern Province.

Facey, William. *Riyadh: The Old City from Its Origins until the 1950s.* London: Immel, 1992.

This title shows the architectural and historical development of the older sections of Riyadh.

Al-Fahad, Abdulaziz H. "From Exclusivism to Accomodation: Doctrinal and Legal Evolution of Wahhabism." *New York University Law Review* 79 (2004).

This account describes events in Wahhabi political life from the first to the third Sa'udi realms. Holds that the Gulf War *fatwa* permitting foreign forces to fight to defend the kingdom was the culmination of gradual accommodations made by Wahhabists, despite the exclusivism of early southern Wahhabism.

Fakhro, Munira. "Gulf Women and Islamic Law." In *Feminism and Islam: Legal and Literary Perspectives*, edited by Mai Yamani. Reading, UK: Garnet, 1996, 251–262.

This essay outlines major problems in Islamic law for women as interpreted in the Gulf states.

Fandy, Mamoun. *Saudi Arabia and the Politics of Dissent.* New York: St. Martin's, 1999.

This book presents the origins, ideas, and experiences of different strands of political opposition in Saudi Arabia, from the Shi'a to the neosalafists.

al-Farsy, Fouad. *Custodian of the Two Holy Mosques: King Fahd bin Abdul Aziz.* New York: Knight Communications, 2001.

A biography and account of King Fahd's accomplishments.

al-Farsy, Fouad. *Modernity and Tradition: The Saudi Equation.* London and New York: Kegan Paul International, 1990.

Like so much of Arab and Western literature at this time, the work views Saudi Arabia as being in transition from traditional modes.

Al-Fassi, Hatoon. *Women in Pre-Islamic Arabia*. Oxford, UK: British Archaeological Reports, Archaeopress, 2007.

An original study of women in pre-Islamic Arabia. Original studies are important because scholars have disagreed about many issues—whether women's roles in ceremonial, political, and war activities were curtailed by Islam or whether they were much more disadvantaged prior to Islam.

Fernea, Elizabeth. *In Search of Islamic Feminism: One Woman's Journey*. New York: Doubleday, 1998.

This book includes a short chapter on the author's visit to the kingdom as part of the author's investigation of Islamic feminism throughout the Middle East, North Africa, and other countries.

Fernea, Elizabeth Warnock, and Robert Fernea. *The Arab World: Personal Encounters*. Garden City, NY: Anchor Books, 1987.

The book concerns the distinguished anthropologist Robert Fernea and author/sociological scholar B. J. (as she was known) Fernea's experiences in various parts of the Arab world. Pertinent to Saudi Arabia are Robert Fernea's letters and notes from the field in Ha'il in 1983 and a short essay on the disappearing opportunities for fieldwork (on pages 293–316).

Field, Michael. *The Merchants: The Big Business Families of Saudi Arabia and the Gulf States*. Woodstock, NY: Overlook, 1985.

Illustrates the details of the families who built business empires in the Gulf states.

Freedman, Lawrence, and Efraim Karsh. *The Gulf Conflict, 1990–1991: Diplomacy and War in the New World Order*. Princeton, NJ: Princeton University Press, 1993.

Explores the implications of the Iraq's occupation of Kuwait and the ensuing Gulf War and discusses the strategic aim of all involved in the conflict, including Saudi Arabia.

al-Fuhayd, Mandil. *Min adabina al-sha'biyya*. Riyadh, Saudi Arabia: Dar al-Yamama li-l-bahth wa tarjuma wa nashr, 1978.

A study of popular (vernacular) oral literature that has become part of the *adab*, or literary tradition of the area.

Fürtig, Henner. *Iran's Rivalry with Saudi Arabia between the Gulf Wars*, Reading, UK: Ithaca, 2002.

A detailed study of the two nations' interactions.

Gause, Gregory F., III. *Oil Monarchies: Domestic and Security Challenges in the Arab Gulf States*. Washington, DC: Council on Foreign Relations, 1994.

Views these monarchies in transition and under modernization.

Gause, Gregory F., III. *Saudi-Yemeni Relations: Domestic Structures and Foreign Influence*. New York: Columbia University Press, 1990.

A comprehensive study of the Sa'udi Arabian role in the Yemeni Civil War and efforts to influence Yemen until the late 1980s.

Al-Ghadeer, Moneera. *Desert Voices: Bedouin Women's Poetry in Saudi Arabia*. London: Tauris Academic Studies, 2009.

A collection of poetry composed by tribal women.

al-Ghadyan, Ahmed A. "The Judiciary in Saudi Arabia." *Arab Law Quarterly* 13, no. 3 (1998), 235–252.

A review of the role and particular features of the judges in Saudi Arabia.

Ghazanfar, Shahina. *Handbook of Arabian Medicinal Plants*. London: CRC, 1994.

A review of the plants, herbs, and spices used as medicine in the Arabian tradition.

Gibb, H A. R. *Arabic Literature: An Introduction*. Oxford and London: Oxford University Press, 1963, 1974.

A classic Orientalist overview of various genres of Arabic literature.

Gordon, Murray. *Slavery in the Arab World*. New York: New Amsterdam Books, 1989.

A study of slavery in the Arab countries.

al-Gosaibi (or al-Qusaybi), Ghazi. "Octopus," "When I am With You," and "Silence." Translated by Sherif Elmusa and Charles Doria. In *Modern Arabic Poetry*, edited by Salma Khadra Jayyusi. New York: Columbia University Press, 1987.

Several poems by the noted writer and government figure.

al-Gosaibi (al-Qusaybi), Ghazi. *Fever*. 1980.

Collection of poetry by the late writer and government figure (whose name is also rendered al-Qusaybi or al-Qusaibi).

al-Gosaibi (al-Qusaybi), Ghazi. *Chosen Poems*. 1980.

Poetry collection.

al-Gosaibi (al-Qusaybi), Ghazi. *You Are My Riyadh*. 1976.

Another of the favorite collections of this author's work.

Grund, F. "Danses d'ailleures: La mâle danse, ceremonies masculines en Arabie Saoudite." *Danser*, no. 269 (September 1998), 26–28.

On men's dances in Saudi Arabia, including the *'ardha*.

Guillaume, Alfred Guillaume, trans. and ed. *The Life of Muhammad: A Translation of [Ibn Hisham's adaptation of] Ishaq's Sirat Rasul Allah*. London: Oxford University Press, 1955.

The most important biographical work on the Prophet Muhammad in English, which actually combines a translation of Ibn Ishaq's *Sirah* (or biography) of the Prophet from Ibn Hisham's recension of that work with material by the historian al-Tabari and others.

Habib, John S. *Saudi Arabia and the American National Interests*. Boca Raton, FL: Universal, 2003.

An examination of the U.S.–Saudi Arabian relationship.

Habib, John S. *Ibn Saud's Warriors of Islam: The Ikhwan of Najd and Their Role in the Creation of the Saudi Kingdom, 1910–1930*. Atlantic Highlands, NJ: Humanities Press, 1978.

An account of the critical role of the Ikhwan in the conquest of the state.

Habib, Mohammed A. "Development of Agriculture in Tihamah: Regional Growth and Development in the Jizan Region." PhD diss., University of Arizona, 1988.

A study of agriculture in Tihamah.

al-Hadhdhal, A. I. *Mukhtarat min al-shi'r al-nabati al-mu'asir*. Riyadh, Saudi Arabia: Matabi' al-shihri, 1392h.

A collection of modern Nabati (oral vernacular) poetry.

Halliday, Fred. *Arabia without Sultans: A Political Survey of Instability in the Arab World*. New York: Vintage Books, 1975.

A study of the Arabian Peninsular countries in the context of the political struggles of the late 1960s and 1970s by a scholar who headed this area of study at the London School of Economics during the latter part of his career.

Hamdan, Amani. "Women and Education in Saudi Arabia: Challenges and Achievements." *International Education Journal* 6, no. 1 (2005), 42–64.

An assessment of women's status in education.

Hamzah, Fuad. *Fi bilad Asir*. Riyadh, Saudi Arabia: Maktabat al-Nasr al-Hadithah, 1968.

The customs and practices of the Asir area are discussed in this book.

Hamzah, Fuad. "Najran." *Journal of the Royal Central Asian Society* 22 (1935), 631–640.

This article concerns Najran in southern Saudi Arabia, captured by the al-Sa'ud from Yemeni rule.

Hansen, Eric. "The Hidden History of a Scented Wood." *Saudi Aramco World* 51, no. 6 (November/December 2000), 2–13.

This essay relates the origins of *'ud* in Southeast Asia. It is burned like incense in Saudi Arabia.

al-Harbi, Abdullah. "The Impact of New Towns in Saudi Arabia: A Case Study of Yanbu." PhD diss., University of Lancaster, 1991.

A dissertation about the changing role and nature of Yanbu in the context of development in Saudi Arabia.

Harrigan, Peter. "New Pieces of Mada'in Saleh's Puzzle." *Saudi Aramco World* 58, no. 4 (July/August 2007), 14–23.

This piece discusses new discoveries about the Nabataean site Mada'in Saleh.

Harrigan, Peter. "Volcanic Arabia." *Saudi-Aramco World*, March/April 2006.

A brief article on the Harrah region and Saudi Arabia's volcanic past.

Harrigan, Peter. "Art Rocks in Saudi Arabia." *Saudi-Aramco World*, March/April 2002.

This piece summarizes findings about the prehistoric drawings on stone sites in Saudi Arabia.

Harrigan, Peter, and Rosalind Mazzawi. "Saudi Arabia's First Olympic Medals." *Saudi-Aramco World*, January/February 2001.

This article gives an account of the first Saudi Arabian athletes' victories at the Olympic Games.

Hart, Parker T. *Saudi Arabia and the United States: Birth of a Security Partnership*. Bloomington: Indiana University Press, 1998.

An account of U.S.–Saudi Arabian relations and their rationale.

Hashim, Najwa. *Al-Safar fi layl al-ahzan*. Jeddah, Saudi Arabia: Al-Dar al-Sa'udiyya li-Nashr wa-Tawzi', 1986.

A collection of stories in a modern style.

al-Hashimi, Muhammad Ali. *The Ideal Muslim Society: As Defined in the Qur'an and Sunnah*. Riyadh, Saudi Arabia: International Islamic Publishing House, 2007.

A work about the Muslim *ummah* in its ideal state. Dr. al-Hashimi, a Syrian, is also known for his books on the idealized Muslim woman and man. He studied in Saudi Arabia and taught in the Faculty of Arabic Language at Imam Muhammad ibn al-Sa'ud Islamic University, and hosted a religious radio program.

al-Hathloul, Saleh Ali, and Narayanan Edadan. *Urban Development in Saudi Arabia*. Riyadh, Saudi Arabia: Dar al-Sahan, 1995.

A study of urban planning and growth in the early 1990s.

Hawali, Safar. *Haqa'iq hawl 'azmat al-khalij*. Cairo: Dar Makka al-Mukarram, 1991.

A strong critique of the al-Sa'ud government, its alliance with the West, and its betrayal of the Saudi Arabian people by one of the best-known Awakening (*sahwa*) shaykhs.

Hayes, John R., ed. *The Genius of Arab Civilization: Source of Renaissance*. New York: New York University Press, 1992.

Scholars noted for their work on Arabic music, art, literature, music, sciences, architecture, military history, history, and philosophy discuss the Arab contributions to these fields.

al-Hazimi, Mansur Ibrahim, Ezzat Khattab, and Salma al-Jayusi, eds. *Beyond the Dunes: An Anthology of Modern Saudi Writers*. London: I. B. Tauris, 2006.

A large anthology of poetry and short stories, introduced by a chronological overview of modern Saudi Arabian literature.

El-Hazmi, M. A., A. R. Al-Swailem, A. S. Warsy, et al. "Consanguinity among the Saudi Arabian Population." *Medical Genetics* 32 (1995), 623–626.

This piece estimates and discusses the medical risks of the large numbers of Saudi Arabians who are typically married to first or second cousins with regard to certain conditions.

Hegghammer, Thomas. *Jihad in Saudi Arabia: Violence and Pan-Islamism since 1979*. Cambridge: Cambridge University Press, 2010.

An account of the global jihadist (al-Qa'ida, also transliterated as al-Qa'ida) movement in Saudi Arabia, primarily from 1998/1999 to early 2009, by a researcher then in the Norwegian defense sector.

Hegghammer, Thomas. "Terrorist Recruitment and Radicalization in Saudi Arabia." *Middle East Policy* 13, no. 4 (Winter 2006), 39–60.

This piece describes the rise of Islamic militants known as al-Qa'ida fi Jazirat al-'Arabiyyah in Saudi Arabia and the government's response.

Hegghammer, Thomas, and Stèphane Lacroix. "Rejectionist Islamism in Saudi Arabia: The Case of Juhayman al-'Utaybi Revisited." *International Journal of Middle East Studies* 39, no. 1 (2007), 103–122.

These two authors, who helped produce the International Crisis Group's reports on Saudi Arabia and are respectively connected to Giles Kepel and the Norwegian defense sector, link the 1979 so-called 'Utaybi movement that took over the Grand Mosque with the contemporary *salafi* (neosalafist) opposition movement.

Helms, Christine M. *The Cohesion of Saudi Arabia*. London: Croom Helm, 1981.

A political study of Saudi Arabia.

Henderson, Simon. "After King Abdullah: Succession in Saudi Arabia." *Policy Focus #96*. Washington, DC: Washington Institute for Near East Policy, 2009.

An updated version of the 1994 study.

Henderson, Simon. *After King Fahd: Succession in Saudi Arabia*. Washington, DC: Washington Institute for Near East Policy, 1994.

A study of the royal family and the succession process.

Herz, Siba Al. *The Others*. Beirut, Lebanon, 2008; New York: Seven Stories, 2009.

A novel, published under a pseudonym, which includes the protagonist's amorous relationships with other women.

High Commission for the Development of Arriyadh, Kingdom of Saudi Arabia. *Al-Riyadh: Abq al-'Asala wa Rawnaq w-al-Hadatha* (*Riyadh: The Redolence of the Original City and the Beauty of the Modern*). Riyadh: High Commission for the Development of Arriyadh, 1424h.

Titled in Arabic and English, this is a book of photographs of Riyadh, juxtaposing those from more than 50 years earlier with others of the contemporary city.

Hilden, Joy [May] Totah. *Bedouin Weaving of Saudi Arabia and Other Countries*. London: Arabian Publishing; Oakfield, CT: David Brown, 2010.

A study of bedouin flat-weave textiles used for dress, tents, rugs, saddlebags, and other items and their history.

Hilden, Joy May. "The Use of Wasm (Animal Brands) in Beduin Weavings." Beduin Weaving. n.d. http://www.beduinweaving.com

A study of the markers indicating tribal ownership by an expert on Bedouin weaving practices.

Hillenbrand, Robert. "Traditional Architecture of the Arabian Peninsula." *Bulletin of the British Society of Middle Eastern Studies* 16, no. 2 (1989), 186–192.

Style and forms of traditional architecture are described.

Hogarth, David George. *Hejaz before World War One: A Handbook*. 2nd ed. Cambridge and New York: Oleander; Naples: Falcon, 1978.

An extremely detailed survey of the physical area, routes, tribes, leaders, politics, and customs of the Hijaz, originally published in Naples by Falcon.

Hogarth, David George. *The Penetration of Arabia: A Record of the Development of Western Knowledge Concerning the Arabian Peninsula*. Beirut, Lebanon: Khayats, 1966.

A reprint of archaeologist Hogarth's 1904 work. Hogarth starts by asking why the Western travelers, including those in very poor health and without funds, like Charles Doughty, were drawn to the region despite various mishaps and dangers and what their explorations tell us.

Holden, David, and Richard Johns. *The House of Saud*. New York: Holt Rinehart and Winston, 1982.

A study of the royal family and Saudi Arabia.

Holes, Clive. *Dialect, Culture and Society in Eastern Arabia: A Glossary*. Leiden, the Netherlands: Brill, 2001.

A very thorough study of the pre-oil dialects of Bahrain and, in some cases, the surrounding area and their social context. Useful for the study of language and culture in eastern Saudi Arabia as well, not least because of the glossary, which explains phrases and various usages. Based in part on personal interviews and recordings.

Hopper, Mathew S. "Pearls, Globalization and the African Diaspora in the Arabian Gulf in the Age of Empire." Paper presented at the 124th Annual Meeting of the American Historical Association, San Diego, January 9, 2010.

An overview of the African slaves' role in the pearl-diving industry and of that industry's demise due to the global depression in the 1930s and the production of cultured pearls.

Hopper, Mathew S. "Slavery and the Slave Trades in the Indian Ocean and Arab Worlds: Global Connections and Disconnections." Paper presented at 10th Annual Gilder Lehrmann International Center Conference, Yale University, November 7–8, 2008.

This conference paper follows on the author's dissertation coverage of slavery and its import in world economic history of the period.

Hopper, Mathew S. "The African Presence in Arabia: Slavery, the World Economy, and the African Diaspora in Eastern Arabia, 1840–1940." PhD diss., University of California, Los Angeles, 2006.

An important review showing that slavery from Africa was essential to agricultural production and pearl diving in this era.

Hopwood, Derek, ed. *The Arabian Peninsula: Society and Politics*. London: Allen and Unwin, 1972.

Studies of Saudi Arabia and its smaller neighbors up to the late 1960s.

Hourani, Albert. *A History of the Arab Peoples*. Cambridge, MA: Harvard University Press, 1989.

A masterful social history of the Islamic and Arab empires and of the Arab world under the Ottomans and in modern times.

Howarth, David. *The Desert King*. New York: McGraw-Hill, 1964.

A biography and study of Ibn Sa'ud.

Hoyland, Robert. *Arabia and the Arabs: From the Bronze Age to the Coming of Islam*. London and New York: Routledge, 2001.

An history of the peninsula in the earliest periods.

Human Rights Watch (HRW). "Saudi Arabia: Women's Rights Promises Broken. Evidence Shows Male Permission Still Being Required for Surgery, Travel." July 8, 2009. http://www.hrw.org/en/news/2009/07/08/saudi-arabia-women-s-rights-promises-broken

Women are required to obtain permissions from their male guardians for surgery, travel, education etc. and this may restrict their individual rights.

Human Rights Watch (HRW). "As If I Am Not Human." July 7, 2008. http://www.hrw.org/en/reports/2008/07/07/if-i-am-not-human-0

This report covers the deplorable situation of non-Saudi Arabian national domestic workers who have been subject to abuse, long hours, and non-payment.

Hume-Griffith, M. E. *Behind the Veil in Persia and Turkish Arabia: An Account of an Eng-lishwoman's Eight Years' Residence amongst the Women of the East.* London: Seeley, 1909.

A Western traveler's account of her experiences in parts of Arabia and Persia that highlights the world of women.

Al Hussain, M., and M. Al Bunyan. "Consanguineous Marriages in a Saudi Population and the Effect of Inbreeding on Perinatal and Postnatal Mortality." *Annual Tropical Paediatrics* 17 (1997), 155–160.

Considers how consanguinity, which is prevalent in Saudi Arabia due to the preference for cousin marriage, affects women's maternal death rates.

Ibn Bishr, 'Uthman. *'Unwan al-majd fi tarikh Najd.* Riyadh, Saudi Arabia: Maktabah al-Riyadh al-Hadithah, n.d.

An account of Muhammad ibn 'Abd al-Wahhab's mission and the first Sa'udi state by a contemporary who approved of 'Abd al-Wahhab. His account is used by many scholars of the movement as it contains information from oral sources from the period.

Ibn Ghannam, Husayn, *Tarikh Najd.* Edited by Nassar Al-Din Assad. Riyadh: 'Abd al-'Aziz ibn Muhammad ibn Ibrahim al-Shaykh, 1982.

An alternate edition of the same work as in Ibn Ghannam's 1961 work.

Ibn Ghannam, Husayn. *Rawdat al-afkar wa al-afham li-murtad hal al-Imam wa-ta'dad ghazawat dhawi al-Islam.* Riyadh, Saudi Arabia, 1381h.

Ibn Ghannam (d. 1810) was a scholar and supporter of 'Abd al-Wahhab and describes his movement in this text. This account also includes information derived from oral sources who differ from those drawn on by Ibn Bishr.

Ibn Ghannam, Husayn. *Tarikh Najd.* Cairo, 1961.

The history of Najd at the time of Muhammad ibn 'Abd al-Wahhab and the first Sa'udi state.

Ibn Hurayyil, S. H. *Diwan al-Nabat al-hadith.* Beirut, Lebanon: Matabi' al-Wafa, 1374h.

A collection of modern oral poetry (Nabati).

Ibn Qasim, 'Abd al-Rahman ibn Muhammad, ed. *al-Durar al-saniyah fi al-ajwiba al-najdiyyah.* 12 vols. Riyadh, Saudi Arabia, 1995.

A collection of writings by 19th-century Nadji *'ulama.*

Ibrahim, Fuad. *The Shi'as of Saudi Arabia.* London: Saqi Books, 2007.

This title describes the historic and contemporary situation of the Shi'a population of Saudi Arabia.

Ibrahim, Mahmood. "Social and Economic Conditions in Pre-Islamic Mecca." *International Journal of Middle East Studies* 14, no. 3 (1982), 343–358.

This article takes a position different from Patricia Crone's.

Ingham, Bruce. *Najdi Arabic: Central Arabian.* Amsterdam: John Benjamin, 1994.

A study of the dialect of Najd.

Ingham, Bruce. *Bedouin of Northern Arabia: Traditions of the Dhafir.* London: Kegan Paul International (KPI), 1986.

An ethnographic description of the Dhafir and their oral traditions.

International Crisis Group. "Saudi Arabia Backgrounder: Who Are the Islamists?" *Middle East Report*, September 21, 2004.

An explanation of the *sahwa* and the neosalafists and events in the first year of conflict with the Saudi Arabian militants.

International Crisis Group. "Can Saudi Arabia Reform Itself?" *ICG Middle East Report,* no. 28, July 14, 2004.

A critique of Saudi Arabia's political ills from a Western perspective, but with useful details about different political currents.

al-'Isa, Mayy bint 'Abd al-'Aziz. *al-Haya al-'ilmiyya fi Najd mundhu qiyam da'wat al-Shaykh Muhammad ibn 'Abd al-Wahhab wa hatta nihayat al-dawla al-Sa'udiyya al-'ula*. Riyadh, Saudi Arabia: Darat al-Malik 'Abd al-'Aziz, 1997.

The *'ulama*'s intellectual output in Najd prior to and following Shaykh Muhammad ibn 'Abd al-Wahhab's movement.

Jabber, Paul. "Oil, Arms, and Regional Diplomacy: Strategic Dimensions of the Saudi-Egyptian Relationship." In *Rich and Poor States in the Middle East: Egypt and the New Arab Order*, edited by Malcolm H. Kerr and El Sayed Yassin. Boulder, CO: Westview, 1982, 415–448.

In this Jabber shows how the Egyptian-Saudi Arabian relationship fits into the volume's exploration of "rich" and "poor" states. Saudi Arabia's first oil boom allowed for weapons purchases and bore on its changing policies toward Egypt, with the most powerful military in the region.

Jacquard, Roland. *In the Name of Osama bin Laden: Global Terrorism and the Bin Laden Brotherhood*. Durham, NC: Duke University Press, 2002.

With an introduction and analysis by Jacquard, original documents issued by Osama bin Laden are provided in this book.

Jargy, Simon. "Sung Poetry in the Arabian Peninsula." In *Garland Encyclopedia of World Music*, edited by Virginia Danielson, Scott Marcus, and Dwight Reynolds. New York: Routledge, 2002, vol. 6, 663–669.

An important review of the role of poetry in popular music.

Jargy, Simon. "Sung Poetry in the Oral Tradition of the Gulf Region and the Arabian Peninsula." *Oral Tradition* 4, no. 1–2 (1989), 175–187.

This title covers certain forms of sung poetry in Saudi Arabia and the smaller Arabian states.

Jargy, Simon. "Comments on the Concept and Characteristics of the Folk Music in the Gulf and Arabian Peninsula." *Ma'thurat al-Sha'biyya* 1, January 1986.

This title describes the unique features of folk music in the Gulf region.

al-Jayyusi, Salma Khadra. *The Literature of Modern Arabia: An Anthology*. London: Kegan Paul, 1988.

An anthology of modern literature.

Al-Jeraisy, Khaled 'Abd al-Rahman, coll. and ed. *Selected Fatwas on Faith Healing and Witchcraft*. Riyadh, Saudi Arabia: Khaled al-Jersaisy Establishment, 1422h.

This works contains *fatawa*, Islamic legal rulings, on the form of folk medicine used in Saudi Arabia and also those forbidding witchcraft.

Al-Jeraisy, Khaled 'Abd al-Rahman. *Raghbah*. Raghbah and Riyadh, Saudi Arabia: Khaled al-Jeraisy, 1420h. (1999/2000).

A complete illustrated study of the city of Raghbah, its history, its environs, and its major families.

Jones, Toby. "Saudi Arabia's Silent Spring." *Foreign Policy*, February 2009. http://www.foreignpolicy.com/story/cms.php?story_id=4718

Discusses King 'Abdullah's reforms announced on the 14th of February, 2009. Despite others' perceiving this as a new age in Saudi Arabia, Jones reminds that women lack suffrage and power is not being shared outside the royal family.

Jones, Toby. "Saudi Arabia's Not So New Anti-Shi'ism." *Middle East Report* 242 (Spring 2007).

On the origins of *salafi* anti-Shi'a sentiments in earlier Wahhabist thought and history.

Joyce, Miriam. *Ruling Shaikhs and Her Majesty's Government 1960–1969*. Portland, OR: Frank Cass, 2003.

This title explains the changing relationships between the British government and the traditional leaders of Gulf nations in the years prior to Britain's withdrawal from the Gulf.

al-Juhany, Uwaidah M. *Najd before the Salafi Reform Movement: Social, Religious and Political Conditions in the Three Centuries Preceding the Rise of the Saudi State*. Reading, UK: Ithaca, 2002.

An important historical description of the conditions leading up to the *salafi* movement of Muhammad ibn 'Abd al-Wahhab.

al-Kamali, Sh. *al-Shi'r 'inda al-badu* [Poetry among the bedouin]. Baghdad: Matba'at al-Irshad, 1964.

A study of oral poetry.

Katakura, Motoko. *Bedouin Village*. Tokyo: University of Tokyo Press, 1977.

A study of the Bedouin lifestyle, customs and changes in that lifestyle as of the 1970s.

Kay, Shirley. *The Bedouin*. North Vancouver, BC, Canada: Douglas David and Charles, 1978.

Kechichian, Joseph A. *Faysal: Saudi Arabia's King for All Seasons*. Gainesville: University Press of Florida, 2008.

An analysis of King Faysal ibn 'Abd al-'Aziz and his era.

Kechichian, Joseph A. *Succession in Saudi Arabia*. New York: Palgrave, 2001.

This title explains the process of determining leadership in Saudi Arabia and how this can be accomplished collectively by the large Sa'udi royal family.

Kerr, Malcolm. *The Arab Cold War: Gamal Abd al-Nasir and His Rivals, 1958–1970*. London: Oxford University Press, 1971.

A study of the polarization between Saudi Arabia and Jordan, Egypt, Syria, and other populist republican regimes that the author calls a cold war. This cold war dominated regional politics in the mid-20th century.

Keynoush, Banafsheh. "The Iranian-Saudi Arabian Relationship: From Ideological Confrontation to Pragmatic Accommodation." PhD diss., Fletcher School, Tufts University, 2007.

An overview of the bilateral relationship from the Khomeinist revolutionary period to later accommodation or cooperation.

King, Geoffrey. *The Traditional Architecture of Saudi Arabia*. London: I. B. Tauris, 1998.

Saudi Arabia's architecture in various regions and how climate, building materials, and various cultural styles have influenced it, with numerous illustrations.

King, Geoffrey. *The Historical Mosques of Saudi Arabia*. New York: Longman, 1986.

An art history and archaeology professor covers the historic mosques of Saudi Arabia.

King, Geoffrey. "Some Notes on Mosques in Eastern and Western Saudi Arabia." *Bulletin of the School of Oriental and African Studies* 42, no. 2 (1980), 251–276.

This article was written when King taught in Saudi Arabia and includes special details of the local mosque architecture.

King, Geoffrey. "Traditional Najdi Mosques." *Bulletin of the School of Oriental and African Studies* 41, no. 3 (1978), 464–498.

On the style of the mosques of Najd, Saudi Arabia's central region.

The King Abdulaziz Historical Centre. Riyadh, Saudi Arabia: Arriyadh Development Authority, 2000.

This title outlines the history of Saudi Arabia, the facilities of the historical center and national museum, and restorations.

Kostiner, Joseph. "The Rise of *Jihadi* Trends in Saudi Arabia: The Post Iraq-Kuwait War Phase." In *Radical Islam and International Security: Challenges and Responses*, edited by Hillel Frisch and Efraim Inbar. New York: Routledge, 2007, 73–92.

This chapter covers the upsurge in newer, more militant individuals and groups in Saudi Arabia after the Gulf War.

Kostiner, Joseph. "The Role of Tribal Groups in State Expansion and Consolidation." In *Changing Nomads in a Changing World*, edited by Joseph Ginat and Anatoly Khazanov. Brighton, UK: Sussex Academic, 1998, 143–155.

This chapter presents a role for tribal groups based on the Saudi Arabian example.

Kostiner, Joseph. "State, Islam and Opposition in Saudi Arabia: The Post Desert-Storm Phase." *Middle East Review of International Affairs* 1, no. 2 (July 1997).

A discussion of the state's reaction to Islamic opposition, under a new *'ulama*, and other figures during the Gulf War.

Kostiner, Joseph. *The Making of Saudi Arabia, 1916–1936*. New York: Oxford University Press, 1993.

Describes the establishment of the modern Saudi Arabia by 'Abd al-'Aziz al-Sa'ud and the Ikhwan.

Kostiner, Joseph. "Transforming Dualities: Tribes and State Formation in Saudi Arabia." In *Tribe and State Formation in the Middle East*, edited by Philip S. Khoury and Joseph Kostiner. Berkeley and Los Angeles: University of California Press, 1991.

This chapter concerns the role of tribes, and tribal chieftaincy in the context of the formation of the Ikhwan and their challenge, in keeping with the volume editors' thesis that tribal (or family) loyalties were a significant aspect of state formation.

Kurpershoek, P. Marcel. *Arabia of the Bedouins*. London: Al Saqi, 2001.

This title covers the author's travels in central Saudi Arabia in the late 1980s and the performance and content of the oral poetry he was collecting and studying.

Kurpershoek, P. Marcel. *Oral Poetry and Narratives from Central Arabia*. Vol. 1. Leiden, the Netherlands: E. J. Brill, 1994.

A study of oral poetry and folk literature.

Lacey, Robert. *Inside the Kingdom: Kings, Clerics, Modernists, Terrorists and the Struggle for Saudi Arabia*. New York: Viking Penguin, 2009.

This book brings to life the contemporary kingdom and the many contradictions in the decades since the author wrote *The Kingdom*.

Lacey, Robert. *The Kingdom*. New York: Harcourt Brace Jovanovich, 1981.

The history and background of Ibn Sa'ud's battle for power and the growth of the Sa'udi state up to the late 1970s is detailed here. One of the most readable treatments but long banned within Saudi Arabia.

Lacroix, Stéphane. *Awakening Islam: Religious Dissent in Contemporary Saudi Arabia*. Translated by George Holoch. Cambridge, MA: Harvard University Press, 2011.

This book is a translation of the volume in French listed below.

Lacroix, Stéphane. *Les islamistes saoudiens. Une insurrection manquée* [Saudi Islamists. A failed uprising]. Paris: Presses Universitaires de France, 2010.

Lacroix, a graduate student of Giles Kepel, analyzes the neosalafist movement as a form of political opposition and considers it to have failed. (In other media comments, he suggests that it may be the main revolutionary force in Saudi Arabia or that it has been bought off). His description of the *sahwa* (Islamic awakening) is based on at least 50 personal interviews. He makes a claim that it was Islamists from Egypt and elsewhere who supposedly radicalized Saudi Arabia, and that they became entrenched in state institutions.

Lacroix, Stéphane. "Islamo-Liberal Politics in Saudi Arabia." In *Saudi Arabia in the Balance*, edited by Paul Aarts and Gerd Nonneman. London: Hurst, 2005, 35–56.

This title is about the influence of two different groups—the so-called *tayyar libarali*, or liberal trend, and the salafists, Islamists who believe religious reform is the proper path and who challenged the Saudi Arabian government in 2003–2004.

Lacroix, Stéphane. "Between Islamists and Liberals: Saudi Arabia's New 'Islamo-Liberal' Reformists." *Middle East Journal* 58, no. 3 (Summer 2004).

An analysis of two different strands of opposition in Saudi Arabia that have arisen since the first Gulf War.

Lambert, Jean. "The Arabian Peninsula: An Overview." In *Garland Encyclopedia of World Music*, edited by Virginia Danielson, Scott Marcus, and Dwight Reynolds. New York: Routledge, 2002, vol. 6, 649–661.

A broad description of unifying aspects of music in the peninsula.

Lancaster, William. *The Rwala Bedouin Today*. Cambridge: Cambridge University Press, 1981; Prospect Heights, IL: Waveland, 1997.

An ethnography of the Rwala Bedouin of the Arabian Peninsula, with whom the author spent several years.

Larsen, Torben B. *The Butterflies of Saudi Arabia and Its Neighbors*. London: Stacey International, 1984.

An illustrated study by an expert on the butterflies of the Middle East.

Larsen, Torben B. "In the Alps of Arabia." *Aramco World*, July/August 1983, 16–21.

This piece describes unique flora of the highlands of Arabia.

Lebkicher, Roy, George Rentz, and Max Steineke. *The Arabia of Ibn Saud*. New York: Russell F. Moore, 1952.

A classic study of Arabia in Ibn Sa'ud's period and about the al-Sa'ud.

Lebling, Robert W., Jr. "The Treasure of Tarthuth." *Saudi Aramco World*, March/April 2003.

Tarthuth (*Cynomorium coccineum* or *Fungus melitensis*) is known as "Maltese mushroom," "desert thumb," or "red thumb." It grows in the al-Dahna Desert in early spring and is eaten and used as medicine.

Lebling, Robert W., and Donna Pepperdine. "Natural Remedies of Arabia." *Saudi Aramco World* 57, no. 5 (September/October 2006).

Excerpt from the book *Natural Remedies of Arabia* on herbs and spices used as medicine in Saudi Arabia.

Lebling, Robert W., and Donna Pepperdine. *Natural Remedies of Arabia*. London: Al-Turath/Stacey International, 2006.

Discusses herbs and spices employed as medicine in Saudi Arabia.

Lecker, Michael. *Muslims, Jews and Pagans: Studies on Early Islamic Medina*. Leiden, the Netherlands: E. J. Brill, 1995.

A study of the political struggles of early Medina from the Arabic sources.

Letter to the West: A Saudi View. Riyadh, Saudi Arabia: www.ghainaa.net, 2005.

A controversial letter written by a group of Saudi Arabian scholars and intellectuals. Available on many different websites in Arabic.

Lewis, Bernard. *Race and Slavery in the Middle East: An Historical Enquiry*. New York: Oxford University Press, 1990.

A work on the issue of race and slavery from classical sources that illustrates instances of racism and counterexamples of cultural and religious tolerance.

Lippmann, Thomas W. *Inside the Mirage: America's Fragile Partnership with Saudi Arabia*. Boulder, CO: Westview, 2004.

The story of U.S.–Saudi Arabian relations from the first journey of Standard Oil of California geologists to the kingdom in 1933 up to the years preceding the September 11, 2001, attacks. Written by a former Middle East bureau head and national security correspondent for the *Washington Post*.

Long, David E. *Culture and Customs of Saudi Arabia*. Westport, CT: Greenwood, 2005.

An introduction to Saudi Arabian customs, etiquette, and culture.

Long, David E. "The Hajj and Its Impact on Saudi Arabia and the Muslim World." *Saudi-Arabian Forum*, February 2003; reposted on SUSRIS (Saudi-U.S. Relations), December 16, 2007. http://www.saudi-us-relations.org/articles/2007/ioi/071216-long-hajj.html

Describes the yearly pilgrimage to Mecca and its effects on Saudi Arabia and the broader Islamic world.

Long, David E. *The United States and Saudi Arabia: Ambivalent Allies*. Boulder, CO: Westview, 1985.

Recounts the U.S.–Saudi Arabian relationship up to the mid-1980s.

Long, David E. *The Hajj Today: A Survey of Contemporary Makkah Pilgrimage*. Albany: State University of New York, 1979.

A study of the pilgrimage in the mid-1970s.

Looney, Robert. *Economic Development in Saudi Arabia: Consequences of the Oil Price Decline*. Greenwich, CT: Jai, 1990.

An important study of Saudi Arabia's "bust" period following the boom of the 1970s.

Louër, Laurence. *Transnational Shia Politics: Religious and Political Networks in the Gulf*. New York: Columbia University Press, 2008.

A study of the networks impacting Shi'a in the Gulf region, including Saudi Arabia.

Lunde, Paul. "Science in the Golden Age" and "Arabs and Astronomy." In "Science: The Islamic Legacy." Special issue, *Aramco World*. Reprint, Leiden and Washington DC: Aramco, ca. 1986, 3–5 and 51–53.

Brief articles on the golden age of the sciences in the medieval Arab world. In an *Aramco World* issue from 1986.

Lunde, Paul. "Saudization: A Useful Tool in the Kingdom's Battle Against Unemployment?" *Journal of South Asian and Middle Eastern Studies* 27, no. 3 (Spring 2004).

This piece questions the progress made in the Saudization policies and how they affect employment.

Ma'ahad al-Dirasat al-Diplumasiyya. *Al-Arshif al-Alaktruniyya li-Isdarat al-Ma'ahad*. 1400–1424 (1980–2004). Riyadh: Diplomatic Institute, Ministry of Foreign Affairs, Saudi Arabia, 2005.

The collected works in this date range on CD by the research/educational unit of the Ministry of Foreign Affairs.

Mababbaya, Mamarinta. *The Role of Multinational Companies in the Middle East: The Case of Saudi Arabia*. London: University of Westminster, 2002.

This title describes how multinational companies are changing consumption and the economic scene in the region and their impact in Saudi Arabia.

Mackey, Sandra. *The Saudis: Inside the Desert Kingdom*. New York and Scarborough, ON, Canada: New American Library, 1987.

A journalistic account of Saudi Arabia from the takeover of the Great Mosque to the new stricter religious polices of the 1980s.

Mahy, Lyn. "Saudi Aramco World Flavored with Tradition: Food from Saudi Arabia." *Aramco World*, November/December 1975.

Food traditions in Saudi Arabia are presented in this article.

Maisal, Sebastien, and John A. Shoup. *Saudi Arabia and the Gulf States Today: An Encyclopedia of Life in the Arab States*. Westport, CT: Greenwood and ABC-CLIO, 2009.

A reference work on Saudi Arabia and the Gulf states covering many topics from culture to politics.

Makky, Abdel Wahed. *Mecca: The Pilgrimage City: A Study of Pilgrim Accommodations*. London: Croom Helm, 1978.

A detailed study of pilgrimage housing in Mecca.

El Mallakh, Raguei. *Saudi Arabia: Rush to Development: Profile of an Energy Economy and Development*. Baltimore, MD: Johns Hopkins University Press, 1982.

This title is an assessment of the Saudi Arabian economy during the first two five-year plans and of the prospects for the third five-year plan.

Malmignati, Countess. *Through Inner Deserts to Medina*. London: Phillip Allan, 1925.

A travel diary of the author's journeys in Arabia, written primarily for the European audience of the time.

al-Mani, Saleh. "The Ideological Dimension in Saudi-Iranian Relations." In *Iran and the Gulf: A Search for Stability*, edited by Jamal S. al-Suwaidi. Abu Dhabi, United Arab Emirates: Emirates Center for Strategic Studies and Research, 1996, 158–174.

This piece describes the political clash between Iran of Khomeini's era and Saudi Arabia, which is a contest for gain in Islamic audiences as much as a strategic issue.

Marcel, Valérie. *Oil Titans: National Oil Companies in the Middle East*. London: Chatham House, 2006.

A study of nationalized oil companies from an economic perspective.

Matthiesen, Toby. "The Shi'a of Saudi Arabia at a Crossroads." *Middle East Report Online*, May 6, 2009. http://www.merip.org/mero050609.html

A report on the Intifadhat of 1430 (2010) and its background.

Mauger, Thierry. *Impressions of Arabia: Architecture and Frescoes of the Asir Region*. Paris: Flammarion-Pere Casto, 1996.

The arts and design of the living environment of the southwestern Asir region. Photographs of the vibrant, colorful designs painted on local houses and buildings.

Melman, Billie. *Women's Orients: English Women and the Middle East, 1718–1918*. Ann Arbor: University of Michigan Press, 1992.

An analysis of travelers' and missionaries' accounts of the Middle East, including the Blunts'.

al-Menaa, Fahad Nasser. "The Causes of Drug Usage, Distribution and Smuggling in Saudi Arabia." PhD diss., Washington State University, 1995.

Drug use is forbidden and strictly punished in Saudi Arabia, yet it has grown and become a public health problem. This study describes what was known of the drug trade and usage at that time.

Ménoret, Pascal. *The Saudi Enigma: A History*. London: Zed Books, 2005.

An important study of Saudi Arabia. Counters the usual idea that colonization has not impacted the kingdom.

Metz, Helen Chapin, ed. Federal Research Division, Library of Congress. *Saudi Arabia: A Country Study*. Washington, DC: Library of Congress, 1993.

A detailed collection on the state of education, history, economics, finance, politics, government, and society up to the early 1990s.

Ministry of Planning, Kingdom of Saudi Arabia. *Eighth Development Plan, 2005–2009*. Riyadh, Saudi Arabia: Ministry of Planning, 2005.

The eighth economic plan for development as produced by the Saudi Arabian government.

Ministry of Planning, Kingdom of Saudi Arabia. *Seventh Development Plan 2000–2004*. Riyadh, Saudi Arabia: Ministry of Planning, 2000.

The seventh official economic plan for development in Saudi Arabia.

Minosa, Tchekoff. *Najran—Desert Garden of Arabia*. Paris: Scorpio Editeur, 1983.

One of the few studies to focus on Najran.

Mobaraki, A. E. H., and B. Soderfeldt. "Gender Inequity in Saudi Arabia and Its Role in Public Health." *Eastern Mediterranean Health Journal* 16, no. 1 (January 2010).

This piece gives examples of direct negative effects on women's health that stem from men's authority over women, polygamy, arranged marriages, and other issues.

Mogassabi, Khalil S. "Modernity and Tradition in the Design of New Towns: Sadat City, Egypt and Yanbu, Saudi Arabia." Master's thesis, Massachusetts Institute of Technology, 1990.

Allusions to the past are included in modern design in these two examples of officially planned cities.

Moinuddin, Hassan. *The Charter of the Islamic Conference and Legal Framework of Economic Cooperation among Its Member States*. New York: Oxford University Press, 1987.

This title is concerned with the formation of the Islamic Conference and the aspirations for the organization and its members.

El Mouzan, M. L, A. A. Al Salloum, A. S. Al Herbish, M. M. Qurachi, and A. A. Al Omar. "Consanguinity and Major Genetic Disorders in Saudi Children: A Community-Based Cross-sectional study." *Annual of Saudi Medicine* 228 (2008), 69–73.

This study denies that major genetic disorders are due to consanguinity but does not actually mention or discuss all of them. However, the study does admit a higher rate of congenital heart failure in the children of close relatives.

Mufti, Muhammad H. *Health Care Development Strategies in the Kingdom of Saudi Arabia*. New York: Kluwer, 2000.

This title covers the then-ongoing process of reengineering health care in Saudi Arabia given the state of various facilities and need for medical workers. It discusses the establishment of the National Health Care Insurance program and the associated costs of providing improved care.

al-Mumayiz, Amin. *Al-Mamlaka al-'Arabiyya kama ' ariftuha: Mudhakkirat diblumasiyya* [The Kingdom of Saudi Arabia as I knew it: Diplomatic memoirs]. Beirut, Lebanon, 1963.

The memoirs of a former official.

al-Munajjed (printed AlMunajjed), Mona. *Women in Saudi Arabia Today*. Basingstoke, UK: Macmillan, 1995.

A preliminary study of women in Saudi Arabia and the progress made in education and other areas.

Munif, 'Abdelrahman. *Mudun al-milh* [Cities of salt]. 5 vols. 9th ed. Beirut, Lebanon: al-Mu'assasah al-'Arabiyyah lil-Dirasat wa-al-Nashr, 1999.

A fictional account of a desert kingdom in moral and spiritual bankruptcy that closely resembles Saudi Arabia, written by an award-winning author in exile. Perhaps best known is the first volume of the series, which appeared in translation as *Variations on Night and Day*, translated by Peter Theroux (New York: Pantheon Books, 1993).

Munif, 'Abdelrahman. *Sharq al-Mutawwasit*. 3rd ed. Beirut, Lebanon: al-Mu'sasah al-'Arabiyyah lil-dirasa wa al-nashr, 1991.

One of Munif's many novels that predated *Mudun al-milh*. It depicts the extraordinary measures taken by an imaginary kingdom to control the activities of its citizens at home and abroad.

Munro, Alan. *An Arabian Affair: Politics and Diplomacy behind the Gulf War*. London: Brassey's, 1996.

A view of the Gulf War from diplomatic history.

Murphy, Caryle. "Analysis: What Is behind Saudi Offensive in Yemen." *Globalpost*, November 14, 2009.

This piece claims that Iran's support for the Houthis is the rationale for the Saudi Arabian offensive in Yemen in the fall of 2009.

Murphy, Keith B., and Sherifa Zuhur. "Qur'an." In *Encyclopedia of U.S. Middle Eastern Wars*, edited by Spencer Tucker. Santa Barbara, CA: ABC-CLIO, 2010, vol. 3, 1013–1015.

A summary of the history of the Qur'an, its transcription, and its importance in the Middle East.

al-Mutawa, Abdullah M. "The Ulama of Najd from the Sixteenth Century to the Mid-Eighteenth Century." PhD diss., University of California, Los Angeles, 1989.

A dissertation that explores the intellectual and political attitudes of the *'ulama* in the period prior to the Wahhabi reform.

al-Najjar, Muhammad Rajab. "Contemporary Trends in the Study of Folklore in the Arab Gulf States." In *Statecraft in the Middle East: Oil, Historical Memory and Popular Culture*, edited by Eric Davis and Nicolas Gavrielides. Miami: Florida International University Press, 1991, 176–201.

The studies of folklore being carried out at the Arab Gulf States Folklore Center at Doha, Qatar, as supported by multiple countries, are described, as are trends in folklore studies.

Nawwab, Ni'mah Ismail. "The Suqs of Asir." *Saudi Aramco World* 49, no. 4 (1998), 2–9.

An illustrated description of the markets of Asir.

Nawwab, Ni'mah Ismail. "The Children's Kingdom." *Aramco World*, November/December 1995, 18–27.

An illustrated article about the annual children's art contest in Saudi Arabia.

Nawwab, Nimah Ismail. *Unfurled*. Vista, CA: Selwa Press, 2004.

Poetry of a modern Saudi Arabian woman written in English.

Nawwab, Ni'mat. "Painting Cultural History." *Aramco World*, January/February 2001, 20–27.

This piece describes the career of the artist Safiya Said Binzagr and a center she established.

Neubauer, Eckard. "Arabic Writings on Music: Eighth to Nineteenth Centuries." In *Garland Encyclopedia of World Music*, edited by Virginia Danielson, Scott Marcus, and Dwight Reynolds. New York: Routledge, 2002, vol. 6, 363–386.

An informative discussion of sources in Arabic on music pertinent to various genres.

Neubauer, Eckhard, and Veronica Doubleday. "Islamic Religious Music." In *The New Grove Dictionary of Music and Musicians*, edited by Stanley Sadie. New York and London: Macmillan, 2001, 599–610.

An overview of some of the styles of religious music and chanting.

Niblock, Tim. *Saudi Arabia: Power, Legitimacy, Survival*. New York: Routledge, 2006.

Saudi Arabia's political structure and trends, and the impact of calls for reform, are detailed here.

Niblock, Tim, ed. *State, Society and Economy in Saudi Arabia.* New York, 1982.

A collection on Saudi Arabia written in the late 1970s and early 1980s.

Niblock, Tim, with Monica Malik. *The Political Economy of Saudi Arabia*. London: Routledge, 2007.

This title covers Saudi Arabia's economic development from 1962 to 2006.

Nicholson, James. *The Hejaz Railway*. London: Stacey International, in association with Riyadh: Al-Turath, 2005.

An illustrated volume focused on the planning and establishment of the Hijaz Railway and its involvement in the events of the Arab Revolt and World War I.

Nicholson, Reynald A. *A Literary History of the Arabs*. Cambridge: Cambridge University Press, 1977. (Reprint of the same work published with T. F. Unwin, 1907.)

An instructive discussion of the literary styles and historical context of early Arab writers.

Nomachi, Ali Kazuyoshi, and Sayed Hossein Nasr. *Mecca, the Blessed, Medina, the Radiant: The Holiest Cities of Islam*. New York: Aperture, 1997.

The meaning of the two Holy Cities and their history for Muslims are described in this book.

Obaid, Nawaf E. *The Oil Kingdom at 100: Petroleum Policymaking in Saudi Arabia*. Washington DC: Washington Institute for Near East Policy, 2000.

An analysis of Saudi Arabian petroleum policymaking and plans to reduce dependence on oil, in addition to a critical look at Saudi Arabian governance.

Ochsenwald, William. "Islam and Loyalty in the Saudi Hijaz: 1926–1939." *Die Welt des Islams* 47, no. 1 (2007), 1–32.

Similar to the author's chapter in Ayoob and Kosebalaban, eds., a description of the effects on religious life of annexing the Hijaz.

Ochsenwald, William. *Religion, Society and the State in Arabia: The Hijaz under Ottoman Control, 1840–1908*. Columbus: Ohio State University Press, 1984.

An important historical study of the Ottomans in the Hijaz.

Okruhlik, Gwenn. "Empowering Civility through Nationalism: Reformist Islam and Belonging in Saudi Arabia." In *Remaking Muslim Politics: Pluralism, Contestation, Democratization*, edited by Robert W. Hefner. Princeton, NJ: Princeton University Press, 2005, 189–212.

This essay describes the process of creating and enhancing a Saudi Arabian political and civil identity while also promoting gradual reform.

Palms and Pomegranates: Traditional Dress of Saudi Arabia. Exhibition catalog. Washington, DC: U.S. Committee for Saudi Arabian Cultural Heritage, n.d. [ca. 1987].

An illustrated exhibition catalog that accompanied a major exhibit of traditional, regional Saudi Arabian dress.

Pampanini, Andrea H. *Cities from the Arabian Desert: The Building of Jubail and Yanbu in Saudi Arabia*. Westport, CT: Praeger, 1997.

The process of planning and building these two port cities is detailed in this book.

Pant, Harsh V. "Saudi Arabia Woos China and India." *Middle East Quarterly*, Fall 2006.

An assessment in a neoconservative (generally anti–Saudi Arabian and pro-Israeli) journal implying a new Saudi Arabian foreign policy due to differences with the United States.

Pellat, Charles. "Jewelers with Words: The Heritage of Arabic Literature." In *Islam and the Arab World: Faith, People, Culture*, edited by Bernard Lewis. New York: Albert Knopf, 1970, 141–160.

A description and analysis of the medieval forms and development of Arabic literature.

Pesce, Angelo. *Jiddah—Portrait of an Arabian City*. Cambridge, UK: Falcon, 1976.

Part of the literature on urban centers of the Arabian Peninsula, this work by the author of *Mecca: A Hundred Years Ago* describes Jeddah's lengthy history, urban landscape, and architecture.

Pesce, Angelo, and Khalid Khidr. *Taif: The Summer Capital of Saudi Arabia*. Jeddah, Saudi Arabia: Immel, 1984.

The historical and architectural setting of Ta'if, long a favored place for retreat and vacations, is detailed here.

Peters, Francis E. *The Arabs and Arabia on the Eve of Islam*. Brookfield, VT: Ashgate, 1999.

The pre-Islamic period from a historical perspective.

Peters, Francis E. *The Hajj: The Muslim Pilgrimage to Mecca and the Holy Places*. Princeton, NJ: Princeton University Press, 1994 and 1996.

Pre-Islamic worship in Mecca up to the demise of the Hashemite Kingdom of the Hijaz in 1926 is described here. It shows the linkages and impact of the pilgrimage on the area, the measures taken to defend the caravans, public health problems, costs and benefits, and the transformations from the traditional to the early modern *hajj*.

Peters, Francis E. *Mecca: A Literary History of the Muslim Holy Land*. Princeton, NJ: Princeton University Press, 1994.

Mecca and the *hajj* are described based on various literary sources.

Peterson, J. E. *Historical Dictionary of Saudi Arabia*. Lanham, MD: Scarecrow Press, 2003.

A summary of information on Saudi Arabia with a detailed bibliography.

Peterson, J. E. *Saudi Arabia and the Illusion of Security*. Adelphi Paper 348. London: Oxford University Press, 2002.

This title defines a Saudi Arabian conception of security in the Gulf and within its borders and introduces the impact of the attacks of September 11, 2001.

Peterson, J. E. *Defending Arabia*. London: Croom Helm, 1986.

This title details the origins of British interests in Arabia and its pursuit of a Gulf security policy through the two world wars and into the postwar era with a detailed assessment of air power and air routes.

Philby, Harry St. John Bridger. *The Empty Quarter: Being a Description of the Great South Desert Known as the Rubʻ al-Khali*. London: Holt, 1933; London: Century, 1986.

This explorer, intelligence officer, figure in British politics in the Middle East, and ornithologist gives his account of the Rubʻ al-Khali region.

Philby, Harry St. John Bridger. *Forty Years in the Wilderness*. London: R. Hale, 1957.

Philby is also known as Jack Philby, or Shaykh ʻAbdullah after his conversion to Islam. These are his memoirs, written in Beirut after he was exiled due to his criticisms of King Saʻud. His Arabian wife and family accompanied him. His archives—other materials and correspondence—were sold by his Arabian family to Aramco and later acquired by the Middle East Centre Archive (formerly known as the Private Papers Collection) at St. Antony's College, Oxford University.

Philby, Harry St. John Bridger. *Saʻudi Arabia*. London: Benn; New York: Praeger, 1955.

Philby was an adviser to Ibn Saʻud on matters pertaining to the United Kingdom and as such had a unique view of the formation of the new state. This book took the new government of King Saʻud to task and caused a scandal.

Philby, Harry St. John Bridger. *Arabian Highlands*. Ithaca, NY: Cornell University Press, 1952.

A large volume on St. John Philby's travels in the highlands of Saudi Arabia (Asir) and their history.

Philby, Harry St. John Bridger. *Arabian Jubilee*. London: R. Hale, 1952.

This title was written to coincide with King ʻAbd al-ʻAziz's Golden Jubilee. As the king had collapsed (due to illness) and the *ʻulama* would not permit the celebrations, the book is one of the few publications marking the event.

Philby, Harry St. John B. *Arabian Days*. London: R. Hale, 1948.

Accounts by Philby of his mission, activities, and travels in Saudi Arabia.

Philby, Henry St. John B. *A Pilgrim in Arabia*. London: R. Hale, 1946.

Philby describes his experiences as a pilgrim on the *hajj* in Saudi Arabia's Holy Cities.

Philby, Harry St. John Bridger. *The Heart of Arabia: A Record of Travel and Exploration*. 2 vols. London: Constable, 1922.

The first travel book by St. John (Jack) Philby, written while on leave at Eastbourne (in the United Kingdom). During its writing he was summoned by Lord Curzon's committee to proceed to Ibn Sa'ud for they had realized that he and his Ikhwan were more likely to prevail in power than Sharif Husayn.

Pierpoli, Paul, and Sherifa Zuhur. "Medina." In *Encyclopedia of the Arab-Israeli Wars*, edited by Spencer Tucker. Santa Barbara, CA: ABC-CLIO, 2008, vol. 2, 673.

A brief article about Medina and its history.

Pint, John. *The Desert Caves of Saudi Arabia*. Riyadh: Saudi Arabia: Saudi Geological Survey, 2003.

A book-length treatment of the cave formations in Saudi Arabia based on the author's explorations.

Pint, John. "Saudi Arabia's Desert Caves." *Aramco World* 51, no. 2 (March/April 2000), 27–38.

A description of these unique caverns, filled with water due to the geological formations of this region.

Poché, Christian. "Music in Ancient Arabia from Archaeological and Written Sources." In *Garland Encyclopedia of World Music*, edited by Virginia Danielson, Scott Marcus, and Dwight Reynolds. New York: Routledge, 2002, vol. 6, 357–362.

This essay summarizes what is known about music in ancient Arabia from art history and written sources.

Powell, William. *Saudi Arabia and Its Royal Family*. Secaucus, NJ: Lyle Stuart, 1982.

A study of Saudi Arabia through the late 1970s.

al-Qabesi, Mohyddin, coll. and ed. *The Holy Quran and the Sword: Selected Addresses, Speeches Memoranda and Interviews by HM the Late King Abdul Aziz al-Saud*. Riyadh: Saudi Desert House for Publishing and Distribution, 1998.

A collection of letters, speeches, interviews, cables, and formal statements of Ibn Sa'ud, illustrated with photographs, together with a brief introduction and a short essay by King Fahd ibn 'Abd al-'Aziz about his father.

al-Qahtani, Fahd. *Sira' al-Ajniha fi al-'A'ila al-Sa'udiyya*. London: Safa, 1988.

This title focuses on the Saudi Arabian royal family.

al-Qarney, Mohsin ibn Farhan. *al-Qura' al-taqlidiyya bi-al-mantaqah al-janubiyah*. Riyadh, Saudi Arabia: King Sa'ud University, 1414h.

This title describes the villages of the southern region of Saudi Arabia and their traditional lifestyle.

Quandt, William. *Saudi Arabia in the 1980s: Foreign Policy, Security, and Oil*. Washington, DC: Brookings, 1981.

Security and foreign policy issues in the 1980s, which explain some of the various conflicting issues in U.S. foreign policy, are described in this title.

Qureshi, Naseem Akhtar, Aladin Hadi al-Amri, Muzamil Hasan Abdelgadir, and Esam Ahmed El-Haraka. "Traditional Cautery among Psychiatric Patients in Saudi Arabia." *Transcultural Psychiatry* 35, no. 1 (March 1998), 75–83.

Traditional healers use cautery, or burning, as a medical technique to treat various ills, including psychiatric problems.

Racy, Ali Jihad. "The Life History of the Lyre (in the Path of the Lyre): The Tanburah of the Gulf Region." *Musiké, International Journal of Ethnomusicological Studies* 2, no. 2 (2006).

The instrument known as the *tanburah* or, on the Red Sea coasts and the Sinai Peninsula, as the *simsimiyya* is related to the ancient *lyra* or lyre and shows musical links between the Red Sea, the Gulf regions, and the coast of Egypt and northeastern Africa.

Racy, Ali Jihad. "Music of the Arabian Desert in the Accounts of Early Western Travelers" (Musiqa al-Badiyah fi Sijillat al-Rahhalah al-Gharbiyyin, translation by the author). In *al-Ma'thurat al-Sha'biyyah*. Doha, Qatar: The GCC Arab Gulf States Folklore Center, 1998.

An important and useful source on the musical genres of the bedouin from the accounts of the early Western travelers.

Racy, Ali Jihad. "Music." In *The Genius of Arab Civilization: Source of Renaissance*, edited by John R. Hayes. New York: New York University Press, 1992, 151–171.

Describes unique and common elements of Arabic music; its structure, history, and appreciation; and the development of various instruments.

Al Rajhi, Ahmed, Abdullah Al-Salamah, Monica Malik, and Rodney Wilson. *Economic Development in Saudi Arabia*. New York: Routledge, 2003.

A collection on the economic condition of Saudi Arabia, given the volatility of the region but also its solid basis in the oil economy.

Al-Rasheed, Madawi, ed. *Kingdom without Borders: Saudi Political, Religious and Media Frontiers*. New York: Columbia University Press, 2008.

Essays on Saudi Arabia explain various problems engendered by the official policies of the Saudi Arabian government, given its aim to control dissidence, the rise of violent Islamic elements, and the expansion of contact with outside media.

Al-Rasheed, Madawi. "Saudi Arabia and the Palestine War: Beyond Official History." In *The War for Palestine: Rewriting the History of 1948 War*, edited by Eugene Rogan and Avi Shlaim. 2nd ed. Cambridge: Cambridge University Press, 2007, 228–247.

Adds to our historical knowledge about the al-Sa'ud government's actions and pragmatic approach to the Palestine War, as its ally, the United States, backed the creation of the state of Israel.

Al-Rasheed, Madawi. *A History of Saudi Arabia*. Cambridge: Cambridge University Press, 2002.

This title begins with her earlier work on the Rashidi dynasty, contrasting it and the Sharifian Hijazi state with the new Wahhabi-Najdi order.

Al-Rasheed, Madawi. "The Shi'a of Saudi Arabia: A Minority in Search of Cultural Authenticity." *British Journal of Middle Eastern Studies* 24, no. 1 (May 1993), 121–138.

An exploration of the Shi'a of Saudi Arabia, who, in the eastern region, had risen up briefly against the government.

al-Rasheed, Madawi. *Politics in an Arabian Oasis: The Rashidi Tribal Dynasty*. London: I. B. Tauris, 1991.

This study focused on the Rashidi history and culture of the premodern era.

al-Rasheed, Madawi, and Robert Vitalis, eds. *Counternarratives: History, Contemporary Society, and Politics in Saudi Arabia and Yemen*. New York: Palgrave Macmillan, 2004.

Both editors have issued highly critical treatments of the al-Sa'ud government and its policies. Al-Rasheed's contribution is about the national imaginaries, or mythologies, created in the 1999 centennial celebration of the capture of Riyadh. Guido Steinberg covers historic trade in Najd, and Gwenn Okruhlik covers some obstacles to the establishment of tourism based on her experiences of guided visits just after the Gulf War.

Raswan, Carl Reinhard. *The Arab and His Horse*. Oakland, CA: By the author, 1955.

This title is considered a key work on the Arabian horse and the Arabian-breeding industry. The author, Carl Reinhard Raswan, renamed himself after a beloved Arabian horse. He went to Egypt and later Arabia and was adopted by a tribe, later moving to the United States and spending many years compiling indexed material on the Arabians. This book was a labor of love and not a financial success. His books were republished in German prior to his death.

Raswan, Carl Reinhard. *Black Tents of Arabia: My Life among the Bedouin*. Boston: Little Brown, 1935. (Published in expanded edition by Xlibris in 2003.)

A travel and adventure story and account of the bedouin as the author lived with them in Arabia. The expanded edition includes some of the author's early articles.

Reed, Jennifer Bond. *The Saudi Royal Family*. New York: Chelsea House, 2006.

With a forward by Arthur M. Schlesinger on leadership, this is a history of Saudi Arabia structured around accounts of the al-Sa'ud rulers.

"Religion in the Middle, Education: The Rich Cultural Attributes of Israel, Saudi Arabia, Turkey and Jordan." Included "God is a Circle," directed by Thomas Pollack, Roger Jackson, and Liz Marks. 2010. For Explore.org. Tribune Media Services. Screened LINKTV, June 16, 2011.

This program, focused on religious ideas in education, included a segment at an excellent new officially funded center for disabled children in Saudi Arabia, intended to give them "as much joy and independence as possible."

Rentz, George Snavely, Jr. "Wahhabism and Saudi Arabia." In *The Arabian Peninsula: Society and Politics*, edited by Derek Hopwood. Totowa, NJ: Rowman and Littlefield, 1972.

A chapter-length account of the Wahhabiyya movement and the Ikhwan's clashes with other elements in Arabia by George S. Rentz, who spent his life and career working on (and in) Saudi Arabia and for many years was located at Aramco's Research Division.

Rentz, George S. *The Birth of the Islamic Reform Movement in Saudi Arabia: Muhammad Ibn Abd al-Wahhab 1703/4–1792 and the Beginning of Unitarian Empire in Saudi Arabia*. Edited and introduced by William Facey. London: Arabian Publishers, 2004.

Published version of Rentz's important thesis that utilizes Ibn Ghannam's and Ibn Bishr's accounts (and many others) of Muhammad ibn 'Abd al-Wahhab's reform movement.

Riedel, Bruce, and Bilal Y. Saab. "Al Qa'ida's Third Front." *Washington Quarterly* 31, no. 2 (Spring 2008), 33–46.

Considers the al-Qa'ida campaign in Saudi Arabia as if it were directly coordinated by bin Laden and Zawahiri, as has been asserted by the authors, Bruce Hoffman, and other Washington sources.

Rihani, Ameen. *Ibn Sa'oud of Arabia*. Boston: Houghton Mifflin, 1928.

Account by a Syrian administrator and courtier of King 'Abd al-'Aziz with important details on his experiences, other figures such as Sharif Husayn and Imam Yahya, and the political intrigues of the time.

Riolo, Amy. *Arabian Delights: Recipes and Princely Entertaining Ideas from the Arabian Peninsula*. Herndon, VA: Capitol Books, 2008.

With a preface on the history of Arabian food, this book includes menus and preparation for great feasts and unique parties centered, for example, on desert truffles, the date harvest, Ramadan, picnics at the sea, and more.

Rougier, Bernard, ed. *Qu'est-ce Que le Salafisme?* Paris: Presses Universitaires de France, 2008.

A collection of essays on salafist trends and the meaning of salafism in contemporary contexts.

Røvsing Olsen, Poul, and Ulrich Wegner. "Arabian Gulf." In *The New Grove Dictionary of Music and Musicians*, edited by Stanley Sadie. New York and London: Macmillan, 2001, vol. 1, 795–797.

An article on the music of the Arabian Gulf region, which includes eastern Saudi Arabia.

Rugh, William. *Arab Mass Media: Newspapers, Radio and Television in Arab Politics*. Westport, CT: Praeger, 2004.

This book by the former U.S. ambassador to Yemen and the United Arab Emirates divides this study of print news media according to political system, treating that of Saudi Arabia as part of the "loyalist press" designed to support the government, in contrast with the "mobilization" press of more radical Arab states. Also contains chapters on radio and television up to the mid-1990s.

Rugh, William. "Education in Saudi Arabia: Tradition, Growth and Reform." *Middle East Journal* 56, no. 3 (2002), 396–414.

This piece describes the changes in Saudi Arabia's educational sector.

Rugh, William. "Education in Saudi Arabia: Choices and Constraints." *Middle East Policy* 9, no. 2 (2002), 40–55.

This piece covers the tensions in Saudi Arabia's goals to preserve its social and religious basis while expanding education.

Rugh, William. "Emergence of a New Middle Class in Saudi Arabia." *Middle East Journal* 27, no. 1 (Winter 1973), 7–20.

This piece explores the growth of a new middle class in Saudi Arabia.

Rush, Alan, ed. *Records of the Hajj: A Documentary History of the Pilgrimage to Mecca*. Slough, UK: Archive Editions, 1993.

A 10-volume series on the *hajj* with extracts from other written works by Western travelers, diplomatic correspondence, and the annual pilgrimage reports prepared by the British government into the 1950s.

Sabini, John. *Armies in the Sand: The Struggle for Mecca*. London: Thames and Hudson, 1981.

A history of the region of the two Holy Cities and a detailed coverage of the Arab Revolt and political struggle over the Hijaz early in the 20th century.

Safran, Nadav. *Saudi Arabia: The Ceaseless Quest for Security*. Cambridge, MA: Belknap Press of Harvard University Press, 1985.

A study of the foreign policy of Saudi Arabia and the development of its security forces and structure.

al-Sahaymi, Abd al-Salam. *The Ideology of Terrorism and Violence in the Kingdom of Saudi Arabia: Origins, Causes for Its Spread and the Solution*. Cairo: Dar al-Minhaj, 2006.

A salafi antiterrorist perspective by a professor in the department of jurisprudence at Madina Islamic University.

Salamah, Ahmad Abdullah. *Shia and Sunni Perspective on Islam: An Objective Comparison of the Shia and Sunni Doctrines Based on the Holy Quran and Hadith*. Jeddah, Saudi Arabia: Abul-Qasim, 1991.

Not an objective presentation but a polemical refutation of Shi'ism from the Sunni perspective; useful in understanding the arguments used against the sect and its beliefs in the Saudi Arabian environment.

Salameh, Ghassan. "Political Power and the Saudi State." In *The Modern Middle East*, edited by Albert Hourani, Philip S. Khoury, and Mary C. Wilson. Berkeley: University of California Press, 1993, 579–600.

An assessment of the political structures of the Saudi Arabian state in a volume that provides contemporary coverage, extending the work on the early-modern period in which the modern Middle Eastern states were founded.

Salameh, Ghassan. *Al-Siyasah al-kharajiyyah al-Sa'udiyyah mundhu 1945: Dirasah fi 'alaqat al-duwwaliyyah*. Beirut, Lebanon: Ma'ahad al-Inma' al-'Arabi, 1980.

An analysis of Saudi Arabia's foreign policy from 1945 to the late 1970s from the perspective of international relations. Salameh later served as Lebanon's minister of culture in the fourth Hariri cabinet.

Salibi, Kamal. *The Bible Came from Arabia*. London: Jonathan Cape, 1985.

This title by an emeritus professor of history and archaeology at the American University in Beirut presents a theory that the land of Israel of the ancient Jewish people was actually located on the Arabian Peninsula, in the Hijaz and Asir, based on analysis of early sources, ancient place-names, and their correlates.

al-Samiri, 'Abd al-Jabbar. "Masadar wa maraji' fi fulklur al-khalij al-'arabi wa al-jazirah: al-raqs al-sha'bi" [Sources and references in the folklore of the Arabian Gulf and the peninsula: Folk dance]. *al-Turath al-sha'bi* 9, no. 7 (1978), 268–270.

This piece focuses on Gulf folk dance and its origins.

el-Sanabary, Nagat. "Women and the Nursing Profession in Saudi Arabia." *Arab Women: between Defiance and Restraint*, edited by Suha Sabbagh. New York: Olive Branch, 1996, 71–83.

This piece discusses covers the problems in expanding women's participation in nursing when nurses are subjected to social suspicion or discouragement for working (at all), especially working in an environment with men and in a profession associated with the lower class. She covers the changes in nursing since the time of Lutfiyya al-Khateeb, a pioneer of public health and nursing in Saudi Arabia, given the revolving-door system of importing nurses and health professionals from outside Saudi Arabia.

el-Sanabary, Nagat. "The Education and Contribution of Women Health Care Professionals in Saudi Arabia." *Social Science and Medicine* 37, no. 11 (1993), 1331–1343.

An article concerning the role and training of women in nursing in Saudi Arabia. A longer version of the 1996 chapter in Sabbagh's book.

el-Sanabary, Nagat. "The Saudi Arabian Model of Female Education and the Reproduction of Gender Divisions." Working Paper no. 16, G. E. von Grunebaum Center for Near Eastern Studies, University of California, Los Angeles, 1992.

This paper that shows that educators were not interested in challenging the reproduction of gender divisions in the separation of women and men in Saudi Arabian schools but rather in improving programs for women within that framework.

Saqqaf, Khayriyya. *Li-Tobhira nahwa al-abad*. Riyadh, Saudi Arabia: Dar al-Ulum, 1982.

A collection of short stories in a dramatic and captivating style.

al-Sa'ud, Norah bint Muhammad, al-Jawhara Muhammad al-'Anqari, and Madeha Muhammad al-'Atroush, eds. *Abha, Bilad Asir: Southwestern Region of the Kingdom of Saudi Arabia.* Riyadh, Saudi Arabia: By the editors, printed by M. A. Ajroush, 1989.

Materials on the southwestern areas of Saudi Arabia with their unique cultural features are featured here.

al-Sa'ud, Sa'ud al-Faisal ibn 'Abd al-'Aziz. "Saudi-European Relations: Towards a Reliable Partnership." Public address, European Policy Center, Brussels, February 19, 2004.

In this speech, Prince Sa'ud described Saudi Arabia's ongoing reforms and the need for cooperation in building approaches to counter terrorism, for the West should not dismiss a 1400-year-old culture and civilization by stigmatizing it as merely a hatchery for terrorism.

al-Sa'ud, Turki al-Faisal ibn 'Abd al-'Aziz. "Saudi Arabian Constitutional Evolution." Keynote address at the 15th Annual Arab-U.S. Policymakers Conference, Washington, DC, October 30, 2006. Available at SUSRIS: http://www.saudi-us-relations.org/articles/2006/ioi/061106-turki-succession.html

A public address that speaks to the growth and regularization of political practices that can be seen as a compact between the Saudi Arabian rulers and their people.

Saudiwoman's Weblog. http://saudiwoman.wordpress.com/

This website covers many women's issues in the kingdom; for instance, at the time of writing, the sentencing of Manal al-Sharif, who has protested the ban on women's driving and posted a video of herself driving on the Internet.

Scheuer, Michael, Stephen Ulph, and John C. K. Daly. *Saudi Arabian Oil Facilities: The Achilles Heel of the Western Economy.* Washington, DC: Jamestown Foundation, May 2006.

A short pamphlet by a former Central Intelligence Agency analyst and author known as Anonymous (Scheuer) and an interpreter of various al-Qa'ida Internet writings (Ulph) with alarming warnings that al-Qa'ida will attack oil facilities in Saudi Arabia. Scheuer's position is that the United States should back away from the alliance with Saudi Arabia (and the one in Israel).

Sedgwick, Mark. "Saudi Sufis: Compromise in the Hijaz 1925–1940." *Die Welt des Islams* 37, no. 3 (1997), 349–368.

This study shows that the Wahhabist conquest did not eradicate other forms of Islam in the Hijaz but that the subsequent Sufi worship was managed and contained via compromise with the rulers.

Al-Semmari, Fahd, ed. *A History of the Arabian Peninsula.* Translated by S. Jayyusi. London: Palgrave Macmillan, 2010.

Essays that condense important insights of the contributing authors are included in this title. Many of these were heretofore unavailable in English.

Serjeant, Robert B. *Customary and Shari'ah Law in Saudi Arabia.* Brookfield, VT: Varorium, 1991.

A study of *'urf* (tribal or customary law) in Saudi Arabia and Islamic law with many examples of procedures and issues.

Serjeant, Robert B. *Saudi Arabian Poetry and Prose of Hadramawt.* London: Taylor's Foreign Press, 1951.

A work on popular poetry and prose of Saudi Arabia and Hadramaut.

Serjeant, Robert B., and G. Rex Smith. *Farmers and Fishermen in Arabia: Studies in Customary Law and Practice.* Brookfield, VT: Varorium, 1995.

This title shows how customary (*'urf*) or tribal law works in practice and is responsive to the material conditions of those living from farming or fishing.

Shaker, Fatna. *Nabt al-Ardh* [The earth's planet]. Jeddah, Saudi Arabia: Tihamah, 1981.

A work by a noted Saudi Arabian woman writer.

al-Shamlan, Sharifa. *Muntahal Hudu'.* Riyadh, Saudi Arabia: Nadi al-Qissa al-Sa'udi. al-Jam'iyya al-'arabiyya lil-thaqafa wa-l-funun, 1989.

A collection of short stories with social aspects.

al-Shayeb, Abdullah A. *Al-Jubail: Saudi Village (Architectural Survey).* Doha, Qatar: Arab Gulf States Folklore Center, 1985.

A survey of al-Jubayl.

Sheikh, Naveed. *The New Politics of Islam: Pan-Islamic Foreign Policy in a World of States.* London: RoutledgeCurzon, 2003.

This title characterizes Saudi Arabian foreign policy as building on Islamic alliances.

Al-Shetaiwi, Abdullah S. "Factors Affecting the Underutilisation of Qualified Saudi Women in the Saudi Private Sector." PhD diss., Loughborough University, 2002.

Social, religious, and economic factors impeding the hiring of Saudi Arabian women are described in this thesis.

Shiloah, Amnon, II. "Folk Music" (section of "Arab Music"). In *The New Grove Dictionary of Music and Musicians*, edited by Stanley Sadie. New York and London: Macmillan, 2001, vol. 1, 824–831.

The second section of the larger entry on Arab music considers popular (or folk) genres and includes aspects that are part of the music of the Arabian Peninsula.

Silsby, Jill. *Inland Birds of Saudi Arabia.* London: Immel, 1980.

A study of the birds of the interior of Saudi Arabia.

Simon, Geoff. *Saudi Arabia: The Shape of a Client Feudalism.* New York: St. Martin's, 1998.

A description of Saudi Arabia's failure to reform that is viciously critical of the royal family and the authoritarianism of the Saudi Arabian government.

Simpson, William. *The Prince: The Secret Story of the World's Most Intriguing Royal: Prince Bandar bin Sultan.* New York: Regan (Harper-Collins), 2006.

The biography of Prince Bandar, former ambassador to the United States.

Snouck Hurgronje, Christaan. *Mekka in the Latter Part of the Nineteenth Century, 1885– 1889.* Translated by James Henry Monahan. Leiden, the Netherlands: Brill, 1931 (reprint, 1970).

An important record of lifestyles in Mecca and the Hijaz; the Dutch author also collected various items, instruments, costumes, and artifacts.

Sowayan, Sa'd Abdullah. "Tonight My Gun Is Loaded: Poetic Dueling in Arabia." *Oral Tradition* 4, no. 1–2 (1989), 151–173.

An article on poetic duels or contests, based on the author's original research on *nabati* poetry and performance.

Sowayan, Sa'd Abdullah. *Nabati Poetry: The Oral Poetry of Arabia.* Berkeley and Los Angeles: University of California Press, 1985.

A title on the development and current tradition of Nabati, oral poetry of Saudi Arabia.

Sowayan, Sa'd Abdullah. *al-Shi'r al-sha'bi fi al-mamlakah al-'arabiyyah al-sa'udiyyah.* Doha, Qatar: Arab Gulf States Folklore Center, 1985.

A discussion of popular, or folk, poetry of Saudi Arabia.

Sultan, Khaled bin, HRH General (with Patrick Seale). *Desert Warrior: A Personal View of the Gulf War by the Joint Forces Commander.* London and New York: HarperCollins, 1995.

A memoir of the Saudi Arabian commander of the coalition forces (and son of the defense minister) in the first Gulf War.

Steinberg, Guido. "The Shiites in the Eastern Province of Saudi Arabia, 1913–1953." In *The Twelver Shia in Modern Times: Religious Culture and Political History*, edited by Rainer Brunner and Werner Ende. Leiden, the Netherlands: Brill, 2001, 236–254.

The history of the Shi'a of the Eastern Province.

Tarabulsi, Mohammed Yusof. *Jeddah: A Story of a City.* Riyadh, Saudi Arabia: King Fahd National Library, 2006.

Jeddah's past and present.

Tasnee Petrochemicals. *Environmental Impact Assessment Ethylene Project. Attachment 4: Environmental Baseline Study.* Al-Jubail, Saudi Arabia: Tasnee Petrochemicals, 2005.

A study that shows the impact of a major ethylene project in accessible language.

Tayash, Fahad. "Sameri Tradition and Zar Dance in Saudi Arabia." *al-Ma'thurat al-Sha'biyya* 9 (1988), 23–36.

An article on the *samri* song and performance format and the *zar*, or performance and music of exorcism.

al-Tayer, 'Abdullah ibn Musa. *Amrika allati qad ta'ud.* Riyadh, Saudi Arabia: Author, 2005 (1426h).

This title is about the troubled Saudi Arabian–American relationship and the idealized America that Saudi Arabians hope will return after the rise of neoconservativism and anti–Saudi Arabian stances following 9/11.

Teitelbaum, Joshua. *Holier Than Thou: Saudi Arabia's Islamic Opposition.* Washington, DC: Washington Institute for Near East Policy, 2000.

This short monograph traces the rise of Islamic opposition to the Saudi Arabian government in the 1990s. This opposition called for an even more stringent application of Islamic law and mores and a different foreign policy, not so beholden to the West.

Teitelbaum, Joshua. *The Rise and Fall of the Hashemite Kingdom of Hejaz.* New York: New York University Press, 2001.

A study of the short-lived kingdom of the Hijaz, which had been backed by Britain until the ascent of Ibn Sa'ud.

al-Thabit, 'Abdullah. *al-Irhabi 20.* Beirut, Lebanon and Damascus, Syria: Dar al-Mada, 2006. (Available in translation as *Terroriste no. 20*, translated by Françoise Neyrod [Paris: Actes Sud Sindbad, 2010].)

An autobiographical work about a young man swept into Islamic militance.

Thesiger, Wilfred. *Crossing the Sands.* Dubai, United Arab Emirates: Motivate, 2006.

This book chronicles the author's travels in the Empty Quarter and the Arabian Peninsula in the 1940s, including his view of the bedouin, and contains excellent photographs.

Topham, John, *Traditional Crafts of Saudi Arabia.* London: Stacey International, 1981.

A study of numerous crafts and folk products and practices of Saudi Arabia with illustrations by one of the most avid collectors of these products.

Trench, R., ed. *Gazetteer of Arabian Tribes.* 18 vols. Farnham Commons, UK: Cambridge Archive Editions, 1996.

A huge survey of information about the tribes of the Arabian Peninsula and Iraq from 19th- and 20th-century sources.

Trofimov, Yaroslav. *The Siege of Mecca: The Forgotten Uprising in Islam's Holiest Shrine and the Birth of Al Qa'ida.* New York: Random House, 2007.

An account of the 1979 uprising and takeover of the Grand Mosque at Mecca. The author explores the connections of the 'Utaybi movement with the growth of al-Qa'ida in Saudi Arabia.

Unger, Craig. *House of Bush, House of Saud: The Secret Relationship between the World's Two Most Powerful Dynasties.* New York: Scribner, 2004.

An exposé of relationships between the Bush family from its corporate dealings with the Sa'udi royal family blaming the latter for Islamic radicalism. I have excluded similar books from the bibliography.

Urkevich, Lisa A. "Saudi Arabia, Kingdom of." In *The New Grove Dictionary of Music and Musicians*, edited by Stanley Sadie. 2nd ed. New York and London: Macmillan, 2001, vol. 22, 324–328.

A very useful overview of nonreligious music in the Kingdom of Saudi Arabia by a specialist on music of the Gulf.

al-'Uthaymin, 'Abd Allah Saleh. *Muhammad ibn Abd al-Wahhab: The Man and His Works.* London: I. B. Tauris, 2009.

This book, based on the author's 1972 dissertation for the University of Edinburgh, covers Muhammad ibn 'Abd al-Wahhab's life and output; the travails of the Wahhabis from their own sources and others; and the debates about 'Abd al-Wahhab's additions to doctrine.

Van der Meulen, Daniel. *The Wells of Ibn Saud.* New York: Praeger, 1957.

The memoirs of a Dutch diplomat stationed in Jeddah in the 1920s and the 1940s.

Vassiliev, Alexei. *The History of Saudi Arabia.* London: Saqi Books, 1998; New York: New York University Press, 2000.

A well-translated thorough history of the kingdom to the late 1990s, with excellent coverage of earlier sources by the former *Pravda* correspondent to Saudi Arabia.

Vincett, Betty A. Lipscombe. *Animal Life in Saudi Arabia.* Cernusco, Italy: Garzanti Editore, 1982.

This title describes the animals of Saudi Arabia, their habits, and their habitats.

Vincett, Betty A. Lipscombe. *Wild Flowers of Central Arabia.* Milan, Italy: Published by the author, 1977.

A work on wildflowers of Najd and the central regions. Each species is photographed, identified with its Latin name, and described.

Vitalis, Robert. *America's Kingdom: Mythmaking on the Saudi Oil Frontier.* New York: Verso, 2009.

This title covers the Aramco venture, as do Brown (1999) and Lippman (2004), but is more critical of American exploitation of Saudi Arabia and the defeat of progressive Saudi Arabians by the royal powers loyal to Fahd who are still in power.

Vogel, Frank. "The Public and Private in Saudi Arabia: Restrictions on the Powers of Committees for Ordering the Good and Forbidding the Evil." *Social Research* 70, no. 3 (2003), 749–768.

An article on the historical role of the *muhtasib* (the official who enforced the *hisba* [the principle of commanding the good and forbidding evil] in the marketplace) and its usurpation by the CPVPV (Committee for the Promotion of Virtue and Prevention of Vice—the "religious police") in Saudi Arabia. Vogel argues for certain restrictions given the intent of the original office; it was not used to spy on private citizens, for example.

Vogel, Frank. *Islamic Law and Legal System: Studies of Saudi Arabia.* Leiden, the Netherlands: Brill, 2000.

A study of applied Islamic law in Saudi Arabia. The author observed such noted judges as Shaykh Sulayman al-Muhanna and Shaykh Ahmad al-'Umari, looks at *fatawa* of the Grand Mufti Shaykh Bin Baz and others, and contrasts the laws of the *madhahib* with those deriving from the royal edicts of the king.

Voll, John. "Muhammad Hayya al-Sindi and Muhammad ibn 'Abd al-Wahhab: An Analysis of an Intellectual Group in Eighteenth-Century Madina." *Bulletin of the School of Oriental and African Studies* 38 (1975), 32–39.

A review of these noted Islamic thinkers and their impact.

Wardak, Ali. "Crime and Social Control in Saudi Arabia." In *Transnational and Comparative Criminology*, edited by James Sheptycki and Ali Wardak. London: Glasshouse, 2005, 91–116.

This title describes the theory of crime and how the laws work to produce social control in Saudi Arabia as part of a comparative study.

Watt, W. Montgomery. *Muhammad at Medina.* Oxford, UK: Oxford University Press, 1951, 1956.

An essential work built on classical sources about the new Muslim community at Medina.

Watt, W. Montgomery. *Muhammad at Mecca.* Oxford, UK: Oxford University Press, 1953.

The pre-Islamic setting and advent of the revelations up to the *hijrah* (the emigration from Mecca to Yathrib/Medina) are described in this title.

Wehry, Frederick, Theodore W. Karasik, Alireza, Nader, Jeremy Ghez, Lydia Hansell, and Robert A. Guffey. *Saudi-Iranian Relations since the Fall of Saddam: Rivalry, Cooperation and Implications for U.S. Policy.* Washington, DC: Rand Corporation (National Security Research Division), 2009.

A lengthy and insightful report on the security and political relationship between Iran and Saudi Arabia after 2003.

Wheeler, Brannon. *Mecca and Eden: Ritual, Relics and Territory in Islam.* Chicago: University of Chicago Press, 2006.

This title uses works of *tafsir* (exegesis) and other texts to explain the sacred and symbolic aspects of Mecca, likening it to Eden.

Winder, R. Bayly. *Saudi Arabia in the Nineteenth Century.* London: Macmillan, 1965.

A classic history that thoroughly covers Muhammad 'Ali Pasha of Egypt's efforts to conquer the Arabian Peninsula for the Ottomans.

Wolfe, Michael. *One Thousand Roads to Mecca: Ten Centuries of Travelers Writing about the Muslim Pilgrimage.* New York: Grove, 1997.

A collection of writings about the *hajj.* A few are by the early Muslim travelers Nasr-e Khosraw, Ibn Jubayr, and Ibn Batuta; some are by European travelers like John Burckhardt and Richard Burton; and others are from Muslims like Sikander, the Begum of Bhopal, Muhammad Asad, and Malcolm X.

Wynbrandt, James. *A Brief History of Saudi Arabia.* New York: Facts on File, 2004.

A brief review of events in the Arabian Peninsula and Saudi Arabia suitable for younger readers.

Yamani, Maha A. Z. *Polygamy and Law in Saudi Arabia.* Reading, UK: Ithaca, 2008.

The scriptural basis of men's claim to multiple wives and other resulting legal implications.

Yamani, Mai. "The Two Faces of Saudi Arabia." *Survival*, February 1, 2008.

This work describes the conflicting views on reform and change to be found in Saudi Arabia.

Yamani, Mai. "The Challenge of Globalization in Saudi Arabia." In *On Shifting Ground: Muslim Women in the Global Era*, edited by Fereshteh Norahie-Simone. New York: Feminist Press, 2005, 80–87.

According to this chapter, the insular Saudi Arabian government does not know how to respond to globalization; its reforms are halfhearted; and radical conservatives are expanding more rapidly than are liberals.

Yamani, Mai. *Cradle of Islam: The Hijaz and the Quest for an Arabian Identity.* London: I. B. Tauris, 2004.

This book chronicles the growth of premodern regional identity in the Hijaz and how this was subsumed by the Najdi and Wahhabi movement establishing the modern state. The author also shows various ways in which those from the Hijaz continue to express their own identity.

Yamani, Mai. *Changed Identities: The Challenge of a New Generation in Saudi Arabia.* London: Royal Institute of International Affairs, 2000.

Based on survey data, the author explores the ideas and worldview of young Saudi Arabians.

Yamani, Mai. "Muslim Women and Human Rights in Saudi Arabia: Aspirations of a New Generation." In *The Rule of Law in the Middle East and the Islamic World: Human Rights and the Judicial Process*, edited by Eugene Cotran and Mai Yamani. London: Tauris, in association with the Centre of Islamic Studies and Middle Eastern Law, SOAS (School of Oriental and African Studies), University of London, 2000, 137–143.

This work details the obstacles to human rights to be found in the laws as applied to women in Saudi Arabia and the hopes of younger women for jobs, the right to drive, and more freedom from social control.

Yamani, Mai. "You Are What You Cook: Cuisine and Class in Mecca." In *A Taste of Thyme: Culinary Cultures in the Middle East,* edited by Sami Zubaida and Richard Tapper. London: Tauris Parke, 2000.

Mecca's unique dishes and their social location are described here.

Yamani, Mai. "Cross-Cultural Marriage within Islam: Ideals and Reality." In *Cross-Cultural Marriage: Identity and Choice*, edited by R. Breger and Rosanna Hill. Oxford, UK: Berg, 1998, 153–169.

An example of a marriage between a Saudi Arabian woman and a Pakistani man is given to illustrate the challenges of cross-cultural marriage, which is a challenge anywhere but a special one in Saudi Arabia.

Yamani, Mai. "Changing the Habits of a Lifetime: The Adaptation of Hejazi Dress to the New Social Order." In *Languages of Dress in the Middle East*, edited by Nancy Lindesfarne-Tapper and Bruce Ingham. Richmond, UK: Curzon, 1997.

The natives of the Hijaz had to adapt to new roles of dress imposed by the Najdi al-Sa'ud government. These impacted women and men.

Yamani, Mai. "Some Observations on Women in Saudi Arabia." In *Feminism and Islam: Legal and Literary Perspectives*, edited by Mai Yamani. Reading, UK: Garnet, 1996, 263–281.

General observations that some women in Saudi Arabia rejected the Western truisms about their "oppression" and had different priorities for change.

Yamani, Mai. "Fasting and Feasting: Some Social Aspects of the Observance of Ramadan in Saudi Arabia." In *The Diversity of the Muslim Community: Anthropological Essays in Memory of Peter Lienhardt*, edited by Ahmed al-Shabi. London: Ithaca, 1987.

This piece addresses certain issues in food consumption and fasting during the month of Ramadan.

Yamani, Sarah. "Toward a National Education Paradigm in the Arab World: A Comparative Study of Saudi Arabia and Qatar." *al-Nakhlah: The Fletcher School Online Journal for Issues Related to Southwest Asia and Islamic Civilization*, Spring 2006. http://fletcher.tufts.edu/al_nakhlah/archives/spring2006.asp

A comparison of the two countries that is critical of Saudi Arabia in that women are not being employed despite their educational attainment.

Al-Yassini, Ayman. *Religion and State in the Kingdom of Saudi Arabia.* Boulder, CO: Westview, 1985.

One of the works that claims that there are two poles of power in Saudi Arabia, the royal family and the Wahhabi religious leaders and that the royal family has used Wahhabism as a means of expanding state control.

Zain al-Abedin, Sohaila. *Masirat al-mar'a al-Sa'udiyya ila ayna?* Jeddah, Saudi Arabia: al-Dar Sa'udiyya li-Nashr wa-Tawzi', 1982.

The writings on the "woman question" by a noted essayist who rejects a Western feminist imprint on Saudi Arabia.

Zain al-Abedin, Sohaila. *Bina' al-usra al-Muslima.* Jeddah, Saudi Arabia: al-Dar Sa'udiyya li-Nashr wa-Tawzi', 1984.

The author asserts that the true Muslim family, the building block of Muslim society, must observe Islamic principles.

Zaydan, Jurji. *Tarikh adab al-lughah al-'arabiyyah.* Cairo: Dar al-Hilal, 1911.

A history of Arabic literature and language written as part of the author's effort to revitalize Arabic.

Zeghidour, Slimane. *La Vie Quotidienne á La Mecque de Mahomet á Nos Jours.* Paris: Hachette, 1989.

The lifestyle of Mecca from ancient times to the 1980s is described here.

Zirinsky, Roni. *Ad-Hoc Arabism: Advertising, Culture and Technology in Saudi Arabia.* New York: Peter Lang, 2005.

A study by an Israeli scholar of motifs in Saudi Arabian advertising and the cultural meaning of these motifs.

Zuhur, Sherifa. *Ideological and Motivational Factors in the Defusing of Radical Islamist Violence.* Carlisle, PA, and Cairo: Institute of Middle Eastern, Islamic, and Strategic Studies, 2010.

Assesses the role of ideology in the defusing of violence by members of the al-Qa'ida movement in Saudi Arabia and in the government's counseling prison program, and reformulations of religious principles (on jihad, for example) that are similar to those in the Egyptian and Libyan militants' self-produced recantations.

Zuhur, Sherifa. "Considerations of Honor Crimes, FGM, Kidnapping/Rape and Early Marriage in Selected Arab Nations." Expert Paper presented at "Good Practices in

Legislation to Address Harmful Practices against Women," United Nations Division for the Advancement of Women and U.N. Economic Commission for Africa, Addis Ababa, May 25–28, 2009. http://www.un.org/womenwatch/daw/vaw/v-egms-gplahpaw .htm

This Expert Paper covers instances of female genital mutilation, kidnapping/rape, and child marriage in Saudi Arabia along with a discussion of legal reforms in other Arab countries to inhibit such practices.

Zuhur, Sherifa. "Decreasing Violence in Saudi Arabia and Beyond." In *Home-Grown Terrorism: Understanding and Addressing the Root Causes of Radicalisation Among Groups with an Immigrant Heritage in Europe*, edited by Thomas M. Pick, Anne Speckhard, and Beatrice Jacuch. Amsterdam: IOS, 2009, 74–98.

This title looks at the role of Islamic principles in decreasing violence or convincing radicals in Saudi Arabia to desist from opposition to the state.

Zuhur, Sherifa. Personal interviews and field notes. Riyadh, Jeddah, Dir'iyyah and other sites, Saudi Arabia, 2005–2008.

Zuhur, Sherifa. "Military Perspectives on the U.S.-Saudi Arabian Relationship and Future of the Global War on Terror" [in Arabic]. Riyadh, Saudi Arabia: Institute of Diplomatic Studies, Ministry of Foreign Affairs, 2005.

Addresses the U.S.–Saudi Arabian relationship in light of the rise of neoconservative influence in American foreign policy making and U.S. projections of a 20-year (or longer) war (dubbed the Long War) on transnational jihadists and all "extreme" Muslims.

Zuhur, Sherifa. *Saudi Arabia: Islamism, Political Reform and the Global War on Terror.* Carlisle, PA: Strategic Studies Institute, 2005.

Describes the rise of Islamic and liberal opposition and forces for reform in Saudi Arabia, the Saudi Arabian government's responses, and appropriate responses by the United States.

Zuhur, Sherifa. "Arabs and Arab Culture." In *Nazar, Photography and Visual Culture of the Arab World*, edited by Wim Melis. Leeuwarden, the Netherlands: Stichting Fotografie Noorderlicht, 2004, 22–24 (English) and 14–16 (Arabic).

Why do Arabs claim a common culture? This essay is included in a collection of photography of and by Arabs to explain the basis of Arab identity in history and the presence of a visual culture.

SELECTED RECORDINGS

Arabie saoudite: Musique de 'Unayzah, Ancienne Cité du Najd. Pierre Bois, dir. Paris: Maison des Cultures du Monde, 1999. Inédit. CD W 260087.

The music of the city of 'Unayzah in Saudi Arabia is featured here.

Ettab-Talal Madah. Performed by 'Itab and Talal Madah, Funun al-Jazeera, FJCD 1109.

The Saudi Arabian female singing star 'Itab and the male star Talal Maddah, who mentored so many other singers and musicians, in some of their best-known songs.

A Musical Anthology of the Arabian Peninsula. Recorded by Simon Jargy and Poul Røvsing Olsen (also cited as: and Ali Zakariyya al-Ansari). 4 vols. Vol. 1, Sung Poetry of the

Bedouins. Vol. 2, Music of the Pearl Divers. Vol. 3, *Sawt*: Music from the City. Vol. 4, Women's Songs. Geneva: Archives Internationales de Musique Populaire de la Musée d'Éthnographie, 1994 (Field recordings made in the Gulf and the Arabian Peninsula from the early 1970s). Distributed by Gary Thal Music Inc. Geneva: 1994, VDE-Gallo CD 758–59–60–61.

This work of music demonstrates many of the musical forms that are described in Chapter 6 of this book.

Musique des bédouins. Bhattacharya, Deben, dir. Paris: Bam. Folkore et Musiques de l'univers, [ca. 1970s]. LD 5783, LP, disk.

Anthropological recordings of bedouin music.

al-Quran al-Karim. Qari' [Reciter]: Mishary bin Rashid Alafasy. Set of 26 CDs. UFI. 1424H. (ca. 2003)

A complete collection of *tajwid*, or the recitation of the Qur'an in a clear and powerful rendition.

Rayigh. Performed by A. Abd al-Majid. Rotana. 397 TC ROT, 1997.

A performance by a noted Saudi Arabian performer.

Rhythms from an Oasis. Comp. Dhafer Kohaji and Aref al-Amer. CD. Saudi Aramco, 2003.

This collection is of entirely instrumental music (without vocals); it plays on traditional forms but with the modern addition of electrified keyboard.

Samra: Songs from Saudi Arabia. Produced by Kay Hardy Campbell. Audiocassette, 1985.

Samra II: More Songs from Saudi Arabia. Produced by Kay Hardy Campbell. Audiocassette, 1986.

Sha'biyyat. Vols. 15–16. Performed by Muhammad 'Abdu, Sawt El Jazira. MACD 528 and MACD 529.

Sha'biyyat Muhammad 'Abduh: Folk Songs. Performed by M. 'Abduh. Sawt El Jezira. MACD 516 and MACD 517, 1991.

Tanburah Music of the Gulf. Coll. A.J. Racy (accompanies volume). Arab Gulf States Folklore Center, 1988.

Al-Tawhîd. Comp. by Siraj Omar, lyrics by Prince Khalid al-Faisal. A modern musical epic with vocals by Talâl Maddâh, Muhammad 'Abduh, 'Abd-al Majîd 'Abd Allah, 'Abd Allah Rashâd, and Râshid al-Mâjid. W 260001, Maison des Cultures du Monde, 1994.

The Very Best of Ettab. Performed by 'Itab. Relax-In REL CD 313, 1989.

The favorite recording of female singing star 'Itab.

Thematic Index

HISTORY

Media, Freedom of Speech, and Censorship

Human Rights

Index